CJ
1945-70 REPAIR MANUAL

CEO Rick Van Dalen
President Dean F. Morgantini, S.A.E.
Vice President–Finance Barry L. Beck
Vice President–Sales Glenn D. Potere

Executive Editor Kevin M. G. Maher, A.S.E.

Manager–Consumer Automotive Richard Schwartz, A.S.E.
Manager–Professional Automotive Richard J. Rivele
Manager–Marine/Recreation James R. Marotta, A.S.E.
Manager–Electronic Fulfillment Will Kessler, A.S.E., S.A.E.

Production Specialists Brian Hollingsworth, Melinda Possinger
Project Managers Thomas A. Mellon, A.S.E., S.A.E., Christine L. Sheeky, S.A.E., Todd W. Stidham, A.S.E., Ron Webb

Schematics Editors Christopher G. Ritchie, A.S.E., S.A.E., S.T.S., Stephanie A. Spunt

Editor George B. Heinrich III, A.S.E., S.A.E.

CHILTON *Automotive Books*
PUBLISHED BY **W. G. NICHOLS, INC.**

Manufactured in USA
© 1997 W. G. Nichols, Inc.
1025 Andrew Drive
West Chester, PA 19380
ISBN 0-8019-8976-0
Library of Congress Catalog Card No. 97-65603
3456789012 9876543210

Chilton is a registered trademark of Cahners Business Information, a division of Reed Elsevier, Inc., and has been licensed to W. G. Nichols, Inc.

www.chiltononline.com

Contents

1 GENERAL INFORMATION AND MAINTENANCE
- 1-2 HOW TO USE THIS BOOK
- 1-3 TOOLS AND EQUIPMENT
- 1-6 SAFETY
- 1-8 FASTENERS
- 1-15 MODEL IDENTIFICATION
- 1-17 ROUTINE MAINTENANCE
- 1-39 FLUIDS AND LUBRICANTS
- 1-59 SPECIFICATIONS CHARTS

2 ENGINE PERFORMANCE AND TUNE-UP
- 2-2 TUNE-UP PROCEDURES
- 2-2 SPECIFICATIONS CHART
- 2-11 FIRING ORDERS
- 2-12 POINT TYPE IGNITION
- 2-16 IGNITION TIMING
- 2-18 VALVE LASH
- 2-21 IDLE SPEED AND MIXTURE ADJUSTMENTS

3 ENGINE AND ENGINE OVERHAUL
- 3-2 BASIC ELECTRICAL THEORY
- 3-5 ENGINE ELECTRICAL
- 3-19 ENGINE MECHANICAL
- 3-23 SPECIFICATIONS CHARTS
- 3-76 EXHAUST SYSTEM

4 EMISSION CONTROLS
- 4-2 AIR POLLUTION
- 4-3 AUTOMOTIVE EMISSIONS
- 4-6 EMISSION CONTROLS

5 FUEL SYSTEM
- 5-2 BASIC FUEL SYSTEM DIAGNOSIS
- 5-2 CARBURETED FUEL SYSTEM
- 5-15 FUEL TANK
- 5-16 SPECIFICATIONS CHART
- 5-16 TROUBLESHOOTING CHART

6 CHASSIS ELECTRICAL
- 6-2 TROUBLESHOOTING ELECTRICAL SYSTEMS
- 6-12 HEATER
- 6-14 TROUBLESHOOTING CHARTS
- 6-14 WINDSHIELD WIPERS
- 6-15 INSTRUMENTS
- 6-17 LIGHTING
- 6-23 WIRING DIAGRAMS

Contents

7 — DRIVE TRAIN

- **7-2** MANUAL TRANSMISSION
- **7-12** CLUTCH
- **7-20** TRANSFER CASE
- **7-21** POWER TAKE-OFF UNIT
- **7-23** DRIVELINE
- **7-27** REAR AXLE
- **7-31** 4WD FRONT DRIVE AXLE
- **7-38** 2WD FRONT AXLE

8 — SUSPENSION AND STEERING

- **8-2** WHEELS
- **8-2** FRONT AND REAR SUSPENSIONS
- **8-8** SPECIFICATIONS CHART
- **8-9** STEERING
- **8-15** TROUBLESHOOTING CHARTS

9 — BRAKES

- **9-2** BRAKE OPERATING SYSTEM
- **9-11** DRUM BRAKES
- **9-17** TRANSMISSION (PARKING) BRAKE
- **9-20** SPECIFICATIONS CHART
- **9-21** TROUBLESHOOTING CHARTS

10 — BODY AND TRIM

- **10-2** EXTERIOR
- **10-8** INTERIOR
- **10-15** STAIN REMOVAL CHART

GLOSSARY

- **10-16** GLOSSARY

MASTER INDEX

- **10-21** MASTER INDEX

SAFETY NOTICE

Proper service and repair procedures are vital to the safe, reliable operation of all motor vehicles, as well as the personal safety of those performing repairs. This manual outlines procedures for servicing and repairing vehicles using safe, effective methods. The procedures contain many NOTES, CAUTIONS and WARNINGS which should be followed, along with standard procedures to eliminate the possibility of personal injury or improper service which could damage the vehicle or compromise its safety.

It is important to note that repair procedures and techniques, tools and parts for servicing motor vehicles, as well as the skill and experience of the individual performing the work vary widely. It is not possible to anticipate all of the conceivable ways or conditions under which vehicles may be serviced, or to provide cautions as to all possible hazards that may result. Standard and accepted safety precautions and equipment should be used when handling toxic or flammable fluids, and safety goggles or other protection should be used during cutting, grinding, chiseling, prying, or any other process that can cause material removal or projectiles.

Some procedures require the use of tools specially designed for a specific purpose. Before substituting another tool or procedure, you must be completely satisfied that neither your personal safety, nor the performance of the vehicle will be endangered.

Although information in this manual is based on industry sources and is complete as possible at the time of publication, the possibility exists that some car manufacturers made later changes which could not be included here. While striving for total accuracy, Nichols Publishing cannot assume responsibility for any errors, changes or omissions that may occur in the compilation of this data.

PART NUMBERS

Part numbers listed in this reference are not recommendations by Nichols Publishing for any product brand name. They are references that can be used with interchange manuals and aftermarket supplier catalogs to locate each brand supplier's discrete part number.

SPECIAL TOOLS

Special tools are recommended by the vehicle manufacturer to perform their specific job. Use has been kept to a minimum, but where absolutely necessary, they are referred to in the text by the part number of the tool manufacturer. These tools can be purchased, under the appropriate part number, from your local dealer or regional distributor, or an equivalent tool can be purchased locally from a tool supplier or parts outlet. Before substituting any tool for the one recommended, read the SAFETY NOTICE at the top of this page.

ACKNOWLEDGMENTS

Nichols Publishing expresses appreciation to Chrysler Corporation for their generous assistance.

Nichols Publishing would like to express thanks to all of the fine companies who participate in the production of our books. Hand tools supplied by Craftsman are used during all phases of our vehicle teardown and photography. Many of the fine specialty tools used in our procedures were provided courtesy of Lisle Corporation. Lincoln Automotive Products (1 Lincoln Way, St. Louis, MO 63120) has provided their industrial shop equipment, including jacks (engine, transmission and floor), engine stands, fluid and lubrication tools, as well as shop presses. Rotary Lifts, the largest automobile lift manufacturer in the world, offering the biggest variety of surface and in-ground lifts available (1-800-640-5438 or www.Rotary-Lift.com), has fulfilled our shop's lift needs. Much of our shop's electronic testing equipment was supplied by Universal Enterprises Inc. (UEI).

No part of this publication may be reproduced, transmitted or stored in any form or by any means, electronic or mechanical, including photocopy, recording, or by information storage or retrieval system, without prior written permission from the publisher.

FASTENERS, MEASUREMENTS AND CONVERSIONS
BOLTS, NUTS AND OTHER
  THREADED RETAINERS 1-8
STANDARD AND METRIC
  MEASUREMENTS 1-13
TORQUE 1-10
FLUIDS AND LUBRICANTS
AUTOMATIC TRANSMISSION 1-43
BODY LUBRICATION AND
  MAINTENANCE 1-53
BRAKE AND CLUTCH MASTER
  CYLINDERS 1-49
CHASSIS GREASING 1-50
COOLING SYSTEM 1-47
DRIVE AXLES 1-45
ENGINE 1-40
FUEL AND OIL
  RECOMMENDATIONS 1-39
MANUAL STEERING GEAR 1-49
MANUAL TRANSMISSION 1-43
POWER STEERING PUMP 1-49
STEERING KNUCKLE 1-50
TRANSFER CASE 1-45
**HISTORY AND MODEL
IDENTIFICATION 1-15**
HOW TO BUY A USED VEHICLE
TIPS 1-57
HOW TO USE THIS BOOK
AVOIDING THE MOST COMMON
  MISTAKES 1-2
AVOIDING TROUBLE 1-2
MAINTENANCE OR REPAIR? 1-2
WHERE TO BEGIN 1-2
JACKING AND HOISTING 1-56
JUMP STARTING A DEAD BATTERY
JUMP STARTING
  PRECAUTIONS 1-55
JUMP STARTING PROCEDURE 1-56
ROUTINE MAINTENANCE
AIR CLEANER 1-17
BATTERY 1-19
BELTS 1-28
EVAPORATIVE CANISTER 1-19
FRONT HUB AND WHEEL
  BEARINGS 1-31
FUEL FILTER 1-18
HEAT RISER 1-19
HOSES 1-30
PCV VALVE 1-19
TIRES AND WHEELS 1-35
WINDSHIELD WIPERS 1-23
SERIAL NUMBER IDENTIFICATION
DRIVE AXLE 1-17
ENGINE 1-15
TRANSFER CASE 1-17
TRANSMISSION 1-16
VEHICLE 1-15
SERVICING YOUR VEHICLE SAFELY
DO'S 1-6
DON'TS 1-7

SPECIFICATIONS CHARTS
CAPACITIES 1-61
ENGINE IDENTIFICATION 1-15
FRONT AND REAR DRIVE AXLE
  APPLICATIONS 1-17
MAINTENANCE INTERVALS 1-59
MANUAL TRANSMISSION
  APPLICATIONS 1-16
STANDARD (ENGLISH) TO METRIC
  CONVERSION CHARTS 1-62
VEHICLE IDENTIFICATION 1-15
TOOLS AND EQUIPMENT
SPECIAL TOOLS 1-6
TOWING THE VEHICLE 1-53
TRAILER TOWING
COOLING 1-54
HANDLING A TRAILER 1-54
HITCH (TONGUE) WEIGHT 1-53
TRAILER WEIGHT 1-53

1

GENERAL INFORMATION AND MAINTENANCE

FASTENERS, MEASUREMENTS
  AND CONVERSIONS 1-8
FLUIDS AND LUBRICANTS 1-39
HISTORY AND MODEL
  IDENTIFICATION 1-15
HOW TO BUY A USED VEHICLE 1-57
HOW TO USE THIS BOOK 1-2
JACKING AND HOISTING 1-56
JUMP STARTING A DEAD
  BATTERY 1-54
ROUTINE MAINTENANCE 1-17
SERIAL NUMBER IDENTIFICATION 1-15
SERVICING YOUR VEHICLE
  SAFELY 1-6
SPECIFICATIONS CHARTS 1-15
TOOLS AND EQUIPMENT 1-3
TOWING THE VEHICLE 1-53
TRAILER TOWING 1-53

1-2　GENERAL INFORMATION AND MAINTENANCE

HOW TO USE THIS BOOK

Chilton's Total Car Care manual for all models 63, 73, 75 and Maverick utility vehicles and CJ-2A, CJ-3A, CJ-3B, CJ-5 and CJ-6 models from 1945-70 is intended to help you learn more about the inner workings of your vehicle while saving you money on its upkeep and operation.

The beginning of the book will likely be referred to the most, since that is where you will find information for maintenance and tune-up. The other sections deal with the more complex systems of your vehicle. Operating systems from engine through brakes are covered to the extent that the average do-it-yourselfer becomes mechanically involved. This book will not explain such things as rebuilding a differential for the simple reason that the expertise required and the investment in special tools make this task uneconomical. It will, however, give you detailed instructions to help you change your own brake pads and shoes, replace spark plugs, and perform many more jobs that can save you money, give you personal satisfaction and help you avoid expensive problems.

A secondary purpose of this book is a reference for owners who want to understand their vehicle and/or their mechanics better. In this case, no tools at all are required.

Where to Begin

Before removing any bolts, read through the entire procedure. This will give you the overall view of what tools and supplies will be required. There is nothing more frustrating than having to walk to the bus stop on Monday morning because you were short one bolt on Sunday afternoon. So read ahead and plan ahead. Each operation should be approached logically and all procedures thoroughly understood before attempting any work.

All sections contain adjustments, maintenance, removal and installation procedures, and in some cases, repair or overhaul procedures. When repair is not considered practical, we tell you how to remove the part and then how to install the new or rebuilt replacement. In this way, you at least save the labor costs. Backyard repair of some components is just not practical.

Avoiding Trouble

Many procedures in this book require you to "label and disconnect . . ." a group of lines, hoses or wires. Don't be lulled into thinking you can remember where everything goes — you won't. If you hook up vacuum or fuel lines incorrectly, the vehicle will run poorly, if at all. If you hook up electrical wiring incorrectly, you may instantly learn a very expensive lesson.

You don't need to know the official or engineering name for each hose or line. A piece of masking tape on the hose and a piece on its fitting will allow you to assign your own label such as the letter A or a short name. As long as you remember your own code, the lines can be reconnected by matching similar letters or names. Do remember that tape will dissolve in gasoline or other fluids; if a component is to be washed or cleaned, use another method of identification. A permanent felt-tipped marker can be very handy for marking metal parts. Remove any tape or paper labels after assembly.

Maintenance or Repair?

It's necessary to mention the difference between maintenance and repair. Maintenance includes routine inspections, adjustments, and replacement of parts which show signs of normal wear. Maintenance compensates for wear or deterioration. Repair implies that something has broken or is not working. A need for repair is often caused by lack of maintenance. Example: draining and refilling the automatic transmission fluid is maintenance recommended by the manufacturer at specific mileage intervals. Failure to do this can ruin the transmission, requiring very expensive repairs. While no maintenance program can prevent items from breaking or wearing out, a general rule can be stated: MAINTENANCE IS CHEAPER THAN REPAIR.

Two basic mechanic's rules should be mentioned here. First, whenever the left side of the vehicle or engine is referred to, it is meant to specify the driver's side. Conversely, the right side of the vehicle means the passenger's side. Second, most screws and bolts are removed by turning counterclockwise, and tightened by turning clockwise.

Safety is always the most important rule. Constantly be aware of the dangers involved in working on an automobile and take the proper precautions. See the information in this section regarding SERVICING YOUR VEHICLE SAFELY and the SAFETY NOTICE on the acknowledgment page.

Avoiding the Most Common Mistakes

Pay attention to the instructions provided. There are 3 common mistakes in mechanical work:

1. Incorrect order of assembly, disassembly or adjustment. When taking something apart or putting it together, performing steps in the wrong order usually just costs you extra time; however, it CAN break something. Read the entire procedure before beginning disassembly. Perform everything in the order in which the instructions say you should, even if you can't immediately see a reason for it. When you're taking apart something that is very intricate, you might want to draw a picture of how it looks when assembled at one point in order to make sure you get everything back in its proper position. We will supply exploded views whenever possible. When making adjustments, perform them in the proper order; often, one adjustment affects another, and you cannot expect even satisfactory results unless each adjustment is made only when it cannot be changed by any other.

2. Overtorquing (or undertorquing). While it is more common for overtorquing to cause damage, undertorquing may allow a fastener to vibrate loose causing serious damage. Especially when dealing with aluminum parts, pay attention to torque specifications and utilize a torque wrench in assembly. If a torque figure is not available, remember that if you are using the right tool to perform the job, you will probably not have to strain yourself to get a fastener tight enough. The pitch of most threads is so slight that the tension you put on

GENERAL INFORMATION AND MAINTENANCE 1-3

the wrench will be multiplied many times in actual force on what you are tightening. A good example of how critical torque is can be seen in the case of spark plug installation, especially where you are putting the plug into an aluminum cylinder head. Too little torque can fail to crush the gasket, causing leakage of combustion gases and consequent overheating of the plug and engine parts. Too much torque can damage the threads or distort the plug, changing the spark gap.

There are many commercial products available for ensuring that fasteners won't come loose, even if they are not torqued just right (a very common brand is Loctite®). If you're worried about getting something together tight enough to hold, but loose enough to avoid mechanical damage during assembly, one of these products might offer substantial insurance. Before choosing a threadlocking compound, read the label on the package and make sure the product is compatible with the materials, fluids, etc. involved.

3. Crossthreading. This occurs when a part such as a bolt is screwed into a nut or casting at the wrong angle and forced. Crossthreading is more likely to occur if access is difficult. It helps to clean and lubricate fasteners, then to start threading with the part to be installed positioned straight in. Then, start the bolt, spark plug, etc. with your fingers. If you encounter resistance, unscrew the part and start over again at a different angle until it can be inserted and turned several times without much effort. Keep in mind that many parts, especially spark plugs, have tapered threads, so that gentle turning will automatically bring the part you're threading to the proper angle, but only if you don't force it or resist a change in angle. Don't put a wrench on the part until it's been tightened a couple of turns by hand. If you suddenly encounter resistance, and the part has not seated fully, don't force it. Pull it back out to make sure it's clean and threading properly.

Always take your time and be patient; once you have some experience, working on your vehicle may well become an enjoyable hobby.

TOOLS AND EQUIPMENT

▶ See Figures 1, 2, 3, 4, 5, 6, 7, 8, 9, 10, 11, 12 and 13

Naturally, without the proper tools and equipment it is impossible to properly service your vehicle. It would also be virtually impossible to catalog every tool that you would need to perform all of the operations in this book. Of course, It would be unwise for the amateur to rush out and buy an expensive set of tools on the theory that he/she may need one or more of them at some time.

The best approach is to proceed slowly, gathering a good quality set of those tools that are used most frequently. Don't be misled by the low cost of bargain tools. It is far better to spend a little more for better quality. Forged wrenches, 6 or 12-point sockets and fine tooth ratchets are by far preferable to their less expensive counterparts. As any good mechanic can tell you, there are few worse experiences than trying to work on a vehicle with bad tools. Your monetary savings will be far outweighed by frustration and mangled knuckles.

Begin accumulating those tools that are used most frequently: those associated with routine maintenance and tune-up. In addition to the normal assortment of screwdrivers and pliers, you should have the following tools:

- Wrenches/sockets and combination open end/box end wrenches in sizes from 1/8-3/4 in. or 3mm-19mm (depending on whether your vehicle uses standard or metric fasteners) and a 13/16 in. or 5/8 in. spark plug socket (depending on plug type).

➡If possible, buy various length socket drive extensions. Universal-joint and wobble extensions can be extremely useful, but be careful when using them, as they can change the amount of torque applied to the socket.

- Jackstands for support.
- Oil filter wrench.
- Spout or funnel for pouring fluids.
- Grease gun for chassis lubrication (unless your vehicle is not equipped with any grease fittings — for details, please refer to information on Fluids and Lubricants found later in this section).
- Hydrometer for checking the battery (unless equipped with a sealed, maintenance-free battery).
- A container for draining oil and other fluids.
- Rags for wiping up the inevitable mess.

In addition to the above items there are several others that are not absolutely necessary, but handy to have around. These include Oil Dry® (or an equivalent oil absorbent gravel — such as cat litter) and the usual supply of lubricants, antifreeze and fluids, although these can be purchased as needed. This is a basic list for routine maintenance, but only your personal needs and desire can accurately determine your list of tools.

After performing a few projects on the vehicle, you'll be amazed at the other tools and non-tools on your workbench. Some useful household items are: a large turkey baster or siphon, empty coffee cans and ice trays (to store parts), ball of twine, electrical tape for wiring, small rolls of colored tape for tagging lines or hoses, markers and pens, a note pad, golf tees (for plugging vacuum lines), metal coat hangers or a roll

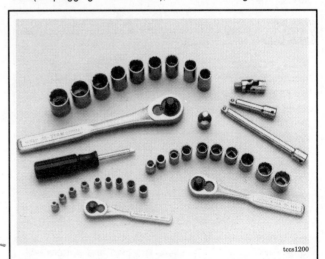

Fig. 1 All but the most basic procedures will require an assortment of ratchets and sockets

1-4 GENERAL INFORMATION AND MAINTENANCE

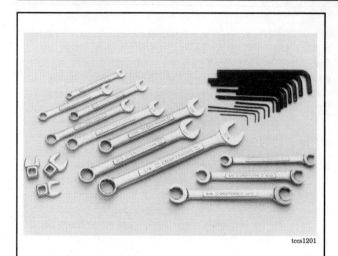

Fig. 2 In addition to ratchets, a good set of wrenches and hex keys will be necessary

Fig. 3 A hydraulic floor jack and a set of jackstands are essential for lifting and supporting the vehicle

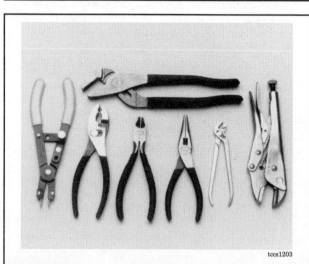

Fig. 4 An assortment of pliers, grippers and cutters will be handy for old rusted parts and stripped bolt heads

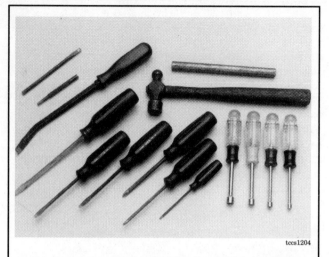

Fig. 5 Various drivers, chisels and prybars are great tools to have in your tool box

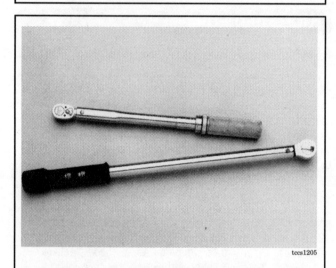

Fig. 6 Many repairs will require the use of a torque wrench to assure the components are properly fastened

of mechanics's wire (to hold things out of the way), dental pick or similar long, pointed probe, a strong magnet, and a small mirror (to see into recesses and under manifolds).

A more advanced set of tools, suitable for tune-up work, can be drawn up easily. While the tools are slightly more sophisticated, they need not be outrageously expensive. There are several inexpensive tach/dwell meters on the market that are every bit as good for the average mechanic as a professional model. Just be sure that it goes to a least 1200-1500 rpm on the tach scale and that it works on 4, 6 and 8-cylinder engines. (If you have one or more vehicles with a diesel engine, a special tachometer is required since diesels don't use spark plug ignition systems). The key to these purchases is to make them with an eye towards adaptability and wide range. A basic list of tune-up tools could include:

- Tach/dwell meter.
- Spark plug wrench and gapping tool.
- Feeler gauges for valve or point adjustment. (Even if your vehicle does not use points or require valve adjustments, a feeler gauge is helpful for many repair/overhaul procedures).

GENERAL INFORMATION AND MAINTENANCE 1-5

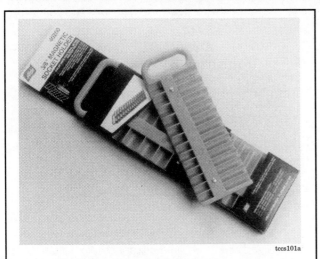

Fig. 7 Tools from specialty manufacturers such as Lisle® are designed to make your job easier . . .

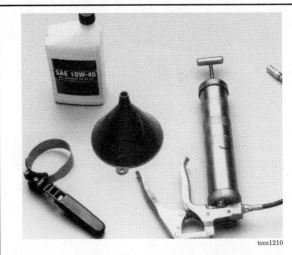

Fig. 10 A few inexpensive lubrication tools will make maintenance easier

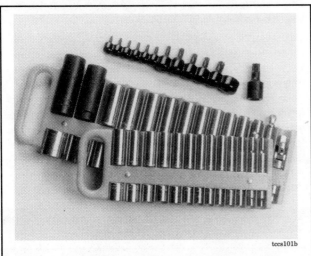

Fig. 8 . . . these Torx® drivers and magnetic socket holders are just 2 examples of such handy products

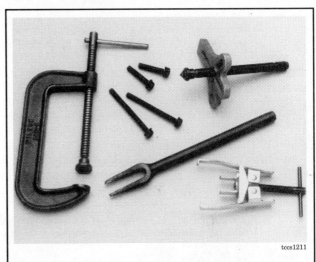

Fig. 11 Various pullers, clamps and separator tools are needed for many larger, more complicated repairs

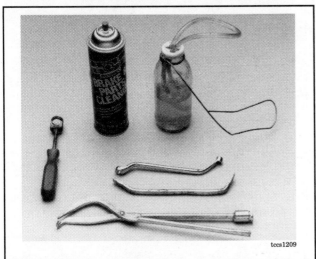

Fig. 9 Although not always necessary, using specialized brake tools will save time

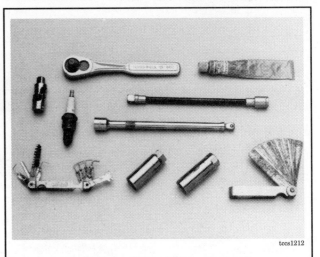

Fig. 12 A variety of tools and gauges should be used for spark plug gapping and installation

1-6 GENERAL INFORMATION AND MAINTENANCE

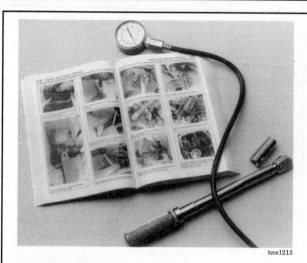

Fig. 13 Proper information is vital, so always have a Chilton Total Car Care manual handy

A tachometer/dwell meter will ensure accurate tune-up work on vehicles without electronic ignition. The choice of a timing light should be made carefully. A light which works on the DC current supplied by the vehicle's battery is the best choice; it should have a xenon tube for brightness. On any vehicle with an electronic ignition system, a timing light with an inductive pickup that clamps around the No. 1 spark plug cable is preferred.

In addition to these basic tools, there are several other tools and gauges you may find useful. These include:
- Compression gauge. The screw-in type is slower to use, but eliminates the possibility of a faulty reading due to escaping pressure.
- Manifold vacuum gauge.
- 12V test light.
- A combination volt/ohmmeter
- Induction Ammeter. This is used for determining whether or not there is current in a wire. These are handy for use if a wire is broken somewhere in a wiring harness.

As a final note, you will probably find a torque wrench necessary for all but the most basic work. The beam type models are perfectly adequate, although the newer click types (breakaway) are easier to use. The click type torque wrenches tend to be more expensive. Also keep in mind that all types of torque wrenches should be periodically checked and/or recalibrated. You will have to decide for yourself which better fits your purpose.

Special Tools

Normally, the use of special factory tools is avoided for repair procedures, since these are not readily available for the do-it-yourself mechanic. When it is possible to perform the job with more commonly available tools, it will be pointed out, but occasionally, a special tool was designed to perform a specific function and should be used. Before substituting another tool, you should be convinced that neither your safety nor the performance of the vehicle will be compromised.

Special tools can usually be purchased from an automotive parts store or from your dealer. In some cases special tools may be available directly from the tool manufacturer.

SERVICING YOUR VEHICLE SAFELY

▶ See Figures 14, 15, 16 and 17

It is virtually impossible to anticipate all of the hazards involved with automotive maintenance and service, but care and common sense will prevent most accidents.

The rules of safety for mechanics range from "don't smoke around gasoline," to "use the proper tool(s) for the job." The trick to avoiding injuries is to develop safe work habits and to take every possible precaution.

Do's

- Do keep a fire extinguisher and first aid kit handy.
- Do wear safety glasses or goggles when cutting, drilling, grinding or prying, even if you have 20-20 vision. If you wear glasses for the sake of vision, wear safety goggles over your regular glasses.
- Do shield your eyes whenever you work around the battery. Batteries contain sulfuric acid. In case of contact with the eyes or skin, flush the area with water or a mixture of water and baking soda, then seek immediate medical attention.
- Do use safety stands (jackstands) for any undervehicle service. Jacks are for raising vehicles; jackstands are for making sure the vehicle stays raised until you want it to come

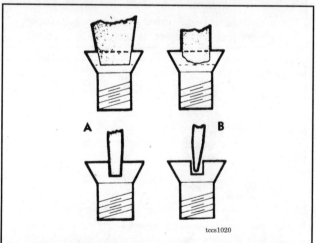

Fig. 14 Screwdrivers should be kept in good condition to prevent injury or damage which could result if the blade slips from the screw

down. Whenever the vehicle is raised, block the wheels remaining on the ground and set the parking brake.
- Do use adequate ventilation when working with any chemicals or hazardous materials. Like carbon monoxide, the asbes-

GENERAL INFORMATION AND MAINTENANCE 1-7

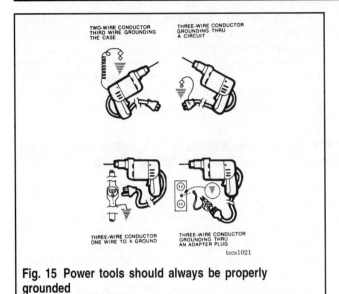

Fig. 15 Power tools should always be properly grounded

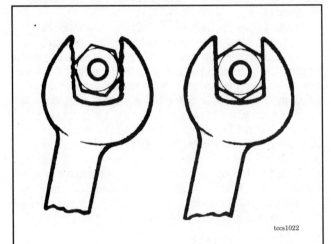

Fig. 16 Using the correct size wrench will help prevent the possibility of rounding off a nut

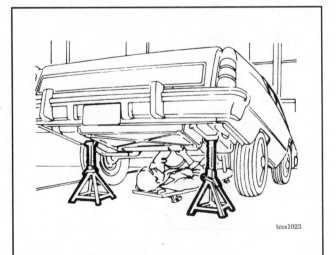

Fig. 17 NEVER work under a vehicle unless it is supported using safety stands (jackstands)

tos dust resulting from some brake lining wear can be hazardous in sufficient quantities.
• Do disconnect the negative battery cable when working on the electrical system. The secondary ignition system contains EXTREMELY HIGH VOLTAGE. In some cases it can even exceed 50,000 volts.
• Do follow manufacturer's directions whenever working with potentially hazardous materials. Most chemicals and fluids are poisonous if taken internally.
• Do properly maintain your tools. Loose hammerheads, mushroomed punches and chisels, frayed or poorly grounded electrical cords, excessively worn screwdrivers, spread wrenches (open end), cracked sockets, slipping ratchets, or faulty droplight sockets can cause accidents.
• Likewise, keep your tools clean; a greasy wrench can slip off a bolt head, ruining the bolt and often harming your knuckles in the process.
• Do use the proper size and type of tool for the job at hand. Do select a wrench or socket that fits the nut or bolt. The wrench or socket should sit straight, not cocked.
• Do, when possible, pull on a wrench handle rather than push on it, and adjust your stance to prevent a fall.
• Do be sure that adjustable wrenches are tightly closed on the nut or bolt and pulled so that the force is on the side of the fixed jaw.
• Do strike squarely with a hammer; avoid glancing blows.
• Do set the parking brake and block the drive wheels if the work requires a running engine.

Don'ts

• Don't run the engine in a garage or anywhere else without proper ventilation — EVER! Carbon monoxide is poisonous; it takes a long time to leave the human body and you can build up a deadly supply of it in your system by simply breathing in a little every day. You may not realize you are slowly poisoning yourself. Always use power vents, windows, fans and/or open the garage door.
• Don't work around moving parts while wearing loose clothing. Short sleeves are much safer than long, loose sleeves. Hard-toed shoes with neoprene soles protect your toes and give a better grip on slippery surfaces. Jewelry such as watches, fancy belt buckles, beads or body adornment of any kind is not safe working around a vehicle. Long hair should be tied back under a hat or cap.
• Don't use pockets for tool boxes. A fall or bump can drive a screwdriver deep into your body. Even a rag hanging from your back pocket can wrap around a spinning shaft or fan.
• Don't smoke when working around gasoline, cleaning solvent or other flammable material.
• Don't smoke when working around the battery. When the battery is being charged, it gives off explosive hydrogen gas.
• Don't use gasoline to wash your hands; there are excellent soaps available. Gasoline contains dangerous additives which can enter the body through a cut or through your pores. Gasoline also removes all the natural oils from the skin so that bone dry hands will suck up oil and grease.
• Don't service the air conditioning system unless you are equipped with the necessary tools and training. When liquid or compressed gas refrigerant is released to atmospheric pressure it will absorb heat from whatever it contacts. This will chill

1-8 GENERAL INFORMATION AND MAINTENANCE

or freeze anything it touches. Although refrigerant is normally non-toxic, R-12 becomes a deadly poisonous gas in the presence of an open flame. One good whiff of the vapors from burning refrigerant can be fatal.

- Don't use screwdrivers for anything other than driving screws! A screwdriver used as an prying tool can snap when you least expect it, causing injuries. At the very least, you'll ruin a good screwdriver.

- Don't use a bumper or emergency jack (that little ratchet, scissors, or pantograph jack supplied with the vehicle) for anything other than changing a flat! These jacks are only intended for emergency use out on the road; they are NOT designed as a maintenance tool. If you are serious about maintaining your vehicle yourself, invest in a hydraulic floor jack of at least a 1½ ton capacity, and at least two sturdy jackstands.

FASTENERS, MEASUREMENTS AND CONVERSIONS

Bolts, Nuts and Other Threaded Retainers

▶ See Figures 18, 19, 20 and 21

Although there are a great variety of fasteners found in the modern car or truck, the most commonly used retainer is the threaded fastener (nuts, bolts, screws, studs, etc). Most threaded retainers may be reused, provided that they are not damaged in use or during the repair. Some retainers (such as stretch bolts or torque prevailing nuts) are designed to deform when tightened or in use and should not be reinstalled.

Whenever possible, we will note any special retainers which should be replaced during a procedure. But you should always inspect the condition of a retainer when it is removed and replace any that show signs of damage. Check all threads for rust or corrosion which can increase the torque necessary to achieve the desired clamp load for which that fastener was originally selected. Additionally, be sure that the driver surface of the fastener has not been compromised by rounding or other damage. In some cases a driver surface may become only partially rounded, allowing the driver to catch in only one direction. In many of these occurrences, a fastener may be installed and tightened, but the driver would not be able to grip and loosen the fastener again. (This could lead to frustration down the line should that component ever need to be disassembled again).

If you must replace a fastener, whether due to design or damage, you must ALWAYS be sure to use the proper replacement. In all cases, a retainer of the same design, material and strength should be used. Markings on the heads of most bolts will help determine the proper strength of the fastener. The same material, thread and pitch must be selected to assure proper installation and safe operation of the vehicle afterwards.

Thread gauges are available to help measure a bolt or stud's thread. Most automotive and hardware stores keep gauges available to help you select the proper size. In a pinch, you can use another nut or bolt for a thread gauge. If the bolt you are replacing is not too badly damaged, you can select a match by finding another bolt which will thread in its place. If you find a nut which threads properly onto the damaged bolt, then use that nut to help select the replacement bolt. If however, the bolt you are replacing is so badly damaged (broken or drilled out) that its threads cannot be used as a gauge, you might start by looking for another bolt (from the same assembly or a similar location on your vehicle) which will thread into the damaged bolt's mounting. If so, the other bolt can be used to select a nut; the nut can then be used to select the replacement bolt.

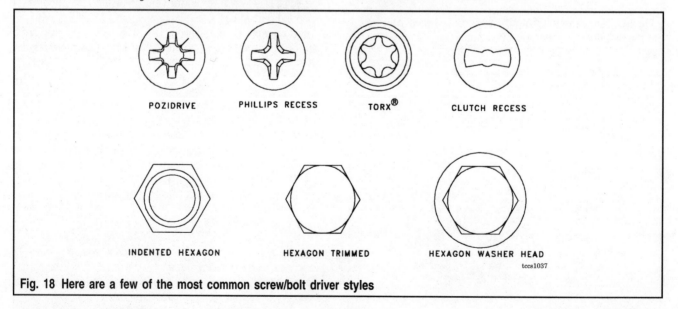

Fig. 18 Here are a few of the most common screw/bolt driver styles

GENERAL INFORMATION AND MAINTENANCE   1-9

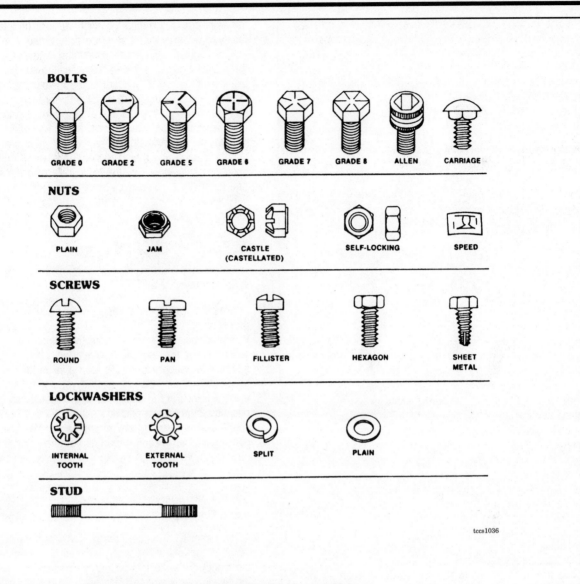

Fig. 19 There are many different types of threaded retainers found on vehicles

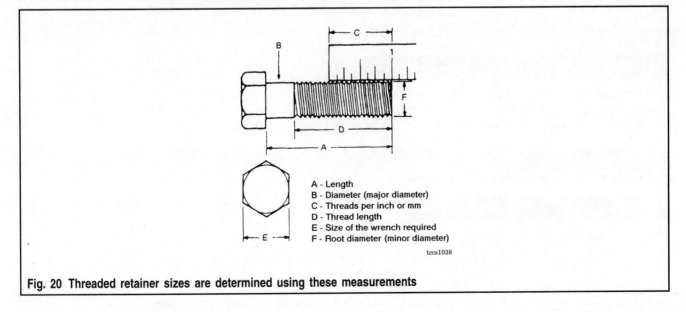

A - Length
B - Diameter (major diameter)
C - Threads per inch or mm
D - Thread length
E - Size of the wrench required
F - Root diameter (minor diameter)

Fig. 20 Threaded retainer sizes are determined using these measurements

1-10 GENERAL INFORMATION AND MAINTENANCE

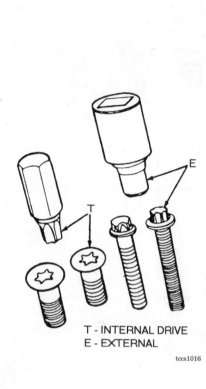

Fig. 21 Special fasteners such as these Torx® head bolts are used by manufacturers to discourage people from working on vehicles without the proper tools

In all cases, be absolutely sure you have selected the proper replacement. Don't be shy, you can always ask the store clerk for help.

✶✶WARNING

Be aware that when you find a bolt with damaged threads, you may also find the nut or drilled hole it was threaded into has also been damaged. If this is the case, you may have to drill and tap the hole, replace the nut or otherwise repair the threads. NEVER try to force a replacement bolt to fit into the damaged threads.

Torque

Torque is defined as the measurement of resistance to turning or rotating. It tends to twist a body about an axis of rotation. A common example of this would be tightening a threaded retainer such as a nut, bolt or screw. Measuring torque is one of the most common ways to help assure that a threaded retainer has been properly fastened.

When tightening a threaded fastener, torque is applied in three distinct areas, the head, the bearing surface and the clamp load. About 50 percent of the measured torque is used in overcoming bearing friction. This is the friction between the bearing surface of the bolt head, screw head or nut face and the base material or washer (the surface on which the fastener is rotating). Approximately 40 percent of the applied torque is used in overcoming thread friction. This leaves only about 10 percent of the applied torque to develop a useful clamp load (the force which holds a joint together). This means that friction can account for as much as 90 percent of the applied torque on a fastener.

TORQUE WRENCHES

♦ See Figures 22 and 23

In most applications, a torque wrench can be used to assure proper installation of a fastener. Torque wrenches come in various designs and most automotive supply stores will carry a variety to suit your needs. A torque wrench should be used any time we supply a specific torque value for a fastener. A torque wrench can also be used if you are following the general guidelines in the accompanying charts. Keep in mind that because there is no worldwide standardization of fasteners, the charts are a general guideline and should be used with caution. Again, the general rule of "if you are using the right tool for the job, you should not have to strain to tighten a fastener" applies here.

Beam Type
♦ See Figure 24

The beam type torque wrench is one of the most popular types. It consists of a pointer attached to the head that runs the length of the flexible beam (shaft) to a scale located near the handle. As the wrench is pulled, the beam bends and the pointer indicates the torque using the scale.

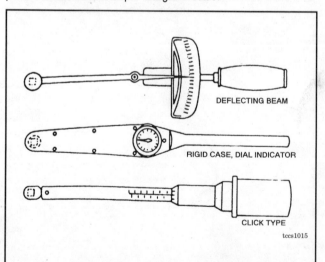

Fig. 22 Various styles of torque wrenches are usually available at your local automotive supply store

GENERAL INFORMATION AND MAINTENANCE

Standard Torque Specifications and Fastener Markings

In the absence of specific torques, the following chart can be used as a guide to the maximum safe torque of a particular size/grade of fastener.
- There is no torque difference for fine or coarse threads.
- Torque values are based on clean, dry threads. Reduce the value by 10% if threads are oiled prior to assembly.
- The torque required for aluminum components or fasteners is considerably less.

U.S. Bolts

SAE Grade Number	1 or 2			5			6 or 7		
Number of lines always 2 less than the grade number.									
Bolt Size (Inches)—(Thread)	Maximum Torque			Maximum Torque			Maximum Torque		
	Ft./Lbs.	Kgm	Nm	Ft./Lbs.	Kgm	Nm	Ft./Lbs.	Kgm	Nm
¼—20	5	0.7	6.8	8	1.1	10.8	10	1.4	13.5
—28	6	0.8	8.1	10	1.4	13.6			
5/16—18	11	1.5	14.9	17	2.3	23.0	19	2.6	25.8
—24	13	1.8	17.6	19	2.6	25.7			
⅜—16	18	2.5	24.4	31	4.3	42.0	34	4.7	46.0
—24	20	2.75	27.1	35	4.8	47.5			
7/16—14	28	3.8	37.0	49	6.8	66.4	55	7.6	74.5
—20	30	4.2	40.7	55	7.6	74.5			
½—13	39	5.4	52.8	75	10.4	101.7	85	11.75	115.2
—20	41	5.7	55.6	85	11.7	115.2			
9/16—12	51	7.0	69.2	110	15.2	149.1	120	16.6	162.7
—18	55	7.6	74.5	120	16.6	162.7			
⅝—11	83	11.5	112.5	150	20.7	203.3	167	23.0	226.5
—18	95	13.1	128.8	170	23.5	230.5			
¾—10	105	14.5	142.3	270	37.3	366.0	280	38.7	379.6
—16	115	15.9	155.9	295	40.8	400.0			
⅞—9	160	22.1	216.9	395	54.6	535.5	440	60.9	596.5
—14	175	24.2	237.2	435	60.1	589.7			
1—8	236	32.5	318.6	590	81.6	799.9	660	91.3	894.8
—14	250	34.6	338.9	660	91.3	849.8			

Metric Bolts

Relative Strength Marking	4.6, 4.8			8.8		
Bolt Markings						
Bolt Size Thread Size x Pitch (mm)	Maximum Torque			Maximum Torque		
	Ft./Lbs.	Kgm	Nm	Ft./Lbs.	Kgm	Nm
6 x 1.0	2–3	.2–.4	3–4	3–6	4–.8	5–8
8 x 1.25	6–8	.8–1	8–12	9–14	1.2–1.9	13–19
10 x 1.25	12–17	1.5–2.3	16–23	20–29	2.7–4.0	27–39
12 x 1.25	21–32	2.9–4.4	29–43	35–53	4.8–7.3	47–72
14 x 1.5	35–52	4.8–7.1	48–70	57–85	7.8–11.7	77–110
16 x 1.5	51–77	7.0–10.6	67–100	90–120	12.4–16.5	130–160
18 x 1.5	74–110	10.2–15.1	100–150	130–170	17.9–23.4	180–230
20 x 1.5	110–140	15.1–19.3	150–190	190–240	26.2–46.9	160–320
22 x 1.5	150–190	22.0–26.2	200–260	250–320	34.5–44.1	340–430
24 x 1.5	190–240	26.2–46.9	260–320	310–410	42.7–56.5	420–550

Fig. 23 Standard and metric bolt torque specifications based on bolt strengths — WARNING: use only as a guide

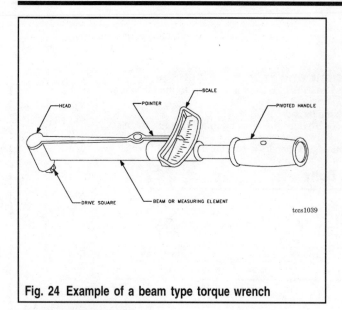

Fig. 24 Example of a beam type torque wrench

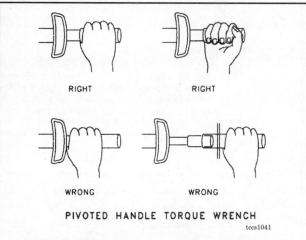

Fig. 26 Torque wrenches with pivoting heads must be grasped and used properly to prevent an incorrect reading

Click (Breakaway) Type
♦ See Figure 25

Another popular design of torque wrench is the click type. To use the click type wrench you pre-adjust it to a torque setting. Once the torque is reached, the wrench has a reflex signalling feature that causes a momentary breakaway of the torque wrench body, sending an impulse to the operator's hand.

Pivot Head Type
♦ See Figures 25 and 26

Some torque wrenches (usually of the click type) may be equipped with a pivot head which can allow it to be used in areas of limited access. BUT, it must be used properly. To hold a pivot head wrench, grasp the handle lightly, and as you pull on the handle, it should be floated on the pivot point. If the handle comes in contact with the yoke extension during the process of pulling, there is a very good chance the torque readings will be inaccurate because this could alter the wrench loading point. The design of the handle is usually such as to make it inconvenient to deliberately misuse the wrench.

➡It should be mentioned that the use of any U-joint, wobble or extension will have an effect on the torque readings, no matter what type of wrench you are using. For the most accurate readings, install the socket directly on the wrench driver. If necessary, straight extensions (which hold a socket directly under the wrench driver) will have the least effect on the torque reading. Avoid any extension that alters the length of the wrench from the handle to the head/driving point (such as a crow's foot). U-joint or Wobble extensions can greatly affect the readings; avoid their use at all times.

Rigid Case (Direct Reading)
♦ See Figure 27

A rigid case or direct reading torque wrench is equipped with a dial indicator to show torque values. One advantage of these wrenches is that they can be held at any position on the wrench without affecting accuracy. These wrenches are often

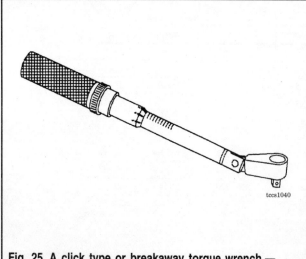

Fig. 25 A click type or breakaway torque wrench — note this one has a pivoting head

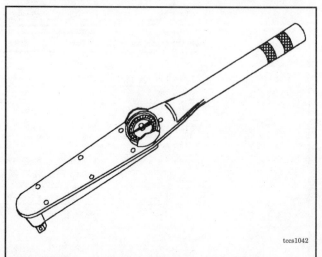

Fig. 27 The rigid case (direct reading) torque wrench uses a dial indicator to show torque

GENERAL INFORMATION AND MAINTENANCE 1-13

preferred because they tend to be compact, easy to read and have a great degree of accuracy.

TORQUE ANGLE METERS

♦ See Figure 28

Because the frictional characteristics of each fastener or threaded hole will vary, clamp loads which are based strictly on torque will vary as well. In most applications, this variance is not significant enough to cause worry. But, in certain applications, a manufacturer's engineers may determine that more precise clamp loads are necessary (such is the case with many aluminum cylinder heads). In these cases, a torque angle method of installation would be specified. When installing fasteners which are torque angle tightened, a predetermined seating torque and standard torque wrench are usually used first to remove any compliance from the joint. The fastener is then tightened the specified additional portion of a turn measured in degrees. A torque angle gauge (mechanical protractor) is used for these applications.

Standard and Metric Measurements

♦ See Figure 29

Throughout this manual, specifications are given to help you determine the condition of various components on your vehicle, or to assist you in their installation. Some of the most common measurements include length (in. or cm/mm), torque (ft. lbs., inch lbs. or Nm) and pressure (psi, in. Hg, kPa or mm Hg). In most cases, we strive to provide the proper measurement as determined by the manufacturer's engineers.

Though, in some cases, that value may not be conveniently measured with what is available in your tool box. Luckily, many of the measuring devices which are available today will have two scales so the Standard or Metric measurements may easily be taken. If any of the various measuring tools which are available to you do not contain the same scale as listed in the specifications, use the accompanying conversion factors to determine the proper value.

The conversion factor chart is used by taking the given specification and multiplying it by the necessary conversion factor. For instance, looking at the first line, if you have a measurement in inches such as "free-play should be 2 in." but your ruler reads only in millimeters, multiply 2 in. by the conversion factor of 25.4 to get the metric equivalent of 50.8mm. Likewise, if the specification was given only in a Metric measurement, for example in Newton Meters (Nm), then look at the center column first. If the measurement is 100 Nm, multiply it by the conversion factor of 0.738 to get 73.8 ft. lbs.

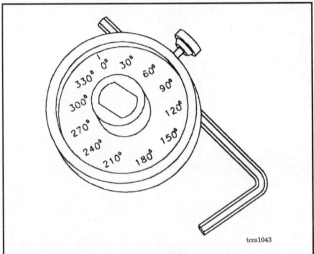

Fig. 28 Some specifications require the use of a torque angle meter (mechanical protractor)

CONVERSION FACTORS

LENGTH-DISTANCE

Inches (in.)	x 25.4	= Millimeters (mm)	x .0394	= Inches
Feet (ft.)	x .305	= Meters (m)	x 3.281	= Feet
Miles	x 1.609	= Kilometers (km)	x .0621	= Miles

VOLUME

Cubic Inches (in3)	x 16.387	= Cubic Centimeters	x .061	= in3
IMP Pints (IMP pt.)	x .568	= Liters (L)	x 1.76	= IMP pt.
IMP Quarts (IMP qt.)	x 1.137	= Liters (L)	x .88	= IMP qt.
IMP Gallons (IMP gal.)	x 4.546	= Liters (L)	x .22	= IMP gal.
IMP Quarts (IMP qt.)	x 1.201	= US Quarts (US qt.)	x .833	= IMP qt.
IMP Gallons (IMP gal.)	x 1.201	= US Gallons (US gal.)	x .833	= IMP gal.
Fl. Ounces	x 29.573	= Milliliters	x .034	= Ounces
US Pints (US pt.)	x .473	= Liters (L)	x 2.113	= Pints
US Quarts (US qt.)	x .946	= Liters (L)	x 1.057	= Quarts
US Gallons (US gal.)	x 3.785	= Liters (L)	x .264	= Gallons

MASS-WEIGHT

Ounces (oz.)	x 28.35	= Grams (g)	x .035	= Ounces
Pounds (lb.)	x .454	= Kilograms (kg)	x 2.205	= Pounds

PRESSURE

Pounds Per Sq. In. (psi)	x 6.895	= Kilopascals (kPa)	x .145	= psi
Inches of Mercury (Hg)	x .4912	= psi	x 2.036	= Hg
Inches of Mercury (Hg)	x 3.377	= Kilopascals (kPa)	x .2961	= Hg
Inches of Water (H_2O)	x .07355	= Inches of Mercury	x 13.783	= H_2O
Inches of Water (H_2O)	x .03613	= psi	x 27.684	= H_2O
Inches of Water (H_2O)	x .248	= Kilopascals (kPa)	x 4.026	= H_2O

TORQUE

Pounds-Force Inches (in-lb)	x .113	= Newton Meters (N·m)	x 8.85	= in-lb
Pounds-Force Feet (ft-lb)	x 1.356	= Newton Meters (N·m)	x .738	= ft-lb

VELOCITY

Miles Per Hour (MPH)	x 1.609	= Kilometers Per Hour (KPH)	x .621	= MPH

POWER

Horsepower (Hp)	x .745	= Kilowatts	x 1.34	= Horsepower

FUEL CONSUMPTION*

Miles Per Gallon IMP (MPG)	x .354	= Kilometers Per Liter (Km/L)
Kilometers Per Liter (Km/L)	x 2.352	= IMP MPG
Miles Per Gallon US (MPG)	x .425	= Kilometers Per Liter (Km/L)
Kilometers Per Liter (Km/L)	x 2.352	= US MPG

*It is common to covert from miles per gallon (mpg) to liters/100 kilometers (1/100 km), where mpg (IMP) x 1/100 km = 282 and mpg (US) x 1/100 km = 235.

TEMPERATURE

Degree Fahrenheit (°F) = (°C x 1.8) + 32
Degree Celsius (°C) = (°F − 32) x .56

Fig. 29 Standard and metric conversion factors chart

GENERAL INFORMATION AND MAINTENANCE

HISTORY AND MODEL IDENTIFICATION

The first "Jeep", as we know it today, was the Model MB Military. It was produced from 1941 through 1945. The distinguishing characteristics were an L-head, 4-cylinder engine, no tailgate, a 6 volt (6V) electrical system, split windshield, rear mounted spare tire, and a timing chain.

The next model was the CJ-2A. It was made from 1945 to 1949 and was the first Jeep made available directly to the public. This is the civilian version of the MB Military. The letters CJ stand for Civilian Jeep. The distinguishing characteristics of this model are the L-head, 4-cylinder engine, split windshield, and 6V electrical system. The civilian version differs from the Model MB Military in that the spare tire is mounted on the side of the vehicle and there is a tailgate.

The CJ-3A was brought out in 1948. The only outward difference between this model and the CJ-2A is that the CJ-3A has a one piece windshield. This model was produced until 1953.

In 1947, Kaiser introduced the Model 2WD and 4WD Truck. This small pick-up was essentially similar to contemporary CJ models, with a 4L-134 engine and 2-piece windshield. it was produced through 1950. At the same time, the Model 4-63 was released. This was a 2WD station wagon version of the pick-up and was produced through 1950. A distinguishing characteristic was the use of a Planar independent front suspension, using a single transverse leaf spring and upper control arms. In 1949, a 4WD version of the 4-63 was introduced, known as the 4x4-63. Conventional front suspension was used. It too was produced through 1950. In 1950, a 6-cylinder version was introduced, known as the 6-73, equipped with the 6-226 engine. It was produced only in 1950.

In 1950 the Models 4-73 and 4x4-73 were introduced in both pick-up and station wagon configurations. They used the 4F-134 and 6-226 engines The were produced through 1951.

The military services received a new model Jeep in 1950: the Model MC-M38 Military. This Jeep had a 24V electrical system, a 4-cylinder L-head engine, no tailgate, brush guards over the headlights, a one piece windshield, and a rear mounted spare tire. This model was produced only until 1951.

In 1951 the Model MF-M38A1 Military replaced the Model MC-M38 Military. The newer model had rounded front fenders and was made until 1968.

A new civilian Jeep, the Model CJ-3B, was introduced in 1953. It can be distinguished by its high flat hood but also had a 4-cylinder, F-head engine, side mounted spare tire, one piece windshield, tailgate, angular fenders (like all of the earlier models), and a 6V or 12V electrical system. The CJ-3B was made until 1964.

In 1956, the model 4-75 4x4 Utility Wagon was introduced. It used the 4F-134, 6-226 and 6-230 engines. It was produced through 1964.

In 1958, a 2WD version of the 4-75 was introduced, named the Maverick. It had "captive air" tires and a 4F-134 engine. It was produced only in 1958.

The CJ-5, a civilian version of the MD-38A1 was released in 1955. It had a tailgate, a 6V or 12V electrical system, and rounded fenders. Two engines were offered for the first time in the Universal series with this introduction. The traditional 4-cylinder F-head was offered, as well as the V6 Buick engine. The V6 was available from 1965 through 1970. The CJ-5's spare is usually mounted on the side.

A longer version of the CJ-5 was also introduced in 1955. This was the CJ-6 with a wheelbase of 101 in. (2.57 m). It was identical to the CJ-5 except for the longer wheelbase.

SERIAL NUMBER IDENTIFICATION

Vehicle

The vehicle serial number is located on a metal plate mounted on the firewall under the hood. It is on the left side on CJ-5, and CJ-6 models and on the right on CJ-3B models. Identification of a specific vehicle requires a prefix plus a serial number. The following chart identifies the Jeep model by the serial number prefix.

Any prefix that is not given here indicates that yours is a special vehicle with differences that are not covered in this book.

Engine

4-134

The engine serial number for the Willys built F-Head 4 cylinder engine is located on the water pump boss at the front of the engine. It consists of a 5 or 6 digit number. The engine code prefix for the F-Head is 4J.

VEHICLE IDENTIFICATION

Model	Prefix
CJ-2A	no prefix
CJ-3A	no prefix
	451-GB1
	452-GB1
	453-GB1
CJ-3B	453-GB2
	454-GB2
	57348
	8105
CJ-5	57548
	8305
CJ-5A	8322
CJ-6	57648
	8405
CJ-6A	8422

It is sometimes necessary to machine oversize or undersize clearances for cylinder blocks and crankshafts. If your engine

1-16 GENERAL INFORMATION AND MAINTENANCE

ENGINE IDENTIFICATION

Engine	Engine Displacement			Type	Mfg. by	Years	Models
	c.i.d.	cc	liters				
4–134	134	2199	2.2	L–Head, Inline 4	Kaiser	1945-53	CJ-2A, CJ-3A
4–134	134	2199	2.2	F–Head, Inline 4	Kaiser	1953-69	CJ-3B, CJ-5, CJ-6
6–225	225	3,691	3.7	OHV, V6	Buick	1966-70	CJ-5, CJ-6
6–226	226	3,706	3.7	L–Head, Inline 6	Kaiser	1950-60	Utility
6–230	230	3,775	3.8	SOHC, Inline 6	Continental	1960-64	Utility

OHV—Overhead Valve

89761c03

is equipped with oversized or undersized parts, it is necessary to order parts that will match the old parts. To find out if your engine is one with odd-sized parts, check the engine code letter or the engine code number itself — which in some cases is followed by a letter or a series of letters. The following list explains just what the letters indicate:
• Letter A (10001-A) indicates 0.010 in. (0.254mm) undersized main and connecting rod bearings.
• Letter B (10001-B) indicates 0.010 in. (0.254mm) oversized cylinder bore.
• Letter AB (l0001-AB) indicates the combination of A and B above.
• Letter C (10001-C) indicates 0.002 in. (0.0508mm) undersized piston pin.
• Letter D (10001-D) indicates 0.010 in. (0.254mm) undersized main bearing journals.
• Letter E (10001-E) indicates 0.010 in. (0.254mm) undersized connecting rod bearing journals.

6-225

The engine number for the Buick built V6-225 engine is located on the right side of the engine, on the crankcase, just below the head. The code is KLH. The codes RU and RV, included in the engine number of 1965 and 1966 engines, indicate manual or automatic transmission, respectively.

It is sometimes necessary to machine oversize or undersize clearances for cylinder blocks and crankshafts. If your engine is equipped with oversized or undersized parts, it is necessary to order parts that will match the old parts. To find out if your engine is one with odd-sized parts, check the engine code letter or the engine code number itself, which in some cases is followed by a letter or a series of letters. The following chart explains just what the letters indicate:
Letter A (10001-A) indicates 0.010 in. (0.254mm) undersized main and connecting rod bearings.
Letter B (10001-B) indicates 0.010 in. (0.254mm) oversized cylinder bore.
Letter AB (l0001-AB) indicates the combination of A and B above.

Letter C (10001-C) indicates 0.002 in. (0.0508mm) undersized piston pin.
Letter D (10001-D) indicates 0.010 in. (0.254mm) undersized main bearing journals.
Letter E (10001-E) indicates 0.010 in. (0.254mm) undersized connecting rod bearing journals.

6-226

The 6-226 engine serial number is stamped on a machined surface near the left front corner of the block, above the generator. The serial number will have a prefix, FW, followed by a 5 digit number.

6-230

The 6-230 engine serial number is stamped on a machined surface on the right front of the block, just behind the ignition coil. The serial number prefixes are:
• NS60C: 2WD, manual transmission, 1 barrel carburetor
• TS60C: 4WD, manual transmission, 1 barrel carburetor
• ND60C: 2WD, manual transmission, 2 barrel carburetor
• TD60C: 4WD, manual transmission, 2 barrel carburetor
• AD60C: Automatic Transmission suffix A, indicates 0.010 in. (0.254mm) oversized main and rod bearings; B indicates 0.010 in. (0.254mm) oversized pistons; AB is a combination of both.

Transmission

There is a tag attached to the transmission case that identifies the manufacturer and model of the transmission. It is necessary to have the information on this tag before ordering parts. When reassembling the transmission, be sure that this tag is replaced on the transmission case so identification can be made in the future.

In some cases, the transmission identification number may be embossed on the transmission housing.

GENERAL INFORMATION AND MAINTENANCE 1-17

MANUAL TRANSMISSION APPLICATIONS

Transmission Model	Speeds	Years	Jeep Models
Warner T-90C ①	3-spd.	1945-70	Standard on all models
Warner T-86	4-spd. ②	1947-58	Optional on 2WD Utility models w/6-226 engines
Warner T-90	3-spd.	1947-58	Standard on 4WD models w/4-134 engines
Warner T-90J	3-spd.	1947-58	Standard on 4WD Utility models w/6-226 engines
Warner T-96	4-spd. ②	1947-58	Optional on 2WD Utility models w/4-134 engines
Warner T-86AA	3-spd.	1955-70	Standard on all models w/6-225 engines
Warner T-98A	4-spd.	1955-70	Optional on all models

① On CJ-2A models up to serial number 38221, the transmission has external linkage.
② Equipped with a Warner R-10B overdrive unit.

Drive Axle

Refer to the accompanying chart for drive axle identification.

Transfer Case

There was only one transfer case available in 4WD models from 1945-70, which was the Spicer 18.

FRONT AND REAR DRIVE AXLE APPLICATIONS

Axle Type	Years	Jeep Models
Front Axle		
Spicer 25	1945-53	CJ-2A, CJ-3A
Spicer 25	1947-64	Utility
Dana 27	1954-70	CJ-3B, CJ-5, CJ-6
Dana 27A	1954-70	CJ-3B, CJ-5, CJ-6
Rear Axle		
Dana/Spicer 23-2	1945-49	CJ-2A before serial number 13453
Dana/Spicer 41-2	1945-49	CJ-2A after serial number 13453
Dana/Spicer 44	1947-64	Utility models w/3700 lb. GVW
	1948-70	CJ-3A, CJ-3B, CJ-5, CJ-6
Dana/Spicer 53	1947-64	Utility models w/4500 lb. GVW
Dana/Spicer 27	1955-64	DJ-3A

GVW - Gross Vehicle Weight.

ROUTINE MAINTENANCE

See the Maintenance Intervals Chart in this section for the recommended maintenance intervals for the components covered here.

Air Cleaner

OIL BATH TYPE

To service the oil bath type air cleaner on the L4-134, F4-134, 6-226 or 6-230, first unscrew the oil cup clamp and remove the oil cup from the cleaner body. Remove the oil from the cup and scrape out all the dirt inside, on the bottom. Wash the cup with a safe solvent. Refill the oil cup and replace it on the air cleaner body. Use the same viscosity of oil as you use in the engine crankcase.

To service the air cleaner body (less the oil cup), loosen the hose clamp and remove the hose form the cleaner. Detach the breather hose from the fitting on the cleaner. Remove the two wing nuts and lift the cleaner from the vehicle. Agitate the cleaner body thoroughly in a cleaning solution to clean the filtering element and then dry the element with compressed air. Reinstall the air cleaner body and replace the oil cup. The air cleaner should be serviced every 2,000 miles.

1-18 GENERAL INFORMATION AND MAINTENANCE

To service the oil bath type air cleaner on V6 engines, first remove the air cleaner from the engine by unscrewing the wing nut on top of the air cleaner. Remove the oil cup from the body of the air cleaner and remove all of the oil from the oil cup. Remove all of the dirt from the inside of the coil cup with a safe solvent. Wash the filter element in solvent, air dry it, and then fill the oil cup to the indicated level with clean oil. Assemble the air cleaner element to the oil cup, making sure that the gasket is in place between the two pieces. Mount the air cleaner assembly in the carburetor, making sure that the gasket between the air cleaner and the carburetor is in place and making a good seal. Secure the air cleaner to the carburetor with the wing nut.

PAPER ELEMENT TYPE

Remove the wing nut or hex nuts on top of the cover. On the 6-225, detach the rubber hose from the engine rocker arm (valve) cover and set the cover aside, being careful not to damage the large diameter hose or hoses to the air cleaner inlet.

If the filter element has a foam wrapper, remove the wrapper and wash it in detergent or a safe solvent. Squeeze and blot dry. Wet the wrapper in engine oil and squeeze it tightly in an absorbent towel or rag to remove the excess.

Clean the dirt from the paper element by rapping it gently against a flat surface. Replace the element as necessary.

Clean the housing and the cover. Replace the oiled wrapper, if any, on the element and reinstall the element in the housing, placing it 180 degrees from its original position.

➡The oiled foam wrapper element is a factory option for some years. It should be available through Jeep parts. There are also aftermarket variations on this, both dry and oiled.

Fuel Filter

REPLACEMENT

Early 4-134 and All 6-226
♦ See Figures 30, 31, 32 and 33

Most of these engines have a fuel pump with a bowl containing a replaceable filter element. Some have only a mesh strainer in the fuel pump.

Late 4-134, 6-225 and 6-230
♦ See Figure 34

All these engines have a throwaway cartridge filter in the line between the fuel pump and the carburetor. To replace it:
1. Remove the air cleaner as necessary.
2. Put an absorbent rag under the filter to catch spillage.
3. Remove the hose clamps.
4. Remove the filter and short attaching hoses.
5. Remove the hoses if they are to be reused.

Fig. 30 The fuel pump/filter assembly is mounted on the lower left-hand side of the engine

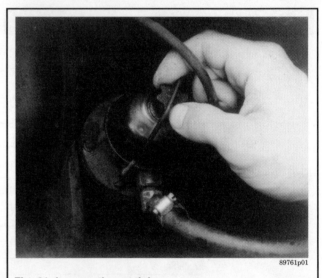

Fig. 31 Loosen the retaining screw . . .

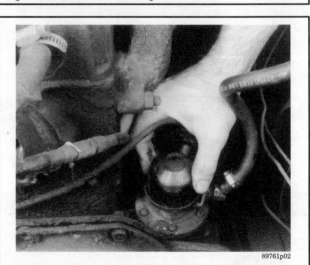

Fig. 32 . . . push the retaining screw and wire off to one side . . .

GENERAL INFORMATION AND MAINTENANCE 1-19

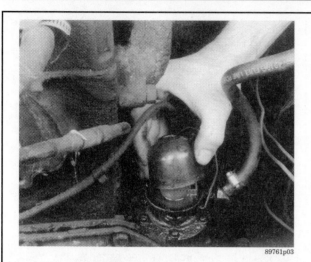

Fig. 33 . . . then lift the cover off of the pump — the screen/filter is under the cover

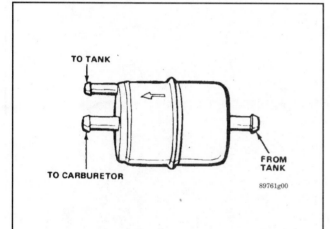

Fig. 34 When installing a new fuel filter, make certain that the fuel flow indicator marks on the filter point in the correct direction

6. Assemble the new filter and hoses.

➡ The original equipment wire hose clamps should be replaced with screw type band clamps for the best results.

7. Install the filter, tighten the clamps, start the engine, and check for leaks. Discard the rag and old filter safely.

PCV Valve

The PCV valve, which is the heart of the positive crankcase ventilation system, should be free of dirt and residue and in working order. As long as the valve is kept clean and is not showing signs of becoming damaged or gummed up, it should work properly. When the valve cannot be cleaned sufficiently or becomes sticky and will not operate freely, it should be replaced.

The PCV filter, which is located at the air filter housing on some 6-cylinder models, should be checked along with the PCV valve. Just blow out the screen with compressed air in the reverse direction of the normal air flow. Check to see that the screen forms a good seal around the edges of the air cleaner housing so no dirt can pass. If the screen is torn or clogged, or if it is seated improperly and cannot be repaired, replace it.

The PCV valve is in the right rocker arm (valve) cover on the V6 engines, in the intake manifold on the 4-cylinder engines, and in the rocker arm cover on the inline 6-cylinder engines.

Heat Riser

The heat riser is a thermostatically operated valve in the exhaust manifold. It closes when the engine is cold, to direct hot exhaust gases to the intake manifold, in order to preheat the incoming fuel/air mixture. If it sticks closed, the result will be a rough idle after the engine warms up. If it sticks open, there will be frequent stalling during warm up, especially in cold and damp weather.

On the V6, the valve is between the exhaust manifold and the exhaust pipe. On inline 6-cylinder engines, it is an integral part of the exhaust manifold. The heat riser counterweight should move freely. If it sticks, apply Jeep Heat Valve Lubricant or something similar (engine cool) to the ends of the shaft. Sometimes rapping the end of the shaft sharply with a hammer (engine hot) will break it loose. If this fails, parts must be removed for repair or replacement.

Evaporative Canister

None of the 1945-70 Jeep models came equipped from the factory with an evaporative canister.

Battery

GENERAL MAINTENANCE

All batteries, regardless of type, should be carefully secured by a battery hold-down device. If this is not done, the battery terminals or casing may crack from stress applied to the battery during vehicle operation. A battery which is not secured may allow acid to leak out, making it discharge faster; such leaking corrosive acid can also eat away components under the hood. A battery that is not sealed must be checked periodically for electrolyte level. You cannot add water to a sealed maintenance-free battery (though not all maintenance-free batteries are sealed), but a sealed battery must also be checked for proper electrolyte level as indicated by the color of the built-in hydrometer "eye."

Keep the top of the battery clean, as a film of dirt can help completely discharge a battery that is not used for long periods. A solution of baking soda and water may be used for cleaning, but be careful to flush this off with clear water. DO

1-20 GENERAL INFORMATION AND MAINTENANCE

NOT let any of the solution into the filler holes. Baking soda neutralizes battery acid and will de-activate a battery cell.

※※CAUTION

Always use caution when working on or near the battery. Never allow a tool to bridge the gap between the negative and positive battery terminals. Also, be careful not to allow a tool to provide a ground between the positive cable/terminal and any metal component on the vehicle. Either of these conditions will cause a short circuit leading to sparks and possible personal injury.

Batteries in vehicles which are not operated on a regular basis can fall victim to parasitic loads (small current drains which are constantly drawing current from the battery). Normal parasitic loads may drain a battery on a vehicle that is in storage and not used for 6-8 weeks. Vehicles that have additional accessories such as a cellular phone, an alarm system or other devices that increase parasitic load may discharge a battery sooner. If the vehicle is to be stored for 6-8 weeks in a secure area and the alarm system, if present, is not necessary, the negative battery cable should be disconnected at the onset of storage to protect the battery charge.

Remember that constantly discharging and recharging will shorten battery life. Take care not to allow a battery to be needlessly discharged.

BATTERY FLUID

▶ See Figures 35, 36 and 37

※※CAUTION

Battery electrolyte contains sulfuric acid. If you should splash any on your skin or in your eyes, flush the affected area with plenty of clear water. If it lands in your eyes, get medical help immediately.

The fluid (sulfuric acid solution) contained in the battery cells will tell you many things about the condition of the battery. Because the cell plates must be kept submerged below the fluid level in order to operate, maintaining the fluid level is extremely important. And, because the specific gravity of the acid is an indication of electrical charge, testing the fluid can be an aid in determining if the battery must be replaced. A battery in a vehicle with a properly operating charging system should require little maintenance, but careful, periodic inspection should reveal problems before they leave you stranded.

Fluid Level

Check the battery electrolyte level at least once a month, or more often in hot weather or during periods of extended vehicle operation. On non-sealed batteries, the level can be checked either through the case on translucent batteries or by removing the cell caps on opaque-cased types. The electrolyte level in each cell should be kept filled to the split ring inside each cell, or the line marked on the outside of the case.

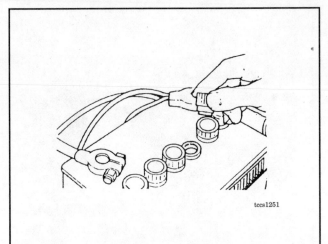

Fig. 35 On non-maintenance free batteries, the level can be checked through the case on translucent batteries; the cell caps must be removed on other models

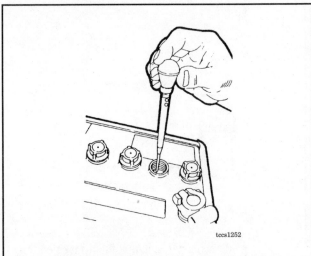

Fig. 36 Check the specific gravity of the battery's electrolyte with a hydrometer

If the level is low, add only distilled water through the opening until the level is correct. Each cell is separate from the others, so each must be checked and filled individually. Distilled water should be used, because the chemicals and minerals found in most drinking water are harmful to the battery and could significantly shorten its life.

If water is added in freezing weather, the vehicle should be driven several miles to allow the water to mix with the electrolyte. Otherwise, the battery could freeze.

Although some maintenance-free batteries have removable cell caps for access to the electrolyte, the electrolyte condition and level on all sealed maintenance-free batteries must be checked using the built-in hydrometer "eye." The exact type of eye varies between battery manufacturers, but most apply a sticker to the battery itself explaining the possible readings.

GENERAL INFORMATION AND MAINTENANCE

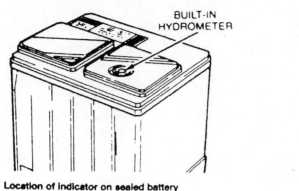

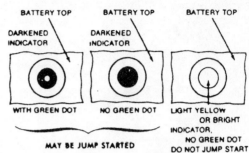

Fig. 37 A typical sealed (maintenance-free) battery with a built-in hydrometer — NOTE that the hydrometer eye may vary between battery manufacturers; always refer to the battery's label

When in doubt, refer to the battery manufacturer's instructions to interpret battery condition using the built-in hydrometer.

➡Although the readings from built-in hydrometers found in sealed batteries may vary, a green eye usually indicates a properly charged battery with sufficient fluid level. A dark eye is normally an indicator of a battery with sufficient fluid, but one which may be low in charge. And a light or yellow eye is usually an indication that electrolyte supply has dropped below the necessary level for battery (and hydrometer) operation. In this last case, sealed batteries with an insufficient electrolyte level must usually be discarded.

Specific Gravity

As stated earlier, the specific gravity of a battery's electrolyte level can be used as an indication of battery charge. At least once a year, check the specific gravity of the battery. It should be between 1.20 and 1.26 on the gravity scale. Most auto supply stores carry a variety of inexpensive battery testing hydrometers. These can be used on any non-sealed battery to test the specific gravity in each cell.

The battery testing hydrometer has a squeeze bulb at one end and a nozzle at the other. Battery electrolyte is sucked into the hydrometer until the float is lifted from its seat. The specific gravity is then read by noting the position of the float. If gravity is low in one or more cells, the battery should be slowly charged and checked again to see if the gravity has come up. Generally, if after charging, the specific gravity between any two cells varies more than 50 points (0.50), the battery should be replaced as it can no longer produce sufficient voltage to guarantee proper operation.

On sealed batteries, the built-in hydrometer is the only way of checking specific gravity. Again, check with your battery's manufacturer for proper interpretation of its built-in hydrometer readings.

CABLES

♦ See Figures 38, 39, 40, 41, 42 and 43

Once a year (or as necessary), the battery terminals and the cable clamps should be cleaned. Loosen the clamps and remove the cables, negative cable first. On batteries with posts on top, the use of a puller specially made for this purpose is recommended. These are inexpensive and available in most auto parts stores. Side terminal battery cables are secured with a small bolt.

Clean the cable clamps and the battery terminal with a wire brush, until all corrosion, grease, etc., is removed and the metal is shiny. It is especially important to clean the inside of the clamp (an old knife is useful here) thoroughly, since a small deposit of foreign material or oxidation there will prevent a sound electrical connection and inhibit either starting or charging. Special tools are available for cleaning these parts, one type for conventional top post batteries and another type for side terminal batteries.

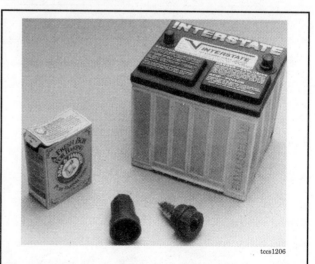

Fig. 38 Maintenance is performed with household items and with special tools like this post cleaner

1-22 GENERAL INFORMATION AND MAINTENANCE

Fig. 39 The underside of this special battery tool has a wire brush to clean post terminals

Fig. 40 Place the tool over the terminals and twist to clean the post

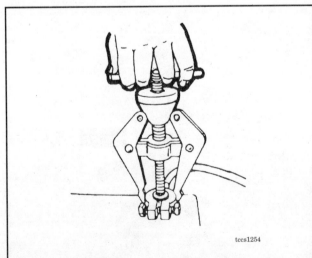

Fig. 41 A special tool is available to pull the clamp from the post

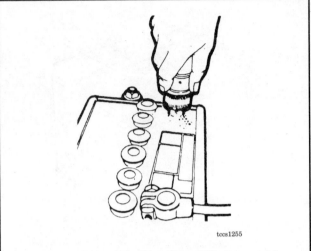

Fig. 42 Clean the battery terminals until the metal is shiny

Fig. 43 The cable ends should be cleaned as well

Before installing the cables, loosen the battery hold-down clamp or strap, remove the battery and check the battery tray. Clear it of any debris, and check it for soundness (the battery tray can be cleaned with a baking soda and water solution). Rust should be wire brushed away, and the metal given a couple coats of anti-rust paint. Install the battery and tighten the hold-down clamp or strap securely. Do not overtighten, as this can crack the battery case.

After the clamps and terminals are clean, reinstall the cables, negative cable last; DO NOT hammer the clamps onto post batteries. Tighten the clamps securely, but do not distort them. Give the clamps and terminals a thin external coating of grease after installation, to retard corrosion.

Check the cables at the same time that the terminals are cleaned. If the cable insulation is cracked or broken, or if the ends are frayed, the cable should be replaced with a new cable of the same length and gauge.

GENERAL INFORMATION AND MAINTENANCE

CHARGING

♦ See Figure 44

✱✱CAUTION

The chemical reaction which takes place in all batteries generates explosive hydrogen gas. A spark can cause the battery to explode and splash acid. To avoid serious personal injury, be sure there is proper ventilation and take appropriate fire safety precautions when connecting, disconnecting, or charging a battery and when using jumper cables.

A battery should be charged at a slow rate to keep the plates inside from getting too hot. However, if some maintenance-free batteries are allowed to discharge until they are almost "dead," they may have to be charged at a high rate to bring them back to "life." Always follow the charger manufacturer's instructions on charging the battery.

REPLACEMENT

When it becomes necessary to replace the battery, select one with a rating equal to or greater than the battery originally installed. Deterioration and just plain aging of the battery cables, starter motor, and associated wires makes the battery's job harder in successive years. The slow increase in electrical resistance over time makes it prudent to install a new battery with a greater capacity than the old.

Battery State of Charge at Room Temperature

Specific Gravity Reading	Charged Condition
1.260–1.280	Fully Charged
1.230–1.250	¾ Charged
1.200–1.220	½ Charged
1.170–1.190	¼ Charged
1.140–1.160	Almost no Charge
1.110–1.130	No Charge

Fig. 44 The specific gravity measured by a hydrometer will indicate the level of charge currently in the battery

Windshield Wipers

ELEMENT (REFILL) CARE AND REPLACEMENT

♦ See Figures 45, 46, 47, 48, 49, 50, 51, 52, 53, 54, 55 and 56

For maximum effectiveness and longest element life, the windshield and wiper blades should be kept clean. Dirt, tree sap, road tar and so on will cause streaking, smearing and blade deterioration if left on the glass. It is advisable to wash the windshield carefully with a commercial glass cleaner at least once a month. Wipe off the rubber blades with the wet rag afterwards. Do not attempt to move wipers across the windshield by hand; damage to the motor and drive mechanism will result.

To inspect and/or replace the wiper blade elements, place the wiper switch in the **LOW** speed position and the ignition switch in the **ACC** position. When the wiper blades are ap-

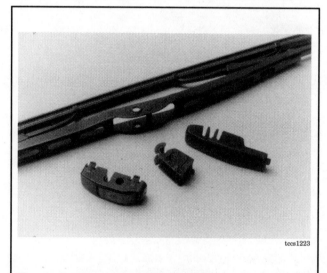

Fig. 45 Bosch® wiper blade and fit kit

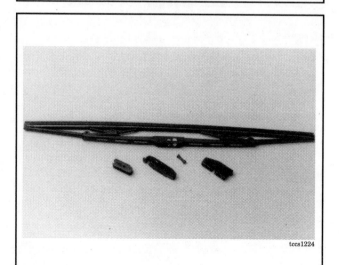

Fig. 46 Lexor® wiper blade and fit kit

1-24 GENERAL INFORMATION AND MAINTENANCE

Fig. 47 Pylon® wiper blade and adaptor

Fig. 48 Trico® wiper blade and fit kit

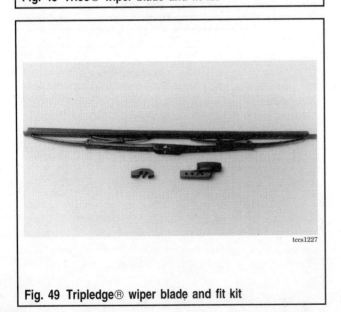

Fig. 49 Tripledge® wiper blade and fit kit

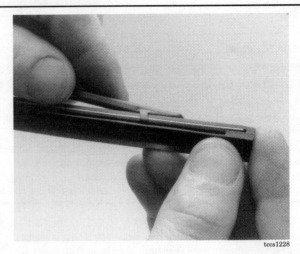

Fig. 50 To remove and install a Lexor® wiper blade refill, slip out the old insert and slide in a new one

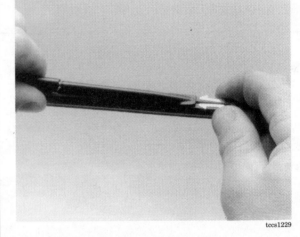

Fig. 51 On Pylon® inserts, the clip at the end has to be removed prior to sliding the insert off

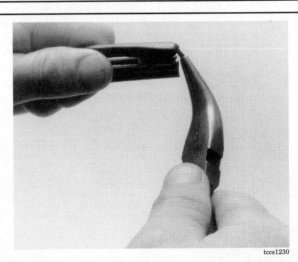

Fig. 52 On Trico® wiper blades, the tab at the end of the blade must be turned up . . .

GENERAL INFORMATION AND MAINTENANCE 1-25

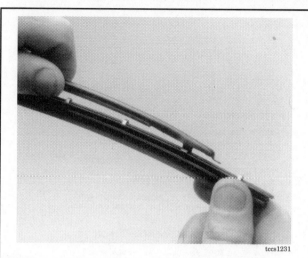

Fig. 53 ... then the insert can be removed. After installing the replacement insert, bend the tab back

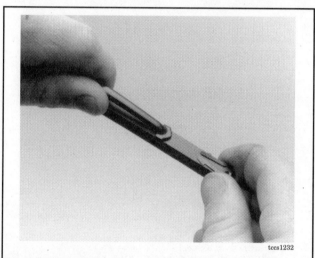

Fig. 54 The Tripledge® wiper blade insert is removed and installed using a securing clip

proximately vertical on the windshield, turn the ignition switch to **OFF**.

Examine the wiper blade elements. If they are found to be cracked, broken or torn, they should be replaced immediately. Replacement intervals will vary with usage, although ozone deterioration usually limits element life to about one year. If the wiper pattern is smeared or streaked, or if the blade chatters across the glass, the elements should be replaced. It is easiest and most sensible to replace the elements in pairs.

If your vehicle is equipped with aftermarket blades, there are several different types of refills and your vehicle might have any kind. Aftermarket blades and arms rarely use the exact same type blade or refill as the original equipment. Here are some typical aftermarket blades; not all may be available for your vehicle:

The Anco® type uses a release button that is pushed down to allow the refill to slide out of the yoke jaws. The new refill slides back into the frame and locks in place.

Some Trico® refills are removed by locating where the metal backing strip or the refill is wider. Insert a small screwdriver blade between the frame and metal backing strip. Press down to release the refill from the retaining tab.

Other types of Trico® refills have two metal tabs which are unlocked by squeezing them together. The rubber filler can then be withdrawn from the frame jaws. A new refill is installed by inserting the refill into the front frame jaws and sliding it rearward to engage the remaining frame jaws. There are usually four jaws; be certain when installing that the refill is engaged in all of them. At the end of its travel, the tabs will lock into place on the front jaws of the wiper blade frame.

Another type of refill is made from polycarbonate. The refill has a simple locking device at one end which flexes downward out of the groove into which the jaws of the holder fit, allowing easy release. By sliding the new refill through all the jaws and pushing through the slight resistance when it reaches the end of its travel, the refill will lock into position.

To replace the Tridon® refill, it is necessary to remove the wiper blade. This refill has a plastic backing strip with a notch about 1 in. (25mm) from the end. Hold the blade (frame) on a hard surface so that the frame is tightly bowed. Grip the tip of the backing strip and pull up while twisting counterclockwise. The backing strip will snap out of the retaining tab. Do this for the remaining tabs until the refill is free of the blade. The length of these refills is molded into the end and they should be replaced with identical types.

Regardless of the type of refill used, be sure to follow the part manufacturer's instructions closely. Make sure that all of the frame jaws are engaged as the refill is pushed into place and locked. If the metal blade holder and frame are allowed to touch the glass during wiper operation, the glass will be scratched.

1-26 GENERAL INFORMATION AND MAINTENANCE

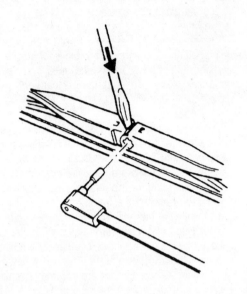

BLADE REPLACEMENT

1. CYCLE ARM AND BLADE ASSEMBLY TO UP POSITION ON THE WINDSHIELD WHERE REMOVAL OF BLADE ASSEMBLY CAN BE PERFORMED WITHOUT DIFFICULTY. TURN IGNITION KEY OFF AT DESIRED POSITION.

2. TO REMOVE BLADE ASSEMBLY, INSERT SCREWDRIVER IN SLOT, PUSH DOWN ON SPRING LOCK AND PULL BLADE ASSEMBLY FROM PIN (VIEW A)

3. TO INSTALL, PUSH THE BLADE ASSEMBLY ON THE PIN SO THAT THE SPRING LOCK ENGAGES THE PIN (VIEW A). BE SURE THE BLADE ASSEMBLY IS SECURELY ATTACHED TO PIN

VIEW A

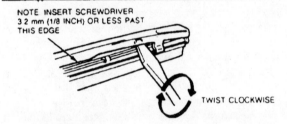

NOTE INSERT SCREWDRIVER 3.2 mm (1/8 INCH) OR LESS PAST THIS EDGE

TWIST CLOCKWISE

ELEMENT REPLACEMENT

1. INSERT SCREWDRIVER BETWEEN THE EDGE OF THE SUPER STRUCTURE AND THE BLADE BACKING DRIP (VIEW B) TWIST SCREWDRIVER SLOWLY UNTIL ELEMENT CLEARS ONE SIDE OF THE SUPER STRUCTURE CLAW

2. SLIDE THE ELEMENT INTO THE SUPER STRUCTURE CLAWS

VIEW B

4. INSERT ELEMENT INTO ONE SIDE OF THE END CLAWS (VIEW D) AND WITH A ROCKING MOTION PUSH ELEMENT UPWARD UNTIL IT SNAPS IN (VIEW E)

VIEW D

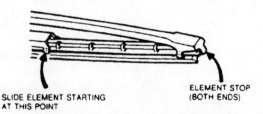

SLIDE ELEMENT STARTING AT THIS POINT

ELEMENT STOP (BOTH ENDS)

3. SLIDE THE ELEMENT INTO THE SUPER STRUCTURE CLAWS, STARTING WITH SECOND SET FROM EITHER END (VIEW C) AND CONTINUE TO SLIDE THE BLADE ELEMENT INTO ALL THE SUPER STRUCTURE CLAWS TO THE ELEMENT STOP (VIEW C)

VIEW C

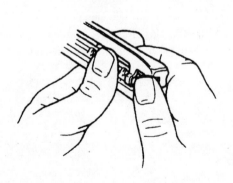

VIEW E

Fig. 55 Trico® wiper blade insert (element) replacement

GENERAL INFORMATION AND MAINTENANCE   1-27

BLADE REPLACEMENT

1. Cycle arm and blade assembly to a position on the windshield where removal of blade assembly can be performed without difficulty. Turn ignition key off at desired position.
2. To remove blade assembly from wiper arm, pull up on spring lock and pull blade assembly from pin (View A). Be sure spring lock is not pulled excessively or it will become distorted.
3. To install, push the blade assembly onto the pin so that the spring lock engages the pin (View A). Be sure the blade assembly is securely attached to pin.

ELEMENT REPLACEMENT

1. In the plastic backing strip which is part of the rubber blade assembly, there is an 11.11mm (7/16 inch) long notch located approximately one inch from either end. Locate either notch.
2. Place the frame of the wiper blade assembly on a firm surface with either notched end of the backing strip visible.
3. Grasp the frame portion of the wiper blade assembly and push down until the blade assembly is tightly bowed.
4. With the blade assembly in the bowed position, grasp the tip of the backing strip firmly, pulling up and twisting C.C.W. at the same time. The backing strip will then snap out of the retaining tab on the end of the frame.
5. Lift the wiper blade assembly from the surface and slide the backing strip down the frame until the notch lines up with the next retaining tab, twist slightly, and the backing strip will snap out. Continue this operation with the remaining tabs until the blade element is completely detached from the frame.
6. To install blade element, reverse the above procedure, making sure all six (6) tabs are locked to the backing strip before installing blade to wiper arm.

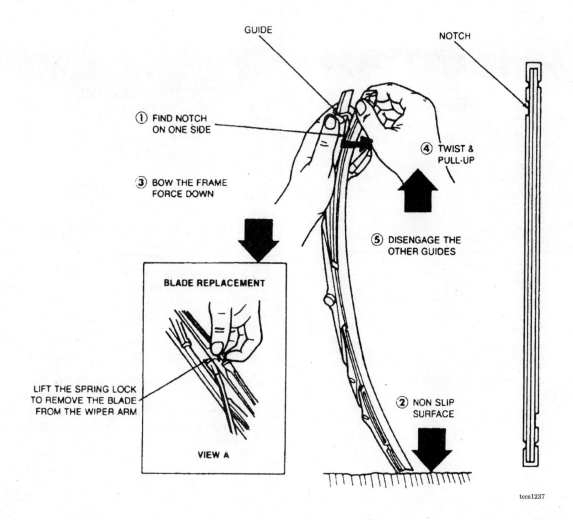

Fig. 56 Tridon® wiper blade insert (element) replacement

1-28 GENERAL INFORMATION AND MAINTENANCE

Belts

INSPECTION

▶ See Figures 57, 58, 59 and 60

The belts which drive the engine accessories such as the alternator, the air pump, power steering pump, air conditioning compressor and water pump are of either the V-belt design or flat, serpentine design. Older belts show wear and damage readily, since their basic design was a belt with a rubber casing. As the casing wore, cracks and fibers were readily apparent. Newer design, caseless belts do not show wear as readily, and many untrained people cannot distinguish between a good, serviceable belt and one that is worn to the point of failure.

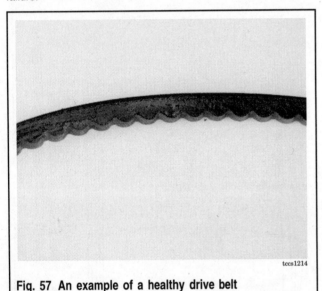

Fig. 57 An example of a healthy drive belt

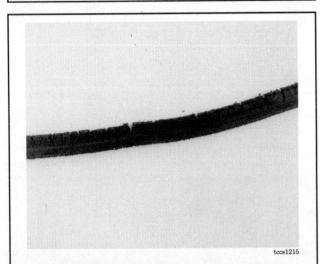

Fig. 58 Deep cracks in this belt will cause flex, building up heat that will eventually lead to belt failure

Fig. 59 The cover of this belt is worn, exposing the critical reinforcing cords to excessive wear

Fig. 60 Installing too wide a belt can result in serious belt wear and/or breakage

It is a good idea, therefore, to visually inspect the belts regularly and replace them, routinely, every two to three years.

ADJUSTING

▶ See Figures 61 and 62

Belts are normally adjusted by loosening the bolts of the accessory being driven and moving that accessory on its pivot points until the proper tension is applied to the belt. The accessory is held in this position while the bolts are tightened. To determine proper belt tension, you can purchase a belt tension gauge or simply use the deflection method. To determine deflection, press inward on the belt at the mid-point of its longest straight run. The belt should deflect (move inward) 3/8-1/2 in. (9.5-12.7mm). Some long V-belts and most serpentine belts have idler pulleys which are used for adjusting purposes. Just loosen the idler pulley and move it to take up tension on the belt.

GENERAL INFORMATION AND MAINTENANCE 1-29

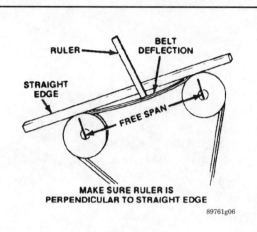

Fig. 61 Accessory drive belt tension can be measured by the amount of deflection present between two of the belt pulleys

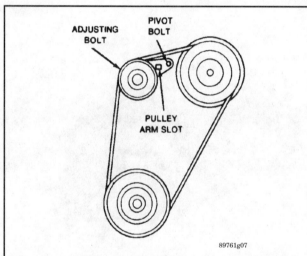

Fig. 62 Some accessory drive pulleys are equipped with a rectangular slot to aid in tensioning the drive belt

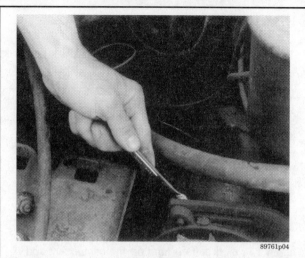

Fig. 63 To remove the belts, first loosen the mounting and adjusting bolts slightly . . .

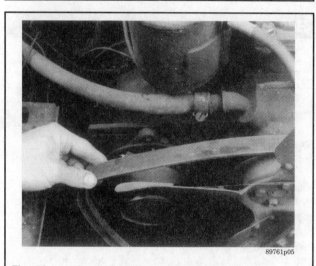

Fig. 64 . . . then push the component toward the engine and slip the belt off of the drive pulley

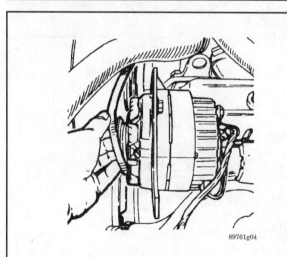

Fig. 65 Position the new belt over all applicable pulleys . . .

REMOVAL & INSTALLATION

♦ See Figures 63, 64, 65 and 66

To remove a drive belt, simply loosen the accessory being driven and move it on its pivot point to free the belt. Then, remove the belt. If an idler pulley is used, it is often necessary, only, to loosen the idler pulley to provide enough slack the remove the belt.

It is important to note, however, that on engines with many driven accessories, several or all of the belts may have to be removed to get at the one to be replaced.

1-30 GENERAL INFORMATION AND MAINTENANCE

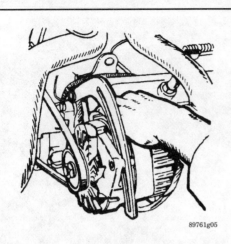

Fig. 66 . . . then pull outward on the component and tighten the bolts — make sure to properly tension the drive belt

Fig. 68 A hose clamp that is too tight can cause older hoses to separate and tear on either side of the clamp

Hoses

INSPECTION

▶ See Figures 67, 68, 69 and 70

Upper and lower radiator hoses along with the heater hoses should be checked for deterioration, leaks and loose hose clamps at least every 15,000 miles (24,000 km). It is also wise to check the hoses periodically in early spring and at the beginning of the fall or winter when you are performing other maintenance. A quick visual inspection could discover a weakened hose which might have left you stranded if it had remained unrepaired.

Whenever you are checking the hoses, make sure the engine and cooling system are cold. Visually inspect for cracking, rotting or collapsed hoses, and replace as necessary. Run your hand along the length of the hose. If a weak or swollen spot is noted when squeezing the hose wall, the hose should be replaced.

Fig. 69 A soft spongy hose (identifiable by the swollen section) will eventually burst and should be replaced

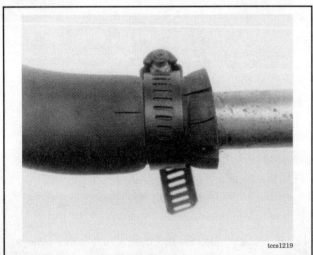

Fig. 67 The cracks developing along this hose are a result of age-related hardening

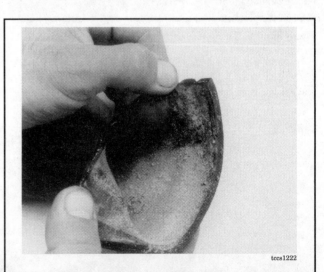

Fig. 70 Hoses are likely to deteriorate from the inside if the cooling system is not periodically flushed

GENERAL INFORMATION AND MAINTENANCE   1-31

REMOVAL & INSTALLATION

1. Remove the radiator pressure cap.

> **✳✳CAUTION**
>
> Never remove the pressure cap while the engine is running, or personal injury from scalding hot coolant or steam may result. If possible, wait until the engine has cooled to remove the pressure cap. If this is not possible, wrap a thick cloth around the pressure cap and turn it slowly to the stop. Step back while the pressure is released from the cooling system. When you are sure all the pressure has been released, use the cloth to turn and remove the cap.

2. Position a clean container under the radiator and/or engine draincock or plug, then open the drain and allow the cooling system to drain to an appropriate level. For some upper hoses, only a little coolant must be drained. To remove hoses positioned lower on the engine, such as a lower radiator hose, the entire cooling system must be emptied.

> **✳✳CAUTION**
>
> When draining coolant, keep in mind that cats and dogs are attracted by ethylene glycol antifreeze, and are quite likely to drink any that is left in an uncovered container or in puddles on the ground. This will prove fatal in sufficient quantity. Always drain coolant into a sealable container. Coolant may be reused unless it is contaminated or several years old.

3. Loosen the hose clamps at each end of the hose requiring replacement. Clamps are usually either of the spring tension type (which require pliers to squeeze the tabs and loosen) or of the screw tension type (which require screw or hex drivers to loosen). Pull the clamps back on the hose away from the connection.

4. Twist, pull and slide the hose off the fitting, taking care not to damage the neck of the component from which the hose is being removed.

➡ If the hose is stuck at the connection, do not try to insert a screwdriver or other sharp tool under the hose end in an effort to free it, as the connection and/or hose may become damaged. Heater connections especially may be easily damaged by such a procedure. If the hose is to be replaced, use a single-edged razor blade to make a slice along the portion of the hose which is stuck on the connection, perpendicular to the end of the hose. Do not cut deep so as to prevent damaging the connection. The hose can then be peeled from the connection and discarded.

5. Clean both hose mounting connections. Inspect the condition of the hose clamps and replace them, if necessary.

To install:

6. Dip the ends of the new hose into clean engine coolant to ease installation.

7. Slide the clamps over the replacement hose, then slide the hose ends over the connections into position.

8. Position and secure the clamps at least ¼ in. (6.35mm) from the ends of the hose. Make sure they are located beyond the raised bead of the connector.

9. Close the radiator or engine drains and properly refill the cooling system with the clean, drained engine coolant or a suitable mixture of ethylene glycol (or other suitable) coolant and water.

10. If available, install a pressure tester and check for leaks. If a pressure tester is not available, run the engine until normal operating temperature is reached (allowing the system to naturally pressurize), then check for leaks.

> **✳✳CAUTION**
>
> If you are checking for leaks with the system at normal operating temperature, BE EXTREMELY CAREFUL not to touch any moving or hot engine parts. Once temperature has been reached, shut the engine OFF, and check for leaks around the hose fittings and connections which were removed earlier.

Front Hub and Wheel Bearings

REMOVAL, REPACKING AND INSTALLATION

Non-Locking Hubs

➡ Sodium-based grease is not compatible with lithium-based grease. Read the package labels and be careful not to mix the two types. If there is any doubt as to the type of grease used, completely clean the old grease from the bearing and hub before replacing.

Before handling the bearings, there are a few things that you should remember to do and not to do.

Remember to DO the following:

- Remove all outside dirt from the housing before exposing the bearing.
- Treat a used bearing as gently as you would a new one.
- Work with clean tools in clean surroundings.
- Use clean, dry canvas gloves, or at least clean, dry hands.
- Clean solvents and flushing fluids are a must.
- Use clean paper when laying out the bearings to dry.
- Protect disassembled bearings from rust and dirt. Cover them up.
- Use clean rags to wipe bearings.
- Keep the bearings in oil-proof paper when they are to be stored or are not in use.
- Clean the inside of the housing before replacing the bearing.

Do NOT do the following:

- Don't work in dirty surroundings.
- Don't use dirty, chipped or damaged tools.
- Try not to work on wooden work benches or use wooden mallets.
- Don't handle bearings with dirty or moist hands.
- Do not use gasoline for cleaning. Use a safe solvent.
- Do not spin-dry bearings with compressed air. They will be damaged.
- Do not spin dirty bearings.

1-32 GENERAL INFORMATION AND MAINTENANCE

- Avoid using cotton waste or dirty cloths to wipe bearings.
- Try not to scratch or nick bearing surfaces.
- Do not allow the bearing to come in contact with dirt or rust at any time.

4-WHEEL DRIVE VEHICLES

▶ See Figures 71, 72, 73, 74, 75, 76, 77 and 78

1. Raise the front of the vehicle and place jackstands under the axle.
2. Remove the wheel.
3. Remove the front hub grease cap and driving hub snapring. On models equipped with locking hubs, remove the retainer knob hub ring, agitator knob, snapring, outer clutch retaining ring and actuating cam body.
4. Remove the splined driving hub and the pressure spring. This may require slight prying with a screwdriver.
5. Remove the external snapring from the spindle shaft and remove the hub shaft drive gear.
6. Remove the wheel bearing locknut, lockring, adjusting nut and inner lockring.
7. On vehicles with drum brakes, remove the hub and drum assembly. This may require that the brake adjusting wheel be backed off a few turns. The outer wheel bearing and spring retainer will come off with the hub.
8. On vehicles with disc brakes, remove the caliper and suspend it out of the way by hanging it from a suspension or frame member with a length of wire. Do not disconnect the brake hose, and be careful to avoid stretching the hose. Remove the rotor and hub assembly. The outer wheel bearing and, on vehicles with locking hubs, the spring collar, will come off with the hub.
9. Carefully drive out the inner bearing and seal from the hub, using a wood block.
10. Inspect the bearing races for excessive wear, pitting or grooves. If they are cracked or grooved, or if pitting and excess wear is present, drive them out with a drift or punch.

Fig. 72 After removing the wheel, loosen the hub nut

Fig. 73 Remove the hub nut and flat washer . . .

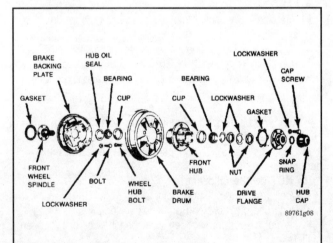

Fig. 71 Exploded view of the front wheel hub and bearings — 4WD models with drum brakes

Fig. 74 . . . followed by the bearing adjusting nut . . .

GENERAL INFORMATION AND MAINTENANCE 1-33

Fig. 75 . . . and the adjusting nut's flat washer

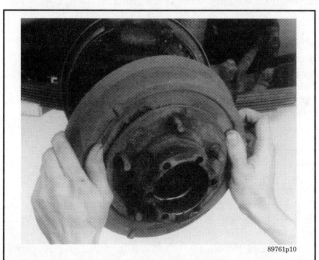

Fig. 76 Remove the outer bearing, then pull the drum off of the axle shaft

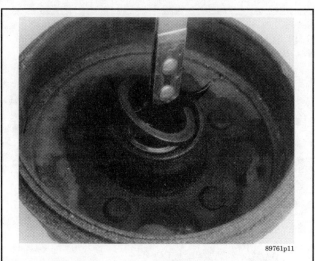

Fig. 77 Use a seal remover to extract the old hub's inner seal

Fig. 78 Once the seal is pried out, the inner bearing can be removed

11. Check the bearing for excess wear, pitting or cracks, or excess looseness.

➡If it is necessary to replace either the bearing or the race, replace both. Never replace just a bearing or a race. These parts wear in a mating pattern. If just one is replaced, premature failure of the new part will result.

12. If the old parts are retained, thoroughly clean them in a safe solvent and allow them to dry on a clean towel. Never spin dry them with compressed air.
13. On vehicles with drum brakes, cover the spindle with a cloth and thoroughly brush all dirt from the brakes. Never blow the dirt off the brakes, due to the presence of asbestos in the dirt, which is harmful to your health when inhaled.
14. Remove the cloth and thoroughly clean the spindle.
15. Thoroughly clean the inside of the hub.
16. Pack the inside of the hub with EP wheel bearing grease. Add grease to the hub until it is flush with the inside diameter of the bearing cup.
17. Pack the bearing with the same grease. A needle-shaped wheel bearing packer is best for this operation. If one is not available, place a large amount of grease in the palm of your hand and slide the edge of the bearing cage through the grease to pick up as much as possible, then work the grease in as best you can with your fingers.
18. If a new race is being installed, very carefully drive it into position until it bottoms all around, using a brass drift. Be careful to avoid scratching the surface.
19. Place the inner bearing in the race and install a new grease seal.
20. Place the hub assembly onto the spindle and install the inner lockring and outer bearing. Install the wheel bearing nut and torque it to 50 ft. lbs. (68 Nm) while turning the wheel back and forth to seat the bearings. Back off the nut about 1/4 turn (90°) maximum.
21. Install the lockwasher with the tab aligned with the keyway in the spindle and turn the inner wheel bearing adjusting nut until the peg on the nut engages the nearest hole in the lockwasher.
22. Install the outer locknut and torque it to 50 ft. lbs. (68 Nm).

1-34 GENERAL INFORMATION AND MAINTENANCE

23. Install the spring collar, drive flange, snapring, pressure spring, and hub cap.
24. Install the caliper over the rotor.

2-WHEEL DRIVE VEHICLES

◆ See Figure 79

1. Raise the front of the vehicle and place jackstands under the axle.
2. Remove the wheel.
3. Remove the front hub grease cap.
4. Remove the cotter pin and locknut.
5. Pull out on the brake drum slightly to free the outer bearing and remove the bearing.
6. Remove the drum and hub.
7. Using an awl, puncture the inner seal and pry it out. Discard the seal.
8. Remove the inner bearing.
9. Inspect the bearing races for excessive wear, pitting or grooves. If they are cracked or grooved, or if pitting and excess wear is present, drive them out with a drift or punch.
10. Check the bearing for excess wear, pitting or cracks, or excess looseness.

➡ **If it is necessary to replace either the bearing or the race, replace both. Never replace just a bearing or a race. These parts wear in a mating pattern. If just one is replaced, premature failure of the new part will result.**

11. If the old parts are retained, thoroughly clean them in a safe solvent and allow them to dry on a clean towel. Never spin dry them with compressed air.
12. On vehicles with drum brakes, cover the spindle with a cloth and thoroughly brush all dirt from the brakes. Never blow the dirt off the brakes, due to the presence of asbestos in the dirt, which is harmful to your health when inhaled.
13. Remove the cloth and thoroughly clean the spindle.
14. Thoroughly clean the inside of the hub.
15. Pack the inside of the hub with EP wheel bearing grease. Add grease to the hub until it is flush with the inside diameter of the bearing cup.
16. Pack the bearing with the same grease. A needle-shaped wheel bearing packer is best for this operation. If one is not available, place a large amount of grease in the palm of your hand and slide the edge of the bearing cage through the grease to pick up as much as possible, then work the grease in as best you can with your fingers.
17. If a new race is being installed, very carefully drive it into position until it bottoms all around, using a brass drift. Be careful to avoid scratching the surface.
18. Place the inner bearing in the race and install a new grease seal.
19. Place the hub assembly onto the spindle and install the outer bearing. Install the wheel bearing nut and tighten it until the hub binds while turning. Back off the nut about $1/6$-$1/4$ turn to free the bearings. Install a new cotter pin.
20. Install the grease cap.
21. Install the wheel.
22. Lower the vehicle and install the hub cap.

Locking Hubs

Jeep vehicles through 1970 were not factory equipped with locking hubs. Locking hubs could often be purchased as a dealer installed option, or as aftermarket components.

The following is a general service procedure that should apply to all types. Locking hubs should be lubricated at least once a year and as soon as possible if running for extended periods submerged in water. The same type of grease should be used in the locking hubs as is used on the wheel bearings. EP lithium based chassis lube is preferred.

1. Remove the lockout screws and washers.
2. Remove the hub ring and knob.
3. Remove the internal snapring from the groove in the hub.
4. Remove the cam body ring and clutch retainer from the hub and disassemble the parts.
5. Remove the axle shaft snapring. It may be necessary to push in on the gear and pull out on the axle with a bolt to make the snapring removal easier.
6. Remove the drive gear and clutch gear. A slight rocking of the hub may make them slide out easier.
7. Remove the coil spring and spring retainer.
8. Clean all the components in a safe solvent. Wipe out the hub with a clean cloth.

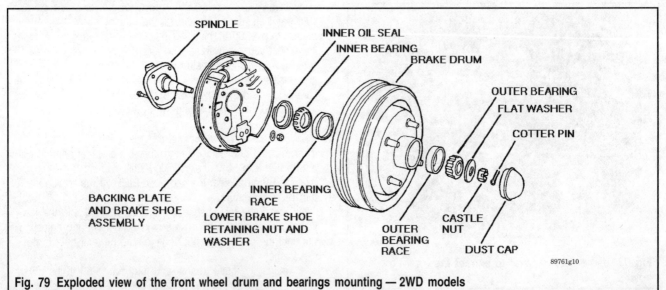

Fig. 79 Exploded view of the front wheel drum and bearings mounting — 2WD models

GENERAL INFORMATION AND MAINTENANCE

9. Grease the inside of the hub liberally.
10. Install the spring retainer ring with the undercut area facing inwards. Be sure it seats against the bearing.
11. Install the coil spring with the large end going in first.
12. Install the axle shaft sleeve and ring and the inner clutch ring with the teeth of both components meshed together in a locked position. It may be necessary to rock the hub to mesh the splines of the axle with those of the axle shaft sleeve and ring. Keep the two gears locked in position.
13. Install the axle shaft snapring. Push in on the gear and pull out on the axle with a bolt to allow the snapring to go into the groove.
14. Install the actuating cam body ring into the outer clutch retaining ring and install them in the hub.
15. Install the internal snapring.
16. Apply a small amount of Lubriplate® grease to the ears of the cam.
17. Assemble the knob in the hub ring and assemble them to the axle with the knob in the locked position. Tighten the screws and washers evenly and alternately, making sure the retainer ring is not cocked in the hub.
18. Torque the screws to 40 inch lbs. (4.5 Nm).

Tires and Wheels

Inspect the tire treads for cuts, bruises and other damage. Check the air valves to be sure that they are tight. Replace any missing valve caps.

The tires should be checked frequently for proper air pressure. A chart in the glove compartment or on the driver's door pillar gives the recommended inflation pressure. Pressures can increase as much as 6 psi due to heat buildup. It is a good idea to have your own accurate gauge, and to check pressures weekly. Not all gauges on service station air pumps can be trusted.

Inspect tires for uneven wear that might indicate the need for front end alignment or tire rotation. Tires should be replaced when a tread wear indicator appears as a solid band across the tread.

When you buy new tires, give some thought to these points, especially if you are switching to larger tires or to another profile series (50, 60, 70, 78):

1. All four tires should be the same. Four wheel drive requires that all tires be the same size, type, and tread pattern to provide even traction on loose surfaces, to prevent driveline bind when conventional part time four wheel drive is used, and to prevent excessive wear on the center differential with full time four wheel drive.
2. The wheels must be the correct width for the tire. Tire dealers have charts of tire and rim compatibility. A mismatch can cause sloppy handling and rapid tread wear. The old rule of thumb is that the tread width should match the rim width (inside bead to inside bead) within an inch. For radial tires, the rim width should be 80% or less of the tire (not tread) width.
3. The height (mounted diameter) of the new tires can greatly change speedometer accuracy, engine speed at a given road speed, fuel mileage, acceleration, and ground clearance. Tire makers furnish full measurement specifications. Speedometer drive gears are available from Jeep parts for correction.

➡**Dimensions of tires marked the same size may vary significantly, even among tires from the same maker.**

4. The spare tire should be usable, at least for low speed operation, with the new tires. You will probably have to remove the side mounted spare for clearance.
5. There shouldn't be any body interference when loaded, on bumps, or in turning.

The only sure way to avoid problems with these points is to stick to tire and wheel sizes available as factory options.

Common sense and good driving habits will afford maximum tire life. Fast starts, sudden stops and hard cornering are hard on tires and will shorten their useful life span. Make sure that you don't overload the vehicle or run with incorrect pressure in the tires. Both of these practices will increase tread wear.

➡**For optimum tire life, keep the tires properly inflated, rotate them often and have the wheel alignment checked periodically.**

Inspect your tires frequently. Be especially careful to watch for bubbles in the tread or sidewall, deep cuts or under-inflation. Replace any tires with bubbles in the sidewall. If cuts are so deep that they penetrate to the cords, discard the tire. Any cut in the sidewall of a radial tire renders it unsafe. Also look for uneven tread wear patterns that may indicate the front end is out of alignment or that the tires are out of balance.

TIRE ROTATION

▶ See Figures 80 and 81

Tires must be rotated periodically to equalize wear patterns that vary with a tire's position on the vehicle. Tires will also wear in an uneven way as the front steering/suspension system wears to the point where the alignment should be reset.

Rotating the tires will ensure maximum life for the tires as a set, so you will not have to discard a tire early due to wear on only part of the tread. Regular rotation is required to equalize wear.

When rotating "unidirectional tires," make sure that they always roll in the same direction. This means that a tire used on the left side of the vehicle must not be switched to the right side and vice-versa. Such tires should only be rotated front-to-rear or rear-to-front, while always remaining on the same side of the vehicle. These tires are marked on the sidewall as to the direction of rotation; observe the marks when reinstalling the tire(s).

Some styled or "mag" wheels may have different offsets front to rear. In these cases, the rear wheels must not be used up front and vice-versa. Furthermore, if these wheels are equipped with unidirectional tires, they cannot be rotated unless the tire is remounted for the proper direction of rotation.

➡**The compact or space-saver spare is strictly for emergency use. It must never be included in the tire rotation or placed on the vehicle for everyday use.**

1-36 GENERAL INFORMATION AND MAINTENANCE

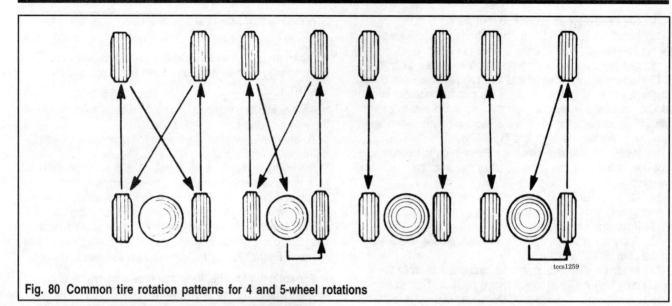

Fig. 80 Common tire rotation patterns for 4 and 5-wheel rotations

Fig. 81 Unidirectional tires are identifiable by sidewall arrows and/or the word "rotation"

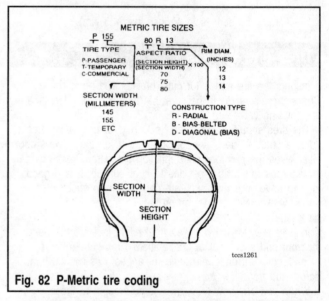

Fig. 82 P-Metric tire coding

TIRE DESIGN

▶ See Figure 82

For maximum satisfaction, tires should be used in sets of four. Mixing of different types (radial, bias-belted, fiberglass belted) must be avoided. In most cases, the vehicle manufacturer has designated a type of tire on which the vehicle will perform best. Your first choice when replacing tires should be to use the same type of tire that the manufacturer recommends.

When radial tires are used, tire sizes and wheel diameters should be selected to maintain ground clearance and tire load capacity equivalent to the original specified tire. Radial tires should always be used in sets of four.

✹✹CAUTION

Radial tires should never be used on only the front axle.

When selecting tires, pay attention to the original size as marked on the tire. Most tires are described using an industry size code sometimes referred to as P-Metric. This allows the exact identification of the tire specifications, regardless of the manufacturer. If selecting a different tire size or brand, remember to check the installed tire for any sign of interference with the body or suspension while the vehicle is stopping, turning sharply or heavily loaded.

Snow Tires

Good radial tires can produce a big advantage in slippery weather, but in snow, a street radial tire does not have sufficient tread to provide traction and control. The small grooves of a street tire quickly pack with snow and the tire behaves like a billiard ball on a marble floor. The more open, chunky tread of a snow tire will self-clean as the tire turns, providing much better grip on snowy surfaces.

To satisfy municipalities requiring snow tires during weather emergencies, most snow tires carry either an M + S designation after the tire size stamped on the sidewall, or the designa-

GENERAL INFORMATION AND MAINTENANCE

tion "all-season." In general, no change in tire size is necessary when buying snow tires.

Most manufacturers strongly recommend the use of 4 snow tires on their vehicles for reasons of stability. If snow tires are fitted only to the drive wheels, the opposite end of the vehicle may become very unstable when braking or turning on slippery surfaces. This instability can lead to unpleasant endings if the driver can't counteract the slide in time.

Note that snow tires, whether 2 or 4, will affect vehicle handling in all non-snow situations. The stiffer, heavier snow tires will noticeably change the turning and braking characteristics of the vehicle. Once the snow tires are installed, you must re-learn the behavior of the vehicle and drive accordingly.

➡ **Consider buying extra wheels on which to mount the snow tires. Once done, the "snow wheels" can be installed and removed as needed. This eliminates the potential damage to tires or wheels from seasonal removal and installation. Even if your vehicle has styled wheels, see if inexpensive steel wheels are available. Although the look of the vehicle will change, the expensive wheels will be protected from salt, curb hits and pothole damage.**

TIRE STORAGE

If they are mounted on wheels, store the tires at proper inflation pressure. All tires should be kept in a cool, dry place. If they are stored in the garage or basement, do not let them stand on a concrete floor; set them on strips of wood, a mat or a large stack of newspaper. Keeping them away from direct moisture is of paramount importance. Tires should not be stored upright, but in a flat position.

INFLATION & INSPECTION

♦ See Figures 83, 84, 85, 86, 87, 88, 89 and 90

The importance of proper tire inflation cannot be overemphasized. A tire employs air as part of its structure. It is designed around the supporting strength of the air at a specified pres-

Fig. 84 Tires with deep cuts, or cuts which show bulging should be replaced immediately

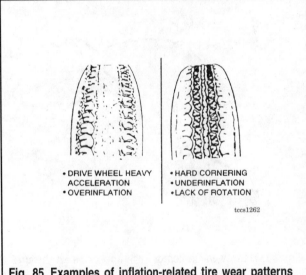
Fig. 85 Examples of inflation-related tire wear patterns

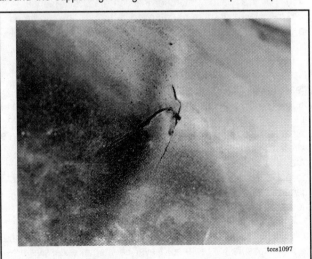
Fig. 83 Tires should be checked frequently for any sign of puncture or damage

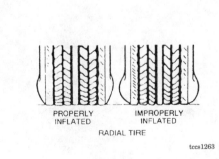
Fig. 86 Radial tires have a characteristic sidewall bulge; don't try to measure pressure by looking at the tire. Use a quality air pressure gauge

1-38 GENERAL INFORMATION AND MAINTENANCE

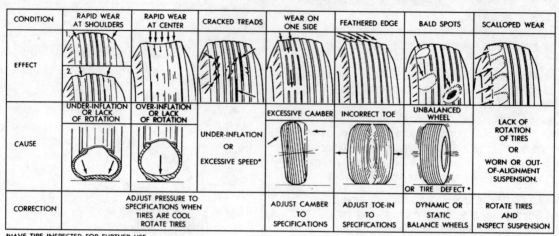

Fig. 87 Common tire wear patterns and causes

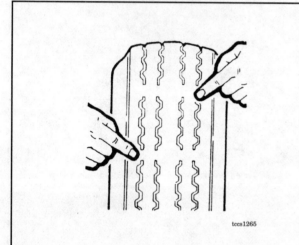

Fig. 88 Tread wear indicators will appear when the tire is worn

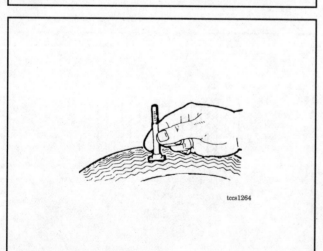

Fig. 89 Accurate tread depth indicators are inexpensive and handy

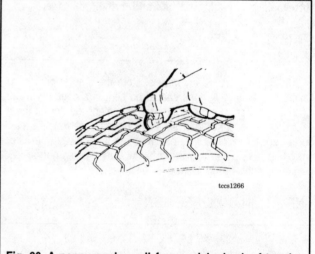

Fig. 90 A penny works well for a quick check of tread depth

sure. For this reason, improper inflation drastically reduces the tires's ability to perform as intended. A tire will lose some air in day-to-day use; having to add a few pounds of air periodically is not necessarily a sign of a leaking tire.

Two items should be a permanent fixture in every glove compartment: an accurate tire pressure gauge and a tread depth gauge. Check the tire pressure (including the spare) regularly with a pocket type gauge. Too often, the gauge on the end of the air hose at your corner garage is not accurate because it suffers too much abuse. Always check tire pressure when the tires are cold, as pressure increases with temperature. If you must move the vehicle to check the tire inflation, do not drive more than a mile before checking. A cold tire is generally one that has not been driven for more than three hours.

A plate or sticker is normally provided somewhere in the vehicle (door post, hood, tailgate or trunk lid) which shows the proper pressure for the tires. Never counteract excessive pres-

GENERAL INFORMATION AND MAINTENANCE

sure build-up by bleeding off air pressure (letting some air out). This will cause the tire to run hotter and wear quicker.

✳✳CAUTION

Never exceed the maximum tire pressure embossed on the tire! This is the pressure to be used when the tire is at maximum loading, but it is rarely the correct pressure for everyday driving. Consult the owner's manual or the tire pressure sticker for the correct tire pressure.

Once you've maintained the correct tire pressures for several weeks, you'll be familiar with the vehicle's braking and handling personality. Slight adjustments in tire pressures can fine-tune these characteristics, but never change the cold pressure specification by more than 2 psi. A slightly softer tire pressure will give a softer ride but also yield lower fuel mileage. A slightly harder tire will give crisper dry road handling but can cause skidding on wet surfaces. Unless you're fully attuned to the vehicle, stick to the recommended inflation pressures.

All tires made since 1968 have built-in tread wear indicator bars that show up as ½ in. (13mm) wide smooth bands across the tire when 1/16 in. (1.5mm) of tread remains. The appearance of tread wear indicators means that the tires should be replaced. In fact, many states have laws prohibiting the use of tires with less than this amount of tread.

You can check your own tread depth with an inexpensive gauge or by using a Lincoln head penny. Slip the Lincoln penny (with Lincoln's head upside-down) into several tread grooves. If you can see the top of Lincoln's head in 2 adjacent grooves, the tire has less than 1/16 in. (1.5mm) tread left and should be replaced. You can measure snow tires in the same manner by using the "tails" side of the Lincoln penny. If you can see the top of the Lincoln memorial, it's time to replace the snow tire(s).

CARE OF SPECIAL WHEELS

If you have invested money in magnesium, aluminum alloy or sport wheels, special precautions should be taken to make sure your investment is not wasted and that your special wheels look good for the life of the vehicle.

Special wheels are easily damaged and/or scratched. Occasionally check the rims for cracking, impact damage or air leaks. If any of these are found, replace the wheel. But in order to prevent this type of damage and the costly replacement of a special wheel, observe the following precautions:

- Use extra care not to damage the wheels during removal, installation, balancing, etc. After removal of the wheels from the vehicle, place them on a mat or other protective surface. If they are to be stored for any length of time, support them on strips of wood. Never store tires and wheels upright; the tread may develop flat spots.
- When driving, watch for hazards; it doesn't take much to crack a wheel.
- When washing, use a mild soap or non-abrasive dish detergent (keeping in mind that detergent tends to remove wax). Avoid cleansers with abrasives or the use of hard brushes. There are many cleaners and polishes for special wheels.
- If possible, remove the wheels during the winter. Salt and sand used for snow removal can severely damage the finish of a wheel.
- Make certain the recommended lug nut torque is never exceeded or the wheel may crack. Never use snow chains on special wheels; severe scratching will occur.

FLUIDS AND LUBRICANTS

Fuel and Oil Recommendations

FUEL

All models through 1970 are designed to use a regular grade of gasoline.

ENGINE OIL

▶ See Figure 91

Many factors help to determine the proper oil for your Jeep. The big question is what viscosity to use and when. The whole question of viscosity revolves around the lowest anticipated ambient temperature to be encountered before your next oil change. The recommended viscosity ratings for temperatures ranging from below 0°F (-18°C) to above +32°F (0°C) are listed in the accompanying chart. They are broken down into multi-viscosities and single viscosities. Multi-viscosity oils are recommended because of their wider range of acceptable temperatures and driving conditions.

The SAE grade number indicates the viscosity of the engine oil, or its ability to lubricate under a given temperature. The lower the SAE grade number, the lighter the oil. The lower the viscosity, the easier it is to crank the engine in cold weather.

The API (American Petroleum Institute) designation indicates the classification of engine oil for use under given operating conditions. For gasoline engines, only oils designated for Service SE/SF, or just SF, should be used. You can find the SE or SF marking either on the top or on the side of the container. The viscosity rating should be in the same place. Select the viscosity rating to be used by your type of driving and the temperature range anticipated before the next oil change.

The multi-viscosity oils offer the advantage of being adaptable to temperature extremes. They allow easy starts at low temperatures, yet still give good protection at high speeds and warm temperatures.

1-40 GENERAL INFORMATION AND MAINTENANCE

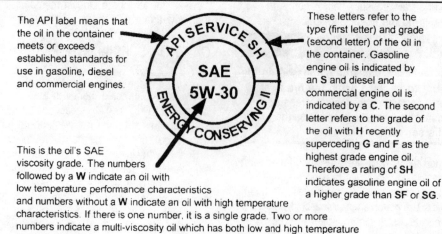

Fig. 91 A label on the oil container will provide important information about the oil

Engine

OIL LEVEL CHECK

Make sure that your vehicle is on a level surface to ensure an accurate reading. Then, raise the hood, position the prop rod, and measure the oil with the dipstick which is on the left side of 4-cylinder and on the right side of 6-cylinder engines. Add oil through the filler pipe on the right side of 4-134 engines, through the valve cover filler hole on 6-225 engines and through the filler pipe on the left side of the 6-226 and 6-230 engines.

If the oil is below the ADD mark, add a 1 qt. (0.947L) of oil, then recheck the level. If the level is still not reading full, add only ½ qt. (0.473L) at a time, until the dipstick reads FULL. Do not overfill the engine. When you check the oil, make sure that you allow sufficient time for all of the oil to drain back into the crankcase after stopping the engine. A minute or so should be enough time.

OIL AND FILTER CHANGE

♦ See Figures 92, 93, 94, 95, 96, 97, 98, 99 and 100

Before draining the oil, make sure that the engine is at operating temperature. Hot oil will hold more impurities in suspension and will flow better, removing more oil and dirt.

Drain the oil into a suitable receptacle. After the drain plug is loosened, unscrew the plug with your fingers, using a rag to shield your fingers from the heat. Push in on the plug as you unscrew it so you can feel when all of the screw threads are out of the hole. You can then remove the plug quickly with the minimum amount of oil running down your arm. You will also have the plug in your hand and not in the bottom of a pan of hot oil.

Change the oil filter every time you change the oil. The engine should be at operating temperature. On the older L4-134 and F4-134 and all 6-226 engines, the oil filter is located on the right side forward part of the top of the engine. To change the element, remove the bolt, remove the lid, and remove and discard the element. Clean out the cup with a clean, dry cloth and flushing oil or clean, light viscosity engine oil. Clean the lid in the same manner and remove and discard the old gasket. Replace it with a new one. Do not use a solvent that could get into the oil and dilute it. Place the new filter element in the cup. Place the lid on the cup and the bolt down through the center. Tighten the bolt to 10-15 ft. lbs. (14-20 Nm). Start the engine and look for leaks. If a leak does develop, turn the engine OFF and remove the oil filter lid. Inspect the gasket to see if it is seated properly. Adjust the gasket if needed. Install the lid, start the engine, and check for leaks. If the leak persists, tighten the bolt further.

On the newer F4-134, 6-225, and 6-230 engines, the oil filter is the spin-on type. On the F4-134 engines, the filter is in the same place as the former cartridge type filter. On the V6 engine, the filter is on the right side of the engine just below the alternator. On the 6-230, it is at the lower left front of the block.

To replace the filter, you will need an oil filter wrench. Loosen the filter with the filter wrench. With a rag wrapped around the filter, unscrew the filter from the oil pump housing. Be careful of hot oil that might run down the side of the filter, especially on the inline 6-cylinder engines. On the F4-134 engines, the filter is mounted with the open side facing downward so you won't have to worry about oil running down on your hand. Make sure that you have a pan under the filter before you start to remove it from the engine so you won't make a mess and, if some of the hot oil does happen to get on you, you will have a place to dump the filter in a hurry. Wipe the base of the mounting plate with a clean, dry cloth. When you install the new filter, smear a small amount of oil on the gasket with your finger, just enough to coat the entire surface where it comes in contact with the mounting plate. When you tighten the filter, turn it only a ¼ turn after it comes in contact with the mounting plate.

GENERAL INFORMATION AND MAINTENANCE

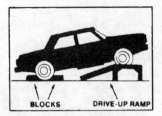
1. Warm the car up before changing your oil. Raise the front end of the car and support it on drive-on ramps or jackstands.

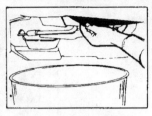
2. Locate the drain plug on the bottom of the oil pan and slide a low flat pan of sufficient capacity under the engine to catch the oil. Loosen the plug with a wrench and turn it out the last few turns by hand. Keep a steady inward pressure on the plug to avoid hot oil from running down your arm.

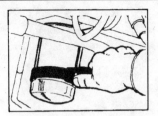
3. Remove the oil filter with a filter wrench. The filter can hold more than a quart of oil, which will be hot. Be sure the gasket comes off with the filter and clean the mounting base on the engine.

4. Lubricate the gasket on the new filter with clean engine oil. A dry gasket may not make a good seal and will allow the filter to leak.

5. Position a new filter on the mounting base and spin it on by hand. Do not use a wrench. When the gasket contacts the engine, tighten it another ½-1 turn by hand.

6. Using a rag, clean the drain plug and the area around the drain hole in the oil pan.

7. Install the drain plug and tighten it finger-tight. If you feel resistance, stop and be sure you are not cross-threading the plug. Finally, tighten the plug with a wrench.

8. Locate the oil cap on the valve cover. An oil spout is the easiest way to add oil, but a funnel will do just as well.

9. Start the engine and check for leaks. The oil pressure warning light will remain on for a few seconds; when it goes out, stop the engine and check the level on the dipstick.

Fig. 92 For Jeep models equipped with a spin-on type oil filter, follow this general procedure to change the oil and filter

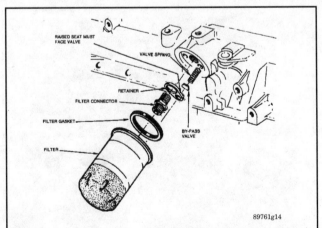
Fig. 93 The inline 6-cylinder engines (6-226 and 6-230) utilize a spin-on type oil filter as shown — always apply a film of clean engine oil to the filter gasket prior to installation

Fig. 94 Remove the oil pan drain plug . . .

1-42 GENERAL INFORMATION AND MAINTENANCE

Fig. 95 . . . and drain the oil into a suitably-sized catch pan

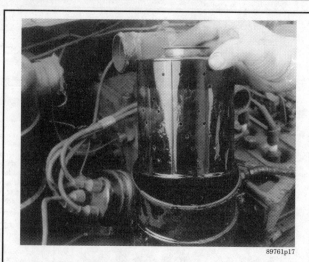

Fig. 98 Remove the filter element from the canister for replacement or cleaning

Fig. 96 While the oil pan drains, remove the oil filter cover hold-down bolt . . .

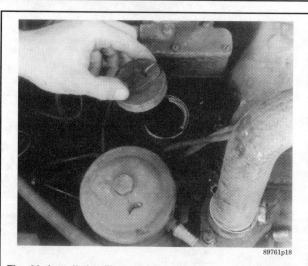

Fig. 99 Install the filter and cover, then remove the oil filler cap

Fig. 97 . . . and remove the oil filter cover

Fig. 100 Install the oil pan drain plug, then fill the engine with clean engine oil

GENERAL INFORMATION AND MAINTENANCE 1-43

Manual Transmission

FLUID LEVEL CHECK

▶ See Figures 101 and 102

The level of lubricant in the transmission should be maintained at the filler hole on all manual transmissions. This hole is on the right side. When you check the level in the transmission, make sure that the vehicle is level so that you get a true reading. When you remove the filler plug, lubricant should run out of the hole. Replace the plug quickly for a minimum loss of lubricant. If lubricant does not run out of the hole when the plug is removed, lubricant should be added until it does. Replace the plug as soon as the lubricant reaches the level of the hole.

FLUID CHANGE

Remove the drain plug which is at the bottom of the transmission or else on the side near the bottom. Allow all the lubricant to run out before reinstalling the plug. Refill the case with the correct viscosity oil. All manual transmissions, except the T4 and T5, use SAE 80W-90 gear oil. The T4 and T5 manual transmissions use Dexron®II Automatic Transmission Fluid (ATF).

Automatic Transmission

FLUID LEVEL CHECK

The fluid level in automatic transmissions is checked with a dipstick in the filler pipe at the right rear of the engine. The fluid level should be maintained between the ADD and FULL marks on the end of the dipstick with the automatic transmission fluid at normal operating temperature. To raise the level from the ADD mark to the FULL mark, requires the addition of 1 pt. (0.473L) of fluid. The fluid level with the fluid at room temperature (75°F) should be approximately ¼ in. (6mm) below the ADD mark.

➡ In checking the Automatic Transmission Fluid (ATF), insert the dipstick in the filler tube with the markings toward the center of the vehicle. Also, remember that the FULL mark on the dipstick is calibrated for normal operating temperature. This temperature is obtained only after at least 15 miles (24 km) of expressway driving or the equivalent of city driving.

1. With the transmission in Park, the engine running at idle speed, the foot brake applied and the vehicle resting on level ground, move the transmission gear selector through each of the gear positions, including Reverse, allowing time for the transmission to engage. Return the shift selector to the Park position and apply the parking brake. Do **NOT** turn the engine **OFF**, but leave it running at idle speed.
2. Clean all dirt from around the transmission dipstick cap and the end of the filler tube.
3. Pull the dipstick out of the tube, wipe it off with a clean cloth, and push it back into the tube all the way, making sure that it seats completely.
4. Pull the dipstick out of the tube again and read the level of the fluid on the stick. The level should be between the ADD and FULL marks. If fluid must be added, add enough fluid through the tube to raise the level to between the ADD and FULL marks. Do not overfill the transmission because this will cause foaming and loss of fluid through the vent.

➡ Use only Dexron® or Dexron®II transmission fluid.

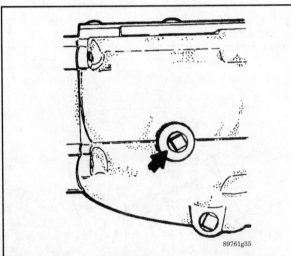

Fig. 101 Most manual transmissions are equipped with both a fill plug (arrow) and a drain plug (bottom plug)

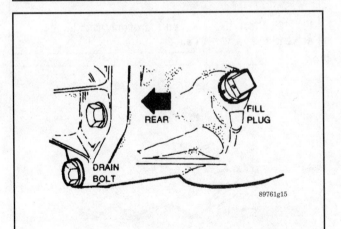

Fig. 102 If your particular transmission does not have a drain plug, remove the lowest tailshaft bolt to drain the fluid

DRAIN, FILTER SERVICE AND REFILL

▶ See Figures 103, 104, 105, 106 and 107

If, when the ATF level is checked, the fluid is noticed to be discolored from a clear red to brown, has a burned smell, or contains water, it should be changed immediately.

1. Drive the vehicle for at least 20 minutes at expressway speeds or the equivalent to raise the temperature of the fluid to its normal operating range.
2. Drain the ATF into an appropriate container before it has cooled. The fluid is drained by loosening the transmission pan and allowing the fluid to run out around the edges. It is best to loosen only one corner of the pan and allow most of the fluid to drain out.
3. Remove the remaining pan screws, and remove the pan and pan gasket.
4. Remove the strainer and discard it.
5. Remove the O-ring seal from the pick-up pipe and discard it.
6. Install a new O-ring seal on the pick-up pipe and install the new strainer and pipe assembly.
7. Thoroughly clean the bottom pan and position a new gasket on the pan mating surface.
8. Install the pan and tighten the attaching screws to 121-158 inch lbs. (14-18 Nm).
9. Pour about 5 qts. (4.74L) of Dexron® or Dexron®II ATF down the dipstick tube. Make sure that the funnel, container, hose or any other item used to assist in filling the transmission is clean.
10. Start the engine with the transmission in Park. Do NOT race it. Allow the engine to idle for a few minutes.
11. After the engine has been running for a few minutes, move the selector lever through all of the gears.
12. With the selector lever in Park, check the transmission fluid level and adjust as necessary. Remember the ATF must be warm when at the Full mark.

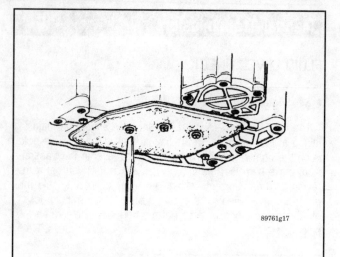

Fig. 104 Once the pan is removed, the filter can be replaced with a new one

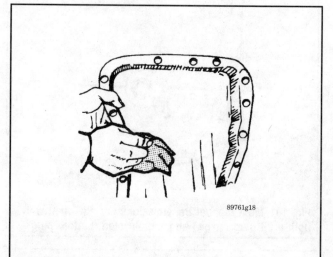

Fig. 105 Clean the fluid pan thoroughly with a safe solvent and allow it to air dry

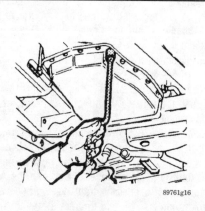

Fig. 103 On automatic transmissions without drain plugs, loosen the pan bolts and allow one corner of the pan to hang so that the fluid will drain out

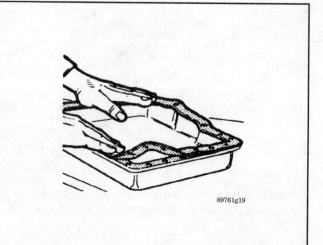

Fig. 106 Install a new pan-to-transmission housing gasket onto the fluid pan and install the pan

GENERAL INFORMATION AND MAINTENANCE 1-45

Fig. 107 Fill the transmission with the proper amount of fluid — do NOT overfill the transmission

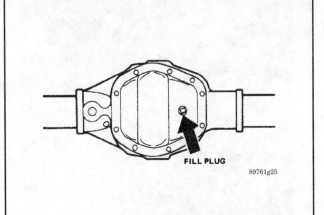

Fig. 108 The fill plugs on both the front and rear drive axles are located in the middle of the differential covers

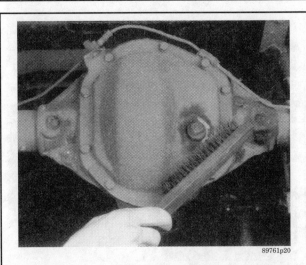

Fig. 109 Before checking and/or draining the differential fluid, brush away dirt from both the drain and fill plugs

Transfer Case

FLUID LEVEL CHECK

The Spicer 18 was the only transfer case available in 4WD models from 1945-70. The transfer case should be checked in the same manner as the manual transmission. The level should be up to the filler hole. Use the same viscosity oil as in the transmission. The filler hole is on the right side. Check the oil level at the top hole. The bottom plug is the drain plug.

➡ Some models may be equipped with a two piece fill plug (a small threaded plug inside a larger one). If your transfer case is so equipped, the fluid level is checked at the bottom of the smaller plug. To remove the smaller plug, hold the larger one firmly with a wrench while removing the smaller plug.

DRAIN & REFILL

All manual transfer cases are to be serviced at the same time and in the same manner as the manual transmissions. The transfer case has its own drain plug which should be opened. Do not rely on the transmission drain plug to completely drain the transfer case, even if they are interconnected. Once the transfer case has been drained, replace the drain plug, remove the fill plug and fill the transfer case. The Spicer 18 uses SAE 80W-90 gear oil. Replace the fill plug.

Drive Axles

FLUID LEVEL CHECK

◆ See Figures 108 and 109

The standard front and rear axle differentials use SAE 80W/90 gear oil. Either is acceptable for use in the differential housing. Powr-Lok® differentials use only Jeep Powr-Lok® Lubricant or its equivalent. In Trac-Lok® axles, use any limited slip gear oil meeting SAE 75W/90, 80W/90 or 85W/90 specifications. Check the level of the oil in the differential housing every 5,000 miles (8,000 km) under normal driving conditions and every 3,000 miles (4,800 km) if the vehicle is used in severe driving conditions. The level should be up to the filler hole. When you remove the filler plug, the oil should start to run out. If it does not, replenish the supply until it does.

The lubricant should be changed every 30,000 miles (48,000 km). If running in deep water, change the lubricant daily.

DRAIN & REFILL

◆ See Figures 108, 109, 110, 111, 112, 113, 114, 115, 116 and 117

1. Use a wire brush or rag to clean the area around the drain and fill plugs.

1-46 GENERAL INFORMATION AND MAINTENANCE

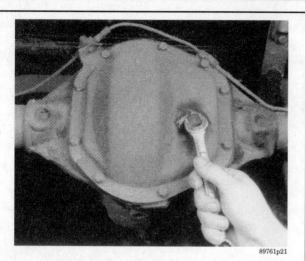

Fig. 110 To drain the differential fluid, first loosen (but do not remove) the fill plug

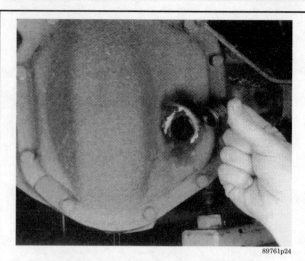

Fig. 113 Remove the fill plug in order to fill the differential case

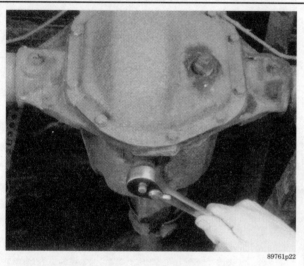

Fig. 111 Remove the drain plug . . .

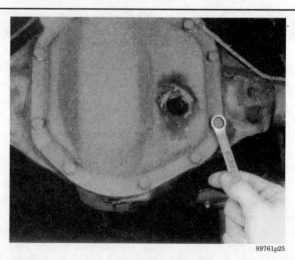

Fig. 114 If the differential cover gasket leaks and must be replaced, remove the retaining bolts

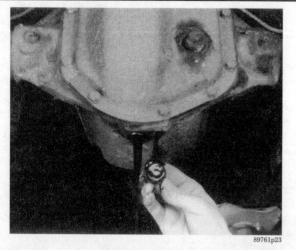

Fig. 112 . . . and allow the differential oil to drain into a catch pan

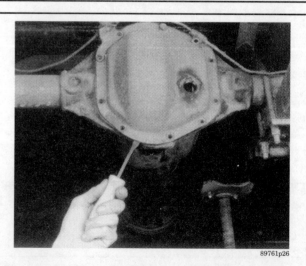

Fig. 115 Gently pry the cover away from the case and allow residual oil to drain

GENERAL INFORMATION AND MAINTENANCE 1-47

Fig. 116 Remove the case cover from the differential and . . .

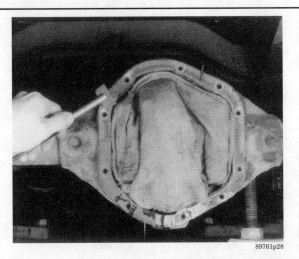

Fig. 117 . . . cover the differential with a shop rag, then remove any old gasket material

2. Loosen (but do not remove) the fill plug, to make sure that it can be turned easily. If necessary, spray penetrating lubricant.
3. Position a suitable catch pan, then loosen and remove the drain plug. Allow the lubricant to empty out.
4. If the differential cover gasket leaks (or differential service is required), perform Steps 4a-4d:
   a. Remove the axle differential housing cover and allow the remaining lubricant to drain into the pan.
   b. Cover the differential with a clean rag, and remove any old gasket material. Remove the rag.
   c. Install the differential housing cover with a new gasket.
   d. Tighten the cover attaching bolts to 15-25 ft. lbs. (20-34 Nm).
5. Install and tighten the drain plug.
6. Remove the fill plug and add new lubricant to the fill hole level.
7. Install and tighten the fill plug.

➡ Trac-Lok® (limited-slip) differentials may be cleaned only by disassembling the unit and wiping with clean, lint-free rags.

Cooling System

LEVEL CHECK

▶ See Figure 118

The coolant level should be maintained about ½ in. (13mm) below the filler neck of the radiator with 4L-134, 4F-134, 6-226 and 6-230 engines.

On the 6-225 engine, the coolant level should be maintained 1½-2 in. (38-51mm) below the bottom of the filler cap when the engine is cold. Since operating temperatures reach as high as 205°F (96°C), coolant could be forced out of the radiator if it is filled too high. The radiator coolant level should be checked regularly, such as every time you refuel the vehicle. Never open the radiator cap of an engine that hasn't had sufficient time to cool or the pressure can blow off the cap and send out a spray of scalding water.

On systems with a coolant recovery tank, maintain the coolant level at the level marks on the recovery bottle.

For best protection against freezing and overheating, maintain an approximate 50% water and 50% ethylene glycol (or other suitable) antifreeze mixture in the cooling system. Do not mix different brands of antifreeze to avoid possible chemical damage to the cooling system.

Avoid using water that is known to have a high alkaline content or is very hard, except in emergency situations. Drain

Fig. 118 An antifreeze tester can be used to determine the freezing and boiling level of the coolant

1-48 GENERAL INFORMATION AND MAINTENANCE

and flush the cooling system as soon as possible after using such water.

> **✻✻CAUTION**
>
> Cover the radiator cap with a thick cloth before removing it from a radiator in a vehicle that is hot. Turn the cap counterclockwise slowly until pressure can be heard escaping. Allow all pressure to escape from the radiator before completely removing the radiator cap. It is best to allow the engine to cool if possible, before removing the radiator cap.

➡ Never add cold water to an overheated engine while the engine is not running.

After filling the radiator, run the engine until it reaches normal operating temperature, to make sure that the thermostat has opened and all the air is bled from the system.

DRAINING, FLUSHING AND REFILLING

▶ See Figures 119, 120 and 121

> **✻✻CAUTION**
>
> When draining coolant, keep in mind that cats and dogs are attracted by ethylene glycol antifreeze, and are quite likely to drink any that is left in an uncovered container or in puddles on the ground. This will prove fatal in sufficient quantity. Always drain the coolant into a sealable container. Coolant should be reused unless it is contaminated or several years old.

To drain the cooling system, allow the engine to cool down **BEFORE ATTEMPTING TO REMOVE THE RADIATOR CAP.**

Fig. 119 The cooling system should be pressure tested once a year

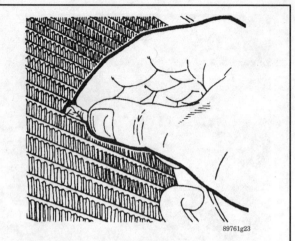

Fig. 120 Whenever servicing your cooling system, take a few moments to clear the radiator fins of debris, to allow your system to provide maximum engine cooling

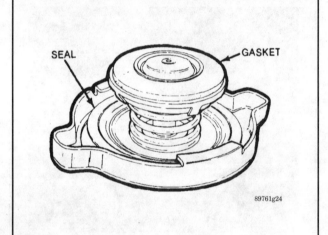

Fig. 121 Inspect the radiator cap rubber gasket and metal seal for any deterioration at least once a year

Then turn the cap until it hisses. Wait until all pressure is off the cap before removing it completely.

> **✻✻CAUTION**
>
> To avoid burns and scalding, always handle a warm radiator cap with a heavy rag.

1. At the dash, set the heater TEMP control lever to the fully HOT position.
2. With the radiator cap removed, drain the radiator by loosening the petcock at the bottom of the radiator. Locate any drain plugs in the block and remove them. Flush the radiator with water until the fluid runs clear.
3. Close the petcock and replace the plug(s), then refill the system with a 50/50 mix of ethylene glycol or other suitable antifreeze. Fill the system to ¾-1¼ in. (19.05-31.75mm) from the bottom of the filler neck. Reinstall the radiator cap.

➡ If equipped with a fluid reservoir tank, fill it up to the MAX level.

GENERAL INFORMATION AND MAINTENANCE 1-49

4. Operate the engine at 2,000 rpm for a few minutes and check the system for signs of leaks.

Radiator Cap Inspection

Allow the engine to cool sufficiently before attempting to remove the radiator cap. Use a rag to cover the cap, then remove by pressing down and turning counterclockwise to the first stop. If any hissing is noted (indicating the release of pressure), wait until the hissing stops completely, then press down again and turn counterclockwise until the cap can be removed.

> **✱✱CAUTION**
>
> **DO NOT attempt to remove the radiator cap while the engine is hot. Severe personal injury from steam burns can result.**

Check the condition of the radiator cap gasket and seal inside of the cap. The radiator cap is designed to seal the cooling system under normal operating conditions which allows the build up of a certain amount of pressure (this pressure rating is stamped or printed on the cap). The pressure in the system raises the boiling point of the coolant to help prevent overheating. If the radiator cap does not seal, the boiling point of the coolant is lowered and overheating will occur. If the cap must be replaced, purchase the new cap according to the pressure rating which is specified for your vehicle.

Prior to installing the radiator cap, inspect and clean the filler neck. If you are reusing the old cap, clean it thoroughly with clear water. After turning the cap on, make sure the arrows align with the overflow hose.

Brake and Clutch Master Cylinders

The master cylinder is located under the floor. To check the level of the brake fluid remove the floor plate. Clean the area of all dirt so that, when you remove the cover, no dirt will fall in and contaminate the brake fluid. Dirt in the hydraulic system could score the inside of the master cylinder or wheel cylinders and cause leakage or brake failure. Unscrew the lid of the master cylinder with a wrench. The fluid level should be within ½ in. (13mm) from the top of the reservoir chamber. Use only heavy duty brake fluid and keep it away from any other fluids or vapors that could contaminate it.

If the master cylinder is less than half full, there is probably a leak somewhere in the hydraulic system. Investigate the problem before driving the vehicle.

Power Steering Pump

FLUID LEVEL CHECK

▶ See Figure 122

The level of the fluid should be at the correct point on the dipstick attached to the inside of the lid of the power steering pump. Replenish the supply with DEXRON®II Automatic Transmission Fluid (ATF).

Manual Steering Gear

FLUID LEVEL CHECK

▶ See Figure 123

There is a fill plug on top of the steering gear box. The level should be maintained at the bottom of the fill plug hole. The correct lubricant is SAE 80W/90 gear oil.

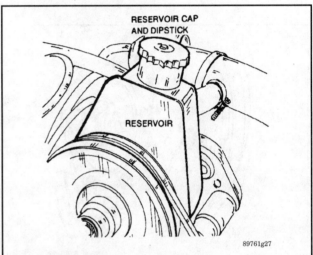

Fig. 122 The power steering fluid dipstick is mounted to the underside of the reservoir cap

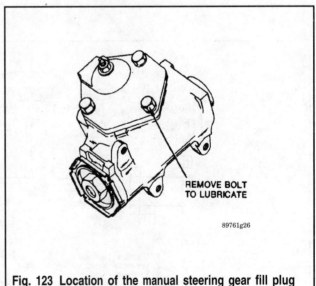

Fig. 123 Location of the manual steering gear fill plug

1-50 GENERAL INFORMATION AND MAINTENANCE

Steering Knuckle

FLUID LEVEL CHECK

♦ See Figure 124

The axle shaft universal joints are located in the steering knuckle and are bathed in oil as they turn. To check the fluid level in the steering knuckle, remove the filler plug from the inside of the knuckle. The fluid should be at the level of the hole. If it is not, replenish the supply. Examine the knuckle for leaks if the level is abnormally low. A leak should be readily visible.

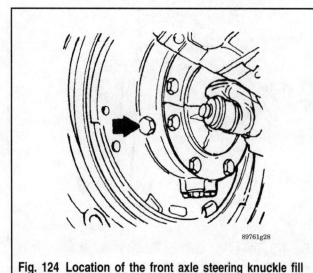

Fig. 124 Location of the front axle steering knuckle fill plug

Chassis Greasing

♦ See Figures 125, 126, 127, 128, 129, 130 and 131

Chassis greasing should be performed every 6 months or 7,500 miles (12,000 km) for Jeeps used in normal or light service. More frequent greasing is recommended for Jeeps in heavy or severe usage: every 3 months or 3,000 miles (4,800 km). Greasing can be performed with a commercial pressurized grease gun or at home by using a hand-operated grease gun. Wipe the grease fittings clean before greasing in order to prevent the possibility of forcing any dirt into the component.

Water resistant EP chassis lubricant (grease) should be used for all chassis grease points. Refer to the accompanying illustrations for the locations of the vehicles' grease points.

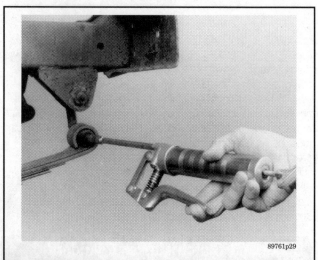

Fig. 125 A hand-operated grease gun can be used to grease the components on your Jeep

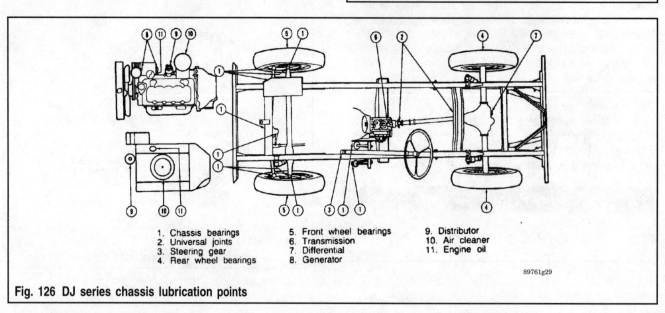

1. Chassis bearings
2. Universal joints
3. Steering gear
4. Rear wheel bearings
5. Front wheel bearings
6. Transmission
7. Differential
8. Generator
9. Distributor
10. Air cleaner
11. Engine oil

Fig. 126 DJ series chassis lubrication points

GENERAL INFORMATION AND MAINTENANCE

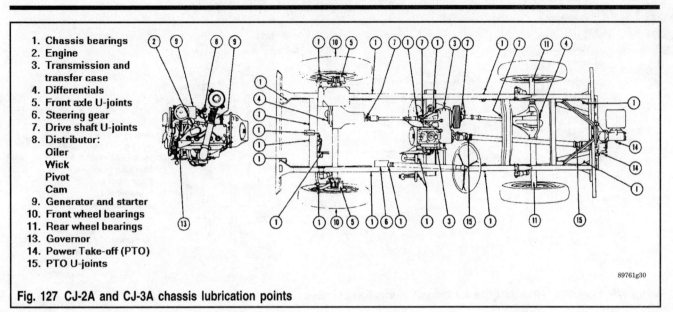

1. Chassis bearings
2. Engine
3. Transmission and transfer case
4. Differentials
5. Front axle U-joints
6. Steering gear
7. Drive shaft U-joints
8. Distributor:
   Oiler
   Wick
   Pivot
   Cam
9. Generator and starter
10. Front wheel bearings
11. Rear wheel bearings
13. Governor
14. Power Take-off (PTO)
15. PTO U-joints

Fig. 127 CJ-2A and CJ-3A chassis lubrication points

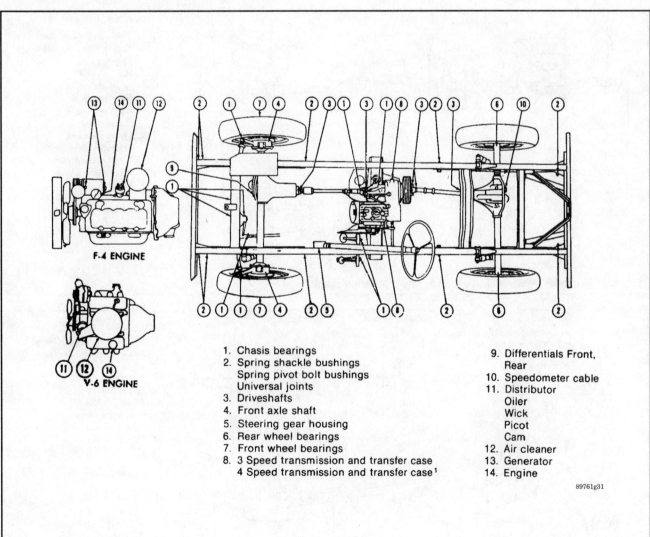

1. Chasis bearings
2. Spring shackle bushings
   Spring pivot bolt bushings
   Universal joints
3. Driveshafts
4. Front axle shaft
5. Steering gear housing
6. Rear wheel bearings
7. Front wheel bearings
8. 3 Speed transmission and transfer case
   4 Speed transmission and transfer case[1]
9. Differentials Front, Rear
10. Speedometer cable
11. Distributor
    Oiler
    Wick
    Picot
    Cam
12. Air cleaner
13. Generator
14. Engine

Fig. 128 CJ-3B, CJ-5 and CJ-6 chassis lubrication points

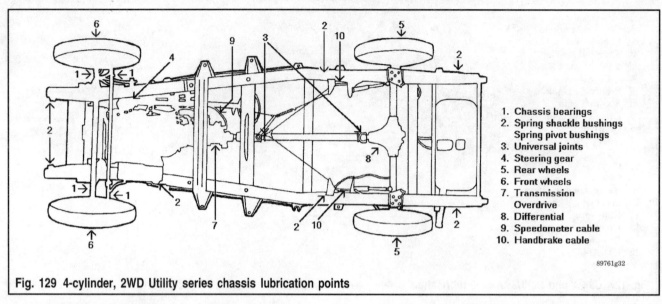

Fig. 129 4-cylinder, 2WD Utility series chassis lubrication points

1. Chassis bearings
2. Spring shackle bushings
   Spring pivot bushings
3. Universal joints
4. Steering gear
5. Rear wheels
6. Front wheels
7. Transmission
   Overdrive
8. Differential
9. Speedometer cable
10. Handbrake cable

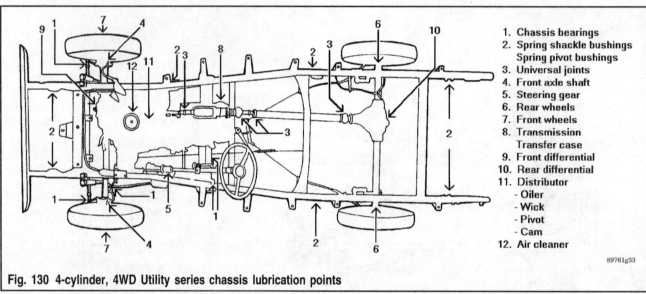

Fig. 130 4-cylinder, 4WD Utility series chassis lubrication points

1. Chassis bearings
2. Spring shackle bushings
   Spring pivot bushings
3. Universal joints
4. Front axle shaft
5. Steering gear
6. Rear wheels
7. Front wheels
8. Transmission
   Transfer case
9. Front differential
10. Rear differential
11. Distributor
    - Oiler
    - Wick
    - Pivot
    - Cam
12. Air cleaner

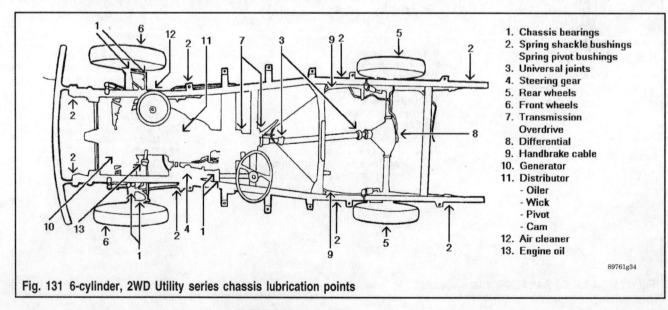

Fig. 131 6-cylinder, 2WD Utility series chassis lubrication points

1. Chassis bearings
2. Spring shackle bushings
   Spring pivot bushings
3. Universal joints
4. Steering gear
5. Rear wheels
6. Front wheels
7. Transmission
   Overdrive
8. Differential
9. Handbrake cable
10. Generator
11. Distributor
    - Oiler
    - Wick
    - Pivot
    - Cam
12. Air cleaner
13. Engine oil

GENERAL INFORMATION AND MAINTENANCE

Body Lubrication and Maintenance

LOCK CYLINDERS

Apply graphite lubricant sparingly through the key slot. Insert the key and operate the lock several times to be sure that the lubricant is worked into the lock cylinder.

DOOR HINGES AND HINGE CHECKS

Spray a silicone lubricant on the hinge pivot points to eliminate any binding conditions. Open and close the door several times to be sure that the lubricant is evenly and thoroughly distributed.

TAILGATE

Spray a silicone lubricant on all of the pivot and friction surfaces to eliminate any squeaks or binds. Work the tailgate to distribute the lubricant

BODY DRAIN HOLES

Be sure that the drain holes in the doors and rocker panels are cleared of obstruction. A small screwdriver can be used to clear them of any debris.

TOWING THE VEHICLE

If your Jeep must be towed, follow these guidelines:
1. A Jeep with a manual transmission can be towed with either all four wheels or either axle on the ground for any distance at a safe speed with both the transmission and transfer case in Neutral.
2. To tow a Jeep with an automatic transmission and Quadra-Trac®, the driveshaft to the axle(s) remaining on the ground must be disconnected. Be sure to index mark the driveshafts and yoke flanges for alignment upon assembly. Also, the driveshafts must be tied securely up out of the way or removed completely while the vehicle is being towed.
3. A Jeep equipped with an automatic transmission and Quadra-Trac® with the optional low range reduction unit can be towed with all four wheels on the ground without disconnecting the driveshafts. Place the transmission shift lever in Park, the low range reduction unit shift lever in Neutral, and the emergency drive control knob in the Normal position. If the emergency drive system was engaged when the engine was shut down, it will have to be restarted and the emergency drive control knob turned to the Normal position to disengage the system since the control mechanism is vacuum operated.

✱✱CAUTION

Never tow the Jeep with the emergency drive system engaged or the reduction unit in low range.

In all cases, unnecessary wear and tear can be avoided by disconnecting the driveshafts at the differentials and either tying them up out of the way or removing them altogether. Be sure to index mark the driveshafts and yoke flanges for proper alignment during assembly. If the Jeep is equipped with free running front hubs (manual transmission only), there is no need to remove the front driveshaft, simply disengage the hubs.

TRAILER TOWING

Jeep vehicles have long been popular as trailer towing vehicles. Their strong construction, 4-wheel drive and wide range of engine/transmission combinations make them ideal for towing campers, boat trailers and utility trailers.

Factory trailer towing packages are available on most Jeep vehicles. However, if you are installing a trailer hitch and wiring on your Jeep, there are a few thing that you ought to know.

Trailer Weight

The weight of the trailer is the most important factor. A good weight-to-horsepower ratio is about 35:1, that is, 35 lbs. of Gross Combined Weight (GCW) for every horsepower your engine develops. Multiply the engine's rated horsepower by 35 and subtract the weight of the vehicle passengers and luggage. The number remaining is the approximate ideal maximum weight you should tow, although a numerically higher axle ratio can help compensate for heavier weight.

Hitch (Tongue) Weight

▶ See Figure 132

Calculate the hitch weight in order to select a proper hitch. The weight of the hitch is usually 9-11% of the trailer gross weight and should be measured with the trailer loaded. Hitches fall into various categories: those that mount on the frame and rear bumper, the bolt-on type, or the weld-on distribution type used for larger trailers. Axle mounted or clamp-on bumper hitches should never be used.

Check the gross weight rating of your trailer. Tongue weight is usually figured as 10% of gross trailer weight. Therefore, a trailer with a maximum gross weight of 2000 lbs. will have a maximum tongue weight of 200 lbs. Class I trailers fall into this category. Class II trailers are those with a gross weight rating of 2000-3000 lbs., while Class III trailers fall into the 3500-6000 lbs. category. Class IV trailers are those over 6000 lbs. and are for use with fifth wheel trucks, only.

When you've determined the hitch that you'll need, follow the manufacturer's installation instructions, exactly, especially when

1-54 GENERAL INFORMATION AND MAINTENANCE

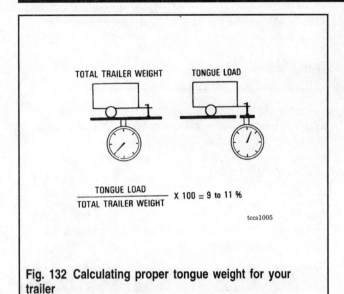

Fig. 132 Calculating proper tongue weight for your trailer

it comes to fastener torques. The hitch will subjected to a lot of stress and good hitches come with hardened bolts. Never substitute an inferior bolt for a hardened bolt.

Cooling

ENGINE

Overflow Tank

One of the most common, if not THE most common, problems associated with trailer towing is engine overheating. If you have a cooling system without an expansion tank, you'll definitely need to get an aftermarket expansion tank kit, preferably one with at least a 2 qt. (1.9L) capacity. These kits are easily installed on the radiator's overflow hose, and come with a pressure cap designed for expansion tanks.

Flex Fan

Another helpful accessory for vehicles using a belt-driven radiator fan is a flex fan. These fans are large diameter units designed to provide more airflow at low speeds, by using fan blades that have deeply cupped surfaces. The blades then flex, or flatten out, at high speed, when less cooling air is needed. These fans are far lighter in weight than stock fans, requiring less horsepower to drive them. Also, they are far quieter than stock fans. If you do decide to replace your stock fan with a flex fan, note that if your vehicle has a fan clutch, a spacer will be needed between the flex fan and water pump hub.

JUMP STARTING A DEAD BATTERY

▶ See Figure 133

Whenever a vehicle is jump started, precautions must be followed in order to prevent the possibility of personal injury.

Oil Cooler

Aftermarket engine oil coolers are helpful for prolonging engine oil life and reducing overall engine temperatures. Both of these factors increase engine life. While not absolutely necessary in towing Class I and some Class II trailers, they are recommended for heavier Class II and all Class III towing. Engine oil cooler systems usually consist of an adapter, screwed on in place of the oil filter, a remote filter mounting and a multi-tube, finned heat exchanger, which is mounted in front of the radiator or air conditioning condenser.

TRANSMISSION

An automatic transmission is usually recommended for trailer towing. Modern automatics have proven reliable and, of course, easy to operate, in trailer towing. The increased load of a trailer, however, causes an increase in the temperature of the automatic transmission fluid. Heat is the worst enemy of an automatic transmission. As the temperature of the fluid increases, the life of the fluid decreases.

It is essential, therefore, that you install an automatic transmission cooler. The cooler, which consists of a multi-tube, finned heat exchanger, is usually installed in front of the radiator or air conditioning compressor, and hooked in-line with the transmission cooler tank inlet line. Follow the cooler manufacturer's installation instructions.

Select a cooler of at least adequate capacity, based upon the combined gross weights of the vehicle and trailer.

Cooler manufacturers recommend that you use an aftermarket cooler in addition to, and not instead of, the present cooling tank in your radiator. If you do want to use it in place of the radiator cooling tank, get a cooler at least two sizes larger than normally necessary.

➡**A transmission cooler can, sometimes, cause slow or harsh shifting in the transmission during cold weather, until the fluid has a chance to come up to normal operating temperature. Some coolers can be purchased with or retrofitted with a temperature bypass valve which will allow fluid flow through the cooler only when the fluid has reached above a certain operating temperature.**

Handling A Trailer

Towing a trailer with ease and safety requires a certain amount of experience. It's a good idea to learn the feel of a trailer by practicing turning, stopping and backing in an open area such as an empty parking lot.

Remember that batteries contain a small amount of explosive hydrogen gas which is a by-product of battery charging. Sparks should always be avoided when working around batter-

GENERAL INFORMATION AND MAINTENANCE 1-55

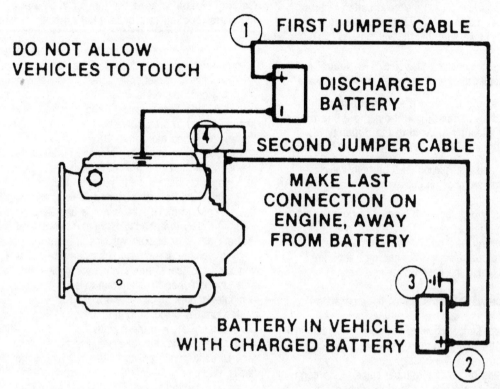

Fig. 133 Connect the jumper cables to the batteries and engine in the order shown

ies, especially when attaching jumper cables. To minimize the possibility of accidental sparks, follow the procedure carefully.

✳✳CAUTION

NEVER hook the batteries up in a series circuit or the entire electrical system will go up in smoke, including the starter!

Vehicles equipped with a diesel engine may utilize two 12 volt batteries. If so, the batteries are connected in a parallel circuit (positive terminal to positive terminal, negative terminal to negative terminal). Hooking the batteries up in parallel circuit increases battery cranking power without increasing total battery voltage output. Output remains at 12 volts. On the other hand, hooking two 12 volt batteries up in a series circuit (positive terminal to negative terminal, positive terminal to negative terminal) increases total battery output to 24 volts (12 volts plus 12 volts).

Jump Starting Precautions

- Be sure that both batteries are of the same voltage. Vehicles covered by this manual, unlike most vehicles on the road today, utilize either a 6, 12 or 24 volt charging system.
- Be sure that both batteries are of the same polarity (have the same terminal, in most cases NEGATIVE grounded).
- Be sure that the vehicles are not touching or a short could occur.
- On serviceable batteries, be sure the vent cap holes are not obstructed.
- Do not smoke or allow sparks anywhere near the batteries.
- In cold weather, make sure the battery electrolyte is not frozen. This can occur more readily in a battery that has been in a state of discharge.
- Do not allow electrolyte to contact your skin or clothing.

1-56 GENERAL INFORMATION AND MAINTENANCE

Jump Starting Procedure

1. Make sure that the voltages of the 2 batteries are the same. The batteries and charging systems in the Jeep models covered by this manual can be of either the 6, 12 or 24 volt variety.
2. Pull the jumping vehicle (with the good battery) into a position so the jumper cables can reach the dead battery and that vehicle's engine. Make sure that the vehicles do NOT touch.
3. Place the transmissions of both vehicles in **Neutral** (MT) or **P** (AT), as applicable, then firmly set their parking brakes.

➡ **If necessary for safety reasons, the hazard lights on both vehicles may be operated throughout the entire procedure without significantly increasing the difficulty of jumping the dead battery.**

4. Turn all lights and accessories OFF on both vehicles. Make sure the ignition switches on both vehicles are turned to the **OFF** position.
5. Cover the battery cell caps with a rag, but do not cover the terminals.
6. Make sure the terminals on both batteries are clean and free of corrosion or proper electrical connection will be impeded. If necessary, clean the battery terminals before proceeding.
7. Identify the positive (+) and negative (-) terminals on both batteries.
8. Connect the first jumper cable to the positive (+) terminal of the dead battery, then connect the other end of that cable to the positive (+) terminal of the booster (good) battery.
9. Connect one end of the other jumper cable to the negative (-) terminal on the booster battery and the final cable clamp to an engine bolt head, alternator bracket or other solid, metallic point on the engine with the dead battery. Try to pick a ground on the engine that is positioned away from the battery in order to minimize the possibility of the 2 clamps touching should one loosen during the procedure. DO NOT connect this clamp to the negative (-) terminal of the bad battery.

✱✱CAUTION

Be very careful to keep the jumper cables away from moving parts (cooling fan, belts, etc.) on both engines.

10. Check to make sure that the cables are routed away from any moving parts, then start the donor vehicle's engine. Run the engine at moderate speed for several minutes to allow the dead battery a chance to receive some initial charge.
11. With the donor vehicle's engine still running slightly above idle, try to start the vehicle with the dead battery. Crank the engine for no more than 10 seconds at a time and let the starter cool for at least 20 seconds between tries. If the vehicle does not start in 3 tries, it is likely that something else is also wrong or that the battery needs additional time to charge.
12. Once the vehicle is started, allow it to run at idle for a few seconds to make sure that it is operating properly.
13. Turn ON the headlights, heater blower and, if equipped, the rear defroster of both vehicles in order to reduce the severity of voltage spikes and subsequent risk of damage to the vehicles' electrical systems when the cables are disconnected. This step is especially important to any vehicle equipped with computer control modules.
14. Carefully disconnect the cables in the reverse order of connection. Start with the negative cable that is attached to the engine ground, then the negative cable on the donor battery. Disconnect the positive cable from the donor battery and finally, disconnect the positive cable from the formerly dead battery. Be careful when disconnecting the cables from the positive terminals not to allow the alligator clips to touch any metal on either vehicle or a short and sparks will occur.

JACKING AND HOISTING

▶ See Figure 134

Scissors jacks or hydraulic jacks are recommended for all Jeep vehicles. To change a tire, place the jack beneath the spring plate, below the axle, near the wheel to be changed.

Make sure that you are on level ground, that the transmission is in Reverse or with automatic transmissions, Park; the parking brake is set, and the tire diagonally opposite to the one to be changed is blocked so that it will not roll. Loosen the lug nuts before you jack the wheel to be changed completely free of the ground.

If you use a hoist, make sure that the pads of the hoist are located in such a way as to lift on the Jeep frame and not on a shock absorber mount, floor boards, oil pan, or any other part that cannot support the full weight of the vehicle.

Fig. 134 When jacking, hoisting or supporting a Jeep, make sure that the support is under the frame

GENERAL INFORMATION AND MAINTENANCE 1-57

HOW TO BUY A USED VEHICLE

Many people believe that a two or three year old used car or truck is a better buy than a new vehicle. This may be true as most new vehicles suffer the heaviest depreciation in the first two years and, at three years old, a vehicle is usually not old enough to present a lot of costly repair problems. But keep in mind, when buying a non-warranted automobile, there are no guarantees. Whatever the age of the used vehicle you might want to purchase, this section and a little patience should increase your chances of selecting one that is safe and dependable.

Tips

1. First decide what model you want, and how much you want to spend.
2. Check the used car lots and your local newspaper ads. Privately owned vehicles are usually less expensive, however, you may not get a warranty that, in many cases, comes with a used vehicle purchased from a lot. Of course, some aftermarket warranties may not be worth the extra money, so this is a point you will have to debate and consider based on your priorities.
3. Never shop at night. The glare of the lights make it easy to miss faults on the body caused by accident or rust repair.
4. Try to get the name and phone number of the previous owner. Contact him/her and ask about the vehicle. If the owner of a lot refuses this information, look for a vehicle somewhere else.

A private seller can tell you about the vehicle and maintenance. But remember, there's no law requiring honesty from private citizens selling used vehicles. There is a law that forbids tampering with or turning back the odometer mileage. This includes both the private citizen and the lot owner. The law also requires that the seller or anyone transferring ownership of the vehicle must provide the buyer with a signed statement indicating the mileage on the odometer at the time of transfer.

5. You may wish to contact the National Highway Traffic Safety Administration (NHTSA) to find out if the vehicle has ever been included in a manufacturer's recall. Write down the year, model and serial number before you buy the vehicle, then contact NHTSA (there should be a 1-800 number that your phone company's information line can supply). If the vehicle was listed for a recall, make sure the needed repairs were made.
6. Refer to the Used Vehicle Checklist in this section and check all the items on the vehicle you are considering. Some items are more important than others. Only you know how much money you can afford for repairs, and depending on the price of the vehicle, may consider performing any needed work yourself. Beware, however, of trouble in areas that will affect operation, safety or emission. Problems in the Used Vehicle Checklist break down as follows:

- Numbers 1-8: Two or more problems in these areas indicate a lack of maintenance. You should beware.
- Numbers 9-13: Problems here tend to indicate a lack of proper care, however, these can usually be corrected with a tune-up or relatively simple parts replacement.
- Numbers 14-17: Problems in the engine or transmission can be very expensive. Unless you are looking for a project, walk away from any vehicle with problems in 2 or more of these areas.

7. If you are satisfied with the apparent condition of the vehicle, take it to an independent diagnostic center or mechanic for a complete check. If you have a state inspection program, have it inspected immediately before purchase, or specify on the bill of sale that the sale is conditional on passing state inspection.
8. Road test the vehicle — refer to the Road Test Checklist in this section. If your original evaluation and the road test agree — the rest is up to you.

USED VEHICLE CHECKLIST

▶ See Figure 135

➡The numbers on the illustrations refer to the numbers on this checklist.

1. Mileage: Average mileage is about 12,000-15,000 miles per year. More than average mileage may indicate hard usage or could indicate many highway miles (which could be less detrimental than half as many tough around town miles).
2. Paint: Check around the tail pipe, molding and windows for overspray indicating that the vehicle has been repainted.
3. Rust: Check fenders, doors, rocker panels, window moldings, wheel wells, floorboards, under floor mats, and in the trunk for signs of rust. Any rust at all will be a problem. There is no way to permanently stop the spread of rust, except to replace the part or panel.

➡If rust repair is suspected, try using a magnet to check for body filler. A magnet should stick to the sheet metal parts of the body, but will not adhere to areas with large amounts of filler.

4. Body appearance: Check the moldings, bumpers, grille, vinyl roof, glass, doors, trunk lid and body panels for general overall condition. Check for misalignment, loose hold-down clips, ripples, scratches in glass, welding in the trunk, severe misalignment of body panels or ripples, any of which may indicate crash work.
5. Leaks: Get down and look under the vehicle. There are no normal leaks, other than water from the air conditioner evaporator.
6. Tires: Check the tire air pressure. One old trick is to pump the tire pressure up to make the vehicle roll easier. Check the tread wear, then open the trunk and check the spare too. Uneven wear is a clue that the front end may need an alignment.
7. Shock absorbers: Check the shock absorbers by forcing downward sharply on each corner of the vehicle. Good shocks will not allow the vehicle to bounce more than once after you let go.
8. Interior: Check the entire interior. You're looking for an interior condition that agrees with the overall condition of the vehicle. Reasonable wear is expected, but be suspicious of new seat covers on sagging seats, new pedal pads, and worn

1-58 GENERAL INFORMATION AND MAINTENANCE

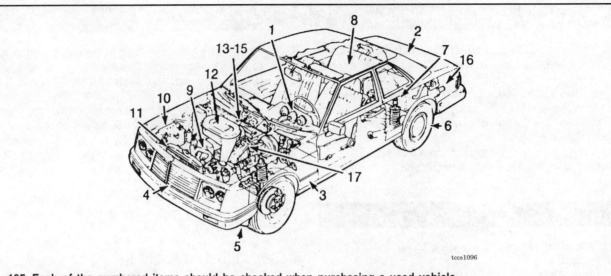

Fig. 135 Each of the numbered items should be checked when purchasing a used vehicle

armrests. These indicate an attempt to cover up hard use. Pull back the carpets and look for evidence of water leaks or flooding. Look for missing hardware, door handles, control knobs, etc. Check lights and signal operations. Make sure all accessories (air conditioner, heater, radio, etc.) work. Check windshield wiper operation.

9. Belts and Hoses: Open the hood, then check all belts and hoses for wear, cracks or weak spots.

10. Battery: Low electrolyte level, corroded terminals and/or cracked case indicate a lack of maintenance.

11. Radiator: Look for corrosion or rust in the coolant indicating a lack of maintenance.

12. Air filter: A severely dirty air filter would indicate a lack of maintenance.

13. Ignition wires: Check the ignition wires for cracks, burned spots, or wear. Worn wires will have to be replaced.

14. Oil level: If the oil level is low, chances are the engine uses oil or leaks. Beware of water in the oil (there is probably a cracked block or bad head gasket), excessively thick oil (which is often used to quiet a noisy engine), or thin, dirty oil with a distinct gasoline smell (this may indicate internal engine problems).

15. Automatic Transmission: Pull the transmission dipstick out when the engine is running. The level should read FULL, and the fluid should be clear or bright red. Dark brown or black fluid that has distinct burnt odor, indicates a transmission in need of repair or overhaul.

16. Exhaust: Check the color of the exhaust smoke. Blue smoke indicates, among other problems, worn rings. Black smoke can indicate burnt valves or carburetor problems. Check the exhaust system for leaks; it can be expensive to replace.

17. Spark Plugs: Remove one or all of the spark plugs (the most accessible will do, though all are preferable). An engine in good condition will show plugs with a light tan or gray deposit on the firing tip.

ROAD TEST CHECKLIST

1. Engine Performance: The vehicle should be peppy whether cold or warm, with adequate power and good pickup. It should respond smoothly through the gears.

2. Brakes: They should provide quick, firm stops with no noise, pulling or brake fade.

3. Steering: Sure control with no binding harshness, or looseness and no shimmy in the wheel should be expected. Noise or vibration from the steering wheel when turning the vehicle means trouble.

4. Clutch (Manual Transmission): Clutch action should give quick, smooth response with easy shifting. The clutch pedal should have free-play before it disengages the clutch. Start the engine, set the parking brake, put the transmission in first gear and slowly release the clutch pedal. The engine should begin to stall when the pedal is $1/2$-$3/4$ of the way up.

5. Automatic Transmission: The transmission should shift rapidly and smoothly, with no noise, hesitation, or slipping.

6. Differential: No noise or thumps should be present. Differentials have no normal leaks.

7. Driveshaft/Universal Joints: Vibration and noise could mean driveshaft problems. Clicking at low speed or coast conditions means worn U-joints.

8. Suspension: Try hitting bumps at different speeds. A vehicle that bounces excessively has weak shock absorbers or struts. Clunks mean worn bushings or ball joints.

9. Frame/Body: Wet the tires and drive in a straight line. Tracks should show two straight lines, not four. Four tire tracks indicate a frame/body bent by collision damage. If the tires can't be wet for this purpose, have a friend drive along behind you and see if the vehicle appears to be traveling in a straight line.

GENERAL INFORMATION AND MAINTENANCE

Maintenance Chart

1945–50

Interval	Item	Service
Every 1,000 miles	Steering linkage	EP chassis lube
	U-Joints	EP chassis lube
	Spring shackles w/fittings	EP chassis lube
	Steering gear level	Check
	Rear wheel bearings w/fittings	Lubricate sparingly
	Manual transmission	Check level
	Transfer case	Check level
	Front axle	Check level
	Rear axle	Check level
	Distributor oiler	Lubricate w/engine oil
	Distributor wick and pivot	Lubricate w/engine oil
	Distributor cam	2cc of silicone grease
	Generator	2–4 drops of engine oil
	6-cyl. heat riser	Lubricate
Every 2,000 miles	Change oil and filter	See oil viscosity chart
	Air cleaner	Clean and refill with engine oil
Every 6,000 miles	Front wheel bearings	Clean and repack
	Fuel filter	Replace
	Oil filler cap	Clean
	Timing and dwell	Check
	Heat riser	Lubricate
	Point, condenser, rotor	Replace
	Spark plugs	Replace
	Drive belts	Check
	Rear wheel bearings wo/fittings	Clean and repack
Every 10,000 miles	Manual transmission	Change fluid
	Transfer case	Change fluid
	Front axle	Change fluid
	Rear axle	Change fluid
Every 12,000 miles	Steering knuckles	Change lubricant
	Speedometer cable	Lubricate
Every 24,000 miles	Engine coolant	Flush and change
	Spark plug wires	Change
Every 300 hours	Power take off	Drain and refill

1951–61

Interval	Item	Service
Every 2,000 miles	Steering linkage	EP chassis lube
	U-joints	EP chassis lube
	Spring shackles w/fittings	EP chassis lube
	Steering gear level	Check
	Rear wheel bearings w/fittings	Lubricate sparingly
	Manual transmission	Check level
	Transfer case	Check level
	Front axle	Check level
	Rear axle	Check level
	Distributor oiler	Lubricate w/engine oil
	Distributor wick and pivot	Lubricate w/engine oil
	Distributor cam	2cc of silicone grease
	Generator	2–4 drops of engine oil
	Change oil and filter (4-134)	See oil viscosity chart
	4-134 air cleaner	Clean and refill with engine oil
Every 6,000 miles	Front wheel bearings	Clean and repack
	Rear wheel bearings wo/fittings	Clean and repack

1-60 GENERAL INFORMATION AND MAINTENANCE

Maintenance Chart (cont.)

1951-61

Interval	Item	Service
Every 10,000 miles	Manual transmission	Change fluid
	Transfer case	Change fluid
	Front axle	Change fluid
	Rear axle	Change fluid
Every 12,000 miles	Steering knuckles	Change lubricant
	Speedometer cable	Lubricate
	Fuel filter	Replace
	PCV valve	Replace
	Oil filler cap	Clean
	Timing and dwell	Check
	Heat riser	Lubricate
	Point, condenser, rotor	Replace
	Spark plugs	Replace
Every 24,000 miles	Spark plug wires	Change
Once a year	Engine coolant	Flush and change

* Severe service

1962-69

Interval	Item	Service
Every 4,000 miles	Engine oil and filter	Change
Every 6,000 miles	Steering gear	Check level
	Differentials	Check level
	King pins	Chassis lube
	Manual transmission	Check level
	Transfer case	Check level
	Clutch cross shaft	Chassis lube
	Air cleaner, dry type	Change filter
	Drive belts	Check
	Air cleaner, oil bath type	Clean and refill
Every 12,000 miles	All chassis lube fittings	EP chassis lube
	Front and rear wheel bearings	Clean and repack
	U-joints	EP chassis lube
	Fuel filter	Replace
	PCV valve	Replace
	Oil filler cap	Clean
	Timing and dwell	Check
	Heat riser	Lubricate
	Point condenser, rotor	Replace
	Spark plugs	Replace
Every 30,000 miles	Differentials	Change fluid
	Manual transmission	Change fluid
	Transfer case	Change fluid
	Spark plug wires	Change

1970

Interval	Item	Service
Every 6,000 miles	Engine oil and filter	Change
	Steering gear	Check level
	Differentials	Check level
	Manual transmission	Check level
	Transfer case	Check level
	Drive belts	Check
	Air cleaner	Change filter
Every 12,000 miles	All chassis lube fittings	EP chassis lube
	Front and rear wheel bearings	Clean and repack
	U-joints	EP chassis lube

Maintenance Chart (cont.)

1970

Interval	Item	Service
Every 12,000 miles	Fuel filter	Replace
	PCV valve	Replace
	Oil filler cap	Clean
	Timing and dwell	Check
	Heat riser	Lubricate
	Point condenser, rotor	Replace
	Spark plugs	Replace
Every 30,000 miles	Differentials	Change fluid
	Manual transmission	Change fluid
	Spark plug wires	Change
	Transfer case	Change fluid

CAPACITIES

Model	Engine	Engine Oil with Filter (qts.)	Transmission (pts.) 3-Spd	4-Spd	Auto.	Transfer Case (pts.)	Drive Axle Front (pts.)	Rear (pts.)	Fuel Tank (gal.)	Cooling System (qts.)
4–63, 4x4–63	4–134	5.0	3.5	—	—	3.5	2.5	2.75	10.5	12.0
6–63	6–226	6.0	①	6.75	—	②	3.0	3.0	22.0	12.0
4–73	4–134	5.0	3.5	—	—	3.5	2.5	2.75	10.5	12.0
	6–226	6.0	①	6.75	—	②	3.0	3.0	22.0	12.0
4–75	4–134	5.0	3.5	—	—	3.5	2.5	2.75	10.5	12.0
	6–226	6.0	①	6.75	—	②	3.0	3.0	22.0	12.0
	6–230	6.0	2.75	6.5	—	3.25	③	3.0	20.0	12.0
CJ–2A	4–134	5.0	3.5	—	—	3.5	2.5	2.75	10.5	12.0
CJ–3A	4–134	5.0	3.5	—	—	3.5	2.5	2.75	10.5	12.0
CJ–3B	4–134	5.0	3.0	—	—	3.5	2.5	2.5	10.5	12.0
CJ–5	4–134	5.0	3.0	6.75	—	3.5	2.5	2.5	10.5	12.0
	6–225	4.0	3.0	6.75	—	3.5	2.5	2.5	10.5	10.0
CJ–6	4–134	5.0	3.0	6.75	—	3.5	2.5	2.5	10.5	12.0
	6–225	4.0	3.0	6.75	—	3.5	2.5	2.5	10.5	12.0

① Transmission and transfer case are filled together, sharing a common sump. Total capacity for the 3-speed with a transfer case is 6.5 pts.
② Transfer case capacity on vehicles with the optional 4-speed transmission is 3.5 pts.
③ Dana 27: 2.5
   Dana 44: 3.0

1-62 GENERAL INFORMATION AND MAINTENANCE

ENGLISH TO METRIC CONVERSION: MASS (WEIGHT)

Current **mass** measurement is expressed in pounds and ounces (lbs. & ozs.). The metric unit of mass (or weight) is the kilogram (kg). Even although this table does not show conversion of masses (weights) larger than 15 lbs, it is easy to calculate larger units by following the data immediately below.

To convert ounces (oz.) to grams (g): multiply th number of ozs. by 28
To convert grams (g) to ounces (oz.): multiply the number of grams by .035

To convert pounds (lbs.) to kilograms (kg): multiply the number of lbs. by .45
To convert kilograms (kg) to pounds (lbs.): multiply the number of kilograms by 2.2

lbs	kg	lbs	kg	oz	kg	oz	kg
0.1	0.04	0.9	0.41	0.1	0.003	0.9	0.024
0.2	0.09	1	0.4	0.2	0.005	1	0.03
0.3	0.14	2	0.9	0.3	0.008	2	0.06
0.4	0.18	3	1.4	0.4	0.011	3	0.08
0.5	0.23	4	1.8	0.5	0.014	4	0.11
0.6	0.27	5	2.3	0.6	0.017	5	0.14
0.7	0.32	10	4.5	0.7	0.020	10	0.28
0.8	0.36	15	6.8	0.8	0.023	15	0.42

ENGLISH TO METRIC CONVERSION: TEMPERATURE

To convert Fahrenheit (°F) to Celsius (°C): take number of °F and subtract 32; multiply result by 5; divide result by 9
To convert Celsius (°C) to Fahrenheit (°F): take number of °C and multiply by 9; divide result by 5; add 32 to total

Fahrenheit (F)		Celsius (C)		Fahrenheit (F)		Celsius (C)		Fahrenheit (F)		Celsius (C)	
°F	°C	°C	°F	°F	°C	°C	°F	°F	°C	°C	°F
−40	−40	−38	−36.4	80	26.7	18	64.4	215	101.7	80	176
−35	−37.2	−36	−32.8	85	29.4	20	68	220	104.4	85	185
−30	−34.4	−34	−29.2	90	32.2	22	71.6	225	107.2	90	194
−25	−31.7	−32	−25.6	95	35.0	24	75.2	230	110.0	95	202
−20	−28.9	−30	−22	100	37.8	26	78.8	235	112.8	100	212
−15	−26.1	−28	−18.4	105	40.6	28	82.4	240	115.6	105	221
−10	−23.3	−26	−14.8	110	43.3	30	86	245	118.3	110	230
−5	−20.6	−24	−11.2	115	46.1	32	89.6	250	121.1	115	239
0	−17.8	−22	−7.6	120	48.9	34	93.2	255	123.9	120	248
1	−17.2	−20	−4	125	51.7	36	96.8	260	126.6	125	257
2	−16.7	−18	−0.4	130	54.4	38	100.4	265	129.4	130	266
3	−16.1	−16	3.2	135	57.2	40	104	270	132.2	135	275
4	−15.6	−14	6.8	140	60.0	42	107.6	275	135.0	140	284
5	−15.0	−12	10.4	145	62.8	44	112.2	280	137.8	145	293
10	−12.2	−10	14	150	65.6	46	114.8	285	140.6	150	302
15	−9.4	−8	17.6	155	68.3	48	118.4	290	143.3	155	311
20	−6.7	−6	21.2	160	71.1	50	122	295	146.1	160	320
25	−3.9	−4	24.8	165	73.9	52	125.6	300	148.9	165	329
30	−1.1	−2	28.4	170	76.7	54	129.2	305	151.7	170	338
35	1.7	0	32	175	79.4	56	132.8	310	154.4	175	347
40	4.4	2	35.6	180	82.2	58	136.4	315	157.2	180	356
45	7.2	4	39.2	185	85.0	60	140	320	160.0	185	365
50	10.0	6	42.8	190	87.8	62	143.6	325	162.8	190	374
55	12.8	8	46.4	195	90.6	64	147.2	330	165.6	195	383
60	15.6	10	50	200	93.3	66	150.8	335	168.3	200	392
65	18.3	12	53.6	205	96.1	68	154.4	340	171.1	205	401
70	21.1	14	57.2	210	98.9	70	158	345	173.9	210	410
75	23.9	16	60.8	212	100.0	75	167	350	176.7	215	414

GENERAL INFORMATION AND MAINTENANCE

ENGLISH TO METRIC CONVERSION: LENGTH

To convert inches (ins.) to millimeters (mm): multiply number of inches by 25.4
To convert millimeters (mm) to inches (ins.): multiply number of millimeters by .04

Inches		Decimals	Milli-meters	Inches to millimeters inches	mm	Inches		Decimals	Milli-meters	Inches to millimeters inches	mm
	1/64	0.051625	0.3969	0.0001	0.00254		33/64	0.515625	13.0969	0.6	15.24
1/32		0.03125	0.7937	0.0002	0.00508	17/32		0.53125	13.4937	0.7	17.78
	3/64	0.046875	1.1906	0.0003	0.00762		35/64	0.546875	13.8906	0.8	20.32
1/16		0.0625	1.5875	0.0004	0.01016	9/16		0.5625	14.2875	0.9	22.86
	5/64	0.078125	1.9844	0.0005	0.01270		37/64	0.578125	14.6844	1	25.4
3/32		0.09375	2.3812	0.0006	0.01524	19/32		0.59375	15.0812	2	50.8
	7/64	0.109375	2.7781	0.0007	0.01778		39/64	0.609375	15.4781	3	76.2
1/8		0.125	3.1750	0.0008	0.02032	5/8		0.625	15.8750	4	101.6
	9/64	0.140625	3.5719	0.0009	0.02286		41/64	0.640625	16.2719	5	127.0
5/32		0.15625	3.9687	0.001	0.0254	21/32		0.65625	16.6687	6	152.4
	11/64	0.171875	4.3656	0.002	0.0508		43/64	0.671875	17.0656	7	177.8
3/16		0.1875	4.7625	0.003	0.0762	11/16		0.6875	17.4625	8	203.2
	13/64	0.203125	5.1594	0.004	0.1016		45/64	0.703125	17.8594	9	228.6
7/32		0.21875	5.5562	0.005	0.1270	23/32		0.71875	18.2562	10	254.0
	15/64	0.234375	5.9531	0.006	0.1524		47/64	0.734375	18.6531	11	279.4
1/4		0.25	6.3500	0.007	0.1778	3/4		0.75	19.0500	12	304.8
	17/64	0.265625	6.7469	0.008	0.2032		49/64	0.765625	19.4469	13	330.2
9/32		0.28125	7.1437	0.009	0.2286	25/32		0.78125	19.8437	14	355.6
	19/64	0.296875	7.5406	0.01	0.254		51/64	0.796875	20.2406	15	381.0
5/16		0.3125	7.9375	0.02	0.508	13/16		0.8125	20.6375	16	406.4
	21/64	0.328125	8.3344	0.03	0.762		53/64	0.828125	21.0344	17	431.8
11/32		0.34375	8.7312	0.04	1.016	27/32		0.84375	21.4312	18	457.2
	23/64	0.359375	9.1281	0.05	1.270		55/64	0.859375	21.8281	19	482.6
3/8		0.375	9.5250	0.06	1.524	7/8		0.875	22.2250	20	508.0
	25/64	0.390625	9.9219	0.07	1.778		57/64	0.890625	22.6219	21	533.4
13/32		0.40625	10.3187	0.08	2.032	29/32		0.90625	23.0187	22	558.8
	27/64	0.421875	10.7156	0.09	2.286		59/64	0.921875	23.4156	23	584.2
7/16		0.4375	11.1125	0.1	2.54	15/16		0.9375	23.8125	24	609.6
	29/64	0.453125	11.5094	0.2	5.08		61/64	0.953125	24.2094	25	635.0
15/32		0.46875	11.9062	0.3	7.62	31/32		0.96875	24.6062	26	660.4
	31/64	0.484375	12.3031	0.4	10.16		63/64	0.984375	25.0031	27	690.6
1/2		0.5	12.7000	0.5	12.70						

ENGLISH TO METRIC CONVERSION: TORQUE

To convert foot-pounds (ft. lbs.) to Newton-meters: multiply the number of ft. lbs. by 1.3
To convert inch-pounds (in. lbs.) to Newton-meters: multiply the number of in. lbs. by .11

in lbs	N-m	in lbs	N-m	in lbs	N-m	in lbs	N-m	in lbs	N-m
0.1	0.01	1	0.11	10	1.13	19	2.15	28	3.16
0.2	0.02	2	0.23	11	1.24	20	2.26	29	3.28
0.3	0.03	3	0.34	12	1.36	21	2.37	30	3.39
0.4	0.04	4	0.45	13	1.47	22	2.49	31	3.50
0.5	0.06	5	0.56	14	1.58	23	2.60	32	3.62
0.6	0.07	6	0.68	15	1.70	24	2.71	33	3.73
0.7	0.08	7	0.78	16	1.81	25	2.82	34	3.84
0.8	0.09	8	0.90	17	1.92	26	2.94	35	3.95
0.9	0.10	9	1.02	18	2.03	27	3.05	36	4.07

ENGLISH TO METRIC CONVERSION: TORQUE

Torque is now expressed as either foot-pounds (ft./lbs.) or inch-pounds (in./lbs.). The metric measurement unit for torque is the Newton-meter (Nm). This unit—the Nm—will be used for all SI metric torque references, both the present ft./lbs. and in./lbs.

ft lbs	N-m	ft lbs	N-m	ft lbs	N-m	ft lbs	N-m
0.1	0.1	33	44.7	74	100.3	115	155.9
0.2	0.3	34	46.1	75	101.7	116	157.3
0.3	0.4	35	47.4	76	103.0	117	158.6
0.4	0.5	36	48.8	77	104.4	118	160.0
0.5	0.7	37	50.7	78	105.8	119	161.3
0.6	0.8	38	51.5	79	107.1	120	162.7
0.7	1.0	39	52.9	80	108.5	121	164.0
0.8	1.1	40	54.2	81	109.8	122	165.4
0.9	1.2	41	55.6	82	111.2	123	166.8
1	1.3	42	56.9	83	112.5	124	168.1
2	2.7	43	58.3	84	113.9	125	169.5
3	4.1	44	59.7	85	115.2	126	170.8
4	5.4	45	61.0	86	116.6	127	172.2
5	6.8	46	62.4	87	118.0	128	173.5
6	8.1	47	63.7	88	119.3	129	174.9
7	9.5	48	65.1	89	120.7	130	176.2
8	10.8	49	66.4	90	122.0	131	177.6
9	12.2	50	67.8	91	123.4	132	179.0
10	13.6	51	69.2	92	124.7	133	180.3
11	14.9	52	70.5	93	126.1	134	181.7
12	16.3	53	71.9	94	127.4	135	183.0
13	17.6	54	73.2	95	128.8	136	184.4
14	18.9	55	74.6	96	130.2	137	185.7
15	20.3	56	75.9	97	131.5	138	187.1
16	21.7	57	77.3	98	132.9	139	188.5
17	23.0	58	78.6	99	134.2	140	189.8
18	24.4	59	80.0	100	135.6	141	191.2
19	25.8	60	81.4	101	136.9	142	192.5
20	27.1	61	82.7	102	138.3	143	193.9
21	28.5	62	84.1	103	139.6	144	195.2
22	29.8	63	85.4	104	141.0	145	196.6
23	31.2	64	86.8	105	142.4	146	198.0
24	32.5	65	88.1	106	143.7	147	199.3
25	33.9	66	89.5	107	145.1	148	200.7
26	35.2	67	90.8	108	146.4	149	202.0
27	36.6	68	92.2	109	147.8	150	203.4
28	38.0	69	93.6	110	149.1	151	204.7
29	39.3	70	94.9	111	150.5	152	206.1
30	40.7	71	96.3	112	151.8	153	207.4
31	42.0	72	97.6	113	153.2	154	208.8
32	43.4	73	99.0	114	154.6	155	210.2

ENGLISH TO METRIC CONVERSION: FORCE

Force is presently measured in pounds (lbs.). This type of measurement is used to measure spring pressure, specifically how many pounds it takes to compress a spring. Our present force unit (the pound) will be replaced in SI metric measurements by the Newton (N). This term will eventually see use in specifications for electric motor brush spring pressures, valve spring pressures, etc.

To convert pounds (lbs.) to Newton (N): multiply the number of lbs. by 4.45

lbs	N	lbs	N	lbs	N	oz	N
0.01	0.04	21	93.4	59	262.4	1	0.3
0.02	0.09	22	97.9	60	266.9	2	0.6
0.03	0.13	23	102.3	61	271.3	3	0.8
0.04	0.18	24	106.8	62	275.8	4	1.1
0.05	0.22	25	111.2	63	280.2	5	1.4
0.06	0.27	26	115.6	64	284.6	6	1.7
0.07	0.31	27	120.1	65	289.1	7	2.0
0.08	0.36	28	124.6	66	293.6	8	2.2
0.09	0.40	29	129.0	67	298.0	9	2.5
0.1	0.4	30	133.4	68	302.5	10	2.8
0.2	0.9	31	137.9	69	306.9	11	3.1
0.3	1.3	32	142.3	70	311.4	12	3.3
0.4	1.8	33	146.8	71	315.8	13	3.6
0.5	2.2	34	151.2	72	320.3	14	3.9
0.6	2.7	35	155.7	73	324.7	15	4.2
0.7	3.1	36	160.1	74	329.2	16	4.4
0.8	3.6	37	164.6	75	333.6	17	4.7
0.9	4.0	38	169.0	76	338.1	18	5.0
1	4.4	39	173.5	77	342.5	19	5.3
2	8.9	40	177.9	78	347.0	20	5.6
3	13.4	41	182.4	79	351.4	21	5.8
4	17.8	42	186.8	80	355.9	22	6.1
5	22.2	43	191.3	81	360.3	23	6.4
6	26.7	44	195.7	82	364.8	24	6.7
7	31.1	45	200.2	83	369.2	25	7.0
8	35.6	46	204.6	84	373.6	26	7.2
9	40.0	47	209.1	85	378.1	27	7.5
10	44.5	48	213.5	86	382.6	28	7.8
11	48.9	49	218.0	87	387.0	29	8.1
12	53.4	50	224.4	88	391.4	30	8.3
13	57.8	51	226.9	89	395.9	31	8.6
14	62.3	52	231.3	90	400.3	32	8.9
15	66.7	53	235.8	91	404.8	33	9.2
16	71.2	54	240.2	92	409.2	34	9.4
17	75.6	55	244.6	93	413.7	35	9.7
18	80.1	56	249.1	94	418.1	36	10.0
19	84.5	57	253.6	95	422.6	37	10.3
20	89.0	58	258.0	96	427.0	38	10.6

ENGLISH TO METRIC CONVERSION: LIQUID CAPACITY

Liquid or fluid capacity is presently expressed as pints, quarts or gallons, or a combination of all of these. In the metric system the liter (l) will become the basic unit. Fractions of a liter would be expressed as deciliters, centiliters, or most frequently (and commonly) as milliliters.

To convert pints (pts.) to liters (l): multiply the number of pints by .47
To convert liters (l) to pints (pts.): multiply the number of liters by 2.1
To convert quarts (qts.) to liters (l): multiply the number of quarts by .95

To convert liters (l) to quarts (qts.): multiply the number of liters by 1.06
To convert gallons (gals.) to liters (l): multiply the number of gallons by 3.8
To convert liters (l) to gallons (gals.): multiply the number of liters by .26

gals	liters	qts	liters	pts	liters
0.1	0.38	0.1	0.10	0.1	0.05
0.2	0.76	0.2	0.19	0.2	0.10
0.3	1.1	0.3	0.28	0.3	0.14
0.4	1.5	0.4	0.38	0.4	0.19
0.5	1.9	0.5	0.47	0.5	0.24
0.6	2.3	0.6	0.57	0.6	0.28
0.7	2.6	0.7	0.66	0.7	0.33
0.8	3.0	0.8	0.76	0.8	0.38
0.9	3.4	0.9	0.85	0.9	0.43
1	3.8	1	1.0	1	0.5
2	7.6	2	1.9	2	1.0
3	11.4	3	2.8	3	1.4
4	15.1	4	3.8	4	1.9
5	18.9	5	4.7	5	2.4
6	22.7	6	5.7	6	2.8
7	26.5	7	6.6	7	3.3
8	30.3	8	7.6	8	3.8
9	34.1	9	8.5	9	4.3
10	37.8	10	9.5	10	4.7
11	41.6	11	10.4	11	5.2
12	45.4	12	11.4	12	5.7
13	49.2	13	12.3	13	6.2
14	53.0	14	13.2	14	6.6
15	56.8	15	14.2	15	7.1
16	60.6	16	15.1	16	7.6
17	64.3	17	16.1	17	8.0
18	68.1	18	17.0	18	8.5
19	71.9	19	18.0	19	9.0
20	75.7	20	18.9	20	9.5
21	79.5	21	19.9	21	9.9
22	83.2	22	20.8	22	10.4
23	87.0	23	21.8	23	10.9
24	90.8	24	22.7	24	11.4
25	94.6	25	23.6	25	11.8
26	98.4	26	24.6	26	12.3
27	102.2	27	25.5	27	12.8
28	106.0	28	26.5	28	13.2
29	110.0	29	27.4	29	13.7
30	113.5	30	28.4	30	14.2

GENERAL INFORMATION AND MAINTENANCE 1-67

ENGLISH TO METRIC CONVERSION: PRESSURE

The basic unit of pressure measurement used today is expressed as pounds per square inch (psi). The metric unit for psi will be the kilopascal (kPa). This will apply to either fluid pressure or air pressure, and will be frequently seen in tire pressure readings, oil pressure specifications, fuel pump pressure, etc.

To convert pounds per square inch (psi) to kilopascals (kPa): multiply the number of psi by 6.89

Psi	kPa	Psi	kPa	Psi	kPa	Psi	kPa
0.1	0.7	37	255.1	82	565.4	127	875.6
0.2	1.4	38	262.0	83	572.3	128	882.5
0.3	2.1	39	268.9	84	579.2	129	889.4
0.4	2.8	40	275.8	85	586.0	130	896.3
0.5	3.4	41	282.7	86	592.9	131	903.2
0.6	4.1	42	289.6	87	599.8	132	910.1
0.7	4.8	43	296.5	88	606.7	133	917.0
0.8	5.5	44	303.4	89	613.6	134	923.9
0.9	6.2	45	310.3	90	620.5	135	930.8
1	6.9	46	317.2	91	627.4	136	937.7
2	13.8	47	324.0	92	634.3	137	944.6
3	20.7	48	331.0	93	641.2	138	951.5
4	27.6	49	337.8	94	648.1	139	958.4
5	34.5	50	344.7	95	655.0	140	965.2
6	41.4	51	351.6	96	661.9	141	972.2
7	48.3	52	358.5	97	668.8	142	979.0
8	55.2	53	365.4	98	675.7	143	985.9
9	62.1	54	372.3	99	682.6	144	992.8
10	69.0	55	379.2	100	689.5	145	999.7
11	75.8	56	386.1	101	696.4	146	1006.6
12	82.7	57	393.0	102	703.3	147	1013.5
13	89.6	58	399.9	103	710.2	148	1020.4
14	96.5	59	406.8	104	717.0	149	1027.3
15	103.4	60	413.7	105	723.9	150	1034.2
16	110.3	61	420.6	106	730.8	151	1041.1
17	117.2	62	427.5	107	737.7	152	1048.0
18	124.1	63	434.4	108	744.6	153	1054.9
19	131.0	64	441.3	109	751.5	154	1061.8
20	137.9	65	448.2	110	758.4	155	1068.7
21	144.8	66	455.0	111	765.3	156	1075.6
22	151.7	67	461.9	112	772.2	157	1082.5
23	158.6	68	468.8	113	779.1	158	1089.4
24	165.5	69	475.7	114	786.0	159	1096.3
25	172.4	70	482.6	115	792.9	160	1103.2
26	179.3	71	489.5	116	799.8	161	1110.0
27	186.2	72	496.4	117	806.7	162	1116.9
28	193.0	73	503.3	118	813.6	163	1123.8
29	200.0	74	510.2	119	820.5	164	1130.7
30	206.8	75	517.1	120	827.4	165	1137.6
31	213.7	76	524.0	121	834.3	166	1144.5
32	220.6	77	530.9	122	841.2	167	1151.4
33	227.5	78	537.8	123	848.0	168	1158.3
34	234.4	79	544.7	124	854.9	169	1165.2
35	241.3	80	551.6	125	861.8	170	1172.1
36	248.2	81	558.5	126	868.7	171	1179.0

GENERAL INFORMATION AND MAINTENANCE

ENGLISH TO METRIC CONVERSION: PRESSURE

The basic unit of pressure measurement used today is expressed as pounds per square inch (psi). The metric unit for psi will be the kilopascal (kPa). This will apply to either fluid pressure or air pressure, and will be frequently seen in tire pressure readings, oil pressure specifications, fuel pump pressure, etc.

To convert pounds per square inch (psi) to kilopascals (kPa): multiply the number of psi by 6.89

Psi	kPa	Psi	kPa	Psi	kPa	Psi	kPa
172	1185.9	216	1489.3	260	1792.6	304	2096.0
173	1192.8	217	1496.2	261	1799.5	305	2102.9
174	1199.7	218	1503.1	262	1806.4	306	2109.8
175	1206.6	219	1510.0	263	1813.3	307	2116.7
176	1213.5	220	1516.8	264	1820.2	308	2123.6
177	1220.4	221	1523.7	265	1827.1	309	2130.5
178	1227.3	222	1530.6	266	1834.0	310	2137.4
179	1234.2	223	1537.5	267	1840.9	311	2144.3
180	1241.0	224	1544.4	268	1847.8	312	2151.2
181	1247.9	225	1551.3	269	1854.7	313	2158.1
182	1254.8	226	1558.2	270	1861.6	314	2164.9
183	1261.7	227	1565.1	271	1868.5	315	2171.8
184	1268.6	228	1572.0	272	1875.4	316	2178.7
185	1275.5	229	1578.9	273	1882.3	317	2185.6
186	1282.4	230	1585.8	274	1889.2	318	2192.5
187	1289.3	231	1592.7	275	1896.1	319	2199.4
188	1296.2	232	1599.6	276	1903.0	320	2206.3
189	1303.1	233	1606.5	277	1909.8	321	2213.2
190	1310.0	234	1613.4	278	1916.7	322	2220.1
191	1316.9	235	1620.3	279	1923.6	323	2227.0
192	1323.8	236	1627.2	280	1930.5	324	2233.9
193	1330.7	237	1634.1	281	1937.4	325	2240.8
194	1337.6	238	1641.0	282	1944.3	326	2247.7
195	1344.5	239	1647.8	283	1951.2	327	2254.6
196	1351.4	240	1654.7	284	1958.1	328	2261.5
197	1358.3	241	1661.6	285	1965.0	329	2268.4
198	1365.2	242	1668.5	286	1971.9	330	2275.3
199	1372.0	243	1675.4	287	1978.8	331	2282.2
200	1378.9	244	1682.3	288	1985.7	332	2289.1
201	1385.8	245	1689.2	289	1992.6	333	2295.9
202	1392.7	246	1696.1	290	1999.5	334	2302.8
203	1399.6	247	1703.0	291	2006.4	335	2309.7
204	1406.5	248	1709.9	292	2013.3	336	2316.6
205	1413.4	249	1716.8	293	2020.2	337	2323.5
206	1420.3	250	1723.7	294	2027.1	338	2330.4
207	1427.2	251	1730.6	295	2034.0	339	2337.3
208	1434.1	252	1737.5	296	2040.8	240	2344.2
209	1441.0	253	1744.4	297	2047.7	341	2351.1
210	1447.9	254	1751.3	298	2054.6	342	2358.0
211	1454.8	255	1758.2	299	2061.5	343	2364.9
212	1461.7	256	1765.1	300	2068.4	344	2371.8
213	1468.7	257	1772.0	301	2075.3	345	2378.7
214	1475.5	258	1778.8	302	2082.2	346	2385.6
215	1482.4	259	1785.7	303	2089.1	347	2392.5

FIRING ORDERS 2-11
IDLE SPEED AND MIXTURE
  ADJUSTMENTS
    IDLE MIXTURE 2-21
    IDLE SPEED 2-21
IGNITION TIMING
    TIMING 2-16
POINT TYPE IGNITION
    BREAKER POINTS AND
      CONDENSER 2-12
SPECIFICATIONS CHARTS
    TROUBLESHOOTING ENGINE
      PERFORMANCE 2-21
    TROUBLESHOOTING THE IGNITION
      SYSTEM 2-2
    TUNE-UP SPECIFICATIONS 2-2
TUNE-UP PROCEDURES
    SPARK PLUGS 2-2
VALVE LASH
    ADJUSTMENT 2-18

2

ENGINE PERFORMANCE AND TUNE-UP

FIRING ORDERS 2-11
IDLE SPEED AND MIXTURE
ADJUSTMENTS 2-21
IGNITION TIMING 2-16
POINT TYPE IGNITION 2-12
SPECIFICATIONS CHARTS 2-2
TUNE-UP PROCEDURES 2-2
VALVE LASH 2-18

2-2 ENGINE PERFORMANCE AND TUNE-UP

TUNE-UP PROCEDURES

In order to extract the full measure of performance and economy from your engine it is essential that it be properly tuned at regular intervals. A regular tune-up will keep your vehicle's engine running smoothly and will prevent the annoying minor breakdowns and poor performance associated with an untuned engine.

A complete tune-up should be performed every 12,000 miles (19,200 km) or twelve months, whichever comes first. This interval should be halved if the vehicle is operated under severe conditions, such as trailer towing, prolonged idling, continual stop and start driving, or if starting or running problems are noticed. It is assumed that the routine maintenance described in Section 1 has been kept up, as this will have a decided effect on the results of a tune-up. All of the applicable steps of a tune-up should be followed in order, as the result is a cumulative one.

If the specifications on the tune-up sticker in the engine compartment disagree with the Tune-Up Specifications chart in this section, the figures on the sticker must be used. The sticker often reflects changes made during the production run.

Spark Plugs

▶ See Figure 1

A typical spark plug consists of a metal shell surrounding a ceramic insulator. A metal electrode extends downward through the center of the insulator and protrudes a small distance. Located at the end of the plug and attached to the side of the outer metal shell is the side electrode. The side electrode bends in at a 90° angle so that its tip is just past and parallel to the tip of the center electrode. The distance between these two electrodes (measured in thousandths of an inch or hundredths of a millimeter) is called the spark plug gap.

The spark plug does not produce a spark but instead provides a gap across which the current can arc. The coil produces anywhere from 20,000 to 50,000 volts (depending on the type and application) which travels through the wires to the spark plugs. The current passes along the center electrode and jumps the gap to the side electrode, and in doing so, ignites the air/fuel mixture in the combustion chamber.

SPARK PLUG HEAT RANGE

▶ See Figure 2

Spark plug heat range is the ability of the plug to dissipate heat. The longer the insulator (or the farther it extends into the engine), the hotter the plug will operate; the shorter the insulator (the closer the electrode is to the block's cooling passages) the cooler it will operate. A plug that absorbs little heat and remains too cool will quickly accumulate deposits of oil and carbon since it is not hot enough to burn them off. This leads to plug fouling and consequently to misfiring. A plug that absorbs too much heat will have no deposits but, due to the excessive heat, the electrodes will burn away quickly and might possibly lead to preignition or other ignition problems. Preignition takes place when plug tips get so hot that they glow sufficiently to ignite the air/fuel mixture before the actual spark occurs. This early ignition will usually cause a pinging during low speeds and heavy loads.

The general rule of thumb for choosing the correct heat range when picking a spark plug is: if most of your driving is long distance, high speed travel, use a colder plug; if most of your driving is stop and go, use a hotter plug. Original equipment plugs are generally a good compromise between the 2 styles and most people never have the need to change their plugs from the factory-recommended heat range.

REMOVAL & INSTALLATION

▶ See Figures 3, 4, 5, 6 and 7

A set of spark plugs usually requires replacement after about 20,000-30,000 miles (32,000-48,000 km), depending on your style of driving. In normal operation plug gap increases about 0.001 in (0.025 mm) for every 2,500 miles (4000 km). As the

ENGINE TUNE-UP SPECIFICATIONS

| Engine | Years | Spark Plugs | | Distributor | | Ignition Timing (deg.) | | Valve Clearance | | Idle Speed | |
		Type	Gap (in.)	Point Gap (in.)	Dwell (deg.)	Manual Trans.	Auto. Trans.	Intake	Exhaust	Manual Trans.	Auto. Trans.
4-134	1945-52	J-8	0.030	①	②	5B	—	0.016	0.016	600	—
	1953-70	J-8	0.030	①	②	5B	—	0.018	0.016	600	—
6-225	1965-70	44S	0.035	0.016	30	5B	—	Hyd.	Hyd.	550	—
6-226	1950-60	J-8	0.030	①	③	5B	—	0.014	0.014	550	—
6-230	1960-64	L-12Y	0.030	0.02	38	5B	—	0.008	0.008	600	—

① Autolite distributor: 0.020
　Delco distributor: 0.022
② Autolite distributor: 42
　Delco distributor: 25-34
③ Autolite distributor: 39
　Delco distributor: 31-37

ENGINE PERFORMANCE AND TUNE-UP 2-3

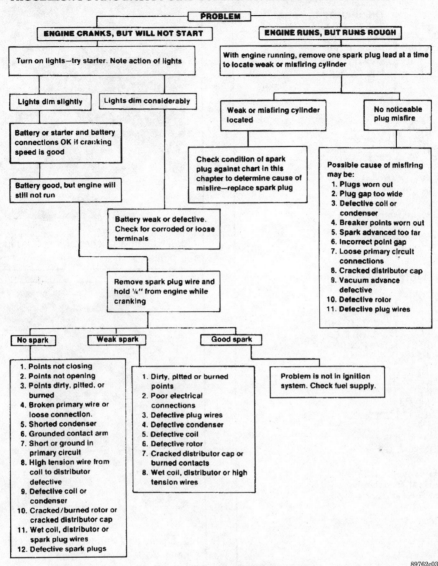

Fig. 1 Cross-section of a spark plug

gap increases, the plug's voltage requirement also increases. It requires a greater voltage to jump the wider gap and about two to three times as much voltage to fire the plug at high speeds than at idle. The improved air/fuel ratio control of modern fuel injection combined with the higher voltage output of modern ignition systems will often allow an engine to run significantly longer on a set of standard spark plugs, but keep in mind that efficiency will drop as the gap widens (along with fuel economy and power).

When you're removing spark plugs, work on one at a time. Don't start by removing the plug wires all at once, because, unless you number them, they may become mixed up. Take a minute before you begin and number the wires with tape.

1. Disconnect the negative battery cable, and if the vehicle has been run recently, allow the engine to thoroughly cool.

2. Carefully twist the spark plug wire boot to loosen it, then pull upward and remove the boot from the plug. Be sure to pull on the boot and not on the wire, otherwise the connector located inside the boot may become separated.

3. Using compressed air, blow any water or debris from the spark plug well to assure that no harmful contaminants are

2-4 ENGINE PERFORMANCE AND TUNE-UP

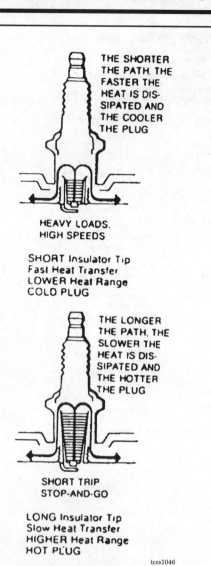

Fig. 2 Spark plug heat range

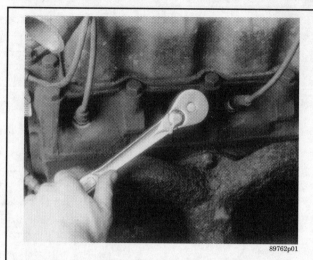

Fig. 4 Using a ratchet and spark plug socket, loosen the plugs . . .

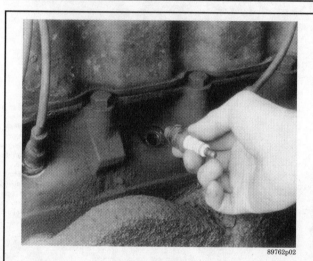

Fig. 5 . . . and remove them from the cylinder head — F-head 4-134 engine shown

Fig. 6 Although spark plugs on the L-head 4-134 engine are mounted on the top of the head, . . .

Fig. 3 Remove the spark plug cable by grasping its boot and twisting/pulling it off the spark plug

ENGINE PERFORMANCE AND TUNE-UP

Fig. 7 ... removal and installation is the same as with the F-head version

allowed to enter the combustion chamber when the spark plug is removed. If compressed air is not available, use a rag or a brush to clean the area.

➡Remove the spark plugs when the engine is cold, if possible, to prevent damage to the threads. If removal of the plugs is difficult, apply a few drops of penetrating oil or silicone spray to the area around the base of the plug, and allow it a few minutes to work.

4. Using a spark plug socket that is equipped with a rubber insert to properly hold the plug, turn the spark plug counterclockwise to loosen and remove the spark plug from the bore.

✱✱WARNING

Be sure not to use a flexible extension on the socket. Use of a flexible extension may allow a shear force to be applied to the plug. A shear force could break the plug off in the cylinder head, leading to costly and frustrating repairs.

To install:

5. Inspect the spark plug boot for tears or damage. If a damaged boot is found, the spark plug wire must be replaced.
6. Using a wire feeler gauge, check and adjust the spark plug gap. When using a gauge, the proper size should pass between the electrodes with a slight drag. The next larger size should not be able to pass while the next smaller size should pass freely.
7. Carefully thread the plug into the bore by hand. If resistance is felt before the plug is almost completely threaded, back the plug out and begin threading again. In small, hard to reach areas, an old spark plug wire and boot could be used as a threading tool. The boot will hold the plug while you twist the end of the wire and the wire is supple enough to twist before it would allow the plug to crossthread.

✱✱WARNING

Do not use the spark plug socket to thread the plugs. Always carefully thread the plug by hand or using an old plug wire to prevent the possibility of crossthreading and damaging the cylinder head bore.

8. Carefully tighten the spark plug. If the plug you are installing is equipped with a crush washer, seat the plug, then tighten about 1/4 turn to crush the washer. If you are installing a tapered seat plug, tighten the plug to specifications provided by the vehicle or plug manufacturer.
9. Apply a small amount of silicone dielectric compound to the end of the spark plug lead or inside the spark plug boot to prevent sticking, then install the boot to the spark plug and push until it clicks into place. The click may be felt or heard, then gently pull back on the boot to assure proper contact.

INSPECTION & GAPPING

▸ See Figures 8, 9, 10, 11, 12, 13, 14, 15, 16, 17, 18 and 19

Check the plugs for deposits and wear. If they are not going to be replaced, clean the plugs thoroughly. Remember that any kind of deposit will decrease the efficiency of the plug. Plugs can be cleaned on a spark plug cleaning machine, which can sometimes be found in service stations, or you can do an acceptable job of cleaning with a stiff brush. If the plugs are cleaned, the electrodes must be filed flat. Use an ignition points file, not an emery board or the like, which will leave deposits. The electrodes must be filed perfectly flat with sharp edges; rounded edges reduce the spark plug voltage by as much as 50%.

Check spark plug gap before installation. The ground electrode (the L-shaped one connected to the body of the plug) must be parallel to the center electrode and the specified size wire gauge (please refer to the Tune-Up Specifications chart for details) must pass between the electrodes with a slight drag.

➡NEVER adjust the gap on a used platinum type spark plug.

Always check the gap on new plugs as they are not always set correctly at the factory. Do not use a flat feeler gauge when measuring the gap on a used plug, because the reading may be inaccurate. A round-wire type gapping tool is the best way to check the gap. The correct gauge should pass through the electrode gap with a slight drag. If you're in doubt, try one size smaller and one larger. The smaller gauge should go through easily, while the larger one shouldn't go through at all. Wire gapping tools usually have a bending tool attached. Use that to adjust the side electrode until the proper distance is obtained. Absolutely never attempt to bend the center electrode. Also, be careful not to bend the side electrode too far or too often as it may weaken and break off within the engine, requiring removal of the cylinder head to retrieve it.

SPARK PLUG CABLES

Inspection

Visually inspect the spark plug cables for burns, cuts, or breaks in the insulation. Check the spark plug boots and the nipples on the distributor cap and coil. Replace any damaged cables. If no physical damage is evident, the cables can be checked with an ohmmeter for excessive resistance.

2-6 ENGINE PERFORMANCE AND TUNE-UP

Tracking Arc
High voltage arcs between a fouling deposit on the insulator tip and spark plug shell. This ignites the fuel/air mixture at some point along the insulator tip, retarding the ignition timing which causes a power and fuel loss.

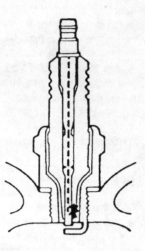

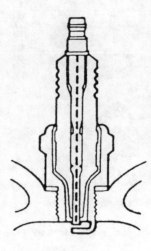

Wide Gap
Spark plug electrodes are worn so that the high voltage charge cannot arc across the electrodes. Improper gapping of electrodes on new or "cleaned" spark plugs could cause a similar condition. Fuel remains unburned and a power loss results.

Flashover
A damaged spark plug boot, along with dirt and moisture, could permit the high voltage charge to short over the insulator to the spark plug shell or the engine. A buttress insulator design helps prevent high voltage flashover.

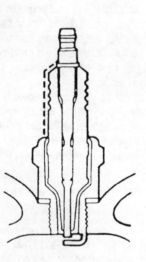

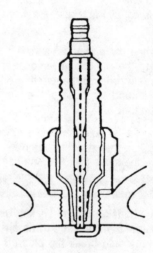

Fouled Spark Plug
Deposits that have formed on the insulator tip may become conductive and provide a "shunt" path to the shell. This prevents the high voltage from arcing between the electrodes. A power and fuel loss is the result.

Bridged Electrodes
Fouling deposits between the electrodes "ground out" the high voltage needed to fire the spark plug. The arc between the electrodes does not occur and the fuel air mixture is not ignited. This causes a power loss and exhausting of raw fuel.

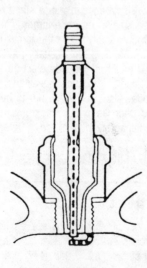

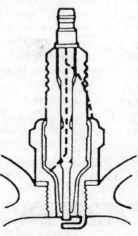

Cracked Insulator
A crack in the spark plug insulator could cause the high voltage charge to "ground out." Here, the spark does not jump the electrode gap and the fuel air mixture is not ignited. This causes a power loss and raw fuel is exhausted.

Fig. 8 Used spark plugs which show damage may indicate engine problems

ENGINE PERFORMANCE AND TUNE-UP

GAP BRIDGED

IDENTIFIED BY DEPOSIT BUILD-UP CLOSING GAP BETWEEN ELECTRODES.

CAUSED BY OIL OR CARBON FOULING. REPLACE PLUG, OR, IF DEPOSITS ARE NOT EXCESSIVE THE PLUG CAN BE CLEANED.

OIL FOULED

IDENTIFIED BY WET BLACK DEPOSITS ON THE INSULATOR SHELL BORE ELECTRODES.

CAUSED BY EXCESSIVE OIL ENTERING COMBUSTION CHAMBER THROUGH WORN RINGS AND PISTONS, EXCESSIVE CLEARANCE BETWEEN VALVE GUIDES AND STEMS, OR WORN OR LOOSE BEARINGS. CORRECT OIL PROBLEM. REPLACE THE PLUG.

CARBON FOULED

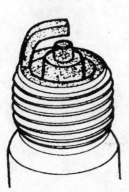

IDENTIFIED BY BLACK, DRY FLUFFY CARBON DEPOSITS ON INSULATOR TIPS, EXPOSED SHELL SURFACES AND ELECTRODES.

CAUSED BY TOO COLD A PLUG, WEAK IGNITION, DIRTY AIR CLEANER, DEFECTIVE FUEL PUMP, TOO RICH A FUEL MIXTURE, IMPROPERLY OPERATING HEAT RISER OR EXCESSIVE IDLING. CAN BE CLEANED.

NORMAL

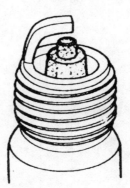

IDENTIFIED BY LIGHT TAN OR GRAY DEPOSITS ON THE FIRING TIP.

PRE-IGNITION

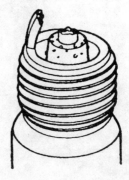

IDENTIFIED BY MELTED ELECTRODES AND POSSIBLY BLISTERED INSULATOR. METALIC DEPOSITS ON INSULATOR INDICATE ENGINE DAMAGE.

CAUSED BY WRONG TYPE OF FUEL, INCORRECT IGNITION TIMING OR ADVANCE, TOO HOT A PLUG, BURNT VALVES OR ENGINE OVERHEATING. REPLACE THE PLUG.

OVERHEATING

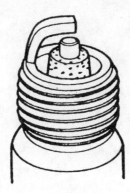

IDENTIFIED BY A WHITE OR LIGHT GRAY INSULATOR WITH SMALL BLACK OR GRAY BROWN SPOTS AND WITH BLUISH-BURNT APPEARANCE OF ELECTRODES.

CAUSED BY ENGINE OVERHEATING, WRONG TYPE OF FUEL, LOOSE SPARK PLUGS, TOO HOT A PLUG, LOW FUEL PUMP PRESSURE OR INCORRECT IGNITION TIMING. REPLACE THE PLUG.

FUSED SPOT DEPOSIT

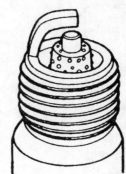

IDENTIFIED BY MELTED OR SPOTTY DEPOSITS RESEMBLING BUBBLES OR BLISTERS.

CAUSED BY SUDDEN ACCELERATION. CAN BE CLEANED IF NOT EXCESSIVE, OTHERWISE REPLACE PLUG.

Fig. 9 Inspect the spark plug to determine engine running conditions

2-8 ENGINE PERFORMANCE AND TUNE-UP

Fig. 10 A normally worn spark plug should have light tan or gray deposits on the firing tip

Fig. 11 A carbon fouled plug, identified by soft, sooty, black deposits, may indicate an improperly tuned vehicle. Check the air cleaner, ignition components and engine control system

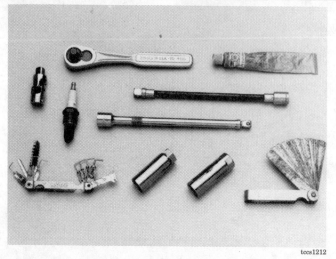

Fig. 12 A variety of tools and gauges are needed for spark plug service

ENGINE PERFORMANCE AND TUNE-UP

Fig. 13 A physically damaged spark plug may be evidence of severe detonation in that cylinder. Watch that cylinder carefully between services, as a continued detonation will not only damage the plug, but could also damage the engine

Fig. 14 An oil fouled spark plug indicates an engine with worn piston rings and/or bad valve seals, allowing excessive oil to enter the chamber

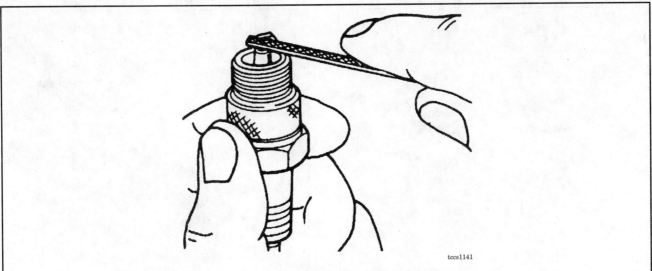

Fig. 15 If the plug is in good condition, the electrodes may be filed flat and the plug reused

2-10 ENGINE PERFORMANCE AND TUNE-UP

Fig. 16 This spark plug has been left in the engine too long, as evidenced by the extreme gap. Plugs with such an extreme gap can cause misfiring and stumbling, accompanied by a noticeable lack of power

Fig. 18 A bridged or almost bridged spark plug, identified by a build-up between the electrodes, caused by excessive carbon or oil build-up on the plug

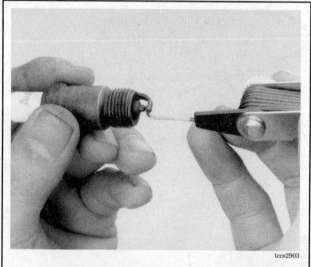

Fig. 17 Checking spark plug gap with a feeler gauge

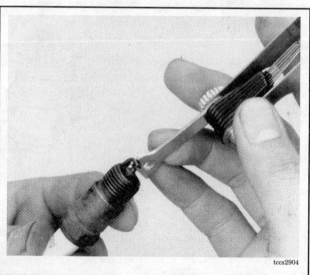

Fig. 19 Adjusting the spark plug gap

ENGINE PERFORMANCE AND TUNE-UP

FIRING ORDERS

▶ See Figures 20, 21, 22 and 23

➡ To avoid confusion, remove and tag the spark plug wires one at a time, for replacement.

If a distributor is not keyed for installation with only one orientation, it could have been removed previously and rewired. The resultant wiring would hold the correct firing order, but could change the relative placement of the plug towers in relation to the engine. For this reason, it is imperative that you label all wires before disconnecting any of them. Also, before removal, compare the current wiring with the accompanying illustrations. If the current wiring does not match, make notes in your book to reflect how your engine is wired.

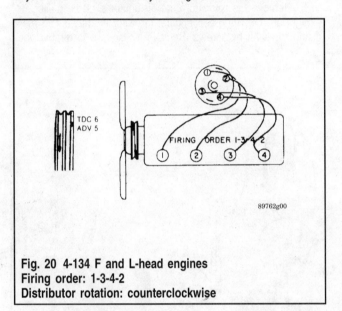

Fig. 20 4-134 F and L-head engines
Firing order: 1-3-4-2
Distributor rotation: counterclockwise

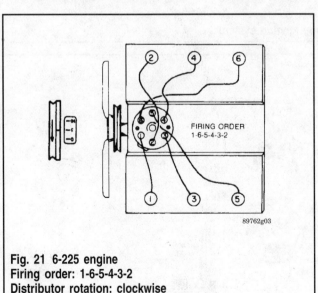

Fig. 21 6-225 engine
Firing order: 1-6-5-4-3-2
Distributor rotation: clockwise

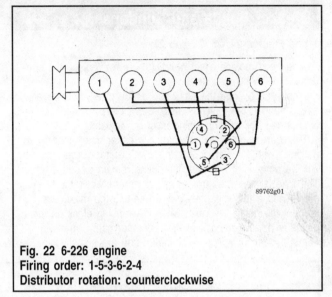

Fig. 22 6-226 engine
Firing order: 1-5-3-6-2-4
Distributor rotation: counterclockwise

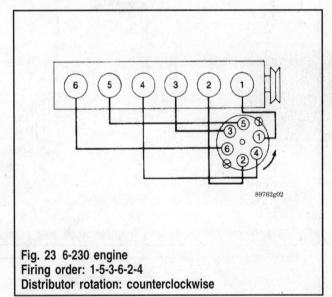

Fig. 23 6-230 engine
Firing order: 1-5-3-6-2-4
Distributor rotation: counterclockwise

2-12 ENGINE PERFORMANCE AND TUNE-UP

POINT TYPE IGNITION

Breaker Points and Condenser

▶ See Figures 24, 25, 26 and 27

When you replace a set of points, always replace the condenser at the same time.

When you change the point gap or the dwell, you will also have changed the ignition timing. So, if the point gap or dwell is changed, the ignition timing must be adjusted.

There are two ways to check the breaker point gap; it can be done with a feeler gauge or a dwell meter. Either way you set the amount of time that the points remain closed or open. The time is measured in degrees of gap between the breaker points with a feeler gauge, you are setting the maximum amount the points will open when the rubbing block on the points is on a high point of the distributor cam. When you adjust the points with a dwell meter, you are adjusting the number of degrees that the points will remain closed before they start to open as a high point of the distributor cam approaches the rubbing block.

INSPECTION

1. Disconnect the high tension wire from the top of the distributor and the coil, and unsnap the distributor retaining caps.
2. Remove the distributor cap by prying off the spring clips on the L- or F-head, or by depressing and turning the hold down screws on the side of the cap on all other engines.
3. Remove the rotor from the distributor shaft by pulling it straight up. On the 6-225 engine, the rotor is attached to the distributor shaft by screws. Remove the screws to remove the rotor.

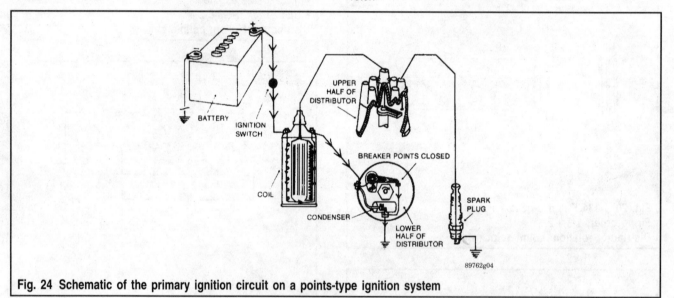

Fig. 24 Schematic of the primary ignition circuit on a points-type ignition system

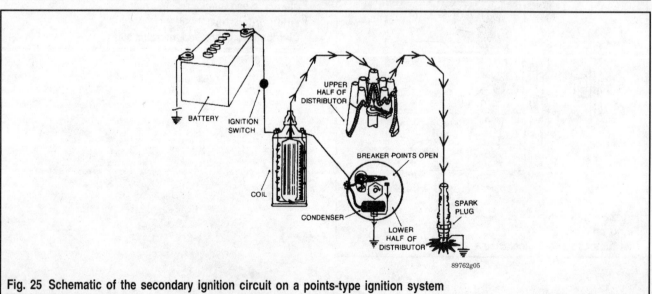

Fig. 25 Schematic of the secondary ignition circuit on a points-type ignition system

ENGINE PERFORMANCE AND TUNE-UP

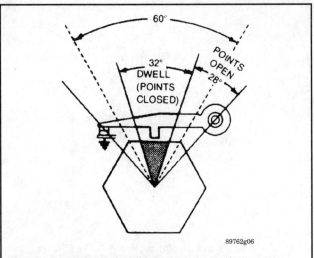

Fig. 26 Rotation of the distributor's actuating cam triggers opening and closing of the breaker points

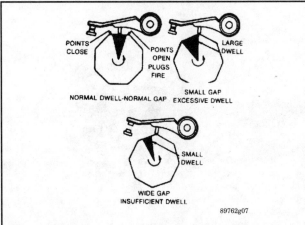

Fig. 27 The adjustment of the points is vital for optimum ignition system operation — otherwise, the breaker points can be held open too long or not long enough

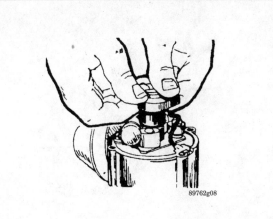

Fig. 28 To remove the rotor, pull it up and off of the distributor shaft — except 6-225 engine with Delco system

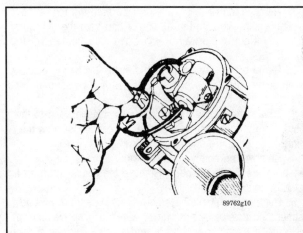

Fig. 29 To remove the condenser wires, unplug them from the distributor housing — except 6-225 engine with Delco system

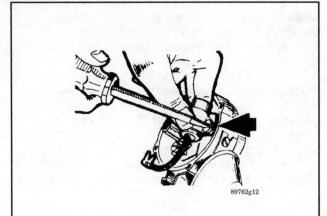

Fig. 30 Using a screwdriver, remove the condenser hold-down screws (arrow) and lift the condenser from the distributor — except 6-225 engine with Delco system

4. Examine the condition of the rotor. If it is cracked or the metal tip is excessively worn or burned, it should be replaced.

5. Pry open the contact points with a small prytool and check the condition of the contacts. If they are excessively worn, burned, or pitted, they should be replaced. 5. If the points are in good condition, adjust them. Then, install the rotor and distributor cap.

6. If the points need to be replaced, perform the following replacement procedure.

REMOVAL & INSTALLATION

▶ See Figures 28, 29, 30, 31, 32, 33, 34 and 35

➡Most 1945-70 vehicles were equipped with Autolite ignition systems. However, beginning in 1954, some were equipped with Delco systems. Never interchange parts from these two systems during removal or installation.

2-14 ENGINE PERFORMANCE AND TUNE-UP

Fig. 31 The points assembly is also retained by a hold-down screw (arrow) — except 6-225 engine with Delco system

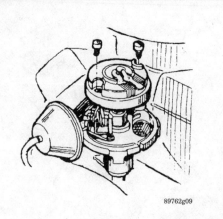

Fig. 32 Remove the 2 rotor retaining screws, then lift the rotor off of the distributor shaft — 6-225 engine with Delco system

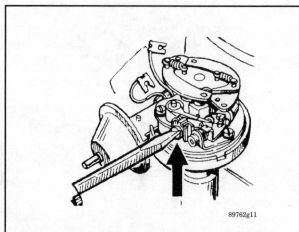

Fig. 33 Loosen the retaining screw to detach the condenser wires from the distributor housing — 6-225 engine with Delco system

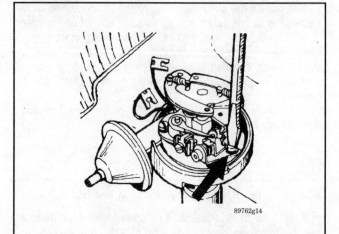

Fig. 34 Loosen, but do not remove the point set hold-down screws, and slide the point set out from under the screws — 6-225 engine with Delco system

1. Remove the coil high tension wire from the top of the distributor cap. Remove the distributor cap from the distributor and place it out of the way. Remove the rotor from the distributor shaft.
2. Remove the dust cover that is in the top of the distributor on some models, covering the points. It is pressed in hand tight.
3. Loosen the screw that holds the condenser lead to the body of the breaker points. Remove the condenser from the points.
4. Remove the screw that holds and grounds the condenser to the distributor body. Remove the condenser from the distributor and discard it.
5. Remove the points assembly attaching screws and adjustment lockscrews. A screwdriver with a holding mechanism will come in handy so you don't drop a screw into the distributor and have to remove the entire distributor to retrieve it.
6. Remove the points by lifting them straight up off the locating dowel on the plate. Wipe off the cam and apply new cam lubricant. Discard the old set of points.
7. Slip the new set of points onto the locating dowel and install the screws that hold the assembly onto the plate. Do not tighten them all the way.
8. Attach the new condenser to the plate with the ground screw.
9. Attach the condenser lead to the points at the proper place. On American Motors engines, and the V6, the primary wire from the coil must now be attached to the points also. Make sure that the connectors for these two wires do not touch the body of the distributor; they will short out the primary circuit of the ignition if they do.
10. Apply a small amount of cam lubricant to the shaft where the rubbing block of the points touches.

ENGINE PERFORMANCE AND TUNE-UP

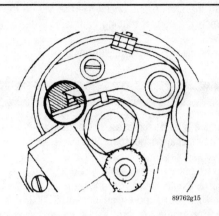

Fig. 35 Once the points are installed, make certain that the contact surfaces are properly aligned — if there is misalignment, correct it by bending the stationary arm, not the moving arm

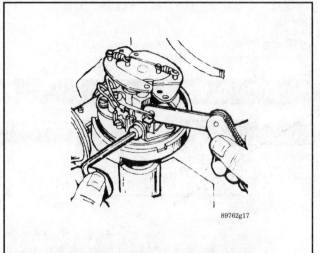

Fig. 37 The Delco distributors, unlike the Autolite distributors, utilize an Allen head adjusting screw

ADJUSTMENT

Using Feeler Gauges
♦ See Figures 36 and 37

1. If the contact points of the assembly are not parallel, bend the stationary contact so they make contact across the entire surface of the contacts. Bend only the bracket part of the point assembly, not the contact surface.
2. Turn the engine until the rubbing block of the points is on one of the high points of the distributor cam. You can do this by either turning the ignition switch to the start position and releasing it quickly or by using a wrench on the bolt that holds the crankshaft pulley to the crankshaft.
3. Place the correct size feeler gauge between the contacts. Make sure it is parallel with the contact surfaces.
4. With your free hand, insert a screwdriver into the notch provided for adjustment or into the eccentric adjusting screw, and then twist the screwdriver to either increase or decrease the gap to the proper setting. The adjusting screws on 6-225 engines have to be turned with an Allen wrench.
5. Tighten the adjustment lockscrew and recheck the contact gap to make sure that it didn't change when the lockscrew was tightened.
6. Replace the rotor, distributor cap, and the high tension wire that connects the top of the distributor and the coil. Make sure that the rotor if firmly seated all the way onto the distributor shaft and that the tab of the rotor is aligned with the notch in the shaft. Align the tab in the base of the distributor cap with the notch in the distributor body. Make sure that the cap is firmly seated on the distributor and that the retainers are in place. Make sure that the end of the high tension wire is firmly placed in the top of the distributor and the coil.

Using a Dwell Meter

➡ Some early models have 6V ignition systems. Make sure your dwell meter has a 6V capability.

1. Adjust the points with a feeler gauge as described above.
2. Connect the dwell meter to the ignition circuit as according to the manufacturer's instructions. One lead of the meter is to be connected to a ground and the other lead is to be connected to the distributor post on the coil. An adapter is usually provided for this purpose.
3. If the dwell meter has a set line on it, adjust the meter to zero the indicator.
4. Start the engine.

➡ Be careful when working on any vehicle while the engine is running. Make sure that the transmission is in neutral and that the parking brake is on. Keep hands, clothing, tools, and the wires of the test instruments clear of the rotating fan blades.

5. Observe the reading on the dwell meter. If the meter does not have a scale for 4-cylinder engines, multiply the 8-cylinder reading by two. If the reading is within the specified range, turn off the engine and remove the dwell meter.
6. If the reading is above the specified range, the breaker point gap is too small. If the reading is below the specified range, the gap is too large. In either case, the engine must be

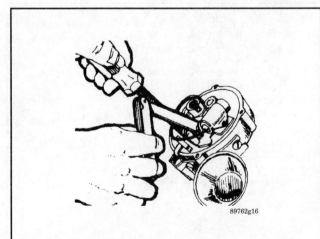

Fig. 36 While gently moving a feeler gauge between the points, slowly tighten the adjusting screw until a drag is felt

2-16 ENGINE PERFORMANCE AND TUNE-UP

stopped and the gap adjusted in the manner previously covered.

➡ On the V6 engine, it is possible to adjust the dwell while the engine is running.

IGNITION TIMING

Timing

GENERAL INFORMATION

▶ See Figure 38

Ignition timing is the measurement, in degrees of crankshaft rotation, of the point at which the spark plugs fire in each of the cylinders. It is measured in degrees before or after Top Dead Center (TDC) of the compression stroke. Ignition timing is controlled by turning the distributor in the engine.

Ideally, the air/fuel mixture in the cylinder will be ignited by the spark plug just as the piston passes TDC of the compression stroke. If this happens, this piston will be beginning the power stroke just as the compressed and ignited air/fuel mixture starts to expand. The expansion of the air/fuel mixture then forces the piston down on the power stroke and turns the crankshaft.

Because it takes a fraction of a second for the spark plug to ignite the gases in the cylinder, the spark plug must fire a little before the piston reaches TDC. Otherwise, the mixture will not be completely ignited as the piston TDC and the full benefit of the explosion will not be used by the engine. The timing measurement is given in degrees of crankshaft rotation before the piston reaches TDC (Before Top Dead Center or BTDC). If the setting for the ignition timing is 5 degrees BTDC, the spark plug must fire 5 degrees before that piston reaches TDC. This only holds true, however, when the engine is at idle speed.

As the engine speed increases, the pistons go faster. The spark plugs have to ignite the fuel even sooner if it is to be completely ignited when the piston reaches TDC. To do this, the distributor has a means to advance the timing of the spark as the engine speed increases. In some 1945-70 Jeep vehicles, the advancing of the spark in the distributor was accomplished by weights alone. Others have a vacuum diaphragm to assist the weights. It is necessary to disconnect the vacuum line to the distributor when the engine is being timed.

If the ignition is set too far advanced (BTDC), the ignition and expansion of the fuel in the cylinder will occur too soon and tend to force the piston down while it is still traveling up. This causes engine ping. If the engine is too far retarded after TDC (After Top Dead Center or ATDC), the piston will have already passed TDC and started on its way down when the fuel is ignited. This will cause the piston to be forced down for only a portion of its travel. This will result in poor engine performance and lack of power.

The timing is best checked with a timing light. This device is connected in series with the No. 1 spark plug. The current that fires the spark plug also causes the light to flash.

There is a notch on the front of the crankshaft pulley on the 4-134 engine. There are also marks to indicate TDC and 5° BTDC on the timing gear cover that will assist you in setting ignition timing.

The 6-225 and 6-226 engines have the scale on the crankshaft pulley and the pointer mark on the engine.

When the engine is running, the timing light should be aimed at the marks on the engine and crankshaft pulley.

There are three basic types of timing lights available. The first is a simple neon bulb with two wire connections. One wire connects to the spark plug terminal and the other plugs into the end of the spark plug wire for the No. 1 cylinder, thus connecting the light in series with the spark plug. This type of light is pretty dim and must be held very close to the timing marks to be seen. Sometimes a dark corner has to be sought out to see the flash at all. This type of light is very inexpen-

7. Start the engine and check the reading on the dwell meter. When the correct reading is obtained, disconnect the dwell meter.
8. Check the adjustment of the ignition timing.

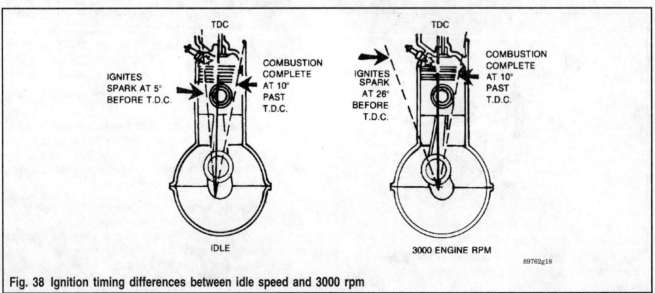

Fig. 38 Ignition timing differences between idle speed and 3000 rpm

ENGINE PERFORMANCE AND TUNE-UP

sive. The second type operates from the car battery, two alligator clips connect to the battery terminals, while an adapter enables a third clip to be connected to the No. 1 spark plug and wire. This type is a bit more expensive, but it provides a nice bright flash that you can see even in bright sunlight. It is the type most often seen in professional shops. The third type replaces the battery power source with 110 volt current.

Timing should be checked at each tune-up and any time the points are adjusted or replaced. The timing marks consist of a notch on the rim of the crankshaft pulley and a graduated scale attached to the engine front (timing) cover. A stroboscopic flash (dynamic) timing light must be used, as a static light is too inaccurate for emission controlled engines.

INSPECTION AND ADJUSTMENT

♦ See Figures 39, 40, 41, 42, 43 and 44

➡Some early engines utilize 6V or 24V ignition systems. Make sure your tach/dwell meter and timing light have 6V or 24V capability.

1. Locate the timing marks on the pulley and on the front of the engine, or on the flywheel on CJ-2A and early CJ-3A engines.
2. Clean off the timing marks so you can see them.
3. Mark the timing marks with a piece of chalk or white paint. Mark the one on the engine that will indicate correct timing when it is aligned with the mark on the pulley or flywheel.
4. Attach a tachometer to the engine.
5. Attach a timing light according to the manufacturer's instructions. If the timing light has three wires, one is attached to the no. 1 spark plug lead with an adapter. The other two are connected to the battery. The red one goes to the positive side of the battery and the black one to the negative terminal.
6. Disconnect the vacuum line to the distributor at the distributor. Plug the end of the hose.
7. Check to make sure that all of the wires clear the fan and then start the engine.
8. If there is an idle speed solenoid, disconnect it.

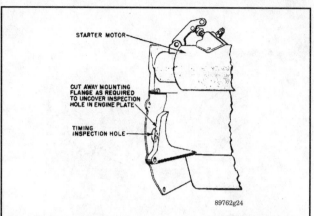

Fig. 40 If a replacement, newer style 4-134 engine block was installed in your CJ-3A Jeep (originally equipped with an early style block), the section of engine block shown must be cut away to use the flywheel mounted timing marks

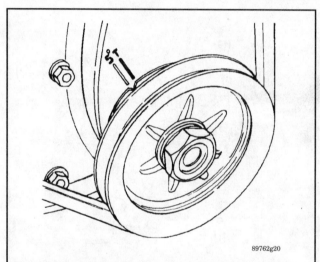

Fig. 41 Timing mark locations on 4-134 F-head engines at the crankshaft pulley

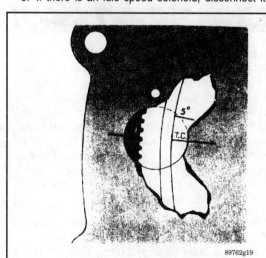

Fig. 39 Timing mark locations on 4-134 L-head engines at the flywheel housing

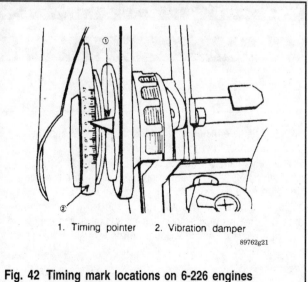

1. Timing pointer   2. Vibration damper

Fig. 42 Timing mark locations on 6-226 engines

2-18 ENGINE PERFORMANCE AND TUNE-UP

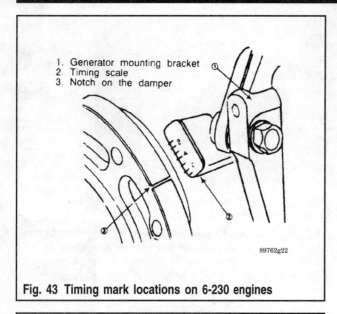

Fig. 43 Timing mark locations on 6-230 engines

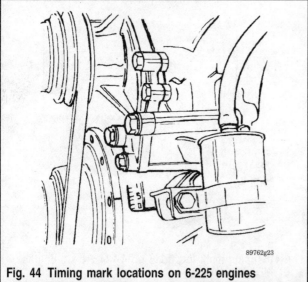

Fig. 44 Timing mark locations on 6-225 engines

9. Aim the timing light at the timing marks. If the marks that you put on the pulley and the engine are aligned, the timing is correct. Turn off the engine and remove the tachometer and the timing light. If the marks are not in alignment, proceed to the following steps.

10. Turn the engine **OFF**.

11. Loosen the distributor lock bolt just enough so that the distributor can be turned with a little effort.

12. Start the engine. Keep the cords of the timing light clear of the fan.

13. With the timing light aimed at the pulley and the marks on the engine, turn the distributor in the direction of rotor rotation to retard the spark, and in the opposite direction of rotor rotation to advance the spark. Line up the marks on the pulley and the engine.

14. When the marks are aligned, tighten the distributor lock bolt and recheck the timing with the timing light to make sure that the distributor did not move when you tightened the distributor lockbolt.

15. Turn the engine **OFF** the engine and remove the timing light.

➡ On CJ-3A models beginning with engine serial No. 130859, a 4½ in. (114.3mm) starter motor was used. To use the larger starter, it was necessary to increase the width of the cylinder block flange, partially covering the flywheel hole. This makes it impossible to use the hole for timing purposes. In this event, use the timing marks on the crankshaft pulley. If a replacement block is installed with the later design in a vehicle originally equipped with the earlier design timing marks, it will be necessary to cut away enough of the flange to allow a view of the timing marks, as no other timing marks exist on these early engines.

VALVE LASH

Adjustment

PROCEDURE

Valve lash determines how far the valves enter into the cylinder and how long they stay open and closed.

If the valve clearance is too large, part of the lift of the camshaft will be used in removing the excessive clearance. The valve will consequently, not be opening as far as it should. This condition has two effects, the valve train components will emit a tapping sound as they take up the excessive clearance and the engine will perform poorly. If the valve clearance is too small, the intake valves and the exhaust valves will open too far and they will not fully seat on the cylinder head when they close. When a valve seats itself on the cylinder head, it does two things; it seals the combustion chamber so that none of the gases in the cylinder escape and it cools itself by transferring some of the heat it absorbs from the combustion in the cylinder to the cylinder head and to the engine's cooling system. If the valve clearance is too small, the engine will run poorly because of the gases escaping from the combustion chamber. The valves will also become overheated and will warp, since they cannot transfer heat unless they are touching the valve seat in the cylinder head.

➡ While all valve adjustments must be made as accurately as possible, it is better to have the value adjustment slightly loose than slightly tight, as burned valves may result from overly tight adjustments.

ENGINE PERFORMANCE AND TUNE-UP

The 4-134 F-head, 6-226 L-head, and the 6-230 engines have adjustable valves. All other engines have hydraulic valve lifters which maintain a zero clearance.

4-134 F-Head Engine

▸ See Figures 45, 46 and 47

The 4-134 L-head designed so that both the intake and exhaust valves are installed in the engine block (a common flat head design — do not confuse the L-head flat head design motor with the F-head engine, which is not a flat head design). Adjustment procedure is the same for all valves. Rotor type exhaust valves were not original equipment, however, some repair kits did supply these. In those cases, follow the specifications for the 4-134 F-head engine.

➡ The engine must be cold when the valves are adjusted.

1. On the 4-134 F-head engine, remove the valve cover. Check all the cylinder head bolts to make sure they are tightened to the correct torque specifications.
2. Remove the valve side cover.

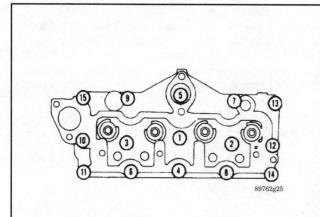

Fig. 45 When double-checking the cylinder head bolts for tightness, use the sequence shown

Fig. 46 Use a feeler gauge between the rocker arm and valve to measure valve clearance . . .

Fig. 47 . . . then turn the adjusting screw to increase or decrease valve clearance

3. Turn the engine until the lifter for the front intake valve is down as far as it will go. The lifter should be resting on the center of the heel (back) of the cam lobe for that valve. You can observe the position of the lifter by looking through the side valve spring cover opening.
4. Put the correct size feeler gauge between the rocker arm and the valve stem. There should be a very slight drag on the feeler gauge when it is pulled through the gap.
   a. If there is a slight drag, the valve is at the correct setting.
   b. If the feeler gauge cannot pass between the rocker arm and the valve stem, the gap between them is too small and must be increased.
   c. If the gauge can be passed through the gap without any drag, the gap is too large and must be decreased.
5. Loosen the locknut on the top of the rocker arm (pushrod side) by turning it counterclockwise.
6. Turn the adjusting screw clockwise to lessen the gap and counterclockwise to increase the gap.
7. When the gap is correct, turn the locknut clockwise (while holding the adjusting screw stationary) to lock the adjusting screw.
8. Follow this procedure for all of the intake valves, making sure that the lifter is all the way down (positioned against the base circle of the camshaft; not sitting on the camshaft lobe) for each adjustment.
9. Turn the engine so that the first exhaust valve is completely closed and the lifter that operates that particular valve is all of the way down and on the base circle of the camshaft that operates it.
10. Insert the correct size feeler gauge between the valve stem of the exhaust valve and the adjusting screw. This is done through the side of the engine in the space that is exposed when the side valve spring cover is removed.
    a. If there is a slight drag on the feeler gauge, the gap should be correct.
    b. If there is too much drag or not enough, turn the adjusting screw clockwise to increase the gap and counterclockwise to decrease the gap.
11. When all of the valves have been adjusted to the proper clearance, replace the covers with new gaskets.

ENGINE PERFORMANCE AND TUNE-UP

6-226 L-Head Engine

◆ See Figure 48

➡ Valves should be adjusted with the engine cold.

1. Remove the fuel pump.
2. Remove the valve cover.
3. Clearance is adjusted by holding the tappet with one wrench and turning the tappet adjuster with another wrench.
4. Check the clearance with a feeler gauge inserted between the tappet and the end of valve stem. Use the accompanying guide to determine the sequence of valve adjustment. Tappets and valves are numbered consecutively from the front of the engine to the back.

6-230 Engine

◆ See Figure 49

Rocker arm adjustment may be made with the engine hot or cold, but the preferred method is with the engine hot and running. The best way of differentiating between the intake and exhaust valves is to simply note which ones are adjacent to the intake manifold tubes and which are adjacent to the exhaust manifold tubes.

COLD METHOD

1. Run the engine to normal operating temperature, then shut it **OFF**.
2. Remove the valve cover.

With These Valves Fully Raised	Adjust These Tappets
1 & 3	10 & 12
8 & 9	4 & 5
2 & 6	7 & 11
10 & 12	1 & 3
4 & 5	8 & 9
7 & 11	2 & 6

Fig. 48 Use this chart for guidance while adjusting the valves in the 6-226 engine

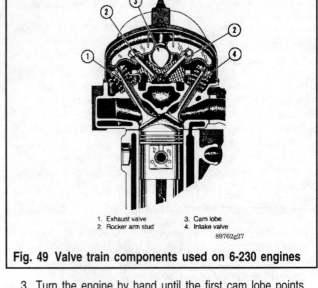

1. Exhaust valve
2. Rocker arm stud
3. Cam lobe
4. Intake valve

Fig. 49 Valve train components used on 6-230 engines

3. Turn the engine by hand until the first cam lobe points to the 6 o'clock position.
4. Insert a feeler gauge between the rocker arm and the top of the valve stem. Refer to the Tune-Up Specifications chart for the correct valve clearance.
5. Use a socket wrench to turn the adjusting nut until the correct clearance is obtained. A slight drag should be felt on the feeler gauge when you try to remove it.
6. Adjust each valve in turn, in this manner, turning the engine so that each camshaft lobe points away from the lifter (6 o'clock position).
7. Install the valve cover, using a new gasket coated with gasket sealer.

HOT METHOD

1. Run the engine to normal operating temperature, then shut it **OFF**.
2. Remove the valve cover.
3. Start the engine and let it idle. If the vehicle is equipped with automatic transmission, set the parking brake, block the wheels and place it in Drive.
4. Proceeding from front to rear, slide the appropriate thickness feeler gauge (see the Tune-Up Specifications chart) between the rocker arm and the top of the valve stem. A slight drag should be felt when withdrawing the gauge.
5. Turn the rocker arm adjusting nut with a socket wrench to give the specified clearance. This is a tricky procedure when done the first time, but it is the most precise way of adjusting the valve lash.

ENGINE PERFORMANCE AND TUNE-UP

IDLE SPEED AND MIXTURE ADJUSTMENTS

Idle Speed

▶ See Figures 50 and 51

This section contains only tune-up adjustment procedures for fuel systems. Descriptions, adjustments, and overhaul procedures for fuel system components can be found in Section 5.

1. Start the engine and run it until it reaches operating temperature.
2. If it hasn't already been done, check and adjust the ignition timing. After you have set the timing, turn off the engine.
3. Attach a tachometer to the engine.
4. Remove the air cleaner. Turn the headlights ON to the high beam position.
5. Start the engine and, with the transmission in Neutral or Park, check the idle speed on the tachometer.
    a. If the reading on the tachometer is correct, turn the engine OFF, then remove the tachometer.
    b. If it is not correct, proceed to the following steps.
6. Turn the idle adjusting screw at the bottom of the carburetor with a screwdriver clockwise to increase idle speed and counterclockwise to decrease it.

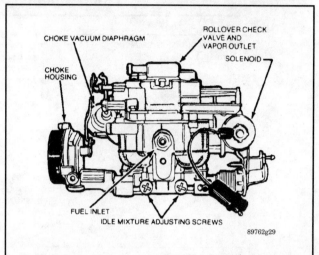

Fig. 51 Identification and location of components on BBD 2-bbl. carburetors

Idle Mixture

The idle mixture screw is located at the very bottom of the carburetor.

1. Turn the screw until it is all the way in. Do not force the screw in any further because it is very easy to damage the needle valve and its seat by screwing the adjusting screw in too tightly.
2. Turn the screw out ¾ to 1¾ turns. This should be the normal adjustment setting. For a richer mixture, turn the screw out. The ideal setting for the mixture adjustment screw results in the maximum engine rpm.

➡ Limiter caps are installed on some engines. These caps limit the amount of adjustment that can be made and should not be removed, if possible.

3. On engines equipped with limiter caps, if a satisfactory idle cannot be obtained perform the following:
    a. Remove the caps by installing a sheet metal screw in the center of the screw and turning clockwise.
    b. After removing the caps, adjust the carburetor in the same manner as described without the caps.
    c. There are special service limiter caps available to replace the ones removed. Install the service limiter caps with the ears positioned against the full rich stops.

➡ Be careful not to disturb the idle setting while installing the caps.

    d. Press the caps squarely and firmly into place.

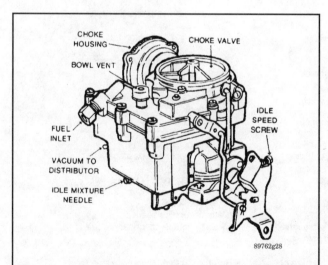

Fig. 50 Identification and location of adjustment points on Rochester 2GC carburetors

ENGINE PERFORMANCE AND TUNE-UP

Troubleshooting Engine Performance

Problem	Cause	Solution
Hard starting (engine cranks normally)	• Binding linkage, choke valve or choke piston	• Repair as necessary
	• Restricted choke vacuum diaphragm	• Clean passages
	• Improper fuel level	• Adjust float level
	• Dirty, worn or faulty needle valve and seat	• Repair as necessary
	• Float sticking	• Repair as necessary
	• Faulty fuel pump	• Replace fuel pump
	• Incorrect choke cover adjustment	• Adjust choke cover
	• Inadequate choke unloader adjustment	• Adjust choke unloader
	• Faulty ignition coil	• Test and replace as necessary
	• Improper spark plug gap	• Adjust gap
	• Incorrect ignition timing	• Adjust timing
	• Incorrect valve timing	• Check valve timing; repair as necessary
Rough idle or stalling	• Incorrect curb or fast idle speed	• Adjust curb or fast idle speed
	• Incorrect ignition timing	• Adjust timing to specification
	• Improper feedback system operation	• Refer to Chapter 4
	• Improper fast idle cam adjustment	• Adjust fast idle cam
	• Faulty EGR valve operation	• Test EGR system and replace as necessary
	• Faulty PCV valve air flow	• Test PCV valve and replace as necessary
	• Choke binding	• Locate and eliminate binding condition
	• Faulty TAC vacuum motor or valve	• Repair as necessary
	• Air leak into manifold vacuum	• Inspect manifold vacuum connections and repair as necessary
	• Improper fuel level	• Adjust fuel level
	• Faulty distributor rotor or cap	• Replace rotor or cap
	• Improperly seated valves	• Test cylinder compression, repair as necessary
	• Incorrect ignition wiring	• Inspect wiring and correct as necessary
	• Faulty ignition coil	• Test coil and replace as necessary
	• Restricted air vent or idle passages	• Clean passages
	• Restricted air cleaner	• Clean or replace air cleaner filter element
	• Faulty choke vacuum diaphragm	• Repair as necessary
Faulty low-speed operation	• Restricted idle transfer slots	• Clean transfer slots
	• Restricted idle air vents and passages	• Clean air vents and passages
	• Restricted air cleaner	• Clean or replace air cleaner filter element
	• Improper fuel level	• Adjust fuel level
	• Faulty spark plugs	• Clean or replace spark plugs
	• Dirty, corroded, or loose ignition secondary circuit wire connections	• Clean or tighten secondary circuit wire connections
	• Improper feedback system operation	• Refer to Chapter 4
	• Faulty ignition coil high voltage wire	• Replace ignition coil high voltage wire
	• Faulty distributor cap	• Replace cap
Exhaust backfire	• Air leak into manifold vacuum	• Check manifold vacuum and repair as necessary
	• Faulty air injection diverter valve	• Test diverter valve and replace as necessary
	• Exhaust leak	• Locate and eliminate leak

ENGINE PERFORMANCE AND TUNE-UP

Troubleshooting Engine Performance (cont.)

Problem	Cause	Solution
Faulty acceleration	• Improper accelerator pump stroke	• Adjust accelerator pump stroke
	• Incorrect ignition timing	• Adjust timing
	• Inoperative pump discharge check ball or needle	• Clean or replace as necessary
	• Worn or damaged pump diaphragm or piston	• Replace diaphragm or piston
	• Leaking carburetor main body cover gasket	• Replace gasket
	• Engine cold and choke set too lean	• Adjust choke cover
	• Improper metering rod adjustment (BBD Model carburetor)	• Adjust metering rod
	• Faulty spark plug(s)	• Clean or replace spark plug(s)
	• Improperly seated valves	• Test cylinder compression, repair as necessary
	• Faulty ignition coil	• Test coil and replace as necessary
	• Improper feedback system operation	• Refer to Chapter 4
Faulty high speed operation	• Incorrect ignition timing	• Adjust timing
	• Faulty distributor centrifugal advance mechanism	• Check centrifugal advance mechanism and repair as necessary
	• Faulty distributor vacuum advance mechanism	• Check vacuum advance mechanism and repair as necessary
	• Low fuel pump volume	• Replace fuel pump
	• Wrong spark plug air gap or wrong plug	• Adjust air gap or install correct plug
	• Faulty choke operation	• Adjust choke cover
	• Partially restricted exhaust manifold, exhaust pipe, catalytic converter, muffler, or tailpipe	• Eliminate restriction
	• Restricted vacuum passages	• Clean passages
	• Improper size or restricted main jet	• Clean or replace as necessary
	• Restricted air cleaner	• Clean or replace filter element as necessary
	• Faulty distributor rotor or cap	• Replace rotor or cap
	• Faulty ignition coil	• Test coil and replace as necessary
	• Improperly seated valve(s)	• Test cylinder compression, repair as necessary
	• Faulty valve spring(s)	• Inspect and test valve spring tension, replace as necessary
	• Incorrect valve timing	• Check valve timing and repair as necessary
	• Intake manifold restricted	• Remove restriction or replace manifold
	• Worn distributor shaft	• Replace shaft
	• Improper feedback system operation	• Refer to Chapter 4
Misfire at all speeds	• Faulty spark plug(s)	• Clean or replace spark plug(s)
	• Faulty spark plug wire(s)	• Replace as necessary
	• Faulty distributor cap or rotor	• Replace cap or rotor
	• Faulty ignition coil	• Test coil and replace as necessary
	• Primary ignition circuit shorted or open intermittently	• Troubleshoot primary circuit and repair as necessary
	• Improperly seated valve(s)	• Test cylinder compression, repair as necessary
	• Faulty hydraulic tappet(s)	• Clean or replace tappet(s)
	• Improper feedback system operation	• Refer to Chapter 4
	• Faulty valve spring(s)	• Inspect and test valve spring tension, repair as necessary
	• Worn camshaft lobes	• Replace camshaft
	• Air leak into manifold	• Check manifold vacuum and repair as necessary
	• Improper carburetor adjustment	• Adjust carburetor
	• Fuel pump volume or pressure low	• Replace fuel pump
	• Blown cylinder head gasket	• Replace gasket
	• Intake or exhaust manifold passage(s) restricted	• Pass chain through passage(s) and repair as necessary
	• Incorrect trigger wheel installed in distributor	• Install correct trigger wheel

2-24 ENGINE PERFORMANCE AND TUNE-UP

Troubleshooting Engine Performance (cont.)

Problem	Cause	Solution
Power not up to normal	• Incorrect ignition timing	• Adjust timing
	• Faulty distributor rotor	• Replace rotor
	• Trigger wheel loose on shaft	• Reposition or replace trigger wheel
	• Incorrect spark plug gap	• Adjust gap
	• Faulty fuel pump	• Replace fuel pump
	• Incorrect valve timing	• Check valve timing and repair as necessary
	• Faulty ignition coil	• Test coil and replace as necessary
	• Faulty ignition wires	• Test wires and replace as necessary
	• Improperly seated valves	• Test cylinder compression and repair as necessary
	• Blown cylinder head gasket	• Replace gasket
	• Leaking piston rings	• Test compression and repair as necessary
	• Worn distributor shaft	• Replace shaft
	• Improper feedback system operation	• Refer to Chapter 4
Intake backfire	• Improper ignition timing	• Adjust timing
	• Faulty accelerator pump discharge	• Repair as necessary
	• Defective EGR CTO valve	• Replace EGR CTO valve
	• Defective TAC vacuum motor or valve	• Repair as necessary
	• Lean air/fuel mixture	• Check float level or manifold vacuum for air leak. Remove sediment from bowl.
Ping or spark knock	• Incorrect ignition timing	• Adjust timing
	• Distributor centrifugal or vacuum advance malfunction	• Inspect advance mechanism and repair as necessary
	• Excessive combustion chamber deposits	• Remove with combustion chamber cleaner
	• Air leak into manifold vacuum	• Check manifold vacuum and repair as necessary
	• Excessively high compression	• Test compression and repair as necessary
	• Fuel octane rating excessively low	• Try alternate fuel source
	• Sharp edges in combustion chamber	• Grind smooth
	• EGR Valve not functioning properly	• Test EGR System and replace as necessary
Surging (at cruising to top speeds)	• Low carburetor fuel level	• Adjust fuel level
	• Low fuel pump pressure or volume	• Replace fuel pump
	• Metering rod(s) not adjusted properly (BBD Model Carburetor)	• Adjust metering rod
	• Improper PCV valve air flow	• Test PCV valve and replace as necessary
	• Air leak into manifold vacuum	• Check manifold vacuum and repair as necessary
	• Incorrect spark advance	• Test and replace as necessary
	• Restricted main jet(s)	• Clean main jet(s)
	• Undersize main jet(s)	• Replace main jet(s)
	• Restricted air vents	• Clean air vents
	• Restricted fuel filter	• Replace fuel filter
	• Restricted air cleaner	• Clean or replace air cleaner filter element
	• EGR valve not functioning properly	• Test EGR System and replace as necessary
	• Improper feedback system operation	• Refer to Chapter 4

BASIC ELECTRICAL THEORY
  BATTERY, STARTING AND
    CHARGING SYSTEMS 3-4
  UNDERSTANDING ELECTRICITY 3-2
ENGINE ELECTRICAL
  ALTERNATOR/GENERATOR 3-9
  BATTERY 3-19
  DISTRIBUTOR 3-7
  IGNITION COIL 3-5
  REGULATOR 3-11
  STARTER 3-12
ENGINE MECHANICAL
  CAMSHAFT 3-66
  COMPRESSION TESTING 3-22
  CRANKSHAFT 3-74
  CRANKSHAFT PULLEY (VIBRATION
    DAMPER) 3-56
  CYLINDER HEAD 3-41
  DESIGN 3-19
  ENGINE 3-25
  ENGINE OVERHAUL TIPS 3-20
  EXHAUST MANIFOLD 3-36
  FLYWHEEL/FLEXPLATE AND RING
    GEAR 3-75
  INTAKE MANIFOLD 3-33
  OIL PAN 3-53
  OIL PUMP 3-53
  PISTONS AND CONNECTING
    RODS 3-67
  RADIATOR 3-37
  REAR MAIN OIL SEAL 3-73
  ROCKER SHAFTS AND ROCKER
    STUDS 3-28
  THERMOSTAT 3-31
  TIMING CHAIN AND
    TENSIONER 3-60
  TIMING CHAIN/GEAR COVER AND
    OIL SEAL 3-57
  TIMING GEARS 3-62
  VALVE GUIDES 3-52
  VALVE SEATS 3-52
  VALVE TIMING 3-64
  VALVES AND SPRINGS 3-48
  WATER PUMP 3-37
EXHAUST SYSTEM
  CATALYTIC CONVERTER 3-78
  FRONT EXHAUST PIPE (HEAD
    PIPE) 3-77
  GENERAL INFORMATION 3-76
  MUFFLER 3-76
  REAR EXHAUST PIPE OR
    TAILPIPE 3-77
SPECIFICATIONS CHARTS
  ALTERNATOR AND REGULATOR
    SPECIFICATIONS 3-5
  CAMSHAFT SPECIFICATIONS 3-23
  CRANKSHAFT AND CONNECTING
    ROD SPECIFICATIONS 3-24
  GENERAL ENGINE
    SPECIFICATIONS 3-23
  GENERATOR AND REGULATOR
    SPECIFICATIONS 3-5
  PISTON AND RING
    SPECIFICATIONS 3-24
  STARTER SPECIFICATIONS 3-5
  TORQUE SPECIFICATIONS 3-24
  TROUBLESHOOTING BASIC
    CHARGING SYSTEM
    PROBLEMS 3-80
  TROUBLESHOOTING BASIC
    STARTING SYSTEM
    PROBLEMS 3-80
  USING A VACUUM GAUGE 3-79
  VALVE SPECIFICATIONS 3-23

3

ENGINE AND ENGINE OVERHAUL

BASIC ELECTRICAL THEORY 3-2
ENGINE ELECTRICAL 3-5
ENGINE MECHANICAL 3-19
EXHAUST SYSTEM 3-76
SPECIFICATIONS CHARTS 3-5

3-2 ENGINE AND ENGINE OVERHAUL

BASIC ELECTRICAL THEORY

Understanding Electricity

For any electrical system to operate, there must be a complete circuit. This simply means that the power flow from the battery must make a full circle. When an electrical component is operating, power flows from the battery to the components, passes through the component (load) causing it to function, and returns to the battery through the ground path of the circuit. This ground may be either another wire or a metal part of the vehicle (depending upon how the component is designed).

BASIC CIRCUITS

▶ See Figures 1 and 2

Perhaps the easiest way to visualize a circuit is to think of connecting a light bulb (with two wires attached to it) to the battery. If one of the two wires was attached to the negative post (-) of the battery and the other wire to the positive post (+), the circuit would be complete and the light bulb would illuminate. Electricity could follow a path from the battery to the bulb and back to the battery. It's not hard to see that with longer wires on our light bulb, it could be mounted anywhere on the vehicle. Further, one wire could be fitted with a switch so that the light could be turned on and off. Various other items could be added to our primitive circuit to make the light flash, become brighter or dimmer under certain conditions, or advise the user that it's burned out.

Ground

Some automotive components are grounded through their mounting points. The electrical current runs through the chassis of the vehicle and returns to the battery through the ground (-) cable; if you look, you'll see that the battery ground cable connects between the battery and the body of the vehicle.

Load

Every complete circuit must include a "load" (something to use the electricity coming from the source). If you were to connect a wire between the two terminals of the battery (DON'T do this, but take our word for it) without the light bulb, the battery would attempt to deliver its entire power supply from one pole to another almost instantly. This is a short circuit. The electricity is taking a short cut to get to ground and is not being used by any load in the circuit. This sudden and uncontrolled electrical flow can cause great damage to other components in the circuit and can develop a tremendous amount of heat. A short in an automotive wiring harness can develop sufficient heat to melt the insulation on all the surrounding wires and reduce a multiple wire cable to one sad lump of plastic and copper. Two common causes of shorts are broken insulation (thereby exposing the wire to contact with surrounding metal surfaces or other wires) or a failed switch (the pins inside the switch come out of place and touch each other).

Switches and Relays

Some electrical components which require a large amount of current to operate also have a relay in their circuit. Since these circuits carry a large amount of current (amperage or amps), the thickness of the wire in the circuit (wire gauge) is also greater. If this large wire were connected from the load to the control switch on the dash, the switch would have to carry the high amperage load and the dash would be twice as large to accommodate wiring harnesses as thick as your wrist. To prevent these problems, a relay is used. The large wires in the circuit are connected from the battery to one side of the relay and from the opposite side of the relay to the load. The relay is normally open, preventing current from passing through the circuit. An additional, smaller wire is connected from the relay to the control switch for the circuit. When the control switch is turned on, it grounds the smaller wire to the relay and completes its circuit. The main switch inside the relay closes, sending power to the component without routing the main

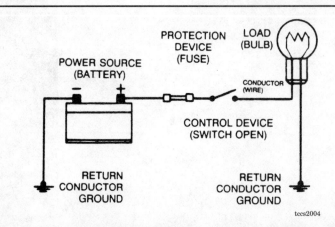

Fig. 1 Here is an example of a simple automotive circuit. When the switch is closed, power from the positive battery terminal flows through the fuse, the switch and then the load (light bulb). The light illuminates and the circuit is completed through the return conductor and the vehicle ground. If the light did not work, the tests could be made with a voltmeter or test light at the battery, fuse, switch or bulb socket

ENGINE AND ENGINE OVERHAUL

TROUBLESHOOTING

▶ See Figures 3, 4 and 5

Electrical problems generally fall into one of three areas:
- The component that is not functioning is not receiving current.
- The component is receiving power but is not using it or is using it incorrectly (component failure).
- The component is improperly grounded.

The circuit can be can be checked with a test light and a jumper wire. The test light is a device that looks like a pointed screwdriver with a wire on one end and a bulb in its handle. A jumper wire is simply a piece of wire with alligator clips or special terminals on each end. If a component is not working,

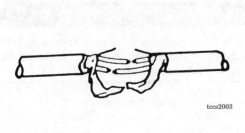

Fig. 2 Damaged insulation can allow wires to break (causing an open circuit) or touch (causing a short circuit)

power through the inside of the vehicle. Some common circuits which may use relays are the horn, headlights, starter and rear window defogger systems.

Protective Devices

It is possible for larger surges of current to pass through the electrical system of your vehicle. If this surge of current were to reach the load in the circuit, it could burn it out or severely damage it. To prevent this, fuses, circuit breakers and/or fusible links are connected into the supply wires of the electrical system. These items are nothing more than a built-in weak spot in the system. It's much easier to go to a known location (the fusebox) to see why a circuit is inoperative than to dissect 15 feet of wiring under the dashboard, looking for what happened.

When an electrical current of excessive power passes through the fuse, the fuse blows (the conductor melts) and breaks the circuit, preventing the passage of current and protecting the components.

A circuit breaker is basically a self repairing fuse. It will open the circuit in the same fashion as a fuse, but when either the short is removed or the surge subsides, the circuit breaker resets itself and does not need replacement.

A fuse link (fusible link or main link) is a wire that acts as a fuse. One of these is normally connected between the starter relay and the main wiring harness under the hood. Since the starter is usually the highest electrical draw on the vehicle, an internal short during starting could direct about 130 amps into the wrong places. Consider the damage potential of introducing this current into a system whose wiring is rated at 15 amps and you'll understand the need for protection. Since this link is very early in the electrical path, it's the first place to look if nothing on the vehicle works, but the battery seems to be charged and is properly connected.

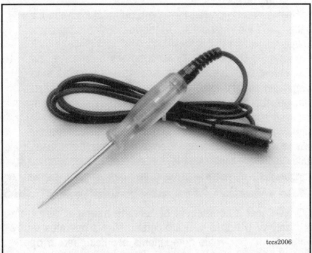

Fig. 3 A 12 volt test light is useful when checking parts of a circuit for power

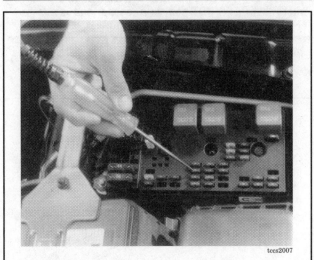

Fig. 4 Here, someone is checking a circuit by making sure there is power to the component's fuse

3-4 ENGINE AND ENGINE OVERHAUL

you must follow a systematic plan to determine which of the three causes is the villain.

1. Turn ON the switch that controls the item not working.

➡ Some items only work when the ignition switch is turned ON.

2. Disconnect the power supply wire from the component.
3. Attach the ground wire of a test light or a voltmeter to a good metal ground.
4. Touch the end probe of the test light (or the positive lead of the voltmeter) to the power wire; if there is current in the wire, the light in the test light will come on (or the voltmeter will indicate the amount of voltage). You have now established that current is getting to the component.
5. Turn the ignition or dash switch OFF and reconnect the wire to the component.

If there was no power, then the problem is between the battery and the component. This includes all the switches, fuses, relays and the battery itself. The next place to look is the fusebox; check carefully either by eye or by using the test light across the fuse clips. The easiest way to check is to simply replace the fuse. If the fuse is blown, and upon replacement, immediately blows again, there is a short between the fuse and the component. This is generally (not always) a sign of an internal short in the component. Disconnect the power wire at the component again and replace the fuse; if the fuse holds, the component is the problem.

✱✱WARNING

DO NOT test a component by running a jumper wire from the battery UNLESS you are certain that it operates on 12 volts. Many electronic components are designed to operate with less voltage and connecting them to 12 volts could destroy them. Jumper wires are best used to bypass a portion of the circuit (such as a stretch of wire or a switch) that DOES NOT contain a resistor and is suspected to be bad.

If all the fuses are good and the component is not receiving power, find the switch for the circuit. Bypass the switch with the jumper wire. This is done by connecting one end of the jumper to the power wire coming into the switch and the other end to the wire leaving the switch. If the component comes to life, the switch has failed.

✱✱WARNING

Never substitute the jumper for the component. The circuit needs the electrical load of the component. If you bypass it, you will cause a short circuit.

Checking the ground for any circuit can mean tracing wires to the body, cleaning connections or tightening mounting bolts for the component itself. If the jumper wire can be connected to the case of the component or the ground connector, you can ground the other end to a piece of clean, solid metal on the vehicle. Again, if the component starts working, you've found the problem.

A systematic search through the fuse, connectors, switches and the component itself will almost always yield an answer. Loose and/or corroded connectors, particularly in ground circuits, are becoming a larger problem in modern vehicles. The computers and on-board electronic (solid state) systems are highly sensitive to improper grounds and will change their function drastically if one occurs.

Remember that for any electrical circuit to work, ALL the connections must be clean and tight.

➡ For more information on Understanding and Troubleshooting Electrical Systems, please refer to Section 6 of this manual.

Battery, Starting and Charging Systems

BASIC OPERATING PRINCIPLES

Battery

The battery is the first link in the chain of mechanisms which work together to provide cranking of the automobile engine. In most modern vehicles, the battery is a lead/acid electrochemical device consisting of six 2V subsections (cells) connected in series so the unit is capable of producing approximately 12V of electrical pressure. Each subsection consists of a series of positive and negative plates held a short distance apart in a solution of sulfuric acid and water.

The two types of plates are of dissimilar metals. This sets-up a chemical reaction, and it is this reaction which produces current flow from the battery when its positive and negative terminals are connected to an electrical accessory such as a lamp or motor. The continued transfer of electrons would eventually convert the sulfuric acid to water, and make the two plates identical in chemical composition. As electrical energy is removed from the battery, its voltage output tends to drop. Thus, measuring battery voltage and battery electrolyte composition are two ways of checking the ability of the unit to supply power. During engine cranking, electrical energy is removed from the battery. However, if the charging circuit is in good condition and the operating conditions are normal, the power removed from the battery will be replaced by the alternator which will force electrons back through the battery, reversing

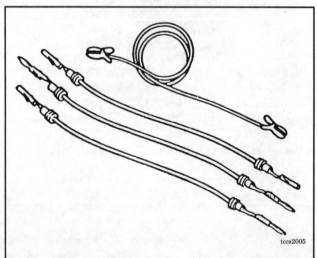

Fig. 5 Jumper wires with various connectors are handy for quick electrical testing

ENGINE AND ENGINE OVERHAUL

the normal flow, and restoring the battery to its original chemical state.

Starting System

The battery and starting motor are linked by very heavy electrical cables designed to minimize resistance to the flow of current. Generally, the major power supply cable that leaves the battery goes directly to the starter, while other electrical system needs are supplied by a smaller cable. During starter operation, power flows from the battery to the starter and is grounded through the vehicle's frame/body or engine and the battery's negative ground strap.

The starter is a specially designed, direct current electric motor capable of producing a great amount of power for its size. One thing that allows the motor to produce a great deal of power is its tremendous rotating speed. It drives the engine through a tiny pinion gear (attached to the starter's armature), which drives the very large flywheel ring gear at a greatly reduced speed. Another factor allowing it to produce so much power is that only intermittent operation is required of it. Thus, little allowance for air circulation is necessary, and the windings can be built into a very small space.

The starter solenoid is a magnetic device which employs the small current supplied by the start circuit of the ignition switch. This magnetic action moves a plunger which mechanically engages the starter and closes the heavy switch connecting it to the battery. The starting switch circuit usually consists of the starting switch contained within the ignition switch, a neutral safety switch or clutch pedal switch, and the wiring necessary to connect these in series with the starter solenoid or relay.

The pinion, a small gear, is mounted to a one way drive clutch. This clutch is splined to the starter armature shaft. When the ignition switch is moved to the **START** position, the solenoid plunger slides the pinion toward the flywheel ring gear via a collar and spring. If the teeth on the pinion and flywheel match properly, the pinion will engage the flywheel immediately. If the gear teeth butt one another, the spring will be compressed and will force the gears to mesh as soon as the starter turns far enough to allow them to do so. As the solenoid plunger reaches the end of its travel, it closes the contacts that connect the battery and starter, then the engine is cranked.

As soon as the engine starts, the flywheel ring gear begins turning fast enough to drive the pinion at an extremely high rate of speed. At this point, the one-way clutch begins allowing the pinion to spin faster than the starter shaft so that the starter will not operate at excessive speed. When the ignition switch is released from the starter position, the solenoid is de-energized, and a spring pulls the gear out of mesh interrupting the current flow to the starter.

Some starters employ a separate relay, mounted away from the starter, to switch the motor and solenoid current on and off. The relay replaces the solenoid electrical switch, but does not eliminate the need for a solenoid mounted on the starter used to mechanically engage the starter drive gears. The relay is used to reduce the amount of current the starting switch must carry.

Charging System

The automobile charging system provides electrical power for operation of the vehicle's ignition system, starting system and all electrical accessories. The battery serves as an electrical surge or storage tank, storing (in chemical form) the energy originally produced by the engine driven generator. The system also provides a means of regulating output to protect the battery from being overcharged and to avoid excessive voltage to the accessories.

The storage battery is a chemical device incorporating parallel lead plates in a tank containing a sulfuric acid/water solution. Adjacent plates are slightly dissimilar, and the chemical reaction of the two dissimilar plates produces electrical energy when the battery is connected to a load such as the starter motor. The chemical reaction is reversible, so that when the generator is producing a voltage (electrical pressure) greater than that produced by the battery, electricity is forced into the battery, and the battery is returned to its fully charged state.

Newer automobiles use alternating current generators or alternators, because they are more efficient, can be rotated at higher speeds, and have fewer brush problems. In an alternator, the field usually rotates while all the current produced passes only through the stator winding. The brushes bear against continuous slip rings. This causes the current produced to periodically reverse the direction of its flow. Diodes (electrical one way valves) block the flow of current from traveling in the wrong direction. A series of diodes is wired together to permit the alternating flow of the stator to be rectified back to 12 volts DC for use by the vehicle's electrical system.

The voltage regulating function is performed by a regulator. The regulator is often built in to the alternator; this system is termed an integrated or internal regulator.

ENGINE ELECTRICAL

➥ **CJ-2A, CJ-3A and some CJ-3B, CJ-5 and CJ-6 models are equipped with 6 volt electrical systems. The easiest way to tell which system your Jeep has is to look at the battery. A 6 volt battery has three cell caps; a 12 volt battery has six cell caps. All systems are negative ground.**

Ignition Coil

REMOVAL & INSTALLATION

1. Disconnect the battery ground.
2. Disconnect the two small and one large wire from the coil.
3. Disconnect the condenser connector from the coil, if equipped.
4. Unbolt and remove the coil.
5. Installation is the reverse of removal.

Generator and Regulator Specifications

6 Volt

Manufacturer	Generator Model No.	Output amps	Brush Spring Tension (oz.)	Regulator Model No.	Regulated Voltage	Regulated Amperage	Cutout Relay Closing Voltage
Autolite	GDZ 4817 GDZ 6001	35	35–53	VRP-6003 VPR-4007 VBO-4601	7.1–7.3	49	6.3–6.8
	GGW 4801 GGW 7404	45	35–53 18–36	VBO-4601C VBE-6105A	7.1–7.3	49	6.3–6.8
Delco-Remy	1102811	45	28	1972063	6.9–7.4	42–47	5.9–6.7

12 Volt

Manufacturer	Generator Model No.	Output amps	Brush Spring Tension (oz.)	Regulator Model No.	Regulated Voltage	Regulated Amperage	Cutout Relay Closing Voltage
Autolite	GJP-7202B GJP-7202A	35	18–36	VRX-6009B VBO-4201E-4E	14.3–14.7	39	12.6–13.6
Delco-Remy	1102096	35	28	197229	13.8–14.8	27–33	11.8–13.5

Alternator and Regulator Specifications

Engine	Year	Alternator Manufacturer	Field Current @ 12v (amps)	Output (amps)	Regulator Manufacturer	Volts @ 75°F
4-134	1966–71	Motorola	1.2–1.7	35	Motorola	14.2–14.6
6-225	1966–71	Motorola	1.2–1.7	35	Delco-Remy	14.2–14.6
6-230	1960–64	Motorola	1.2–1.7	35 ①	Motorola	14.2–14.6

① -Optional 40 Amp.

Starter Specifications

Engine	Year	Manufacturer	Lock Test Amps	Lock Test Volts	Torque (ft. lb.)	No-Load Test Amps	No-Load Test Volts	No-Load Test RPM	Brush Spring Tension (oz.)
4-134	1945–65	Autolite 6v	335	2.0	6.0	65	5.0	4,300	42–53
		Autolite 12v	280	4.0	6.2	50	10.0	5,300	31–47
		Delco 6v	600	3.0	15.0	60	5.0	6,000	35 min.
		Delco 12v	435	5.8	10.5	75	10.3	6,900	24 min.
	1966–71	Autolite	①	4.0	②	50	10.0	4,400	31–47
		Delco	435	5.8	1.5	75	10.3	6,900	24 min.
		Prestolite	405	N.A.	9.0	50	10.0	5,300	32–40
6-225	1966–71	Delco	Not Recommended			75	10.6	6,200	32–40
6-226	1950–60	Autolite 6v	335	2.0	6.0	65	5.0	4,300	42–53
		Autolite 12v	280	4.0	6.2	50	10.0	5,300	31–47
		Delco 6v	600	3.0	15.0	60	5.0	6,000	35 min.
		Delco 12v	435	5.8	10.5	75	10.3	6,900	24 min.
6-230	1960–64	Prestolite	405	4.0	9.0	60	10.0	4,200	42–53

N.A.: Information Not Available
min.: minimum
① Starter #MDU7004: 280
All others: 170
② Starter #MDU7004: 6.2
All others: 1.5

ENGINE AND ENGINE OVERHAUL 3-7

Distributor

▶ See Figures 6, 7 and 8

REMOVAL

Except 6-226 Engine

1. Remove the high-tension wires from the distributor cap terminal towers, noting their positions to assure correct reassembly. For diagrams of firing orders and distributor wiring, refer to the tune-up and troubleshooting section.
2. Remove the primary lead from the terminal post at the side of the distributor.
3. Disconnect the vacuum line if there is one.
4. Remove the two distributor cap retaining hooks or screws and remove the distributor cap.
5. Note the position of the rotor in relation to the base. Scribe a mark on the base of the distributor and on the engine block to facilitate reinstallation. Align the marks with the direction the metal tip of the rotor is pointing.
6. Remove the bolt that holds the distributor to the engine.
7. Lift the distributor assembly from the engine.

6-226 Engine

1. Remove the vacuum line and primary lead from the distributor.
2. Remove the distributor cap.
3. Note the position of the rotor in relation to the base. Scribe a mark on the base of the distributor and on the engine head to facilitate installation. Align the marks with the direction the metal tip of the rotor is pointing.
4. Remove the bolt and lock washer which retain the advance arm to the adapter. Lift out the distributor.

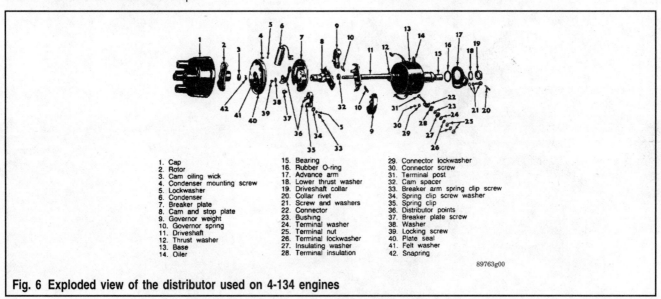

Fig. 6 Exploded view of the distributor used on 4-134 engines

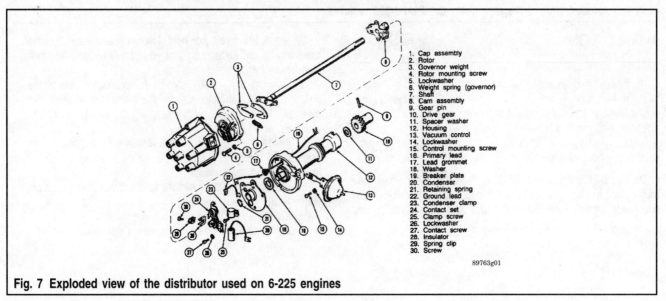

Fig. 7 Exploded view of the distributor used on 6-225 engines

3-8 ENGINE AND ENGINE OVERHAUL

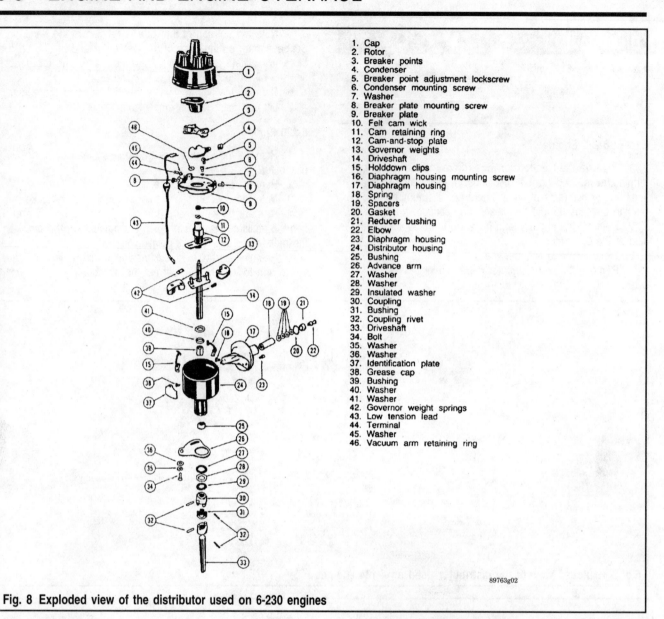

Fig. 8 Exploded view of the distributor used on 6-230 engines

1. Cap
2. Rotor
3. Breaker points
4. Condenser
5. Breaker point adjustment lockscrew
6. Condenser mounting screw
7. Washer
8. Breaker plate mounting screw
9. Breaker plate
10. Felt cam wick
11. Cam retaining ring
12. Cam-and-stop plate
13. Governor weights
14. Driveshaft
15. Holddown clips
16. Diaphragm housing mounting screw
17. Diaphragm housing
18. Spring
19. Spacers
20. Gasket
21. Reducer bushing
22. Elbow
23. Diaphragm housing
24. Distributor housing
25. Bushing
26. Advance arm
27. Washer
28. Washer
29. Insulated washer
30. Coupling
31. Bushing
32. Coupling rivet
33. Driveshaft
34. Bolt
35. Washer
36. Washer
37. Identification plate
38. Grease cap
39. Bushing
40. Washer
41. Washer
42. Governor weight springs
43. Low tension lead
44. Terminal
45. Washer
46. Vacuum arm retaining ring

INSTALLATION

1. Insert the distributor shaft and assembly into the engine. Line up the mark on the distributor and the one on the engine with the metal tip of the rotor. Make sure that the vacuum advance diaphragm is pointed in the same direction as it was pointed originally. This will be done automatically if the marks on the engine and the distributor are line up with the rotor.

➡ On the 6-225, 6-226 and F4-134, the distributor shaft fits into a slot in the end of the oil pump shaft. Therefore, the rotor won't turn when the distributor is pressed into place.

2. Install the distributor hold-down bolt and clamp. Leave the screw loose enough so that you can move the distributor with heavy hand pressure.

3. Connect the primary wire to the distributor side of the coil. Install the distributor cap on the distributor housing. Secure the distributor cap with the spring clips or the screw type retainers, whichever is used.

4. Install the spark plug wires. Make sure that the wires are pressed all of the way into the top of the distributor cap and firmly onto the spark plugs.

5. Adjust the point cam dwell and set the ignition timing. Refer to the tune-up section.

If the engine was turned while the distributor was removed, or if matchmarks were not made during removal, it will be

ENGINE AND ENGINE OVERHAUL 3-9

necessary to initially time the engine. Perform the following procedure.

➡ Design of the V6 engine requires a special form of distributor cam. The distributor may be serviced in the regular way and should cause no more problems than any other distributor, if the firing plan is thoroughly understood. The distributor cam is not ground to standard 6-cylinder indexing intervals. This particular form requires that the original pattern of spark plug wiring be used. The engine will not run in balance if the No. 1 spark plug wire is inserted into the No. 6 distributor cap tower, even though each wire in the firing sequence is advanced to the next distributor tower. There is a difference between the firing intervals of each succeeding cylinder through the 720° engine cycle.

INSTALLATION

Engine Rotated

1. If the engine has been rotated while the distributor was out, you'll have to first position the engine on No. 1 cylinder at Top Dead Center (TDC) firing position, as follows:
   a. You can either remove the valve cover or No. 1 spark plug to determine engine position.
   b. Rotate the engine with a socket wrench on the nut at the center of the front pulley in the normal direction of rotation.
   c. Either feel for air being expelled forcefully through the spark plug hole or watch for the engine to rotate up to the TDC mark without the valves moving (both valves will be closed).
   d. For 4-134 F-head engines, stop turning the engine when either the 5 degree mark on the flywheel is in the middle of the flywheel inspection opening, or the marks on the crankshaft pulley and the timing gear cover are in alignment.
   e. If the valves are moving as you approach TDC, or there is no air being expelled through the plug hole, turn the engine another full turn until you get the appropriate indication as the engine approaches TDC position.
2. Start the distributor into the engine with the matchmarks between the distributor body and the engine lined up. Turn the rotor slightly until the matchmarks on the bottom of the distributor body and the bottom of the distributor shaft near the gear are aligned.

➡ On the 4-134, 6-225 and 6-226, the distributor shaft indexes with the oil pump driveshaft. Then, insert the distributor all the way into the engine. If you have trouble getting the distributor and camshaft gears to mesh, turn the rotor back and forth very slightly until the distributor can be inserted easily. If the rotor is not now lined up with the position of No. 1 plug terminal, you'll have to pull the distributor back out slightly, shift the position of the rotor appropriately, and then reinstall it.

3. Align the matchmarks between the distributor and engine.
4. Install the distributor mounting bolt and tighten it finger-tight.

5. Reattach the vacuum advance line and distributor wiring connector, and reinstall the gasket and cap.
6. Reconnect the negative battery cable.
7. Adjust the ignition timing as described in Section 2.
8. Tighten the distributor mounting bolt securely.

➡ A CJ-5 and CJ-6 4-134 F-head distributor (IAD 4041) is identical to the distributor used on CJ-3B's (IAD 4008A), with the exception of the hold-down arm. The CJ-5 and CJ-6 distributor was originally installed in the CJ-3B. It is necessary to remove the oil pump in order to install a newer distributor in the CJ-3B. Place the distributor in the correct timing position and install the hold-down screw. Engage the distributor drive and carefully mesh the gears without disturbing the correct timing position of the distributor, and then replace the oil pump.

Alternator/Generator

GENERAL INFORMATION

◆ See Figure 9

All Jeep vehicles through 1964 had DC generators. In 1965, alternators were installed on the Tuxedo Park versions of the CJ-5 and CJ-6. These models were known respectively as the CJ-5A and CJ-6A. Starting in 1966, all Jeep vehicles came with alternators.

An alternator differs from a conventional DC shunt generator in that the armature is stationary, and is called the stator, while the field rotates and is called the rotor. The higher current values in the alternator's stator are conducted to the external circuit through fixed leads and connections, rather than through a rotating commutator and brushes as in a DC generator. This eliminates a major point of maintenance.

The alternator employs a 3-phase stator winding. The rotor consists of a field coil encased between 6-poled, interleaved sections producing a 12-pole magnetic field with alternating north and south poles. By rotating the rotor inside the stator, and alternating current is induced in the stator windings. This alternating current is changed to direct current by diodes and is routed out of the alternator through the output terminal. Diode rectifiers act as one way electrical valves. Half of the diodes have a negative polarity and are grounded. The other half of the diodes have a positive polarity and are connected to the output terminal.

Since the diodes have a high resistance to the flow of current in one direction, and a low resistance in the opposite direction, they are connected in a manner which allows current to flow from the alternator to the battery in the low resistance direction.

The high resistance in the other direction prevents the flow of current from the battery to the alternator. Because of this feature, there is no need for a circuit breaker between the alternator and the battery.

Residual magnetism in the rotor field poles is minimal. The starting field current must, therefore, be supplied by the battery. It is connected to the field winding through the ignition switch and the charge indicator lamp or ammeter.

As in the DC shunt generator, the alternator voltage is regulated by varying the field current. This is accomplished elec-

3-10 ENGINE AND ENGINE OVERHAUL

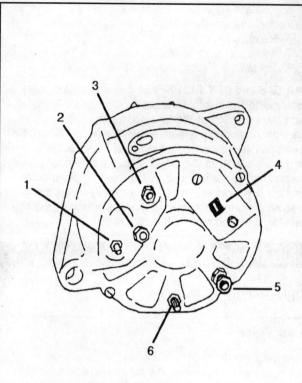

1. Auxiliary terminal
2. Output terminal
3. Auxiliary terminal
4. Field terminal
5. Ground terminal
6. Ground terminal

Fig. 9 Alternator terminal identification for Motorola alternators used through 1970

tronically in the transistorized voltage regulator. No current regulator is required because all alternators have self-limiting current characteristics.

An alternator is better that a conventional, DC shunt generator because it is lighter and more compact, because it is designed to supply the battery and accessory circuits through a wide range of engine speeds, and because it eliminates the necessary maintenance of replacing brushes and servicing commutators.

The transistorized voltage regulator is an electronic switching device. It senses the voltage at the auxiliary terminal of the alternator and supplies the necessary field current for maintaining the system voltage at the output terminal. The output current is determined by the battery electrical load, such as operating headlights or heater blower.

The transistorized voltage regulator is a sealed unit that has no adjustments and must be replaced as a complete unit when it ceases to operate.

ALTERNATOR PRECAUTIONS

To prevent damage to the alternator and regulator, the following precautionary measures must be taken when working with the electrical system.

1. Never reverse battery connections. Always check the battery polarity visually. This is to be done before any connections are made to be sure that all of the connections correspond to the battery ground polarity of the Jeep.
2. Booster batteries for starting must be connected properly. Make sure that the positive cable of the booster battery is connected to the positive terminal of the battery that is getting the boost. This applies to both negative and ground cables.
3. Disconnect the battery cables before using a fast charger. The charger has a tendency to force current through the diodes in the opposite direction for which they were designed. This burns out the diodes.
4. Never use a fast charger as a booster for starting the vehicle.
5. Never disconnect the voltage regulator while the engine is running.
6. Do not ground the alternator output terminal.
7. Do not operate the alternator on an open circuit with the field energized.
8. Do not attempt to polarize an alternator.

REMOVAL & INSTALLATION

1. Remove all of the electrical connections from the alternator or generator. Label all of the wires so that you can install them correctly.
2. Remove all of the attaching nuts, bolts and washers noting different sized threads or nuts and bolts that go in certain holes.
3. Remove the alternator carefully.
4. To install, reverse the removal procedure and adjust the belt as described later.
5. Tighten the mounting bolts to 25-30 ft. lbs. (34-41 Nm) and the sliding adjusting bolt to 20 ft. lbs. (27 Nm).

BELT TENSION ADJUSTMENT

The fan belt drives the generator/alternator and the water pump. If it is too loose, it will slip and the generator/alternator will not be able to produce the rated current. if the belt is too loose, the water pump would not be driven and the engine could overheat. Check the tension of the fan belt by pushing your thumb down on the longest span of belt midway between the pulleys. If the belt flexes more than ½ in. (13mm), it should be tightened. Loosen the bolt on the adjusting bracket and pivot bolt and move the alternator or generator away from the engine to tighten the belt. Do not apply pressure to the rear of the case aluminum housing of an alternator; it might break. Tighten the adjusting bolts when the proper tension is reached.

ENGINE AND ENGINE OVERHAUL 3-11

Regulator

The voltage regulators that are used with alternators are transistorized and cannot be serviced. If the voltage regulator is not operating properly, it must be replaced.

The voltage regulators that are used with shunt type generators are serviceable and can be adjusted. These regulators have three units: the circuit breaker, the voltage regulator and the current limiting regulator. Each performs a separate function.

VOLTAGE REGULATOR

The function of the voltage regulator unit is to hold the generated voltage at a predetermined value as long as the circuit values allow the voltage to build to the operating load.

The electromagnet of the voltage regulator unit has a winding of many turns of fine wire and is connected across the charging circuit so that the system voltage controls the amount of magnetism. The contacts of the voltage regulator unit are connected in the generator field circuit so that the field circuit is completed through the contacts when they are closed and through a resistor when the contacts are opened.

When the voltage rises to a predetermined amount, there is sufficient magnetism created by the regulator winding to pull the armature down. This opens the contacts and inserts resistance in the field circuit of the generator, thus reducing the field current. The generated voltage immediately drops, reducing the pull on the armature to the point where the spring closes the contacts. The output again rises and the cycle is repeated.

These cycles occur at sufficiently high frequencies to hold the generated voltage at a constant level and they will continue as long as the voltage of the circuit is high enough to keep the voltage regulator unit in operation. When there is a current load that is great enough to lower the battery voltage below the operating voltage of the voltage regulating unit, the contacts will remain closed and the generator will maintain a charging rate that is limited by its speed and capacity output.

CURRENT LIMITING REGULATOR

The function of the current limiting regulator is to limit the output of the generator to its maximum safe output.

The electromagnet of the current regulator unit consists of a winding of heavy wire connected in a series with the generator output. When the generator output reaches a predetermined level, the current in the winding produces enough magnetism to overcome spring tension and pull the armature down. This opens the contacts and inserts resistance in the field circuit of the generator. With the field current reduced by the resistance, the generator output falls and there is no longer sufficient magnetism to hold the contacts open. As soon as the spring closes the contacts, the output and the cycle is repeated. These cycles occur at a high enough frequency to limit the output to a minimum fluctuation.

VOLTAGE TESTS & ADJUSTMENTS

Circuit Breaker

The circuit breaker is the unit with the heavy wire windings and is located on the end of the unit.

1. Connect an ammeter in series with the regulator **B** (battery) terminal and the lead that is removed from that terminal. Connect a voltmeter from the regulator **A** (armature) terminal to the regulator base.
2. Disconnect the field lead from the regulator **F** terminal and insert a variable resistance between the lead and the regulator terminal.
3. Run the generator at about 1000 rpm. Insert all of the resistance in the field circuit. Slowly reduce the resistance, noting the voltage reading just before the change caused by the closing of the circuit breaker. Increase the charging rate to the figure specified for the regulator being tested, then reduce the charging rate by inserting resistance into the field circuit. Note the charging rate just before the circuit breaker opens and the ammeter reading drops to 0. The closing voltage and the opening voltage or current should be within the limits specified.
4. To adjust the closing voltage, change the armature spring tension by bending the hanger at the lower end of the spring. Increase the spring tension to raise the closing voltage or decrease the tension to lower the voltage. To adjust the opening voltage, raise or lower the stationary contact, keeping the contacts perfectly aligned. Increasing the contact gap lowers the opening voltage. Change the contact gap by expanding or contracting the contact gap by expanding or contracting the stationary contact bracket, keeping the contacts aligned. Do not adjust the gap between the contacts to less than the specified minimum.

Voltage Regulator

The voltage regulator unit is the one with the fine wire winding.

1. Connect the ammeter as noted in the previous procedure and connect the voltmeter between regulator **B** terminal and the regulator base. Remove the variable resistance from the field circuit.
2. Run the generator at ½ maximum output for 15 minutes to make sure the regulator is at normal operating temperature. Have the cover on the unit during this warm up period and also when taking the readings.
3. Stop the engine, then bring it to approximately 2,500 generator rpm. Adjust the amperage to one half of the maximum output by turning on lights or accessories and then note the voltmeter reading. This reading should be within the limits specified for the voltage regulator.
4. To adjust the operating voltage, change the armature spring tension by bending the hanger at the lower end of the armature spring. After each adjustment, stop the engine and then restart it. Bring it up to speed and adjust the current before taking a reading. The clicks of the opening and closing of the contacts should be regular and clear without irregularities. If the tone is not clear and regular, remove the regulator cover and inspect the contacts. The contacts should be flat and not burned excessively, and should be aligned to make

3-12 ENGINE AND ENGINE OVERHAUL

full face contact. Refer to the section on cleaning the contacts if necessary.

Current Regulator

The current regulator is the unit in the middle of the unit with the heavy wire winding.

1. Connect the regulator and instruments as described in the previous procedures for the voltage regulator and run the generator at approximately 3,000 generator rpm. Turn on lights and accessories so the generator must charge at its maximum rate. The ammeter should show a reading within the specified limits.
2. To adjust the opening amperage, change the armature spring tension by bending the hanger at the lower end of the armature spring. Stop the engine after each adjustment and then restart it. Bring the engine to speed and take an ammeter reading. Keep the cover on the unit when taking the readings. The clocks of the points closing and opening should be clear in tone and regular in frequency without irregularities or misses. If this is not the case, the contacts will have to be serviced.

Contacts

The contacts should be inspected on all three of the units inside the cover of the voltage regulator. The contacts will become grayed and slightly worn during normal use. If the contacts are burned or dirty, or if they are not smooth or aligned properly, they should be adjusted and cleaned. File the contacts smooth. Just file enough so that there is a smooth surface presented to each contact. It is not necessary to file out every trace of pitting. After filing, dampen a clean cloth with carbon tetrachloride and pull the cloth between the contacts of each of the three units. Repeat with a clean dry cloth.

➡ Keep in mind that after filing the points, the gap might have been changed enough to affect the performance of the three units. Check the three units and perform the adjustments. It might be a good idea to examine the contacts before making any adjustments. If the contacts need to be serviced, do it before adjusting spring tensions, etc.

REMOVAL & INSTALLATION

If the voltage regulator still does not function properly, after all of the checks and adjustments, replace the entire unit as described in the following procedure:

1. Remove all of the electrical connections. Label them as you remove them so you can replace them in the correct order on the replacement unit.
2. Remove all of the hold-down screws and then remove the unit from the vehicle.
3. Install the new voltage regulator using the hold-down screws from the old one, or new ones if they are provided with the replacement regulator. Tighten down the hold-down screws.
4. Connect the armature lead to the armature terminal of the voltage regulator.
5. Connect the battery lead to the battery terminal of the voltage regulator.
6. Momentarily touch the field lead to the battery terminal of the voltage regulator. This polarizes the generator and voltage regulator so they have the same polarization as the rest of the electrical system. This has to be done every time all of the leads are disconnected from the generator voltage regulator.
7. Connect the field lead to the field terminal of the voltage regulator.

Starter

REMOVAL & INSTALLATION

▶ See Figures 10, 11, 12, 13, 14, 15, 16, 17 and 18

The starter on the 4-134 L and F-head engines and 6-226 engines can be removed from the top of the engine. The starter motor on all other engines must be removed from beneath the vehicle.

1. Disconnect the negative battery cable.

Fig. 10 To remove the starter motor, first loosen . . .

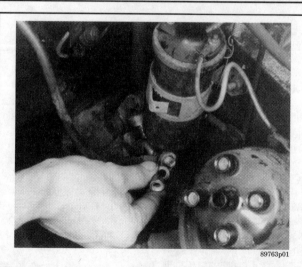

Fig. 11 . . . and remove the wiring's retaining nut and washer . . .

ENGINE AND ENGINE OVERHAUL 3-13

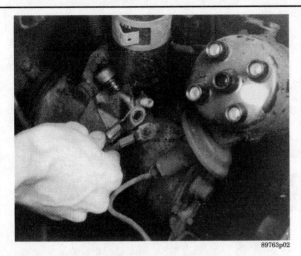

Fig. 12 . . . then remove all wires from the starter motor terminal — 4-134 engine shown

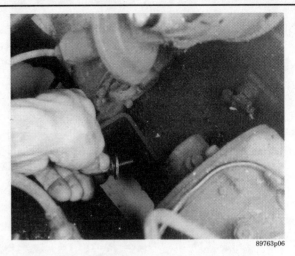

Fig. 15 . . . then remove the starter motor rear mounting bracket bolt

Fig. 13 Detach the starter drive return spring from the drive arm

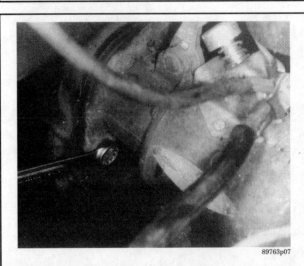

Fig. 16 Loosen the starter motor's lower mounting bolt . . .

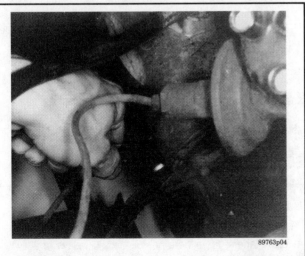

Fig. 14 Remove the starter motor's side mounting bracket retaining bolt . . .

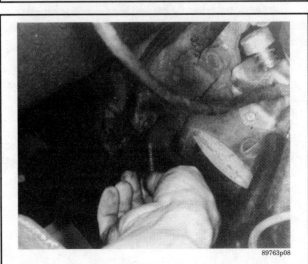

Fig. 17 . . . then remove it from the starter motor and engine block

3-14 ENGINE AND ENGINE OVERHAUL

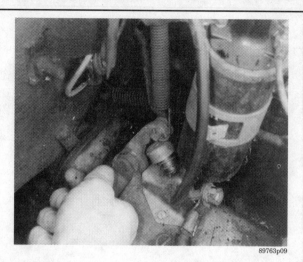

Fig. 18 Support the motor and remove the other mounting bolt

2. On Jeep models equipped with either the 6-225 and 6-230 engines, raise and safely support the vehicle on jackstands.
3. Remove all wires from the starter and tag them for installation.
4. Remove all but one upper attaching bolt, support the starter (it's heavier than it looks) and remove the last bolt.
5. Pull the starter from the engine.
6. Installation is the reverse of removal. Tighten the mounting bolts to:
   - 4-134 and 6-225 engines — 25 ft. lbs. (34 Nm)
   - 6-226 and 6-230 engines — 30 ft. lbs. (41 Nm)

STARTER DRIVE REPLACEMENT

Autolite

1. Remove the cover of the starter drive's actuating lever arm.
2. Remove the through-bolts, starter drive gear housing, and the return spring of the driver gear's actuating lever.
3. Remove the pivot pin, which retains the starter gear actuating lever, then remove the lever and armature.
4. Remove the stop ring retainer. Remove and discard the stop ring which holds the drive gear to the armature shaft, then remove the drive gear assembly.

To install:

5. Lightly lubricate the armature shaft splines with Lubriplate® and install the starter drive gear assembly on the shaft.
6. Install a new stop ring and stop ring retainer.
7. Position the starter drive gear actuating lever to the frame and starter drive assembly. Install the pivot pin.
8. Fill the starter drive gear housing ¼ full of grease.
9. Position the drive actuating lever return spring and the drive gear housing to the frame, then install and tighten the through-bolts.

➡ Be sure that the stop ring retainer is properly seated in the drive housing.

Delco-Remy

1. Remove the through-bolts.
2. Remove the starter drive housing.
3. Slide the two piece thrust collar off the end of the armature shaft.
4. Slide a standard ½ in. (13mm) pipe coupling, or other spacer, onto the shaft so that the end of the coupling butts against the edge of the retainer.
5. Tap the end of the coupling with a hammer, driving the retainer toward the armature end of the snapring.
6. Remove the snapring from its groove in the shaft with pliers. Slide the retainer and the starter drive from the armature.

To install:

7. Lubricate the drive end of the shaft with silicone lubricant.
8. Slide the drive gear assembly onto the shaft, with the gear facing outward.
9. Slide the retainer onto the shaft with the cupped surface facing away from the gear.
10. Stand the whole starter assembly on a block of wood with the snapring positioned on the upper end of the shaft. Drive the snapring down with a small block of wood and a hammer. Slide the snapring into its groove.
11. Install the thrust collar onto the shaft with the shoulder next to the snapring.
12. With the retainer on one side of the snapring and the thrust collar on the other side, squeeze them together with a pair of pliers until the ring seats in the retainer. On models without a thrust collar, use a washer. Remember to remove the washer before installing the starter in the engine.

Prestolite

1. Slide the thrust collar off the armature shaft.
2. Using a standard ½ in. (13mm) pipe connector, drive the snapring retainer off the shaft.
3. Remove the snapring from the groove, and then remove the drive assembly.

To install:

4. Lubricate the drive end and splines with Lubriplate®.
5. Install the clutch assembly onto the shaft.
6. Install the snapring retainer with the cupped surface facing toward the end of the shaft.
7. Install the snapring into the groove. Use a new snapring, if necessary.
8. Install the thrust collar onto the shaft with the shoulder against the snapring.
9. Force the retainer over the snapring in the same manner as was used for the Delco-Remy starters.

SOLENOID OR RELAY REPLACEMENT

Autolite

On the early CJ-2A, CJ-3A, CJ-3B, CJ-5, and CJ-6 with Autolite starters, there were no solenoids or relays to activate the starter drive. The starter drive activated itself by the centrifugal force of the starter motor and deactivated itself in the normal way (by the centrifugal force of the engine's flywheel).

ENGINE AND ENGINE OVERHAUL 3-15

Autolite starters were installed with solenoids mounted on the starter housing beginning in 1960.

To remove the solenoid from the starter, remove all of the leads to the solenoid, remove the connecting lever, and remove the attaching bolts that hold the solenoid assembly to the starter housing. Remove the solenoid assembly from the starter housing.

To install the solenoid assembly, reverse the removal procedure.

Delco-Remy

1. Remove the leads from the solenoid.
2. Remove the drive housing from the starter motor.
3. Remove the shift lever pin and bolt from the shift lever.
4. Remove the attaching bolts that hold the solenoid assembly to the housing of the starter motor.
5. Remove the starter solenoid from the starter housing.
6. To install the solenoid, reverse the removal procedure.

Prestolite

1. Remove the leads from the solenoid assembly.
2. Remove the attaching bolts that hold the solenoid to the starter housing.
3. Remove the bolt form the shift lever.
4. Remove the solenoid assembly from the starter housing.
5. Reverse the procedure for installation.

STARTER OVERHAUL

▶ See Figures 19, 20 and 21

Autolite/Motorcraft

DISASSEMBLY

1. Remove the cover screw, the cover through-bolts, the starter drive end housing and the starter drive plunger lever return spring.
2. Remove the starter gear plunger lever pivot pin, the lever and the armature. Remove the stop ring retainer and the stop ring from the armature shaft (discard the ring), then the starter drive gear assembly.
3. Remove the brush end-plate, the insulator assembly and the brushes from the plastic holder, then lift out the brush holder. For reassembly, note the position of the brush holder with respect to the end terminal.
4. Remove the two ground brush-to-frame screws.
5. Bend up the sleeve's edges which are inserted in the frame's rectangular hole, then remove the sleeve and the retainer. Detach the field coil ground wire from the copper tab.
6. Remove the three coil retaining screws. Cut the field coil connection at the switch post lead, then remove the pole shoes and the coils from the frame.
7. Cut the positive brush leads from the field coils (as close to the field connection point as possible).
8. Check the armature and the armature windings for broken or burned insulation, open circuits or grounds.
9. Check the commutator for run-out. If it is rough, has flat spots or is more than 0.005 in. (0.127mm) out-of-round, reface the commutator face.
10. Inspect the armature shaft and the two bearings for scoring and excessive wear, then replace it (if necessary).
11. Inspect the starter drive. If the gear teeth are pitted, broken or excessively worn, replace the starter drive.

➡ The factory brush length is ½ in. (13mm); the wear limit is ¼ in. (6mm).

ASSEMBLY

1. Install the starter terminal, the insulator, the washers and the nut in the frame.

➡ **Be sure to position the screw slot perpendicular to the frame end surface.**

2. Position the coils and the pole pieces, with the coil leads in the terminal screw slot, then install the screws. When tightening the pole screws, strike the frame with several sharp hammer blows to align the pole shoes, then stake the screws.
3. Install the solenoid coil and the retainer, then bend the tabs to hold the coils to the frame.
4. Using resin-core solder and a 300 watt iron, solder the field coils and the solenoid wire to the starter terminal. Check for continuity and ground connections of the assembled coils.
5. Position the solenoid coil ground terminal over the nearest ground screw hole and the ground brushes-to-starter frame, then install the screws.
6. Apply a thin coating of Lubriplate® on the armature shaft splines. Install the starter motor drive gear assembly-to-armature shaft, followed by a new stop ring and retainer. Install the armature in the starter frame.
7. Position the starter drive gear plunger lever to the frame and the starter drive assembly, then install the pivot pin. Place some grease into the end housing bore. Fill it about ¼ full, then position the drive end housing to the frame.
8. Install the brush holder and the brush springs. The positive brush leads should be positioned in their respective brush holder slots, to prevent grounding problems.
9. Install the brush end-plate. Be certain that the end-plate insulator is in the proper position on the end-plate.
10. Install the two starter frame through-bolts and tighten them to 55-75 inch lbs. (6.2-8.4 Nm).
11. Install the starter drive plunger lever cover and tighten the retaining screw.

Delco-Remy

DISASSEMBLY

1. Detach the field coil connectors from the motor solenoid terminal. If equipped, remove solenoid mounting screws.
2. Remove the through-bolts, the commutator end frame, the field frame and the armature assembly from drive housing.
3. Remove the over-running clutch from the armature shaft as follows:
   a. Slide the two piece thrust collar off the end of the armature shaft.
   b. Slide a standard ½ in. (13mm) pipe coupling or other spacer onto the shaft, so that the coupling end butts against the retainer edge.
   c. Using a hammer, tap the coupling end, driving the retainer towards the armature end of the snapring.
   d. Using snapring pliers, remove the snapring from its groove in the shaft, then slide the retainer and the clutch from the shaft.

3-16 ENGINE AND ENGINE OVERHAUL

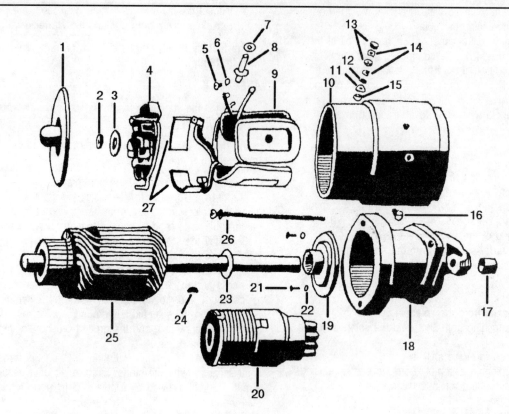

1. End plate
2. Plug
3. Thrust washer
4. Brush plate assembly
5. Screw
6. Lock washer
7. Insulating washer
8. Terminal
9. Field coil and pole shoe set
10. Frame
11. Insulating washer
12. Washer
13. Nut
14. Lockwasher
15. Insulating bushing
16. Pole shoe screw
17. Sleeve bearing
18. Drive end frame
19. Intermediate bearing
20. Bendix drive
21. Screw
22. Lockwasher
23. Thrust washer
24. Key
25. Armature
26. Through bolt
27. Insulator

Fig. 19 Exploded view of the starter motor used on 4-134 engines

4. Disassemble the field frame brush assembly by releasing the V-spring and removing the support pin. The brush holders, the brushes and the springs can now be pulled out as a unit and the leads disconnected.

➡On the integral frame units, remove the brush holder from the brush support and the brush screw.

5. If equipped, separate the solenoid from the lever housing.

CLEANING AND INSPECTION

1. Clean the parts with a rag. Do not immerse the parts in a solvent.

✵✵WARNING

Immersion in a solvent will dissolve the grease that is packed in the clutch mechanism. It will damage the armature and the field coil insulation.

2. Test the over-running clutch action. The pinion should turn freely in the overrunning direction but must not slip in the cranking direction. Check that the pinion teeth have not been chipped, cracked or excessively worn. Replace the unit (if necessary).

3. Inspect the armature commutator. If the commutator is rough or out of round, it should be machined and undercut.

➡Undercut the insulation between the commutator bars by 1/32 in. (0.794mm). The undercut must be the full width of the insulation and flat at the bottom. A triangular groove will not be satisfactory. Most late model starter motor use a molded armature commutator design. No attempt to undercut the insulation should be made or serious damage may result to the commutator.

ASSEMBLY

1. Install the brushes into the holders, then install the solenoid (if equipped).

2. Assemble the insulated and the grounded holder together.

ENGINE AND ENGINE OVERHAUL   3-17

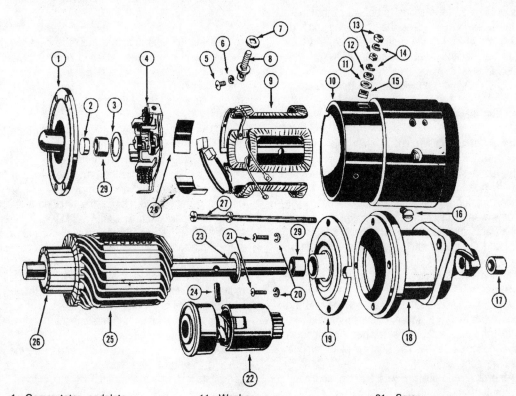

1. Commutator endplate
2. Plug
3. Thrust washer
4. Brush holder
5. Screw
6. Lockwasher
7. Washer
8. Terminal stud
9. Field coil and pole shoe
10. Motor frame
11. Washer
12. Insulator washer
13. Terminal stud nut
14. Lockwasher
15. Insulator washer
16. Screw
17. Bearing
18. Drive end frame
19. Intermediate bearing plate
20. Lockwasher
21. Screw
22. Bendix Folo-Thru® drive
23. Thrust washer
24. Holding pin
25. Armature
26. Commutator
27. Through bolt
28. Insulator
29. Bushing

Fig. 20 Exploded view of the starter motor used on 6-230 engines

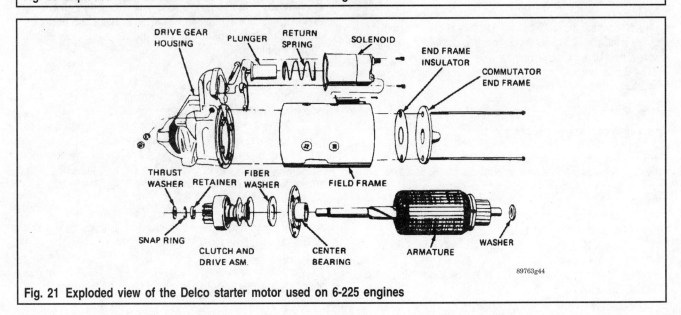

Fig. 21 Exploded view of the Delco starter motor used on 6-225 engines

ENGINE AND ENGINE OVERHAUL

3. Using the V-spring, position and assemble the unit on the support pin.
4. Push the holders and the spring to bottom of the support, then rotate the spring to engage the slot in the support.
5. Attach the ground wire to the grounded brush and the field lead wire to the insulated brush, then repeat this procedure for other brush sets.
6. Assemble the over-running clutch to the armature shaft as follows:
   a. Lubricate the drive end of the shaft with silicone lubricant.
   b. Slide the clutch assembly onto the shaft with the pinion outward.
   c. Slide the retainer onto the shaft with the cupped surface facing away from the pinion.
   d. Stand the armature up on a wood surface with the commutator downward. Position the snapring on the upper end of the shaft and drive it onto the shaft with a small block of wood and a hammer, then slide the snapring into groove.
   e. Install the thrust collar onto the shaft with the shoulder next to snapring.
   f. With the retainer on one side of the snapring and the thrust collar on the other side, squeeze two sets together (with pliers) until the ring seats in the retainer. On models without a thrust collar use a washer. Remember to remove the washer before continuing.
7. Lubricate the drive end bushing with silicone lubricant, then slide the armature and the clutch assembly into place, while engaging the shift lever with the clutch.

➡ On the non-integral starters, the shift lever may be installed in the drive gear housing first.

8. Position the field frame over the armature and apply sealer (silicone) between the frame and the solenoid case. Position the frame against the drive housing, making sure the brushes are not damaged in the process.
9. Lubricate the commutator end bushing with silicone lubricant, place a washer on the armature shaft and slide the commutator end frame onto the shaft. Install the through-bolts and tighten.
10. Reconnect the field coil connections to the solenoid motor terminal. Install the solenoid mounting screws (if equipped).
11. Check the pinion clearance. It should be 0.010–0.140 in. (0.254–3.556mm) with the pinion in the cranking position, on all models.

Prestolite

DISASSEMBLY AND ASSEMBLY

1. To remove the solenoid, remove the screw from the field coil connector and solenoid mounting screws. Rotate the solenoid 90 degrees and remove it along with the plunger return spring.
2. For further service, remove the two through-bolts, then remove the commutator end frame and washer.
3. To replace the clutch and drive assembly proceed as follows:
   a. Remove the thrust washer or the collar from the armature shaft.
   b. Slide a 5/8 in. deep socket or a piece of pipe of suitable size over the shaft and against the retainer as a driving tool.
   c. Tap the tool to remove the retainer off the snapring.
   d. Remove the snapring from the groove in the shaft. Check and make sure the snapring isn't distorted. If it is, it will be necessary to replace it with a new one upon reassembly.
   e. Remove the retainer and clutch assembly from the armature shaft.
4. The shift lever may be disconnected from the plunger at this time by removing the roll pin.
5. On models with the standard starter, the brushes may be removed by removing the brush holder pivot pin which positions one insulated and one grounded brush. Remove the brush and spring and replace the brushes as necessary.
6. On models with the smaller 5MT starter, remove the brush and holder from the brush support, then remove the screw from the brush holder and separate the brush and holder. Replace the brushes as necessary.
7. Installation is the reverse of removal. Assemble the armature and clutch and drive assembly as follows:
   a. Lubricate the drive end of the armature shaft and slide the clutch assembly onto the armature shaft with the pinion away from the armature.
   b. Slide the retainer onto the shaft with the cupped side facing the end of the shaft.
   c. Install the snapring into the groove on the armature shaft.
   d. Install the thrust washer on the shaft.
   e. Position the retainer and thrust washer with the snapring in between. Using two pliers, grip the retainer and thrust washer or collar and squeeze until the snapring is forced into the retainer and is held securely in the groove in the armature shaft.
   f. Lubricate the drive gear housing bushing.
   g. Engage the shift lever yoke with the clutch and slide the complete assembly into the drive gear housing.

➡ When the starter motor is disassembled or the solenoid is replaced, it is necessary to check the pinion clearance. Pinion clearance must be correct to prevent the buttons on the shift lever yoke from rubbing on the clutch collar during cranking.

CHECKING PINION CLEARANCE

1. Disengage the motor field coil connector from the solenoid motor terminal and insulate it carefully.
2. Connect one 12 volt battery lead to the solenoid switch terminal and the other to the starter frame.
3. Flash a jumper lead momentarily from the solenoid motor terminal to the starter frame. This will shift the pinion into cranking position and it will remain there until the battery is disconnected.
4. Push the pinion back as far as possible to take up any movement, and check the clearance with a feeler gauge. The clearance should be 0.010–0.140 in. (0.254–3.556mm).
5. There are no means for adjusting pinion clearance on the starter motor. If clearance does not fall within the limits, check for improper installation and replace all worn parts.

ENGINE AND ENGINE OVERHAUL   3-19

Battery

REMOVAL & INSTALLATION

1. Remove the hold-down screws from the battery box. Loosen the nuts that secure the cable ends to the battery terminals. Lift the battery cables from the terminals with a twisting motion.
2. If there is a battery cable puller available, make use of it. Lift the battery from the vehicle.
3. Before installing the battery in the vehicle, make sure that the battery terminals are clean and free from corrosion. Use a battery terminal cleaner on the terminals and on the inside of the battery cable ends. If a cleaner is not available, use a heavy sandpaper to remove the corrosion. A mixture of baking soda and water will neutralize any acid.
4. Place the battery in the vehicle.
5. Install the cables on the terminals.
6. Tighten the nuts on the cable ends.
7. Smear a light coating of grease on the cable ends and the tops of the terminals. This will prevent buildup of oxidized acid on the terminals and the cable ends. Install and tighten the nuts of the battery box.

ENGINE MECHANICAL

Design

4-134 L-HEAD ENGINE

The model L4-134 engine is an L-head 4-cylinder engine. The cylinder block and crankcase are cast integrally. Both intake and exhaust valves are mounted in the cylinder block with through water jacketing to provide effective cooling. The valves are operated by conventional valve tappets. The engine is equipped with a fully counterbalanced crankshaft supported by three main bearings. To better control balance, the counterweights are independently forged and permanently attached to the crankshaft with dowels and capscrews that are tack welded. Crankshaft end-play is adjusted by shims placed between the crankshaft thrust shims placed between the crankshaft thrust washer and the shoulder on the crankshaft.

Aluminum pistons, forged steel connecting rods, and replaceable main and connecting rod bearings are used in this engine. The camshaft on current production engines is gear driven from the crankshaft (chain driven on early production engines).

The water pump is mounted on the front of the cylinder block, and is belt driven by the crankshaft. Circulation of the coolant is controlled by a thermostat installed in the water outlet which is mounted on top of the cylinder head.

The engine is pressure lubricated. An oil pump, gear driven by the camshaft, is mounted externally on the left side of the crankcase. The pump forces the lubricant through oil channels and drilled passages in the crankshaft to efficiently lubricate the main and connecting rod bearings. Lubricant is also force fed to the camshaft bearings and timing gears. Cylinder walls and piston pins are lubricated from spurt holes in the 'follow' side of the connecting rods.

The carburetor is mounted on top of the intake manifold. The intake and exhaust manifolds are mounted on the left side of the cylinder block. A thermostatically controlled valve in the exhaust manifold controls the temperature of fuel/air mixture in the intake manifold.

4-134 F-HEAD ENGINE

The F4-134, 4-cylinder engine is of a combination valve-in-head and valve-in-block construction. The intake valves are mounted in the head and are operated by pushrods through rocker arms. The intake manifold is cast as an integral part of the cylinder head and is completely water jacketed. This type of construction transfers heat from the cooling system to the intake passages and assists in vaporizing the fuel when the engine is cold. Therefore, there is no heat control valve (heat riser) needed in the exhaust manifold.

The exhaust valves are mounted in the block with thorough water jacketing to provide effective cooling of the valves.

The engine is pressure lubricated. An oil pump which is driven by the camshaft forces the lubricant through oil channels and drilled passages in the crankshaft to efficiently lubricate the main and connecting rod bearings. Lubricant is also force fed to the camshaft bearings, rocker arms, and timing gears. Cylinder walls and piston pins are lubricated from spurt holes in the 'follow' side of the connecting rods.

The circulation of the coolant is controlled by a thermostat in the water outlet elbow which is cast as part of the cylinder head.

The engine is equipped with a fully counterbalanced crankshaft that is supported by three main bearings. The counterweights of the crankshaft are independently forged and are permanently attached to the crankshaft with dowels and cap screws that are tack welded. Crankshaft end-play is adjusted by placing shims between the crankshaft thrust washer and the shoulder on the crankshaft.

The pistons have an extra groove directly above the top ring which acts as a heat dam or insulator.

The engine was available in compression ratios ranging from 6.3:1 to 7.8:1, which permits the use of regular octane gas.

The displacement of the F4-134 engine is 134.2 cu. in. (2199.5cc).

V6-225 ENGINE

The V6 engine has a displacement of 225 cu. in. (3687.75cc) and a compression ratio of 9.0:1, which permits the use of regular octane gas.

3-20 ENGINE AND ENGINE OVERHAUL

The engine is designed with two banks of three cylinders each. The banks of cylinders are opposed to one another at a 90 degree angle. The left bank of cylinders, as viewed from the driver's seat, is set forward of the right bank so that the connecting rods of opposite pairs of pistons and rods can be attached to the same crank pin.

The crankshaft counterbalance weights are cast as an integral part of the crankshaft. All of the crankshaft bearings are identical in diameter, except for No. 2 bearing which is the thrust bearing. It is larger than the rest.

The cast iron heads are interchangeable. The camshaft, which is located above the crankshaft, between the two banks, operates hydraulic valve lifters. The rocker arms are not adjustable.

6-226 L-HEAD ENGINE

This Kaiser-built engine is used in the Utility Series trucks. It is of the valve-in-block, or flat head, design. The head and block are cast iron. With this arrangement, there are no moving parts in the cylinder head. The crankshaft is supported by four main bearings.

6-230 ENGINE

The overhead camshaft 6-230, built by the Continental Engine Corp. was a fairly radical design for its day, incorporating features found in more modern engines. The camshaft is equipped with only six lobes, with the same camshaft lobe operating both intake and exhaust valves on each cylinder. The cylinders and crankcase are integrally cast, forming a rigid unit. The fully balanced crankshaft is supported by four, unusually large, main bearings. The cylinder head employs a cross-flow design with hemispherical combustion chambers.

Engine Overhaul Tips

Most engine overhaul procedures are fairly standard. In addition to specific parts replacement procedures and specifications for your individual engine, this section is also a guide to acceptable rebuilding procedures. Examples of standard rebuilding practice are given and should be used along with specific details concerning your particular engine.

Competent and accurate machine shop services will ensure maximum performance, reliability and engine life. In most instances it is more profitable for the do-it-yourself mechanic to remove, clean and inspect the component, buy the necessary parts and deliver these to a shop for actual machine work.

On the other hand, much of the rebuilding work (crankshaft, block, bearings, piston rods, and other components) is well within the scope of the do-it-yourself mechanic's tools and abilities. You will have to decide for yourself the depth of involvement you desire in an engine repair or rebuild.

TOOLS

The tools required for an engine overhaul or parts replacement will depend on the depth of your involvement. With a few exceptions, they will be the tools found in a mechanic's tool kit (see Section 1 of this manual). More in-depth work will require some or all of the following:

- A dial indicator (reading in thousandths) mounted on a universal base
- Micrometers and telescope gauges
- Jaw and screw-type pullers
- Scraper
- Valve spring compressor
- Ring groove cleaner
- Piston ring expander and compressor
- Ridge reamer
- Cylinder hone or glaze breaker
- Plastigage®
- Engine stand

The use of most of these tools is illustrated in this section. Many can be rented for a one-time use from a local parts jobber or tool supply house specializing in automotive work.

Occasionally, the use of special tools is called for. See the information on Special Tools and the Safety Notice in the front of this book before substituting another tool.

INSPECTION TECHNIQUES

Procedures and specifications are given in this section for inspecting, cleaning and assessing the wear limits of most major components. Other procedures such as Magnaflux® and Zyglo® can be used to locate material flaws and stress cracks. Magnaflux® is a magnetic process applicable only to ferrous materials. The Zyglo® process coats the material with a fluorescent dye penetrant and can be used on any material.

Checking for suspected surface cracks can be more readily made using spot check dye. The dye is sprayed onto the suspected area, wiped off and the area sprayed with a developer. Cracks will show up brightly.

OVERHAUL TIPS

Aluminum has become extremely popular for use in engines, due to its low weight. Observe the following precautions when handling aluminum parts:

- Never hot tank aluminum parts (the caustic hot tank solution will eat the aluminum.
- Remove all aluminum parts (identification tag, etc.) from engine parts prior to the tanking.
- Always coat threads lightly with engine oil or anti-seize compounds before installation, to prevent seizure.
- Never overtorque bolts or spark plugs especially in aluminum threads.

Stripped threads in any component can be repaired using any of several commercial repair kits (Heli-Coil®, Microdot®, Keenserts®, etc.).

When assembling the engine, any parts that will be exposed to frictional contact must be prelubed to provide lubrication at initial start-up. Any product specifically formulated for this purpose can be used, but engine oil is not recommended as a prelube in most cases.

When semi-permanent (locked, but removable) installation of bolts or nuts is desired, threads should be cleaned and coated

ENGINE AND ENGINE OVERHAUL

with Loctite® or another similar, commercial non-hardening sealant.

REPAIRING DAMAGED THREADS

♦ See Figures 22, 23, 24, 25 and 26

Several methods of repairing damaged threads are available. Heli-Coil® (shown here), Keenserts® and Microdot® are among the most widely used. All involve basically the same principle — drilling out stripped threads, tapping the hole and installing a prewound insert — making welding, plugging and oversize fasteners unnecessary.

Two types of thread repair inserts are usually supplied: a standard type for most inch coarse, inch fine, metric course and metric fine thread sizes and a spark lug type to fit most spark plug port sizes. Consult the individual tool manufacturer's catalog to determine exact applications. Typical thread repair kits will contain a selection of prewound threaded inserts, a tap (corresponding to the outside diameter threads of the insert)

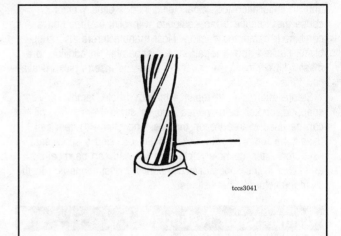

Fig. 24 Drill out the damaged threads with the specified size bit. Be sure to drill completely through the hole or to the bottom of a blind hole

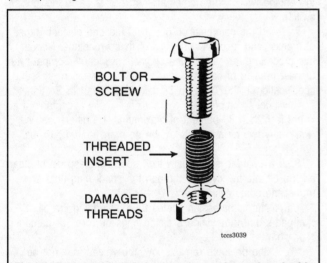

Fig. 22 Damaged bolt hole threads can be replaced with thread repair inserts

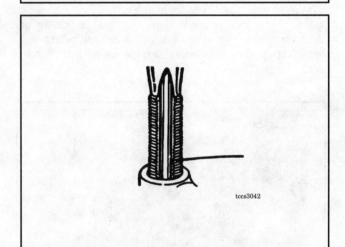

Fig. 25 Using the kit, tap the hole in order to receive the thread insert. Keep the tap well oiled and back it out frequently to avoid clogging the threads

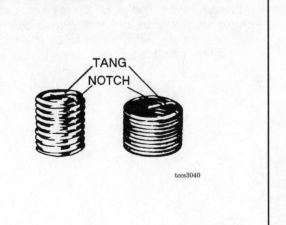

Fig. 23 Standard thread repair insert (left), and spark plug thread insert

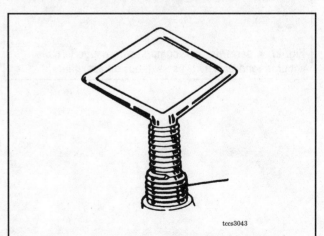

Fig. 26 Screw the insert onto the installer tool until the tang engages the slot. Thread the insert into the hole until it is 1/4-1/2 turn below the top surface, then remove the tool and break off the tang using a punch

3-22 ENGINE AND ENGINE OVERHAUL

and an installation tool. Spark plug inserts usually differ because they require a tap equipped with pilot threads and a combined reamer/tap section. Most manufacturers also supply blister-packed thread repair inserts separately in addition to a master kit containing a variety of taps and inserts plus installation tools.

Before attempting to repair a threaded hole, remove any snapped, broken or damaged bolts or studs. Penetrating oil can be used to free frozen threads. The offending item can usually be removed with locking pliers or using a screw/stud extractor. After the hole is clear, the thread can be repaired, as shown in the series of accompanying illustrations and in the kit manufacturer's instructions.

Compression Testing

▶ See Figure 27

A noticeable lack of engine power, excessive oil consumption and/or poor fuel mileage measured over an extended period are all indicators of internal engine war. Worn piston rings, scored or worn cylinder bores, blown head gaskets, sticking or burnt valves and worn valve seats are all possible culprits here. A check of each cylinder's compression will help you locate the problems.

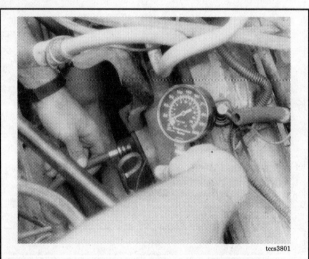

Fig. 27 A screw-in type compression gauge is more accurate and easier to use without an assistant

As mentioned in the Tools and Equipment portion of Section 1, a screw-in type compression gauge is more accurate that the type which is simply held against the spark plug hole, although it takes slightly longer to use. It's worth it to obtain a more accurate reading. Perform the following procedure:

1. Warm up the engine to normal operating temperature.
2. Remove all spark plugs.
3. Disconnect the high tension lead from the ignition coil.
4. Fully open the throttle either by operating the carburetor throttle linkage by hand or by having an assistant floor the accelerator pedal.
5. Screw the compression gauge into the No. 1 spark plug hole until the fitting is snug.

➡ Be careful not to cross thread the plug hole. On aluminum cylinder heads use extra care, as the threads in these heads are easily ruined.

6. Ask an assistant to depress the accelerator pedal fully on both carbureted and fuel injected Jeep vehicles. Then, while reading the compression gauge, have the assistant crank the engine two or three times in short bursts using the ignition switch.
7. Read the compression gauge at the end of each series of cranks, and record the highest of these readings. Repeat this procedure for each of the engine's cylinders. Compare the highest reading of each cylinder to the compression pressure specification in the Tune-Up Specifications chart in Section 1.

A cylinder's compression pressure is usually acceptable if it is not less than 80 percent of maximum. The difference between any two cylinders should be no more than 12-14 lbs. (26-31 kg).

8. If a cylinder is unusually low, pour a tablespoon of clean engine oil into the cylinder through the spark plug hole and repeat the compression test.

   a. If the compression comes up after adding the oil, it appears that the cylinder's piston rings or bore are damaged or worn.

   b. If the pressure remains low, the valves may not be seating properly (a valve job is needed), or the head gasket may be blown near that cylinder.

   c. If compression in any two adjacent cylinders is low, and if the addition of oil doesn't help the compression, there is leakage past the head gasket. Oil and coolant water in the combustion chamber can result from this problem. There may be evidence of water droplets on the engine dipstick when a head gasket has blown.

ENGINE AND ENGINE OVERHAUL 3-23

General Engine Specifications

Engine	Years	Fuel System Type	SAE net Horsepower @ rpm	SAE net Torque ft. lb. @ rpm	Bore x Stroke	Comp. Ratio	Oil Press. (psi.) @ 2000 rpm
4-134	1945–52	1-bbl	60 @ 4,000	105 @ 2,000	3.125 x 4.375	7.0:1	35
	1953–67	1-bbl	75 @ 4,000	114 @ 2,000	3.125 x 4.375	7.4:1	35
	1968–71	1-bbl	75 @ 4,000	114 @ 2,000	3.125 x 4.375	6.7:1	35
6-225	1965–71	2-bbl	160 @ 4,200	235 @ 3,500	3.750 x 3.400	9.0:1	33
6-226	1950–60	1-bbl	105 @ 3,600	190 @ 1,400	3.312 x 4.375	6.86:1	35
6-230	1960–64	1-bbl	140 @ 4,400	210 @ 1,750	3.343 x 4.375	8.5:1	45

1-bbl: one barrel carburetor
2-bbl: two barrel carburetor

Camshaft Specifications
(All specifications in inches)

Engine	Journal Diameter 1	2	3	4	5	Bearing Clearance	Lobe Lift Int.	Exh.	End Play
4-134 L-Head	2.1860–2.1855	2.1225–2.1215	2.0600–2.0590	1.6230–1.6225	—	0.0010–0.0025	0.3510	0.3510	0.004–0.007
4-134 F-Head	2.1860–2.1855	2.1225–2.1215	2.0600–2.0590	1.6230–1.6225	—	0.0010–0.0025	0.2600	0.3510	0.004–0.007
6-225	1.7560–1.7550	1.7260–1.7250	1.6960–1.6950	1.6660–1.6650	—	0.0015–0.0040	N.A.	N.A.	N.A.
6-226	1.8725–1.8735	1.8095–1.8105	1.7472–1.7485	1.2475–1.2485	—	0.0010–0.0030	0.2840	0.2840	0.003–0.007
6-230	1.9975–1.9965	1.8725–1.8715	1.7505–1.7495	1.3755–1.3745	—	0.0020–0.0040	0.3750	0.3750	0.007–0.008

N.A.: Information not available

Valve Specifications

Engine	Seat Angle (deg)	Face Angle (deg)	Spring Test Pressure (lbs. @ in.)	Spring Installed Height (in.)	Stem to Guide Clearance (in.) Intake	Exhaust	Stem Diameter (in.) Intake	Exhaust
4-134 L-Head	45	45	120 @ 1.750	2.109	0.0007–0.0022	0.0025–0.0045	0.3730	0.3715
4-134 F-Head	45	45	①	1.660	0.0007–0.0022	0.0025–0.0045	0.3733–0.3738	0.3710–0.3720
6-225	45	45	168 @ 1.260	1.640	0.0012–0.0032	0.0015–0.0035 ②	0.3415–0.3427	0.3402–0.3412
6-226	③	④	107 @ 1.312	1.672	0.0012–0.0030	0.0032–0.0050	0.3402–0.3410	0.3382–0.3390
6-230	45	45	130 @ 0.886	1.260	0.0010–0.0030	0.0025–0.0045	0.3400–0.3410	0.3385–0.3395

① Intake: 153 @ 1.400
　Exhaust: 120 @ 1.750
② Measured at the top
③ Intake: 30
　Exhaust: 45
④ Intake: 60
　Exhaust: 45

ENGINE AND ENGINE OVERHAUL

Crankshaft and Connecting Rod Specifications
(All specifications in inches)

Engine	Crankshaft				Connecting Rod		
	Main Bearing Journal Dia.	Main Bearing Oil Clearance	Shaft End Play	Thrust on No.	Journal Dia.	Oil Clearance	Side Clearance
4-134	2.3331–2.3341	0.0003–0.0029	0.0040–0.0060	1	1.9375–1.9383	0.0001–0.0019	0.004–0.010
6-225	2.4993–2.4997	0.0005–0.0021	0.0040–0.0080	2	1.9998–2.0002	0.0020–0.0023	0.006–0.017
6-226	2.3740–2.3750	0.0008–0.0028	0.0030–0.0070	4	2.0623	0.0007–0.0025	0.006–0.011
6-230	2.3747–2.3755	0.0005–0.0025	0.0030–0.0070	4	2.0619–2.0627	0.0006–0.0025	Snug

Piston and Ring Specifications
(All specifications in inches)

Engine	Ring Gap			Ring Side Clearance			Piston* Clearance
	#1 Compr.	#2 Compr.	Oil Control	#1 Compr.	#2 Compr.	Oil Control	
4-134	0.0070–0.0170	0.0070–0.0170	0.0070–0.0170	0.0020–0.0040	0.0015–0.0035	0.0010–0.0025	0.0025–0.0045
6-225	0.0100–0.0200	0.0100–0.0200	0.0150–0.0350	0.0020–0.0035	0.0030–0.0050	0.0015–0.0085	0.0005–0.0011
6-226	0.0080–0.0180	0.0080–0.0160	0.0080–0.0160	0.0020–0.0040	0.0030–0.0070	0.0060–0.0100	0.0007–0.0017
6-230	0.0100–0.0450	0.1000–0.0450	0.0150–0.0550	0.0020–0.0031	0.0020–0.0031	Snug	0.0007–0.0017

*Measured at the skirt

Torque Specifications
(All specifications in ft. lb.)

Engine	Cyl. Head	Conn. Rod	Main Bearing	Crankshaft Damper	Flywheel	Manifold	
						Intake	Exhaust
4-134	60–70	35–45	65–75	65–75	35–41	29–35 ①	20–35
6-225	65–85	30–40	85–95	140–150	50–65	45–55	14–20
6-226	35–45	40–45	85–95	100–130	35–40	30–35	
6-230	80–95	40–45	85–95	100–130	40–45	15–20	35–40

① L-Head only

ENGINE AND ENGINE OVERHAUL 3-25

Engine

REMOVAL & INSTALLATION

4-134 Engine

L-HEAD MODEL

1. Drain the cooling system by opening the drain cocks on the bottom of the radiator and the lower right side of the block.

> **⁕⁕CAUTION**
>
> When draining coolant, keep in mind that cats and dogs are attracted by ethylene glycol antifreeze, and are quite likely to drink any that is left in an uncovered container or in puddles on the ground. This will prove fatal in sufficient quantity. Always drain the coolant into a sealable container. Coolant should be reused unless it is contaminated or several years old.

2. Disconnect the battery cables.
3. Remove the upper and lower radiator hoses and the heater hoses.
4. Remove the four bolts securing the fan hub and blades.
5. Remove the four radiator attaching screws and lift out the radiator.
6. Disconnect the fuel line and the windshield wiper hose at the fuel pump.
7. Remove the air cleaner from the carburetor.
8. Disconnect the choke and throttle controls.
9. Disconnect the cables at the starter and remove the starter.
10. Disconnect the generator wires.
11. Disconnect the wires from the coil, oil pressure sender and temperature sender.
12. Disconnect the exhaust pipe from the manifold.
13. Place a jack under the crankshaft pulley, disconnect and remove the two front engine supports, and slightly lower the engine. This will allow access to the two top bolts on the bell housing.
14. Install a lifting sling and shop crane on the engine and take up all slack.
15. Unbolt the engine from the bell housing.
16. Pull the engine forward or roll the vehicle backwards until the clutch clears the bell housing. Then, lift the engine up and out of the vehicle.

To install:

17. Lower the engine into the vehicle. Push the engine backwards until the clutch enters the bell housing.
18. Bolt the engine to the bell housing.
19. Let the engine down, onto the two front supports.
20. Bolt the engine to the supports.
21. Connect the exhaust pipe to the manifold.
22. Connect the wires to the coil, oil pressure sender and temperature sender.
23. Connect the generator wires.
24. Install the starter and connect the cables at the starter.
25. Connect the choke and throttle controls.
26. Install the air cleaner on the carburetor.
27. Connect the fuel line, and the windshield wiper hose at the fuel pump.
28. Install the radiator.
29. Install the four bolts securing the fan hub and blades.
30. Install the upper and lower radiator hoses and the heater hoses.
31. Connect the battery cables.
32. Fill the cooling system.

F-HEAD MODEL

1. Drain the cooling system by opening the drain cocks at the bottom of the radiator and the lower right side of the cylinder block.

> **⁕⁕CAUTION**
>
> When draining coolant, keep in mind that cats and dogs are attracted by ethylene glycol antifreeze, and are quite likely to drink any that is left in an uncovered container or in puddles on the ground. This will prove fatal in sufficient quantity. Always drain the coolant into a sealable container. Coolant should be reused unless it is contaminated or several years old.

2. Disconnect the battery at the positive terminal to avoid the possibility of a short circuit.
3. Remove the air cleaner horn from the carburetor and disconnect the breather hose at the oil filler pipe.
4. Disconnect the carburetor choke and throttle controls by loosening the clamp bolts and setscrews.
5. Disconnect the fuel tank-to-fuel pump line at the fuel pump by unscrewing the connecting nut.
6. Plug the fuel line to prevent leakage. Disconnect the windshield wiper vacuum hose at the fuel pump.
7. Remove the radiator stay bar on the CJ3B.
8. Remove the upper and lower radiator hoses. Remove the heater hoses, if so equipped, from the water pump and the rear of the cylinder head.
9. Remove the fan hub and fan blades.
10. Remove the four radiator attaching screws and remove the radiator and shroud as one unit.
11. Remove the starter motor cables and remove the starter motor.
12. Disconnect the wires from the alternator or the generator. Disconnect the ignition primary wire at the ignition coil.
13. Disconnect the oil pressure and temperature sending unit wires at the units.
14. Disconnect the exhaust pipe at the exhaust manifold by removing the stud nuts.
15. Remove the spark plug wires from the cable bracket that is mounted to the rocker arm cover. Remove the cable bracket by removing the stud nuts.
16. Remove the rocker arm cover by removing the attaching stud nuts.
17. Attach a lifting bracket to the engine using the head bolts. Be sure that the bolts selected will hold the engine with the weight balanced. Attach the lifting bracket to a boom hoist, or other lifting device, and take up all of the slack.
18. Remove the two nuts and bolts from each front engine support. Disconnect the engine ground strap. Remove the engine supports. Lower the engine slightly to permit access to the two top bolts on the flywheel housing.

3-26 ENGINE AND ENGINE OVERHAUL

19. Remove the bolts that attach the flywheel housing to the engine.
20. Pull the engine forward, or roll the vehicle backward, until the clutch clears the flywheel housing. Lift the engine from the vehicle.

To install:
21. Lower the engine into the vehicle. Push the engine backwards until the clutch enters the bell housing.
22. Bolt the engine to the bell housing.
23. Let the engine down, onto the two front supports.
24. Bolt the engine to the supports.
25. Install the rocker arm cover.
26. Install the spark plug wires on the cable bracket that is mounted to the rocker arm cover. Install the cable bracket by installing the stud nuts.
27. Connect the exhaust pipe at the exhaust manifold by installing the stud nuts.
28. Connect the oil pressure and temperature sending unit wires at the units.
29. Connect the wires from the alternator or the generator. Connect the ignition primary wire at the ignition coil.
30. Install the starter motor and install the starter motor cables.
31. Install the radiator and shroud as one unit.
32. Install the fan hub and fan blades.
33. Install the upper and lower radiator hoses. Install the heater hoses, if so equipped, on the water pump and the rear of the cylinder head.
34. Install the radiator stay bar on the CJ3B.
35. Connect the windshield wiper vacuum hose at the fuel pump.
36. Connect the fuel tank-to-fuel pump line at the fuel pump.
37. Connect the carburetor choke and throttle controls.
38. Install the air cleaner horn on the carburetor and connect the breather hose at the oil filler pipe.
39. Connect the battery at the positive terminal.
40. Fill the cooling system.

6-225 Engine

1. Remove the hood.
2. Disconnect the battery ground cable from the engine and the battery.
3. Remove the air cleaner.
4. Drain the coolant from the radiator and engine.

✱✱CAUTION

When draining coolant, keep in mind that cats and dogs are attracted by ethylene glycol antifreeze, and are quite likely to drink any that is left in an uncovered container or in puddles on the ground. This will prove fatal in sufficient quantity. Always drain the coolant into a sealable container. Coolant should be reused unless it is contaminated or several years old.

5. Disconnect the alternator wiring harness from the connector at the regulator.
6. Disconnect the upper and lower radiator hoses from the engine.
7. Remove the right and left radiator support bars.
8. Remove the radiator from the vehicle.
9. Disconnect the engine wiring harnesses from the connectors which are located on the fire wall.
10. Disconnect the battery cable and wiring from the engine starter assembly.
11. Remove the starter assembly from the engine.
12. Disconnect the engine fuel hoses from the fuel lines at the right fame rails.
13. Plug the fuel lines.
14. Disconnect the throttle linkage and the choke cable from the carburetor and remove the cable support bracket that is mounted on the engine.
15. Disconnect the exhaust pipes from the right and left sides of the engine.
16. Place a jack under the transmission and support the weight of the transmission.
17. Remove the bolts that secure the engine to the front motor mounts.
18. Attach a suitable sling to the engine lifting eyes and, using a hoist, lift the engine just enough to support its weight.
19. Remove the bolts that secure the engine to the flywheel housing.
20. Raise the engine slightly and slide the engine forward to remove the transmission main shaft form the clutch plate splines.

➡ **The engine and the transmission must be raised slightly to release the spline from the clutch plate while sliding the engine forward.**

21. When the engine is free of the transmission shaft, raise the engine and remove it from the vehicle.

To install:
22. Lower the engine into the vehicle.
23. Slide the engine rearward to install the transmission main shaft in the clutch plate splines.
24. Install the bolts that secure the engine to the flywheel housing. Tighten the bolts to 30-40 ft. lbs. (41-54 Nm).
25. Install the bolts that secure the engine to the front motor mounts. Tighten the bolts to 75 ft. lbs. (102 Nm).
26. Connect the exhaust pipes to the right and left sides of the engine.
27. Connect the throttle linkage and the choke cable to the carburetor and Install the cable support bracket that is mounted on the engine.
28. Connect the engine fuel hoses to the fuel lines at the right fame rails.
29. Install the starter assembly on the engine. Tighten the starter-to-block bolts to 30-40 ft. lbs. (41-54 Nm) the bracket bolts to 10-12 ft. lbs. (14-16 Nm).
30. Connect the battery cable and wiring to the engine starter assembly.
31. Connect the engine wiring harnesses to the connectors which are located on the firewall.
32. Install the radiator.
33. Install the right and left radiator support bars.
34. Connect the upper and lower radiator hoses to the engine.
35. Connect the alternator wiring harness to the connector at the regulator.
36. Fill the cooling system.
37. Install the air cleaner.
38. Connect the battery ground cable to the engine and the battery.

ENGINE AND ENGINE OVERHAUL

39. Install the hood.

6-226 Engine

1. Drain the cooling system.

> **✴✴CAUTION**
>
> When draining coolant, keep in mind that cats and dogs are attracted by ethylene glycol antifreeze, and are quite likely to drink any that is left in an uncovered container or in puddles on the ground. This will prove fatal in sufficient quantity. Always drain the coolant into a sealable container. Coolant should be reused unless it is contaminated or several years old.

2. Remove the hood.
3. Remove the radiator and heater hoses, and all other cooling system hoses.
4. Remove the radiator.
5. Disconnect the battery.
6. Remove the coolant surge tank.
7. Remove the air cleaner and air cleaner bracket.
8. Remove the rear heater hose support bracket.
9. Remove the vacuum line which runs between the carburetor and distributor.
10. Tag and remove the spark plug wires from the distributor.
11. Remove the coil lead from the distributor.
12. Remove the distributor cap.
13. Rotate the engine so that the No.1 cylinder is at TDC of the compression stroke.
14. Mark the relationship of the rotor and distributor body.
15. Mark the relationship of the distributor body and head.
16. Remove the hold-down clamp.
17. Remove the distributor.
18. Disconnect the choke cable and wire.
19. Disconnect the throttle control wire at the carburetor.
20. Disconnect the accelerator cable at the distributor adapter.
21. Disconnect the fuel line at the carburetor.
22. Remove the carburetor.
23. Remove the oil filler tube by pulling it straight out of the block.
24. Tag the coil wires and disconnect them.
25. Remove the ignition coil.
26. Disconnect the oil filter hoses.
27. Remove the filter and bracket.
28. Disconnect the wire at the temperature sending unit.
29. Disconnect the wires at the starter. Tag them.
30. Remove the generator housing.
31. Remove the generator and bracket.
32. Remove the generator idler pulley and bracket.
33. Remove the fan belt.
34. Remove the fan.

➡ Early models used a four-bladed fan. Willys recommended that owners of these vehicles replace the fan with the later six-bladed unit. If the original fan was attacked with hex nuts and lock washers, the new fan should be installed using elastic stop nuts.

35. Disconnect the radiator brace at the engine mount and swing it out of the way.
36. Disconnect the vacuum line at the fuel pump.
37. Disconnect the fuel lines at the fuel pump.
38. Disconnect the exhaust pipe at the manifold.
39. Disconnect the transfer case linkage.
40. Disconnect the wire at the oil pressure sending unit.
41. Disconnect the engine ground strap.
42. Disconnect the transmission shift rods at the transmission and secure them out of the way.
43. Disconnect the clutch cable at the cross shaft.
44. Remove the cross shaft.
45. Disconnect the hand brake release spring.
46. Disconnect the hand brake cable and conduit and move it out of the way.
47. Disconnect the front driveshaft at the transfer case and axle.
48. Disconnect the rear driveshaft at the transfer case.
49. Disconnect the speedometer cable at the transfer case.
50. Attach a lifting bracket, using existing head bolts.
51. Take up the weight of the engine with a shop crane.
52. Support the transmission with a jackstand.
53. Remove the front engine mount bolts.
54. Place a floor jack under the rear engine support crossmember.
55. Remove the crossmember attaching bolts.
56. Remove the engine-to-bell housing attaching bolts.
57. Raise the engine slightly to free it from the front mounts.
58. Remove the floor jack.
59. Slide the engine forward to free it from the transmission.
60. Raise the engine clear of the truck.
61. Place the engine on a work stand or dolly. Never let it rest on the oil pan.

To install:

62. Lower the engine into the truck.
63. Slide the engine rearward to engage the transmission.
64. Lower the engine onto the front mounts.
65. Install the engine-to-bell housing attaching bolts. Tighten them to 40 ft. lbs. (54 Nm).
66. Install the crossmember attaching bolts. Tighten them to 30 ft. lbs. (41 Nm).
67. Install the front engine mount bolts. Tighten them to 50 ft. lbs. (68 Nm).
68. Connect the speedometer cable at the transfer case.
69. Connect the front driveshaft at the axle and transfer case.
70. Connect the rear driveshaft at the transfer case.
71. Connect the hand brake cable and conduit.
72. Connect the hand brake release spring.
73. Install the cross shaft.
74. Connect the clutch cable at the cross shaft.
75. Connect the transmission shift rods at the transmission.
76. Adjust the linkage.
77. Connect the engine ground strap.
78. Connect the wire at the oil pressure sending unit.
79. Connect the transfer case linkage.
80. Connect the exhaust pipe at the manifold. Tighten the nuts to 50 ft. lbs. (68 Nm).
81. Connect the vacuum line and fuel lines at the fuel pump.
82. Connect the radiator brace at the engine mount.
83. Install the fan and belt.
84. Adjust the belt.
85. Install the generator idler pulley and bracket.

3-28 ENGINE AND ENGINE OVERHAUL

86. Install the generator and bracket. Tighten the bolts to 25 ft. lbs. (34 Nm).
87. Install the generator housing.
88. Connect the wires at the starter.
89. Connect the wire at the temperature sending unit.
90. Install the filter and bracket.
91. Connect the oil filter hoses.
92. Install the ignition coil.
93. Install the oil filler tube.
94. Install the carburetor.
95. Connect the filet line at the carburetor.
96. Connect the throttle control wire at the carburetor.
97. Connect the accelerator cable at the distributor adapter.
98. Connect the choke cable and wire.
99. Install the distributor, aligning all the matchmarks.
100. Install the distributor cap and connect all the wires.
101. Install the vacuum line which runs between the carburetor and distributor.
102. Install the rear heater hose support bracket.
103. Install the air cleaner and air cleaner bracket.
104. Install the coolant surge tank.
105. Connect the battery.
106. Install the radiator.
107. Install the radiator and heater hoses, and all other cooling system hoses.
108. Install the hood.
109. Fill the cooling system.

6-230 Engine

1. Raise and support the truck on jackstands.
2. Drain the oil from the engine.
3. Remove the oil filter.
4. Drain the coolant.

❊❊CAUTION

When draining the coolant, keep in mind that cats and dogs are attracted by the ethylene glycol antifreeze, and are quite likely to drink any that is left in an uncovered container or in puddles on the ground. This will prove fatal in sufficient quantity. Always drain the coolant into a sealable container. Coolant should be reused unless it is contaminated or several years old.

5. Disconnect the hydraulic line at the clutch slave cylinder.
6. Remove the hood.
7. Remove the upper and lower radiator hoses.
8. Disconnect the automatic transmission cooler lines.
9. Remove the heater hoses.
10. Remove the radiator.
11. Disconnect and tag all wires attached to the engine.
12. Disconnect and tag any remaining hoses attached to the engine.
13. Remove the drive belts.
14. Remove the alternator.
15. Remove the fan and spacer.
16. Remove the battery and tray.
17. Unbolt the exhaust pipe from the manifold.
18. Remove the exhaust pipe from the bracket at the clutch housing.
19. Remove the carburetor.
20. Disconnect the fuel line at the frame.
21. Remove the front engine support bolts.
22. Take up the weight of the engine with a shop crane.
23. Remove the transfer case.
24. Remove the transmission.
25. Raise the engine slightly, pull it forward to clear the fire wall and lift it out of the vehicle.
26. Lower the engine into the vehicle and slide it rearward slightly.
27. Install the front engine support bolts. Tighten the engine mount bolts to 25-30 ft. lbs. (34-41 Nm).
28. Install the transmission. Tighten the bell housing-to-engine bolts to 40-50 ft. lbs. (54-68 Nm).
29. Install the transfer case.
30. Remove the shop crane.
31. Connect the fuel line at the frame.
32. Install the carburetor. Tighten the nuts to 146-182 inch lbs. (16-20 Nm).
33. Install the exhaust pipe to the bracket at the clutch housing.
34. Connect the hydraulic line at the clutch slave cylinder.
35. Connect the exhaust pipe to the manifold.
36. Install the battery and tray.
37. Install the fan and spacer.
38. Install the alternator. Tighten mounting bolts to 40-45 ft. lbs. (54-61 Nm) and the adjusting bolt to 146-182 inch lbs. (16-20 Nm).
39. Install the drive belts.
40. Install the radiator.
41. Install the heater hoses.
42. Install the upper and lower radiator hoses.
43. Connect the automatic transmission cooler lines.
44. Connect any remaining hoses to the engine.
45. Connect all wires to the engine.
46. Fill the cooling system.
47. Install the oil filter.
48. Fill the crankcase.
49. Install the hood.

Rocker Shafts and Rocker Studs

REMOVAL & INSTALLATION

4-134 Engine

F-HEAD MODEL

► See Figures 28, 29, 30, 31, 32, 33 and 34

1. Remove the rocker arm cover attaching bolts and remove the rocker arm cover.
2. Remove the nuts from the rocker arm shaft support studs.
3. Remove the intake valve pushrods from the engine.
4. Install in the reverse order. Tighten the rocker arm retaining bolts to 30-33 ft. lbs. (41-45 Nm).

6-225 Engine

1. Remove the crankcase ventilator valve from the right side valve cover.
2. Remove the four attaching bolts from the right and left side valve covers and remove both of the valve covers.

ENGINE AND ENGINE OVERHAUL   3-29

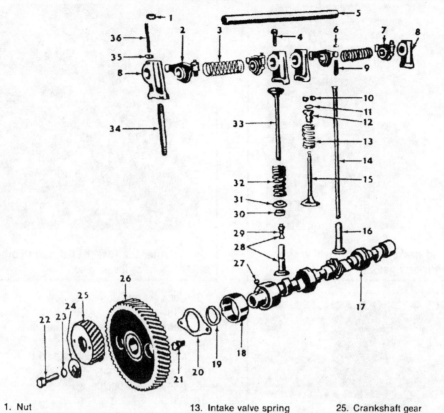

1. Nut
2. Left rocker arm
3. Rocker arm shaft spring
4. Rocker shaft lock screw
5. Rocker shaft
6. Nut
7. Right rocker arm
8. Rocker arm shaft bracket
9. Intake valve tappet adjusting screw
10. Intake valve upper retainer lock
11. Oil seal
12. Intake valve spring upper retainer
13. Intake valve spring
14. Intake valve push rod
15. Intake valve
16. Intake valve tappet
17. Camshaft
18. Camshaft front bearing
19. Camshaft thrust plate spacer
20. Camshaft thrust plate
21. Bolt and lock washer
22. Bolt
23. Lockwasher
24. Camshaft gear washer
25. Crankshaft gear
26. Camshaft gear
27. Woodruff key No. 9
28. Exhaust valve tappet
29. Tappet adjusting screw
30. Spring retainer lock
31. Roto cap assembly
32. Exhaust valve spring
33. Exhaust valve
34. Rocker shaft support stud
35. Washer
36. Rocker arm cover stud

Fig. 28 Exploded view of the camshaft and related valve train components — 4-134 F-head engine

Fig. 29 Remove the rocker arm cover hold-down screws . . .

Fig. 30 . . . then lift the cover off of the cylinder head

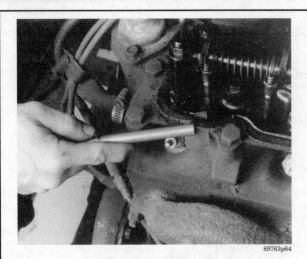

Fig. 31 Remove the old gasket before installing the rocker arm cover with a new gasket

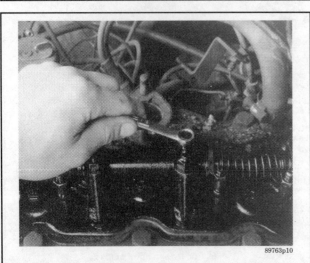

Fig. 32 After removing the rocker arm cover, remove the shaft hold-down nuts . . .

Fig. 33 . . . then carefully lift the shaft assembly off of the cylinder head

Fig. 34 After the rocker shaft is removed, remove the pushrods from the engine

3. Unscrew, but do not remove, the bolts that attach the rocker arm assemblies to the cylinder heads.
4. Remove the rocker arm assemblies, with the bolts in place, from the cylinder heads.
5. Mark each of the pushrods so that they can be installed in their original positions.
6. Remove the pushrods.

To install:
7. Install the pushrods.
8. Install the rocker arm assemblies. Install in the reverse order. Tighten the bolts to 30 ft. lbs. (41 Nm), a little at a time.
9. Clean the mating surfaces of the covers and heads.
10. Install the valve covers using new gaskets. Tighten the bolts to 36-60 inch lbs. (4.0-6.7 Nm).
11. Install the crankcase ventilator valve from the right side valve cover.

6-230 Engine
♦ See Figure 35

1. Remove the rocker arm cover.
2. Remove the rocker arm-to-stud nuts and lift off the rocker arms and balls.

To install:
3. Install the rocker arm and ball on the stud.
4. Install, but do not tighten, the rocker arm nut.
5. When all removed arms are installed, adjust the valves, being VERY CAREFUL to precisely align the rocker arms while tightening the nut!
6. Clean the mating surfaces of the rocker arm cover and head.
7. Install the rocker arm cover, using a new gasket. Tighten the bolts to 36-60 inch lbs. (4.0-6.7 Nm).

ENGINE AND ENGINE OVERHAUL   3-31

1. Exhaust valve
2. Valve guide
3. Valve guide seal
4. Valve spring
5. Valve spring retainer
6. Rocker arm
7. Rocker arm stud
8. Rocker arm ball
9. Rocker arm guide
10. Camshaft
11. Cam bearing support deck
12. Rocker arm
13. Rocker arm cover
14. Oil tube
15. Valve spring retainer
16. Valve spring
17. Valve guide seal
18. Valve guide
19. Intake valve
20. Intake manifold

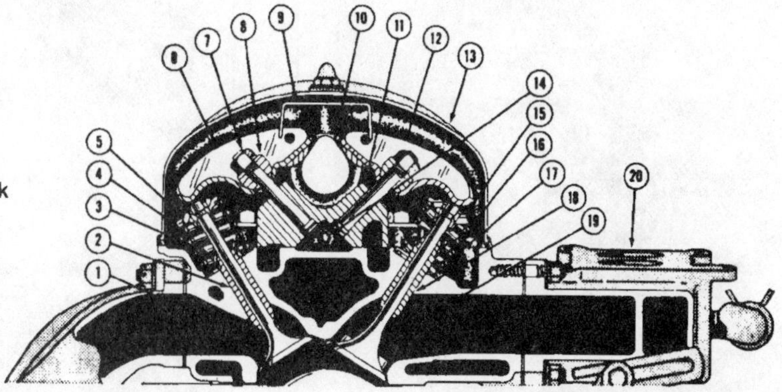

Fig. 35 Cross-section view of the cylinder head, showing the valve train components utilized by the 6-230 engine

Thermostat

REMOVAL & INSTALLATION

▶ See Figures 36, 37, 38, 39, 40, 41, 42, 43, 44, 45, 46 and 47

The thermostat is located in the water outlet housing at the front or on top of the engine. On the 6-225 V6 the water outlet housing is located in the front of the intake manifold.

✱✱CAUTION

When draining coolant, keep in mind that cats and dogs are attracted by ethylene glycol antifreeze, and are quite likely to drink any that is left in an uncovered container or in puddles on the ground. This will prove fatal in sufficient quantity. Always drain the coolant into a sealable container. Coolant should be reused unless it is contaminated or several years old.

To remove the thermostats from all of these engines, first drain the cooling system. It is not necessary to disconnect or remove any of the hoses. Remove the two attaching screws and lift the housing from the engine. Remove the thermostat and the gasket. To install, place the thermostat in the housing with the spring inside the engine. Install a new gasket with a small amount of sealing compound applied to both sides. Install the water outlet and tighten the attaching bolts to 30 ft. lbs. (41 Nm). Refill the cooling system.

Fig. 36 Locate and loosen the cooling system draincock valve . . .

Fig. 37 . . . allowing the coolant to drain into a catch pan

3-32 ENGINE AND ENGINE OVERHAUL

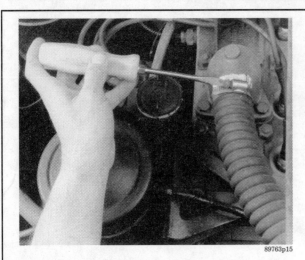
Fig. 38 Loosen the upper radiator hose clamp, then detach the hose from the neck

Fig. 41 Remove the thermostat form the recess in the cylinder head

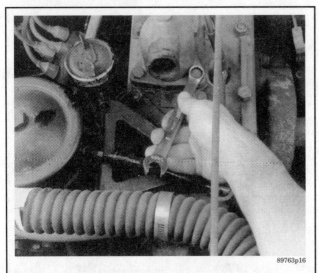
Fig. 39 Remove the waterneck retaining bolts . . .

Fig. 42 Scrape the old gasket material from the head — L-head 4-134 engine shown

Fig. 40 . . . then lift the waterneck off the cylinder head

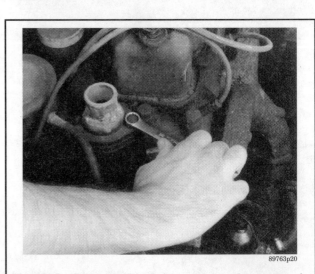
Fig. 43 On F-head 4-134 engines, remove the waterneck hold-down bolts . . .

ENGINE AND ENGINE OVERHAUL 3-33

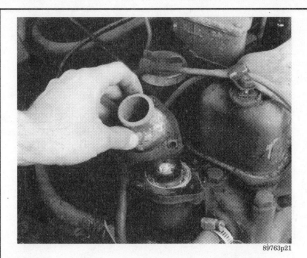

Fig. 44 . . . and lift the waterneck from the cylinder head

Fig. 45 Remove the used gasket with a scraper, if necessary

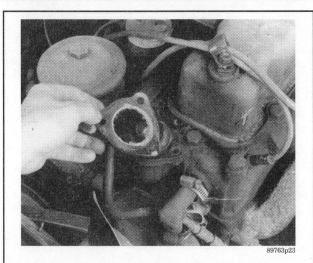

Fig. 46 The gasket must be removed, because the thermostat is mounted under the gasket

Fig. 47 Pull the thermostat out of the cylinder head — F-head 4-134 engine shown

Intake Manifold

REMOVAL & INSTALLATION

4-134 Engine

L-HEAD MODEL

▶ See Figures 48, 49, 50, 51, 52, 53, 54, 55 and 56

The intake and exhaust manifolds are bolted together and are easiest removed as an assembly.

1. On models so equipped, remove the crankcase ventilator tube which runs from the ventilator valve mounted in the intake manifold to an elbow mounted on the valve cover plate.
2. Remove the seven nuts from the manifold-to-block studs.
3. Pull the manifolds off the studs. Discard the gasket.

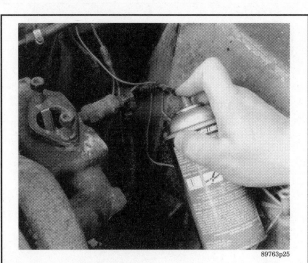

Fig. 48 If necessary, spray the ventilator tube fitting with a penetrating lubrication . . .

3-34 ENGINE AND ENGINE OVERHAUL

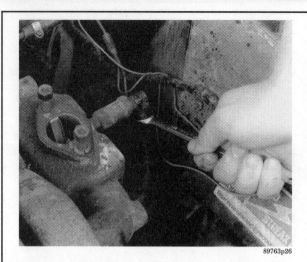

Fig. 49 . . . then detach the ventilator tube from the manifold

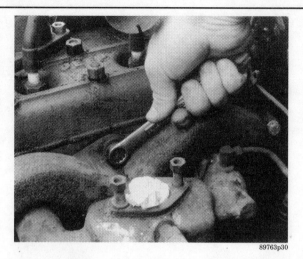

Fig. 52 . . . then remove the manifold-to-engine block mounting bolts

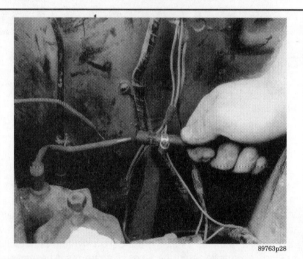

Fig. 50 Detach all vacuum connections from the intake/exhaust manifold

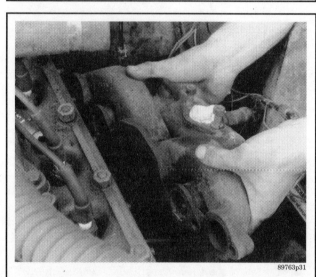

Fig. 53 Pull the manifold off of the engine block . . .

Fig. 51 Remove the manifold-to-exhaust pipe mounting nuts . . .

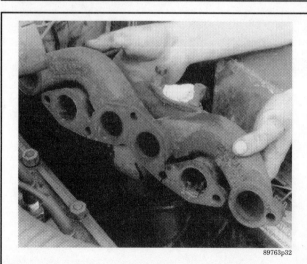

Fig. 54 As can be seen, the intake and exhaust manifolds are fastened together

ENGINE AND ENGINE OVERHAUL 3-35

Fig. 55 To separate the manifolds, remove the mounting bolts

Fig. 56 Once the manifold is removed, access to the side cover can be gained

To install:

4. If the studs were removed for replacement, coat the new studs with a sealer such as Permatex No. 2, prior to installation.

5. Place a new gasket in position on the studs and carefully slide the manifolds on. Tighten to 29-35 ft. lbs. (39-48 Nm). in a circular pattern from the ends toward the center.

F-HEAD MODEL

On the F4-134 engine the intake manifold is cast as an integral part of the head.

6-225 Engine

▶ See Figure 57

1. Drain the cooling system.

> **✲✲CAUTION**
>
> When draining coolant, keep in mind that cats and dogs are attracted by ethylene glycol antifreeze, and are quite likely to drink any that is left in an uncovered container or in puddles on the ground. This will prove fatal in sufficient quantity. Always drain the coolant into a sealable container. Coolant should be reused unless it is contaminated or several years old.

2. Disconnect the crankcase vent hose, distributor vacuum hose, and the fuel line from the carburetor.
3. Disconnect the two distributor leads from the coil.
4. Disconnect the wire from the temperature sending unit.
5. Remove the ten cap bolts that hold the intake manifold to the cylinder head. They must be replaced in their original location.
6. Remove the intake manifold assembly and gasket from the engine.
7. Reverse the removal procedure for installation. Tighten the bolts to the correct torque, and in the proper sequence.

6-226 Engine

➡ The intake and exhaust manifolds are removed as a unit, then separated.

1. Remove the engine cover and housing.
2. Remove the air cleaner and carburetor.
3. Disconnect the exhaust pipe at the manifold.
4. Unbolt and remove the manifolds.
5. Installation is the reverse of removal. Retainers are used under the retaining nuts on all studs except the top ends and lower center. Plain washers are used under these nuts. It is possible, if you're not careful, to install the manifold assembly so that it interferes with the fit of the valve chamber cover at the upper rear corner of the cover. Leakage would result in

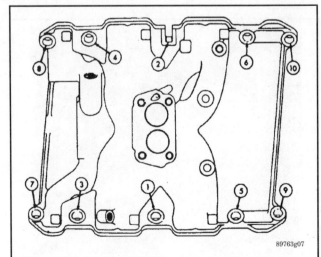

Fig. 57 Intake manifold tightening sequence for the 6-225 engine

3-36 ENGINE AND ENGINE OVERHAUL

this case. Tighten the nuts, from the center towards the ends, to 30-35 ft. lbs. (41-48 Nm).

6-230 Engine

1. Disconnect and tag any hoses, wires or cables attached to the manifold or carburetor.
2. Remove the air cleaner.
3. Remove the carburetor.
4. Remove the nut and lock washer that attaches the manifold and dipstick tube to the lower center stud on the head.
5. Remove the dipstick and tube.
6. Support the manifold and remove the four remaining nuts and lock washers that attach it to the head and manifold.
7. Discard the gasket and thoroughly clean the mating surfaces of the head and manifold.
8. Installation is the reverse of removal. Always use a new gasket. Note that the gasket overlaps the intake port openings slightly. This is a calculated overlap designed to assist in air/fuel distribution. Do not attempt to cut the gasket to make it larger. Tighten the manifold nuts to 15-20 ft. lbs. (20-27 Nm).

Exhaust Manifold

REMOVAL & INSTALLATION

4-134 Engine

L-HEAD MODEL

Refer to the Intake Manifold procedure, earlier in this section.

F-HEAD MODEL

▶ See Figures 58 and 59

1. Remove the air delivery hose from the air injection tube assembly if the engine is so equipped. If not, proceed to Step 2.
2. Remove the five nuts from the manifold studs.

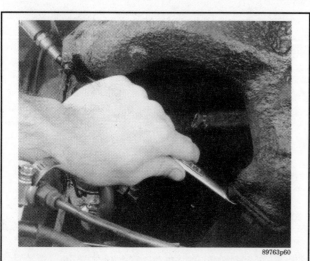

Fig. 58 Remove the exhaust manifold-to-exhaust pipe retaining nuts and separate the two

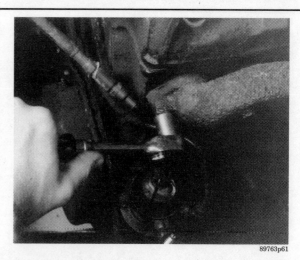

Fig. 59 Remove the exhaust manifold bolts and remove the manifold from the engine

3. Pull the manifold from the mounting studs. Be careful not to damage the air injection tubes if the engine is equipped with an air pump.
4. Remove the gaskets from the cylinder block.
5. If the exhaust manifold is to be replaced it will be necessary to remove the air injection tubes from the exhaust manifold. The application of heat may be necessary to aid removal.

To install:

6. Use new gaskets when replacing the exhaust manifold. Make sure that the cylinder head are clean. Tighten the attaching nuts to the correct torque specification.
7. If the exhaust manifold was be replaced, install the air injection tubes. The application of heat may be necessary to aid installation.
8. Install the air delivery hose on the air injection tube assembly if the engine is so equipped.

6-225 Engine

▶ See Figure 60

1. Remove the five attaching screws, one nut, and exhaust manifold from the side of the cylinder head.
2. Use a new gasket when replacing the exhaust manifolds. Make sure that the mating surfaces of the manifold and the cylinder head are clean. Tighten the manifold nuts and bolts to the correct torque value.

6-226 Engine

The exhaust manifold is removed as an assembly with the intake manifold. See the appropriate intake manifold procedure, located earlier in this section.

6-230 Engine

1. Disconnect the exhaust pipe at the manifold.
2. Remove the ten nuts, eight flat washers and two retainers that attach the manifold to the head.
3. Lift off the manifold and remove and discard the gasket.
4. Clean the mating surfaces thoroughly and install the manifold, using a new gasket. Tighten the nuts to 35-40 ft. lbs. (48-54 Nm).
5. Attach the exhaust pipe.

ENGINE AND ENGINE OVERHAUL 3-37

Fig. 60 Exhaust manifold used on the left-hand side of the engine — the right-hand manifold is similar

Radiator

REMOVAL & INSTALLATION

♦ See Figures 61, 62 and 63

1. Drain the radiator by opening the drain cock and removing the radiator pressure cap.

✱✱CAUTION

When draining coolant, keep in mind that cats and dogs are attracted by ethylene glycol antifreeze, and are quite likely to drink any that is left in an uncovered container or in puddles on the ground. This will prove fatal in sufficient quantity. Always drain the coolant into a sealable container. Coolant should be reused unless it is contaminated or several years old.

2. Remove the upper and lower hose clamps and hoses at the radiator.
3. Disconnect the automatic transmission oil cooler lines at the radiator, if so equipped. Remove the radiator shroud from the radiator, if so equipped.
4. Remove all attaching screws that secure the radiator to the radiator body support.
5. Remove the radiator.
6. Replace in reverse order of the removal procedure.

Water Pump

REMOVAL & INSTALLATION

4-134 Engine

♦ See Figures 61, 64, 65, 66, 67 and 68

1. Drain the cooling system.

✱✱CAUTION

When draining coolant, keep in mind that cats and dogs are attracted by ethylene glycol antifreeze, and are quite likely to drink any that is left in an uncovered container or in puddles on the ground. This will prove fatal in sufficient quantity. Always drain the coolant into a sealable container. Coolant should be reused unless it is contaminated or several years old.

2. Disconnect the hoses at the pump.
3. Remove the fan belt.
4. Unbolt the fan and hub assembly.
5. Unbolt and remove the pump.
6. Installation is the reverse of removal. Tighten the pump bolts to 17 ft. lbs. (23 Nm). Always use a new gasket coated with sealer.

6-225 Engine

♦ See Figure 62

1. Drain the cooling system.

✱✱CAUTION

When draining coolant, keep in mind that cats and dogs are attracted by ethylene glycol antifreeze, and are quite likely to drink any that is left in an uncovered container or in puddles on the ground. This will prove fatal in sufficient quantity. Always drain the coolant into a sealable container. Coolant should be reused unless it is contaminated or several years old.

2. Disconnect all hoses at the pump.
3. Remove the drive belts.
4. Remove the fan and hub assembly.
5. Unbolt and remove the water pump along with the alternator adjustment bracket.
6. Installation is the reverse of removal. Always use a new gasket coated with sealer. Tighten the water pump bolts to 73-97 inch lbs. (8.2-10.9 Nm).

3-38 ENGINE AND ENGINE OVERHAUL

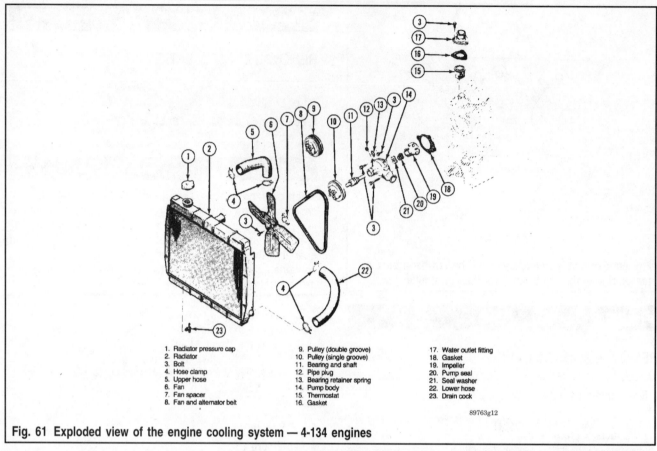

1. Radiator pressure cap
2. Radiator
3. Bolt
4. Hose clamp
5. Upper hose
6. Fan
7. Fan spacer
8. Fan and alternator belt
9. Pulley (double groove)
10. Pulley (single groove)
11. Bearing and shaft
12. Pipe plug
13. Bearing retainer spring
14. Pump body
15. Thermostat
16. Gasket
17. Water outlet fitting
18. Gasket
19. Impeller
20. Pump seal
21. Seal washer
22. Lower hose
23. Drain cock

Fig. 61 Exploded view of the engine cooling system — 4-134 engines

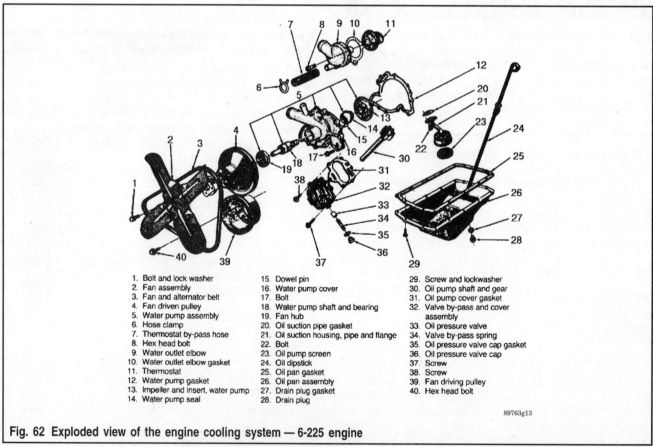

1. Bolt and lock washer
2. Fan assembly
3. Fan and alternator belt
4. Fan driven pulley
5. Water pump assembly
6. Hose clamp
7. Thermostat by-pass hose
8. Hex head bolt
9. Water outlet elbow
10. Water outlet elbow gasket
11. Thermostat
12. Water pump gasket
13. Impeller and insert, water pump
14. Water pump seal
15. Dowel pin
16. Water pump cover
17. Bolt
18. Water pump shaft and bearing
19. Fan hub
20. Oil suction pipe gasket
21. Oil suction housing, pipe and flange
22. Bolt
23. Oil pump screen
24. Oil dipstick
25. Oil pan gasket
26. Oil pan assembly
27. Drain plug gasket
28. Drain plug
29. Screw and lockwasher
30. Oil pump shaft and gear
31. Oil pump cover gasket
32. Valve by-pass and cover assembly
33. Oil pressure valve
34. Valve by-pass spring
35. Oil pressure valve cap gasket
36. Oil pressure valve cap
37. Screw
38. Screw
39. Fan driving pulley
40. Hex head bolt

Fig. 62 Exploded view of the engine cooling system — 6-225 engine

ENGINE AND ENGINE OVERHAUL 3-39

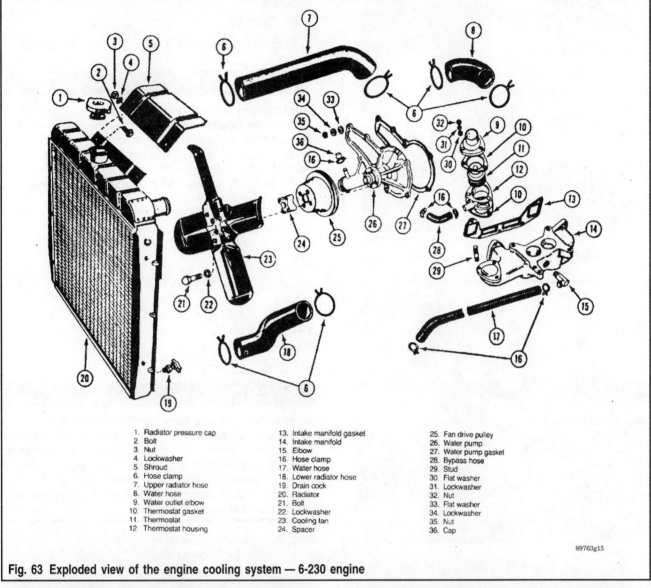

1. Radiator pressure cap
2. Bolt
3. Nut
4. Lockwasher
5. Shroud
6. Hose clamp
7. Upper radiator hose
8. Water hose
9. Water outlet elbow
10. Thermostat gasket
11. Thermostat
12. Thermostat housing
13. Intake manifold gasket
14. Intake manifold
15. Elbow
16. Hose clamp
17. Water hose
18. Lower radiator hose
19. Drain cock
20. Radiator
21. Bolt
22. Lockwasher
23. Cooling fan
24. Spacer
25. Fan drive pulley
26. Water pump
27. Water pump gasket
28. Bypass hose
29. Stud
30. Flat washer
31. Lockwasher
32. Nut
33. Flat washer
34. Lockwasher
35. Nut
36. Cap

Fig. 63 Exploded view of the engine cooling system — 6-230 engine

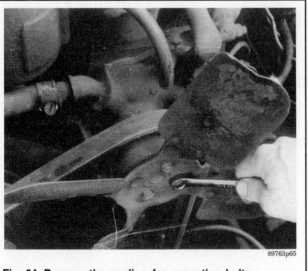

Fig. 64 Remove the cooling fan mounting bolts . . .

Fig. 65 . . . then remove the cooling fan from the water pump pulley

3-40 ENGINE AND ENGINE OVERHAUL

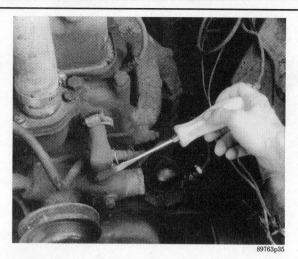

Fig. 66 Detach all cooling system hoses from the water pump . . .

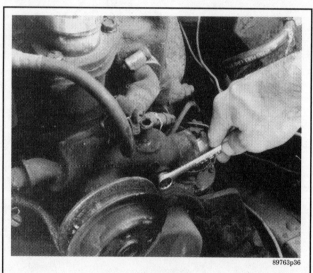

Fig. 67 . . . then remove all water pump mounting bolts

Fig. 68 Pull the water pump off of the front of the engine block — F-head model shown

6-226 Engine

♦ See Figure 69

1. Disconnect the hoses at the pump. Drain the cooling system.

> **✻✻CAUTION**
>
> When draining coolant, keep in mind that cats and dogs are attracted by ethylene glycol antifreeze, and are quite likely to drink any that is left in an uncovered container or in puddles on the ground. This will prove fatal in sufficient quantity. Always drain the coolant into a sealable container. Coolant should be reused unless it is contaminated or several years old.

2. Remove the fan belt.
3. Remove the fan and hub.
4. Unbolt and remove the pump.
5. Installation is the reverse of removal. Always use a new gasket coated with sealer. Tighten the pump bolts to 17 ft. lbs. (23 Nm).

6-230 Engine

♦ See Figure 63

1. Drain the cooling system.

> **✻✻CAUTION**
>
> When draining coolant, keep in mind that cats and dogs are attracted by ethylene glycol antifreeze, and are quite likely to drink any that is left in an uncovered container or in puddles on the ground. This will prove fatal in sufficient quantity. Always drain the coolant into a sealable container. Coolant should be reused unless it is contaminated or several years old.

2. Disconnect the hoses at the pump.
3. Remove the fan and pulley.

ENGINE AND ENGINE OVERHAUL   3-41

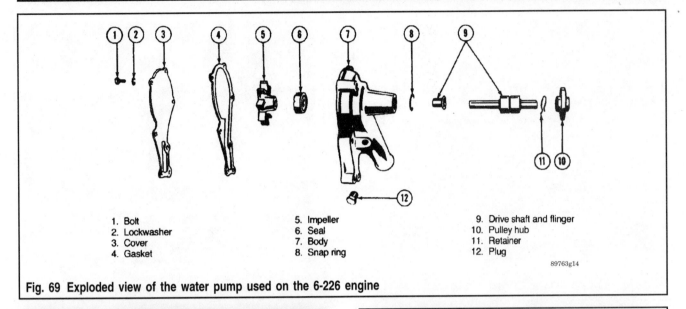

1. Bolt
2. Lockwasher
3. Cover
4. Gasket
5. Impeller
6. Seal
7. Body
8. Snap ring
9. Drive shaft and flinger
10. Pulley hub
11. Retainer
12. Plug

Fig. 69 Exploded view of the water pump used on the 6-226 engine

Cylinder Head

REMOVAL & INSTALLATION

♦ See Figure 70

➡ It is important to note that each engine has its own head bolt tightening sequence and torque. Incorrect tightening procedure may cause head warpage and compression loss. Correct sequence and torque for each engine model is shown in this section.

4-134 Engine

L-HEAD MODEL

♦ See Figures 71, 72, 73, 74, 75, 76, 77, 78, 79, 80, 81, 82, 83, 84, 85 and 86

1. Remove the spark plugs.

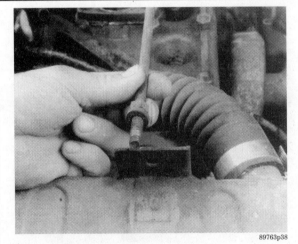

Fig. 71 For added clearance, removal of the crossbrace may be necessary

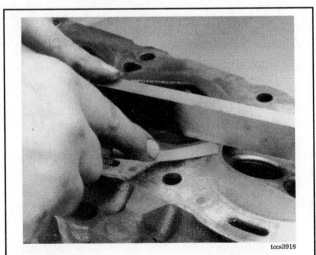

Fig. 70 Check the cylinder head for flatness across the head surface

Fig. 72 Using a flare nut wrench, loosen . . .

3-42 ENGINE AND ENGINE OVERHAUL

Fig. 73 . . . then remove the water temperature sender

Fig. 76 . . . then set it aside

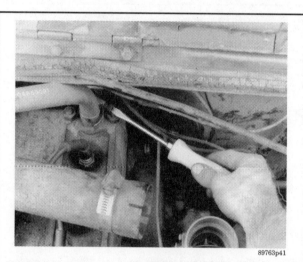

Fig. 74 Remove the heater hoses from the cylinder head

Fig. 77 Make certain to maintain the oil filter in an upright position so that no oil will leak

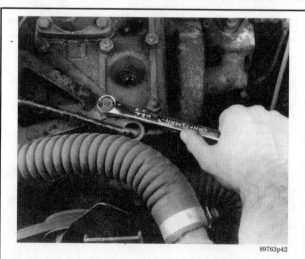

Fig. 75 Remove the cylinder head nuts retaining the oil filter bracket . . .

Fig. 78 Remove the air filter inlet tube and spark plug wires from the cylinder head

ENGINE AND ENGINE OVERHAUL 3-43

Fig. 79 It may be easier to remove the distributor cap along with the spark plug wires

Fig. 82 Remove the old gasket from the engine block

Fig. 80 Remove any remaining cylinder head nuts . . .

Fig. 83 On L-head engines, all valves are mounted in the engine block . . .

Fig. 81 . . . then lift the cylinder head off of the engine block

Fig. 84 . . . and the cylinder head only forms the combustion chambers

3-44 ENGINE AND ENGINE OVERHAUL

Fig. 85 Make certain to tighten the cylinder head nuts to the proper torque value

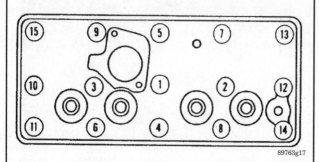

Fig. 86 To prevent cylinder head warpage and to ensure adequate cylinder sealing, it is essential that the cylinder head mounting bolts be tightened in the sequence shown

2. Drain the cooling system.

✴✴CAUTION

When draining coolant, keep in mind that cats and dogs are attracted by ethylene glycol antifreeze, and are quite likely to drink any that is left in an uncovered container or in puddles on the ground. This will prove fatal in sufficient quantity. Always drain the coolant into a sealable container. Coolant should be reused unless it is contaminated or several years old.

3. Remove the temperature sending unit.
4. Remove the head nuts.
5. Lift the head from the block.

➡ Do not use a sharp instrument such as a chisel or screwdriver to break the head from the block. If the head sticks, screw lifting hooks into the No. 1 and 4 spark plug holes.

6. Thoroughly clean the gasket mating surfaces. Remove all traces of old gasket material. Remove all carbon deposits from the combustion chambers. Lay a straightedge across the head and check for flatness; total warpage should not exceed 0.001 in. (0.0254mm).
7. Install the head, using a new gasket. Make sure the head and block surfaces are clean. Tighten the head to 60-70 ft. lbs. (82-95 Nm).

F-HEAD MODEL

♦ See Figures 87, 88, 89, 90, 91, 92, 93 and 94

1. Drain the coolant.

✴✴CAUTION

When draining coolant, keep in mind that cats and dogs are attracted by ethylene glycol antifreeze, and are quite likely to drink any that is left in an uncovered container or in puddles on the ground. This will prove fatal in sufficient quantity. Always drain the coolant into a sealable container. Coolant should be reused unless it is contaminated or several years old.

2. Remove the upper radiator hose.
3. Remove the carburetor.
4. On early engines remove the by-pass hose on the front of the cylinder head.
5. Remove the rocker arm cover.
6. Remove the rocker arm attaching stud nuts and rocker arm shaft assembly.
7. Remove the cylinder head bolts. One of the bolts is located below the carburetor mounting, inside the intake manifold.
8. Lift off the cylinder head.
9. Thoroughly clean the gasket mating surfaces. Remove all traces of old gasket material. Remove all carbon deposits from the combustion chambers. Lay a straightedge across the head and check for flatness. Total deviation should not exceed 0.001 in. (0.0254mm).

Fig. 87 Remove the oil filter and bracket from the cylinder head

ENGINE AND ENGINE OVERHAUL 3-45

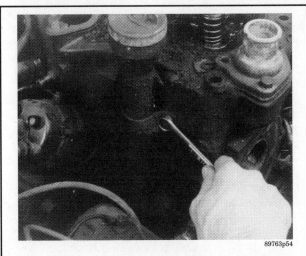
Fig. 88 Detach the oil filler bracket from the cylinder head

Fig. 89 If not already done, label and remove the pushrods

Fig. 90 Remove all cylinder head mounting bolts — one bolt is located in the intake manifold

Fig. 91 Lift the cylinder head from the engine block . . .

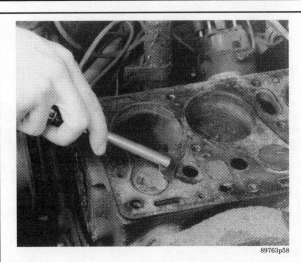
Fig. 92 . . . then remove the old gasket from the engine block

Fig. 93 Use a torque wrench to tighten the cylinder head bolts to the proper value

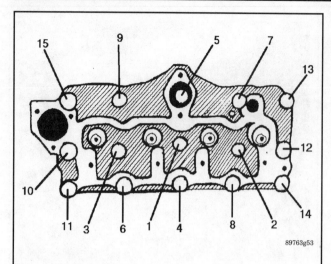

Fig. 94 Make certain to tighten the cylinder head bolts in the sequence shown

10. Reverse the procedure to install the cylinder head. Tighten the head bolts first to 40 ft. lbs. (54 Nm), then to the specified torque in the correct sequence.

6-225 Engine

▶ See Figure 95

1. Drain the cooling system.

✲✲CAUTION

When draining coolant, keep in mind that cats and dogs are attracted by ethylene glycol antifreeze, and are quite likely to drink any that is left in an uncovered container or in puddles on the ground. This will prove fatal in sufficient quantity. Always drain the coolant into a sealable container. Coolant should be reused unless it is contaminated or several years old.

2. Remove the intake manifold.
3. Remove the rocker cover.
4. Remove the exhaust pipes at the flanges.

5. Remove the alternator in order to remove the right head.
6. Remove the dipstick and power steering pump, if so equipped, in order to remove the left head.
7. Remove the valve cover and the rocker assemblies. Mark these parts so that they can be reinstalled in exactly the same positions.
8. Unbolt the head bolts and lift off the cylinder head(s). It is very important that the inside of the engine be protected from dirt. The hydraulic lifters are particularly susceptible to being damaged by dirt.

To install:

9. Thoroughly clean the gasket mating surfaces. Remove all traces of old gasket material. Remove all carbon deposits from the combustion chambers. Lay a straightedge across the head and check for flatness. Total deviation should not exceed 0.001 in. (0.0254mm).
10. Do not apply sealant to the head or block. Coat both sides of the gasket with sealer. The gasket should be stamped TOP for installation. Place the gasket on the block.
11. Install the head on the block. Insert the bolts and tighten them, in sequence, to the 65-85 ft. lbs. (88-116 Nm), in three progressive passes.
12. Install the rocker assemblies and the valve covers. Tighten the rocker arm assemblies to 25-35 ft. lbs. (34-48 Nm) and the valve covers to 36-60 inch lbs. (4.0-6.7 Nm).
13. Install the dipstick and power steering pump, if so equipped.
14. Install the alternator. Tighten the bracket-to-head bolts to 30-40 ft. lbs. (41-54 Nm), the bracket to water pump bolts to 15-25 ft. lbs. (20-34 Nm).
15. Install the exhaust pipes at the flanges. Tighten the nuts to 20 ft. lbs. (27 Nm).
16. Install the intake manifold. Tighten the bolts to 45-55 ft. lbs. (61-75 Nm).
17. Fill the cooling system.

6-226 Engine

▶ See Figure 96

1. Remove the hood.
2. Remove the carburetor.
3. Remove the intake and exhaust manifold assembly.

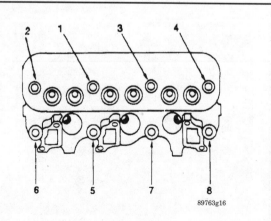

Fig. 95 Make certain to tighten the cylinder head mounting bolts in the sequence shown to ensure proper cylinder sealing and to prevent damage to the cylinder head

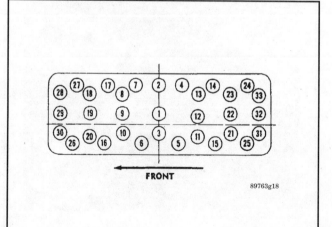

Fig. 96 Tighten the cylinder head mounting bolts only in the sequence shown

ENGINE AND ENGINE OVERHAUL

4. Drain the cooling system.

> **✴✴CAUTION**
>
> When draining coolant, keep in mind that cats and dogs are attracted by ethylene glycol antifreeze, and are quite likely to drink any that is left in an uncovered container or in puddles on the ground. This will prove fatal in sufficient quantity. Always drain the coolant into a sealable container. Coolant should be reused unless it is contaminated or several years old.

5. Remove the water pump.
6. Remove the surge tank, water outlet and thermostat.
7. Remove the distributor and plug wires. Tag the wires for installation.
8. Remove the oil filter and bracket and position it out of the way.
9. Remove the coil.
10. Unbolt the oil filler tube from the head.
11. Remove and tag any wires connected to the head.
12. Remove the head bolts. There is a partially hidden head bolt next to the distributor adapter.
13. Lift off the head. Discard the head gasket.

To install:
14. Inspect the head for cracks, leaks or other damage. Replace leaky core plugs. Lay a straightedge across the head and check for flatness. Total deviation should not exceed 0.031 in. (0.7874mm). Localized deviation, between any two points, should not exceed 0.010 in. (0.254mm). Unevenness between the head and block, at any given point should not exceed 0.015 in. (0.381mm). If deviation is not within acceptable limits, the head should be replaced.
15. Thoroughly clean the mating surfaces of the head and block.
16. Check the head bolt holes for proper depth. To do this, place the head on the block, without the gasket. Insert the bolts into the holes, without the washers. Turn each bolt down, by hand. The bolts should be free enough to be turned all the way down by hand. The head of each bolt must tighten down on the head surface. If a bolt does not turn freely, clean and/or retap the hole as necessary. If a bolt will not turn all the way down, check for foreign matter in the hole. If there is no foreign matter, the hole will have to be deepened by retapping.
17. Obtain two bolts which are the thread size as the head bolts, but are at least 5 in. (127mm) longer. Cut the heads off the bolts and file screwdriver slots in each one. Install these bolts in positions 24 and 26, in the illustration.
18. Coat both sides of the new gasket with sealer. Position the gasket on the block. Make sure that the bolt holes line up.
19. Lower the head onto the block, using the guide bolts.
20. Coat the threads of the head bolts with sealer and install them. Turn the bolts down snugly, in the proper sequence. Remove the guide bolts and install bolts 24 and 26. Tighten all bolts, in the proper sequence, to 45 ft. lbs. (61 Nm).
21. Install any wires connected to the head.
22. Attach the oil filler tube to the head.
23. Install the coil.
24. Install the oil filter and bracket.
25. Install the distributor and plug wires.
26. Install the surge tank, water outlet and thermostat.

27. Install the water pump.
28. Install the intake and exhaust manifold assembly.
29. Install the carburetor.
30. Install the hood.
31. Fill the cooling system.
32. Start the engine and let it reach normal operating temperature. Shut off the engine and retighten the bolts to 45 ft. lbs. (61 Nm), in sequence. Recheck the bolt torque at 500 miles (800km) and 1,000 miles (1600km) after service.

6-230 Engine

▶ See Figure 97

➡ This procedure requires a special tool.

1. Remove the rocker arm cover.
2. Install camshaft sprocket remover W-268, or its equivalent, as shown. Tighten the nut to relieve tension on the camshaft.
3. Remove the capscrew, lock washer, flat washer and fuel pump eccentric from the camshaft sprocket.
4. Pull forward on the sprocket to remove it from the shaft. With the sprocket still engaged in the chain, release the tension on the tool by loosening the nut. Gently allow the sprocket to rest on the bosses in the cover.

➡ **Do not rotate the crankshaft while the camshaft sprocket is removed in this manner. Do not attempt to remove the camshaft sprocket from the chain.**

5. Disconnect the lubrication tube from the head and block.
6. Remove the two timing chain cover-to-head bolts.
7. Remove the head bolts. Note that there are three short head bolts and eleven long ones. All bolts have flat washers.
8. Lift off the head and discard the gasket.

To install:
9. Inspect the head for cracks, leaks or other damage. Replace leaky core plugs. Lay a straightedge across the head and check for flatness. Total deviation should not exceed 0.003 in. (0.0762mm).
10. Thoroughly clean the mating surfaces of the head and block. Remove all carbon from the combustion chambers and tops of pistons. Clean all water and oil gallery holes.

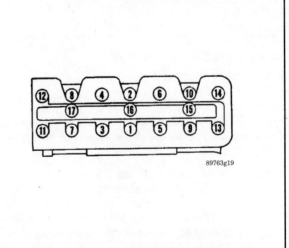

Fig. 97 Make sure that the cylinder head bolts are tightened according to the sequence shown

11. Coat both sides of the new gasket with sealer. Position the gasket on the block. Make sure that the bolt holes line up.
12. Obtain two bolts which are the thread size as the head bolts, but are at least 5 ½ in. (139.7mm). Cut the heads off the bolts and file screwdriver slots in each one.
13. Using a hoist, lower the head to within ¼ in. (6mm) of the block.
14. Install the two modified bolts in bolt holes 12 and 14 in the head (see the torque sequence illustration) and screw them into the block to act as guide pins. This procedure is important, as these guide pins will prevent damage to the timing cover, chain and sprocket.
15. Lower the head into position and install the head bolts, with the exception of the No. 12 and No. 14 bolts, finger-tight. Leave the guide pins in holes 12 and 14.
16. Start the timing cover-to-head bolts into the head.
17. Tighten the 12 installed head bolts, in the sequence illustrated, to 35 ft. lbs. (48 Nm). Then, remove the guide pins and install the two head bolts in their places. Tighten them to 35 ft. lbs. (48 Nm) also.

➡ Late production engines have zinc plated bolts for these two locations. Make sure that these special bolts are used.

18. Tighten all bolts, in the sequence shown, to 95 ft. lbs. (129 Nm).
19. Connect the lubrication tube from the head and block.
20. Install the camshaft sprocket and chain.
21. Install the capscrew, lock washer, flat washer and fuel pump eccentric on the camshaft sprocket.
22. Remove camshaft sprocket tool W-268.
23. Install the rocker arm cover.

Valves and Springs

➡ Fabricate a valve arrangement board to use when you remove the valves, which will indicate the port in which each valve was originally installed (and which cylinder head on the V6 engine). Also note that the valve keys, rotators, caps, etc. should be arranged in a manner which will allow you to install them on the valve on which they were originally used.

REMOVAL

Valves Installed in Cylinder Head

▶ See Figures 98, 99 and 100

1. The head must be removed from the engine.

➡ In all but the 4-134, all the valves are in the head. In the 4-134, just the intakes are in the head. The exhaust valves are in the block.

2. Remove the rocker arm assemblies.
3. Using a spring compressor, compress the valve springs and remove the keepers (locks). Relax the compressor and remove the washers or rotators, the springs, and the lower washers (on some engines). Keep all parts in order.

Valves Installed in Engine Block

4-134 ENGINE

▶ See Figures 101, 102 and 103

1. Remove the attaching bolts from the side valve spring cover. Remove the side valve spring cover and gasket.
2. Use rags to block off the three holes in the exhaust chamber to prevent the valve retaining locks from falling into the crankcase should they be accidentally dropped.
3. Using a valve spring compressor, compress the valve springs only on those valves which are in the closed position (valve seated against the head). Remove the valve spring retainer locks, the retainer, and the exhaust valve spring. Close the other valves by rotating the camshaft and repeat the previous steps for the remaining valves.
4. Lift all of the valves from the cylinder block. If the valve cannot be removed from the block, pull the valve upward as far as possible and remove the spring. Lower the valve and remove any carbon deposits from the valve stem. This will permit removal of the valve.

6-226 ENGINE

1. Remove the cylinder head.
2. Remove the valve chamber cover from the side of the block. Look for evidence of oil seepage past the cover bolt seals.
3. Remove the two valve tappet oil shields. They are held in place by spring clips and may be lifted out with your fingers, or pried out.
4. Use shop rags to block off the holes in the valve chamber, to prevent the valve locks from falling into the crankcase.
5. Using a spring compressor on those valves which are closed compress the valve springs and remove the locks. Relax the compressor and remove the retainer and spring. Lift the valve from the block and mark it for assembly. Rotate the crankshaft and close each valve in turn, performing the removal procedure.

INSPECTION & REFACING

▶ See Figures 104, 105 and 106

1. Clean the valves with a wire wheel.
2. Inspect the valves for warping, cracks or wear.
3. The valves may be refaced if not worn or pitted excessively.
4. Using a valve guide cleaner chucked into a drill, clean all of the valve guides. Check the valve stem diameter and the guide diameter with micrometers. Valve guides on the 4-134, 6-226 and 6-230 are replaceable. On the other engines, the guide must be reamed and an insert pressed in, or they may be knurled to bring up interior metal, restoring their diameter. Oversized valve stems are available to compensate for wear.
5. Install each valve into its respective port (guide) of the cylinder head.
6. Mount a dial indicator so that the stem is at 90 degrees to the valve stem, as close to the valve guide as possible.
7. Move the valve off its seat, and measure the valve guide-to-stem clearance by rocking the stem back and forth to actuate the dial indicator.

ENGINE AND ENGINE OVERHAUL 3-49

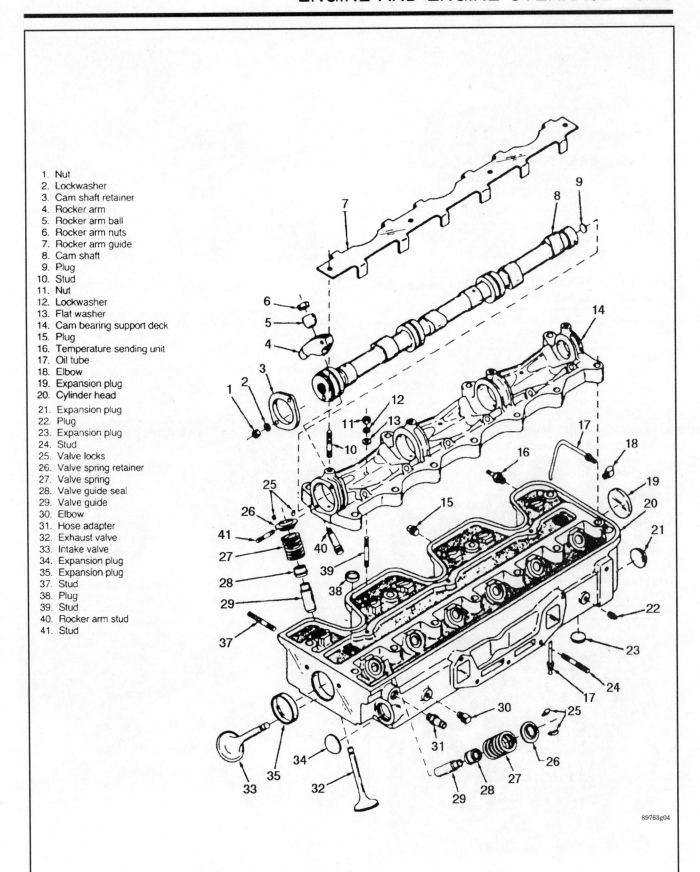

1. Nut
2. Lockwasher
3. Cam shaft retainer
4. Rocker arm
5. Rocker arm ball
6. Rocker arm nuts
7. Rocker arm guide
8. Cam shaft
9. Plug
10. Stud
11. Nut
12. Lockwasher
13. Flat washer
14. Cam bearing support deck
15. Plug
16. Temperature sending unit
17. Oil tube
18. Elbow
19. Expansion plug
20. Cylinder head
21. Expansion plug
22. Plug
23. Expansion plug
24. Stud
25. Valve locks
26. Valve spring retainer
27. Valve spring
28. Valve guide seal
29. Valve guide
30. Elbow
31. Hose adapter
32. Exhaust valve
33. Intake valve
34. Expansion plug
35. Expansion plug
37. Stud
38. Plug
39. Stud
40. Rocker arm stud
41. Stud

Fig. 98 Exploded view of the valve train utilized by the 6-230 engine

3-50 ENGINE AND ENGINE OVERHAUL

Fig. 99 Invert the cylinder head and withdraw the valve from the cylinder head bore

Fig. 100 A wire wheel may be used to clean the combustion chambers of carbon deposits

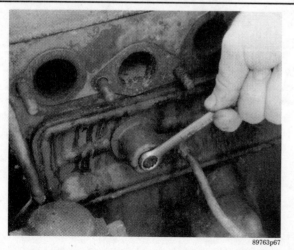
Fig. 101 Remove the side cover retaining bolts/breather assemblies . . .

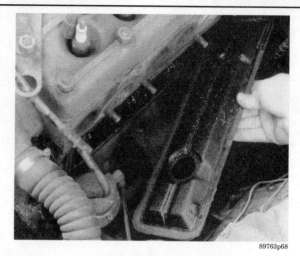
Fig. 102 . . . then pull the side cover off of the engine block

Fig. 103 Once the cover is removed, access to the springs can be gained

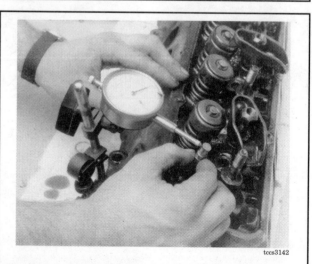
Fig. 104 A dial gauge may be used to check valve stem-to-guide clearance

ENGINE AND ENGINE OVERHAUL 3-51

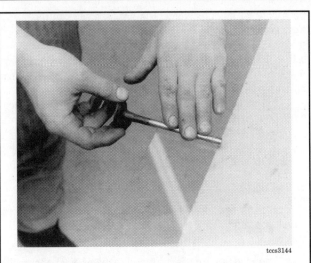

Fig. 105 Valve stems may be rolled on a flat surface to check for bends

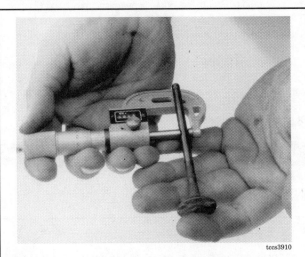

Fig. 106 Use a micrometer to check the valve stem diameter

8. In short, the refacing of valves and other such head work is most easily done at a machine shop. The quality and time saved easily justifies the cost.

9. Inspect the springs for obvious signs of wear. Check their installed height and tension using the values in the Valve Specifications Chart in this section.

REFACING

Using a valve grinder, resurface the valves according to specifications in this section.

➡All machine work should be performed by a competent, professional machine shop.

✱✱CAUTION

Valve face angle is not always identical to valve seat angle. A minimum margin of $1/32$ in. (0.794mm) should remain after grinding the valve. The valve stem top should also be squared and resurfaced, by placing the stem in the V-block of the grinder, and turning it while pressing lightly against the grinding wheel. Be sure to chamfer the edge of the tip so that the squared edges do not dig into the rocker arm or camshaft.

LAPPING

This procedure should be performed after the valves and seats have been machined, to insure that each valve mates to each seat precisely.

1. Invert the cylinder head, lightly lubricate the valve stems, and install the valves in the head as numbered.
2. Coat valve seats with fine grinding compound, and attach the lapping tool suction cup to a valve head.

➡Moisten the suction cup.

3. Rotate the tool between your palms, changing position and lifting the tool often to prevent grooving.
4. Lap the valve until a smooth, polished seat is evident.
5. Remove the valve and tool, and rinse away all traces of grinding compound.

VALVE SPRING TESTING

▶ See Figures 107 and 108

Place the spring on a flat surface next to a square. Measure the height of the spring, and rotate it against the edge of the square to measure distortion. If spring height varies (by comparison) by more than $1/16$ in. (1.588mm) or if distortion exceeds $1/16$ in. (1.588mm), replace the spring.

In addition to evaluating the spring as indicated earlier, test the spring pressure at the installed and compressed (installed height minus valve lift) height using a valve spring tester. Spring pressure should be within 1 lb. (2.2kg) of all other springs in either position.

INSTALLATION

1. Coat all parts with clean engine oil. Install all parts in their respective locations. The spring is installed with the closely wound coils toward the valve head. Always use new valve seals.
2. Use a spring compressor to install the keepers and slowly release the compressor after the keepers are in place.

➡Coat the locks, on the 6-226, with chassis grease to hold them in place until you release the spring compressor.

3. Release the spring compressor. Tap the end of the stem with a wood mallet to insure that the keepers are securely in place.
4. Install all other parts in reverse order of removal.

3-52 ENGINE AND ENGINE OVERHAUL

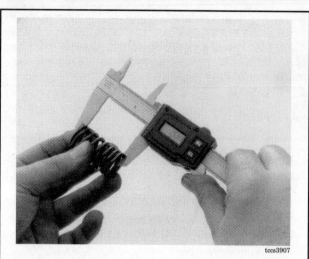

Fig. 107 Use a caliper gauge to check the valve spring free-length

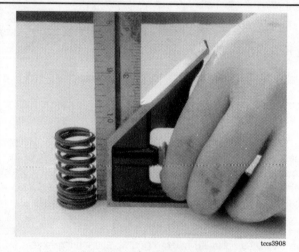

Fig. 108 Check the valve spring for squareness on a flat surface; a carpenter's square can be used

Valve Guides

REMOVAL & INSTALLATION

4-134 and 6-230 Engines

➡A press is used for removal and installation of guides.

1. Place the head in the press and press the old guide out through the bottom and the new one in through the top. On the 6-230, all the guides are the same. On the 4-134, the only guides in the head are the intakes.
2. Once the new guide is in place, check its protrusion. On the 6-230, the guide should protrude 0.45 in. (11.43mm) above the head surface. On the 4-134, the guide should be flush with the head surface.
3. The exhaust valve guides on the 4-134 are also replaceable. These guides are located in the block. A press is not necessary for this procedure. The engine should be removed from the vehicle. The head, oil pan and crankshaft should be removed. The guides are driven out of their bores from above, with a driver made for the purpose. The new guides are then driven in with the same tool, until their tops are 1 in. (25.4mm) below the block surface.

4. On all three engines, after the guides are in place, they must be reamed:
- 6-230 — 0.342-0.343 in. (8.6868-8.7122mm)
- 4-134 — Intake: 0.3740-0.3760 in. (9.4996-9.5504mm); Exhaust: 0.3735-0.3765 in. (9.4869-9.5631mm)

6-226 Engine

➡A press is not necessary for this procedure. The engine should be removed from the vehicle. The cylinder head and oil pan should be removed.

1. The guides are pulled out of their bores from above, with a tool made for the purpose.
2. Check the valve guide bore and the outside diameter of the new guide. Ream the bore, if necessary, to obtain a 0.0005-0.0030 in. (0.0127-0.0762mm) press fit. Guides are available in 0.0005 in. (0.0127mm) and 0.0055 in. (0.1397mm) oversizes.
3. The new guides are then pulled into place with the same tool, until their tops are $1^7/_{32}$ in. (30.96mm) below the block surface.
4. Ream the new guides to a diameter of 0.3423-0.3432 in. (8.694-8.717mm).

Valve Seats

INSPECTION & REFACING

♦ See Figures 109 and 110

The exhaust valve seats on the 4-134 and 6-226 are replaceable. All others have integral seats. Check the condition of the seats for excessive wear, pitting or cracks. Remove all traces of deposits from the seats. The seats may be refaced

Fig. 109 Check the valve seat concentricity with a specially designed dial indicator

ENGINE AND ENGINE OVERHAUL 3-53

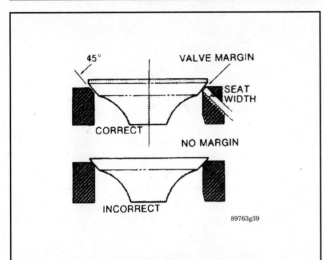

Fig. 110 When seating the valves on the seats, make certain to maintain a proper seat width

with a special grinding tool, to the dimensions shown in the Valve Specifications Chart.

You can replace the exhaust valve seats by driving them out from the bottom with a driver made for the purpose. This requires removal of the engine from the truck. Removal of the head, crankshaft, camshaft and pistons and rods. The new seats should be chilled with dry ice and installed immediately. They are driven into place with a seat installation tool. After installation, they should be ground to a 45° angle.

Oil Pan

REMOVAL & INSTALLATION

4-134 and 6-225 Engines

▶ See Figures 111, 112, 113, 114, 115 and 116

To remove the oil pan on these engines, remove the oil pan attaching bolts and remove the oil pan. Clean all of the attaching surfaces and install new gaskets.

6-226 Engine

1. Remove the engine from the truck.
2. Place the engine on a work stand and turn it upside down.
3. Remove the oil pan attaching bolts and remove the oil pan.
4. Clean all the mating surfaces and install a new gasket coated with sealer on the pan.
5. Position the oil pan, install the bolts and tighten them to 109 inch lbs. (12 Nm).
6. Install the engine.

6-230 Engine

▶ See Figure 117

1. Unbolt and remove the pan.
2. Pull the ends of the pan gasket from the front and rear filler blocks.

3. Insert gasket aligning dowels in the holes on each side of the block at the front.
4. Place the new gasket on top of the old gasket. With the gaskets held in place by the dowels, make a cut through both gaskets, ³⁄₃₂ in. (2.38mm) from the front filler block, or ⁵⁄₁₆ in. (8mm) from the edge of the nearest hole. The cut must be so that the triangular end of the oil pan seal will cover the splice.
5. Remove both gaskets and discard the old one.
6. Clean the gasket mating surfaces thoroughly.
7. Coat both sides of the new gaskets with sealer, and the splice near the front filler block. With the dowels in the holes, position the gaskets on the block. Replace the ends of the oil pan seal at both filler blocks.
8. Coat the filler block seals with clean engine oil.
9. Install the pan and hand-tighten the bolts.
10. Working from the center bolts toward the ends, and alternating from side to side, tighten the bolts to 146-182 inch lbs. (16-20 Nm).

Oil Pump

REMOVAL & INSTALLATION

4-134 Engines

▶ See Figure 118

1. Set No. 1 piston at Top Dead Center (TDC) in order to reinstall the oil pump without disturbing the ignition timing.
2. Remove the distributor cover and note the position of the rotor. Keep the rotor in that position when the oil pump is installed.
3. Remove the cap screws and lock washers that attach the oil pump to the cylinder block. Carefully slide the oil pump and its driveshaft out of the cylinder block.

The oil pump is driven by the camshaft by means of a spiral gear. The distributor in turn is driven by the oil pump by means of a tongue on the end of the distributor shaft which engages a slot in the end of the oil pump shaft. Because the tongue and the slot are both machined off center, the two shafts can be meshed in only one position. Since the position of the distributor shaft determines the timing of the engine, and is controlled by the oil pump shaft, the position of the oil pump shaft with respect to the camshaft is important. If only the oil pump has been removed, install it so that the slot in the end of the shaft lines up with the tip of the distributor shaft and allows that shaft to slip into it without disturbing the original position of the distributor. If the engine has been disturbed or both the distributor and the oil pump have been removed, perform the following procedure:

4. Turn the crankshaft to align the timing marks on the crankshaft and camshaft timing gears.
5. Install the oil pump gasket on the pump.
6. With the wider side of the slot on top start the oil pump driveshaft into the opening in the cylinder keeping the mounting holes in the body of the pump in alignment with the holes in the cylinder block.
7. Insert a long blade screwdriver into the distributor shaft opening in the side of the cylinder block and engage the slot in the oil pump shaft. Turn the shaft so that the slot is posi-

3-54 ENGINE AND ENGINE OVERHAUL

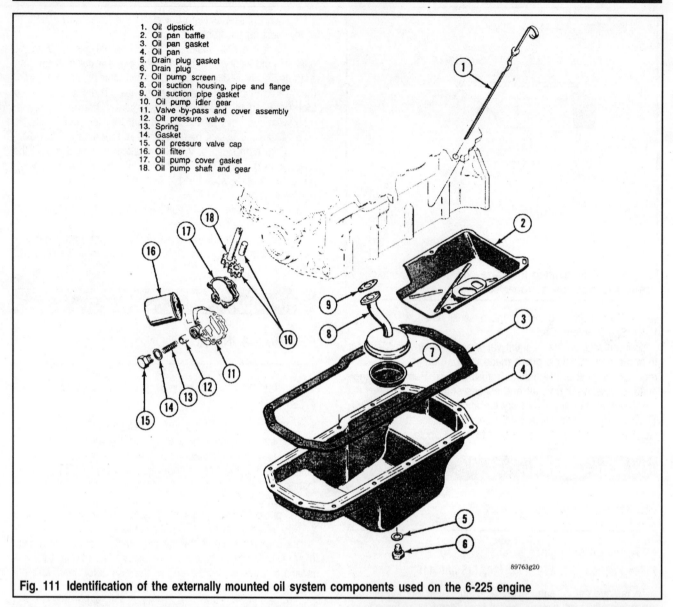

Fig. 111 Identification of the externally mounted oil system components used on the 6-225 engine

1. Oil dipstick
2. Oil pan baffle
3. Oil pan gasket
4. Oil pan
5. Drain plug gasket
6. Drain plug
7. Oil pump screen
8. Oil suction housing, pipe and flange
9. Oil suction pipe gasket
10. Oil pump idler gear
11. Valve by-pass and cover assembly
12. Oil pressure valve
13. Spring
14. Gasket
15. Oil pressure valve cap
16. Oil filter
17. Oil pump cover gasket
18. Oil pump shaft and gear

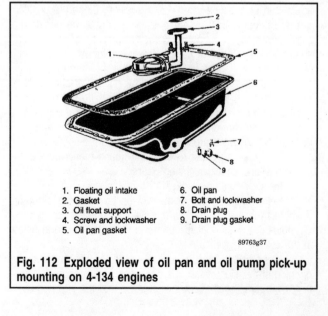

1. Floating oil intake
2. Gasket
3. Oil float support
4. Screw and lockwasher
5. Oil pan gasket
6. Oil pan
7. Bolt and lockwasher
8. Drain plug
9. Drain plug gasket

Fig. 112 Exploded view of oil pan and oil pump pick-up mounting on 4-134 engines

Fig. 113 Remove the oil pan retaining bolts . . .

ENGINE AND ENGINE OVERHAUL 3-55

Fig. 114 ... then lower the oil pan from the engine block

Fig. 115 Once the pan is removed, access to the oil pick-up can be gained

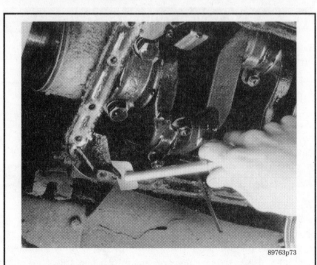

Fig. 116 Remove the old gasket from the oil pan mounting surface — 4-134 engine

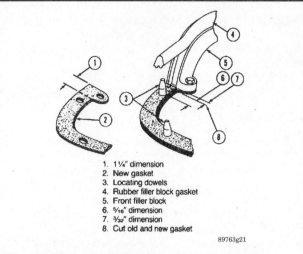

1. 1¼" dimension
2. New gasket
3. Locating dowels
4. Rubber filler block gasket
5. Front filler block
6. ⁵⁄₁₆" dimension
7. ³⁄₃₂" dimension
8. Cut old and new gasket

Fig. 117 When installing a new oil pan gasket, the gasket must be trimmed to fit

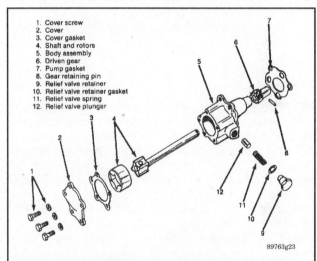

1. Cover screw
2. Cover
3. Cover gasket
4. Shaft and rotors
5. Body assembly
6. Driven gear
7. Pump gasket
8. Gear retaining pin
9. Relief valve retainer
10. Relief valve retainer gasket
11. Relief valve spring
12. Relief valve plunger

Fig. 118 Exploded view of the oil pump used on late model L-head and all F-head 4-134 engines

tioned at what would be roughly the nine-thirty position on a clock face.

8. Remove the screwdriver and observe the position of the slot in the end of the oil pump shaft to make certain it is properly positioned.

9. Replace the screwdriver and, while turning the screwdriver clockwise to guide the oil pump driveshaft gear into engagement with the camshaft gear, press against the oil pump to force it into position.

10. Remove the screwdriver and again observe the position of the slot. If installation was properly made, the slot will be in a position roughly equivalent to the 11 o'clock position on the face of a clock, with the wider side of the slot still on the top. If the slot is improperly positioned, remove the oil pump and repeat the operation.

11. Coat the threads of the capscrews with gasket cement and secure the oil pump in place.

6-225 Engine

1. Remove the oil filter.

3-56 ENGINE AND ENGINE OVERHAUL

2. Disconnect the wire from the oil pressure indicator switch in the filter by-pass pump cover assembly to the timing chain cover.
3. Remove the screws that attach the oil pump cover assembly to the timing chain cover.
4. Remove the cover assembly and slide out the oil pump.
5. Install in reverse order of the removal procedure.

6-226 Engine

1. Remove the engine from the truck.
2. Remove the oil pan.
3. Remove the lock wire from the rear intermediate main bearing bolts.
4. Unbolt the pump from the bearing cap.
5. Turn the engine so that No.1 piston is at Top Dead Compression (TDC) on the compression stroke.
6. Install the distributor. Rotate the oil pump driveshaft so that when the oil pump is installed, the pump driveshaft tongue engages the slot in the lower end of the distributor driveshaft. The slot at the top of the distributor shaft must be roughly parallel with the side of the block.
7. Install the pump and tighten the attaching nuts to 35 ft. lbs. (48 Nm).

6-230 Engine

▶ See Figure 119

1. Remove the fan.
2. Remove the three nuts that attach the pump to the timing case cover.
3. Pull the pump straight up and out of the cover. Discard the gasket.
4. Prime the pump with clean engine oil prior to installation. Always use a new gasket.
5. If the engine was not rotated during pump removal, simply install the pump, engaging the drive slots.
6. If the engine was rotated, turn the crankshaft until No. 1 piston is at Top Dead Center (TDC) on the compression stroke and the pointer on the timing marks is aligned with the 0 mark.
7. Position the pump and gasket on the mounting studs. Do not install the pump far enough to engage the drive gear. Insert a long screwdriver into the distributor shaft opening in the opposite side of the cover and engage the slot in the oil pump shaft. Turn the shaft so that the slot is in the 4 and 10 o'clock position with the narrow side of the shaft up. Remove the screwdriver and, with a light, look in the hole to see if the slot is properly positioned. Install the screwdriver again, and turn the screwdriver counterclockwise to guide the oil pump drive gear into engagement with the crankshaft. Press against the pump gear to force it into engagement. Remove the screwdriver and again observe the slot. If correctly positioned, it will be in the 3 and 9 o'clock position, with the narrow side still on top. Install the nuts.

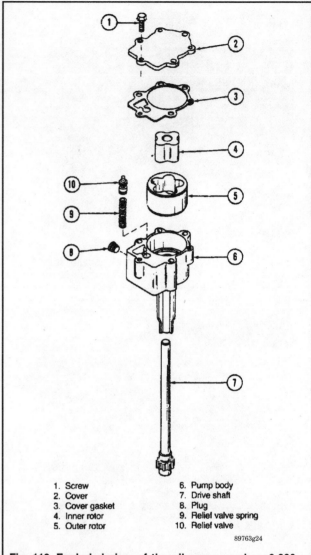

1. Screw
2. Cover
3. Cover gasket
4. Inner rotor
5. Outer rotor
6. Pump body
7. Drive shaft
8. Plug
9. Relief valve spring
10. Relief valve

Fig. 119 Exploded view of the oil pump used on 6-230 engines

Crankshaft Pulley (Vibration Damper)

REMOVAL & INSTALLATION

▶ See Figure 120

1. Remove the fan shroud, as required. If necessary, drain the cooling system and remove the radiator. Remove drive belts from pulley.

✱✱CAUTION

When draining coolant, keep in mind that cats and dogs are attracted by ethylene glycol antifreeze, and are quite likely to drink any that is left in an uncovered container or in puddles on the ground. This will prove fatal in sufficient quantity. Always drain the coolant into a sealable container. Coolant should be reused unless it is contaminated or several years old.

ENGINE AND ENGINE OVERHAUL

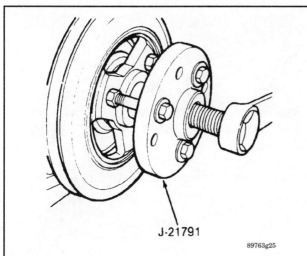

Fig. 120 A puller, such as J-21791, is necessary to remove the crankshaft damper

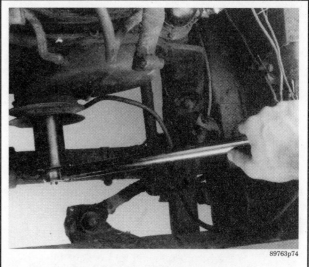

Fig. 121 Remove the lower pulley retaining nut . . .

2. On those engines with a separate pulley, remove the retaining bolts and separate the pulley from the vibration damper.
3. Remove the vibration damper/pulley retaining bolt from the crankshaft end.
4. Using a puller, remove the damper/pulley from the crankshaft.
5. Upon installation, align the key slot of the pulley hub to the crankshaft key. Complete the assembly in the reverse order of removal. Tighten the retaining bolts to specifications.

Timing Chain/Gear Cover and Oil Seal

REMOVAL & INSTALLATION

4-134 Engines

♦ See Figures 121, 122, 123, 124, 125, 126, 127 and 128

1. Remove the drive belts and crankshaft pulley.
2. Remove the attaching bolts, nuts and lock washers that hold the timing gear cover to the engine.
3. Remove the timing gear cover.
4. Remove the timing pointer.
5. Remove the timing gear cover gasket.
6. Remove and discard the crankshaft oil seal from the timing gear cover.
7. Replace in reverse order of the removal procedure. Replace the crankshaft oil seal. Use a new timing gear cover gasket.

6-225 Engine

♦ See Figure 129

1. Remove the water pump and crankshaft pulley.
2. Remove the two bolts that attach the oil pan to the timing chain cover.
3. Remove the five bolts that attach the timing chain cover to the engine block.
4. Remove the cover and gasket.
5. Remove the crankshaft front oil seal.

Fig. 122 . . . and slide the pulley off of the crankshaft

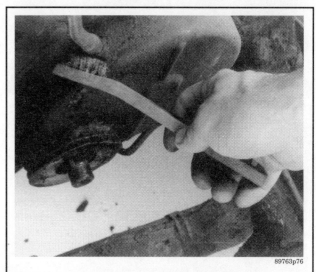

Fig. 123 Clean around the breather tube fitting . . .

3-58 ENGINE AND ENGINE OVERHAUL

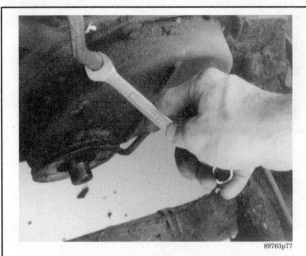

Fig. 124 ... then remove the fitting from the front cover

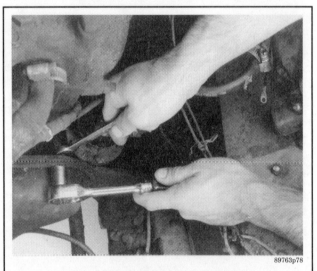

Fig. 125 Remove the front cover mounting bolts ...

Fig. 126 ... then remove the oil pan-to-front cover bolts

Fig. 127 Use a small prytool to separate the cover from the engine block ...

Fig. 128 ... then pull the cover off of the engine block

6. From the rear of the timing chain cover, coil new packing around the crankshaft hole in the cover so that the ends of the packing are at the top. Drive in the new packing with a punch. It will be necessary to ream out the hole to obtain clearance for the crankshaft vibration damper hub.

6-226 Engine

➡ Special tools are needed for this job.

1. Drain the cooling system.

✱✱CAUTION

When draining coolant, keep in mind that cats and dogs are attracted by ethylene glycol antifreeze, and are quite likely to drink any that is left in an uncovered container or in puddles on the ground. This will prove fatal in sufficient quantity. Always drain the coolant into a sealable container. Coolant should be reused unless it is contaminated or several years old.

ENGINE AND ENGINE OVERHAUL

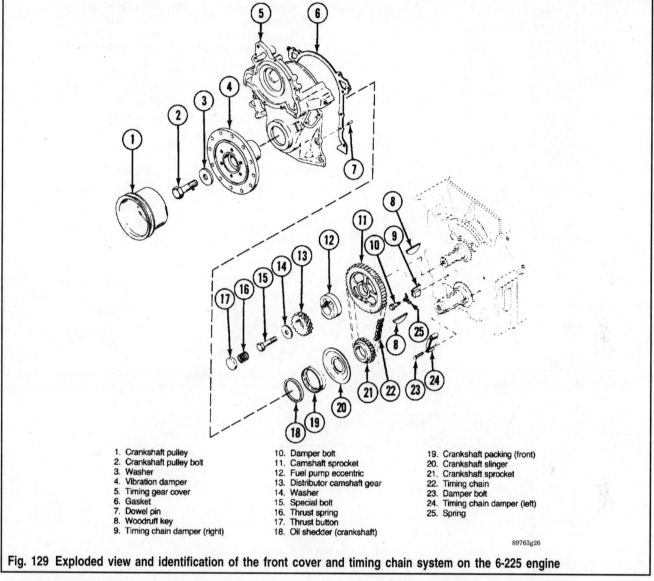

1. Crankshaft pulley
2. Crankshaft pulley bolt
3. Washer
4. Vibration damper
5. Timing gear cover
6. Gasket
7. Dowel pin
8. Woodruff key
9. Timing chain damper (right)
10. Damper bolt
11. Camshaft sprocket
12. Fuel pump eccentric
13. Distributor camshaft gear
14. Washer
15. Special bolt
16. Thrust spring
17. Thrust button
18. Oil shedder (crankshaft)
19. Crankshaft packing (front)
20. Crankshaft slinger
21. Crankshaft sprocket
22. Timing chain
23. Damper bolt
24. Timing chain damper (left)
25. Spring

Fig. 129 Exploded view and identification of the front cover and timing chain system on the 6-225 engine

2. Remove the radiator.
3. Remove the vibration damper and timing pointer.
4. Unbolt and remove the cover. Discard the gasket.
5. Brace the cover and drive out the old seal.
6. Drive the new seal into place, making sure that it is flush and not cocked. Lubricate the inner seal surface with clean engine oil.
7. Coat both sides of a new gasket with sealer and position it on the block.
8. Position the cover on the block, and if one is available, use an aligning tool to aid in positioning the cover.
9. Install the bolts and tighten them to 182 inch lbs. (20 Nm).
10. Install all other parts in reverse order of removal. Fill the cooling system.

6-230 Engine

♦ See Figures 130 and 131

➡ Special tools are needed for this job.

1. Remove the fan, hub and drive pulley.
2. Remove the water pump.
3. Remove the oil pump.
4. Remove the distributor.
5. Remove the thermostat and housing.
6. Remove the bolt and pilot washer that attach the vibration damper to the crankshaft. Later model engines have a lock plate on the damper.
7. Using a puller, remove the damper from the crankshaft.
8. Using seal remover W-286, pull the front seal from the case.
9. Remove the hose from the water port of the cover.
10. Unbolt and remove the cover from the front plate.
11. Make sure that the mating surfaces of the cover and block are clean.
12. Coat both sides of the new gaskets with sealer and position them on the block.
13. Place the cover on the block and install and tighten the bolts. Tighten the 5/16 in. bolts to 146-182 inch lbs. (16-20 Nm) and the 3/8 in. bolts to 15-20 ft. lbs. (20-27 Nm).

3-60 ENGINE AND ENGINE OVERHAUL

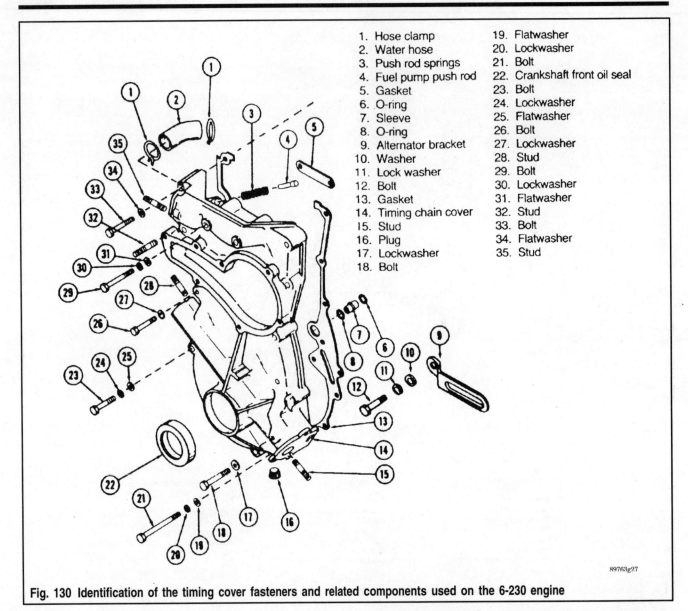

Fig. 130 Identification of the timing cover fasteners and related components used on the 6-230 engine

1. Hose clamp
2. Water hose
3. Push rod springs
4. Fuel pump push rod
5. Gasket
6. O-ring
7. Sleeve
8. O-ring
9. Alternator bracket
10. Washer
11. Lock washer
12. Bolt
13. Gasket
14. Timing chain cover
15. Stud
16. Plug
17. Lockwasher
18. Bolt
19. Flatwasher
20. Lockwasher
21. Bolt
22. Crankshaft front oil seal
23. Bolt
24. Lockwasher
25. Flatwasher
26. Bolt
27. Lockwasher
28. Stud
29. Bolt
30. Lockwasher
31. Flatwasher
32. Stud
33. Bolt
34. Flatwasher
35. Stud

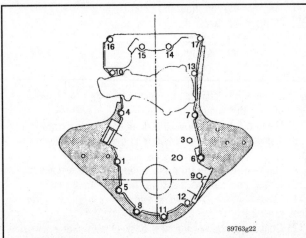

Fig. 131 Make certain to tighten the timing cover retaining bolts in the proper sequence so that adequate sealing is maintained

14. Using a seal driver, install a new front seal. Apply sealer to the outer rim of the seal and clean engine oil to the seal lips prior to installation.
15. Install all other parts in reverse order of removal. The vibration damper may be pressed on by reversing the removal tool. Tighten the damper bolt to 100-130 ft. lbs. (136-177 Nm). If a damper lock is used, tighten the bolts to 40-50 ft. lbs. (54-68 Nm).

Timing Chain and Tensioner

REMOVAL & INSTALLATION

L4-134 Engines Before Serial No. 175402 in CJ-2A Models

1. Remove the timing chain cover.
2. Pull the sprocket forward alternately and evenly until they are free.
3. On installation, align the timing marks on the sprockets. Check the end float between the crankshaft sprocket and the

ENGINE AND ENGINE OVERHAUL   3-61

thrust plate. Clearance should be 0.004-0.008 in. (0.1016-0.2032mm). Camshaft gear-to-thrust plate clearance is 0.003-0.055 in. (0.0762-1.397mm). Both clearances are adjustable by shim packs. Check, also, the running clearances between the gears. Proper clearance is 0.000-0.002 in. (0.0000-0.0508mm).

4. Turn the crankshaft so that Nos. 1 and 4 piston are at Top Dead Center (TDC) as indicated by the Top Center (TC) mark on the flywheel seen through the timing hole in the right side of the flywheel housing.

5. Place the camshaft sprocket on the shaft and turn the shaft until the punch mark on the rim of the sprocket faces the punch mark on the crankshaft sprocket.

6. Remove the camshaft sprocket and install the sprocket and timing chain. Timing is correct when a line drawn through the sprocket centers, intersects the timing marks on both sprockets.

6-225 Engine

▶ See Figure 129

1. Remove the timing chain cover.
2. Make sure that the timing marks on the crankshaft and the camshaft sprockets are aligned. This will make installing the parts easier.

➡ It is not necessary to remove the timing chain dampers (tensioners) unless they are worn or damaged and require replacement.

3. Remove the front crankshaft oil slinger.
4. Remove the bolt and the special washer that hold the camshaft distributor drive gear and fuel pump eccentric at the forward end of the camshaft. Remove the eccentric and the gear from the camshaft.
5. Alternately pry forward the camshaft sprocket and then the crankshaft sprocket until the camshaft sprocket is pried from the camshaft.
6. Remove the camshaft sprocket, sprocket key, and timing chain from the engine.
7. Pry the crankshaft sprocket from the crankshaft.

To install:

8. If the engine has not been disturbed proceed to step Number 4 for installation procedures.
9. If the engine has been disturbed turn the crankshaft so that number one piston is at top dead center.
10. Temporarily install the sprocket key and the camshaft sprocket on the camshaft. Turn the camshaft so that the index mark of the sprocket is downward. Remove the key and sprocket from the camshaft.
11. Assemble the timing chain and sprockets. Install the keys, sprockets, and chain assembly on the camshaft and crankshaft so that the index marks of both the sprockets are aligned.

➡ It will be necessary to hold the spring loaded timing chain damper out of the way while installing the timing chain and sprocket assembly.

12. Install the front oil slinger on the crankshaft with the inside diameter against the sprocket (concave side toward the front of the engine).

13. Install the fuel pump eccentric on the camshaft and the key, with the oil groove of the eccentric forward.
14. Install the distributor drive gear on the camshaft. Secure the gear and eccentric to the camshaft with the retaining washer and bolt.
15. Tighten the bolt to 40-55 ft. lbs. (54-75 Nm).

6-226 Engine

1. Remove the timing chain cover.
2. Before removing the parts, check for timing chain stretch. Press inward on the chain at a point midway between the gears. If the chain deflects more than ½ in. (13mm), it is overly stretched and must be discarded.
3. Bend up the lock tabs and the camshaft gear retaining bolt and remove the bolt.
4. Pry, alternately, behind each gear until both are free.
5. Inspect both gears. If either appears to be excessively worn, or if either are chipped or cracked, both gears and the chain must be replaced. If only the chain is defective, then, only the chain needs replacement. Inspect the cover. If it is bent or damaged, replace it.
6. Place the two gears into the chain so that there are exactly nine links, or ten pins, between the timing marks on the gears.
7. If either the camshaft or crankshaft was rotated while the gears were off, position the shafts so that the keyways are positioned as illustrated.
8. Slide the gears onto the shafts. If everything is aligned properly, the gears should slip into place with finger pressure.
9. If the camshaft has to be tapped into place, check that the camshaft bearing journals are not contacting the sides of Nos. 1, 5, or 9 tappets. This sometimes occurs when the camshaft is pushed backwards during gear installation. If this does occur, hold the camshaft forward to prevent tappet damage.
10. When the gears are fully seated, place the lock plate on the camshaft, with the tab in the hole of the gear.
11. Install the camshaft gear nut and tighten it to 40 ft. lbs. (54 Nm). Bend the lock plate to secure the nut.
12. Install the oil slinger on the crankshaft.
13. Install the remaining parts in reverse order of removal.

6-230 Engine

▶ See Figures 130, 131 and 132

➡ Special tools are needed for this job.

1. Remove the timing chain cover. Measure across the gap between the chain sides. If the gap is less than 3.38 in. (85.85mm), the chain is stretched and should be replaced.
2. Install the camshaft sprocket remover tool as shown under the Cylinder Head Removal and Installation procedure.
3. Remove the sprocket with the tool as described under the cylinder head procedure.
4. Slide the chain from the sprocket.
5. Remove the chain tensioner pin to release tension on the tensioner blade. Remove the blade assembly and spring.
6. Remove the chain guide bracket.
7. The crank sprocket may now be removed.
8. Install the tensioner bracket on the front plate with the rubber covered leg positioned between the chain and the front plate.

3-62 ENGINE AND ENGINE OVERHAUL

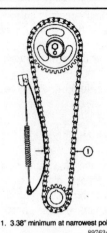

1. 3.38" minimum at narrowest point

Fig. 132 When the timing chain is properly tensioned, dimension (1) should be a minimum of 3.38 in. (85.9mm)

9. Install the two capscrews and washers and two new 5/16-24 seal nuts. Hold these seal nuts from turning when tightening the bolts.
10. Position the tensioner blade assembly and spring on the anchor stud on the front engine plate. Bend the blade so that the hook at the upper end of the spring is aligned with the notch in the top of the blade.
11. Insert the tensioner pin so that it engages the spring and blade. Position the top of the tensioner in the bracket.
12. Rotate the engine so that No. 1 piston is at TDC compression. Air will be forced out the spark plug hole when this occurs.
13. With the engine at Top Dead Center (TDC) on the No. 1 cylinder, the key ways in the crankshaft should be in the 12 o'clock position.
14. Temporarily install the camshaft sprocket and turn the camshaft until the nose of the No. 1 camshaft lobe, and the dowel hole on the camshaft, are pointing downward to the 6 o'clock position. Remove the sprocket.
15. Install a key in the crankshaft key way nearest the block.
16. Install the camshaft sprocket remover tool as before.
17. Position the chain on the sprockets so that the key way of the crank sprocket is up and the key way of the camshaft sprocket is down. The copper links of the chain should be aligned with the timing marks on the sprockets. When properly assembled, there should be 1½ chain units, comprising 31 steel links between the copper links.
18. Lift the assembled chain and sprockets and slide the crank sprocket into position until it is fully seated.
19. Using the camshaft sprocket tool, tighten the nut to pull tension on the chain and align the sprocket with the end of the shaft. Push the sprocket off the tool and onto the shaft, aligning the key and key slot.
20. Position the fuel pump eccentric on the camshaft sprocket. Install the capscrew, lock washer and flat washer.
21. Remove the camshaft tool.

Timing Gears

REMOVAL & INSTALLATION

L4-134 Engines After No. 175402 and All F4-134 Engines
▶ See Figures 133, 134, 135, 136, 137, 138, 139, 140 and 141

1. Remove the timing gear cover.
2. Use a puller to remove both the crankshaft and the camshaft gear from the engine after removing all attaching nuts and bolts.
3. Remove the Woodruff keys.

To install:
4. Install the Woodruff key in the longer of the two key ways on the front end of the crankshaft.

Fig. 133 Remove the crankshaft pulley's Woodruff key and retain for installation

Fig. 134 Slide the outer cover off of the crankshaft gear . . .

ENGINE AND ENGINE OVERHAUL

Fig. 135 . . . then slide the crankshaft gear spacer off of the crankshaft

Fig. 138 Remove the camshaft gear retaining bolt . . .

Fig. 136 Use a puller to loosen the crankshaft gear . . .

Fig. 139 . . . then slide the washer/spacer off of the camshaft gear

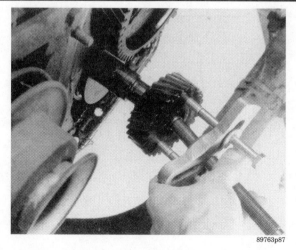
Fig. 137 . . . then slide the crankshaft gear off of the crankshaft

Fig. 140 Sometime during this procedure, be sure to clean the old gasket off the block

3-64 ENGINE AND ENGINE OVERHAUL

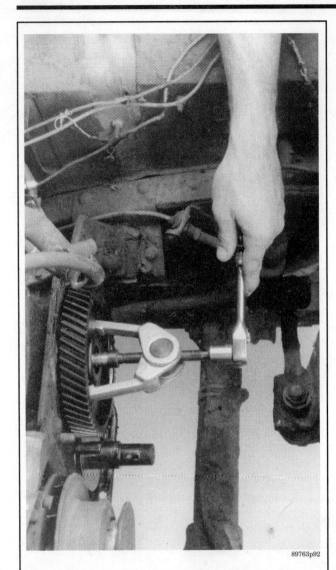

Fig. 141 Use a puller to remove the camshaft gear from the camshaft

5. Install the crankshaft timing gear on the front end of the crankshaft with the timing mark facing away from the cylinder block.
6. Align the key way in the gear with the Woodruff key and then drive or press the gear onto the crankshaft firmly against the thrust washer.
7. Turn the camshaft or the crankshaft as necessary so that the timing marks on the two gears will be together after the camshaft gear is installed.
8. Install the Woodruff key in the key way on the front of the camshaft.
9. Start the large timing gear on the camshaft with the timing mark facing out.

➡ Do not drive the gear onto the camshaft as the camshaft may drive the plug out of the rear of the engine and cause an oil leak.

10. Install the camshaft retaining screw and tighten it to 30–40 ft. lbs. (41–54 Nm). This will draw the gear onto the camshaft as the screw is tightened. Standard running tolerance between the timing gears is 0.000–0.002 in. (0.00–0.05mm).

11. Install the timing gears with the marks aligned as shown.
12. Set the intake valve clearance to 0.020 in. (0.5mm) on the No. 1 cylinder.
13. Rotate the crankshaft until the No. 1 cylinder intake valve is ready to open as indicated by the IO mark on the flywheel. The mark should be centered in the hole.

➡ Some later models do not have an IO mark. TC and 5 degrees are the only marks. On these engines, the intake value opens at 9 degrees BTC. To estimate valve opening, measure the distance between TC and 5 degrees and measure about that distance further on. On CJ-3A models beginning with engine No. 130859, a 4½ in. (114.3mm) starter motor was used. To use the larger starter, it was necessary to increase the width of the cylinder block flange, partially covering the flywheel hole. This makes it impossible to use the hole for timing purposes. In this event, use the timing marks on the crankshaft pulley. If a replacement block is installed with the later design in a vehicle originally equipped with the earlier design timing marks, it will be necessary to cut away enough of the flange to allow a view of the timing marks, as no other timing marks exist on the these early engines.

Valve Timing

L4-134 ENGINES BEFORE NO. 175402 IN CJ-2A MODELS

▶ See Figures 142 and 143

1. Turn the crankshaft so that pistons Nos. 1 and 4 are positioned at Top Dead Center (TDC) as indicated by the TC mark on the flywheel seen through the timing hole in the right side of the flywheel housing.
2. Place the camshaft sprocket on the shaft and turn the shaft until the punch mark on the rim of the sprocket faces the punch mark on the crankshaft sprocket.
3. Remove the camshaft sprocket and install the sprocket and timing chain. Timing is correct when a line drawn through

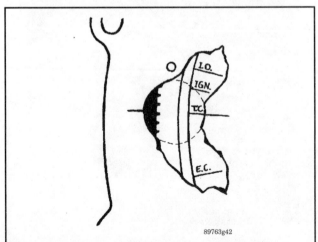

Fig. 142 View of the timing marks located on the flywheel and as seen through the view hole in the engine case — L4-134 engines before no. 175402

ENGINE AND ENGINE OVERHAUL　3-65

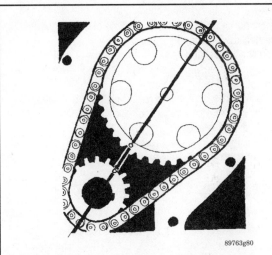

Fig. 143 Make certain that the timing gear marks are aligned as shown

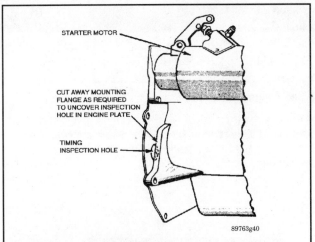

Fig. 145 If a replacement engine block was installed along with the original flywheel, the mounting flange on the engine must be cut away

the sprocket centers, intersects the timing marks on both sprockets.

L4-134 ENGINES AFTER ENGINE NO. 175402 AND ALL F4-134 ENGINES

▶ See Figures 144, 145 and 146

1. Install the timing gears with the marks aligned as shown.
2. Set the intake valve clearance to 0.020 in. (0.5mm) on the No. 1 cylinder.
3. Rotate the crankshaft until the No. 1 cylinder intake valve is ready to open as indicated by the IO mark on the flywheel. The mark should be centered in the hole.

➡Some later models do not have an IO mark. TC and 5 degrees are the only marks. On these engines, the intake valve opens at 9 degrees BTC. To estimate valve opening,

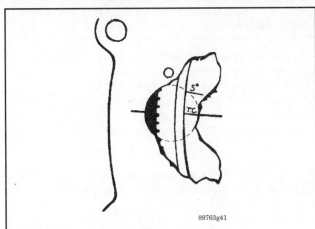

Fig. 144 View of the timing marks located on the flywheel and as seen through the view hole in the engine case — L4-134 engines after no. 175402 and all F4-134 engines

Fig. 146 Make certain, when installing the timing gears or setting the engine at TDC, that the timing marks are as close to each other as possible (as shown)

measure the distance between TC and 5 degrees and measure about that distance further on. On CJ-3A models beginning with engine No. 130859, a 4½ in. (114.3mm) starter motor was used. To use the larger starter, it was necessary to increase the width of the cylinder block flange, partially covering the flywheel hole. This makes it impossible to use the hole for timing purposes. In this event, use the timing marks on the crankshaft pulley. If a replacement block is installed with the later design in a vehicle originally equipped with the earlier design timing marks, it will be necessary to cut away enough of the flange to allow a view of the timing marks, as no other timing marks exist on the these early engines.

3-66 ENGINE AND ENGINE OVERHAUL

Camshaft

REMOVAL & INSTALLATION

♦ See Figures 147 and 148

➡Caution must be taken when performing this procedure. Camshaft bearings are coated with babble material, which can be damaged by scraping the camshaft lobes across the bearing.

4-134 Engines

1. Remove the engine.
2. Remove the exhaust manifold.
3. Remove the oil pump and the distributor.
4. Remove the crankshaft pulley.
5. Remove the cylinder head.
6. Remove the exhaust valves.
7. Remove the timing gear cover and the crankshaft and camshaft timing gears.
8. Remove the front end-plate.
9. Push the intake and exhaust valve lifters into the cylinder block as far as possible so that the ends of the lifters are not in contact with the camshaft.
10. Secure each tappet in the raised position by installing a clip type clothes pin on the shank of each tappet or tie them up in the plate and spacer.
11. Remove the crankshaft thrust plate attaching screws. Remove the camshaft thrust plate and spacer.
12. Pull the camshaft forward out of the cylinder block being careful to prevent damage to the camshaft bearing surfaces.

To install:

13. Slide the camshaft into the cylinder block being careful to prevent damage to the camshaft bearing surfaces.
14. Install the crankshaft thrust plate attaching screws. Install the camshaft thrust plate and spacer.
15. Remove the clothes pins.
16. Install the front end-plate.
17. Install the timing gear cover and the crankshaft and camshaft timing gears.
18. Install the exhaust valves.
19. Install the cylinder head.
20. Install the crankshaft pulley.
21. Install the oil pump and the distributor.
22. Install the exhaust manifold.
23. Install the engine.

6-225 Engine

1. Remove the engine.

✳✳CAUTION

When draining coolant, keep in mind that cats and dogs are attracted by ethylene glycol antifreeze, and are quite likely to drink any that is left in an uncovered container or in puddles on the ground. This will prove fatal in sufficient quantity. Always drain the coolant into a sealable container. Coolant should be reused unless it is contaminated or several years old.

2. Remove the intake manifold and carburetor assembly.
3. Remove the distributor.
4. Remove the fuel pump.
5. Remove the alternator, drive belts, cooling fan, fan pulley and water pump.
6. Remove the crankshaft pulley and the vibration damper.
7. Remove the oil pump.
8. Remove the timing chain cover.
9. Remove the timing chain and the camshaft sprocket, along with the distributor drive gear and the fuel pump eccentric.
10. Remove the rocker arm assemblies.

➡The pushrods need not be removed. But if they are, be sure that they are replaced in their original Positions.

11. Lift the tappets up so that they are not in contact with the camshaft. Use wire clips or clip type pins to hold the tappets up.
12. Carefully guide the camshaft forward out of the engine. Avoid marring the bearing surfaces.

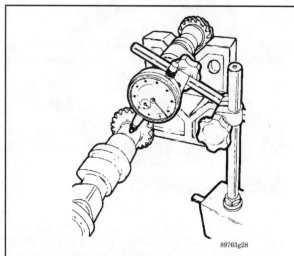

Fig. 147 A dial indicator mounted on a base can be used to check for camshaft straightness

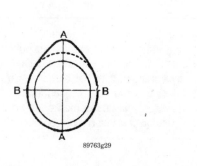

Fig. 148 To determine camshaft lobe height, subtract dimension B from dimension A

ENGINE AND ENGINE OVERHAUL 3-67

13. Coat all moving parts with an engine oil supplement, such as STP or its equivalent.
14. Slide the camshaft, carefully, into position. Avoid marring the bearing surfaces.
15. Drop the tappets back onto the camshaft.
16. Install the rocker arm assemblies.
17. Install the timing chain and the camshaft sprocket, along with the distributor drive gear and the fuel pump eccentric.
18. Install the timing chain cover.
19. Install the oil pump.
20. Install the crankshaft pulley and the vibration damper.
21. Install the alternator, drive belts, cooling fan, fan pulley and water pump.
22. Install the fuel pump.
23. Install the distributor.
24. Install the intake manifold and carburetor assembly.
25. Install the engine.

6-226 Engine

1. Drain the cooling system and remove the radiator.

✱✱CAUTION

When draining coolant, keep in mind that cats and dogs are attracted by ethylene glycol antifreeze, and are quite likely to drink any that is left in an uncovered container or in puddles on the ground. This will prove fatal in sufficient quantity. Always drain the coolant into a sealable container. Coolant should be reused unless it is contaminated or several years old.

2. Remove the timing chain and gears as described earlier.
3. Remove the fuel pump.
4. Remove the cylinder head.
5. Remove the oil pan.
6. Remove the oil pump.
7. Remove the tappet chamber cover.
8. Remove the valves and springs as described earlier.
9. Pull the tappets up and hold them in the up position with spring-type clothes pins.
10. Remove the camshaft thrust plate from the front of the block.
11. Pull the camshaft from the front of the block, being **very** careful to avoid damaging the journals and bearings.
12. Thoroughly clean the camshaft in a safe solvent.
13. Check the journals with a micrometer. If any journal is more than 0.001 in. (0.0254mm) out of round, the camshaft should be replaced.
14. Camshaft faces should not show any wear or scoring. Total camshaft run-out should not exceed 0.002 in. (0.0508mm). Replace the camshaft if it is at all suspect.
15. With an inside micrometer, check the bearing diameter. If any bearing is more than 0.004 in. (0.1016mm) oversize, it should be replaced. **All bearings must be replaced as a set, if any one is worn or damaged.**
16. To remove the bearings, remove the core plug at the rear of the block and insert a bearing puller. Remove the bearings one at a time.
17. When installing new bearings, replace them one at a time, making sure that the oil holes are aligned. When installing the front bearing, the small groove from the oil hole must be toward the front of the engine. Coat the rim of the core plug with gasket sealer before installing it.
18. Coat the camshaft with clean engine oil and slide it into place. Install the thrust plate and tighten the bolts to 182 inch lbs. (20 Nm).
19. Drop the tappets onto the camshaft.
20. Install the valves and springs as described earlier.
21. Install the tappet chamber cover.
22. Install the oil pump.
23. Install the oil pan.
24. Install the cylinder head.
25. Install the fuel pump.
26. Install the timing chain and gears as described earlier.
27. Install the radiator.
28. Fill the cooling system and road test the car.

6-230 Engine

1. Remove the cylinder head.
2. Lift the rocker arm guide from the head.
3. Check the rocker arms to determine which ones do not have tension against them. Turn these parallel to the camshaft.
4. Remove tension on the remaining rocker arms by backing off on the adjusting nuts. Then, turn these parallel to the camshaft.
5. Unbolt the camshaft retainer from the camshaft bearing support deck. Remove the retainer. Some engines have a shim between the retainer and deck. Do not lose it!
6. Pull forward on the camshaft to remove it from the deck.
7. Unbolt and remove the camshaft bearing support deck from the head.
8. Inspect the camshaft for wear or damage. Camshaft runout should not exceed 0.0005 in. (0.0127mm). Camshaft bearing clearance should not exceed 0.004 in. (0.1016mm).
9. Coat all parts with engine oil supplement prior to installation. Do not forget the shim, if one was there to begin with. If a new camshaft bearing support deck is being installed, determine if a shim is needed. To do this, measure the distance between the centerline of the camshaft bearing deck front mounting holes and the retainer surface on the deck. If the dimension is 0.810 in. (20.574mm), the retainer is to be installed without a shim. If the dimension is 0.780 in. (19.812mm), a shim is required.
10. Install the camshaft bearing support deck on the head. Tighten the nuts to 146-182 inch lbs. (16-20 Nm).
11. Slide the camshaft into the deck.
12. Install the retainer. Some engines have a shim between the retainer and deck. Tighten the nuts to 146-182 inch lbs. (16-20 Nm).
13. Adjust the valves.
14. Install the rocker arm guide on the head.
15. Install the cylinder head.

Pistons and Connecting Rods

REMOVAL

▶ See Figures 149, 150, 151, 152, 153, 154, 155 and 156

➡In most cases, this procedure is easier with the engine out of the vehicle

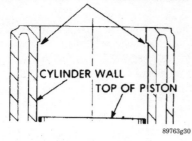

Fig. 149 Before removal of the piston is possible, the ridge must be ground down with a ridge reamer

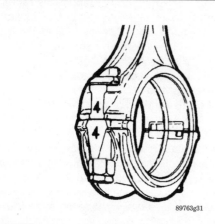

Fig. 150 When removing the piston/connecting rod assemblies, make certain to matchmark the rod bearing caps with the rods

Fig. 151 Place rubber hose over the connecting rod studs to protect the crank and bores from damage

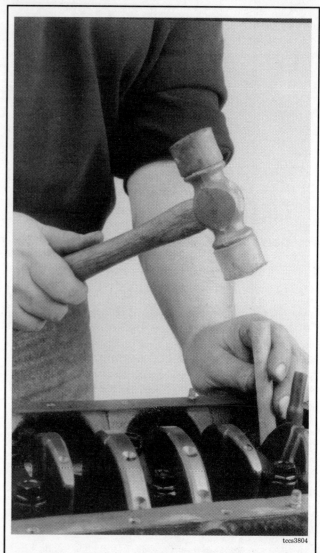

Fig. 152 Carefully tap the piston out of the bore using a wooden dowel

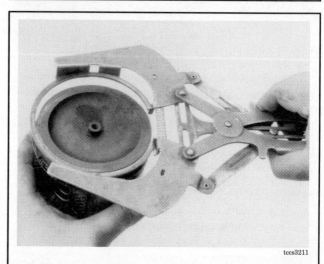

Fig. 153 Use a ring expander tool to remove the piston rings

ENGINE AND ENGINE OVERHAUL 3-69

Fig. 154 Clean the piston grooves using a ring groove cleaner

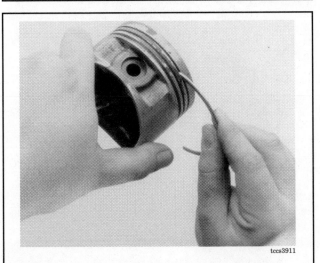

Fig. 155 You can use a piece of an old ring to clean the piston grooves, BUT be careful, the ring is sharp

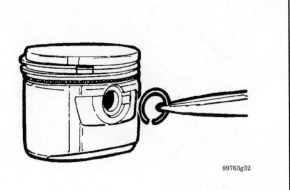

Fig. 156 To separate the pistons from the connecting rods on some engines, remove the piston pin lockrings (if applicable)

1. Remove the head(s).
2. Remove the oil pan.
3. Rotate the engine to bring each piston, in turn, to the bottom of its stroke. With the piston bottomed, use a ridge reamer to remove the ridge at the top of the cylinder. **Do not cut too deeply!**
4. Matchmark the rods and caps. If the pistons are to be removed from the connecting rod, mark the cylinder number on the piston with a silver pencil or quick drying paint for proper cylinder identification and cap-to-rod location. Remove the connecting rod cap nuts and lift off the rod caps, keeping them in order. Install a guide hose over the threads of the rod bolts. This is to prevent damage to the bearing journal and rod bolt threads.
5. Using a hammer handle, push the piston and rod assemblies up out of the block.

PISTON PIN REPLACEMENT

Use care at all times when handling and servicing connecting rods and pistons. To prevent possible damage to these units, do not clamp the rod or piston in a vise since they may become distorted. Do not allow the pistons to strike against one another, against hard objects or bench surfaces, since distortion of the piston contour or nicks in the soft aluminum material may result.

1. Remove the piston rings using a suitable piston ring remover.
2. Remove the piston pin lock ring, if used. Install the guide bushing of the piston pin removing and installing tool.
3. Install the piston and connecting rod assembly on a support, and place the assembly in an arbor press. Press the pin out of the connecting rod, using the appropriate piston pin tool.
4. Assembly is the reverse of disassembly. Use new lock rings where needed.

INSPECTION

Cylinder Block

Check the cylinder walls for evidence of rust, which would indicate a cracked block. Check the block face for distortion with a straightedge. Maximum distortion variance is 0.005 in. (0.127mm). The block cannot be planed, so it will have to be replaced if too distorted. Using a micrometer, check the cylinders for out-of-roundness.

Connecting Rods and Bearings
▶ See Figures 157 and 158

Wash connecting rods in cleaning solvent and dry with compressed air. Check for twisted or bent rods and inspect for nicks or cracks. Replace connecting rods that are damaged.
Inspect journals for roughness and wear. Slight roughness may be removed with a fine grit polishing cloth saturated with engine oil. Burrs may be removed with a fine oil stone by moving the stone on the journal circumference. Do not move the stone back and forth across the journal. If the journals are scored or ridged, the crankshaft must be replaced.

3-70 ENGINE AND ENGINE OVERHAUL

The connecting rod journals should be checked for out-of-round and correct size with a micrometer.

➡ Crankshaft rod journals will normally be standard size. If any undersized bearings are used, the size will be stamped on a counterweight. If plastic gauging material is to be used:

1. Clean oil from the journal bearing cap, connecting rod and outer and inner surfaces of the bearing inserts. Position the insert so that the tang is properly aligned with the notch in the rod and cap.
2. Place a piece of plastic gauging material in the center of lower bearing shell.
3. Remove the bearing cap and determine the bearing clearances by comparing the width of the flattened plastic gauging material at its widest point with the graduation on the container. The number within the graduation on the envelope indicates the clearance in thousandths of an inch or millimeters. If this clearance is excessive, replace the bearing and recheck the clearance with the plastic gauging material. Lubricate the bearing with engine oil before installation. Repeat the procedure on the remaining connecting rod bearings. All rods must be connected to their journals when rotating the crankshaft, to prevent engine damage.

Pistons

▶ See Figure 159

Clean varnish from piston skirts and pins with a cleaning solvent. **Do not wire brush any part of the piston.** Clean the ring grooves with a groove cleaner and make sure oil ring holes and slots are clean.

Inspect the piston for cracked ring lands, skirts or pin bosses, wavy or worn ring lands, scuffed or damaged skirts, eroded areas at the top of the piston. Replace pistons that are damaged or show signs of excessive wear. Inspect the grooves for nicks or burrs that might cause the rings to hang up.

Measure piston skirt (across center line of piston pin) and check piston clearance.

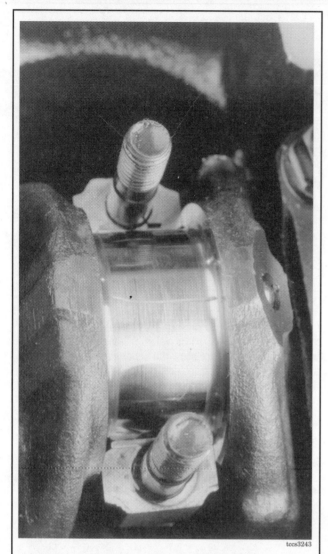

Fig. 157 Apply a strip of gauging material to the bearing journal, then install and torque the cap

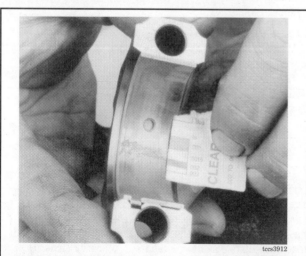

Fig. 158 After the cap is removed again, use the scale supplied with the gauge material to check clearances

Fig. 159 Measure the piston's outer diameter using a micrometer

ENGINE AND ENGINE OVERHAUL 3-71

MEASURING THE OLD PISTONS

♦ See Figure 160

Check used piston-to-cylinder bore clearance as follows:
1. Measure the cylinder bore diameter with a telescope gauge.
2. Measure the piston diameter. When measuring the pistons for size or taper, measurements must be made with the piston pin removed.
3. Subtract the piston diameter from the cylinder bore diameter to determine piston-to-bore clearance.
4. Compare the piston-to-bore clearances obtained with those clearances recommended. Determine if the piston-to-bore clearance is in the acceptable range.
5. When measuring taper, the largest reading must be at the bottom of the skirt.

SELECTING NEW PISTONS

1. If the used piston is not acceptable, check the service piston size and determine if a new piston can be selected. (Service pistons are available in standard, high limit and standard oversize.
2. If the cylinder bore must be reconditioned, measure the new piston diameter, then hone the cylinder bore to obtain the preferred clearance.
3. Select a new piston and mark the piston to identify the cylinder for which it was fitted. On some vehicles, oversize pistons may be found. These pistons will be 0.010 in. (0.254mm) oversize.

CYLINDER HONING

♦ See Figures 161 and 162

1. When cylinders are being honed, follow the manufacturer's recommendations for the use of the hone.
2. Occasionally, during the honing operation, the cylinder bore should be thoroughly cleaned and the selected piston checked for correct fit.
3. When finish-honing a cylinder bore, the hone should be moved up and down at a sufficient speed to obtain a very fine

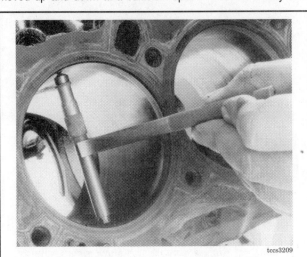

Fig. 160 A telescoping gauge may be used to measure the cylinder bore diameter

Fig. 161 Using a ball type cylinder hone is an easy way to hone the cylinder bore

Fig. 162 A properly cross-hatched cylinder bore

uniform surface finish in a cross-hatch pattern of approximately 45-65 degrees included angle. The finish marks should be clean but not sharp, free from imbedded particles and torn or folded metal.
4. Permanently mark the piston for the cylinder to which it has been fitted and proceed to hone the remaining cylinders.

➡Handle the pistons with care. Do not attempt to force the pistons through the cylinders until the cylinders have been honed to the correct size. Pistons can be distorted through careless handling.

5. Thoroughly clean the bores with hot water and detergent. Scrub well with a stiff bristle brush and rinse thoroughly with hot water. It is extremely essential that a good cleaning operation be performed. If any of the abrasive material is allowed to remain in the cylinder bores, it will rapidly wear the new rings and cylinder bores. The bores should be swabbed several times with light engine oil and a clean cloth and then wiped with a clean dry cloth. **Cylinders should not be cleaned with kerosene or gasoline.** Clean the remainder of the

3-72 ENGINE AND ENGINE OVERHAUL

cylinder block to remove the excess material spread during the honing operation.

CHECKING CYLINDER BORE

♦ See Figure 160

Cylinder bore size can be measured with inside micrometers or a cylinder gauge. The most wear will occur at the top of the ring travel.

Reconditioned cylinder bores should be held to not more than 0.001 in. (0.025mm) taper.

If the cylinder bores are smooth, the cylinder walls should not be deglazed. If the cylinder walls are scored, the walls may have to be honed before installing new rings. It is important that reconditioned cylinder bores be thoroughly washed with a soap and water solution to remove all traces of abrasive material to eliminate premature wear.

RING TOLERANCES

When installing new rings, ring gap and side clearance should be checked as follows:

Piston Ring and Rail Gap

Each ring and rail gap must be measured with the ring or rail positioned squarely and at the bottom of the ring travel area of the bore.

Side Clearance

♦ See Figure 163

Each ring must be checked for side clearance in its respective piston groove by inserting a feeler gauge between the ring and its upper land. The piston grooves must be cleaned before checking the ring for side clearance specifications. To check oil ring side clearance, the oil rings must be installed on the piston.

PISTON RING REPLACEMENT

For service ring specifications and detailed installation productions, refer to the instructions furnished with the parts package.

PISTON ASSEMBLY & INSTALLATION

♦ See Figures 164, 165, 166 and 167

1. Using a ring expander, install new rings in the grooves, with their gaps staggered to be 270° apart.
2. Using a straightedge, check the rods for straightness. Check, also, for cracks. Before assembling the block, it's a good idea to have the block checked for cracks with Magnaflux® or its equivalent.
3. Install the pins and retainers.
4. Coat the pistons with clean engine oil and apply a ring compressor. Position the assembly over the cylinder bore and slide the piston into the cylinder slowly, taking care to avoid

Fig. 163 Checking the ring side clearance

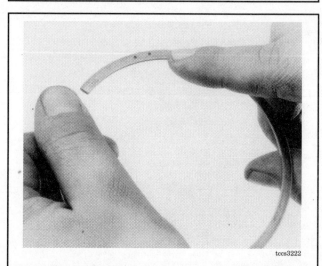

Fig. 164 Most rings are marked to show which side should face upward

ENGINE AND ENGINE OVERHAUL 3-73

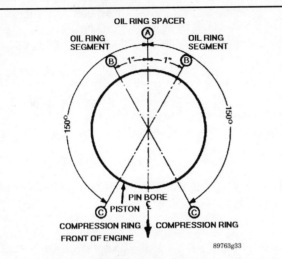

Fig. 165 When installing the piston rings, make certain to position the ring gaps as shown

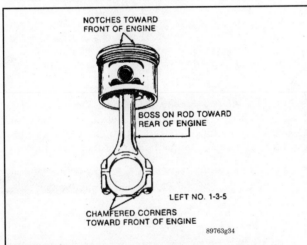

Fig. 166 When installing the piston/connecting rods on the left bank of the 6-225 engine, take note of the directional markings as shown

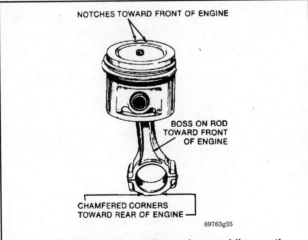

Fig. 167 The piston/connecting rod assemblies on the right bank of the 6-225 engine share the same directional markings

nicking the walls. The pistons will have a mark on the crown, such as a groove or notch or stamped symbol. This mark indicates the side of the piston which should face front. Lower the piston slowly, until it bottoms on the crankshaft. A good idea is to cover the rod studs with length of rubber hose to avoid nicking the crank journals. Assemble the rod caps at this time. Check the rod bearing clearances using Plastigage®, going by the instructions on the package.

5. Install the bearing caps with the stamped numbers matched. Tighten the caps to the figure shown in the Torque Specifications Chart. See the accompanying illustrations for proper piston and rod installation.

Rear Main Oil Seal

REPLACEMENT

4-134 Engines

♦ See Figure 168

➡On early L-head 4-134 engines, the rear bearing is sealed by a wick packing. This packing is installed in a groove machined into the rear main bearing cap. On later L-head 4-134 and all F-head 4-134 engines, a steel-backed lip seal is used. This seal can be used to replace the older wick seal, and can be replaced without removing the crankshaft.

WICK-TYPE SEALS

1. Remove the engine from the vehicle.
2. Remove the timing chain cover and crankshaft timing gear.
3. Remove the oil pan and pick-up unit.
4. Slide the thrust washers and adjusting shims off the front end of the crankshaft.
5. Move the two pieces of the rear main cap packing away from the sides of the cap.
6. Note the numbers of the main caps and block for position when installing.

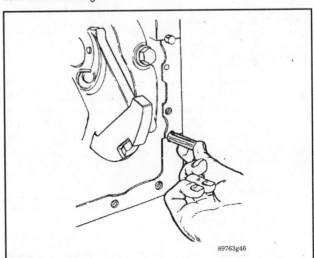

Fig. 168 Rear bearing cap packing used in late L-head and all F-head 4-134 engines

ENGINE AND ENGINE OVERHAUL

7. Unbolt and remove the main bearing caps.

※※WARNING

Take great care in removing the caps. Lift them evenly and avoid binding on the dowels. If you suspect that any of the dowels were bent during removal, replace them.

8. Unbolt and remove the connecting rod caps, taking care to note their position for installation.
9. Lift out the crankshaft.
10. Remove the rear main seal wicking from the grooves.
11. If a steel-backed lip-type seal is being used to replace the older style wicking, go on to the next procedure for later L4-134 and all F4-134 engines. If a wick-type seal is being used, clean the seal grooves, and insert the seal in the grooves with your fingers.
12. Using a round piece of wood, roll the seal tightly into the groove starting at one end and working toward the center, then the other end toward the center.
13. A small portion of the packing will protrude above the surface of the cap. This should be cut off flush with the cap at each end.

LIP-TYPE SEALS

The following procedure should be used for later L4-134 and all F4-134 engines with steel-backed lip type seals.

1. Raise and support the vehicle on jackstands.
2. Remove the oil pan.
3. Remove the rear main bearing cap.
4. Using a center punch, drive the upper seal out of its groove just far enough to grasp it with a pliers, and pull it the rest of the way.
5. Apply a light film of chassis grease to the lower seal and install it in the cap.
6. Install the rubber packings in the upper crankcase half. The packings are of a predetermined length to allow about $1/4$ in. (6mm) protrusion. This protrusion is necessary for a positive seal. **Do not trim these seals!**
7. Apply a small amount of RTV sealant to both sides and face of the bearing cap and install it.
8. Tighten the cap to the figure shown in the torque specifications chart.
9. Install the oil pan.

6-225 Engine

➡ **For removal of both upper and lower seals, the crankshaft must be removed from the engine. Crankshaft removal is easiest with the engine out of the vehicle.**

1. Remove the engine form the vehicle as described earlier in this section.
2. Remove the timing case and gears, and any spacers and shims from the front of the crankshaft.
3. Remove the oil pan and oil pick-up.
4. Note the mating of crankshaft and main caps. Matchmark them with an indelible ink marker.
5. Unbolt the No. 1 main bearing cap. Using a prybar, carefully lift the cap from the dowels. Take great care to avoid damaging the dowels. Any bent dowels must be replaced.
6. In the same manner, remove the next two caps.
7. To remove the rear cap, rear main bearing bolt remover, special tool W-323 or its equivalent must be used.
8. Matchmark the connecting rod caps and remove them.
9. Lift out the crankshaft.
10. Remove the braided seal from the inner groove of the cap and the neoprene seals from the outer grooves.
11. Using a center punch, drive the block seal out just far enough to grasp with a pliers and pull out.
12. Dip a new block seal in engine oil and force it into place in the block.
13. Insert the new braided cap seal into the groove in the cap and coat it with engine oil.
14. Cut the ends of the braided seals flush with the cap and block surfaces.
15. The new neoprene seals are installed after the cap is tightened in place. These seals are supposed to project about $1/16$ in. (1.5875mm) above the cap. **Do not cut these seals flush with the cap!** Before installation, dip the neoprene seals in kerosene for about 12 minutes. After installation squirt some more kerosene on the protruding ends of the seals. Then, peen the ends of the seals with a hammer to make sure of a tight seal at the upper parting line between the cap and block.
16. Installation of the crankshaft and remaining parts is the reverse of removal. Tighten the main cap bolts evenly, one side then the other, a little at a time until the torque value is reached.

➡ **Whenever the second cap is removed, the thrust surfaces must be aligned. To do this, pry the crankshaft back and forth several times throughout its end travel with the cap bolts of the second main cap only finger-tight.**

Crankshaft

REMOVAL

4-134 Engines

1. Remove the engine from the vehicle.
2. Remove the fan, hub, timing cover, pulleys and timing gears from the engine.
3. Slide the thrust washers and adjusting shims from the front end of the crankshaft. Be careful to avoid losing or mismatching the washers and shims!
4. Remove the oil pan and pick-up.
5. Pull the two pieces of the rear main cap packing out from the sides of the cap.
6. Note the matchmarks on the bearing caps and remove the nuts and washers from the cap dowels.
7. Using a prybar under the ends of each main cap, carefully lift the caps off the dowels. Take great care to avoid damage to the caps or dowels, as bent dowels must be replaced.
8. Note the matchmarks on the connecting rod caps and remove the bearing caps from the rods.
9. Lift the crankshaft from the block.

6-225 Engine

1. Remove the engine and mount it on a work stand.
2. Remove the flywheel.

ENGINE AND ENGINE OVERHAUL 3-75

3. Remove the fan and hub.
4. Remove the crankshaft pulley and vibration damper.
5. Remove the timing chain and sprocket.
6. Remove the oil pan, and pick-up.
7. Remove the connecting rod caps, marking them for reassembly.
8. Mark the main bearing caps.
9. Remove the two bolts from the cap and carefully lift it off with the aid of a prybar. Similarly remove the next two caps.
10. To remove the last cap, a special tool, main bearing bolt remover W-323 is necessary.
11. Lift the crankshaft from the block.

INSPECTION

1. Check the crankshaft for wear or damage to the bearing surfaces of the journals. Crankshafts that are damaged can be reconditioned by a professional machine shop.
2. Using a dial indicator, check the crankshaft journal run-out. Measure the crankshaft journals with a micrometer to determine the correct size rod and main bearings to be used. Whenever a new or reconditioned crankshaft is installed, new connecting rod bearings and main bearings should be installed.
3. Clean all oil passages in the block (and crankshaft if it is being reused).

➡ **A new rear main seal should be installed any time the crankshaft is removed or replaced.**

4. Wipe the oil from the crankshaft journal and the outer and inner surfaces of the bearing shell.
5. Place a piece of plastic gauging material in the center of the bearing.
6. Use a floor jack or other means to hold the crankshaft against the upper bearing shell. This is necessary to obtain accurate clearance readings when using plastic gauging material.
7. Install the bearing cap and bearing. Place engine oil on the cap bolts and install. Tighten the bolts to specification.
8. Remove the bearing cap and determine the bearing clearance by comparing the width of the flattened plastic gauging material at its widest point with the graduations on the gauging material container. The number within the graduation on the envelope indicates the clearance in millimeters or thousandths of an inch. If the clearance is greater than allowed, **replace both bearing shells as a set**. Recheck the clearance after replacing the shells.

INSTALLATION

➡ **Main bearing clearances must be corrected by the use of selective upper and lower shells. UNDER NO CIRCUMSTANCES should the use of shims behind the shells to compensate for wear be attempted.**

1. Install new bearing upper halves in the block. If the crankshaft has been turned to resurface the journals, undersized bearing must be used to compensate. Lay the crankshaft in the block.
2. Install the lower bearing halves in the caps.

3. Use Plastigage® to check bearing fit.
4. When the bearings are properly fitted, install and tighten the bearing caps.
5. Check crankshaft end-play to determine the need for thrust washers.
6. While you're at it, it's a good idea to replace the rear main seal at this time.
7. Install sufficient oil pan bolts in the block to align with the connecting rod bolts. Use rubber bands between the bolts to position the connecting rods as required. Connecting rod position can be adjusted by increasing the tension on the rubber bands with additional turns around the pan bolts or thread protectors.
8. Position the upper half of main bearings in the block and lubricate them with engine oil.
9. Position crankshaft key way in the same position as removed and lower it into block. The connecting rods will follow the crank pins into the correct position as the crankshaft is lowered.
10. Lubricate the thrust flanges with clean engine oil or engine rebuilding oil. Install caps with the lower half of the bearings lubricated with engine oil. Lubricate the cap bolts with engine oil and install, but do not tighten.
11. With a block of wood, bump the shaft in each direction to align the thrust flanges of the main bearing. After bumping the shaft in each direction, wedge the shaft to the front and hold it while torquing the thrust bearing cap bolts.

➡ **In order to prevent the possibility of cylinder block and/or main bearing cap damage, the main bearing caps are to be tapped into their cylinder block cavity using a wood or rubber mallet before the bolts are installed. Do not use attaching bolts to pull the main bearing caps into their seats. Failure to observe this information may damage the cylinder block or a bearing cap.**

12. Tighten all main bearing caps to specification. Check crankshaft end-play, using a flat feeler gauge.
13. Remove the connecting rod bolt thread protectors and lubricate the connecting rod bearings with engine oil.
14. Install the connecting rod bearing caps in their original position. Tighten the nuts to specification.
15. Install all parts in reverse order of removal. See related procedures in this section for component installation.

Flywheel/Flexplate and Ring Gear

➡ **Flexplate is the term for a flywheel mated with an automatic transmission.**

REMOVAL & INSTALLATION

All Engines

➡ **The ring gear is replaceable only on engines mated with a manual transmission. Engine with automatic transmissions have ring gears which are welded to the flexplate.**

1. Remove the transmission and transfer case.
2. Remove the clutch, if equipped, or torque converter from the flywheel. The flywheel bolts should be loosened a little at a time in a cross pattern to avoid warping the flywheel. On Jeep

3-76 ENGINE AND ENGINE OVERHAUL

vehicles with manual transmission, replace the pilot bearing in the end of the crankshaft if removing the flywheel.

3. The flywheel should be checked for cracks and glazing. It can be resurfaced by a machine shop.

4. If the ring gear is to be replaced, drill a hole in the gear between two teeth, being careful not to contact the flywheel surface. Using a cold chisel at this point, crack the ring gear and remove it.

5. Polish the inner surface of the new ring gear and heat it in an oven to about 600°F (316°C). Quickly place the ring gear on the flywheel and tap it into place, making sure that it is fully seated.

→Never heat the ring gear past 800°F (426°C), or the tempering will be destroyed

6. Position the flywheel on the end of the crankshaft. Tighten the bolts a little at a time, in a cross pattern, to the torque figure shown in the Torque Specifications Chart.

7. Install the clutch or torque converter.

8. Install the transmission and transfer case.

EXHAUST SYSTEM

General Information

♦ See Figure 169

→Safety glasses should be worn at all times when working on or near the exhaust system. Older exhaust systems will almost always be covered with loose rust particles which will shower you when disturbed. These particles are more than a nuisance and could injure your eye.

Whenever working on the exhaust system always keep the following in mind:

- Check the complete exhaust system for open seams, holes loose connections, or other deterioration which could permit exhaust fumes to seep into the passenger compartment.
- The exhaust system is usually supported by free-hanging rubber mountings which permit some movement of the exhaust system, but does not permit transfer of noise and vibration into the passenger compartment. Do not replace the rubber mounts with solid ones.
- Before removing any component of the exhaust system, ALWAYS squirt a liquid rust dissolving agent onto the fasteners for ease of removal. A lot of knuckle skin will be saved by following this rule. It may even be wise to spray the fasteners and allow them to sit overnight.

✳✳CAUTION

Allow the exhaust system to cool sufficiently before spraying a solvent exhaust fasteners. Some solvents are highly flammable and could ignite when sprayed on hot exhaust components.

- Annoying rattles and noise vibrations in the exhaust system are usually caused by misalignment of the parts. When aligning the system, leave all bolts and nuts loose until all parts are properly aligned, then tighten, working from front to rear.
- When installing exhaust system parts, make sure there is enough clearance between the hot exhaust parts and pipes and hoses that would be adversely affected by excessive heat. Also make sure there is adequate clearance from the floor pan to avoid possible overheating of the floor.

Muffler

REMOVAL & INSTALLATION

→The following applies to exhaust systems using clamped joints. Most later model, original equipment systems use welded joints at the muffler. These joints will, of course, have to be cut.

1. Raise and support the rear end on jackstands, placed under the frame, so that the axle hangs freely.
2. Remove the muffler clamps.
3. Remove the tail pipe hanger clamp.
4. Spray the joint liberally with a penetrant/rust dissolver compound such as Liquid Wrench®, WD-40®, or equivalent.
5. If the tail pipe cannot be pulled or twisted free from the muffler, drive a chisel between the muffler and tail pipe at several places to free it.
6. Disconnect the muffler hanger.
7. If the pipe leading into the muffler is not to be replaced, and cannot be pulled free of the muffler, heat the joint with an oxyacetylene torch until it is cherry red. Place a block of wood against the front of the muffler and drive it rearward to disengage it from the pipe. If the pipe is being replaced, use a chisel to free it.

✳✳CAUTION

When using a torch, make certain that no combustibles, brake or fuel lines are in the immediate area of the torch.

8. When installing the new muffler, make sure that the locator slot and tab at the tail pipe joint index each other.
9. Drive the muffler onto the front pipe.
10. Position the system, without muffler clamps, under the Jeep and install the hangers. Make certain that there is sufficient clearance between the system components and the floor pan and axle. Then, install the muffler clamps and tighten the hangers.

→Install the muffler clamps so that the shafts of the U-bolts covers the slots in the joint flanges.

ENGINE AND ENGINE OVERHAUL

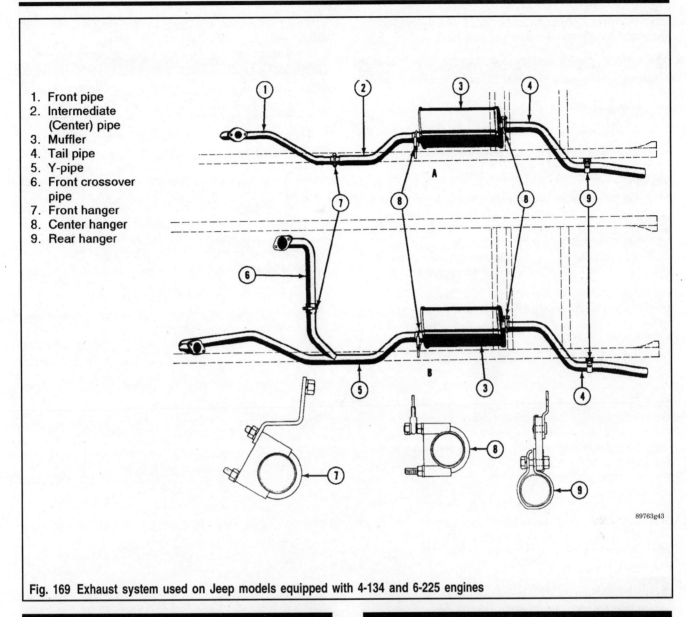

1. Front pipe
2. Intermediate (Center) pipe
3. Muffler
4. Tail pipe
5. Y-pipe
6. Front crossover pipe
7. Front hanger
8. Center hanger
9. Rear hanger

Fig. 169 Exhaust system used on Jeep models equipped with 4-134 and 6-225 engines

Front Exhaust Pipe (Head Pipe)

REMOVAL & INSTALLATION

1. Raise and support the front end on jackstands.
2. Disconnect any oxygen sensor wires or air injection pipes.
3. Disconnect the front pipe at the manifold(s).
4. Disconnect the rear end of the pipe from the muffler or catalytic converter.
5. Installation is the reverse of removal. Tighten the pipe-to-manifold nuts to 17 ft. lbs. (23 Nm) on 4-cylinder engines, or 20 ft. lbs. (27 Nm). on the 6-225 engine. Make sure the pipe is properly aligned.

Rear Exhaust Pipe or Tailpipe

REMOVAL & INSTALLATION

➡ Some vehicles use an intermediate pipe, also called a rear exhaust pipe. This pipe connects the front pipe with the muffler, or runs between the converter and muffler.

1. Raise and support the rear end on jackstands.
2. If just the intermediate pipe is being replaced, cut it at the joints and collapse and remove the remainder from the front pipe and muffler or converter. If adjoining parts are also being replaced, the pipe may be chiseled off.
3. If just the tail pipe is being replaced, cut it just behind the muffler and collapse and remove the remainder from the muffler flange. Remove the tail pipe hanger.
4. When installing any pipe, position it in the system and make sure that it is properly aligned and has sufficient clearance at the floor pan. Position U-bolts so that the bolt shafts

ENGINE AND ENGINE OVERHAUL

cover any slots in the pipe flanges. When the system is correctly aligned, tighten all U-bolts and hangers.

Catalytic Converter

REMOVAL & INSTALLATION

1. Raise and support the rear end on jackstands.
2. Disconnect the downstream air injection tube at the converter.
3. On the 4-cylinder engine, the front pipe is bolted to the converter at a facing flange. On the 6-225 engine, the front pipe and converter are clamped together at a slip-fit joint. On all engines, the rear joint of the converter is a slip-fit.
4. To avoid damaging any components, it will probably be necessary to heat any slip-fit joint with an oxyacetylene torch, until the joint is cherry red. Then, place a block of wood against the converter and drive it off of the pipe.

✴✴CAUTION

When using a torch, make certain that no combustibles or brake or fuel lines are in the immediate area of the torch.

5. Position the replacement converter in the system and install the rear clamp. Hand tighten the nuts.
6. On 4-cylinder engines: bolt the flanges together at the front end. Tighten the bolts to 25 ft. lbs. (34 Nm). Tighten the rear clamp nuts to 45 ft. lbs. (61 Nm).
7. On the 6-225 engine, install the front clamp, make sure that the converter is properly positioned and tighten the front and rear clamp nuts to 45 ft. lbs. (61 Nm).
8. Install the downstream air injection tube and tighten the clamps to 36-48 inch lbs. (4.0-5.4 Nm).
9. Lower the Jeep.

ENGINE AND ENGINE OVERHAUL 3-79

USING A VACUUM GAUGE

White needle = steady needle   Dark needle = drifting needle

The vacuum gauge is one of the most useful and easy-to-use diagnostic tools. It is inexpensive, easy to hook up, and provides valuable information about the condition of your engine.

Indication: Normal engine in good condition

Gauge reading: Steady, from 17–22 in./Hg.

Indication: Sticking valve or ignition miss

Gauge reading: Needle fluctuates from 15–20 in./Hg. at idle

Indication: Late ignition or valve timing, low compression, stuck throttle valve, leaking carburetor or manifold gasket.

Gauge reading: Low (15–20 in./Hg.) but steady

Indication: Improper carburetor adjustment, or minor intake leak at carburetor or manifold

NOTE: *Bad fuel injector O-rings may also cause this reading.*

Gauge reading: Drifting needle

Indication: Weak valve springs, worn valve stem guides, or leaky cylinder head gasket (vibrating excessively at all speeds).

NOTE: *A plugged catalytic converter may also cause this reading.*

Gauge reading: Needle fluctuates as engine speed increases

Indication: Burnt valve or improper valve clearance. The needle will drop when the defective valve operates.

Gauge reading: Steady needle, but drops regularly

Indication: Choked muffler or obstruction in system. Speed up the engine. Choked muffler will exhibit a slow drop of vacuum to zero.

Gauge reading: Gradual drop in reading at idle

Indication: Worn valve guides

Gauge reading: Needle vibrates excessively at idle, but steadies as engine speed increases

Troubleshooting Basic Charging System Problems

Problem	Cause	Solution
Noisy alternator	• Loose mountings • Loose drive pulley • Worn bearings • Brush noise • Internal circuits shorted (High pitched whine)	• Tighten mounting bolts • Tighten pulley • Replace alternator • Replace alternator • Replace alternator
Squeal when starting engine or accelerating	• Glazed or loose belt	• Replace or adjust belt
Indicator light remains on or ammeter indicates discharge (engine running)	• Broken fan belt • Broken or disconnected wires • Internal alternator problems • Defective voltage regulator	• Install belt • Repair or connect wiring • Replace alternator • Replace voltage regulator
Car light bulbs continually burn out—battery needs water continually	• Alternator/regulator overcharging	• Replace voltage regulator/alternator
Car lights flare on acceleration	• Battery low • Internal alternator/regulator problems	• Charge or replace battery • Replace alternator/regulator
Low voltage output (alternator light flickers continually or ammeter needle wanders)	• Loose or worn belt • Dirty or corroded connections • Internal alternator/regulator problems	• Replace or adjust belt • Clean or replace connections • Replace alternator or regulator

Troubleshooting Basic Starting System Problems

Problem	Cause	Solution
Starter motor rotates engine slowly	• Battery charge low or battery defective • Defective circuit between battery and starter motor • Low load current • High load current	• Charge or replace battery • Clean and tighten, or replace cables • Bench-test starter motor. Inspect for worn brushes and weak brush springs. • Bench-test starter motor. Check engine for friction, drag or coolant in cylinders. Check ring gear-to-pinion gear clearance.
Starter motor will not rotate engine	• Battery charge low or battery defective • Faulty solenoid • Damage drive pinion gear or ring gear • Starter motor engagement weak • Starter motor rotates slowly with high load current • Engine seized	• Charge or replace battery • Check solenoid ground. Repair or replace as necessary. • Replace damaged gear(s) • Bench-test starter motor • Inspect drive yoke pull-down and point gap, check for worn end bushings, check ring gear clearance • Repair engine
Starter motor drive will not engage (solenoid known to be good)	• Defective contact point assembly • Inadequate contact point assembly ground • Defective hold-in coil	• Repair or replace contact point assembly • Repair connection at ground screw • Replace field winding assembly
Starter motor drive will not disengage	• Starter motor loose on flywheel housing • Worn drive end busing • Damaged ring gear teeth • Drive yoke return spring broken or missing	• Tighten mounting bolts • Replace bushing • Replace ring gear or driveplate • Replace spring
Starter motor drive disengages prematurely	• Weak drive assembly thrust spring • Hold-in coil defective	• Replace drive mechanism • Replace field winding assembly
Low load current	• Worn brushes • Weak brush springs	• Replace brushes • Replace springs

ENGINE AND ENGINE OVERHAUL

Troubleshooting Engine Mechanical Problems

Problem	Cause	Solution
External oil leaks	Fuel pump gasket broken or improperly seated	Replace gasket
	Cylinder head cover RTV sealant broken or improperly seated	Replace sealant; inspect cylinder head cover sealant flange and cylinder head sealant surface for distortion and cracks
	Oil filler cap leaking or missing	Replace cap
	Oil filter gasket broken or improperly seated	Replace oil filter
	Oil pan side gasket broken, improperly seated or opening in RTV sealant	Replace gasket or repair opening in sealant; inspect oil pan gasket flange for distortion
	Oil pan front oil seal broken or improperly seated	Replace seal; inspect timing case cover and oil pan seal flange for distortion
	Oil pan rear oil seal broken or improperly seated	Replace seal; inspect oil pan rear oil seal flange; inspect rear main bearing cap for cracks, plugged oil return channels, or distortion in seal groove
	Timing case cover oil seal broken or improperly seated	Replace seal
	Excess oil pressure because of restricted PCV valve	Replace PCV valve
	Oil pan drain plug loose or has stripped threads	Repair as necessary and tighten
	Rear oil gallery plug loose	Use appropriate sealant on gallery plug and tighten
	Rear camshaft plug loose or improperly seated	Seat camshaft plug or replace and seal, as necessary
	Distributor base gasket damaged	Replace gasket
Excessive oil consumption	Oil level too high	Drain oil to specified level
	Oil with wrong viscosity being used	Replace with specified oil
	PCV valve stuck closed	Replace PCV valve
	Valve stem oil deflectors (or seals) are damaged, missing, or incorrect type	Replace valve stem oil deflectors
	Valve stems or valve guides worn	Measure stem-to-guide clearance and repair as necessary
	Poorly fitted or missing valve cover baffles	Replace valve cover
	Piston rings broken or missing	Replace broken or missing rings
	Scuffed piston	Replace piston
	Incorrect piston ring gap	Measure ring gap, repair as necessary
	Piston rings sticking or excessively loose in grooves	Measure ring side clearance, repair as necessary
	Compression rings installed upside down	Repair as necessary
	Cylinder walls worn, scored, or glazed	Repair as necessary
	Piston ring gaps not properly staggered	Repair as necessary
	Excessive main or connecting rod bearing clearance	Measure bearing clearance, repair as necessary
No oil pressure	Low oil level	Add oil to correct level
	Oil pressure gauge, warning lamp or sending unit inaccurate	Replace oil pressure gauge or warning lamp
	Oil pump malfunction	Replace oil pump
	Oil pressure relief valve sticking	Remove and inspect oil pressure relief valve assembly
	Oil passages on pressure side of pump obstructed	Inspect oil passages for obstruction
	Oil pickup screen or tube obstructed	Inspect oil pickup for obstruction
	Loose oil inlet tube	Tighten or seal inlet tube

ENGINE AND ENGINE OVERHAUL

Troubleshooting Engine Mechanical Problems (cont.)

Problem	Cause	Solution
Low oil pressure	• Low oil level • Inaccurate gauge, warning lamp or sending unit • Oil excessively thin because of dilution, poor quality, or improper grade • Excessive oil temperature • Oil pressure relief spring weak or sticking • Oil inlet tube and screen assembly has restriction or air leak • Excessive oil pump clearance • Excessive main, rod, or camshaft bearing clearance	• Add oil to correct level • Replace oil pressure gauge or warning lamp • Drain and refill crankcase with recommended oil • Correct cause of overheating engine • Remove and inspect oil pressure relief valve assembly • Remove and inspect oil inlet tube and screen assembly. (Fill inlet tube with lacquer thinner to locate leaks.) • Measure clearances • Measure bearing clearances, repair as necessary
High oil pressure	• Improper oil viscosity • Oil pressure gauge or sending unit inaccurate • Oil pressure relief valve sticking closed	• Drain and refill crankcase with correct viscosity oil • Replace oil pressure gauge • Remove and inspect oil pressure relief valve assembly
Main bearing noise	• Insufficient oil supply • Main bearing clearance excessive • Bearing insert missing • Crankshaft end play excessive • Improperly tightened main bearing cap bolts • Loose flywheel or drive plate • Loose or damaged vibration damper	• Inspect for low oil level and low oil pressure • Measure main bearing clearance, repair as necessary • Replace missing insert • Measure end play, repair as necessary • Tighten bolts with specified torque • Tighten flywheel or drive plate attaching bolts • Repair as necessary
Connecting rod bearing noise	• Insufficient oil supply • Carbon build-up on piston • Bearing clearance excessive or bearing missing • Crankshaft connecting rod journal out-of-round • Misaligned connecting rod or cap • Connecting rod bolts tightened improperly	• Inspect for low oil level and low oil pressure • Remove carbon from piston crown • Measure clearance, repair as necessary • Measure journal dimensions, repair or replace as necessary • Repair as necessary • Tighten bolts with specified torque
Piston noise	• Piston-to-cylinder wall clearance excessive (scuffed piston) • Cylinder walls excessively tapered or out-of-round • Piston ring broken • Loose or seized piston pin • Connecting rods misaligned • Piston ring side clearance excessively loose or tight • Carbon build-up on piston is excessive	• Measure clearance and examine piston • Measure cylinder wall dimensions, rebore cylinder • Replace all rings on piston • Measure piston-to-pin clearance, repair as necessary • Measure rod alignment, straighten or replace • Measure ring side clearance, repair as necessary • Remove carbon from piston
Valve actuating component noise	• Insufficient oil supply	• Check for: (a) Low oil level (b) Low oil pressure (c) Plugged push rods (d) Wrong hydraulic tappets

ENGINE AND ENGINE OVERHAUL 3-83

Troubleshooting Engine Mechanical Problems (cont.)

Problem	Cause	Solution
Valve actuating component noise (cont.)		(e) Restricted oil gallery (f) Excessive tappet to bore clearance
	• Push rods worn or bent	• Replace worn or bent push rods
	• Rocker arms or pivots worn	• Replace worn rocker arms or pivots
	• Foreign objects or chips in hydraulic tappets	• Clean tappets
	• Excessive tappet leak-down	• Replace valve tappet
	• Tappet face worn	• Replace tappet; inspect corresponding cam lobe for wear
	• Broken or cocked valve springs	• Properly seat cocked springs; replace broken springs
	• Stem-to-guide clearance excessive	• Measure stem-to-guide clearance, repair as required
	• Valve bent	• Replace valve
	• Loose rocker arms	• Tighten bolts with specified torque
	• Valve seat runout excessive	• Regrind valve seat/valves
	• Missing valve lock	• Install valve lock
	• Push rod rubbing or contacting cylinder head	• Remove cylinder head and remove obstruction in head
	• Excessive engine oil (four-cylinder engine)	• Correct oil level

Troubleshooting the Cooling System

Problem	Cause	Solution
High temperature gauge indication—overheating	• Coolant level low	• Replenish coolant
	• Fan belt loose	• Adjust fan belt tension
	• Radiator hose(s) collapsed	• Replace hose(s)
	• Radiator airflow blocked	• Remove restriction (bug screen, fog lamps, etc.)
	• Faulty radiator cap	• Replace radiator cap
	• Ignition timing incorrect	• Adjust ignition timing
	• Idle speed low	• Adjust idle speed
	• Air trapped in cooling system	• Purge air
	• Heavy traffic driving	• Operate at fast idle in neutral intermittently to cool engine
	• Incorrect cooling system component(s) installed	• Install proper component(s)
	• Faulty thermostat	• Replace thermostat
	• Water pump shaft broken or impeller loose	• Replace water pump
	• Radiator tubes clogged	• Flush radiator
	• Cooling system clogged	• Flush system
	• Casting flash in cooling passages	• Repair or replace as necessary. Flash may be visible by removing cooling system components or removing core plugs.
	• Brakes dragging	• Repair brakes
	• Excessive engine friction	• Repair engine
	• Antifreeze concentration over 68%	• Lower antifreeze concentration percentage
	• Missing air seals	• Replace air seals
	• Faulty gauge or sending unit	• Repair or replace faulty component
	• Loss of coolant flow caused by leakage or foaming	• Repair or replace leaking component, replace coolant
	• Viscous fan drive failed	• Replace unit
Low temperature indication—undercooling	• Thermostat stuck open	• Replace thermostat
	• Faulty gauge or sending unit	• Repair or replace faulty component

Troubleshooting the Cooling System (cont.)

Problem	Cause	Solution
Coolant loss—boilover	• Overfilled cooling system	• Reduce coolant level to proper specification
	• Quick shutdown after hard (hot) run	• Allow engine to run at fast idle prior to shutdown
	• Air in system resulting in occasional "burping" of coolant	• Purge system
	• Insufficient antifreeze allowing coolant boiling point to be too low	• Add antifreeze to raise boiling point
	• Antifreeze deteriorated because of age or contamination	• Replace coolant
	• Leaks due to loose hose clamps, loose nuts, bolts, drain plugs, faulty hoses, or defective radiator	• Pressure test system to locate source of leak(s) then repair as necessary
	• Faulty head gasket	• Replace head gasket
	• Cracked head, manifold, or block	• Replace as necessary
	• Faulty radiator cap	• Replace cap
Coolant entry into crankcase or cylinder(s)	• Faulty head gasket	• Replace head gasket
	• Crack in head, manifold or block	• Replace as necessary
Coolant recovery system inoperative	• Coolant level low	• Replenish coolant to FULL mark
	• Leak in system	• Pressure test to isolate leak and repair as necessary
	• Pressure cap not tight or seal missing, or leaking	• Repair as necessary
	• Pressure cap defective	• Replace cap
	• Overflow tube clogged or leaking	• Repair as necessary
	• Recovery bottle vent restricted	• Remove restriction
Noise	• Fan contacting shroud	• Reposition shroud and inspect engine mounts
	• Loose water pump impeller	• Replace pump
	• Glazed fan belt	• Apply silicone or replace belt
	• Loose fan belt	• Adjust fan belt tension
	• Rough surface on drive pulley	• Replace pulley
	• Water pump bearing worn	• Remove belt to isolate. Replace pump.
	• Belt alignment	• Check pully alignment. Repair as necessary.
No coolant flow through heater core	• Restricted return inlet in water pump	• Remove restriction
	• Heater hose collapsed or restricted	• Remove restriction or replace hose
	• Restricted heater core	• Remove restriction or replace core
	• Restricted outlet in thermostat housing	• Remove flash or restriction
	• Intake manifold bypass hole in cylinder head restricted	• Remove restriction
	• Faulty heater control valve	• Replace valve
	• Intake manifold coolant passage restricted	• Remove restriction or replace intake manifold

NOTE: *Immediately after shutdown, the engine enters a condition known as heat soak. This is caused by the cooling system being inoperative while engine temperature is still high. If coolant temperature rises above boiling point, expansion and pressure may push some coolant out of the radiator overflow tube. If this does not occur frequently it is considered normal.*

ENGINE AND ENGINE OVERHAUL 3-85

Troubleshooting the Serpentine Drive Belt

Problem	Cause	Solution
Tension sheeting fabric failure (woven fabric on outside circumference of belt has cracked or separated from body of belt)	• Grooved or backside idler pulley diameters are less than minimum recommended • Tension sheeting contacting (rubbing) stationary object • Excessive heat causing woven fabric to age • Tension sheeting splice has fractured	• Replace pulley(s) not conforming to specification • Correct rubbing condition • Replace belt • Replace belt
Noise (objectional squeal, squeak, or rumble is heard or felt while drive belt is in operation)	• Belt slippage • Bearing noise • Belt misalignment • Belt-to-pulley mismatch • Driven component inducing vibration • System resonant frequency inducing vibration	• Adjust belt • Locate and repair • Align belt/pulley(s) • Install correct belt • Locate defective driven component and repair • Vary belt tension within specifications. Replace belt.
Rib chunking (one or more ribs has separated from belt body)	• Foreign objects imbedded in pulley grooves • Installation damage • Drive loads in excess of design specifications • Insufficient internal belt adhesion	• Remove foreign objects from pulley grooves • Replace belt • Adjust belt tension • Replace belt
Rib or belt wear (belt ribs contact bottom of pulley grooves)	• Pulley(s) misaligned • Mismatch of belt and pulley groove widths • Abrasive environment • Rusted pulley(s) • Sharp or jagged pulley groove tips • Rubber deteriorated	• Align pulley(s) • Replace belt • Replace belt • Clean rust from pulley(s) • Replace pulley • Replace belt
Longitudinal belt cracking (cracks between two ribs)	• Belt has mistracked from pulley groove • Pulley groove tip has worn away rubber-to-tensile member	• Replace belt • Replace belt
Belt slips	• Belt slipping because of insufficient tension • Belt or pulley subjected to substance (belt dressing, oil, ethylene glycol) that has reduced friction • Driven component bearing failure • Belt glazed and hardened from heat and excessive slippage	• Adjust tension • Replace belt and clean pulleys • Replace faulty component bearing • Replace belt
"Groove jumping" (belt does not maintain correct position on pulley, or turns over and/or runs off pulleys)	• Insufficient belt tension • Pulley(s) not within design tolerance • Foreign object(s) in grooves • Excessive belt speed • Pulley misalignment • Belt-to-pulley profile mismatched • Belt cordline is distorted	• Adjust belt tension • Replace pulley(s) • Remove foreign objects from grooves • Avoid excessive engine acceleration • Align pulley(s) • Install correct belt • Replace belt
Belt broken (Note: identify and correct problem before replacement belt is installed)	• Excessive tension • Tensile members damaged during belt installation • Belt turnover • Severe pulley misalignment • Bracket, pulley, or bearing failure	• Replace belt and adjust tension to specification • Replace belt • Replace belt • Align pulley(s) • Replace defective component and belt

Troubleshooting the Serpentine Drive Belt (cont.)

Problem	Cause	Solution
Cord edge failure (tensile member exposed at edges of belt or separated from belt body)	• Excessive tension • Drive pulley misalignment • Belt contacting stationary object • Pulley irregularities • Improper pulley construction • Insufficient adhesion between tensile member and rubber matrix	• Adjust belt tension • Align pulley • Correct as necessary • Replace pulley • Replace pulley • Replace belt and adjust tension to specifications
Sporadic rib cracking (multiple cracks in belt ribs at random intervals)	• Ribbed pulley(s) diameter less than minimum specification • Backside bend flat pulley(s) diameter less than minimum • Excessive heat condition causing rubber to harden • Excessive belt thickness • Belt overcured • Excessive tension	• Replace pulley(s) • Replace pulley(s) • Correct heat condition as necessary • Replace belt • Replace belt • Adjust belt tension

AIR POLLUTION
  AUTOMOTIVE POLLUTANTS 4-2
  INDUSTRIAL POLLUTANTS 4-2
  NATURAL POLLUTANTS 4-2
AUTOMOTIVE EMISSIONS
  CRANKCASE EMISSIONS 4-5
  EVAPORATIVE EMISSIONS 4-5
  EXHAUST GASES 4-3
EMISSION CONTROLS
  AIR INJECTION SYSTEM 4-6
  CARBURETOR 4-6
  ELECTRICALLY ASSISTED
    CHOKE 4-9
  EMISSION CONTROL CHECKS 4-10
  FUEL RETURN SYSTEM 4-10
  FUEL TANK VAPOR EMISSION
    CONTROL SYSTEM 4-10
  POSITIVE CRANKCASE VENTILATION
    (PCV) SYSTEM 4-6

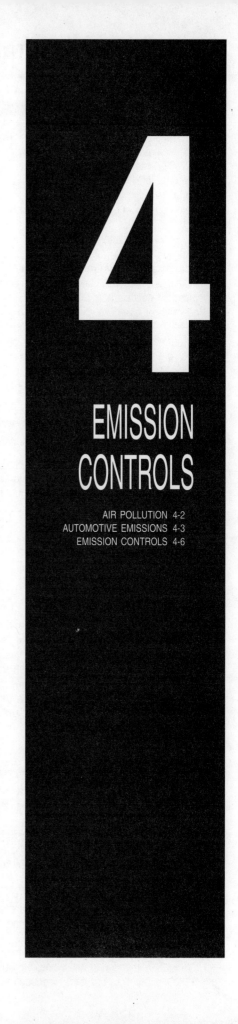

4

EMISSION CONTROLS

AIR POLLUTION 4-2
AUTOMOTIVE EMISSIONS 4-3
EMISSION CONTROLS 4-6

AIR POLLUTION

The earth's atmosphere, at or near sea level, consists approximately of 78 percent nitrogen, 21 percent oxygen and 1 percent other gases. If it were possible to remain in this state, 100 percent clean air would result. However, many varied sources allow other gases and particulates to mix with the clean air, causing our atmosphere to become unclean or polluted.

Some of these pollutants are visible while others are invisible, with each having the capability of causing distress to the eyes, ears, throat, skin and respiratory system. Should these pollutants become concentrated in a specific area and under certain conditions, death could result due to the displacement or chemical change of the oxygen content in the air. These pollutants can also cause great damage to the environment and to the many man made objects that are exposed to the elements.

To better understand the causes of air pollution, the pollutants can be categorized into 3 separate types, natural, industrial and automotive.

Natural Pollutants

Natural pollution has been present on earth since before man appeared and continues to be a factor when discussing air pollution, although it causes only a small percentage of the overall pollution problem. It is the direct result of decaying organic matter, wind born smoke and particulates from such natural events as plain and forest fires (ignited by heat or lightning), volcanic ash, sand and dust which can spread over a large area of the countryside.

Such a phenomenon of natural pollution has been seen in the form of volcanic eruptions, with the resulting plume of smoke, steam and volcanic ash blotting out the sun's rays as it spreads and rises higher into the atmosphere. As it travels into the atmosphere the upper air currents catch and carry the smoke and ash, while condensing the steam back into water vapor. As the water vapor, smoke and ash travel on their journey, the smoke dissipates into the atmosphere while the ash and moisture settle back to earth in a trail hundreds of miles long. In some cases, lives are lost and millions of dollars of property damage result.

Industrial Pollutants

Industrial pollution is caused primarily by industrial processes, the burning of coal, oil and natural gas, which in turn produce smoke and fumes. Because the burning fuels contain large amounts of sulfur, the principal ingredients of smoke and fumes are sulfur dioxide and particulate matter. This type of pollutant occurs most severely during still, damp and cool weather, such as at night. Even in its less severe form, this pollutant is not confined to just cities. Because of air movements, the pollutants move for miles over the surrounding countryside, leaving in its path a barren and unhealthy environment for all living things.

Working with Federal, State and Local mandated regulations and by carefully monitoring emissions, big business has greatly reduced the amount of pollutant introduced from its industrial sources, striving to obtain an acceptable level. Because of the mandated industrial emission clean up, many land areas and streams in and around the cities that were formerly barren of vegetation and life, have now begun to move back in the direction of nature's intended balance.

Automotive Pollutants

The third major source of air pollution is automotive emissions. The emissions from the internal combustion engines were not an appreciable problem years ago because of the small number of registered vehicles and the nation's small highway system. However, during the early 1950's, the trend of the American people was to move from the cities to the surrounding suburbs. This caused an immediate problem in transportation because the majority of suburbs were not afforded mass transit conveniences. This lack of transportation created an attractive market for the automobile manufacturers, which resulted in a dramatic increase in the number of vehicles produced and sold, along with a marked increase in highway construction between cities and the suburbs. Multi-vehicle families emerged with a growing emphasis placed on an individual vehicle per family member. As the increase in vehicle ownership and usage occurred, so did pollutant levels in and around the cities, as suburbanites drove daily to their businesses and employment, returning at the end of the day to their homes in the suburbs.

It was noted that a smoke and fog type haze was being formed and at times, remained in suspension over the cities, taking time to dissipate. At first this "smog," derived from the words "smoke" and "fog," was thought to result from industrial pollution but it was determined that automobile emissions shared the blame. It was discovered that when normal automobile emissions were exposed to sunlight for a period of time, complex chemical reactions would take place.

It is now known that smog is a photo chemical layer which develops when certain oxides of nitrogen (NOx) and unburned hydrocarbons (HC) from automobile emissions are exposed to sunlight. Pollution was more severe when smog would become stagnant over an area in which a warm layer of air settled over the top of the cooler air mass, trapping and holding the cooler mass at ground level. The trapped cooler air would keep the emissions from being dispersed and diluted through normal air flows. This type of air stagnation was given the name "Temperature Inversion."

TEMPERATURE INVERSION

In normal weather situations, surface air is warmed by heat radiating from the earth's surface and the sun's rays. This causes it to rise upward, into the atmosphere. Upon rising it will cool through a convection type heat exchange with the cooler upper air. As warm air rises, the surface pollutants are carried upward and dissipated into the atmosphere.

When a temperature inversion occurs, we find the higher air is no longer cooler, but is warmer than the surface air, causing the cooler surface air to become trapped. This warm air

EMISSION CONTROLS 4-3

blanket can extend from above ground level to a few hundred or even a few thousand feet into the air. As the surface air is trapped, so are the pollutants, causing a severe smog condition. Should this stagnant air mass extend to a few thousand feet high, enough air movement with the inversion takes place to allow the smog layer to rise above ground level but the pollutants still cannot dissipate. This inversion can remain for days over an area, with the smog level only rising or lowering from ground level to a few hundred feet high. Meanwhile, the pollutant levels increase, causing eye irritation, respiratory problems, reduced visibility, plant damage and in some cases, even disease.

This inversion phenomenon was first noted in the Los Angeles, California area. The city lies in terrain resembling a basin and with certain weather conditions, a cold air mass is held in the basin while a warmer air mass covers it like a lid.

Because this type of condition was first documented as prevalent in the Los Angeles area, this type of trapped pollution was named Los Angeles Smog, although it occurs in other areas where a large concentration of automobiles are used and the air remains stagnant for any length of time.

HEAT TRANSFER

Consider the internal combustion engine as a machine in which raw materials must be placed so a finished product comes out. As in any machine operation, a certain amount of wasted material is formed. When we relate this to the internal combustion engine, we find that through the input of air and fuel, we obtain power during the combustion process to drive the vehicle. The by-product or waste of this power is, in part, heat and exhaust gases with which we must dispose.

The heat from the combustion process can rise to over 4000°F (2204°C). The dissipation of this heat is controlled by a ram air effect, the use of cooling fans to cause air flow and a liquid coolant solution surrounding the combustion area to transfer the heat of combustion through the cylinder walls and into the coolant. The coolant is then directed to a thin-finned, multi-tubed radiator, from which the excess heat is transferred to the atmosphere by 1 of the 3 heat transfer methods, conduction, convection or radiation.

The cooling of the combustion area is an important part in the control of exhaust emissions. To understand the behavior of the combustion and transfer of its heat, consider the air/fuel charge. It is ignited and the flame front burns progressively across the combustion chamber until the burning charge reaches the cylinder walls. Some of the fuel in contact with the walls is not hot enough to burn, thereby snuffing out or quenching the combustion process. This leaves unburned fuel in the combustion chamber. This unburned fuel is then forced out of the cylinder and into the exhaust system, along with the exhaust gases.

Many attempts have been made to minimize the amount of unburned fuel in the combustion chambers due to quenching, by increasing the coolant temperature and lessening the contact area of the coolant around the combustion area. However, design limitations within the combustion chambers prevent the complete burning of the air/fuel charge, so a certain amount of the unburned fuel is still expelled into the exhaust system, regardless of modifications to the engine.

AUTOMOTIVE EMISSIONS

Before emission controls were mandated on internal combustion engines, other sources of engine pollutants were discovered along with the exhaust emissions. It was determined that engine combustion exhaust produced approximately 60 percent of the total emission pollutants, fuel evaporation from the fuel tank and carburetor vents produced 20 percent, with the final 20 percent being produced through the crankcase as a by-product of the combustion process.

Exhaust Gases

The exhaust gases emitted into the atmosphere are a combination of burned and unburned fuel. To understand the exhaust emission and its composition, we must review some basic chemistry.

When the air/fuel mixture is introduced into the engine, we are mixing air, composed of nitrogen (78 percent), oxygen (21 percent) and other gases (1 percent) with the fuel, which is 100 percent hydrocarbons (HC), in a semi-controlled ratio. As the combustion process is accomplished, power is produced to move the vehicle while the heat of combustion is transferred to the cooling system. The exhaust gases are then composed of nitrogen, a diatomic gas (N_2), the same as was introduced in the engine, carbon dioxide (CO_2), the same gas that is used in beverage carbonation, and water vapor (H_2O). The nitrogen (N_2), for the most part, passes through the engine unchanged, while the oxygen (O_2) reacts (burns) with the hydrocarbons (HC) and produces the carbon dioxide (CO_2) and the water vapors (H_2O). If this chemical process would be the only process to take place, the exhaust emissions would be harmless. However, during the combustion process, other compounds are formed which are considered dangerous. These pollutants are hydrocarbons (HC), carbon monoxide (CO), oxides of nitrogen (NOx) oxides of sulfur (SOx) and engine particulates.

HYDROCARBONS

Hydrocarbons (HC) are essentially fuel which was not burned during the combustion process or which has escaped into the atmosphere through fuel evaporation. The main sources of incomplete combustion are rich air/fuel mixtures, low engine temperatures and improper spark timing. The main sources of hydrocarbon emission through fuel evaporation on most vehicles used to be the vehicle's fuel tank and carburetor float bowl.

To reduce combustion hydrocarbon emission, engine modifications were made to minimize dead space and surface area in the combustion chamber. In addition, the air/fuel mixture was made more lean through the improved control which feedback carburetion and fuel injection offers and by the addition of external controls to aid in further combustion of the hydrocarbons outside the engine. Two such methods were the

4-4 EMISSION CONTROLS

addition of air injection systems, to inject fresh air into the exhaust manifolds and the installation of catalytic converters, units that are able to burn traces of hydrocarbons without affecting the internal combustion process or fuel economy.

To control hydrocarbon emissions through fuel evaporation, modifications were made to the fuel tank to allow storage of the fuel vapors during periods of engine shut-down. Modifications were also made to the air intake system so that at specific times during engine operation, these vapors may be purged and burned by blending them with the air/fuel mixture.

CARBON MONOXIDE

Carbon monoxide is formed when not enough oxygen is present during the combustion process to convert carbon (C) to carbon dioxide (CO_2). An increase in the carbon monoxide (CO) emission is normally accompanied by an increase in the hydrocarbon (HC) emission because of the lack of oxygen to completely burn all of the fuel mixture.

Carbon monoxide (CO) also increases the rate at which the photo chemical smog is formed by speeding up the conversion of nitric oxide (NO) to nitrogen dioxide (NO_2). To accomplish this, carbon monoxide (CO) combines with oxygen (O_2) and nitric oxide (NO) to produce carbon dioxide (CO_2) and nitrogen dioxide (NO_2). ($CO + O_2 + NO = CO_2 + NO_2$).

The dangers of carbon monoxide, which is an odorless and colorless toxic gas are many. When carbon monoxide is inhaled into the lungs and passed into the blood stream, oxygen is replaced by the carbon monoxide in the red blood cells, causing a reduction in the amount of oxygen supplied to the many parts of the body. This lack of oxygen causes headaches, lack of coordination, reduced mental alertness and, should the carbon monoxide concentration be high enough, death could result.

NITROGEN

Normally, nitrogen is an inert gas. When heated to approximately 2500°F (1371°C) through the combustion process, this gas becomes active and causes an increase in the nitric oxide (NO) emission.

Oxides of nitrogen (NOx) are composed of approximately 97-98 percent nitric oxide (NO). Nitric oxide is a colorless gas but when it is passed into the atmosphere, it combines with oxygen and forms nitrogen dioxide (NO_2). The nitrogen dioxide then combines with chemically active hydrocarbons (HC) and when in the presence of sunlight, causes the formation of photo-chemical smog.

Ozone

To further complicate matters, some of the nitrogen dioxide (NO_2) is broken apart by the sunlight to form nitric oxide and oxygen. (NO_2 + sunlight = NO + O). This single atom of oxygen then combines with diatomic (meaning 2 atoms) oxygen (O_2) to form ozone (O_3). Ozone is one of the smells associated with smog. It has a pungent and offensive odor, irritates the eyes and lung tissues, affects the growth of plant life and causes rapid deterioration of rubber products. Ozone can be formed by sunlight as well as electrical discharge into the air.

The most common discharge area on the automobile engine is the secondary ignition electrical system, especially when inferior quality spark plug cables are used. As the surge of high voltage is routed through the secondary cable, the circuit builds up an electrical field around the wire, which acts upon the oxygen in the surrounding air to form the ozone. The faint glow along the cable with the engine running that may be visible on a dark night, is called the "corona discharge." It is the result of the electrical field passing from a high along the cable, to a low in the surrounding air, which forms the ozone gas. The combination of corona and ozone has been a major cause of cable deterioration. Recently, different and better quality insulating materials have lengthened the life of the electrical cables.

Although ozone at ground level can be harmful, ozone is beneficial to the earth's inhabitants. By having a concentrated ozone layer called the "ozonosphere," between 10 and 20 miles (16-32 km) up in the atmosphere, much of the ultra violet radiation from the sun's rays are absorbed and screened. If this ozone layer were not present, much of the earth's surface would be burned, dried and unfit for human life.

OXIDES OF SULFUR

Oxides of sulfur (SOx) were initially ignored in the exhaust system emissions, since the sulfur content of gasoline as a fuel is less than $^1/_{10}$ of 1 percent. Because of this small amount, it was felt that it contributed very little to the overall pollution problem. However, because of the difficulty in solving the sulfur emissions in industrial pollutions and the introduction of catalytic converter to the automobile exhaust systems, a change was mandated. The automobile exhaust system, when equipped with a catalytic converter, changes the sulfur dioxide (SO_2) into sulfur trioxide (SO_3).

When this combines with water vapors (H_2O), a sulfuric acid mist (H_2SO_4) is formed and is a very difficult pollutant to handle since it is extremely corrosive. This sulfuric acid mist that is formed, is the same mist that rises from the vents of an automobile battery when an active chemical reaction takes place within the battery cells.

When a large concentration of vehicles equipped with catalytic converters are operating in an area, this acid mist may rise and be distributed over a large ground area causing land, plant, crop, paint and building damage.

PARTICULATE MATTER

A certain amount of particulate matter is present in the burning of any fuel, with carbon constituting the largest percentage of the particulates. In gasoline, the remaining particulates are the burned remains of the various other compounds used in its manufacture. When a gasoline engine is in good internal condition, the particulate emissions are low but as the engine wears internally, the particulate emissions increase. By visually inspecting the tail pipe emissions, a determination can be made as to where an engine defect may exist. An engine with light gray or blue smoke emitting from

EMISSION CONTROLS 4-5

the tail pipe normally indicates an increase in the oil consumption through burning due to internal engine wear. Black smoke would indicate a defective fuel delivery system, causing the engine to operate in a rich mode. Regardless of the color of the smoke, the internal part of the engine or the fuel delivery system should be repaired to prevent excess particulate emissions.

Diesel and turbine engines emit a darkened plume of smoke from the exhaust system because of the type of fuel used. Emission control regulations are mandated for this type of emission and more stringent measures are being used to prevent excess emission of the particulate matter. Electronic components are being introduced to control the injection of the fuel at precisely the proper time of piston travel, to achieve the optimum in fuel ignition and fuel usage. Other particulate afterburning components are being tested to achieve a cleaner emission.

Good grades of engine lubricating oils should be used, which meet the manufacturers specification. Cut-rate oils can contribute to the particulate emission problem because of their low flash or ignition temperature point. Such oils burn prematurely during the combustion process causing emission of particulate matter.

The cooling system is an important factor in the reduction of particulate matter. The optimum combustion will occur, with the cooling system operating at a temperature specified by the manufacturer. The cooling system must be maintained in the same manner as the engine oiling system, as each system is required to perform properly in order for the engine to operate efficiently for a long time.

Crankcase Emissions

Crankcase emissions are made up of water, acids, unburned fuel, oil fumes and particulates. These emissions are classified as hydrocarbons (HC) and are formed by the small amount of unburned, compressed air/fuel mixture entering the crankcase from the combustion area (between the cylinder walls and piston rings) during the compression and power strokes. The head of the compression and combustion help to form the remaining crankcase emissions.

Since the first engines, crankcase emissions were allowed into the atmosphere through a road draft tube, mounted on the lower side of the engine block. Fresh air came in through an open oil filler cap or breather. The air passed through the crankcase mixing with blow-by gases. The motion of the vehicle and the air blowing past the open end of the road draft tube caused a low pressure area (vacuum) at the end of the tube. Crankcase emissions were simply drawn out of the road draft tube into the air.

To control the crankcase emission, the road draft tube was deleted. A hose and/or tubing was routed from the crankcase to the intake manifold so the blow-by emission could be burned with the air/fuel mixture. However, it was found that intake manifold vacuum, used to draw the crankcase emissions into the manifold, would vary in strength at the wrong time and not allow the proper emission flow. A regulating valve was needed to control the flow of air through the crankcase.

Testing, showed the removal of the blow-by gases from the crankcase as quickly as possible, was most important to the longevity of the engine. Should large accumulations of blow-by gases remain and condense, dilution of the engine oil would occur to form water, soots, resins, acids and lead salts, resulting in the formation of sludge and varnishes. This condensation of the blow-by gases occurs more frequently on vehicles used in numerous starting and stopping conditions, excessive idling and when the engine is not allowed to attain normal operating temperature through short runs.

Evaporative Emissions

Gasoline fuel is a major source of pollution, before and after it is burned in the automobile engine. From the time the fuel is refined, stored, pumped and transported, again stored until it is pumped into the fuel tank of the vehicle, the gasoline gives off unburned hydrocarbons (HC) into the atmosphere. Through the redesign of storage areas and venting systems, the pollution factor was diminished, but not eliminated, from the refinery standpoint. However, the automobile still remained the primary source of vaporized, unburned hydrocarbon (HC) emissions.

Fuel pumped from an underground storage tank is cool but when exposed to a warmer ambient temperature, will expand. Before controls were mandated, an owner might fill the fuel tank with fuel from an underground storage tank and park the vehicle for some time in warm area, such as a parking lot. As the fuel would warm, it would expand and should no provisions or area be provided for the expansion, the fuel would spill out of the filler neck and onto the ground, causing hydrocarbon (HC) pollution and creating a severe fire hazard. To correct this condition, the vehicle manufacturers added overflow plumbing and/or gasoline tanks with built in expansion areas or domes.

However, this did not control the fuel vapor emission from the fuel tank. It was determined that most of the fuel evaporation occurred when the vehicle was stationary and the engine not operating. Most vehicles carry 5-25 gallons (19-95 liters) of gasoline. Should a large concentration of vehicles be parked in one area, such as a large parking lot, excessive fuel vapor emissions would take place, increasing as the temperature increases.

To prevent the vapor emission from escaping into the atmosphere, the fuel systems were designed to trap the vapors while the vehicle is stationary, by sealing the system from the atmosphere. A storage system is used to collect and hold the fuel vapors from the carburetor (if equipped) and the fuel tank when the engine is not operating. When the engine is started, the storage system is then purged of the fuel vapors, which are drawn into the engine and burned with the air/fuel mixture.

4-6 EMISSION CONTROLS

EMISSION CONTROLS

There are three types of automotive pollutants: crankcase fumes, exhaust gases and gasoline evaporation. The equipment that is used to limit these pollutants is commonly called emission control equipment.

Carburetor

The carburetors used on engines equipped with emission controls have specific flow characteristics that differ from the carburetors used on vehicles not equipped with emission control devices. The carburetors are identified by number. The correct carburetor should be used when replacement is necessary.

A carburetor dashpot is used on the 4-134 to control throttle closing speed.

➡ Refer to Section 5 of this manual for the dashpot, and other carburetor adjustment procedures.

Positive Crankcase Ventilation (PCV) System

OPERATION

▸ See Figure 1

The crankcase emission control equipment consists of a positive crankcase ventilation valve (PCV), a closed or open oil filler cap and hoses to connect this equipment.

When the engine is running, a small portion of the gases which are formed in the combustion chamber during combustion, leak by the piston rings and enter the crankcase. Since these gases are under pressure, they tend to escape from the crankcase and enter the atmosphere. If these gases were allowed to remain in the crankcase for any length of time, they would contaminate the engine oil and cause sludge to build up. If the gases were allowed to escape into the atmosphere, they would pollute the air, as they contain unburned hydrocarbons. The crankcase emission control equipment recycles these gases back into the engine combustion chamber where they are burned.

Crankcase gases are recycled in the following manner: while the engine is running, clean filtered air is drawn into the crankcase either directly through the oil filler cap, or through the carburetor air filter and then through a hose leading to the oil filler cap. As the air passes through the crankcase, it picks up the combustion gases and carries them out of the crankcase, up through the PCV valve and into the intake manifold. After they enter the intake manifold, they are drawn into the combustion chamber and burned.

The most critical component in the system is the PCV valve. This vacuum controlled valve regulates the amount of gases which are recycled into the combustion chamber. At low engine speeds, the valve is partially closed, limiting the flow of gases into the intake manifold. As engine speed increases, the valve opens to admit greater quantities of the gases into the intake manifold. If the valve should become blocked or plugged, the gases will be prevented from escaping from the crankcases by the normal route. Since these gases are under pressure, they will find their own way out of the crankcase. This alternate route is usually a weak oil seal or gasket in the engine. As the gas escapes by the gasket, it also creates an oil leak. Besides causing oil leaks, a clogged PCV valve also allows these gases to remain in the crankcase for an extended period of time, promoting the formation of sludge in the engine.

The above explanation and the troubleshooting procedure which follows applies to all engines with PCV systems.

TESTING

With the engine running, pull the PCV valve and hose from the engine. Block off the end of the valve with your finger. The engine speed should drop at least 50 rpm when the end of the valve is blocked. If the engine speed does not drop at least 50 rpm, then the valve is defective and should be replaced.

REMOVAL & INSTALLATION

1. Pull the PCV valve and hose from the engine.
2. Remove the PCV valve from the hose. Inspect the inside of the PCV valve from the hose. If it is dirty, disconnect if from the intake manifold and clean it.
3. If the PCV valve hose was removed, connect it to the intake manifold.
4. Connect the PCV valve to its hose.
5. Install the PCV valve on the engine.

Air Injection System

OPERATION

▸ See Figures 2 and 3

All of the gasoline engines used in these Jeep vehicles, except the 6-226, have, at one time or another, incorporated the air injection system for controlling the emission of exhaust gases into the atmosphere. Since this type of emission control system is common to most of the engines, it will be explained here.

The exhaust emission air injection system consists of a belt driven air pump which directs compressed air through connecting hoses to a steel distribution manifold into stainless steel injection tubes in the exhaust port adjacent to each exhaust valve. The air, with its normal oxygen content, reacts with the hot, but incompletely burned exhaust gases and permits further combustion in the exhaust port or manifold.

Air Pump

The air injection pump is a positive displacement vane type which is permanently lubricated and requires little periodic maintenance. The only serviceable parts on the air pump are

EMISSION CONTROLS 4-7

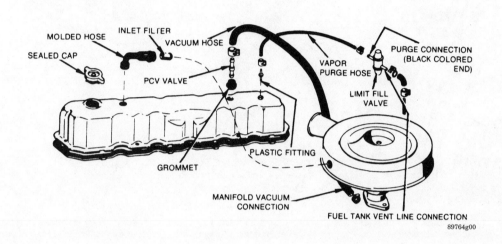

Fig. 1 View of the typical PCV system, which was used on all 1965-70 engines

the filter, exhaust tube, and relief valve. The relief valve relieves the air flow when the pump pressure reaches a preset level. This occurs at high engine rpm. This serves to prevent damage to the pump and to limit maximum exhaust manifold temperatures.

Pump Air Filter

The air filter attached to the pump is a replaceable element type. The filter should be replaced every 12,000 miles (19,200 km) under normal conditions and sooner under off-road use. Some models draw their air supply through the carburetor air filter.

Air Delivery Manifold

The air delivery manifold distributes the air from the pump to each of the air delivery tubes in a uniform manner. A check valve is integral with the air delivery manifold. Its function is to prevent the reverse flow of exhaust gases to the pump should the pump fail. This reverse flow would damage the air pump and connecting hose.

Air Injection Tubes

The air injection tubes are inserted into the exhaust ports. The tubes project into the exhaust ports, directing air into the vicinity of the exhaust valve.

Anti-Backfire Valve

The anti-backfire diverter valve prevents engine backfire by briefly interrupting the air being injected into the exhaust manifold during periods of deceleration or rapid throttle closure. On the 4-134 engines, the valve opens when a sudden increase in manifold vacuum overcomes the diaphragm spring tension. With the valve in the open position, the air flow from the air pump is directed to the atmosphere.

On the 6-225 engine, the anti-backfire valve is what is commonly called a gulp valve. During rapid deceleration the valve is opened by the sudden high vacuum condition in the intake manifold and gulps air into the intake manifold.

Both of these valves prevent backfiring in the exhaust manifold. Both valves also prevent an over right fuel mixture from

4-8 EMISSION CONTROLS

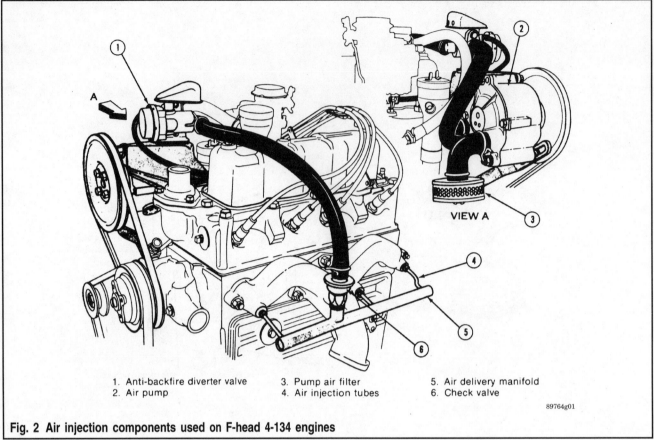

1. Anti-backfire diverter valve
2. Air pump
3. Pump air filter
4. Air injection tubes
5. Air delivery manifold
6. Check valve

Fig. 2 Air injection components used on F-head 4-134 engines

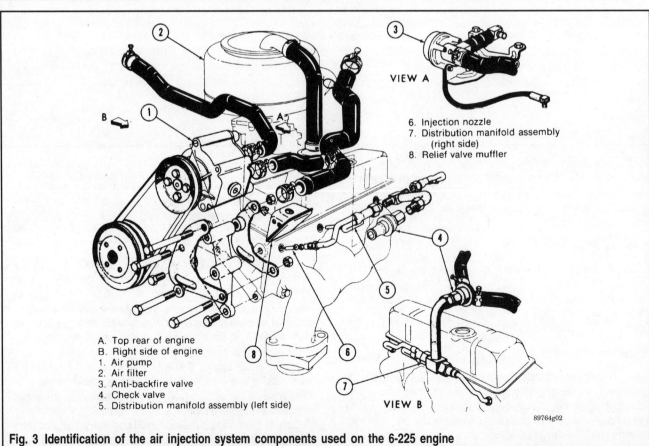

A. Top rear of engine
B. Right side of engine
1. Air pump
2. Air filter
3. Anti-backfire valve
4. Check valve
5. Distribution manifold assembly (left side)
6. Injection nozzle
7. Distribution manifold assembly (right side)
8. Relief valve muffler

Fig. 3 Identification of the air injection system components used on the 6-225 engine

EMISSION CONTROLS 4-9

being burned in the exhaust manifold, which would cause backfiring and possible damage to the engine.

MAINTENANCE & SERVICE

Efficient performance of the exhaust emission control system is dependent upon precise maintenance.

Carburetor

Check the carburetor for the proper application. Check the dashpot for proper operation and adjust as required. When the throttle is released quickly, the arm of the dashpot should fully extend itself and should catch the throttle lever, letting it back to idle position gradually.

Proper idle mixture adjustment is imperative for best exhaust emission control. The idle adjustment should be made with the engine at normal operating temperature and the air cleaner in place. All lights and accessories must be turned off and the transmission must be in Neutral. Refer to Section 2 of this manual for adjustment procedures.

Distributor

Check the distributor number for proper application. Check the distributor cam dwell angle and point condition and adjust to specifications or replace as required. Refer to Section 2 of this manual for adjustment procedures.

Anti-Backfire Diverter Valve

On the 4-134 engines, the anti-backfire valve remains open except when the throttle is closed rapidly from an open position.

To check the valve for proper operation, accelerate the engine in neutral, allowing the throttle to close rapidly. The valve is operating satisfactorily when no exhaust system backfire occurs. A further check can be made by removing the large hose that runs from the anti-backfire valve to the check valve and accelerating the engine and allowing the throttle to close rapidly. If there is an audible momentary interruption of the flow of air, then it can be assumed that the valve is working correctly.

To check the valve on the 6-225 engine, listen for backfire when the throttle is released quickly. If none exists, the valve is doing its job. To check further, remove the large hose that connects the valve with the air pump. Place a finger over the open end of the hose, not the valve, and accelerate the engine, allowing the throttle to close rapidly. The valve is operating satisfactorily if there is a momentary audible rush of air.

Check Valve

The check valve in the air distribution manifold prevents the reverse flow of exhaust gases to the pump in the event the pump should become inoperative or should exhaust pressure ever exceed the pump pressure.

To check this valve for proper operation, remove the air supply hose from the pump at the distribution manifold. With the engine running, listen for exhaust leakage where the check valve is connected to the distribution manifold. If leakage is audible, the valve is not operating correctly.

Air Pump

Check for the proper drive belt tension and adjust as necessary. Do not pry on the die cast pump housing. Check to see if the pump is discharging air. Remove the air outlet hose at the pump. With the engine running, air should be felt at the pump outlet opening.

REMOVAL & INSTALLATION

Air Pump

1. Loosen the air pump adjusting bracket bolts.
2. Remove the drive belt.
3. Remove the air pump intake and discharge hoses.
4. Remove the air pump from the engine.
5. To install, reverse the above procedure.

Anti-Backfire Valve

To remove the anti-backfire valve, disconnect the hoses and bracket-to-engine attaching screws. Install in the reverse order of removal.

Air Distribution Manifold and Air Injection Tubes

It is necessary to remove the exhaust manifold only on the 4-134 engines prior to removing the air distribution manifold and the air injection tubes. On all the other engines, these components can be removed with the manifolds on the engine.

1. Disconnect the air delivery hose from the air injection manifold. Remove the exhaust manifold on the 4-134.
2. Remove the air distribution manifold from the air injection tubes on the 4-134 only.
3. Unscrew the air injection tube from the exhaust manifold or the head. Some resistance may be encountered because of the normal buildup of carbon. The application of heat may be helpful in removing the air injection tubes.
4. Install in the reverse order of removal.

➥There are two lengths of tubes used with the 4-134. The shorter tubes are installed in number 1 and 4 cylinders. The air injection tubes must be installed on the exhaust manifold prior to installing the exhaust manifold on the engine.

Electrically Assisted Choke

OPERATION

An electric assist choke is used to more accurately match the choke operation to engine requirements. It provides extra heat to the choke bimetal spring to speed up the choke valve opening after the underhood air temperature reaches 80-110°F (27-43°C). Its purpose is to reduce the emission of carbon monoxide (CO) during the engine's warm-up period.

A special AC terminal is provided at the alternator to supply a 7 volt power source for the electric choke. A thermostatic switch within the choke cover closes when the underhood air temperature reaches 80-110°F (27-43°C) and allows current to flow to a ceramic heating element. The circuit is completed through the choke cover ground strap and choke housing to the engine. As the heating element warms up, heat is absorbed by an attached metal plate which in turn heats the coke bimetal spring.

After the engine is turned off, the thermostatic switch remains closed until the underhood temperature drops below approximately 65°F (18°C). Therefore, the heating element will immediately begin warming up when the engine is restarted, if the underhood temperature is above 65°F (18°C).

Fuel Tank Vapor Emission Control System

OPERATION

A closed fuel tank system is used on some models through 1970 to route fuel vapor from the fuel tank into the PCV system (6-cylinder engines), where it is burned along with the fuel-air mixture. The system prevents raw fuel vapors from entering the atmosphere.

The fuel vapor system consists of internal fuel tank venting, a vacuum-pressure fuel tank filler cap, an expansion tank or charcoal filled canister, liquid limit fill valve, and internal carburetor venting.

Fuel vapor pressure in the fuel tank forces the vapor through vent lines to the expansion tank or charcoal filled storage canister. The vapor then travels through a single vent line to the limit fill valve, which regulates the vapor flow to the valve cover or air cleaner.

Limit Fill Valve

This valve is essentially a combination vapor flow regulator and pressure relief valve. It regulates vapor flow from the fuel tank vent line into the valve cover. The valve consists of a housing, a spring loaded diaphragm and a diaphragm cover. As tank vent pressure increases, the diaphragm lifts, permitting vapor to flow through. The pressure at which this occurs is 0.17 psi (1.14 kPa). This action regulates the flow of vapors under severe conditions, but generally prohibits the flow of vapor during normal temperature operation, thus minimizing driveability problems.

Liquid Check Valve

The liquid check valve prevents liquid fuel from entering the vapor lines leading to the storage canister. The check valve incorporates a float and needle valve assembly. If liquid fuel should enter the check valve, the float will rise and force the needle upward to close the vent passage. With no liquid fuel present in the check valve, fuel vapors pass freely from the tank, through the check valve, and on to the storage canister.

Fuel Return System

The purpose of the fuel return system is to reduce high temperature fuel vapor problems. The system consists of a fuel return line to the fuel tank and special fuel filter with an extra outlet nipple to which the return line is connected. During normal operation, a small amount of fuel is returned to the fuel tank. During periods of high underhood temperatures, vaporized fuel in the fuel line is returned to the fuel tank and not passed through the carburetor.

➡ **The extra nipple on the special fuel filter should be positioned upward to ensure proper operation of the system.**

Emission Control Checks

ANTI-BACKFIRE DIVERTER VALVE

On the F-head 4-134 engine, the anti-backfire valve remains open except when the throttle is closed rapidly from an open position.

To check the valve for proper operation, accelerate the engine in neutral, allowing the throttle to close rapidly. The valve is operating satisfactorily when no exhaust system backfire occurs. A further check can be made by removing the large hose that runs from the anti-backfire valve to the check valve and accelerating the engine and allowing the throttle to close rapidly. If there is an audible momentary interruption of the flow of air then it can be assumed that the valve is working correctly.

To check the valve on a the 6-225 engine, listen for backfire when the throttle is released quickly. If none exists, the valve is doing its job. To check further, remove the large hose that connects the valve with the air pump. Place a finger over the open end of the hose, not the valve, and accelerate the engine, allowing the throttle to close rapidly. The valve is operating satisfactorily if there is a momentary audible rush of air.

CHECK VALVE

The check valve in the air distribution manifold prevents the reverse flow of exhaust gases to the pump in the event the pump should become inoperative or should exhaust pressure ever exceed the pump pressure.

To check this valve for proper operation, remove the air supply hose from the pump at the distribution manifold. With the engine running, listen for exhaust leakage where the check valve is connected to the distribution manifold. If leakage is audible, the valve is not operating correctly. A small amount of leakage is normal.

AIR PUMP

Check for the proper drive belt tension and adjust as necessary. Do not pry on the die cast pump housing. Check to see if the pump is discharging air. Remove the air outlet hose at the pump. With the engine running, air should be felt at the pump outlet opening.

BASIC FUEL SYSTEM DIAGNOSIS 5-2
CARBURETED FUEL SYSTEM
  CARBURETORS 5-4
  FUEL PUMP 5-2
  GOVERNOR 5-14
FUEL TANK
  TANK ASSEMBLY 5-15
SPECIFICATIONS CHARTS
  CARBURETOR
    SPECIFICATIONS 5-16
  TROUBLESHOOTING BASIC FUEL
    SYSTEM PROBLEMS 5-16

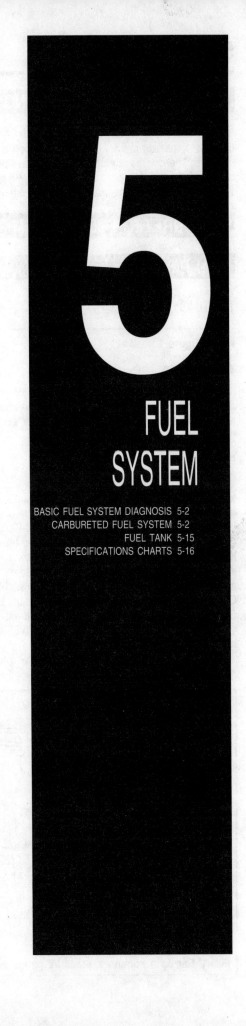

5

FUEL SYSTEM

BASIC FUEL SYSTEM DIAGNOSIS 5-2
CARBURETED FUEL SYSTEM 5-2
FUEL TANK 5-15
SPECIFICATIONS CHARTS 5-16

5-2 FUEL SYSTEM

BASIC FUEL SYSTEM DIAGNOSIS

When there is a problem starting or driving a vehicle, two of the most important checks involve the ignition and the fuel systems. The questions most mechanics attempt to answer first, "is there spark?" and "is there fuel?" will often lead to solving most basic problems. For ignition system diagnosis and testing, please refer to the information on engine electrical components and ignition systems found earlier in this manual. If the ignition system checks out (there is spark), then you must determine if the fuel system is operating properly (is there fuel?).

CARBURETED FUEL SYSTEM

Fuel Pump

TESTING

▶ See Figure 1

Volume Check

Disconnect the fuel line from the carburetor. Place the open end in a suitable container. Start the engine and operate it at normal idle speed. The pump should deliver at least 1 pt. (0.473L) in 30 seconds.

Pressure Check

Disconnect the fuel line at the carburetor. Disconnect the fuel return line from the fuel filter if so equipped, and plug the nipple on the filter. Install a tee fitting on the open end of the fuel line and refit the line to the carburetor. Plug a pressure gauge into the remaining opening of the tee fitting. The hose leading to the pressure gauge should not be any longer than 6 in. (15cm). Start the engine and let it run at idle speed. Bleed any air out of the hose between the gauge and the tee fitting. On pumps with a fuel return line, the line must be plugged. Start the engine. Fuel pressures are as follows:

- 4-134 engine — 2.50-3.75 psi (17.24-25.85 kPa) @ 1,800 rpm
- 6-225 engine — 3.75 psi (25.85 kPa) minimum @ 600 rpm
- 6-226 engine — 3.50-5.50 psi (24.13-37.92 kPa) @ 1,800 rpm
- 6-230 engine — 3.50-5.50 psi (24.13-37.92 kPa) @ 600 rpm

REMOVAL & INSTALLATION

▶ See Figures 2, 3, 4 and 5

All Engines

1. Disconnect the inlet and outlet fuel lines, and any vacuum lines.
2. Remove the two fuel pump body attaching nuts and lockwashers.
3. Pull the pump and gasket, or O-ring, free of the engine. Make sure that the mating surfaces of the fuel pump and the engine are clean.
4. Cement a new gasket to the mounting flange of the fuel pump.
5. Position the fuel pump on the engine block so that the lever of the fuel pump rests on the fuel pump cam of the camshaft.
6. Secure the fuel pump to the block with the two cap screws and lock washers.
7. Connect the intake and outlet fuel lines to the fuel pump, and any vacuum lines.

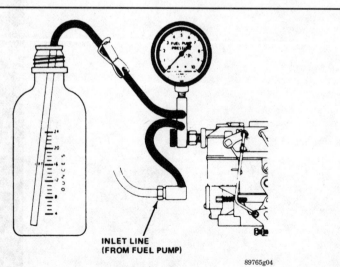

Fig. 1 Set up a container, pressure gauge and fuel lines as shown for the pressure and volume tests

FUEL SYSTEM 5-3

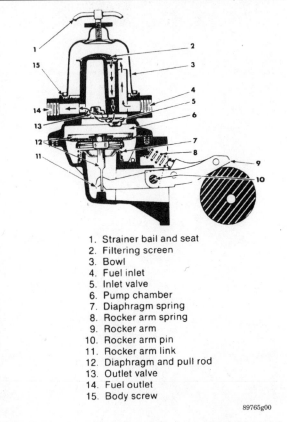

Fig. 2 Cross-section view of the internal workings of the screen-type filter fuel pump used on early L-head 4-134 engines

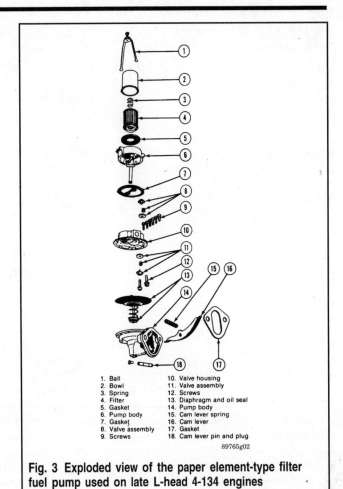

Fig. 3 Exploded view of the paper element-type filter fuel pump used on late L-head 4-134 engines

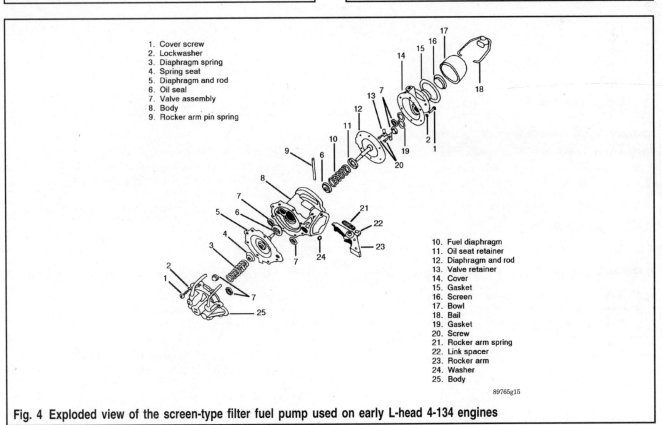

Fig. 4 Exploded view of the screen-type filter fuel pump used on early L-head 4-134 engines

5-4 FUEL SYSTEM

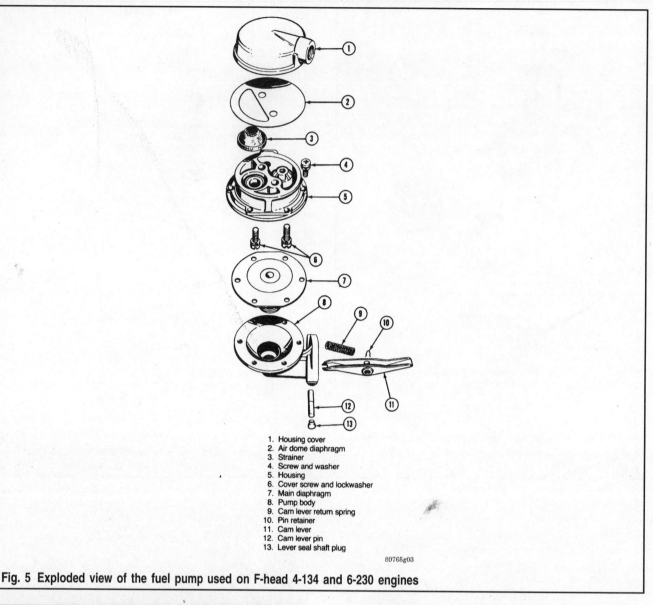

1. Housing cover
2. Air dome diaphragm
3. Strainer
4. Screw and washer
5. Housing
6. Cover screw and lockwasher
7. Main diaphragm
8. Pump body
9. Cam lever return spring
10. Pin retainer
11. Cam lever
12. Cam lever pin
13. Lever seal shaft plug

Fig. 5 Exploded view of the fuel pump used on F-head 4-134 and 6-230 engines

Carburetors

ADJUSTMENTS

Float and Fuel Level

4-134 ENGINES

➡The 4-134 engines utilize the Carter YF carburetor.

1. Remove and invert the bowl cover.
2. Remove the bowl cover gasket.
3. Allow the weight of the float to rest on the needle and spring. Be sure that there is no compression of the spring other than by the weight of the float.
4. Adjust the level by bending the float arm lip that contacts the needle (not the arm) to provide:
   - CJ-2A, CJ-3A models — 3/8 in. (9.5mm)
   - 1945-67 CJ-3B, CJ-5 and CJ-6 models — 5/16 in. (7.9mm)
   - 1968-70 CJ-5 and CJ-6 models — 17/64 in. (6.75mm)

6-225 ENGINE

▶ See Figures 6 and 7

➡The 6-225 engine utilizes the Rochester 2G carburetor.

The procedure for adjusting the float level of the two barrel carburetor installed on the V6 is the same as the procedure for the 4-134 up to Step 4.

The actual measurement is taken from the air horn gasket to the lip at the toe of the float. This distance should be 5/32 in. (4mm). To adjust the float level, bend the float arm as required.

The float drop adjustment is accomplished in the following manner: with the bowl cover turned in the upright position, measure the distance from the gasket to the notch at the toe

FUEL SYSTEM 5-5

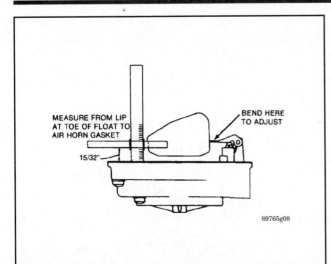

Fig. 6 Bend the float rod to adjust the float level to the specified value

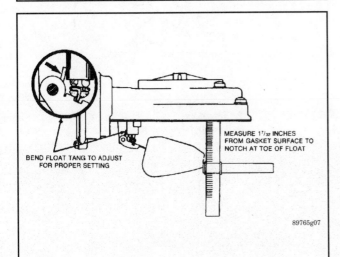

Fig. 7 Invert the air horn to measure the amount of float drop

of the float. Bend the tang as required to obtain a measurement of 1 7/32 in. (30.96mm).

6-226 ENGINE WITH CARTER MODEL YF

1. Remove and invert the bowl cover.
2. Remove the bowl cover gasket.
3. Allow the weight of the float to rest on the needle and spring. Be sure that there is no compression of the spring other than by the weight of the float.
4. Adjust the level by bending the float arm lip that contacts the needle (not the arm) to provide 9/32 in. (7.14mm).

6-226 ENGINE WITH CARTER MODEL WCD

1. Remove the bowl cover and turn it upside down.
2. Remove the gasket.
3. With the tip of the float resting on the needle, measure the distance between the top of the float and the machined surface of the bowl casting. The gap should be 3/16 in. (4.76mm).
4. If not, adjust it by bending the float arms.

6-226 ENGINE WITH CARTER MODEL WGD

1. Remove the bowl cover and turn it upside down.
2. Remove the gasket.
3. With the tip of the float resting on the needle, measure the distance between the top of the float and the machined surface of the bowl casting. The gap should be 9/32 in. (7.14mm).
4. If not, adjust it by bending the float arms.

6-230 ENGINE WITH HOLLEY 1920

1. Remove the carburetor.
2. Slide float gauge J-10238 into position at the economizer body baffle and check the setting. The float should just touch the gauge.
3. If necessary, bend the float tab with needle nosed pliers. Do not allow the float tab to contact the float needle during this operation. Recheck the setting.
4. Slide the economizer diaphragm into position, making sure that the vacuum holes are aligned and that the stem is on the power valve.
5. Install and tighten the cover screws.

6-230 ENGINE WITH HOLLEY 2415

1. Park the vehicle on level ground and run the engine until it is idling at normal operating temperature.
2. With the engine idling, remove the fuel level check plug. The fuel level should be within 1/16 in. (1.6mm) of the bottom of the check plug port.
3. To adjust the level, loosen the fuel valve seat lock screw slightly with a screwdriver and turn the adjusting nut with a 5/8 in. wrench. Turn the nut clockwise to lower, and counterclockwise to raise, the fuel level. A 1/6 turn equals a 1/16 in. (1.6mm) change in the lever.
4. After adjustment, tighten the lockscrew and recheck the level.

Fast Idle Linkage

➡ This adjustment is performed with the air cleaner removed.

4-134 ENGINE

➡ The 4-134 engines use the Carter YF carburetor.

With the choke held in the wide open position, the lip on the fast idle rod should contact the boss on the body casting. Adjust it by bending the fast idle link at the offset in the link.

6-225 ENGINE WITH ROCHESTER 2G

No fast idle speed adjustment is required. Fast idle is controlled by the curb adjustment screw. If the curb idle speed is set correctly and the choke rod is properly adjusted, fast idle speed will be correct.

6-226 ENGINE WITH CARTER MODEL WCD

1. Loosen the choke lever clamp screw on the choke shaft.
2. Insert a 0.04 in. (1.01mm) feeler gauge between the lip of the fast idle cam and the boss of the flange.
3. Hold the choke valve closed tightly and take the slack out of the linkage by pressing the choke lever toward the closed position.
4. Hold it in this position and tighten the clamp screw.

5-6 FUEL SYSTEM

5. With the choke valve tightly closed, tighten the fast idle adjusting screw until there is a gap of 0.016 in. (0.406mm) between the throttle valve and the air horn wall. Make sure that the fast idle screw is on the high step of the cam during this adjustment.

6-226 ENGINE WITH CARTER MODEL WGD

1. Remove the choke coil housing, gasket and baffle plate.
2. Crack the throttle and hold the choke plate closed. Then, close the throttle.
3. At this point, there should be a gap of 0.018–0.023 in. (0.457–0.584mm) between the throttle valve and air horn wall, opposite the idle port.
4. Adjust the gap by bending the choke connecting rod at the lower angle.

6-230 ENGINE

1. Connect a tachometer according to the manufacturer's instructions.
2. On vehicles equipped with a manual choke, adjust the choke wire to give maximum operation of the choke valve. With the engine off the choke fully open, adjust the fast idle screw to obtain a 0.030 in. (0.762mm) gap between the end of the screw and the cam.
3. On vehicles equipped with an automatic choke, run the engine to normal operating temperature. With the choke valve fully open and the engine idling in neutral, open the throttle slightly and rotate the fast idle cam until the fast idle screw contacts the second step of the fast idle cam. Release the throttle. The linkage pullback spring will cause the fast idle adjusting screw to hold the cam in this position. The tachometer should read 2100 rpm. If not, turn the adjusting screw until it does.

Initial Choke Valve Clearance

▶ See Figure 8

1. Position the fast idle screw on the top step of the fast idle cam.
2. Using a vacuum pump, seat the choke vacuum break.
3. Apply light closing pressure in the choke plate to position the plate as far closed as possible without forcing it.
4. Measure the distance between the air horn wall and the choke plate. If it is not that specified in the Carburetor Specifications Chart, bend the choke vacuum break link until it is.

Choke Setting

4-134 AND 6-225 ENGINES

The choke is manually operated by a cable that runs from the dash mounted control pull knob to the set screw on the choke actuating arm. To adjust the choke, loosen the set screw at the choke actuating lever and push in the dash knob as far as it will go. Open the choke plate as far as it will go and hold it with your finger while the set screw is tightened.

6-226 ENGINE

Loosen the choke cover screws and turn the cover, clockwise, until the indicator on the housing aligns with the notch on the casting. Tighten the screws.

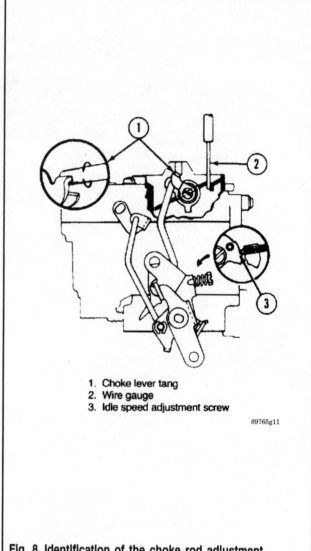

1. Choke lever tang
2. Wire gauge
3. Idle speed adjustment screw

Fig. 8 Identification of the choke rod adjustment components — Rochester 2GV carburetor

Choke Unloader

4-134 AND 6-225 ENGINES

▶ See Figure 9

With the throttle held fully open, apply pressure on the choke valve toward the closed position and measure the clearance between the lower edge of the choke valve and the air horn wall. The setting should be ¼ in. (6mm). Adjust by bending the tang on the fast idle lever, which is located on the throttle linkage.

Dashpot

INLINE 6-CYLINDER ENGINES

With the throttle set at curb idle position fully depress the dashpot stem and measure the clearance between the stem and the throttle lever. Adjust by loosening the lock nut and turning the dashpot.

FUEL SYSTEM 5-7

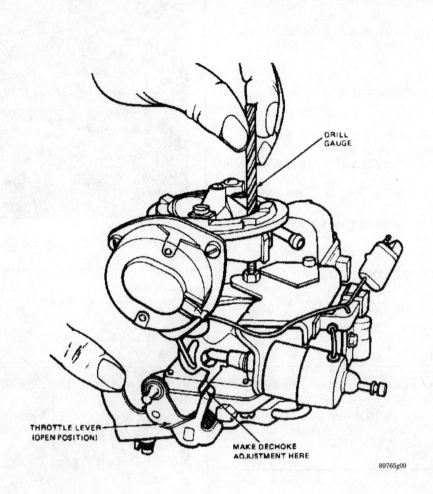

Fig. 9 Use a ¼ in. diameter drill bit as a gauge between the choke plate and throttle bore wall

INLINE 4-CYLINDER AND V6 ENGINES
▶ See Figure 10

The adjustment is made with the engine idling. Loosen the dashpot locknut and turn the assembly until the plunger contacts the throttle lever without being depressed. Then, turn the assembly 2½ turns against the lever, depressing the plunger. Tighten the locknut.

Accelerator Pump

6-226 ENGINE

1. Place the pump connector link in the outer hole of the pump arm.
2. Back out the throttle lever setscrew until the throttle plates seat in their bores. Make certain that the fast idle adjusting screw is not holding the throttle open.
3. Place pump travel gauge, T109-117S, or its equivalent, inverted on the edge of the dust cover boss on the bowl cover.

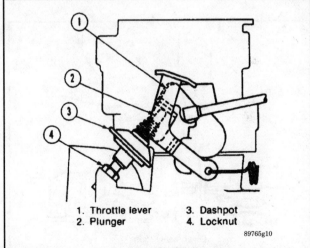

Fig. 10 Identification of the dashpot adjustment components — Rochester 2GV carburetor

5-8 FUEL SYSTEM

4. Turn the knurled nut of the gauge until the finger just touches the upper end of the plunger shaft. The measured distance should be ½ in. (13mm) from the dust cover boss to the top of the plunger. This corresponds to an indicated gauge number of 33. Adjust by bending the link at the upper bend.

Metering Rod

6-226 ENGINE WITH CARTER MODEL WCD

▶ See Figure 11

1. Perform a pump adjustment.
2. Counting the number of threads involved, back out the throttle lever screw until the throttle plates are seated in their bores.
3. Press down on the vacumeter link until the metering rods bottom.
4. In this position, move the metering rod arm until the lip contacts the vacumeter link.
5. Hold it in place and tighten the metering rod setscrew.

6-226 ENGINE WITH CARTER MODEL WGD

1. Perform a pump adjustment.
2. Counting the number of threads involved, back out the throttle lever screw until the throttle plates are seated in their bores.
3. Press down on the vacumeter link until the metering rods bottom.
4. In this position, move the metering rod arm until the lip contacts the vacumeter link.
5. Hold it in place and tighten the metering rod setscrew.

REMOVAL & INSTALLATION

All Engines

▶ See Figures 12, 13, 14, 15, 16, 17, 18, 19, 20, 21, 22, 23 and 24

1. Remove the air cleaner from the top of the carburetor.
2. Remove all lines and hoses, noting their positions to facilitate installation.

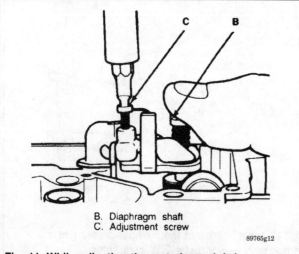

Fig. 11 While adjusting the metering rod, it is necessary to depress the diaphragm shaft

B. Diaphragm shaft
C. Adjustment screw

Fig. 12 For L-head 4-134 engines, disconnect the fuel line from the carburetor . . .

Fig. 13 . . . then detach the throttle cable from the throttle lever

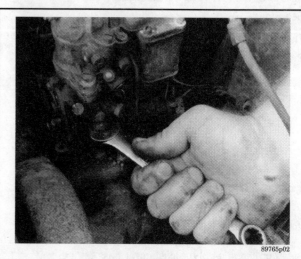

Fig. 14 Remove the rear hold-down nut and loosen the front hold-down nut . . .

FUEL SYSTEM 5-9

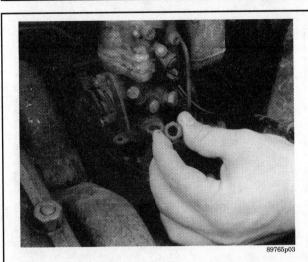
Fig. 15 . . . then remove the front nut while lifting the carburetor off the manifold

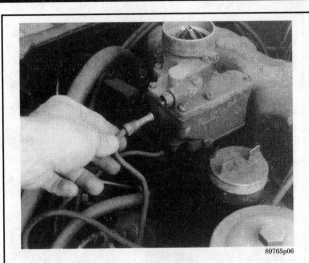
Fig. 18 . . . then pull the fuel line from the carburetor inlet fitting

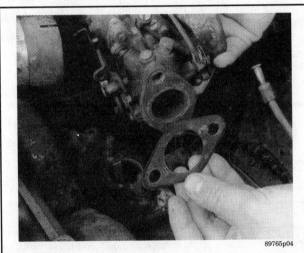
Fig. 16 Make certain to remove the old gasket from the carburetor or manifold

Fig. 19 If equipped, detach the vacuum wiper booster line from the carburetor base

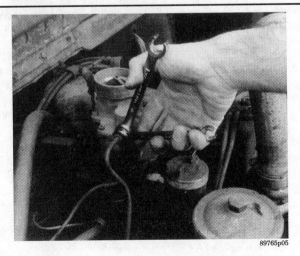
Fig. 17 On F-head 4-134 engines, use 2 wrenches to loosen the fuel line fitting . . .

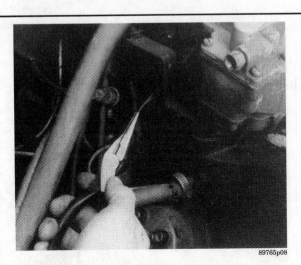
Fig. 20 Remove the cotter pin to detach the throttle cable from the carburetor lever

Fig. 21 Loosen the choke cable clamp screw . . .

Fig. 22 . . . then slide the cable out of the carburetor lever

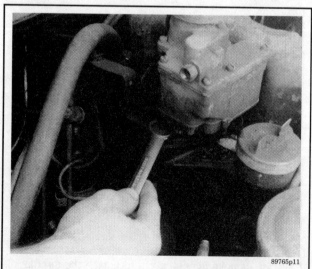

Fig. 23 Remove the carburetor mounting nuts . . .

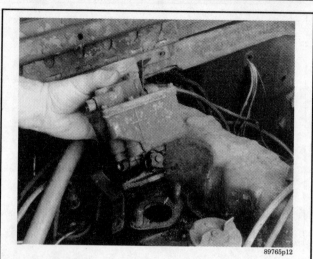

Fig. 24 . . . and lift the carburetor off of the manifold/cylinder head

3. Remove all throttle and choke linkage at the carburetor.
4. Remove the carburetor attaching nuts which hold it to the intake manifold.
5. Lift the carburetor from the engine along with the carburetor base gasket. Discard the gasket.
6. Install the carburetor in the reverse order of removal, using a new base gasket.

➡To avoid any distortion of the carburetor body, always tighten the nuts alternately, in a crisscross pattern to 182 inch lbs. (20 Nm).

OVERHAUL

◆ See Figures 25, 26 and 27

Efficient carburetion depends greatly on careful cleaning and inspection during overhaul, since dirt, gum, water, or varnish in or on the carburetor parts are often responsible for poor performance.

Overhaul your carburetor in a clean, dust-free area. Carefully disassemble the carburetor, referring often to the exploded views. Keep all similar and look-alike parts segregated during disassembly and cleaning to avoid accidental interchange during assembly. Make a note of all jet sizes.

When the carburetor is disassembled, wash all parts (except diaphragms, electric choke units, pump plunger, and any other plastic, leather, fiber or rubber parts) in clean carburetor solvent. Do not leave parts in the solvent any longer than is necessary to sufficiently loosen the deposits. Excessive cleaning may remove the special finish from the float bowl and choke valve bodies, leaving these parts unfit for service. Rinse all parts in clean solvent and blow them dry with compressed air or allow them to air dry. Wipe clean all cork, plastic, leather and fiber parts with a clean, lint-free cloth.

Blow out all passages and jets with compressed air and be sure that there are not restrictions or blockages. Never use wire or similar tools to clean jets, fuel passages, or air bleeds. Clean all jets and valves separately to avoid accidental interchange.

FUEL SYSTEM 5-11

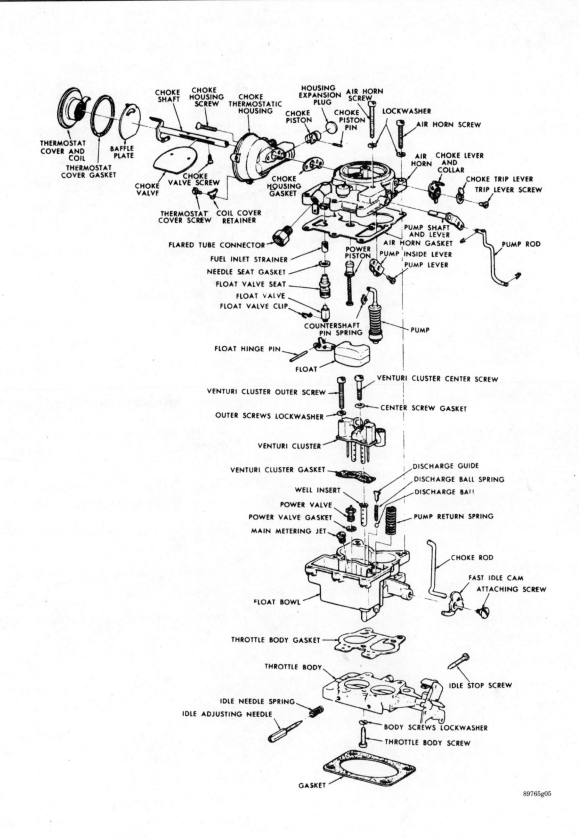

Fig. 25 Exploded view of the Rochester 2GC carburetor used on 6-225 engines

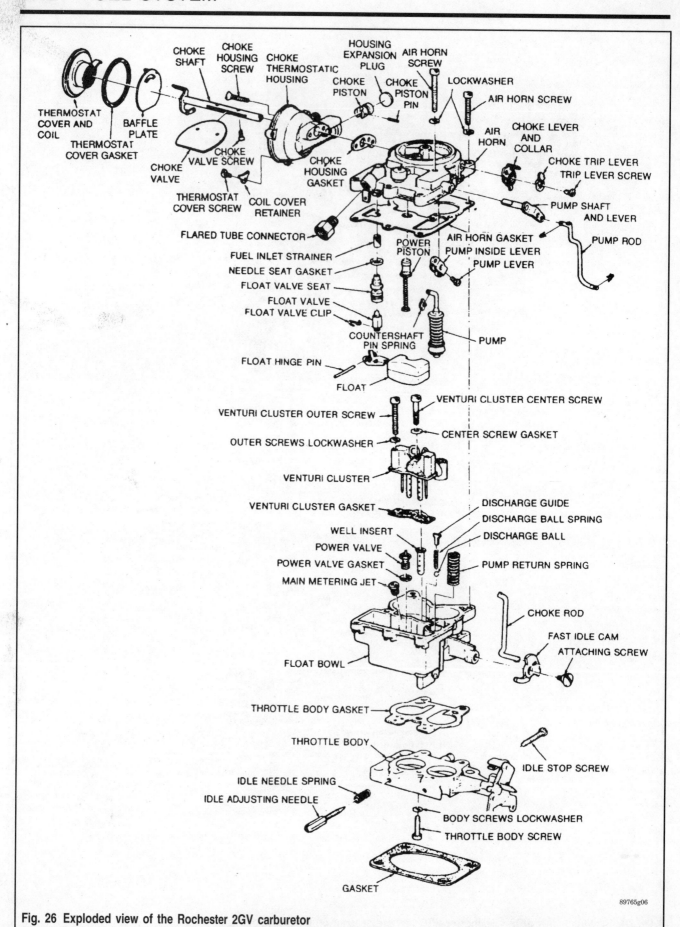

Fig. 26 Exploded view of the Rochester 2GV carburetor

FUEL SYSTEM 5-13

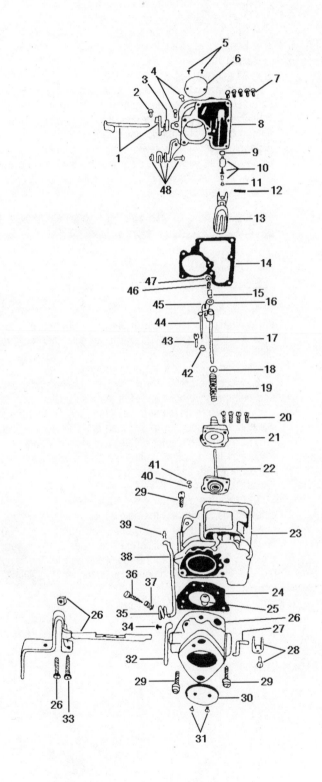

1. Choke shaft and lever
2. Screw
3. Choke lever spring
4. Screw and washer
5. Choke valve screw
6. Choke valve
7. Screw and washer
8. Air horn
9. Needle seat gasket
10. Needle spring and seat
11. Needle pin
12. Float pin
13. Float
14. Gasket
15. Pump spring
16. Metering rod arm
17. Pump link
18. Pump spring retainer
19. Vacuum diaphragm spring
20. Screw and washer
21. Diaphragm housing
22. Diaphragm
23. Body
24. Gasket
25. Idle port plug
26. Throttle body lever and shaft assembly
27. Pump link connector
28. Throttle shaft arm
29. Screw and washer
30. Throttle valve
31. Throttle valve screw
32. Fast idle arm
33. Adjusting screw
34. Body flange plug
35. Clevis clip
36. Idle adjusting screw
37. Idle screw spring
38. Fast idle connector rod
39. Pin spring
40. Ball check valve
41. Ball check valve retainer ring
42. Metering rod jet
43. Low speed jet
44. Metering rod
45. Metering rod spring
46. Inner pump spring
47. Pump spring retainer
48. Bracket and clamp assembly (choke and throttle)

Fig. 27 Exploded view of the Carter YF carburetor used on 4-134 engines

5-14 FUEL SYSTEM

Check all parts for wear or damage. If wear or damage is found, replace the defective parts. Especially check the following:

- Check the float needle and seat for wear. If wear is found, replace the complete assembly.
- Check the float hinge pin for wear and the float(s) for dents or distortion. Replace the float if fuel has leaked into it.
- Check the throttle and choke shaft bores for wear or an out-of-round condition. Damage or wear to the throttle arm, shaft, or shaft bore will often require replacement of the throttle body. These parts require a close tolerance of fit. Wear may allow air leakage, which could affect starting and idling.

➡ **Throttle shafts and bushings are not included in overhaul kits. They can be purchased separately.**

- Inspect the idle mixture adjusting needles for burrs or grooves. Any such condition requires replacement of the needle, since you will not be able to obtain a satisfactory idle.
- Test the accelerator pump check valves. They should pass air one way but not the other. Test for proper seating by blowing and sucking on the valve. Replace the valve if necessary. If the valve is satisfactory, wash the valve again to remove breath moisture.
- Check the bowl cover for warped surfaces with a straightedge.
- Closely inspect the valves and seats for wear and damage, replacing as necessary.
- After the carburetor is assembled, check the choke valve for freedom of operation.

Carburetor overhaul kits are recommended for each overhaul. These kits contain all gaskets and new parts to replace those that deteriorate most rapidly. Failure to replace all parts supplied with the kit (especially gaskets) can result in poor performance later.

Carburetor manufacturers supply overhaul kits of three basic types: minor repair, major repair, and gasket kits. Basically, they contain the following:

Minor Repair Kits:
- All gaskets
- Float needle valve
- Volume control screw
- All diaphragms
- Spring for the pump diaphragm

Major Repair Kits:
- All jets and gaskets
- All diaphragms
- Float needle valve
- Volume control screw
- Pump ball valve
- Main jet carrier
- Float
- Complete intermediate rod
- Intermediate pump lever
- Complete injector tube
- Some cover hold-down screws and washers

Gasket Kits:
- All gaskets

After cleaning and checking all components, reassemble the carburetor, using new parts and referring to the exploded view. When reassembling, make sure that all screws and jets are tight in their seats, but do not overtighten, as the tips will be distorted. Tighten all screws gradually, in rotation. Do not tighten needle valves into their seats; uneven jetting will result. Always use new gaskets. Be sure to adjust the float level when reassembling.

Governor

ADJUSTMENT

1. Connect a tachometer to the engine. Adjust the carburetor to obtain a smooth idle at 600 rpm. Shut off the engine.
2. Check the throttle linkage to be sure that the throttle plate can be set at the wide open position. Make sure that the throttle and governor linkage are operating freely.
3. Place the carburetor in the wide open throttle position and pull the governor handle all the way out.
4. Adjust the governor-to-bell crank rod so that the linkage will hold the carburetor in the wide open throttle position.
5. Close the governor control and start the engine.
6. Pull the governor control out to the last notch and adjust the cable length at the adjusting yoke so that the engine will run at 2,600 rpm.
7. Close the governor control and make sure that the engine returns to the 600 rpm idle speed. Check that the linkage operates freely. If the engine does not return to the 600 rpm figure, loosen the locknut, at the dash panel, which retains the governor hand control to the rod, and back off the handle until the idle speed adjusting screw rests on the stop. Tighten the locknut.

FUEL SYSTEM 5-15

FUEL TANK

Tank Assembly

REMOVAL & INSTALLATION

1945-69 Models

♦ See Figures 28 and 29

1. Make sure that the tank is either completely drained or that the level is at least below any of the vent lines or filler openings so that when these lines are disconnected fuel will not run out.
2. Remove the driver's seat from the vehicle.
3. Disconnect all of the vent line hoses, the fuel gauge electrical lead, the fill hose and the fuel outlet line at the tank.
4. Remove the tank hold-down screws from the mounting brackets, or the hold-down strap, and lift the tank from the vehicle.
5. If there is still gas in the tank, be careful not to spill any fuel when lifting it out of the vehicle. Also, empty the tank of all fuel and flush it with water before soldering or welding the tank.
6. Install the tank in the reverse order of removal.

1970 Model

The fuel tank is attached to the frame by brackets and bolts. The brackets are attached to the tank at the seam flange or the skid plate.

Before removing the fuel tank, make sure that the level of the fuel inside the tank is at least below any of the various hoses connected. It is best to either drain or siphon the majority of fuel out of the tank to make it easier to handle while removing it.

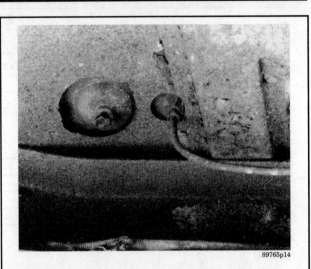

Fig. 28 Some early models are equipped with a fuel tank drain plug under the tank

Fig. 29 Draining the tank prior to removal can make this procedure much easier

5-16 FUEL SYSTEM

CARBURETOR SPECIFICATIONS

All measurements given in inches except where noted

Engine	Years	Carburetor Model	Float Level	Float Drop	Dashpot Setting	Fast Idle	Choke Unloader	Initial Choke Valve Clearance	Automatic Choke Setting
4–134	1945-64	Carter YF	0.3125	—	—	1,500	—	—	—
	1966-70	Carter YF	0.4531	1.25	0.09375	1,600	0.2969	0.2344	Notch
6–225	1966-68	Rochester 2G	1.156	1.875	—	1,800	0.03125	0.25	—
		Rochester 2GV	1.156	1.875	—	1,800	0.03125	0.25	—
	1969-70	Rochester 2G	1.156	1.875	—	1,800	0.04688	0.25	—
6–226	All	Carter WCD	0.1875	—	—	0.04 in.	0.125	—	Index
		Carter WGD	0.28125	—	—	0.018-0.023 in.	0.125	—	Index
6–230	All	Holley 1920	①	—	—	2,100	—	—	—
		Holley 2415	0.0625	—	—	2,100	—	—	—

① Gauge J-10238 should be used to set the float level.

Troubleshooting Basic Fuel System Problems

Problem	Cause	Solution
Engine cranks, but won't start (or is hard to start) when cold	• Empty fuel tank • Incorrect starting procedure • Defective fuel pump • No fuel in carburetor • Clogged fuel filter • Engine flooded • Defective choke	• Check for fuel in tank • Follow correct procedure • Check pump output • Check for fuel in the carburetor • Replace fuel filter • Wait 15 minutes; try again • Check choke plate
Engine cranks, but is hard to start (or does not start) when hot— (presence of fuel is assumed)	• Defective choke	• Check choke plate
Rough idle or engine runs rough	• Dirt or moisture in fuel • Clogged air filter • Faulty fuel pump	• Replace fuel filter • Replace air filter • Check fuel pump output
Engine stalls or hesitates on acceleration	• Dirt or moisture in the fuel • Dirty carburetor • Defective fuel pump • Incorrect float level, defective accelerator pump	• Replace fuel filter • Clean the carburetor • Check fuel pump output • Check carburetor
Poor gas mileage	• Clogged air filter • Dirty carburetor • Defective choke, faulty carburetor adjustment	• Replace air filter • Clean carburetor • Check carburetor
Engine is flooded (won't start accompanied by smell of raw fuel)	• Improperly adjusted choke or carburetor	• Wait 15 minutes and try again, without pumping gas pedal • If it won't start, check carburetor

CIRCUIT PROTECTION
  FUSES 6-22
  FUSIBLE LINKS 6-22
HEATER
  BLOWER MOTOR 6-12
  HEATER CORE 6-13
INSTRUMENTS AND SWITCHES
  IGNITION LOCK CYLINDER 6-15
  IGNITION SWITCH 6-15
  INSTRUMENT CLUSTER 6-15
LIGHTING
  HEADLIGHTS 6-17
  TURN SIGNALS 6-18
SPECIFICATIONS CHARTS
  FUSE APPLICATIONS 6-22
  LIGHT BULB APPLICATIONS 6-19
  TROUBLESHOOTING BASIC DASH
    GAUGE PROBLEMS 6-16
  TROUBLESHOOTING BASIC
    LIGHTING PROBLEMS 6-20
  TROUBLESHOOTING BASIC TURN
    SIGNAL AND FLASHER
    PROBLEMS 6-21
  TROUBLESHOOTING BASIC
    WINDSHIELD WIPER
    PROBLEMS 6-15
  TROUBLESHOOTING THE
    HEATER 6-14
TRAILER WIRING 6-22
**UNDERSTANDING AND
  TROUBLESHOOTING ELECTRICAL
  SYSTEMS**
  ADD-ON ELECTRICAL
    EQUIPMENT 6-12
  SAFETY PRECAUTIONS 6-2
  TROUBLESHOOTING 6-3
  UNDERSTANDING BASIC
    ELECTRICITY 6-2
  WIRING HARNESSES 6-8
WINDSHIELD WIPERS
  WIPER BLADES AND ARMS 6-14
  WIPER LINKAGE 6-14
  WIPER MOTOR 6-14
WIRING DIAGRAMS 6-23

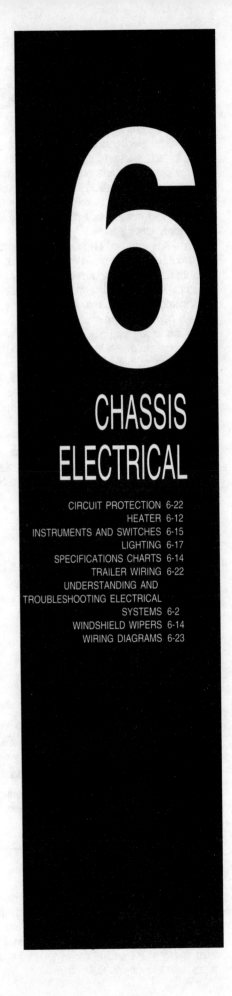

6

CHASSIS ELECTRICAL

CIRCUIT PROTECTION 6-22
HEATER 6-12
INSTRUMENTS AND SWITCHES 6-15
LIGHTING 6-17
SPECIFICATIONS CHARTS 6-14
TRAILER WIRING 6-22
UNDERSTANDING AND
TROUBLESHOOTING ELECTRICAL
SYSTEMS 6-2
WINDSHIELD WIPERS 6-14
WIRING DIAGRAMS 6-23

6-2 CHASSIS ELECTRICAL

UNDERSTANDING AND TROUBLESHOOTING ELECTRICAL SYSTEMS

Over the years import and domestic manufacturers have incorporated electronic control systems into their production lines. In fact, electronic control systems are so prevalent that all new cars and trucks built today are equipped with at least one on-board computer. These electronic components (with no moving parts) should theoretically last the life of the vehicle, provided that nothing external happens to damage the circuits or memory chips.

While it is true that electronic components should never wear out, in the real world malfunctions do occur. It is also true that any computer-based system is extremely sensitive to electrical voltages and cannot tolerate careless or haphazard testing/service procedures. An inexperienced individual can literally cause major damage looking for a minor problem by using the wrong kind of test equipment or connecting test leads/connectors with the ignition switch **ON**. When selecting test equipment, make sure the manufacturer's instructions state that the tester is compatible with whatever type of system is being serviced. Read all instructions carefully and double check all test points before installing probes or making any test connections.

The following section outlines basic diagnosis techniques for dealing with automotive electrical systems. Along with a general explanation of the various types of test equipment available to aid in servicing modern automotive systems, basic repair techniques for wiring harnesses and connectors are also given. Read the basic information before attempting any repairs or testing. This will provide the background of information necessary to avoid the most common and obvious mistakes that can cost both time and money. Although the replacement and testing procedures are simple in themselves, the systems are not, and unless one has a thorough understanding of all components and their function within a particular system, the logical test sequence these systems demand cannot be followed. Minor malfunctions can make a big difference, so it is important to know how each component affects the operation of the overall system in order to find the ultimate cause of a problem without replacing good components unnecessarily. It is not enough to use the correct test equipment; the test equipment must be used correctly.

Safety Precautions

✴✴CAUTION

Whenever working on or around any electrical or electronic systems, always observe these general precautions to prevent the possibility of personal injury or damage to electronic components.

- Never install or remove battery cables with the key **ON** or the engine running. Jumper cables should be connected with the key **OFF** to avoid power surges that can damage electronic control units. Engines equipped with computer controlled systems should avoid both giving and getting jump starts due to the possibility of serious damage to components from arcing in the engine compartment if connections are made with the ignition **ON**.

- Always remove the battery cables before charging the battery. Never use a high output charger on an installed battery or attempt to use any type of "hot shot" (24 volt) starting aid.

- Exercise care when inserting test probes into connectors to insure good contact without damaging the connector or spreading the pins. Always probe connectors from the rear (wire) side, NOT the pin side, to avoid accidental shorting of terminals during test procedures.

- Never remove or attach wiring harness connectors with the ignition switch **ON**, especially to an electronic control unit.

- Do not drop any components during service procedures and never apply 12 volts directly to any component (like a solenoid or relay) unless instructed specifically to do so. Some component electrical windings are designed to safely handle only 4 or 5 volts and can be destroyed in seconds if 12 volts are applied directly to the connector.

- Remove the electronic control unit if the vehicle is to be placed in an environment where temperatures exceed approximately 176°F (80°C), such as a paint spray booth or when arc/gas welding near the control unit location.

Understanding Basic Electricity

Understanding the basic theory of electricity makes electrical troubleshooting much easier. Several gauges are used in electrical troubleshooting to see inside the circuit being tested. Without a basic understanding, it will be difficult to understand testing procedures.

THE WATER ANALOGY

Electricity is the flow of electrons — hypothetical particles thought to constitute the basic stuff of electricity. Many people have been taught electrical theory using an analogy with water. In a comparison with water flowing in a pipe, the electrons would be the water. As the flow of water can be measured, the flow of electricity can be measured. The unit of measurement is amperes, frequently abbreviated amps. An ammeter will measure the actual amount of current flowing in the circuit.

Just as the water pressure is measured in units such as pounds per square inch, electrical pressure is measured in volts. When a voltmeter's two probes are placed on two live portions of an electrical circuit with different electrical pressures, current will flow through the voltmeter and produce a reading which indicates the difference in electrical pressure between the two parts of the circuit.

While increasing the voltage in a circuit will increase the flow of current, the actual flow depends not only on voltage, but on the resistance of the circuit. The standard unit for measuring circuit resistance is an ohm, measured by an ohmmeter. The ohmmeter is somewhat similar to an ammeter, but incorporates its own source of power so that a standard voltage is always present.

CHASSIS ELECTRICAL 6-3

CIRCUITS

An actual electric circuit consists of four basic parts. These are: the power source, such as a generator or battery; a hot wire, which conducts the electricity under a relatively high voltage to the component supplied by the circuit; the load, such as a lamp, motor, resistor or relay coil; and the ground wire, which carries the current back to the source under very low voltage. In such a circuit the bulk of the resistance exists between the point where the hot wire is connected to the load, and the point where the load is grounded. In an automobile, the vehicle's frame or body, which is made of steel, is used as a part of the ground circuit for many of the electrical devices.

Remember that, in electrical testing, the voltmeter is connected in parallel with the circuit being tested (without disconnecting any wires) and measures the difference in voltage between the locations of the two probes; that the ammeter is connected in series with the load (the circuit is separated at one point and the ammeter inserted so it becomes a part of the circuit); and the ohmmeter is self-powered, so that all the power in the circuit should be off and the portion of the circuit to be measured contacted at either end by one of the probes of the meter.

For any electrical system to operate, it must make a complete circuit. This simply means that the power flow from the battery must make a complete circle. When an electrical component is operating, power flows from the battery to the component, passes through the component causing it to perform it to function (such as lighting a light bulb) and then returns to the battery through the ground of the circuit. This ground is usually (but not always) the metal part of the vehicle on which the electrical component is mounted.

Perhaps the easiest way to visualize this is to think of connecting a light bulb with two wires attached to it to your vehicle's battery. The battery in your vehicle has two posts (negative and positive). If one of the two wires attached to the light bulb was attached to the negative post of the battery and the other wire was attached to the positive post of the battery, you would have a complete circuit. Current from the battery would flow out one post, through the wire attached to it and then to the light bulb, where it would pass through causing it to light. It would then leave the light bulb, travel through the other wire, and return to the other post of the battery.

AUTOMOTIVE CIRCUITS

The normal automotive circuit differs from this simple example in two ways. First, instead of having a return wire from the bulb to the battery, the light bulb return the current to the battery through the chassis of the vehicle. Since the negative battery cable is attached to the chassis and the chassis is made of electrically conductive metal, the chassis of the vehicle can serve as a ground wire to complete the circuit. Secondly, most automotive circuits contain switches to turn components on and off.

Some electrical components which require a large amount of current to operate also have a relay in their circuit. Since these circuits carry a large amount of current, the thickness of the wire in the circuit (gauge size) is also greater. If this large wire were connected from the component to the control switch on the instrument panel, and then back to the component, a voltage drop would occur in the circuit. To prevent this potential drop in voltage, an electromagnetic switch (relay) is used. The large wires in the circuit are connected from the vehicle battery to one side of the relay, and from the opposite side of the relay to the component. The relay is normally open, preventing current from passing through the circuit. An additional, smaller wire is connected from the relay to the control switch for the circuit. When the control switch is turned on, it grounds the smaller wire from the relay and completes the circuit.

SHORT CIRCUITS

If you were to disconnect the light bulb (from the previous example of a light-bulb being connected to the battery by two wires) from the wires and touch the two wires together (please take our word for this; don't try it), the result will be a shower of sparks. A similar thing happens (on a smaller scale) when the power supply wire to a component or the electrical component itself becomes grounded before the normal ground connection for the circuit. To prevent damage to the system, the fuse for the circuit blows to interrupt the circuit — protecting the components from damage. Because grounding a wire from a power source makes a complete circuit — less the required component to use the power — the phenomenon is called a short circuit. The most common causes of short circuits are: the rubber insulation on a wire breaking or rubbing through to expose the current carrying core of the wire to a metal part of the car, or a shorted switch.

Some electrical systems on the vehicle are protected by a circuit breaker which is, basically, a self-repairing fuse. When either of the described events takes place in a system which is protected by a circuit breaker, the circuit breaker opens the circuit the same way a fuse does. However, when either the short is removed from the circuit or the surge subsides, the circuit breaker resets itself and does not have to be replaced as a fuse does.

Troubleshooting

When diagnosing a specific problem, organized troubleshooting is a must. The complexity of a modern automobile demands that you approach any problem in a logical, organized manner. There are certain troubleshooting techniques that are standard:

1. Establish when the problem occurs. Does the problem appear only under certain conditions? Were there any noises, odors, or other unusual symptoms?

2. Isolate the problem area. To do this, make some simple tests and observations; then eliminate the systems that are working properly. Check for obvious problems such as broken wires, dirty connections or split/disconnected vacuum hoses. Always check the obvious before assuming something complicated is the cause.

3. Test for problems systematically to determine the cause once the problem area is isolated. Are all the components functioning properly? Is there power going to electrical switches and motors? Is there vacuum at vacuum switches and/or actuators? Is there a mechanical problem such as bent linkage

6-4 CHASSIS ELECTRICAL

or loose mounting screws? Performing careful, systematic checks will often turn up most causes on the first inspection without wasting time checking components that have little or no relationship to the problem.

4. Test all repairs after the work is done to make sure that the problem is fixed. Some causes can be traced to more than one component, so a careful verification of repair work is important in order to pick up additional malfunctions that may cause a problem to reappear or a different problem to arise. A blown fuse, for example, is a simple problem that may require more than another fuse to repair. If you don't look for a problem that caused a fuse to blow, a shorted wire (for example) may go undetected.

Experience has shown that most problems tend to be the result of a fairly simple and obvious cause, such as loose or corroded connectors or air leaks in the intake system. This makes careful inspection of components during testing essential to quick and accurate troubleshooting.

BASIC TROUBLESHOOTING THEORY

Electrical problems generally fall into one of three areas:
- The component that is not functioning is not receiving current.
- The component itself is not functioning.
- The component is not properly grounded.

Problems that fall into the first category are by far the most complicated. It is the current supply system to the component which contains all the switches, relay, fuses, etc.

The electrical system can be checked with a test light and a jumper wire. A test light is a device that looks like a pointed screwdriver with a wire attached to it. It has a light bulb in its handle. A jumper wire is a piece of insulated wire with an alligator clip attached to each end.

If a light bulb is not working, you must follow a systematic plan to determine which of the three causes is the villain.

1. Turn on the switch that controls the inoperable bulb.
2. Disconnect the power supply wire from the bulb.
3. Attach the ground wire to the test light to a good metal ground.
4. Touch the probe end of the test light to the end of the power supply wire that was disconnected from the bulb. If the bulb is receiving current, the test light will go on.

➡If the bulb is one which works only when the ignition key is turned on (turn signal), make sure the key is turned on.

If the test light does not go on, then the problem is in the circuit between the battery and the bulb. As mentioned before, this includes all the switches, fuses, and relays in the system. Turn to a wiring diagram and find the bulb on the diagram. Follow the wire that runs back to the battery. The problem is an open circuit between the battery and the bulb. If the fuse is blown and, when replaced, immediately blows again, there is a short circuit in the system which must be located and repaired. If there is a switch in the system, bypass it with a jumper wire. This is done by connecting one end of the jumper wire to the power supply wire into the switch and the other end of the jumper wire to the wire coming out of the switch. If the test light illuminates with the jumper wire installed, the switch or whatever was bypassed is defective.

➡Never substitute the jumper wire for the bulb, as the bulb is the component required to use the power from the power source.

5. If the bulb in the test light goes on, then the current is getting to the bulb that is not working in the car. This eliminates the first of the three possible causes. Connect the power supply wire and connect a jumper wire from the bulb to a good metal ground. Do this with the switch which controls the bulb works with jumper wire installed, then it has a bad ground. This is usually caused by the metal area on which the bulb mounts to the vehicle being coated with some type of foreign matter.
6. If neither test located the source of the trouble, then the light bulb itself is defective.

The previous test procedure can be applied to any of the components of the chassis electrical system by substituting the component that is not working for the light bulb. Remember that for any electrical system to work, all connections must be clean and tight.

TEST EQUIPMENT

➡Pinpointing the exact cause of trouble in an electrical system can sometimes only be accomplished by the use of special test equipment. The following describes different types of commonly used test equipment and explains how to use them in diagnosis. In addition to the information covered later, the tool manufacturer's instructions booklet (provided with the tester) should be read and clearly understood before attempting any test procedures.

Jumper Wires
▶ See Figures 1 and 2

Jumper wires are simple, yet extremely valuable, pieces of test equipment. They are basically test wires which are used to bypass sections of a circuit. The simplest type of jumper

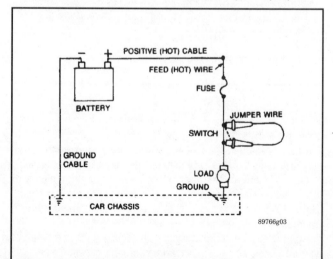

Fig. 1 Example of using a jumper wire to bypass a switch during a diagnostic test

CHASSIS ELECTRICAL   6-5

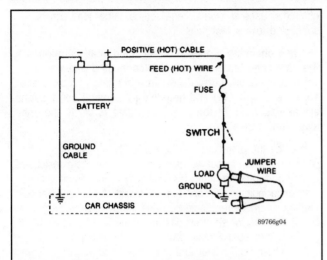

Fig. 2 Checking for a bad ground connection with a jumper wire

wire is a length of multi-strand wire with an alligator clip at each end. Jumper wires are usually fabricated from lengths of standard automotive wire and whatever type of connector (alligator clip, spade connector or pin connector) that is required for the particular vehicle being tested. The well equipped tool box will have several different styles of jumper wires in several different lengths. Some jumper wires are made with three or more terminals coming from a common splice for special purpose testing. In cramped, hard-to-reach areas it is advisable to have insulated boots over the jumper wire terminals in order to prevent accidental grounding, sparks, and possible fire, especially when testing fuel system components.

Jumper wires are used primarily to locate open electrical circuits, on either the ground (-) side of the circuit or on the hot (+) side. If an electrical component fails to operate, connect the jumper wire between the component and a good ground. If the component operates only with the jumper installed, the ground circuit is open. If the ground circuit is good, but the component does not operate, the circuit between the power feed and component may be open. By moving the jumper wire successively back from the lamp toward the power source, you can isolate the area of the circuit where the open is located. When the component stops functioning, or the power is cut off, the open is in the segment of wire between the jumper and the point previously tested.

You can sometimes connect the jumper wire directly from the battery to the hot terminal of the component, but first make sure the component uses 12 volts in operation. Some electrical components, such as fuel injectors, are designed to operate on about 4 volts and running 12 volts directly to the injector terminals can cause damage.

By inserting an in-line fuse holder between a set of test leads, a fused jumper wire can be used for bypassing open circuits. Use a 5 amp fuse to provide protection against voltage spikes. When in doubt, use a voltmeter to check the voltage input to the component and measure how much voltage is normally being applied.

✼✼CAUTION

Never use jumpers made from wire that is of lighter gauge than that which is used in the circuit under test. If the jumper wire is of too small a gauge, it may overheat and possibly melt. Never use jumpers to bypass high resistance loads in a circuit. Bypassing resistances, in effect, creates a short circuit. This may, in turn, cause damage and fire. Jumper wires should only be used to bypass lengths of wire.

Unpowered Test Lights

The 12 volt test light is used to check circuits and components while electrical current is flowing through them. It is used for voltage and ground tests. Twelve volt test lights come in different styles but all have three main parts; a ground clip, a probe, and a light. The most commonly used 12 volt test lights have pick-type probes. To use a 12 volt test light, connect the ground clip to a good ground and probe wherever necessary with the pick. The pick should be sharp so that it can be probed into tight spaces.

✼✼WARNING

Do not use a test light to probe electronic ignition spark plug or coil wires. Never use a pick-type test light to probe wiring on computer controlled systems unless specifically instructed to do so. Any wire insulation that is pierced by the test light probe should be taped and sealed with silicone after testing.

Like the jumper wire, the 12 volt test light is used to isolate opens in circuits. But, whereas the jumper wire is used to bypass the open to operate the load, the 12 volt test light is used to locate the presence of voltage in a circuit. If the test light glows, you know that there is power up to that point; if the 12 volt test light does not glow when its probe is inserted into the wire or connector, you know that there is an open circuit (no power). Move the test light in successive steps back toward the power source until the light in the handle does glow. When it glows, the open is between the probe and point which was probed previously.

➡The test light does not detect that 12 volts (or any particular amount of voltage) is present; it only detects that some voltage is present. It is advisable before using the test light to touch its terminals across the battery posts to make sure the light is operating properly.

Self-Powered Test Lights

The self-powered test light usually contains a 1.5 volt penlight battery. One type of self-powered test light is similar in design to the 12 volt unit. This type has both the battery and the light in the handle, along with a pick-type probe tip. The second type has the light toward the open tip, so that the light illuminates the contact point. The self-powered test light is a dual purpose piece of test equipment. It can be used to test for either open or short circuits when power is isolated from the circuit (continuity test). A powered test light should not be used on any computer controlled system or component unless specifically instructed to do so. Many engine sensors can be destroyed by even this small amount of voltage applied directly to the terminals.

Voltmeters

A voltmeter is used to measure voltage at any point in a circuit, or to measure the voltage drop across any part of a circuit. It can also be used to check continuity in a wire or circuit by indicating current flow from one end to the other. Analog voltmeters usually have various scales on the meter dial and a selector switch to allow the selection of different voltages. The voltmeter has a positive and a negative lead. To avoid damage to the meter, always connect the negative lead to the negative (-) side of the circuit (to ground or nearest the ground side of the circuit) and connect the positive lead to the positive (+) side of the circuit (to the power source or the nearest power source). Note that the negative voltmeter lead will always be black and that the positive voltmeter will always be some color other than black (usually red).

Depending on how the voltmeter is connected into the circuit, it has several uses. A voltmeter can be connected either in parallel or in series with a circuit and it has a very high resistance to current flow. When connected in parallel, only a small amount of current will flow through the voltmeter current path; the rest will flow through the normal circuit current path and the circuit will work normally. When the voltmeter is connected in series with a circuit, only a small amount of current can flow through the circuit. The circuit will not work properly, but the voltmeter reading will show if the circuit is complete or not.

Ohmmeters

The ohmmeter is designed to read resistance (which is measured in ohms or Ω) in a circuit or component. Although there are several different styles of ohmmeters, all analog meters will usually have a selector switch which permits the measurement of different ranges of resistance (usually the selector switch allows the multiplication of the meter reading by 10, 100, 1000, and 10,000). A calibration knob allows the meter to be set at zero for accurate measurement. Since all ohmmeters are powered by an internal battery, the ohmmeter can be used as a self-powered test light. When the ohmmeter is connected, current from the ohmmeter flows through the circuit or component being tested. Since the ohmmeter's internal resistance and voltage are known values, the amount of current flow through the meter depends on the resistance of the circuit or component being tested.

The ohmmeter can be used to perform a continuity test for opens or shorts (either by observation of the meter needle or as a self-powered test light), and to read actual resistance in a circuit. It should be noted that the ohmmeter is used to check the resistance of a component or wire while there is no voltage applied to the circuit. Current flow from an outside voltage source (such as the vehicle battery) can damage the ohmmeter, so the circuit or component should be isolated from the vehicle electrical system before any testing is done. Since the ohmmeter uses its own voltage source, either lead can be connected to any test point.

➡ **When checking diodes or other solid state components, the ohmmeter leads can only be connected one way in order to measure current flow in a single direction. Make sure the positive (+) and negative (-) terminal connections are as described in the test procedures to verify the one-way diode operation.**

In using the meter for making continuity checks, do not be concerned with the actual resistance readings. Zero resistance, or any ohm reading, indicates continuity in the circuit. Infinite resistance indicates an open in the circuit. A high resistance reading where there should be none indicates a problem in the circuit. Checks for short circuits are made in the same manner as checks for open circuits except that the circuit must be isolated from both power and normal ground. Infinite resistance indicates no continuity to ground, while zero resistance indicates a dead short to ground.

Ammeters

An ammeter measures the amount of current flowing through a circuit in units called amperes or amps. Amperes are units of electron flow which indicate how fast the electrons are flowing through the circuit. Since Ohms Law dictates that current flow in a circuit is equal to the circuit voltage divided by the total circuit resistance, increasing voltage also increases the current level (amps). Likewise, any decrease in resistance will increase the amount of amps in a circuit. At normal operating voltage, most circuits have a characteristic amount of amperes, called "current draw" which can be measured using an ammeter. By referring to a specified current draw rating, measuring the amperes, and comparing the two values, one can determine what is happening within the circuit to aid in diagnosis. An open circuit, for example, will not allow any current to flow so the ammeter reading will be zero. More current flows through a heavily loaded circuit or when the charging system is operating.

An ammeter is always connected in series with the circuit being tested. All of the current that normally flows through the circuit must also flow through the ammeter; if there is any other path for the current to follow, the ammeter reading will not be accurate. The ammeter itself has very little resistance to current flow and therefore will not affect the circuit, but it will measure current draw only when the circuit is closed and electricity is flowing. Excessive current draw can blow fuses and drain the battery, while a reduced current draw can cause motors to run slowly, lights to dim and other components to not operate properly. The ammeter can help diagnose these conditions by locating the cause of the high or low reading.

Multimeters

Different combinations of test meters can be built into a single unit designed for specific tests. Some of the more common combination test devices are known as Volt/Amp testers, Tach/Dwell meters, or Digital Multimeters. The Volt/Amp tester is used for charging system, starting system or battery tests and consists of a voltmeter, an ammeter and a variable resistance carbon pile. The voltmeter will usually have at least two ranges for use with 6, 12 and/or 24 volt systems. The ammeter also has more than one range for testing various levels of

CHASSIS ELECTRICAL 6-7

battery loads and starter current draw. The carbon pile can be adjusted to offer different amounts of resistance. The Volt/Amp tester has heavy leads to carry large amounts of current and many later models have an inductive ammeter pick-up that clamps around the wire to simplify test connections. On some models, the ammeter also has a zero-center scale to allow testing of charging and starting systems without switching leads or polarity. A digital multimeter is a voltmeter, ammeter and ohmmeter combined in an instrument which gives a digital readout. These are often used when testing solid state circuits because of their high input impedance (usually 10 megohms or more).

The tach/dwell meter that combines a tachometer and a dwell (cam angle) meter is a specialized kind of voltmeter. The tachometer scale is marked to show engine speed in rpm and the dwell scale is marked to show degrees of distributor shaft rotation. In most electronic ignition systems, dwell is determined by the control unit, but the dwell meter can also be used to check the duty cycle (operation) of some electronic engine control systems. Some tach/dwell meters are powered by an internal battery, while others take their power from the vehicle battery in use. The battery powered testers usually require calibration (much like an ohmmeter) before testing.

TESTING

Open Circuits

To use the self-powered test light or a multimeter to check for open circuits, first isolate the circuit from the vehicle's 12 volt power source by disconnecting the battery or wiring harness connector. Connect the test light or ohmmeter ground clip to a good ground and probe sections of the circuit sequentially with the test light. (start from either end of the circuit). If the light is out/or there is infinite resistance, the open is between the probe and the circuit ground. If the light is on/or the meter shows continuity, the open is between the probe and end of the circuit toward the power source.

Short Circuits

By isolating the circuit both from power and from ground, and using a self-powered test light or multimeter, you can check for shorts to ground in the circuit. Isolate the circuit from power and ground. Connect the test light or ohmmeter ground clip to a good ground and probe any easy-to-reach test point in the circuit. If the light comes on or there is continuity, there is a short somewhere in the circuit. To isolate the short, probe a test point at either end of the isolated circuit (the light should be on/there should be continuity). Leave the test light probe engaged and open connectors, switches, remove parts, etc., sequentially, until the light goes out/continuity is broken. When the light goes out, the short is between the last circuit component opened and the previous circuit opened.

➡ **The battery in the test light and does not provide much current. A weak battery may not provide enough power to illuminate the test light even when a complete circuit is made (especially if there are high resistances in the circuit). Always make sure that the test battery is strong. To check the battery, briefly touch the ground clip to the probe; if the light glows brightly the battery is strong enough for testing. Never use a self-powered test light to perform checks for opens or shorts when power is applied to the electrical system under test. The 12 volt vehicle power will quickly burn out the light bulb in the test light.**

Available Voltage Measurement

Set the voltmeter selector switch to the 20V position and connect the meter negative lead to the negative post of the battery. Connect the positive meter lead to the positive post of the battery and turn the ignition switch **ON** to provide a load. Read the voltage on the meter or digital display. A well charged battery should register over 12 volts. If the meter reads below 11.5 volts, the battery power may be insufficient to operate the electrical system properly. This test determines voltage available from the battery and should be the first step in any electrical trouble diagnosis procedure. Many electrical problems, especially on computer controlled systems, can be caused by a low state of charge in the battery. Excessive corrosion at the battery cable terminals can cause a poor contact that will prevent proper charging and full battery current flow.

Normal battery voltage is 12 volts when fully charged. When the battery is supplying current to one or more circuits it is said to be "under load." When everything is off the electrical system is under a "no-load" condition. A fully charged battery may show about 12.5 volts at no load; will drop to 12 volts under medium load; and will drop even lower under heavy load. If the battery is partially discharged the voltage decrease under heavy load may be excessive, even though the battery shows 12 volts or more at no load. When allowed to discharge further, the battery's available voltage under load will decrease more severely. For this reason, it is important that the battery be fully charged during all testing procedures to avoid errors in diagnosis and incorrect test results.

Voltage Drop

When current flows through a resistance, the voltage beyond the resistance is reduced (the larger the current, the greater the reduction in voltage). When no current is flowing, there is no voltage drop because there is no current flow. All points in the circuit which are connected to the power source are at the same voltage as the power source. The total voltage drop always equals the total source voltage. In a long circuit with many connectors, a series of small, unwanted voltage drops due to corrosion at the connectors can add up to a total loss of voltage which impairs the operation of the normal loads in the circuit. The maximum allowable voltage drop under load is critical, especially if there is more than one high resistance problem in a circuit because all voltage drops are cumulative. A small drop is normal due to the resistance of the conductors.

INDIRECT COMPUTATION OF VOLTAGE DROPS

1. Set the voltmeter selector switch to the 20 volt position.
2. Connect the meter negative lead to a good ground.
3. While operating the circuit, probe all loads in the circuit with the positive meter lead and observe the voltage readings. A drop should be noticed after the first load. But, there should be little or no voltage drop before the first load.

6-8 CHASSIS ELECTRICAL

DIRECT MEASUREMENT OF VOLTAGE DROPS

1. Set the voltmeter switch to the 20 volt position.
2. Connect the voltmeter negative lead to the ground side of the load to be measured.
3. Connect the positive lead to the positive side of the resistance or load to be measured.
4. Read the voltage drop directly on the 20 volt scale.

Too high a voltage indicates too high a resistance. If, for example, a blower motor runs too slowly, you can determine if perhaps there is too high a resistance in the resistor pack. By taking voltage drop readings in all parts of the circuit, you can isolate the problem. Too low a voltage drop indicates too low a resistance. Take the blower motor for example again. If a blower motor runs too fast in the MED and/or LOW position, the problem might be isolated in the resistor pack by taking voltage drop readings in all parts of the circuit to locate a possibly shorted resistor.

HIGH RESISTANCE TESTING

1. Set the voltmeter selector switch to the 4 volt position.
2. Connect the voltmeter positive lead to the positive post of the battery.
3. Turn on the headlights and heater blower to provide a load.
4. Probe various points in the circuit with the negative voltmeter lead.
5. Read the voltage drop on the 4 volt scale. Some average maximum allowable voltage drops are:
   - FUSE PANEL: 0.7 volts
   - IGNITION SWITCH: 0.5 volts
   - HEADLIGHT SWITCH: 0.7 volts
   - IGNITION COIL (+): 0.5 volts
   - ANY OTHER LOAD: 1.3 volts

➡ **Voltage drops are all measured while a load is operating; without current flow, there will be no voltage drop.**

Resistance Measurement

The batteries in an ohmmeter will weaken with age and temperature, so the ohmmeter must be calibrated or "zeroed" before taking measurements. To zero the meter, place the selector switch in its lowest range and touch the two ohmmeter leads together. Turn the calibration knob until the meter needle is exactly on zero.

➡ **All analog (needle) type ohmmeters must be zeroed before use, but some digital ohmmeter models are automatically calibrated when the switch is turned on. Self-calibrating digital ohmmeters do not have an adjusting knob, but its a good idea to check for a zero readout before use by touching the leads together. All computer controlled systems require the use of a digital ohmmeter with at least 10 megohms impedance for testing. Before any test procedures are attempted, make sure the ohmmeter used is compatible with the electrical system or damage to the on-board computer could result.**

To measure resistance, first isolate the circuit from the vehicle power source by disconnecting the battery cables or the harness connector. Make sure the key is **OFF** when disconnecting any components or the battery. Where necessary, also isolate at least one side of the circuit to be checked in order to avoid reading parallel resistances. Parallel circuit resistances will always give a lower reading than the actual resistance of either of the branches. When measuring the resistance of parallel circuits, the total resistance will always be lower than the smallest resistance in the circuit. Connect the meter leads to both sides of the circuit (wire or component) and read the actual measured ohms on the meter scale. Make sure the selector switch is set to the proper ohm scale for the circuit being tested to avoid misreading the ohmmeter test value.

✲✲WARNING

Never use an ohmmeter with power applied to the circuit. Like the self-powered test light, the ohmmeter is designed to operate on its own power supply. The normal 12 volt automotive electrical system current could damage the meter!

Wiring Harnesses

The average automobile contains about ½ mile of wiring, with hundreds of individual connections. To protect the many wires from damage and to keep them from becoming a confusing tangle, they are organized into bundles, enclosed in plastic or taped together and called wiring harnesses. Different harnesses serve different parts of the vehicle. Individual wires are color coded to help trace them through a harness where sections are hidden from view.

Automotive wiring or circuit conductors can be in any one of three forms:

1. Single strand wire
2. Multi-strand wire
3. Printed circuitry

Single strand wire has a solid metal core and is usually used inside such components as alternators, motors, relays and other devices. Multi-strand wire has a core made of many small strands of wire twisted together into a single conductor. Most of the wiring in an automotive electrical system is made up of multi-strand wire, either as a single conductor or grouped together in a harness. All wiring is color coded on the insulator, either as a solid color or as a colored wire with an identification stripe. A printed circuit is a thin film of copper or other conductor that is printed on an insulator backing. Occasionally, a printed circuit is sandwiched between two sheets of plastic for more protection and flexibility. A complete printed circuit, consisting of conductors, insulating material and connectors for lamps or other components is called a printed circuit board. Printed circuitry is used in place of individual wires or harnesses in places where space is limited, such as behind instrument panels.

Since automotive electrical systems are very sensitive to changes in resistance, the selection of properly sized wires is critical when systems are repaired. A loose or corroded connection or a replacement wire that is too small for the circuit will add extra resistance and an additional voltage drop to the circuit. A ten percent voltage drop can result in slow or erratic motor operation, for example, even though the circuit is complete. The wire gauge number is an expression of the cross-section area of the conductor. The most common system for expressing wire size is the American Wire Gauge (AWG) system.

CHASSIS ELECTRICAL 6-9

Gauge numbers are assigned to conductors of various cross-section areas. As gauge number increases, area decreases and the conductor becomes smaller. A 5 gauge conductor is smaller than a 1 gauge conductor and a 10 gauge is smaller than a 5 gauge. As the cross-section area of a conductor decreases, resistance increases and so does the gauge number. A conductor with a higher gauge number will carry less current than a conductor with a lower gauge number.

➡ **Gauge wire size refers to the size of the conductor, not the size of the complete wire. It is possible to have two wires of the same gauge with different diameters because one may have thicker insulation than the other.**

12 volt automotive electrical systems generally use 10, 12, 14, 16 and 18 gauge wire. Main power distribution circuits and larger accessories usually use 10 and 12 gauge wire. Battery cables are usually 4 or 6 gauge, although 1 and 2 gauge wires are occasionally used. Wire length must also be considered when making repairs to a circuit. As conductor length increases, so does resistance. An 18 gauge wire, for example, can carry a 10 amp load for 10 feet without excessive voltage drop; however if a 15 foot wire is required for the same 10 amp load, it must be a 16 gauge wire.

An electrical schematic shows the electrical current paths when a circuit is operating properly. It is essential to understand how a circuit works before trying to figure out why it doesn't. Schematics break the entire electrical system down into individual circuits and show only one particular circuit. In a schematic, no attempt is made to represent wiring and components as they physically appear on the vehicle; switches and other components are shown as simply as possible. Face views of harness connectors show the cavity or terminal locations in all multi-pin connectors to help locate test points.

If you need to backprobe a connector while it is on the component, the order of the terminals must be mentally reversed. The wire color code can help in this situation, as well as a keyway, lock tab or other reference mark.

WIRING REPAIR

Soldering is a quick, efficient method of joining metals permanently. Everyone who has the occasion to make wiring repairs should know how to solder. Electrical connections that are soldered are far less likely to come apart and will conduct electricity much better than connections that are only "pig-tailed" together. The most popular (and preferred) method of soldering is with an electrical soldering gun. Soldering irons are available in many sizes and wattage ratings. Irons with higher wattage ratings deliver higher temperatures and recover lost heat faster. A small soldering iron rated for no more than 50 watts is recommended, especially on electrical systems where excess heat can damage the components being soldered.

There are three ingredients necessary for successful soldering; proper flux, good solder and sufficient heat. A soldering flux is necessary to clean the metal of tarnish, prepare it for soldering and to enable the solder to spread into tiny crevices. When soldering, always use a rosin core solder which is non-corrosive and will not attract moisture once the job is finished. Other types of flux (acid core) will leave a residue that will attract moisture and cause the wires to corrode. Tin is a unique metal with a low melting point. In a molten state, it dissolves and alloys easily with many metals. Solder is made by mixing tin with lead. The most common proportions are 40/60, 50/50 and 60/40, with the percentage of tin listed first. Low priced solders usually contain less tin, making them very difficult for a beginner to use because more heat is required to melt the solder. A common solder is 40/60 which is well suited for all-around general use, but 60/40 melts easier and is preferred for electrical work.

Soldering Techniques

Successful soldering requires that the metals to be joined be heated to a temperature that will melt the solder, usually 360-460°F (182-238°C). Contrary to popular belief, the purpose of the soldering iron is not to melt the solder itself, but to heat the parts being soldered to a temperature high enough to melt the solder when it is touched to the work. Melting flux-cored solder on the soldering iron will usually destroy the effectiveness of the flux.

➡ **Soldering tips are made of copper for good heat conductivity, but must be "tinned" regularly for quick transference of heat to the project and to prevent the solder from sticking to the iron. To "tin" the iron, simply heat it and touch the flux-cored solder to the tip; the solder will flow over the hot tip. Wipe the excess off with a clean rag, but be careful as the iron will be hot.**

After some use, the tip may become pitted. If so, simply dress the tip smooth with a smooth file and "tin" the tip again. Flux-cored solder will remove oxides but rust, bits of insulation and oil or grease must be removed with a wire brush or emery cloth. For maximum strength in soldered parts, the joint must start off clean and tight. Weak joints will result in gaps too wide for the solder to bridge.

If a separate soldering flux is used, it should be brushed or swabbed on only those areas that are to be soldered. Most solders contain a core of flux and separate fluxing is unnecessary. Hold the work to be soldered firmly. It is best to solder on a wooden board, because a metal vise will only rob the piece to be soldered of heat and make it difficult to melt the solder. Hold the soldering tip with the broadest face against the work to be soldered. Apply solder under the tip close to the work, using enough solder to give a heavy film between the iron and the piece being soldered, while moving slowly and making sure the solder melts properly. Keep the work level or the solder will run to the lowest part and favor the thicker parts, because these require more heat to melt the solder. If the soldering tip overheats (the solder coating on the face of the tip burns up), it should be retinned. Once the soldering is completed, let the soldered joint stand until cool. Tape and seal all soldered wire splices after the repair has cooled.

Wire Harness Connectors

Most connectors in the engine compartment or that are otherwise exposed to the elements are protected against moisture and dirt which could create oxidation and deposits on the terminals.

These special connectors are weather-proof. All repairs require the use of a special terminal and the tool required to service it. This tool is used to remove the pin and sleeve terminals. If removal is attempted with an ordinary pick, there is a good chance that the terminal will be bent or deformed. Unlike standard blade type terminals, these weather-proof terminals cannot be straightened once they are bent. Make certain that the connectors are properly seated and all of the sealing rings are in place when connecting leads. On some models, a hinge-type flap provides a backup or secondary locking feature for the terminals. Most secondary locks are used to improve connector reliability by retaining the terminals if the small terminal lock tangs are not positioned properly.

Molded-on connectors require complete replacement of the connection. This means splicing a new connector assembly into the harness. All splices should be soldered to insure proper contact. Use care when probing the connections or replacing terminals in them as it is possible to short between opposite terminals. If this happens to the wrong terminal pair, it is possible to damage certain components. Always use jumper wires between connectors for circuit checking and never probe through weatherproof seals.

Open circuits are often difficult to locate by sight because corrosion or terminal misalignment are hidden by the connectors. Merely wiggling a connector on a sensor or in the wiring harness may correct the open circuit condition. This should always be considered when an open circuit or a failed sensor is indicated. Intermittent problems may also be caused by oxidized or loose connections. When using a circuit tester for diagnosis, always probe connections from the wire side. Be careful not to damage sealed connectors with test probes.

All wiring harnesses should be replaced with identical parts, using the same gauge wire and connectors. When signal wires are spliced into a harness, use wire with high temperature insulation only. It is seldom necessary to replace a complete harness. If replacement is necessary, pay close attention to insure proper harness routing. Secure the harness with suitable plastic wire clamps to prevent vibrations from causing the harness to wear in spots or contact any hot components.

➡ **Weatherproof connectors cannot be replaced with standard connectors. Instructions are provided with replacement connector and terminal packages. Some wire harnesses have mounting indicators (usually pieces of colored tape) to mark where the harness is to be secured.**

In making wiring repairs, its important that you always replace damaged wires with wiring of the same gauge as the wire being replaced. The heavier the wire, the smaller the gauge number. Wires are color-coded to aid in identification and whenever possible the same color coded wire should be used for replacement. A wire stripping and crimping tool is necessary to install solderless terminal connectors. Test all crimps by pulling on the wires; it should not be possible to pull the wires out of a good crimp.

Wires which are open, exposed or otherwise damaged are repaired by simple splicing. Where possible, if the wiring harness is accessible and the damaged place in the wire can be located, it is best to open the harness and check for all possible damage. In an inaccessible harness, the wire must be bypassed with a new insert, usually taped to the outside of the old harness.

When replacing fusible links, be sure to use fusible link wire, NOT ordinary automotive wire. Make sure the fusible segment is of the same gauge and construction as the one being replaced and double the stripped end when crimping the terminal connector for a good contact. The melted (open) fusible link segment of the wiring harness should be cut off as close to the harness as possible, then a new segment spliced in as described. In the case of a damaged fusible link that feeds two harness wires, the harness connections should be replaced with two fusible link wires so that each circuit will have its own separate protection.

➡ **Most of the problems caused in the wiring harness are due to bad ground connections. Always check all vehicle ground connections for corrosion or looseness before performing any power feed checks to eliminate the chance of a bad ground affecting the circuit.**

Hard-Shell Connectors

Unlike molded connectors, the terminal contacts in hard-shell connectors can be replaced. Weatherproof hard-shell connectors with the leads molded into the shell have non-replaceable terminal ends. Replacement usually involves the use of a special terminal removal tool that depresses the locking tangs (barbs) on the connector terminal and allows the connector to be removed from the rear of the shell. The connector shell should be replaced if it shows any evidence of burning, melting, cracks, or breaks. Replace individual terminals that are burnt, corroded, distorted or loose.

➡ **The insulation crimp must be tight to prevent the insulation from sliding back on the wire when the wire is pulled. The insulation must be visibly compressed under the crimp tabs, and the ends of the crimp should be turned in for a firm grip on the insulation.**

The wire crimp must be made with all wire strands inside the crimp. The terminal must be fully compressed on the wire strands with the ends of the crimp tabs turned in to make a firm grip on the wire. Check all connections with an ohmmeter to insure a good contact. There should be no measurable resistance between the wire and the terminal when connected.

Fusible Links

▶ See Figure 3

The fuse link is a short length of special, Hypalon (high temperature) insulated wire, integral with the engine compartment wiring harness and should not be confused with standard wire. It is several wire gauges smaller than the circuit which it protects. Under no circumstances should a fuse link replacement repair be made using a length of standard wire cut from bulk stock or from another wiring harness.

To repair any blown fuse link use the following procedure:

1. Determine which circuit is damaged, its location and the cause of the open fuse link. If the damaged fuse link is one of three fed by a common No. 10 or 12 gauge feed wire, determine the specific affected circuit.
2. Disconnect the negative battery cable.
3. Cut the damaged fuse link from the wiring harness and discard it. If the fuse link is one of three circuits fed by a single feed wire, cut it out of the harness at each splice end and discard it.
4. Identify and procure the proper fuse link with butt connectors for attaching the fuse link to the harness.

➡ **Heat shrink tubing must be slipped over the wire before crimping and soldering the connection.**

CHASSIS ELECTRICAL 6-11

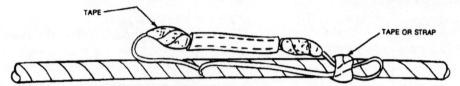
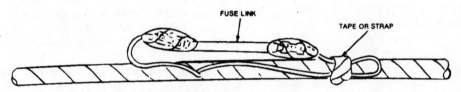
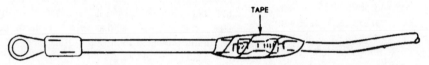
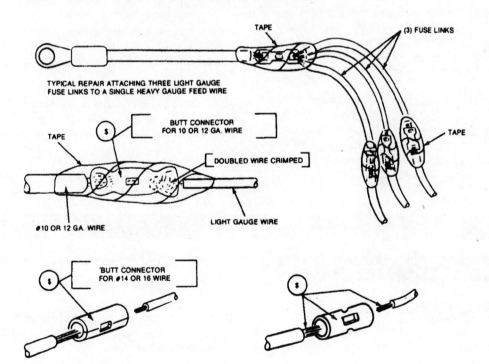

Fig. 3 General fusible link repair — never replace a fusible link with regular wire or a fusible link rated at a higher amperage than the one being replaced

CHASSIS ELECTRICAL

5. To repair any fuse link in a 3-link group with one feed:

   a. After cutting the open link out of the harness, cut each of the remaining undamaged fuse links close to the feed wire weld.

   b. Strip approximately ½ in. (13mm) of insulation from the detached ends of the two good fuse links. Insert two wire ends into one end of a butt connector, then carefully push one stripped end of the replacement fuse link into the same end of the butt connector and crimp all three firmly together.

➡ Care must be taken when fitting the three fuse links into the butt connector as the internal diameter is a snug fit for three wires. Make sure to use a proper crimping tool. Pliers, side cutters, etc. will not apply the proper crimp to retain the wires and withstand a pull test.

   c. After crimping the butt connector to the three fuse links, cut the weld portion from the feed wire and strip approximately ½ in. (13mm) of insulation from the cut end. Insert the stripped end into the open end of the butt connector and crimp very firmly.

   d. To attach the remaining end of the replacement fuse link, strip approximately ½ in. (13mm) of insulation from the wire end of the circuit from which the blown fuse link was removed, and firmly crimp a butt connector or equivalent to the stripped wire. Then, insert the end of the replacement link into the other end of the butt connector and crimp firmly.

   e. Using rosin core solder with a consistency of 60 percent tin and 40 percent lead, solder the connectors and the wires at the repairs then insulate with electrical tape or heat shrink tubing.

6. To replace any fuse link on a single circuit in a harness, cut out the damaged portion, strip approximately ½ in. (13mm) of insulation from the two wire ends and attach the appropriate replacement fuse link to the stripped wire ends with two proper size butt connectors. Solder the connectors and wires, then insulate.

7. To repair any fuse link which has an eyelet terminal on one end such as the charging circuit, cut off the open fuse link behind the weld, strip approximately ½ in. (13mm) of insulation from the cut end and attach the appropriate new eyelet fuse link to the cut stripped wire with an appropriate size butt connector. Solder the connectors and wires at the repair, then insulate.

8. Connect the negative battery cable to the battery and test the system for proper operation.

➡ Do not mistake a resistor wire for a fuse link. The resistor wire is generally longer and has print stating, "Resistor-don't cut or splice."

When attaching a single No. 16, 17, 18 or 20 gauge fuse link to a heavy gauge wire, always double the stripped wire end of the fuse link before inserting and crimping it into the butt connector for positive wire retention.

Add-On Electrical Equipment

The electrical system in your vehicle is designed to perform under reasonable operating conditions without interference between components. Before any additional electrical equipment is installed, it is recommended that you consult your dealer or a reputable repair facility that is familiar with the vehicle and its systems.

If the vehicle is equipped with mobile radio equipment and/or mobile telephone, it may have an effect upon the operation of any on-board computer control modules. Radio Frequency Interference (RFI) from the communications system can be picked up by the vehicle's wiring harnesses and conducted into the control module, giving it the wrong messages at the wrong time. Although well shielded against RFI, the computer should be further protected by taking the following measures:

- Install the antenna as far as possible from the control module. For instance, if the module is located behind the center console area, then the antenna should be mounted at the rear of the vehicle.
- Keep the antenna wiring a minimum of eight inches away from any wiring running to control modules and from the module itself. NEVER wind the antenna wire around any other wiring.
- Mount the equipment as far from the control module as possible. Be very careful during installation not to drill through any wires or short a wire harness with a mounting screw.
- Insure that the electrical feed wire(s) to the equipment are properly and tightly connected. Loose connectors can cause interference.
- Make certain that the equipment is properly grounded to the vehicle. Poor grounding can damage expensive equipment.

HEATER

Blower Motor

REMOVAL & INSTALLATION

All Models
♦ See Figure 4

1. Disconnect the negative battery cable. Detach any interfering control cables.

2. Disengage the following electrical connections:
   a. Heater switch
   b. Ground wire
   c. Battery connector

3. Remove the screws that hold the motor to the heater assembly and remove the blower motor housing and motor.

4. Remove fan and blower motor from blower motor housing.

5. Installation is the reverse of the removal procedure.

CHASSIS ELECTRICAL   6-13

Heater Core

REMOVAL & INSTALLATION

All Models
► See Figure 4

1. Drain the cooling system.

✴✴CAUTION

When draining coolant, keep in mind that cats and dogs are attracted by ethylene glycol antifreeze, and are quite likely to drink any that is left in an uncovered container or in puddles on the ground. This will prove fatal in sufficient quantity. Always drain the coolant into a sealable container. Coolant should be reused unless it is contaminated or several years old.

2. Mark the duct halves to be sure they are reassembled properly.
3. Remove the screws that fasten the two halves of the duct together.
4. Remove the screws that secure the heater core to the duct.
5. Remove the heater core from the vehicle.
6. Install in the reverse order of the removal procedure.

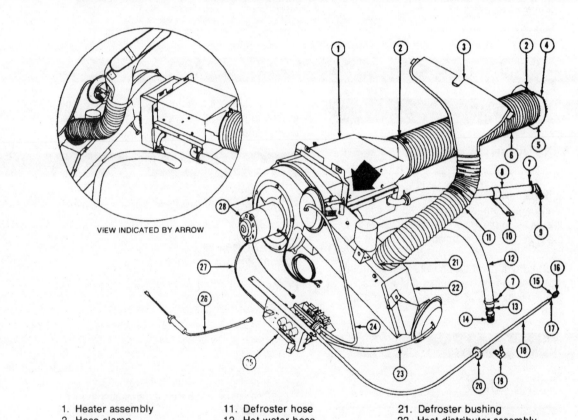

1. Heater assembly
2. Hose clamp
3. Defroster nozzle
4. Air duct screen
5. Air duct and heater collar
6. Air duct intake tube
7. Hose clamp
8. Straight hot water hose
9. Heater tube elbow
10. Heater hose support bracket
11. Defroster hose
12. Hot water hose
13. Heater nipple
14. Reducing bushing
15. Inverted flared tube nut
16. Inverted flared tube connector
17. Heater vacuum to engine tube
18. Heater control tube
19. Clip
20. Grommet
21. Defroster bushing
22. Heat distributor assembly
23. Heater control tube
24. Heater control tube
25. Heater control assembly
26. Fuse holder assembly
27. Bowden wire (control panel to heater)
28. Blower and air inlet assembly

Fig. 4 Identification of the heater system components used in later models — early systems are less complicated

6-14 CHASSIS ELECTRICAL

Troubleshooting the Heater

Problem	Cause	Solution
Blower motor will not turn at any speed	• Blown fuse • Loose connection • Defective ground • Faulty switch • Faulty motor • Faulty resistor	• Replace fuse • Inspect and tighten • Clean and tighten • Replace switch • Replace motor • Replace resistor
Blower motor turns at one speed only	• Faulty switch • Faulty resistor	• Replace switch • Replace resistor
Blower motor turns but does not circulate air	• Intake blocked • Fan not secured to the motor shaft	• Clean intake • Tighten security
Heater will not heat	• Coolant does not reach proper temperature • Heater core blocked internally • Heater core air-bound • Blend-air door not in proper position	• Check and replace thermostat if necessary • Flush or replace core if necessary • Purge air from core • Adjust cable
Heater will not defrost	• Control cable adjustment incorrect • Defroster hose damaged	• Adjust control cable • Replace defroster hose

89766c03

WINDSHIELD WIPERS

Wiper Blades and Arms

REMOVAL & INSTALLATION

To remove the blade, pull it away from the windshield. Push against the tip of the wiper arm to compress the locking spring and disengage the retaining pin. Pivot the blade clockwise to unhook it from the arm. To install the blade, just snap it into position.

To remove the arm, pry it off of the mounting stud carefully. When installing the arm, position the arm so that it does not make contact the rubber molding at either edge of the windshield while running.

Wiper Motor

REMOVAL & INSTALLATION

Except Utility Models

1. Disconnect the negative battery cable.
2. Remove the windshield wiper assembly from the pivot shaft.
3. Remove the vacuum hose or wire from the motor.
4. Remove all attaching screws that hold the motor to the windshield assembly and remove the motor from the vehicle.
5. Install in the reverse order.

Utility Models

A vacuum type wiper motor is used and is located on the firewall in the engine compartment, directly behind the engine. Release the tension on the cables by loosening the nut attaching the tensioner to the mounting bracket. Then, unbolt and remove the motor.

After installing the motor, adjust the cable tension as described in the Wiper Linkage Removal & Installation procedure later in this section.

Wiper Linkage

REMOVAL & INSTALLATION

➡ 1945-70 Jeep vehicles, except for Utility models, have no windshield wiper linkage.

Utility Models

These vehicles employ a cable system to actuate the wiper arms.

1. Release the tension on the cable by loosening the tension attaching nut.
2. Disengage the ferrule at the end of the cable from the wiper arm and remove the cable.
3. The cable is installed by engaging the ferrule in the slot in the wiper arm and passing the cable through the slot.
4. Once the cable is installed, adjust it as follows:
   a. Be sure that the tensioner attaching bolts are tight. The left and right tensioners are not interchangeable.
   b. Loosen, but do not remove the tensioner locknut on the bracket.
   c. When the locknuts are loosened, the tensioners should, automatically, take up the cable slack. It may be necessary to tap the stud to free the tensioner locknut. In some cases, it may help to pry the bracket outwards to get the tensioners to take up the slack.
   d. Tighten the locknuts firmly. If there is still slack, proceed to Step 4e.
   e. Using a file, elongate the holes in the tensioner bracket, toward the center of the vehicle, an additional $1/16$ in. (1.6mm). This should provide enough tensioner movement.
   f. If slack is still present, replace the cables.

CHASSIS ELECTRICAL 6-15

Troubleshooting Basic Windshield Wiper Problems

Problem	Cause	Solution
Electric Wipers		
Wipers do not operate—Wiper motor heats up or hums	• Internal motor defect • Bent or damaged linkage • Arms improperly installed on linking pivots	• Replace motor • Repair or replace linkage • Position linkage in park and reinstall wiper arms
Wipers do not operate—No current to motor	• Fuse or circuit breaker blown • Loose, open or broken wiring • Defective switch • Defective or corroded terminals • No ground circuit for motor or switch	• Replace fuse or circuit breaker • Repair wiring and connections • Replace switch • Replace or clean terminals • Repair ground circuits
Wipers do not operate—Motor runs	• Linkage disconnected or broken	• Connect wiper linkage or replace broken linkage
Vacuum Wipers		
Wipers do not operate	• Control switch or cable inoperative • Loss of engine vacuum to wiper motor (broken hoses, low engine vacuum, defective vacuum/fuel pump) • Linkage broken or disconnected • Defective wiper motor	• Repair or replace switch or cable • Check vacuum lines, engine vacuum and fuel pump • Repair linkage • Replace wiper motor
Wipers stop on engine acceleration	• Leaking vacuum hoses • Dry windshield • Oversize wiper blades • Defective vacuum/fuel pump	• Repair or replace hoses • Wet windshield with washers • Replace with proper size wiper blades • Replace pump

INSTRUMENTS AND SWITCHES

Instrument Cluster

REMOVAL & INSTALLATION

All Models

1. Disconnect the negative battery cable.
2. Separate the speedometer cable from the speedometer head.
3. Remove the cluster-to-dash attaching nuts.
4. Remove the gauge wires and remove the cluster assembly.
5. Install in the reverse order. After installing the cluster, connect the battery and check all of the lights and gauges for proper operation.

SPEEDOMETER CABLE REPLACEMENT

1. Reach up behind the center of the speedometer head. The cable is connected by a threaded ring. Unscrew the ring and pull the cable sheath from the head.
2. The cable core can be pulled from the sheath.
3. If the core is broken, detach the other end of the sheath from the transmission. Pull out the broken end.
4. When installing the cable, apply a very small amount of speedometer cable graphite lubricant to the cable.

Ignition Switch

REMOVAL & INSTALLATION

1. Disconnect the battery ground cable.
2. Unscrew the nut from the front of the instrument panel and remove the switch. Some early production Utility models had a switch held in place by a bezel and tension spring, rather than a threaded bezel.
3. Lower the switch and detach the wiring.
4. Reverse the procedure for installation.

Ignition Lock Cylinder

REMOVAL & INSTALLATION

CJ Models

1. Remove the ignition switch.
2. Put the key in the lock and turn it to the **ON** position.
3. Insert a heavy paper clip wire or something similar through the release hole in the side of the switch. Push in the retaining ring until the lock cylinder can be pulled out.

To install:

4. Align the tang on the cylinder with the slot in the case and push the cylinder in.
5. Install the switch.

Utility Models

1. Turn the key to the left, to the AUXILIARY position.
2. Insert a piece of heavy wire or unbent paper clip into the release hole in the lock cylinder. This will compress the cylinder retainer.
3. Pull the cylinder out with the key.
4. Installation is the reverse of removal.

CHASSIS ELECTRICAL

Troubleshooting Basic Dash Gauge Problems

Problem	Cause	Solution
Coolant Temperature Gauge		
Gauge reads erratically or not at all	• Loose or dirty connections • Defective sending unit	• Clean/tighten connections • Bi-metal gauge: remove the wire from the sending unit. Ground the wire for an instant. If the gauge registers, replace the sending unit.
	• Defective gauge	• Magnetic gauge: Disconnect the wire at the sending unit. With ignition ON gauge should register COLD. Ground the wire; gauge should register HOT.
Ammeter Gauge—Turn Headlights ON (do not start engine). Note reaction		
Ammeter shows charge	• Connections reversed on gauge	• Reinstall connections
Ammeter shows discharge	• Ammeter is OK	• Nothing
Ammeter does not move	• Loose connections or faulty wiring • Defective gauge	• Check/correct wiring • Replace gauge
Oil Pressure Gauge		
Gauge does not register or is inaccurate	• On mechanical gauge, Bourdon tube may be bent or kinked	• Check tube for kinks or bends preventing oil from reaching the gauge
	• Low oil pressure	• Remove sending unit. Idle the engine briefly. If no oil flows from sending unit hole, problem is in engine.
	• Defective gauge	• Remove the wire from the sending unit and ground it for an instant with the ignition ON. A good gauge will go to the top of the scale.
	• Defective wiring	• Check the wiring to the gauge. If it's OK and the gauge doesn't register when grounded, replace the gauge.
	• Defective sending unit	• If the wiring is OK and the gauge functions when grounded, replace the sending unit
All Gauges		
All gauges do not operate	• Blown fuse • Defective instrument regulator	• Replace fuse • Replace instrument voltage regulator
All gauges read low or erratically	• Defective or dirty instrument voltage regulator	• Clean contacts or replace
All gauges pegged	• Loss of ground between instrument voltage regulator and car • Defective instrument regulator	• Check ground • Replace regulator
Warning Lights		
Light(s) do not come on when ignition is ON, but engine is not started	• Defective bulb • Defective wire	• Replace bulb • Check wire from light to sending unit
	• Defective sending unit	• Disconnect the wire from the sending unit and ground it. Replace the sending unit if the light comes on with the ignition ON.
Light comes on with engine running	• Problem in individual system • Defective sending unit	• Check system • Check sending unit (see above)

CHASSIS ELECTRICAL 6-17

LIGHTING

Headlights

REMOVAL & INSTALLATION

All Models
◆ See Figures 5, 6, 7, 8, 9 and 10

1. Remove the one lower attaching screw from the headlight trim ring. Pull out slightly at the bottom and push up to disengage the upper retaining tab.
2. Remove the trim ring.
3. Remove the three retaining screws from the retaining ring.
4. Pull the headlamp out and disconnect the wire harness.

➡ **When installing the headlamp, the number 2 is placed at the top of the lamp.**

5. Install in reverse order of the removal procedure. Check for proper seating of the lamp in its mounting ring and check for proper alignment.

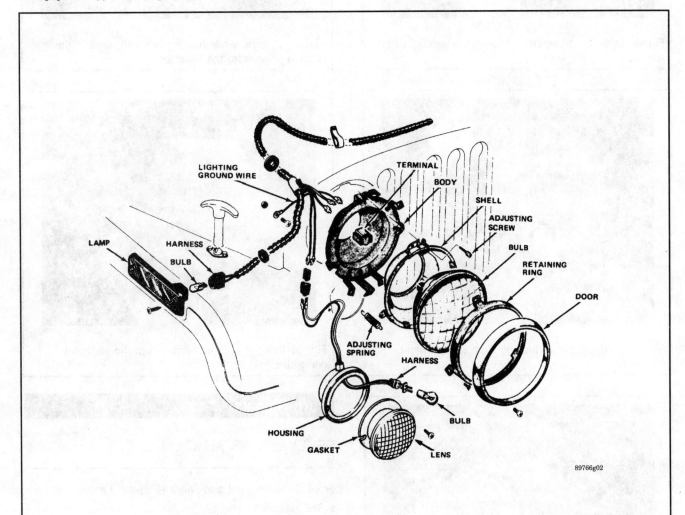

Fig. 5 Exploded view of the headlight, turn signal and side marker light mounting — all models

6-18 CHASSIS ELECTRICAL

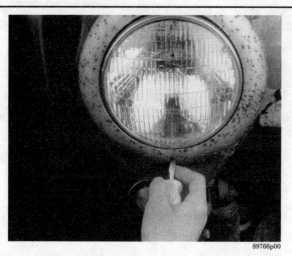

Fig. 6 Unfasten the screws retaining the headlight trim ring . . .

Fig. 9 . . . then, while holding the bulb, remove the retaining ring from the assembly

Fig. 7 . . . then remove the ring from the headlight assembly

Fig. 10 Pull the bulb out and detach the electrical connector from its backside

Turn Signals

REMOVAL & INSTALLATION

Front Grille-Mounted and Fender-Mounted Lamps
▶ See Figures 11 and 12

1. Disconnect the negative battery cable.
2. Remove the lens cover retaining screws, then pull the lens off of the lamp assembly.
3. Remove the light bulb by one of the following methods, depending on the type of light bulb socket used on the vehicle:
   a. Method 1 — depress the bulb slightly, and twist it 1/8 turn counterclockwise, then pull it up and out of the socket.
   b. Method 2 — simply pull it straight out of the socket.
4. Installation is the reverse of the removal procedure.

Fig. 8 Unfasten the headlight retaining ring mounting screws . . .

CHASSIS ELECTRICAL 6-19

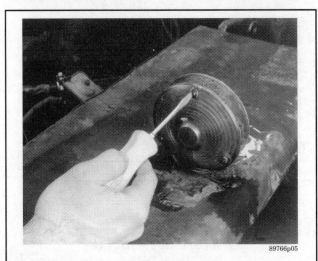

Fig. 11 On fender-mounted lamps, remove the lens retaining screws . . .

Fig. 12 . . . then remove the turn signal lamp lens. Depress and twist the bulb slightly to remove it

Light Bulb Applications

Item	6 Volt Models	12 Volt Models Early 4-134 ①	Late 4-134, 6-225 ②
External Lights;			
Headlights	5040S/6006	5400S/6012	6012
Front parking	63	67	1157
Front signal	1158	1176/1034	1157
Stop/tail/signal	1158	1034	1157
License plate	—	—	1155
Back-up	—	—	1156
4-way flasher	—	—	1157
Side marker	63	67	1157
Interior Lights;			
High beam	51	53/57	53/57
Turn signals	51	53	53
Charge indicator	51	53/57	53/57
Oil pressure	51	57	57
Instrument cluster	55	57	57
Heater controls	—	—	57
Parking brake warning	—	—	57

① This includes all L-head and early F-head 4-134 engines equipped with 12 volt electrical systems.
② This includes late F-head 4-134 and all V6 6-225 engines.

Troubleshooting Basic Lighting Problems

Problem	Cause	Solution
Lights		
One or more lights don't work, but others do	• Defective bulb(s) • Blown fuse(s) • Dirty fuse clips or light sockets • Poor ground circuit	• Replace bulb(s) • Replace fuse(s) • Clean connections • Run ground wire from light socket housing to car frame
Lights burn out quickly	• Incorrect voltage regulator setting or defective regulator • Poor battery/alternator connections	• Replace voltage regulator • Check battery/alternator connections
Lights go dim	• Low/discharged battery • Alternator not charging • Corroded sockets or connections • Low voltage output	• Check battery • Check drive belt tension; repair or replace alternator • Clean bulb and socket contacts and connections • Replace voltage regulator
Lights flicker	• Loose connection • Poor ground • Circuit breaker operating (short circuit)	• Tighten all connections • Run ground wire from light housing to car frame • Check connections and look for bare wires
Lights "flare"—Some flare is normal on acceleration—if excessive, see "Lights Burn Out Quickly"	• High voltage setting	• Replace voltage regulator
Lights glare—approaching drivers are blinded	• Lights adjusted too high • Rear springs or shocks sagging • Rear tires soft	• Have headlights aimed • Check rear springs/shocks • Check/correct rear tire pressure
Turn Signals		
Turn signals don't work in either direction	• Blown fuse • Defective flasher • Loose connection	• Replace fuse • Replace flasher • Check/tighten all connections
Right (or left) turn signal only won't work	• Bulb burned out • Right (or left) indicator bulb burned out • Short circuit	• Replace bulb • Check/replace indicator bulb • Check/repair wiring
Flasher rate too slow or too fast	• Incorrect wattage bulb • Incorrect flasher	• Flasher bulb • Replace flasher (use a variable load flasher if you pull a trailer)
Indicator lights do not flash (burn steadily)	• Burned out bulb • Defective flasher	• Replace bulb • Replace flasher
Indicator lights do not light at all	• Burned out indicator bulb • Defective flasher	• Replace indicator bulb • Replace flasher

CHASSIS ELECTRICAL 6-21

Troubleshooting Basic Turn Signal and Flasher Problems

Most problems in the turn signals or flasher system, can be reduced to defective flashers or bulbs, which are easily replaced. Occasionally, problems in the turn signals are traced to the switch in the steering column, which will require professional service.

F = Front   R = Rear   • = Lights off   o = Lights on

Problem		Solution
Turn signals light, but do not flash		• Replace the flasher
No turn signals light on either side		• Check the fuse. Replace if defective. • Check the flasher by substitution • Check for open circuit, short circuit or poor ground
Both turn signals on one side don't work		• Check for bad bulbs • Check for bad ground in both housings
One turn signal light on one side doesn't work		• Check and/or replace bulb • Check for corrosion in socket. Clean contacts. • Check for poor ground at socket
Turn signal flashes too fast or too slow		• Check any bulb on the side flashing too fast. A heavy-duty bulb is probably installed in place of a regular bulb. • Check the bulb flashing too slow. A standard bulb was probably installed in place of a heavy-duty bulb. • Check for loose connections or corrosion at the bulb socket
Indicator lights don't work in either direction		• Check if the turn signals are working • Check the dash indicator lights • Check the flasher by substitution
One indicator light doesn't light		• On systems with 1 dash indicator: See if the lights work on the same side. Often the filaments have been reversed in systems combining stoplights with taillights and turn signals. Check the flasher by substitution • On systems with 2 indicators: Check the bulbs on the same side Check the indicator light bulb Check the flasher by substitution

6-22 CHASSIS ELECTRICAL

TRAILER WIRING

Wiring the vehicle for towing is fairly easy. There are a number of good wiring kits available and these should be used, rather than trying to design your own.

All trailers will need brake lights and turn signals as well as tail lights and side marker lights. Most areas require extra marker lights for overwide trailers. Also, most areas have recently required back-up lights for trailers, and most trailer manufacturers have been building trailers with back-up lights for several years.

Additionally, some Class I, most Class II and just about all Class III trailers will have electric brakes. Add to this number an accessories wire, to operate trailer internal equipment or to charge the trailer's battery, and you can have as many as seven wires in the harness.

Determine the equipment on your trailer and buy the wiring kit necessary. The kit will contain all the wires needed, plus a plug adapter set which includes the female plug, mounted on the bumper or hitch, and the male plug, wired into, or plugged into the trailer harness.

When installing the kit, follow the manufacturer's instructions. The color coding of the wires is usually standard throughout the industry. One point to note: some domestic vehicles, and most imported vehicles, have separate turn signals. On most domestic vehicles, the brake lights and rear turn signals operate with the same bulb. For those vehicles with separate turn signals, you can purchase an isolation unit so that the brake lights won't blink whenever the turn signals are operated, or, you can go to your local electronics supply house and buy four diodes to wire in series with the brake and turn signal bulbs. Diodes will isolate the brake and turn signals. The choice is yours. The isolation units are simple and quick to install, but far more expensive than the diodes. The diodes, however, require more work to install properly, since they require the cutting of each bulb's wire and soldering in place of the diode.

One, final point, the best kits are those with a spring loaded cover on the vehicle mounted socket. This cover prevents dirt and moisture from corroding the terminals. Never let the vehicle socket hang loosely; always mount it securely to the bumper or hitch.

CIRCUIT PROTECTION

Fuses

The electrical system in all Jeep vehicles is protected from electrical surges by fuses, devices which are designed to break the circuit when a certain amount of amperage is pushed through the fuse. The fuses are designed to break the circuit so that no damage will occur in the electrical components located along the circuit. The amperages, at which the fuses break the circuits, are dependant on the particular circuit being protected; varying components from one circuit to another require different amounts of current for optimal performance.

Refer to the accompanying Fuse Applications chart for proper fuse ratings of the particular vehicle.

Fusible Links

In addition to fuses, the wiring harness incorporates fusible links to protect the wiring. Links are used rather than a fuse, in wiring circuits that are not normally fused, such as the ignition circuit.

Fusible links are sections of wire, with special insulation, designed to melt under electrical overload. There is usually one in the main wire from the battery, and near the alternator output side. If one melts, it must be replaced with a new link of the correct amperage rating. Never replace a melted link with ordinary wire; you run the risk of melting your entire wiring harness.

Fusible links are color coded red in the charging and load circuits to match the color of the circuits they protect. Each link is four gauges smaller than the cable it protects, and is marked on the insulation with the gauge size because the insulation makes it appear heavier than it really is.

Fuse Applications

Item	6 Volt Models	12 Volt Models
Turn signal	14 Amp	①
Tail and stop lights	20 Amp	20 Amp
4-way flasher	14 Amp	14 Amp
Heater	14 Amp	14 Amp
Windshield wipers	14 Amp	14 Amp

① Early 12 volt systems: 9 Amp.
　Late 12 volt systems: 14 Amp.

CHASSIS ELECTRICAL 6-23

WIRING DIAGRAMS

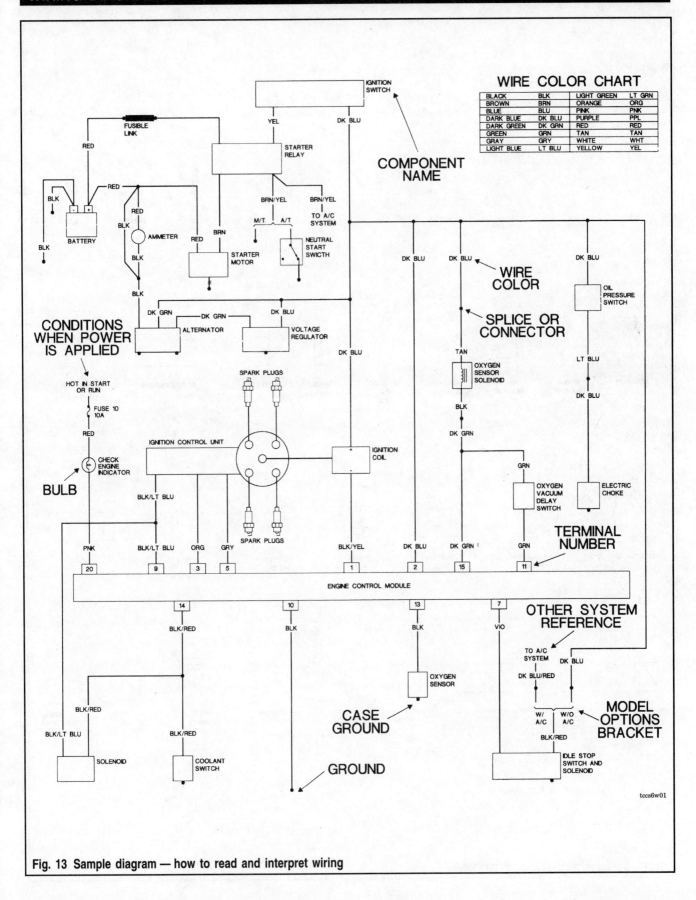

Fig. 13 Sample diagram — how to read and interpret wiring

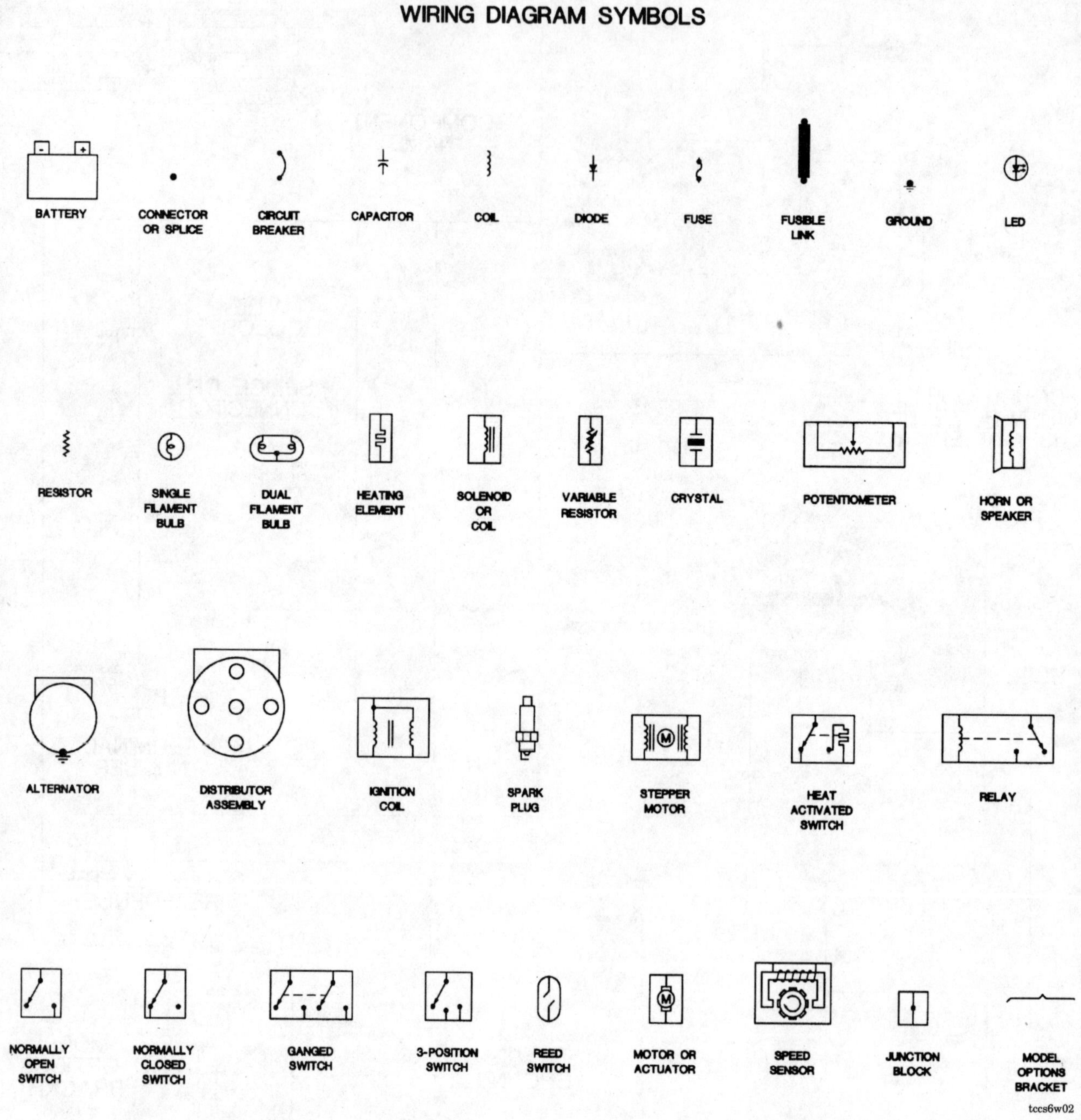

6-24 CHASSIS ELECTRICAL

WIRING DIAGRAM SYMBOLS

BATTERY	CONNECTOR OR SPLICE	CIRCUIT BREAKER	CAPACITOR	COIL	DIODE	FUSE	FUSIBLE LINK	GROUND	LED
RESISTOR	SINGLE FILAMENT BULB	DUAL FILAMENT BULB	HEATING ELEMENT	SOLENOID OR COIL	VARIABLE RESISTOR	CRYSTAL	POTENTIOMETER	HORN OR SPEAKER	
ALTERNATOR	DISTRIBUTOR ASSEMBLY	IGNITION COIL	SPARK PLUG	STEPPER MOTOR	HEAT ACTIVATED SWITCH	RELAY			
NORMALLY OPEN SWITCH	NORMALLY CLOSED SWITCH	GANGED SWITCH	3-POSITION SWITCH	REED SWITCH	MOTOR OR ACTUATOR	SPEED SENSOR	JUNCTION BLOCK	MODEL OPTIONS BRACKET	

Fig. 14 Common wiring diagram symbols

CHASSIS ELECTRICAL 6-25

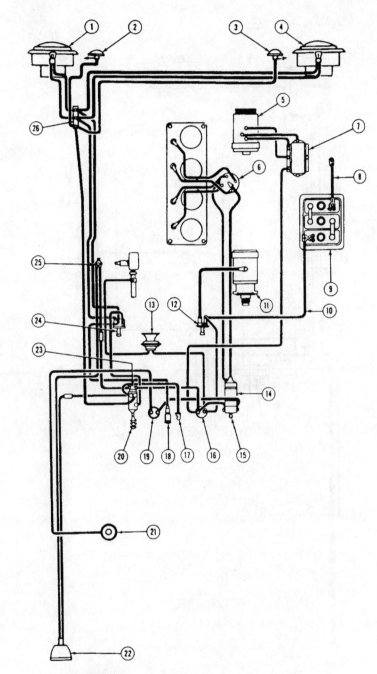

1. Left headlamp
2. Left parking lamp
3. Right parking lamp
4. Right headlamp
5. Generator
6. Distributor
7. Voltage regulator
8. Negative ground cable
9. Battery
10. Positive cable
11. Starting motor
12. Starting switch
13. Horn
14. Ignition coil
15. Ignition switch
16. Ammeter
17. Dash light
18. Tell-tale light
19. Fuel gauge
20. Light switch
21. Fuel gauge sending unit
22. Tail and stop light
23. Light switch circuit breaker
24. Dimmer switch
25. Stop light switch
26. Junction block

Fig. 15 Vehicle wiring diagram — CJ-2A models (6 volt system)

6-26 CHASSIS ELECTRICAL

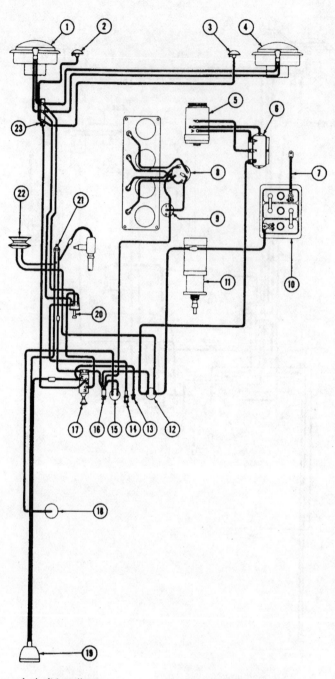

1. Left headlamp
2. Left parking lamp
3. Right parking lamp
4. Right headlamp
5. Generator
6. Voltage regulator
7. Negative ground cable
8. Distributor
9. Ignition coil
10. Battery
11. Starting motor
12. Ammeter
13. Dash light
14. Tell-tale light
15. Fuel gauge
16. Ignition switch
17. Light switch
18. Fuel gauge sending unit
19. Tail and stop light
20. Dimmer switch
21. Stop light switch
22. Horn
23. Junction block

Fig. 16 Vehicle wiring diagram — CJ-3A models (6 volt system)

CHASSIS ELECTRICAL 6-27

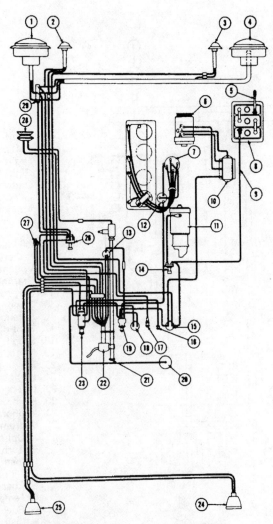

1. Left headlamp
2. Left parking lamp
3. Right parking lamp
4. Right headlamp
5. Negative ground cable
6. Generator
7. Distributor
8. Battery
9. Positive cable
10. Voltage regulator
11. Starting motor
12. Ignition coil
13. Signal flasher
14. Starting switch
15. Ammeter
16. Dash light
17. Tell-tale light
18. Fuel gauge
19. Ignition switch
20. Fuel gauge sending unit
21. Horn button
22. Directional signal switch
23. Light switch
24. Right tail and stop lamp
25. Left tail and stop lamp
26. Dimmer switch
27. Stop light switch
28. Horn
29. Junction block

Fig. 17 Vehicle wiring diagram — CJ-3B models through serial No. 35522 (6 volt system)

6-28 CHASSIS ELECTRICAL

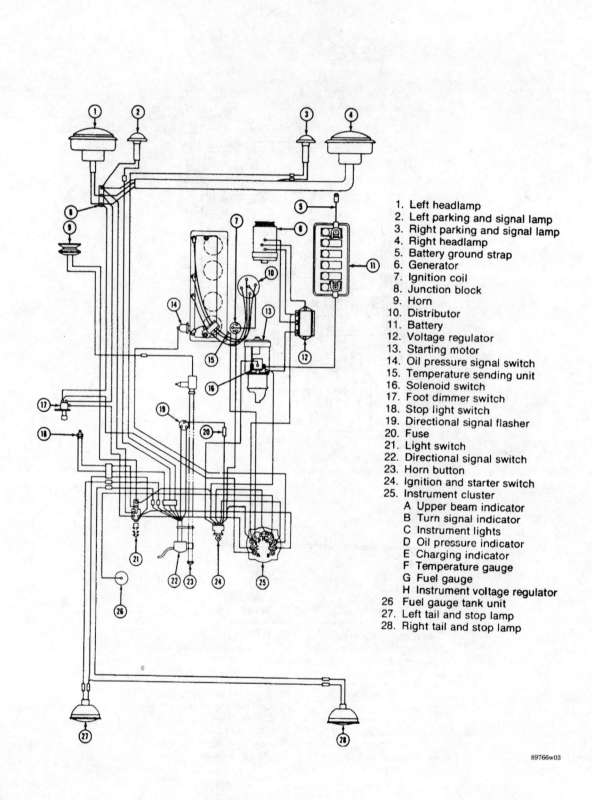

1. Left headlamp
2. Left parking and signal lamp
3. Right parking and signal lamp
4. Right headlamp
5. Battery ground strap
6. Generator
7. Ignition coil
8. Junction block
9. Horn
10. Distributor
11. Battery
12. Voltage regulator
13. Starting motor
14. Oil pressure signal switch
15. Temperature sending unit
16. Solenoid switch
17. Foot dimmer switch
18. Stop light switch
19. Directional signal flasher
20. Fuse
21. Light switch
22. Directional signal switch
23. Horn button
24. Ignition and starter switch
25. Instrument cluster
    A Upper beam indicator
    B Turn signal indicator
    C Instrument lights
    D Oil pressure indicator
    E Charging indicator
    F Temperature gauge
    G Fuel gauge
    H Instrument voltage regulator
26 Fuel gauge tank unit
27. Left tail and stop lamp
28. Right tail and stop lamp

Fig. 18 Vehicle wiring diagram — CJ-3B models after serial No. 35522 (12 volt system)

CHASSIS ELECTRICAL 6-29

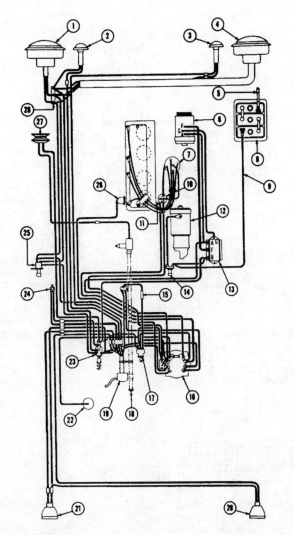

1. Left headlamp
2. Left parking lamp
3. Right parking lamp
4. Right headlamp
5. Negative ground cable
6. Generator
7. Distributor
8. Battery
9. Positive cable
10. Ignition coil
11. Temperature sending unit
12. Starting motor
13. Voltage regulator
14. Starting switch
15. Fuse
16. Instrument switch
17. Ignition switch
18. Horn button
19. Directional signal switch
20. Right tail and stop lamp
21. Left tail and stop lamp
22. Fuel gauge sending unit
23. Light switch
24. Stop light switch
25. Dimmer switch
26. Oil pressure sending unit
27. Horn
28. Junction block

Fig. 19 Vehicle wiring diagram — L-head and early F-head 4-134 equipped CJ-5 models through serial No. 49248 and CJ-6 models through serial No. 12577

6-30 CHASSIS ELECTRICAL

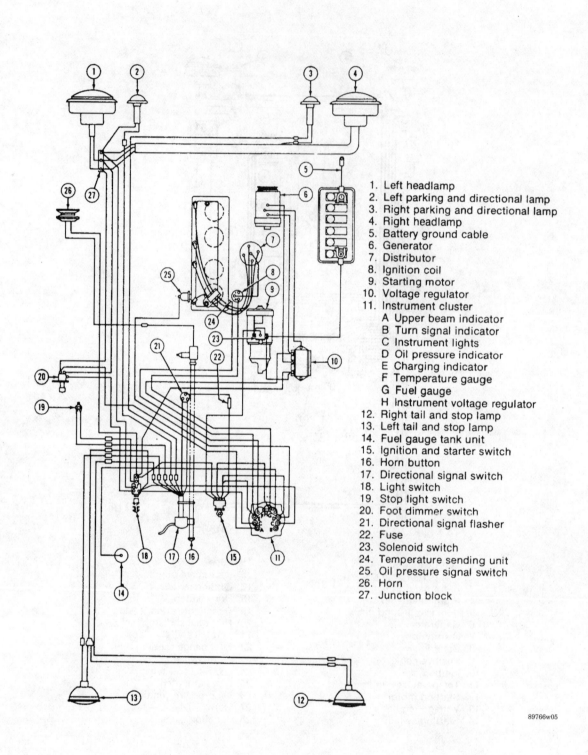

1. Left headlamp
2. Left parking and directional lamp
3. Right parking and directional lamp
4. Right headlamp
5. Battery ground cable
6. Generator
7. Distributor
8. Ignition coil
9. Starting motor
10. Voltage regulator
11. Instrument cluster
    A Upper beam indicator
    B Turn signal indicator
    C Instrument lights
    D Oil pressure indicator
    E Charging indicator
    F Temperature gauge
    G Fuel gauge
    H Instrument voltage regulator
12. Right tail and stop lamp
13. Left tail and stop lamp
14. Fuel gauge tank unit
15. Ignition and starter switch
16. Horn button
17. Directional signal switch
18. Light switch
19. Stop light switch
20. Foot dimmer switch
21. Directional signal flasher
22. Fuse
23. Solenoid switch
24. Temperature sending unit
25. Oil pressure signal switch
26. Horn
27. Junction block

Fig. 20 Vehicle wiring diagram — L-head and early F-head 4-134 equipped CJ-5 models after serial No. 49248 and CJ-6 models after serial No. 12577

CHASSIS ELECTRICAL 6-31

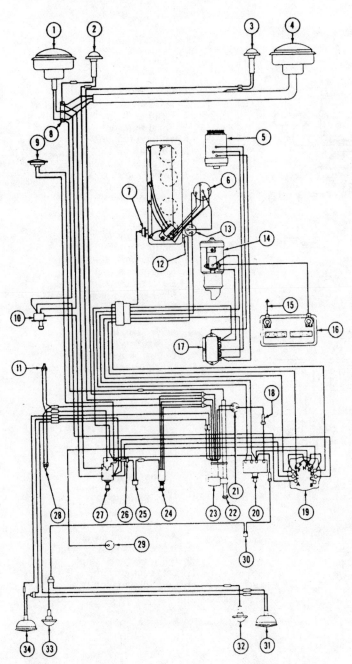

1. Left headlamp
2. Left parking and signal lamp
3. Right parking and signal lamp
4. Right headlamp
5. Generator
6. Ignition distributor
7. Oil pressure sending unit
8. Junction block
9. Horn
10. Foot dimmer switch
11. Stop light switch—front
12. Temperature sending unit
13. Ignition coil
14. Starting motor
15. Battery ground cable
16. Battery
17. Voltage regulator
18. Fuse
19. Instrument cluster
   A Hi-beam indicator
   B Auxiliary
   C Instrument lights
   D Oil pressure indicator
   E Charging indicator
   F Temperature indicator
   G Fuel gauge
   H Instrument voltage regulator
20. Ignition and starter switch
21. Flasher (directional signal)
22. Horn button
23. Directional signal switch
24. 4-Way flasher switch
25. Flasher (4-way)
26. Fuse
27. Main light switch
28. Stop light switch—rear
29. Fuel gauge tank unit
30. Back-up light switch
31. Right tail and stop lamp
32. Right back-up lamp
33. Left back-up lamp
34. Left tail and stop lamp

Fig. 21 Vehicle wiring diagram — late F-head 4-134 equipped CJ-5 and CJ-6 models

6-32 CHASSIS ELECTRICAL

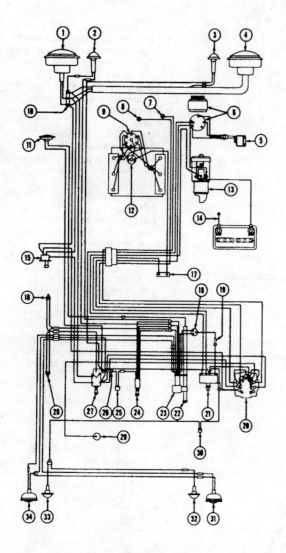

1. Left headlamp
2. Left parking and signal lamp
3. Right parking and signal lamp
4. Right headlamp
5. Voltage regulator
6. Alternator
7. Oil pressure sender
8. Temperature sender
9. Ignition distributor
10. Junction block
11. Horn
12. Ignition coil
13. Starting motor
14. Battery ground cable
15. Foot dimmer switch
16. Stop light switch—front
17. Ballast
18. Flasher (directional signal)
19. Fuse
20. Instrument cluster
    A Hi-beam indicator
    B Auxiliary
    C Instrument lights
    D Oil pressure indicator
    E Charging indicator
    F Temperature indicator
    G Fuel gauge
    H Instrument voltage regulator
21. Ignition and starter switch
22. Horn button
23. Directional signal switch
24. 4-Way flasher switch
25. Flasher (4-way)
26. Fuse
27. Main light switch
28. Stop light switch—rear
29. Fuel gauge tank unit
30. Back-up light switch
31. Right tail and stop lamp
32. Right back-up lamp
33. Left back-up lamp
34. Left tail and stop lamp

Fig. 22 Vehicle wiring diagram — V6 6-225 equipped CJ-5 and CJ-6 models

2WD FRONT AXLE
  FRONT HUB AND WHEEL
    BEARINGS 7-40
  PIVOT PINS 7-38
4WD FRONT DRIVE AXLE
  AXLE SHAFT, BEARING AND
    SEAL 7-31
  FRONT AXLE UNIT 7-34
  FRONT HUB AND WHEEL
    BEARINGS 7-34
  PINION SEAL AND YOKE 7-34
CLUTCH
  ADJUSTMENTS 7-12
  DRIVEN DISC AND PRESSURE
    PLATE 7-13
  UNDERSTANDING THE CLUTCH 7-12
DRIVE AXLES
  DETERMINING AXLE RATIO 7-27
  UNDERSTANDING DRIVE
    AXLES 7-27
DRIVELINE
  FRONT AND REAR
    DRIVESHAFTS 7-23
  U-JOINTS 7-24
MANUAL TRANSMISSION
  ADJUSTMENTS 7-2
  BACK-UP LIGHT SWITCH 7-3
  OVERDRIVE UNIT 7-11
  T-86AA 3-SPEED OVERHAUL 7-6
  T-90C 3-SPEED OVERHAUL 7-6
  T-98A 4-SPEED OVERHAUL 7-9
  TRANSMISSION 7-3
  UNDERSTANDING THE MANUAL
    TRANSMISSION 7-2
POWER TAKE-OFF (PTO) UNIT
  PULLEY DRIVE UNIT 7-22
  SHAFT DRIVE UNIT 7-21
  SHIFT ASSEMBLY 7-21
REAR AXLE
  AXLE SHAFT 7-29
  AXLE SHAFT BEARING 7-29
  PINION OIL SEAL 7-27
  REAR AXLE UNIT 7-30
SPECIFICATIONS CHARTS
  DRIVELINE NOISE DIAGNOSIS 7-26
  MANUAL TRANSMISSION
    APPLICATIONS 7-2
  POWER TAKE-OFF GEAR AND
    SPEED SPECIFICATIONS 7-22
  REAR AXLE APPLICATIONS 7-27
  TROUBLESHOOTING THE MANUAL
    TRANSMISSION AND TRANSFER
    CASE 7-18
TRANSFER CASE
  ADJUSTMENTS 7-20
  TRANSFER CASE 7-20

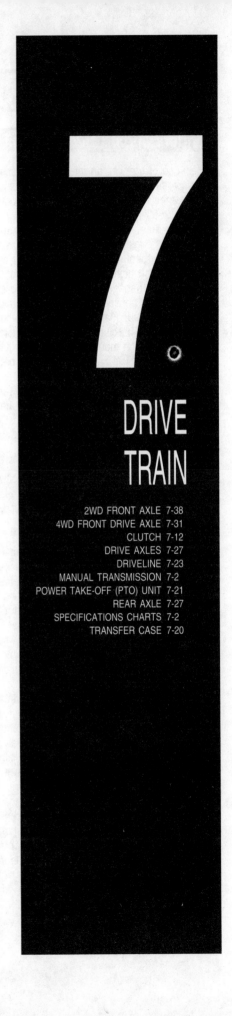

7.
DRIVE TRAIN

2WD FRONT AXLE 7-38
4WD FRONT DRIVE AXLE 7-31
CLUTCH 7-12
DRIVE AXLES 7-27
DRIVELINE 7-23
MANUAL TRANSMISSION 7-2
POWER TAKE-OFF (PTO) UNIT 7-21
REAR AXLE 7-27
SPECIFICATIONS CHARTS 7-2
TRANSFER CASE 7-20

7-2 DRIVE TRAIN

MANUAL TRANSMISSION

Understanding the Manual Transmission

Because of the way an internal combustion engine breathes, it can produce torque (or twisting force) only within a narrow speed range. Most overhead valve pushrod engines must turn at about 2500 rpm to produce their peak torque. Often by 4500 rpm, they are producing so little torque that continued increases in engine speed produce no power increases.

The torque peak on overhead camshaft engines is, generally, much higher, but much narrower.

The manual transmission and clutch are employed to vary the relationship between engine rpm and the speed of the wheels so that adequate power can be produced under all circumstances. The clutch allows engine torque to be applied to the transmission input shaft gradually, due to mechanical slippage. The vehicle can, consequently, be started smoothly from a full stop.

The transmission changes the ratio between the rotating speeds of the engine and the wheels by the use of gears. 4-speed or 5-speed transmissions are most common. The lower gears allow full engine power to be applied to the rear wheels during acceleration at low speeds.

The clutch driveplate is a thin disc, the center of which is splined to the transmission input shaft. Both sides of the disc are covered with a layer of material which is similar to brake lining and which is capable of allowing slippage without roughness or excessive noise.

The clutch cover is bolted to the engine flywheel and incorporates a diaphragm spring which provides the pressure to engage the clutch. The cover also houses the pressure plate. When the clutch pedal is released, the driven disc is sandwiched between the pressure plate and the smooth surface of the flywheel, thus forcing the disc to turn at the same speed as the engine crankshaft.

The transmission contains a mainshaft which passes all the way through the transmission, from the clutch to the driveshaft. This shaft is separated at one point, so that front and rear portions can turn at different speeds.

Power is transmitted by a countershaft in the lower gears and reverse. The gears of the countershaft mesh with gears on the mainshaft, allowing power to be carried from one to the other. Countershaft gears are often integral with that shaft, while several of the mainshaft gears can either rotate independently of the shaft or be locked to it. Shifting from one gear to the next causes one of the gears to be freed from rotating with the shaft and locks another to it. Gears are locked and unlocked by internal dog clutches which slide between the center of the gear and the shaft. The forward gears usually employ synchronizers; friction members which smoothly bring gear and shaft to the same speed before the toothed dog clutches are engaged.

Adjustments

SHIFT LINKAGE

CJ-2A and 2WD Utility Models

First disconnect the shift rods from the remote control levers. Check for binding of the remote control shaft on the steering column and make the necessary adjustments to eliminate any binding condition.

If the shift is not smooth and positive, first make sure that the transmission is in Neutral and then remove the shift rods at the transmission by removing the clevis pins. Slip a short piece of snug fitting $1/4$ in. (6mm) aligning rod through the gearshift levers and housing.

This places the shift lever and clutch assemblies in the Neutral position. Adjust the shift rod yokes at the transmission end so that the clevis pins can be installed freely without moving the shift levers on the transmission. Remove the alignment pin.

If shifting from First to Second is difficult or the transmission hangs up in First gear, shorten the Low and Reverse rod one turn at a time until the condition is corrected. Usually three turns are required. Should the fault continue after completing the above adjustment, check further as follows:

First, remove the lubricating fitting from the shifter housing. Use a narrow feeler gauge which will enter the opening for the lubricator and check the clearance between the faces of the shifting clutches. The clearance should be 0.015-0.031 in. (0.381-0.787mm). If the clearance is greater, the assembly must be removed for adjustment. The shift dog which engages the clutch slots should not have more than 0.009 in. (0.2286mm) clearance in the slots. If the clearance between the clutch grooves and cross pins is too great, these parts must be replaced.

To remove the remote control housing from the steering column for repairs, the following procedure is suggested:

1. Remove the shifting rods from the transmission and also from the steering column remove control clutch levers.
2. Remove the gearshift lever fulcrum pin and the gearshift lever.
3. Remove the plates on the toe board of the steering post.
4. Remove the two screws that hold the remote control housing to the steering post and lift the housing from the positioning pin.
5. Remove the assembly down through the floor pan.
6. Remove the lower clutch and shift lever from the housing by turning counterclockwise.
7. Remove the upper clutch and shift lever in the same manner.

To assemble:

8. Wash all of the parts in a suitable cleaning solution and replace all worn parts before reassembling.
9. Assemble the upper clutch assembly in the housing making sure that the alignment hole in the housing faces the engine. Turn the upper lever assembly in as far as it will go

MANUAL TRANSMISSION APPLICATIONS

Transmission Types	Years	Models
Warner T-86 4-sp OD	1947-58	Optional on 2WD Utility models with 6-226 engines
Warner T-86AA 3-sp	1955-70	Standard on all 6-225 engines
Warner T-90 3-sp	1947-58	Standard on 4WD models with 4-134 engines
Warner T-90C 3-sp	1945-70	Standard on all models
Warner T-90J 3-sp	1947-58	Standard on 4WD Utility models with 6-226 engines
Warner T-96 4-sp OD	1947-58	Optional on 2WD Utility models with 4-134 engines
Warner T-98A 4-sp	1955-70	Optional on all models

OD – Over Drive equipped models.
2WD – 2 Wheel Drive models.
4WD – 4 Wheel Drive models.
3-sp – 3-speed transmissions.
4-sp – 4-speed transmissions.

and then back off one full turn until the hole in the clutch lever aligns with the hole in the housing.

10. Assemble the lower clutch lever assembly in the housing until the faces of the clutches contact, then back off not more than ½ of a turn which should bring the aligning hole in the lever in line with the hole in the housing. If the ½ turn does not bring the alignment hole into the proper position, it will be necessary to grind off the face of the lower clutch so that it can be backed off ½ turn from contact with the upper clutch. The proper clearance of 0.015 in. (0.381mm) is obtained when the lower clutch is backed off ½ turn.

11. Assemble the unit to the steering post in the reverse order of removal and adjust the remote control rods.

12. If, after assembly, the shifter dog catches on the edge of the slot in the clutch when moving the lever up and down, disconnect the shift rod at the transmission end and either lengthen or shorten it slightly to correct this condition.

Back-Up Light Switch

REMOVAL & INSTALLATION

The switch is threaded into the transmission and is removed by unscrewing it. No adjustments are possible.

Transmission

REMOVAL & INSTALLATION

Except Utility Models

✴✴CAUTION

The clutch driven disc may contain asbestos, which has been determined to be a cancer causing agent. Never clean clutch surfaces with compressed air! Avoid inhaling any dust from any clutch surface! When cleaning clutch surfaces, use a commercially available brake cleaning fluid.

1. Raise and support the vehicle on jackstands.
2. Drain the transmission and transfer case.
3. Remove the shift lever and shift housing. On CJ-2A models up to serial No. 38221 remove the remote linkage as follows:
    a. Remove the shift rods from the transmission and from the steering remote control clutch levers.
    b. Remove the shift lever fulcrum pin and remove the shift lever.
    c. Remove the toe plates from the floor pan at the steering column.
    d. Remove the 2 screws holding the linkage housing to the steering column, and lift the housing from the positioning pin.
    e. Remove the shift assembly down through the floor pan.
    f. Remove the lower clutch and shift lever from the housing by turning counterclockwise.
    g. Remove the upper clutch and shift lever in the same manner.
4. Remove the set screw from the transfer case shift lever pivot pin. Remove the pivot pin, shift levers, and shift lever springs.
5. If the vehicle is equipped with Power Take-Off (PTO), remove the shift lever plate screws and lift out the lever.
6. Disconnect the front and rear driveshafts from the transfer case. If the vehicle is equipped with PTO, disconnect the transfer case end of the PTO driveshaft.
7. Disconnect the speedometer cable at the transfer case.
8. Disconnect the hand brake cable.
9. Disconnect the clutch cable at the bell crank.
10. Place jacks under the transmission and engine. Protect the oil pan with a wood block.
11. Remove the nuts holding the rear mount to the crossmember.
12. Remove the transfer case-to-crossmember bolt.

7-4 DRIVE TRAIN

13. Remove the frame center crossmember-to-frame side rail bolts and remove the crossmember. Remove the transmission-to-bell housing bolts.
14. Force the transmission to the right to disengage the clutch control lever tube ball joint.
15. Lower the engine and transmission. Slide the transmission and transfer case assemblies toward the rear until they clear the clutch.
16. Remove the 6 screws and lockwashers attaching the transfer case rear cover and remove the cover. If the vehicle is equipped with PTO, remove the PTO shift unit.
17. Remove the cotter pin, nut, and washer holding the transfer case main drive gear on the rear end of the transmission mainshaft. If possible, remove the main drive gear. If that's not possible, refer to Step 19.
18. Remove the transmission-to-transfer case bolts.
19. Install a transmission mainshaft retaining plate tool W-194 to prevent the mainshaft from pulling out of the case. If this tool is not available, loop a piece of wire around the mainshaft directly in back of the second speed gear. Install the shift housing right and left bolts part way into the case. Attach each end of the wire to the bolts. Support the transfer case, and with a soft mallet, tap lightly on the end of the mainshaft to loosen the gear and separate the two units.
20. Join the transfer case and transmission. Remove the wire or special holding tool. Remove the shift housing right and left bolts.
21. Install the transmission-to-transfer case bolts. Tighten them to 35 ft. lbs. (48 Nm).
22. Install the main drive gear. Install the cotter pin, nut, and washer holding the transfer case main drive gear on the rear end of the transmission mainshaft.
23. Install the transfer case rear cover and Install the cover.
24. For vehicles equipped with PTO, install the PTO shift unit.
25. Slide the transmission and transfer case assemblies forward until they engage the clutch.
26. Force the transmission to the right to engage the clutch control lever tube ball joint.
27. Install the transmission-to-bell housing bolts. Tighten them to 30 ft. lbs. (41 Nm).
28. Install the frame center crossmember. Tighten the bolts to 50 ft. lbs. (68 Nm).
29. Install the transfer case-to-crossmember bolt. Tighten it to 45 ft. lbs. (61 Nm).
30. Install the nuts holding the rear mount to the crossmember. Tighten them to 40 ft. lbs. (54 Nm).
31. Connect the clutch cable at the bell crank.
32. Connect the hand brake cable.
33. Connect the speedometer cable at the transfer case.
34. Connect the front and rear driveshafts to the transfer case. If the vehicle is equipped with PTO, connect the transfer case end of the PTO driveshaft.
35. If the vehicle is equipped with PTO, install the shift lever.
36. Install the set screw in the transfer case shift lever pivot pin. Install the pivot pin, shift levers, and shift lever springs.
37. Install the shift lever and shift housing. On CJ-2A models up to serial No. 38221, install the remote linkage as follows:
    a. Install the upper clutch and shift lever on the housing by turning counterclockwise.
    b. Install the lower clutch and shift lever on the housing by turning counterclockwise.
    c. Install the shift assembly down through the floor pan.
    d. Install the two screws holding the linkage housing to the steering column, and lower the housing onto the positioning pin.
    e. Install the toe plates on the floor pan at the steering column.
    f. Install the shift lever. Install the shift lever fulcrum pin.
    g. Install the shift rods at the transmission and the steering remote control clutch levers.
38. Fill the transmission and transfer case.

Utility Models

2-WHEEL DRIVE

➡ The following applies to models both with and without overdrive.

✳✳CAUTION

The clutch driven disc may contain asbestos, which has been determined to be a cancer causing agent. Never clean clutch surfaces with compressed air! Avoid inhaling any dust from any clutch surface! When cleaning clutch surfaces, use a commercially available brake cleaning fluid.

1. Raise and support the front end on jackstands.
2. Disconnect the negative battery cable.
3. Remove the remote linkage as follows:
    a. Remove the shift rods from the transmission and from the steering remote control clutch levers.
    b. Remove the shift lever fulcrum pin and remove the shift lever.
    c. Remove the toe plates from the floor pan at the steering column.
    d. Remove the two screws holding the linkage housing to the steering column, and lift the housing from the positioning pin.
    e. Remove the shift assembly down through the floor pan.
    f. Remove the lower clutch and shift lever from the housing by turning counterclockwise.
    g. Remove the upper clutch and shift lever in the same manner.
4. Disconnect and tag the wires at the overdrive solenoid.
5. Disconnect and tag the wires at the overdrive rail switch.
6. Matchmark and disconnect the driveshaft at the transmission or overdrive.
7. Disconnect the speedometer cable at the transmission or overdrive. Plug the hole.
8. Disconnect the overdrive control cable.
9. Remove the support at the rear of the overdrive. Keep the spacers together.
10. Remove the overdrive governor.
11. Place a jack under the bell housing and take up the weight of the engine. Protect the oil pan with a block of wood.
12. Place a floor jack under the transmission and support it without lifting the engine.
13. Remove the transmission-to-bell housing bolts.
14. Pull the transmission back about ¾ in. (19mm).

15. Insert a thin prybar through the opening in the side of the bell housing and pry the clutch release fork from engagement with the clutch release bearing carrier.
16. Pull the transmission back until it clears the bell housing and remove it with the clutch release bearing carrier mounted in the main drive gear bearing retainer.
17. Raise the transmission and slide it into place in the bell housing. Make sure that the clutch release bearing engages the release fork.
18. Install the transmission-to-bell housing bolts. Tighten the bolts to 30 ft. lbs. (41 Nm).
19. Install the overdrive governor.
20. Install the support at the rear of the overdrive. Keep the spacers together.
21. Connect the overdrive control cable.
22. Connect the speedometer cable at the transmission or overdrive.
23. Connect the driveshaft at the transmission or overdrive.
24. Connect the wires at the overdrive rail switch.
25. Connect tag the wires at the overdrive solenoid.
26. Install the remote linkage as follows:
   a. Install the upper clutch and shift lever on the housing by turning counterclockwise.
   b. Install the lower clutch and shift lever on the housing by turning counterclockwise.
   c. Install the shift assembly down through the floor pan.
   d. Install the two screws holding the linkage housing to the steering column, and lower the housing onto the positioning pin.
   e. Install the toe plates on the floor pan at the steering column.
   f. Install the shift lever. Install the shift lever fulcrum pin.
   g. Install the shift rods at the transmission and the steering remote control clutch levers.
27. Connect the negative battery cable.

4-WHEEL DRIVE

> **✲✲CAUTION**
>
> The clutch driven disc may contain asbestos, which has been determined to be a cancer causing agent. Never clean clutch surfaces with compressed air! Avoid inhaling any dust from any clutch surface! When cleaning clutch surfaces, use a commercially available brake cleaning fluid.

1. Raise and safely support the vehicle on jackstands.
2. Drain the transmission and transfer case into a catch pan. Dispose of the fluids properly.
3. Remove the shift lever and shift housing.
4. Remove the set screw from the transfer case shift lever pivot pin. Remove the pivot pin, shift levers, and shift lever springs.
5. If the vehicle is equipped with Power Take-Off (PTO), remove the shift lever plate screws and lift out the lever.
6. Disconnect the front and rear driveshafts from the transfer case. If the vehicle is equipped with PTO, disconnect the transfer case end of the PTO driveshaft.
7. Disconnect the speedometer cable at the transfer case.
8. Disconnect the hand brake cable.
9. Disconnect the clutch cable at the bell crank.
10. Place floor jacks under the transmission and engine. Protect the oil pan with a wooden block.
11. Remove the nuts holding the rear mount to the crossmember.
12. Remove the transfer case-to-crossmember bolt.
13. Remove the frame center crossmember-to-frame side rail bolts, then remove the crossmember. Remove the transmission-to-bell housing bolts.
14. Force the transmission to the right to disengage the clutch control lever tube ball joint.
15. Lower the engine and transmission. Slide the transmission and transfer case assemblies toward the rear until they clear the clutch.
16. Remove the 6 screws and lockwashers attaching the transfer case rear cover and remove the cover. If equipped, remove the PTO shift unit.
17. Remove the cotter pin, nut, and washer holding the transfer case main drive gear on the rear end of the transmission mainshaft. If possible, remove the main drive gear. If that's not possible, refer to Step 19.
18. Remove the transmission-to-transfer case bolts.
19. Install a transmission mainshaft retaining plate tool W-194 to prevent the mainshaft from pulling out of the case. If this tool is not available, loop a piece of wire around the mainshaft directly in back of the second speed gear. Install the shift housing right and left bolts part way into the case. Attach each end of the wire to the bolts. Support the transfer case, and with a soft mallet, tap lightly on the end of the mainshaft to loosen the gear and separate the two units.
20. Join the transfer case and transmission. Remove the wire or special holding tool. Remove the shift housing right and left bolts.
21. Install the transmission-to-transfer case bolts. Tighten them to 35 ft. lbs. (48 Nm).
22. Install the main drive gear. Install the cotter pin, nut, and washer holding the transfer case main drive gear on the rear end of the transmission mainshaft.
23. Install the transfer case rear cover and Install the cover. If equipped, install the PTO shift unit.
24. Slide the transmission and transfer case assemblies forward until they engage the clutch.
25. Force the transmission to the right to engage the clutch control lever tube ball joint.
26. Install the transmission-to-bell housing bolts. Tighten them to 30 ft. lbs. (41 Nm).
27. Install the frame center crossmember. Tighten the bolts to 50 ft. lbs. (68 Nm).
28. Install the transfer case-to-crossmember bolt. Tighten it to 45 ft. lbs. (61 Nm).
29. Install the nuts holding the rear mount to the crossmember. Tighten them to 40 ft. lbs. (54 Nm).
30. Connect the clutch cable at the bell crank.
31. Connect the hand brake cable.
32. Connect the speedometer cable at the transfer case.
33. Connect the front and rear driveshafts to the transfer case. If equipped, connect the transfer case end of the PTO driveshaft.
34. If the vehicle is equipped with PTO, install the shift lever.
35. Install the set screw in the transfer case shift lever pivot pin. Install the pivot pin, shift levers, and shift lever springs.
36. Install the shift lever and shift housing.

7-6 DRIVE TRAIN

37. Fill the transmission and transfer case.

T-86AA 3-Speed Overhaul

DISASSEMBLY

♦ See Figure 1

1. Drain the lubricant.
2. Remove the transfer case rear cover.
3. If so equipped, remove the pto shift unit.
4. Remove the cotter pin, nut and washer and remove the transfer case main drive gear.
5. Remove the transmission shift cover.
6. Loop a piece of wire around the mainshaft just behind 2nd gear. Twist the wire and attach one end to the right front cover screw and the other end to the left front cover screw. Tighten the wire to prevent the mainshaft from pulling out of the case when the transfer case is removed. If the mainshaft pulls out, the synchronizer parts will drop to the bottom of the case.
7. Remove the transfer case screws, then tap lightly on the end of the mainshaft to separate the two units. The transmission mainshaft bearing should slide out of the transfer case and stay with the mainshaft.
8. Remove the front main drive gear bearing retainer and gasket.
9. Remove the oil collector screws.
10. Remove the lockplate from the reverse idler shaft and countershaft at the rear of the case.
11. Using a dummy shaft and hammer, drive the countershaft out through the rear of the case.
12. Remove the mainshaft assembly through the rear opening, followed by the main drive gear.
13. Remove the countershaft gear set and 3 thrust washers from the case. Dismantle the countershaft gear assembly.
14. Drive out the reverse idler shaft and gear.

ASSEMBLY

1. Drive in the reverse idler shaft and gear.
2. Assemble the countershaft gear set. End-play, controlled by the thickness of the rear steel thrust washer, should be 0.012-0.018 in. (0.30-0.45mm). Assemble the large bronze washer with the lip entered in the slot in the case. The bronze-faced steel washer is placed next to the gear at the rear end and the steel washer is next to the case. Use a dummy shaft to assemble the countershaft bearing rollers. Hold the rollers in place with grease. The use of a loading sleeve will make the job easier.
3. Install the countershaft gear set and 3 thrust washers from the case.
4. When assembling the mainshaft gears, low and reverse gear is installed with the shoe shoe groove towards the front.
5. Install the mainshaft assembly and main drive gear.
6. When assembling the synchronizer unit, install the 2 springs in the high and intermediate clutch hub with the tensions opposed.
7. Drive the countershaft in through the rear of the case.

8. Install the lockplate on the reverse idler shaft and countershaft.
9. Install the oil collector screws.
10. Install the front main drive gear bearing retainer and gasket.
11. Join the transfer case and transmission. Install the transfer case screws.
12. Install the transmission shift cover.
13. Install the transfer case main drive gear.
14. If so equipped, install the pto shift unit.
15. Install the transfer case rear cover.
16. Fill the case with lubricant.

T-90C 3-Speed Overhaul

DISASSEMBLY

♦ See Figure 2

1. Drain the lubricant.
2. Remove the transfer case rear cover.
3. If so equipped, remove the pto shift unit.
4. Remove the cotter pin, nut and washer and remove the transfer case main drive gear.
5. Remove the transmission shift cover.
6. Loop a piece of wire around the mainshaft just behind 2nd gear. Twist the wire and attach one end to the right front cover screw and the other end to the left front cover screw. Tighten the wire to prevent the mainshaft from pulling out of the case when the transfer case is removed. If the mainshaft pulls out, the synchronizer parts will drop to the bottom of the case.
7. Remove the transfer case screws, then tap lightly on the end of the mainshaft to separate the two units. The transmission mainshaft bearing should slide out of the transfer case and stay with the mainshaft.
8. Remove the front main drive gear bearing retainer and gasket.
9. Remove the oil collector screws.
10. Remove the lockplate from the reverse idler shaft and countershaft at the rear of the case.
11. Using a dummy shaft and hammer, drive the countershaft out through the rear of the case.
12. Remove the mainshaft assembly through the rear opening, followed by the main drive gear.
13. Remove the countershaft gear set and 3 thrust washers from the case. Dismantle the countershaft gear assembly.
14. Drive out the reverse idler shaft and gear.

ASSEMBLY

1. Drive in the reverse idler shaft and gear.
2. Assemble the countershaft gear set. End-play, controlled by the thickness of the rear steel thrust washer, should be 0.012-0.018 in. (0.30-0.45mm). Assemble the large bronze washer with the lip entered in the slot in the case. The bronze-faced steel washer is placed next to the gear at the rear end and the steel washer is next to the case. Use a dummy shaft to assemble the countershaft bearing rollers. Hold

DRIVE TRAIN 7-7

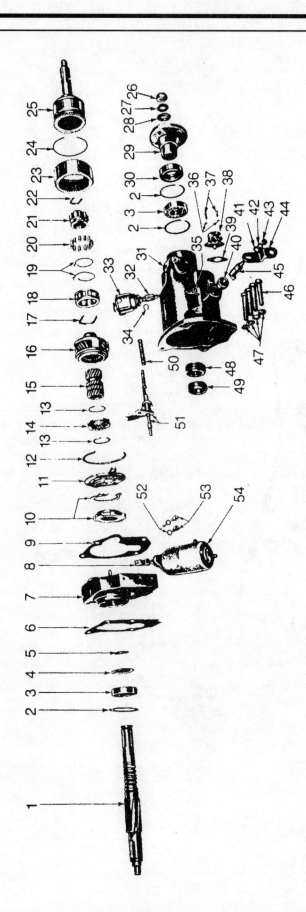

1. Transmission mainshaft
2. Mainshaft bearing snapring
3. Mainshaft bearing
4. Mainshaft oil baffle
5. Mainshaft snapring
6. Adapter to transmission gasket
7. Overdrive housing adapter
8. Sun gear pawl
9. Housing to adapter gasket
10. Balk ring and gear plate
11. Overdrive cover plate
12. Cover plate snapring
13. Sun gear snapring
14. Sun gear shifting collar
15. Sun gear
16. Planetary gear cage
17. Roller retainer clip
18. Freewheel roller retainer
19. Roller retainer spring
20. Freewheel roller
21. Freewheel cam
22. Cam retainer clip
23. Overdrive ring gear
24. Ring gear snapring
25. Mainshaft
26. Mainshaft nut
27. Mainshaft lockwasher
28. Mainshaft washer
29. Coupling flange
30. Mainshaft oil seal
31. Housing
32. Governor driven gear
33. Governor
34. Driven gear retaining ring
35. Control shaft pin
36. Rail switch lockwasher
37. Rail switch screw
38. Rail switch
39. Rail switch gasket
40. Control shaft oil seal
41. Control lever washer
42. Control lever lockwasher
43. Control lever nut
44. Control lever
45. Control shaft
46. Housing to transmission bolt
47. Housing to transmission lockwasher
48. Speedometer drive gear
49. Governor drive gear
50. Shift retractor spring
51. Shift rail and fork
52. Solenoid lockwasher
53. Solenoid bolt
54. Solenoid

Fig. 1 Exploded view of a common T-86/T-96 series transmission with overdrive

7-8 DRIVE TRAIN

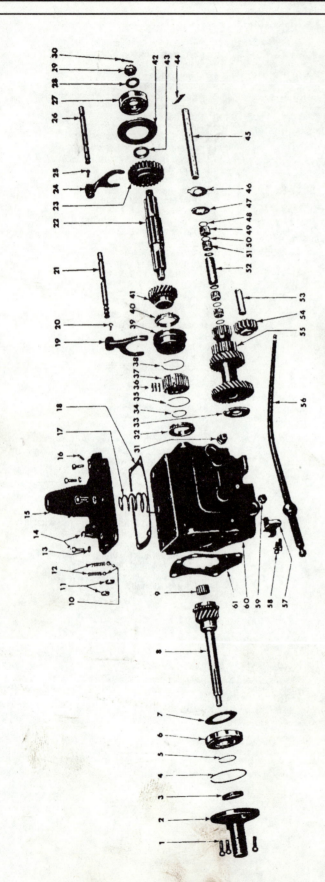

1. Bearing retainer bolt
2. Bearing retainer
3. Bearing retainer oil seal
4. Bearing snapring
5. Main drive gear snapring
6. Main drive gear bearing
7. Front bearing washer
8. Main drive gear
9. Pilot roller bearing
10. Poppet ball
11. Shift rail cap
12. Poppet spring
13. Lockwasher
14. Shift housing bolt
15. Shift housing
16. Interlock plunger
17. Shift lever spring
18. Shift housing gasket
19. High and intermediate shift fork
20. Shift fork pin
21. High and intermediate shift rail
22. Mainshaft
23. Sliding gear
24. Low and reverse shift fork
25. Shift fork pin
26. Low and reverse shift rail
27. Rear bearing
28. Mainshaft washer
29. Mainshaft nut
30. Cotter pin
31. Filler plug
32. Blocking ring
33. Front countershaft thrust washer
34. Clutch hub snapring
35. Synchronizer spring
36. Synchronizer plate
37. Clutch hub
38. Synchronizer spring
39. Clutch sleeve
40. Blocking ring
41. Second speed gear
42. Rear bearing adapter
43. Bearing spacer
44. Lockplate
45. Countershaft
46. Rear countershaft thrust washer
47. Rear countershaft thrust washer
48. Countershaft bearing washer
49. Countershaft bearing rollers
50. Countershaft bearing washer
51. Countershaft bearing rollers
52. Countershaft bearing spacer
53. Reverse gear shaft
54. Reverse idler gear
55. Countershaft gear set
56. Shift lever
57. Oil collector
58. Oil collector screw
59. Drain plug
60. Transmission case
61. Bearing retainer gasket

Fig. 2 Exploded view of a typical T-90 series transmission

DRIVE TRAIN 7-9

the rollers in place with grease. The use of a loading sleeve will make the job easier.

3. Install the countershaft gear set and 3 thrust washers from the case.
4. When assembling the mainshaft gears, low and reverse gear is installed with the shoe shoe groove towards the front.
5. Install the mainshaft assembly and main drive gear.
6. When assembling the synchronizer unit, install the 2 springs in the high and intermediate clutch hub with the tensions opposed.
7. Drive the countershaft in through the rear of the case.
8. Install the lockplate on the reverse idler shaft and countershaft.
9. Install the oil collector screws.
10. Install the front main drive gear bearing retainer and gasket.
11. Join the transfer case and transmission. Install the transfer case screws.
12. Install the transmission shift cover.
13. Install the transfer case main drive gear.
14. If so equipped, install the pto shift unit.
15. Install the transfer case rear cover.
16. Fill the case with lubricant.

T-98A 4-Speed Overhaul

DISASSEMBLY

◆ See Figure 3

1. After draining the transmission and removing the parking brake drum (or shoe assembly), lock the transmission in two gears and remove the U-joint flange, oil seal, speedometer driven gear and bearing assembly. Lubricant capacity is 6½ pints.
2. Remove the output shaft bearing retainer and the speedometer drive gear and spacer.
3. Remove the output shaft bearing snapring, and remove the bearing.
4. Remove the countershaft and idler shaft retainer and the power take-off cover.
5. After removing the input shaft bearing retainer, remove the snaprings from the bearing and the shaft.
6. Remove the input shaft bearing and oil baffle.
7. Drive out the countershaft (from the front). Keep the dummy shaft in contact with the countershaft to avoid dropping any rollers.
8. After removing the input shaft and the synchronizer blocking ring, pull the idler shaft.
9. Remove the reverse gear shifter arm, the output shaft assembly, the idler gear, and the cluster gear. When removing the cluster, do not lose any of the rollers.

Output Shaft

1. Remove the third- and high-speed synchronizer hub snapring from the output shaft, and slide the third- and high-speed synchronizer assembly and the third-speed gear off the shaft. Remove the synchronizer sleeve and the inserts from the hub. Before removing the two snaprings from the ends of the hub, check the end play of the second-speed gear. End-play should be 0.005-0.024 in. (0.13-0.60mm).
2. Remove the second-speed synchronizer snapring. Slide the second-speed synchronizer hub gear off the hub. Do not lose any of the balls, springs, or plates. Pull the hub off the shaft, and remove the second-speed synchronizer from the second-speed gear. Remove the snapring from the rear of the second-speed gear, and remove the gear, spacer, roller bearings, and thrust washer from the output shaft. Remove the remaining snapring from the shaft.

Cluster Gear

Remove the dummy shaft, pilot bearing rollers, bearing spacers, and center spacer from the cluster gear.

Reverse Idler Gear

Rotate the reverse idler gear on the shaft, and if it turns freely and smoothly, disassembly of the unit is not necessary. If any roughness is noticed, disassemble the unit.

Gear Shift Housing

1. Remove the housing cap and lever. Be sure all shafts are in neutral before disassembly.
2. Tap the shifter shafts out of the housing while holding one hand over the holes in the housing to prevent loss of the springs and balls. Remove the two shaft lock plungers from the housing.

Cluster Gear Assembly

Slide the long bearing spacer into the cluster gear bore, and insert the dummy shaft in the spacer. Hold the cluster gear in a vertical position, and install one of the bearing spacers. Position the 22 pilot bearing rollers in the cluster gear bore. Place a spacer on the rollers, and install 22 more rollers and another spacer. Hold a large thrust washer against the end of cluster gear and turn the assembly over. Install the rollers and spacers in the other end of the gear.

Reverse Idler Gear Assembly

1. Install a snapring in one end of the idler gear, and set the gear on end, with the snapring at the bottom.
2. Position a thrust washer in the gear on top of the snapring. Install the bushing on top of the washer, insert the 37 bearing rollers, and then a spacer followed by 37 more rollers. Place the remaining thrust washer on the rollers, and install the other snapring.

Output Shaft Assembly

1. Install the second speed gear thrust washer and snapring on the output shaft. Hold the shaft vertically, and slide on the second speed gear. Insert the bearing rollers in the second-speed gear, and slide the spacer into the gear. Install the snapring on the output shaft at the rear of the second-speed gear. Position the blocking ring on the second-speed gear. Do not invert the shaft because the bearing rollers will slide out of the gear.
2. Press the second-speed synchronizer hub onto the shaft, and install the snapring. Position the shaft vertically in a soft-jawed vise. Position the springs and plates in the second-speed synchronizer hub, and place the hub gear on the hub.

7-10 DRIVE TRAIN

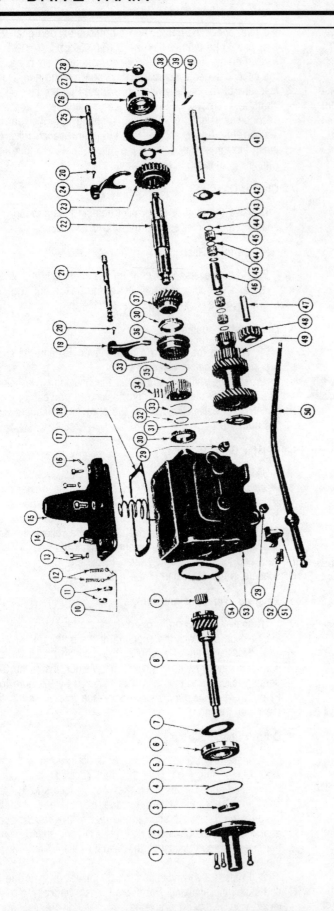

1. Bearing retainer bolt
2. Bearing retainer
3. Bearing retainer oil seal
4. Bearing snapring
5. Main drive gear snapring
6. Main drive gear bearing
7. Front bearing washer
8. Main drive gear
9. Pilot roller bearing
10. Poppet ball
11. Shift rail cap
12. Poppet spring
13. Lockwasher
14. Shift housing bolt
15. Control housing
16. Interlock plunger
17. Shift lever spring
18. Shift tower gasket
19. High and intermediate shift fork
20. Shift fork pin
21. High and intermediate shift rail
22. Mainshaft
23. Sliding gear
24. Low and reverse shift fork
25. Low and reverse shift rail
26. Rear bearing
27. Mainshaft washer
28. Mainshaft nut
29. Filler plug
30. Blocking ring
31. Front countershaft thrust washer
32. Clutch hub snapring
33. Synchronizer spring
34. Synchronizer plate
35. Clutch hub
36. Clutch sleeve
37. Second speed gear
38. Rear bearing adapter
39. Bearing spacer
40. Lockplate
41. Countershaft
42. Rear countershaft thrust washer
43. Rear countershaft thrust washer
44. Countershaft bearing washer
45. Countershaft bearing
46. Countershaft bearing spacer
47. Reverse gear shaft
48. Reverse idler gear
49. Countershaft gear set
50. Shift lever
51. Oil collector
52. Oil collector screw
53. Transmission case
54. Bearing retainer gasket

Fig. 3 Exploded view of a common T-98 series transmission

DRIVE TRAIN 7-11

3. Install the first speed gear and snapring on the shaft and press on the reverse gear.

4. Hold the gear above the hub spring and ball holes, and position one ball at a time in the hub, and slide the hub gear downward to hold the ball in place. Push the plate upward, and insert a small block to hold the plate in position, thereby holding the ball in the hub. Follow these procedures for the remaining balls.

5. Install the third speed gear and synchronizer blocking ring on the shaft.

6. Install the snaprings at both ends of the third and high-speed synchronizer hub. Stagger the openings of the snaprings so that they are not aligned. Place the inserts in the synchronizer sleeve, and position the sleeve on the hub.

7. Slide the synchronizer assembly onto the output shaft. The slots in the blocking ring must be in line with the synchronizer inserts. Install the snapring at the front of the synchronizer assembly.

Gear Shift Housing

1. Place the spring on the reverse gear shifter shaft gate plunger, and install the spring and plunger in the reverse gate. Press the plunger through the gate, and fasten it with the clip. Place the spring and ball in the reverse gate poppet hole. Compress the spring and install the cotter pin.

2. Place the spring and ball in the reverse shifter shaft hole in the gear shift housing. Press down on the ball, and position the reverse shifter shaft so that the reverse shifter arm notch does not slide over the ball. Insert the shaft part way into the housing.

3. Slide the reverse gate onto the shaft, and drive the shaft into the housing until the ball snaps into the groove of the shaft. Install the lock screw lock wire to the gate.

4. Insert the two interlocking plungers in the pockets between the shifter shaft holes. Place the spring and ball in the low and second shifter shaft hole. Press down on the ball, and insert the shifter shaft part way into the housing.

5. Slide the low and second shifter shaft gate onto the shaft, and install the corresponding shifter fork on the shaft so that the offset of the fork is toward the rear of the housing. Push the shaft all the way into the housing until the ball engages the shaft groove. Install the lock screw and wire that fastens the fork to the shaft. Install the third and high shifter shaft in the same manner. Check the interlocking system. Install new expansion plugs in the shaft bores.

CASE ASSEMBLY

1. Coat all parts, especially the bearings, with transmission lubricant to prevent scoring during initial operation.

2. Position the cluster gear assembly in the case. Do not lose any rollers.

3. Place the idler gear assembly in the case, and install the idler shaft. Position the slot in the rear of the shaft so that it can engage the retainer. Install the reverse shifter arm.

4. Drive out the cluster gear dummy shaft by installing the countershaft from the rear. Position the slot in the rear of the shaft so that it can engage the retainer. Use thrust washers as required to get 0.006-0.020 in. (0.15-0.50mm) cluster gear end play. Install the countershaft and idler shaft retainer.

5. Position the input shaft pilot rollers and the oil baffle, so that the baffle will not rub the bearing race. Install the input shaft and the blocking ring in the case.

6. Install the output shaft assembly in the case, and use a special tool to prevent jamming the blocking ring when the input shaft bearing is installed.

7. Drive the input shaft bearing onto the shaft. Install the thickest select-fit snapring that will fit on the bearing. Install the input shaft snapring.

8. Install the output shaft bearing.

9. Install the input shaft bearing without a gasket, and tighten the bolts only enough to bottom the retainer on the bearing snapring. Measure the clearance between the retainer and the case, and select a gasket (or gaskets) that will seal in the oil and prevent end play between the retainer and the snapring. Torque the bolts to specification.

10. Position the speedometer drive gear and spacer, and install a new output shaft bearing retainer seal.

11. Install the output shaft bearing retainer. Torque the bolts to specification, and install safety wire.

12. Install the brake shoe (or drum), and torque the bolts to specification. Install the U-joint flange. Lock the transmission in two gears and torque the nut to specification.

13. Install the power take-off cover plates with new gaskets. Fill the transmission according to specifications.

Overdrive Unit

2WD Utility models were offered with an optional Warner R10B planetary overdrive unit. The unit is electrically engaged at the discretion of the driver. It provides a reduction of about 30%.

REMOVAL & INSTALLATION

➡ Because the unit is essentially a 4th gear, removal is the same as disassembly.

1. Raise and safely support the front end on jackstands.
2. Drain both the transmission and overdrive housings.
3. Remove the two solenoid attaching bolts. Turn the solenoid ¼ turn to the right and pull it out of the unit.
4. Unbolt and remove the overdrive rail switch.

➡ This switch was used only on vehicles with 4-134 engines up to and including vehicle serial Nos. 54747-10084 and 54874-10096.

5. Remove the governor from the right side.
6. Disconnect the speedometer cable.
7. Unbolt and remove the transmission cover from the housing.
8. Shift the transmission into 1st gear.
9. Place transmission mainshaft retaining plate tool W-194 on the rear of the 1st/reverse sliding gear. Attach the tool with two of the cover bolts. If the tool is not available, loop a piece of wire around the mainshaft, just behind the gear and secure the wire to two of the front cover bolts.
10. Remove the nut attaching the companion flange to the overdrive mainshaft. Hold the flange with a holding tool, if necessary.

7-12 DRIVE TRAIN

11. Remove the companion flange, using a puller, if necessary.
12. Using a punch, drive the overdrive control shaft tapered pin out, from the bottom.
13. Pull out the control shaft to disengage the shaft rail.
14. Remove the bolts attaching the overdrive housing and adapter to the transmission.
15. Pull the overdrive housing rearward, while, at the same time, pushing forward on the overdrive mainshaft to prevent the mainshaft from coming off with the housing.

To install:

16. Slide the overdrive housing into place, while holding the mainshaft.
17. Install the bolts attaching the overdrive housing and adapter to the transmission. Tighten them to 30 ft. lbs. (41 Nm).
18. Push in the control shaft to engage the shaft rail.
19. Drive the overdrive control shaft tapered pin into place from the top.
20. Install the companion flange.
21. Install the nut attaching the companion flange to the overdrive mainshaft. Hold the flange with a holding tool, if necessary. Tighten the nut to 75 ft. lbs. (102 Nm).
22. Remove transmission mainshaft retaining plate tool W-194 or the wire.
23. Install the transmission cover.
24. Connect the speedometer cable.
25. Install the governor.
26. If applicable, install the overdrive rail switch.
27. Push the solenoid into the unit and turn it ¼ turn to the left. Install the two solenoid attaching bolts.
28. Fill both the transmission and overdrive housings.
29. Lower the front end.

CLUTCH

Understanding the Clutch

The purpose of the clutch is to disconnect and connect engine power at the transmission. A vehicle at rest requires a lot of engine torque to get all that weight moving. An internal combustion engine does not develop a high starting torque (unlike steam engines) so it must be allowed to operate without any load until it builds up enough torque to move the vehicle. To a point, torque increases with engine rpm. The clutch allows the engine to build up torque by physically disconnecting the engine from the transmission, relieving the engine of any load or resistance.

The transfer of engine power to the transmission (the load) must be smooth and gradual; if it weren't, drive line components would wear out or break quickly. This gradual power transfer is made possible by gradually releasing the clutch pedal. The clutch disc and pressure plate are the connecting link between the engine and transmission. When the clutch pedal is released, the disc and plate contact each other (the clutch is engaged) physically joining the engine and transmission. When the pedal is pushed in, the disc and plate separate (the clutch is disengaged) disconnecting the engine from the transmission.

Most clutch assemblies consists of the flywheel, the clutch disc, the clutch pressure plate, the throw out bearing and fork, the actuating linkage and the pedal. The flywheel and clutch pressure plate (driving members) are connected to the engine crankshaft and rotate with it. The clutch disc is located between the flywheel and pressure plate, and is splined to the transmission shaft. A driving member is one that is attached to the engine and transfers engine power to a driven member (clutch disc) on the transmission shaft. A driving member (pressure plate) rotates (drives) a driven member (clutch disc) on contact and, in so doing, turns the transmission shaft.

There is a circular diaphragm spring within the pressure plate cover (transmission side). In a relaxed state (when the clutch pedal is fully released) this spring is convex; that is, it is dished outward toward the transmission. Pushing in the clutch pedal actuates the attached linkage. Connected to the other end of this is the throw out fork, which hold the throw out bearing. When the clutch pedal is depressed, the clutch linkage pushes the fork and bearing forward to contact the diaphragm spring of the pressure plate. The outer edges of the spring are secured to the pressure plate and are pivoted on rings so that when the center of the spring is compressed by the throw out bearing, the outer edges bow outward and, by so doing, pull the pressure plate in the same direction - away from the clutch disc. This action separates the disc from the plate, disengaging the clutch and allowing the transmission to be shifted into another gear. A coil type clutch return spring attached to the clutch pedal arm permits full release of the pedal. Releasing the pedal pulls the throw out bearing away from the diaphragm spring resulting in a reversal of spring position. As bearing pressure is gradually released from the spring center, the outer edges of the spring bow outward, pushing the pressure plate into closer contact with the clutch disc. As the disc and plate move closer together, friction between the two increases and slippage is reduced until, when full spring pressure is applied (by fully releasing the pedal) the speed of the disc and plate are the same. This stops all slipping, creating a direct connection between the plate and disc which results in the transfer of power from the engine to the transmission. The clutch disc is now rotating with the pressure plate at engine speed and, because it is splined to the transmission shaft, the shaft now turns at the same engine speed.

The clutch is operating properly if:

1. It will stall the engine when released with the vehicle held stationary.
2. The shift lever can be moved freely between 1st and reverse gears when the vehicle is stationary and the clutch disengaged.

Adjustments

CLUTCH LINKAGE

As the clutch facings wear out the free travel of the clutch pedal diminishes. When sufficient wear occurs, the pedal clearance must be adjusted to 1-1½ in. (25.4-38.1mm) on CJ models, or to 1 in. (25.4mm) on Utility models. The free pedal clearance is adjusted by lengthening or shortening the clutch fork cable.

To make this adjustment on all but 6-226 engines, loosen the jam nut on the cable clevis and lengthen or shorten the cable to obtain the proper clearance at the pedal pad, then tighten the jam nut.

To make this adjustment on 6-226 engines, loosen the 2 locknuts on the pedal adjusting rod. Turn the nuts forward to increase, or backwards to decrease the free travel. Tighten the locknuts.

➡ On some older Jeep vehicles, a side movement of the clutch and brake pedals may develop. This is the result of wear on the pedals, shafts, and bushings. One way to compensate for this wear is to install a pedal slack adjuster kit.

Driven Disc and Pressure Plate

REMOVAL & INSTALLATION

▶ See Figures 4, 5, 6, 7, 8, 9, 10, 11, 12, 13, 14, 15, 16, 17, 18 and 19

4-134 Engines

✲✲CAUTION

The clutch driven disc may contain asbestos, which has been determined to be a cancer causing agent. Never clean clutch surfaces with compressed air! Avoid inhaling any dust from any clutch surface! When cleaning clutch surfaces, use a commercially available brake cleaning fluid.

1. Remove the transmission and transfer case from the vehicle.
2. Remove the flywheel housing.
3. Matchmark the clutch pressure plate to the engine flywheel with a center punch so the clutch assembly may be

Fig. 5 Loosen and remove the pressure plate retaining bolts evenly, a little at a time . . .

Fig. 6 . . . then carefully remove the driven disc and pressure plate assembly from the flywheel

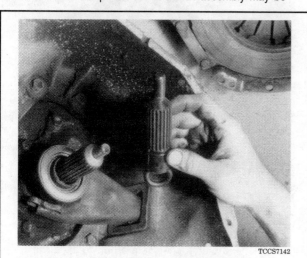

Fig. 4 Typical clutch alignment tool; note how the splines match the transmission's input shaft

Fig. 7 Check across the flywheel surface; it should be flat

7-14 DRIVE TRAIN

Fig. 8 If necessary, lock the flywheel in place and unfasten the retaining bolts . . .

Fig. 9 . . . then remove the flywheel from the crankshaft, in order replace it or have it machined

Fig. 10 Upon installation, it is usually a good idea to apply a threadlocking compound to the flywheel bolts

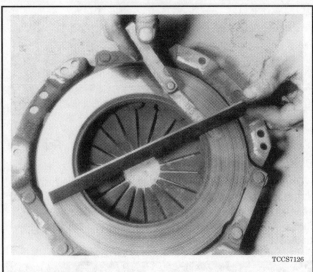

Fig. 11 Check the pressure plate for excessive wear

Fig. 12 Be sure that the flywheel surface is clean, before installing the clutch

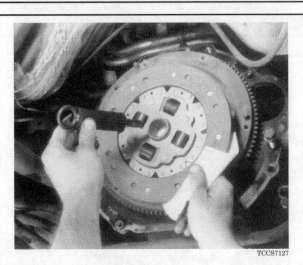

Fig. 13 Install a clutch alignment arbor, to align the clutch assembly during installation

DRIVE TRAIN 7-15

Fig. 14 Clutch plate (driven disc) installed with the arbor in place

Fig. 17 You may want to use a threadlocking compound on the clutch assembly bolts

Fig. 15 Driven disc and pressure plate installed with the alignment arbor in place

Fig. 18 Install the clutch assembly bolts and tighten in steps, using an X pattern

Fig. 16 Pressure plate-to-flywheel bolt holes should align

Fig. 19 Be sure to use a torque wrench to tighten all bolts

7-16 DRIVE TRAIN

installed in the same position after adjustments or replacement are complete.

4. Loosen the clutch pressure plate retaining bolts equally, a little at a time, to prevent distortion and relieve the clutch springs' tension evenly. Remove the bolts.

5. Remove the pressure plate assembly (bracket and pressure plate) and driven disc from the flywheel. The driven disc will just be resting on the pressure plate housing, since it usually is mounted on the input shaft of the transmission, which has been removed. Be careful that it does not fall and cause injury.

To install:

6. The clutch release bearing (throwout bearing) is lubricated at time of assembly and no attempt should be made to lubricate it. Put a small amount of grease in the pilot bushing.

7. Install the driven disc with the short end of the hub toward the flywheel. Use a spare transmission mainshaft or an aligning arbor to align the pressure plate assembly and the driven disc.

8. Leave the arbor in place while tightening the pressure plate bolts evenly a turn or two at a time. Tighten the bolts to 25 ft. lbs. (34 Nm).

9. Install the flywheel housing. Tighten the bolts to 40-50 ft. lbs. (54-68 Nm).

10. Install the transmission and transfer case.

6-225 Engine

▶ See Figures 20 and 21

✳✳CAUTION

The clutch driven disc may contain asbestos, which has been determined to be a cancer causing agent. Never clean clutch surfaces with compressed air! Avoid inhaling any dust from any clutch surface! When cleaning clutch surfaces, use a commercially available brake cleaning fluid.

1. Remove the transmission and transfer case.

2. Remove the clutch throwout bearing and pedal return spring from the clutch fork.

3. Remove the flywheel housing from the engine.

4. Disconnect the clutch form from the ball stud by forcing it toward the center of the vehicle.

5. Matchmark the clutch cover to the flywheel with a center punch so that the cover an later be installed in the same position on the flywheel. This is necessary to maintain engine balance.

6. Loosen the clutch attaching bolts alternately, one turn at a time to avoid distorting the clutch cover flange, until the diaphragm spring tension is released.

7. Support the pressure plate and cover assembly while removing the last of the bolts; remove the pressure plate and driven disc from the flywheel.

8. If it is necessary to disassemble the pressure plate assembly, note the position of the grooves on the edge of the pressure plate and cover. These marks must be aligned during assembly to maintain balance. The clutch diaphragm spring and two pivot rings are riveted to the clutch cover. Inspect the spring, rings and cover for excessive wear or damage. If there is a defect, replace the complete cover assembly.

9. Replace the clutch assembly in reverse order of the removal procedure, taking note of the following:

   a. Use extreme care at all times not to get the clutch driven disc dirty in any way.

   b. Lightly lubricate the inside of the clutch driven disc's spline with a coat of wheel bearing grease. Do the same to the input shaft of the transmission. Wipe off all excess grease so that none will fly off and get onto the driven disc.

   c. Lubricate the throwout bearing collar, the ball stud and the clutch fork with wheel bearing grease.

   d. Use a pilot shaft or a spare transmission main shaft to align the driven shaft and the clutch pressure plate when attaching the assembly to the flywheel.

   e. Tighten down on the clutch-to-flywheel attaching bolts alternately so that the clutch is drawn squarely into position on the flywheel. Each bolt must be tightened one turn at a time to avoid bending the clutch cover flange. Tighten the bolts to 30-40 ft. lbs. (41-54 Nm).

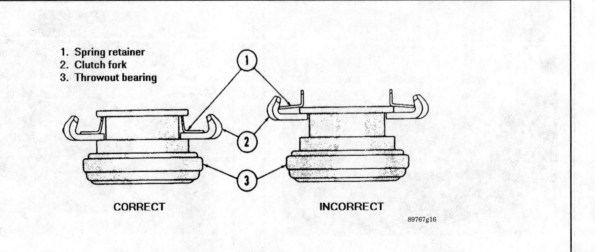

Fig. 20 Correct and incorrect throwout bearing installation on 6-225 engines

DRIVE TRAIN 7-17

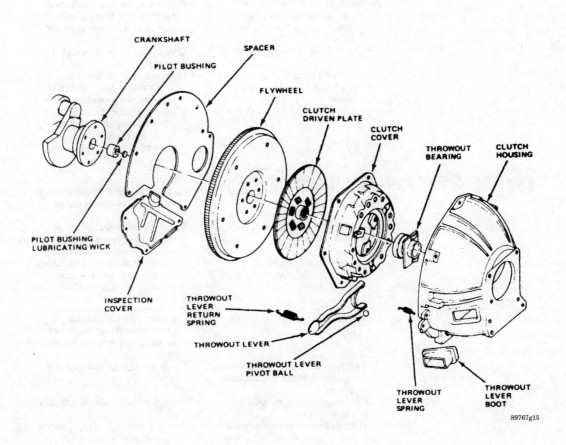

Fig. 21 Exploded view of a typical clutch unit used on 6-cylinder engines

Troubleshooting the Manual Transmission and Transfer Case

Problem	Cause	Solution
Transmission shift hard	• Clutch adjustment incorrect • Clutch linkage or cable binding • Shift rail binding	• Adjust clutch • Lubricate or repair as necessary • Check for mispositioned selector arm roll pin, loose cover bolts, worn shift rail bores, worn shift rail, distorted oil seal, or extension housing not aligned with case. Repair as necessary.
	• Internal bind in transmission caused by shift forks, selector plates, or synchronizer assemblies • Clutch housing misalignment • Incorrect lubricant • Block rings and/or cone seats worn	• Remove, dissemble and inspect transmission. Replace worn or damaged components as necessary. • Check runout at rear face of clutch housing • Drain and refill transmission • Blocking ring to gear clutch tooth face clearance must be 0.030 inch or greater. If clearance is correct it may still be necessary to inspect blocking rings and cone seats for excessive wear. Repair as necessary.
Gear clash when shifting from one gear to another	• Clutch adjustment incorrect • Clutch linkage or cable binding • Clutch housing misalignment • Lubricant level low or incorrect lubricant • Gearshift components, or synchronizer assemblies worn or damaged	• Adjust clutch • Lubricate or repair as necessary • Check runout at rear of clutch housing • Drain and refill transmission and check for lubricant leaks if level was low. Repair as necessary. • Remove, disassemble and inspect transmission. Replace worn or damaged components as necessary.
Transmission noisy	• Lubricant level low or incorrect lubricant • Clutch housing-to-engine, or transmission-to-clutch housing bolts loose • Dirt, chips, foreign material in transmission • Gearshift mechanism, transmission gears, or bearing components worn or damaged • Clutch housing misalignment	• Drain and refill transmission. If lubricant level was low, check for leaks and repair as necessary. • Check and correct bolt torque as necessary • Drain, flush, and refill transmission • Remove, disassemble and inspect transmission. Replace worn or damaged components as necessary. • Check runout at rear face of clutch housing
Transfer case noisy in all drive modes	• Insufficient or incorrect lubricant	• Drain and refill to edge of fill hole with SAE 85W-90 gear lubricant only. Check for leaks and repair if necessary.
		Note: If unit is still noisy after drain and refill, disassembly and inspection may be required to locate source of noise.

DRIVE TRAIN 7-19

Troubleshooting the Manual Transmission and Transfer Case (cont.)

Problem	Cause	Solution
Jumps out of gear	• Clutch housing misalignment	• Check runout at rear face of clutch housing
	• Gearshift lever loose	• Check lever for worn fork. Tighten loose attaching bolts.
	• Offset lever nylon insert worn or lever attaching nut loose	• Remove gearshift lever and check for loose offset lever nut or worn insert. Repair or replace as necessary.
	• Gearshift mechanism, shift forks, selector plates, interlock plate, selector arm, shift rail, detent plugs, springs or shift cover worn or damaged	• Remove, disassemble and inspect transmission cover assembly. Replace worn or damaged components as necessary.
	• Clutch shaft or roller bearings worn or damaged	• Replace clutch shaft or roller bearings as necessary
	• Gear teeth worn or tapered, synchronizer assemblies worn or damaged, excessive end play caused by worn thrust washers or output shaft gears	• Remove, disassemble, and inspect transmission. Replace worn or damaged components as necessary.
	• Pilot bushing worn	• Replace pilot bushing
Will not shift into one gear	• Gearshift selector plates, interlock plate, or selector arm, worn, damaged, or incorrectly assembled	• Remove, disassemble, and inspect transmission cover assembly. Repair or replace components as necessary.
	• Shift rail detent plunger worn, spring broken, or plug loose	• Tighten plug or replace worn or damaged components as necessary
	• Gearshift lever worn or damaged	• Replace gearshift lever
	• Synchronizer sleeves or hubs, damaged or worn	• Remove, disassemble and inspect transmission. Replace worn or damaged components.
Locked in one gear—cannot be shift out	• Shift rail(s) worn or broken, shifter fork bent, setscrew loose, center detent plug missing or worn	• Inspect and replace worn or damaged parts
	• Broken gear teeth on countershaft gear, clutch shaft, or reverse idler gear	• Inspect and replace damaged part
	Gearshift lever broken or worn, shift mechanism in cover incorrectly assembled or broken, worn damaged gear train components	• Disassemble transmission. Replace damaged parts or assemble correctly.
Transfer case difficult to shift or will not shift into desired range	• Vehicle speed too great to permit shifting	• Stop vehicle and shift into desired range. Or reduce speed to 3–4 km/h (2–3 mph) before attempting to shift.
	• If vehicle was operated for extended period in 4H mode on dry paved surface, driveline torque load may cause difficult shifting	• Stop vehicle, shift transmission to neutral, shift transfer case to 2H mode and operate vehicle in 2H on dry paved surfaces
	• Transfer case external shift linkage binding	• Lubricate or repair or replace linkage, or tighten loose components as necessary
	• Insufficient or incorrect lubricant	• Drain and refill to edge of fill hole with SAE 85W-90 gear lubricant only
	• Internal components binding, worn, or damaged	• Disassemble unit and replace worn or damaged components as necessary

7-20 DRIVE TRAIN

Troubleshooting the Manual Transmission and Transfer Case (cont.)

Problem	Cause	Solution
Noisy in—or jumps out of four wheel drive low range	• Transfer case not completely engaged in 4L position	• Stop vehicle, shift transfer case in Neutral, then shift back into 4L position
	• Shift linkage loose or binding	• Tighten, lubricate, or repair linkage as necessary
	• Shift fork cracked, inserts worn, or fork is binding on shift rail	• Disassemble unit and repair as necessary
Lubricant leaking from output shaft seals or from vent	• Transfer case overfilled • Vent closed or restricted • Output shaft seals damaged or installed incorrectly	• Drain to correct level • Clear or replace vent if necessary • Replace seals. Be sure seal lip faces interior of case when installed. Also be sure yoke seal surfaces are not scored or nicked. Remove scores, nicks with fine sandpaper or replace yoke(s) if necessary.
Abnormal tire wear	• Extended operation on dry hard surface (paved) roads in 4H range	• Operate in 2H on hard surface (paved) roads

89767c02

TRANSFER CASE

Adjustments

SHIFT LINKAGE

Spicer 18 Model

This linkage should be adjusted to give ½ in. (13mm) clearance between the floor pan and the lever when in four wheel drive, low range.

Transfer Case

REMOVAL & INSTALLATION

The transfer case can be removed without removing the transmission.

1. Drain the transfer case and transmission and replace the drain plugs.
2. Disconnect the brake cable.
3. Disconnect the front and rear driveshafts at the transfer case.
4. Disconnect the speedometer cable at the transfer case.
5. Disconnect the transfer case shift levers. On vehicles equipped with two shift levers loosen the set screw and remove the pivot pin. Use a prying tool to pry the shift lever springs away from the shift levers. On models equipped with a single shift lever remove the pivot pin cotter key and the adjusting rod attaching nut to remove the shift lever.
6. Remove the cover plate on the rear face of the transfer case or Power Take-Off (PTO) shift unit. Remove the cotter key, nut and washer from the transmission main shaft.
7. If possible, remove the transfer case main drive gear from the transmission main shaft. If it is not possible, continue on.
8. Remove the transmission-to-transfer case mounting bracket bolt and nut.
9. Remove the transmission-to-transfer case attaching bolts.
10. Remove the transfer case. If the transfer case main drive gear has not been removed in Step 7, proceed as follows:
    a. Brace the end of the transmission main shaft so that it cannot be moved in the transmission, then pull the transfer case to the rear to loosen the gear.
    b. Remove the gear.
    c. When separating the two housings, be careful that the transmission main shaft bearing, which bears in both housings, remains in the transmission case.
11. If the transfer case is being removed from the transmission with the two units out of the vehicle, use the above procedure starting from Step 6 and replacing Step 10 with the following procedure:
    a. Remove the transmission shift housing.
    b. Install a transmission mainshaft retaining plate, tool W-194, to prevent the mainshaft from pulling out of the transmission case.
    c. Should this tool be unavailable, loop a piece of wire around the mainshaft directly in back of the mainshaft second speed gear.
    d. Install the transmission shift housing right and left front attaching bolts part way into the transmission case.
    e. Twist the wire and attach each end to one of the screws.
    f. Tighten the wire.
    g. With the mainshaft securely in place, support the transfer case and with a rawhide mallet or brass drift and hammer, then tap lightly on the end of the mainshaft to loosen the gear and separate the two units.

To install:

12. Install the transfer case. If the transfer case main drive gear was not removed in Step 7, proceed as follows:
    a. Install the gear.

DRIVE TRAIN 7-21

b. When separating the two housings, be careful that the transmission mainshaft bearing, which bears in both housings, remains in the transmission case. When installing the transfer case gear on the transmission rear splined driveshaft, tighten the large gear nut securely and insert the cotter pin. Sink the cotter pin well into the nut slots so it will clear the PTO drive, if so equipped.

c. Brace the end of the transmission main shaft so that it cannot be moved in the transmission, then pull the transfer case to the rear to loosen the gear.

13. Remove transmission mainshaft retaining plate, tool W-194, or the wire.
14. Install the transmission shift housing. When installing the rear adapter plate on a 4-speed transmission, be sure that the cap screw heads do not protrude beyond the adapter plate face and that they do not interfere with the transfer case fitting tightly against the rear adapter plate.
15. Install the transmission-to-transfer case attaching bolts.
16. Install the transmission-to-transfer case mounting bracket bolt and nut.
17. Install the transfer case main drive gear on the transmission main shaft.
18. Install the cotter key, nut and washer from the transmission main shaft.
19. Install the cover plate on the rear face of the transfer case or PTO shift unit.
20. Connect the transfer case shift levers. On vehicles equipped with two shift levers loosen the set screw and Install the pivot pin. On models equipped with a single shift lever install the pivot pin cotter key and the adjusting rod attaching nut to install the shift lever.
21. Connect the speedometer cable at the transfer case.
22. Connect the front and rear driveshafts at the transfer case.
23. Connect the brake cable.
24. Fill the transfer case and transmission.

POWER TAKE-OFF (PTO) UNIT

Jeep vehicles were available with an optional Power Take-Off (PTO) unit. The PTO consists of four assemblies:
1. The shift unit, mounted on the transfer case.
2. The driveshaft and U-joints.
3. The shaft drive assembly.
4. The pulley drive assembly.

The shaft drive exits the rear of the vehicle and is designed to operate trailed equipment. The pulley drive is driven by the shaft drive and is designed to operate stationary equipment by a belt drive. The shaft drive assembly was installed far more frequently than was the pulley drive assembly.

Shift Assembly

REMOVAL & INSTALLATION

Drive for the PTO is taken from the transfer case main drive gear through an internal sliding gear. The sliding gear is mounted in the shift housing.

1. Remove the bolts in the driveshaft companion flange at the PTO front U-joint.
2. Unbolt and remove the shift lever.
3. Remove the five bolts securing the shift unit to the transfer case and pull it rearward from the case.
4. Installation is the reverse of removal.

DISASSEMBLY & ASSEMBLY

1. Carefully pry the shift rail and fork froward to clear the poppet ball and spring. Be careful to avoid damaging or losing the ball and spring. Remove the shifting sleeve.
2. Remove the attaching nut and the companion flange.
3. Drive the shaft forward out of the housing.
4. Remove the spacer and bearing from the shaft.
5. Remove the bearing from the housing.
6. Clean and inspect all parts and assemble in reverse of disassembly.

Shaft Drive Unit

REMOVAL & INSTALLATION

The standard 6-splined 1⅜ in. (34.93mm) diameter output shaft is driven through two helical cut gears mounted in a housing attached to the vehicle at the center of the frame rear crossmember.

1. Disconnect the rear U-joint at the companion flange.
2. Remove the retaining screw and the flange.
3. Unbolt and remove the assembly from the vehicle.
4. Installation is the reverse of removal.

DISASSEMBLY & ASSEMBLY

1. Drain the oil from the unit.
2. Remove the rear bearing cover.
3. Remove the nut and lockwasher from the input shaft.
4. Unbolt and remove the input shaft bearing retainer and remove the bearing. Take care not to lose the shims between the gear and the bearing case.
5. Remove the bearing cone, cup and snapring.
6. Remove the oil seal retainer and pilot assembly.
7. Press the shaft through the housing, removing the bearing cone, oil seal and retainer as an assembly.
8. Remove the input shaft gear through the rear opening. Push out the bearing cup and remove the snapring. Remove the bearing cone and oil seal from the shaft.
9. Remove the output shaft in the same manner as the input shaft.
10. Adjustment of the tapered roller bearings on both shafts is accomplished by shim packs placed between the gear hubs and bearing cones.
11. Assembly is the reverse of disassembly. Fill the unit with 90W gear oil.

7-22 DRIVE TRAIN

Pulley Drive Unit

REMOVAL & INSTALLATION

This procedure is accomplished simply by unbolting and removing the unit.

DISASSEMBLY & ASSEMBLY

1. Remove the unit from the vehicle.
2. Drain the oil and clean the unit.
3. Remove the retaining nut and remove the pulley.
4. Unbolt and remove the pulley shaft housing from the gear housing. Do not lose the shims.
5. Press the pulley shaft through the housing, removing the inner bearing cone, spacer and shim pack.
6. Remove the oil seal and outer bearing cone.
7. Remove the bearing retaining cover from the gear housing, then remove the shim pack.
8. Using a brass drift, tap the shaft through the housing; the bearing and gear will come out with it. Be careful not to lose the shim pack.
9. Clean and inspect all parts. Assembly is the reverse of disassembly. Fill the unit with 90W gear oil.

Power Take-Off Chart and Vehicle Ground Speeds
All Gearshift Positions
Miles Per Hour

Governor Control Position	Transfer In	PTO 1 to 1 Gear Ratio						Engine Speed rpm
		Transmission Gear In						
		Low		Intermediate		High		
		PTO Shaft rpm	Jeep Speed mph	PTO Shaft rpm	Jeep Speed mph	PTO Shaft rpm	Jeep Speed mph	
1	Low	358	2.22	644	4.01	1,000	6.22	1,000
	High	358	5.40	644	9.75	1,000	15.13	
2	Low	428	2.67	773	4.81	1,200	7.47	1,200
	High	428	6.48	773	11.71	1,200	18.15	
3	Low	500	3.11	902	5.62	1,400	8.72	1,400
	High	500	7.56	902	13.66	1,400	21.17	
4	Low	571	3.56	1,301	6.42	1,600	9.96	1,600
	High	571	8.65	1,301	15.61	1,600	24.20	
5	Low	643	4.00	1,160	7.22	1,800	12.08	1,800
	High	643	9.73	1,160	17.56	1,800	27.22	
6	Low	714	4.44	1,289	8.02	2,000	12.45	2,000
	High	714	11.89	1,289	19.51	2,000	30.25	
7	Low	786	4.89	1,418	8.83	2,200	13.70	2,200
	High	786	11.89	1,418	21.46	2,200	33.27	
8	Low	857	5.34	1,547	9.63	2,400	14.84	2,400
	High	857	12.97	1,547	23.41	2,400	36.31	
9	Low	929	5.78	1,657	10.43	2,600	16.19	2,600
	High	929	14.05	1,657	25.36	2,600	39.33	

DRIVE TRAIN

DRIVELINE

Front and Rear Driveshafts

▶ See Figures 22, 23, 24, 25, 26 and 27

REMOVAL & INSTALLATION

In order to remove the front and rear driveshafts, unscrew the holding nuts from the universal joint's U-bolts, remove the U-bolts and slide the shaft forward or backward toward the slip joint. The shaft can then be removed from the end yokes and removed from under the vehicle.

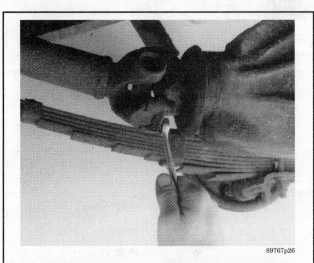

Fig. 22 After matchmarking the driveshaft and yokes, remove the U-bolt nuts . . .

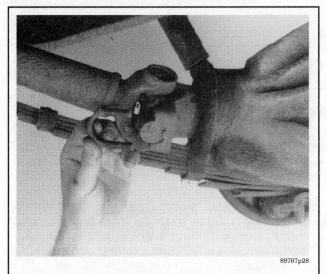

Fig. 23 . . . then remove the U-bolts from the U-joints

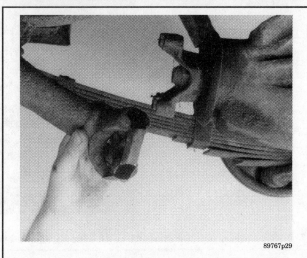

Fig. 24 Slide the driveshaft toward the slip joint and lower it from the yoke

Fig. 25 While supporting the back end of the driveshaft, remove the flange nuts . . .

7-24 DRIVE TRAIN

Fig. 26 . . . then pull the driveshaft off of the parking brake drum flange

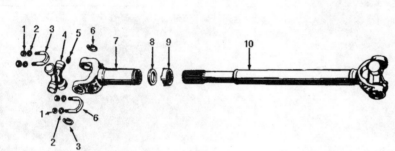

1. U-bolt nut
2. U-bolt washer
3. U-bolt
4. Universal joint journal
5. Lubrication fitting
6. Snap ring
7. Universal joint sleeve yoke
8. Rubber washer
9. Dust cap
10. Propeller shaft tube

Fig. 27 Exploded view of the driveshaft and universal joint used in all 1945-70 Jeep models

Each shaft is equipped with a splined slip joint at one end to allow for variations in length caused by vehicle spring action. Some slip joints are marked with arrows at the spline and sleeve yoke. When installing, align the arrows. If the slip joint is not marked with arrows, align the yokes at the front and rear of the shaft in the same horizontal plane. This is necessary in order to avoid vibration in the drive train. Tighten the U-bolt nuts to 15 ft. lbs. (20 Nm).

U-Joints

Most Jeep vehicles use a conventional universal joint at both ends of both driveshafts. Universal joints are held together by snaprings on the outside of the bearing caps.

On 1945-70 vehicles, 3 types of front axle U-joints were used; the Bendix type and the Rzeppa type, used on Axle models 25 and 27, and the more familiar single cross Cardan type used on axle model 27AF.

OVERHAUL

Single Cross Cardan Type

1. Remove the snaprings by pinching the ends together with a pair of pliers. If the rings do not readily snap out of the groove, tap the end of the bearing lightly to relieve pressure against the rings.
2. After removing the snaprings, press on the end of one bearing until the opposite bearing is pushed from the yoke arm. Turn the joint over and press the first bearing back out of that arm by pressing on the exposed end of the journal shaft. To drive it out, use a soft drift with a flat face, about $1/32$ in. (0.794mm) smaller in diameter than the hole in the yoke; otherwise there is danger of damaging the bearing.
3. Repeat the procedure for the other two bearings, then lift out the journal assembly by sliding it to one side.
4. Wash all parts in cleaning solvent and inspect the parts after cleaning. Replace the journal assembly if it is worn exten-

sively. Make sure that the grease channel in each journal trunnion is open.

5. Pack all of the bearing caps 1/3 full of grease and install the rollers (bearings).

6. Press one of the cap/bearing assemblies into one of the yoke arms just far enough so that the cap will remain in position.

7. Place the journal in position in the installed cap, with a cap/bearing assembly placed on the opposite end.

8. Position the free cap so that when it is driven from the opposite end it will be inserted into the opening of the yoke. Repeat this operation for the other two bearings.

9. Install the retaining clips. If the U-joint binds when it is assembled, tap the arms of the yoke slightly to relieve any pressure on the bearings at the end of the journal.

Bendix Type

▶ See Figure 28

With ordinary shop equipment it is nearly impossible to satisfactorily rebuild this unit. For this reason, the factory no longer supplies parts. After considerable mileage, a joint may pull apart upon removal from the vehicle. This does not mean that the joint is no longer usable. To assemble the axle shaft and universal:

1. Place the differential half of the shaft in a vise with the ground portion above the jaws.

2. Install the center ball (the one with the drilled hole) in the socket in the shaft, with the hole and groove visible.

3. Drop the center ball pin into the drilled hole in the wheel half of the shaft.

4. Place the wheel half of the shaft on the center ball. Slip the three balls into the races.

5. Turn the center ball until the groove lines up with the race for the remaining ball. Slip the ball into the race and straighten the wheel end of the shaft.

6. Turn the center ball until the pin drops into the hole in the ball.

7. Install the lock pin and center punch both ends to secure it.

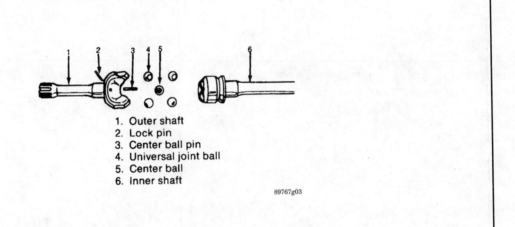

Fig. 28 Identification of the components which comprise a Bendix type front axle U-joint

1. Outer shaft
2. Lock pin
3. Center ball pin
4. Universal joint ball
5. Center ball
6. Inner shaft

Rzeppa Type

▶ See Figures 29, 30 and 31

With the joint removed, determine the method of attachment of the axle to the joint. If 3 bolts are used, start the procedure with Step 1; if there are no mounting bolts, skip Step 1 and proceed to Step 2.

1. Remove the three bolts securing the front axle to the joint. Pull the shaft free of the splined inner race. Remove the retaining ring and remove the axle shaft retainer.

2. To remove the axle shaft from the joint, use a wooden pry, and exert force in the direction of the axis of the axle shaft. Use a mallet, if necessary, to exert enough force to drive the retaining ring, installed on the end of the shaft, into its groove in the spline, permitting the joint to be slipped off the shaft.

3. Push down on various points of the inner race and cage until the balls can be removed with the help of a small prytool.

4. There are two large rectangular holes in the cage as well as four small holes. Turn the cage so that the two bosses in the spindle shaft will drop onto the rectangular holes and lift out the cage.

5. To remove the inner race, turn it so that one of the bosses will drop into a rectangular hole in its cage and shift the race to one side. Lift it out.

6. Assembly is the reverse of disassembly. Take care to keep all parts as clean as possible.

7-26 DRIVE TRAIN

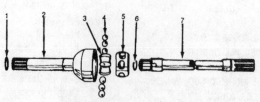

1. Outer axle shaft snap ring
2. Outer shaft
3. Universal joint inner race
4. Ball
5. Cage
6. Axle shaft retainer snap ring
7. Inner shaft

Fig. 29 Identification of the components which comprise a Rzeppa type front axle U-joint

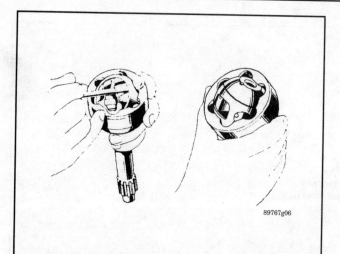

Fig. 30 Use a small prytool to remove the balls from the U-joint cage

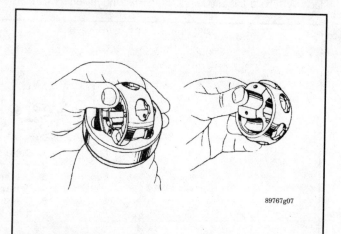

Fig. 31 Once all of the balls are removed, turn the cage 90 degrees from its normal resting position and pull it out of the joint housing

NOISE DIAGNOSIS

The Noise Is	Most Probably Produced By
• Identical under Drive or Coast	• Road surface, tires or front wheel bearings
• Different depending on road surface	• Road surface or tires
• Lower as the car speed is lowered	• Tires
• Similar with car standing or moving	• Engine or transmission
• A vibration	• Unbalanced tires, rear wheel bearing, unbalanced driveshaft or worn U-joint
• A knock or click about every 2 tire revolutions	• Rear wheel bearing
• Most pronounced on turns	• Damaged differential gears
• A steady low-pitched whirring or scraping, starting at low speeds	• Damaged or worn pinion bearing
• A chattering vibration on turns	• Wrong differential lubricant or worn clutch plates (limited slip rear axle)
• Noticed only in Drive, Coast or Float conditions	• Worn ring gear and/or pinion gear

DRIVE TRAIN 7-27

DRIVE AXLES

Understanding Drive Axles

The drive axle is a special type of transmission that reduces the speed of the drive from the engine and transmission and divides the power to the wheels. Power enters the axle from the driveshaft via the companion flange. The flange is mounted on the drive pinion shaft. The drive pinion shaft and gear which carry the power into the differential turn at engine speed. The gear on the end of the pinion shaft drives a large ring gear the axis of rotation of which is 90 degrees away from the of the pinion. The pinion and gear reduce the gear ratio of the axle, and change the direction of rotation to turn the axle shafts which drive both wheels. The axle gear ratio is found by dividing the number of pinion gear teeth into the number of ring gear teeth.

The ring gear drives the differential case. The case provides the two mounting points for the ends of a pinion shaft on which are mounted two pinion gears. The pinion gears drive the two side gears, one of which is located on the inner end of each axle shaft.

By driving the axle shafts through the arrangement, the differential allows the outer drive wheel to turn faster than the inner drive wheel in a turn.

The main drive pinion and the side bearings, which bear the weight of the differential case, are shimmed to provide proper bearing preload, and to position the pinion and ring gears properly.

➡**The proper adjustment of the relationship of the ring and pinion gears is critical. It should be attempted only by those with extensive equipment and/or experience.**

Limited-slip differentials include clutches which tend to link each axle shaft to the differential case. Clutches may be engaged either by spring action or by pressure produced by the torque on the axles during a turn. During turning on a dry pavement, the effects of the clutches are overcome, and each wheel turns at the required speed. When slippage occurs at either wheel, however, the clutches will transmit some of the power to the wheel which has the greater amount of traction. Because of the presence of clutches, limited-slip units require a special lubricant.

Determining Axle Ratio

The drive axle is said to have a certain axle ratio. This number (usually a whole number and a decimal fraction) is actually a comparison of the number of gear teeth on the ring gear and the pinion gear. For example, a 4.11 rear means that theoretically, there are 4.11 teeth on the ring gear and one tooth on the pinion gear or, put another way, the driveshaft must turn 4.11 times to turn the wheels once. Actually, on a 4.11 rear, there might be 37 teeth on the ring gear and 9 teeth on the pinion gear. By dividing the number of teeth on the pinion gear into the number of teeth on the ring gear, the numerical axle ratio (4.11) is obtained. This also provides a good method of ascertaining exactly what axle ratio one is dealing with.

Another method of determining gear ratio is to jack up and support the car so that both rear wheels are off the ground. Make a chalk mark on the rear wheel and the driveshaft. Put the transmission in neutral. Turn the rear wheel one complete turn and count the number of turns that the driveshaft makes. The number of turns that the driveshaft makes in one complete revolution of the rear wheel is an approximation of the rear axle ratio.

REAR AXLE

➡**Two different types of shafts have been used: the tapered shaft and the flanged shaft. The differences are obvious. The terms, tapered and flanged, refer to the outer end of the shaft. The tapered shaft has a single retaining nut on the outer end of the axle shaft. The flanged shaft has a mounting flange for the brake drum on the outer end of the shaft and the shaft is held in place by a retaining plate. One other important point: some tapered and flanged axles have an inner oil seal fitted in the axle shaft housing, inboard of the bearing; some do not. If your axle does not have one, don't install one when replacing the bearing! Axles with an inner seal rely on chassis lube for bearing lubrication and must be prelubed prior to installation. Axles without an inner seal rely on differential oil to lubricate the bearing.**

Pinion Oil Seal

REMOVAL & INSTALLATION

▶ See Figures 32 and 33

With Tapered Shafts

➡Special tools are needed for this job.

1. Raise and support the vehicle and remove the rear wheels and brake drums.
2. Mark the driveshaft and yoke for reassembly and disconnect the driveshaft from the rear yoke.
3. With a socket on the pinion nut and an inch pound torque wrench, rotate the drive pinion several revolutions. Check and record the torque required to turn the drive pinion.
4. Remove the pinion nut. Use a flange holding tool to hold the flange while removing the pinion nut. Discard the pinion nut.

7-28 DRIVE TRAIN

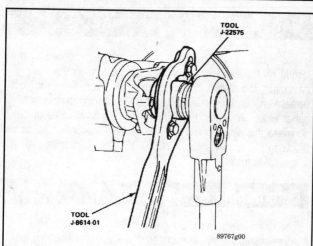

Fig. 32 Use the special holding tool J-8614-01, or its equivalent, to hold the yoke steady while removing the pinion nut

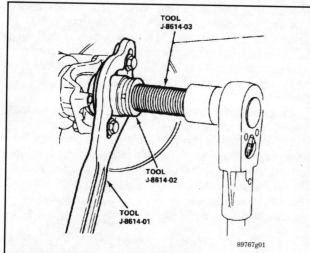

Fig. 33 Use tool J-8614-03, or equivalent, to pull the yoke out of the differential — all axles

5. Matchmark the yoke to the drive pinion shaft for reassembly reference.
6. Remove the rear yoke with a puller.
7. Inspect the seal surface of the yoke and replace it with a new one if the seal surface is pitted, grooved, or otherwise damaged.
8. Remove the pinion oil seal using tool J-9233.

To install:

9. Before installing the new seal, coat the lip of the seal with rear axle lubricant.
10. Install the seal, driving it into place with tool J-22661.
11. Install the yoke on the pinion shaft. Align the marks made on the pinion shaft and yoke during disassembly.
12. Install a new pinion nut. Tighten the nut until end-play is removed from the pinion bearing. Do not overtighten.
13. Check the torque required to turn the drive pinion. The pinion must be turned several revolutions to obtain an accurate reading.
14. Tighten the pinion nut to obtain the torque reading observed during disassembly (Step 3) plus 5 inch lbs. (0.56 Nm). Tighten the nut minimally each time, to avoid overtightening. Do not loosen and then retighten the nut.

➡ If the desired torque is exceeded a new collapsible pinion spacer sleeve must be installed and the pinion gear preload reset.

15. Install the driveshaft, aligning the matchmarks made during disassembly. Install the rear brake drums and wheels.

With Flanged Shafts

1. Raise and safely support the vehicle on jackstands.
2. Matchmark driveshaft to the yoke for reference during assembly and disconnect the driveshaft at the yoke.
3. Remove the pinion shaft nut and washer.
4. Remove the yoke from the pinion shaft, using a puller.
5. Remove the pinion shaft oil seal with tool J-25180.

To install:

6. Install the new seal with a suitable driver.
7. Install the pinion shaft washer and nut. Tighten the nut to 210 ft. lbs. (285 Nm).

Rear Axle Application Chart

Axle Type	Years	Models
DanaSpicer 23-2	1945–49	CJ-2A before serial #13453
Dana/Spicer 27	1955–64	DJ-3A
Dana/Spicer 41-2	1945–49	CJ-2A after serial #13453
Dana/Spicer 44	1947–64	Utility Models w/3700 lb GVW
	1948–70	CJ-3A, CJ-3B, CJ-5, CJ-6
Dana/Spicer 53	1947–64	Utility Models w/4500 lb GVW

DRIVE TRAIN 7-29

8. Align the matchmarks on the driveshaft and yoke and install the driveshaft. Tighten the attaching bolts or nuts to 16 ft. lbs. (22 Nm).

9. Remove the supports and lower the vehicle.

Axle Shaft

REMOVAL & INSTALLATION

Tapered Shafts

1. Raise and safely support the vehicle on jackstands, then remove the hub cap.
2. Remove the wheel.
3. Remove the axle nut dust cap.
4. Remove the axle shaft cotter pin, castle nut and flat washer.
5. Back off the brake adjustment.
6. Use a puller to remove the wheel hub.
7. Remove the screws attaching the brake dust protector, grease and bearing retainers, brake assembly and shim to the housing.
8. Remove the hydraulic line from the brake assembly.
9. Remove the dust shield and oil seal.

➡If both shafts are being removed, keep the shims separated. Axle shaft end-play is adjusted at the left side only.

10. Use a puller to remove the axle shaft.
11. Install the axle shaft in the reverse order of removal, using a new grease seal and installing the hub assembly before the woodruff key. Tighten the axle shaft nut to 150 ft. lbs. (204 Nm). Some axles have and inner oil seal fitted in the axle shaft housing, inboard of the bearing; some do not. If your axle does not have one, do not install one when replacing the bearing! Axles with an inner seal rely on chassis lube for bearing lubrication and must be prelubed prior to installation. Axles without an inner seal rely on differential oil to lubricate the bearing.

➡Should the axle shaft be broken, the inner end can usually be drawn out of the housing with a wire loop after the outer oil seal is removed. However, if the broken end is less than 8 in. (20cm) long, it usually is necessary to remove the differential assembly.

Flanged Shafts

1. Raise and safely support the vehicle on jackstands, then remove the wheels.
2. Remove the brake drum spring locknuts and remove the drum.
3. Remove the axle shaft flange cup plug by piercing the center with a sharp tool and prying it out.
4. Using the access hole in the axle shaft flange, remove the nuts which attach the backing plate and retainer to the axle tube flange.
5. Remove the axle shaft from the housing with an axle puller.

6. Install in reverse order of removal. Tighten the bearing retainer bolts to 50 ft. lbs. (68 Nm) in a crisscross pattern.

➡Some axles have an inner oil seal fitted in the axle shaft housing, inboard of the bearing; some do not. If your axle is not equipped with one, do not install one when replacing the bearing. Axles with an inner seal rely on chassis lube for bearing lubrication and must be prelubed prior to installation. Axles without an inner seal rely on differential oil to lubricate the bearing.

Axle Shaft Bearing

REMOVAL & INSTALLATION

Tapered Shafts

♦ See Figure 34

➡An arbor press is necessary for this procedure.

1. Remove the axle shaft as described earlier in this section.
2. With the aid of an arbor press, remove the bearing from the axle shaft.
3. The new bearing must be installed with the same press as used during removal, or bearing replacing tool J-2995.
4. If an inner seal in the axle housing was present during axle shaft removal, make sure to replace it with a new inner seal and pack the bearing with wheel bearing grease. When packing the bearing, make sure the grease fills the cavities between the bearing rollers.

➡If there was no inner seal, do not install one. Do not pack the bearing with grease. The lack of an inner seal indicates that the bearing is lubed with axle lubricant.

5. Measure axle shaft end-play as follows:
    a. Axle shaft end-play can be measured by installing the hub retaining nut on the shaft so that it can be pushed and pulled with relative ease.

Fig. 34 Rear axle play is adjusted by adding or subtracting shims

b. Strike the end of each axle shaft with a lead hammer to seat the bearing cups against the support plate.

c. Mount a dial indicator on the left side support plate with the stylus resting on the end of the axle shaft.

d. Check the end-play while pushing and pulling on the axle shaft.

e. End-play should be within 0.004-0.008 in. (0.1016-0.2032mm), with 0.006 in. (0.1524mm) as the preferred value.

f. Add shims to increase end-play. Remove the hub retaining nut when finished checking end-play.

➡ When a new axle shaft is installed, a new hub must also be installed. However, a new hub can be installed on an original axle shaft if the serrations on the shaft are not worn or damaged. The procedures for installing an original hub and a new hub are different.

6. Install an original hub in the following manner:
    a. Align the keyway in the hub with the axle shaft key.
    b. Slide the hub onto the axle shaft as far as possible.
    c. Install the axle shaft nut and washer.
    d. Install the drum, drum retaining screws, and wheel.
    e. Lower the vehicle onto its wheels and tighten the axle shaft nut to 250 ft. lbs. (340 Nm). If the cotter pin hole is not aligned, tighten the nut to the next castellation and install the pin. Do not loosen the nut to align the cotter pin hole.

7. Install a new hub in the following manner:
    a. Align the keyway in the hub with the axle shaft key.
    b. Slide the hub onto the axle shaft as far as possible.
    c. Install two well lubricated thrust washers and the axle shaft nut.
    d. Install the brake drum, drum retaining screws, and wheel.
    e. Lower the vehicle onto its wheels.
    f. Tighten the axle shaft nut until the distance from the outer face of the hub to the outer end of the axle shaft is 1$^{5}/_{16}$ in. (33.34mm). Pressing the hub onto the axle to the specified distance is necessary to form the hub serrations properly.
    g. Remove the axle shaft nut and one thrust washer.
    h. Install the axle shaft nut and tighten it to 250 ft. lbs. (340 Nm). If the cotter pin hole is not aligned, tighten the nut to the next castellation and install the pin. Do not loosen the nut to install the cotter pin.

8. Connect the brake line to the wheel cylinder and bleed the brake hydraulic system and adjust the brake shoes.

Flanged Shaft

➡ An arbor press is necessary for this procedure.

1. Remove the axle shaft as described earlier in this section.
2. Position the axle shaft in a vise.
3. Remove the retaining ring by drilling a ¼ in. (6mm) hole about ¾ of the way through the ring, then using a cold chisel over the hole, split the ring.
4. Remove the bearing with an arbor press, discard the seal and remove the retainer plate.
5. Installation is the reverse of removal. The new bearing must be pressed on. Make sure it is squarely seated.

Rear Axle Unit

REMOVAL & INSTALLATION

1. Raise the vehicle and safely support it on jackstands.
2. Remove the rear wheels.
3. Place an indexing mark on the rear yoke and driveshaft, and disconnect the shaft.
4. Disconnect the shock absorbers from the axle tubes. Disconnect the track bar at the axle bracket, on vehicles so equipped.
5. Disconnect the brake hose from the tee fitting on the axle housing. Disconnect the vent tube at the axle.
6. Disconnect the parking brake cable at the frame mounting.
7. Remove the U-bolts. On vehicles with the spring mounted above the axle, disconnect the spring at the rear shackle.
8. Support the axle on a jack, remove the spring clips, and remove the axle assembly from under the vehicle.

To install:

9. Raise the axle on a jack and install the spring clips. Tighten the spring pivot bolts to 30 ft. lbs. (41 Nm) on CJ-2A, CJ-3A, CJ-3B and Utility models, or to 100 ft. lbs. (136 Nm) on CJ-5 and CJ-6 models. On CJ-5 and CJ-6 models also tighten the spring shackle nuts to 24 ft. lbs. (33 Nm).
10. Install the U-bolts. On vehicles with the spring mounted above the axle, connect the spring at the rear shackle. Tighten the U-bolt nuts to the following values:
    - ⁷⁄₁₆ in. U-bolts — 55 ft. lbs. (75 Nm)
    - ½ in. U-bolts — CJ-2A, CJ-3A, CJ-3B and Utility models: 80 ft. lbs. (109 Nm); CJ-5 and CJ-6 models: 55 ft. lbs. (75 Nm)
    - ⁹⁄₁₆ in. U-bolts — 100 ft. lbs. (136 Nm)
11. Connect the parking brake cable at the frame mounting.
12. Connect the brake hose at the tee fitting on the axle housing.
13. Connect the vent tube at the axle.
14. Connect the track bar at the axle bracket, on vehicles so equipped.
15. Connect the shock absorbers to the axle tubes. Tighten the shock stud nut to 45 ft. lbs. (61 Nm).
16. Connect the driveshaft.
17. Install the rear wheels.
18. Lower the vehicle.

➡ Bleed and adjust the brakes accordingly.

DRIVE TRAIN 7-31

4WD FRONT DRIVE AXLE

Axle Shaft, Bearing and Seal

REMOVAL & INSTALLATION

▶ See Figures 35, 36, 37, 38, 39, 40, 41, 42, 43, 44, 45, 46, 47 and 48

The front axle shaft and universal joint assembly is removed as an assembly.

➡ Refer to the U-joint portion of this section for a description of the three types used on these axles.

1. Remove the wheel.
2. Remove the hub with a puller. If there are locking hubs, remove them as described in Section 1.

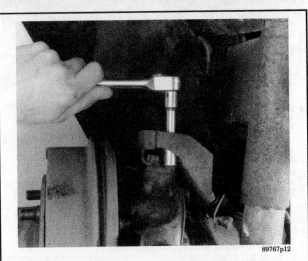

Fig. 36 Another way to remove the axle is to first loosen the brake hose cover bolt . . .

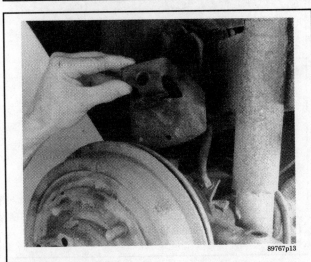

Fig. 37 . . . then remove the brake hose cover from the knuckle assembly

3. Remove the axle shaft driving flange bolts.
4. Apply the foot brakes and remove the axle shaft flange with a puller.
5. Release the locking lip on the lockwasher and remove the outer nut, lockwasher, adjusting nut, and bearing lockwasher.
6. Remove the wheel hub and drum assembly with the bearings. Be careful not to damage the oil seal.
7. Remove the hydraulic brake tube and the brake backing plate screws.
8. Remove the spindle.
9. Remove axle shaft and universal joint assembly.

To install:

10. Single cross Cardan type installation is the reverse of the removal procedure.

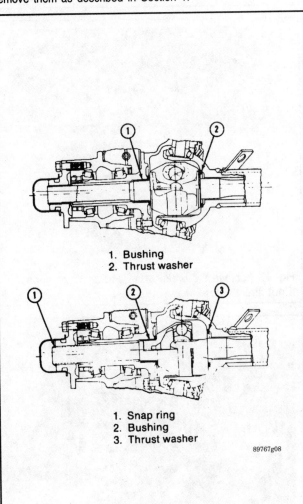

Fig. 35 Cross-sectional views of Bendix type joint (top) and Rzeppa type joint (bottom) front axle shafts

7-32 DRIVE TRAIN

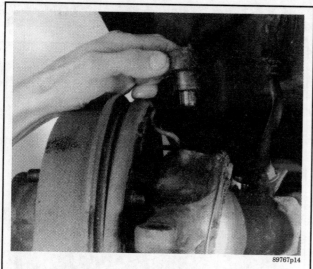

Fig. 38 Remove the upper pivot pin . . .

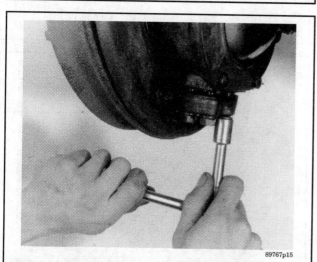

Fig. 39 . . . loosen the lower pivot pin retaining plate bolts . . .

Fig. 40 . . . then remove the lower pivot pin from the knuckle

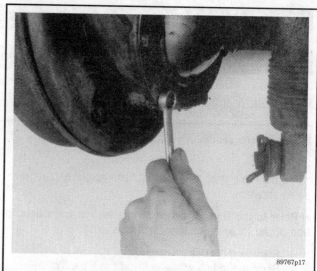

Fig. 41 Remove the knuckle seal plate retaining bolts

Fig. 42 Remove the brake drum and brake components, if not already done

Fig. 43 Remove the spindle from the axle assembly . . .

DRIVE TRAIN 7-33

Fig. 44 . . . then remove the pivot pin bearings from the joint

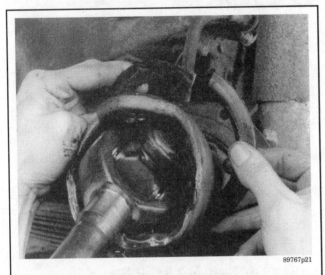

Fig. 45 Remove the knuckle's rubber seal . . .

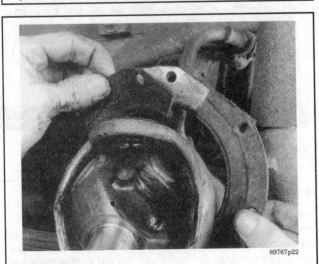

Fig. 46 . . . and also remove the larger gasket from the seal plates

Fig. 47 If necessary, remove the seal plates from the axle housing

Fig. 48 Slide the axle shaft out of the axle housing

11. Bendix type installation is as follows:
   a. Insert the U-joint and shaft assembly into the housing. Mesh the splined end of the shaft with the differential and push it into place.
   b. Install the wheel bearing spindle.
   c. Install the brake tube and backing plate.
   d. Grease and assemble the wheel bearings, hub and drum on the spindle. Install the bearing washer and adjusting nut. Tighten the nut until a slight drag is felt, then back it off $1/6$ turn (one flat of the nut). Install remaining parts.

12. Early Rzeppa type requires a shimming procedure. Installation is the same as the Bendix type except that a shim pack must be installed between the driving flange and the wheel hub to determine the proper operating clearance for the U-joint. To do this:
   a. Install the drive flange on the axle splines without shims.
   b. Install the axle nut and tighten it snugly.
   c. Install two opposite flange bolts snugly.

d. Use a feeler gauge to measure the gap between the outer end of the hub and the inner face of the driving flange. This determines the amount of shimming to be used. It is necessary to install shims of a thickness equal to the measured gap plug 0.015-0.050 in. (0.381-1.27mm). If no gap is found, install a 0.010 in. (0.254mm) shim.

e. Install the correct amount of shims, replace the flange and install the 6 bolts. Install the axle shaft nut and make sure that the proper end-float has been obtained. To do this, back off the shaft nut so that a 0.050 in. (1.27mm) feeler gauge will fit between the nut and driving flange. Tap the end of the shaft with a soft mallet which will force in the shaft the amount of end-float. Measure the clearance between the nut and driving flange. Clearance should be 0.015-0.050 in. (0.381-1.27mm).

13. Late Rzeppa type installation is the same as the Bendix type except that a snapring is used to secure the outer end of the shaft controlling the end-float.

Pinion Seal and Yoke

REMOVAL & INSTALLATION

1. Raise and safely support the front end of the vehicle on jackstands.
2. Matchmark the driveshaft and yoke, then disconnect the driveshaft.
3. Using a holding tool (such as J-8614-01) on the yoke, remove the pinion nut.
4. Remove the yoke, using tools J-8614-01, -02, and -03, or their equivalents.
5. Using tool J-9233 or J-7583, or their equivalents, remove the seal.

To install:

6. Coat the outer rim of the new seal with sealer and install it using a seal driver.
7. Install the yoke, pinion washer and a new pinion nut. Tighten the nut to 210 ft. lbs. (286 Nm).
8. Connect the driveshaft.

Front Axle Unit

REMOVAL & INSTALLATION

1. Raise and support the vehicle safely on jackstands, then remove the wheels.
2. Index the driveshaft to the differential yoke for the proper alignment upon installation. Disconnect the driveshaft at the axle yoke and secure the shaft to the frame rail.
3. Disconnect the steering linkage from the steering knuckles. Disconnect the shock absorbers at the axle housing.
4. If the vehicle is equipped with a stabilizer bar, remove the nuts attaching the stabilizer bar connecting links to the spring tie plates.
5. On vehicles equipped with a sway bar, remove the nuts attaching the sway bar connecting links to the spring tie plates.
6. Disconnect the breather tube from the axle housing. Disconnect the stabilizer bar link bolts at the spring clips.
7. Remove the brake calipers, or drums, hub and rotor, or brake shoes, and the brake shield.
8. Remove the U-bolts and the tie plates.
9. Support the assembly on a jack and loosen the nuts securing the rear shackles, but do not remove the bolts.
10. Remove the front spring shackle bolts. Lower the springs to the floor.
11. Pull the jack and axle housing from underneath the vehicle.

To install:

➡ Tighten the various fasteners to the specified values listed after the procedure.

12. Raise the axle into position.
13. Install the front spring shackle bolts.
14. Tighten the nuts securing the rear shackles.
15. Install the U-bolts and the tie plates.
16. Install the brake calipers, or drums, hub and rotor, or brake shoes, and the brake shield.
17. Connect the breather tube to the axle housing.
18. Connect the stabilizer bar link bolts at the spring clips.
19. On vehicles equipped with a sway bar, install the nuts attaching sway bar connecting links to the spring tie plates.
20. If the vehicle is equipped with a stabilizer bar, install the nuts attaching the stabilizer bar connecting links to the spring tie plates.
21. Connect the steering linkage to the steering knuckles.
22. Connect the shock absorbers at the axle housing.
23. Connect the driveshaft at the axle yoke.
24. Install the wheels.
25. Lower the vehicle.
26. Tighten the suspension fasteners to the following specifications:

CJ-2A, CJ-3A, CJ-3B and Utility models —
- $7/16$ in. spring U-bolt nuts: 55 ft. lbs. (75 Nm)
- All other spring U-bolt nuts: 80 ft. lbs. (109 Nm)
- Spring pivot bolts: 30 ft. lbs. (41 Nm)

CJ-5 and CJ-6 models —
- Connecting rod ball studs: 60 ft. lbs. (82 Nm) minimum
- Spring shackle bolts: 24 ft. lbs. (33 Nm)
- Shock absorber lower mounting nut: 45 ft. lbs. (61 Nm)
- Spring pivot bolts: 100 ft. lbs. (136 Nm)
- $9/16$ in. spring U-bolt nuts: 100 ft. lbs. (136 Nm)
- $1/2$ in. spring U-bolt nuts: 55 ft. lbs. (75 Nm)

Front Hub and Wheel Bearings

ADJUSTMENT

▶ See Figures 49, 50, 51, 52, 53, 54, 55, 56, 57 and 58

➡ Sodium-based grease is not compatible with lithium-based grease. Read the package labels and be careful not to mix the two types. If there is any doubt as to the type of grease used, completely clean the old grease from the bearing and hub before replacing.

Before handling the bearings, there are a few things that you should remember to do and not to do:

DRIVE TRAIN 7-35

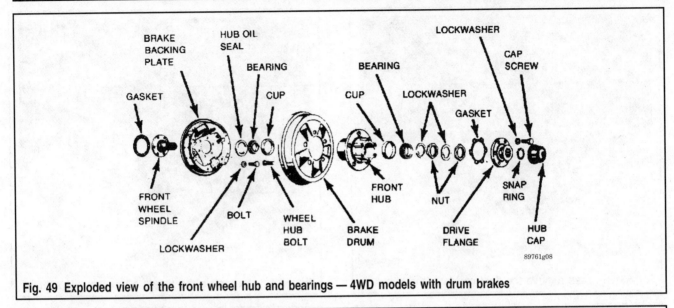

Fig. 49 Exploded view of the front wheel hub and bearings — 4WD models with drum brakes

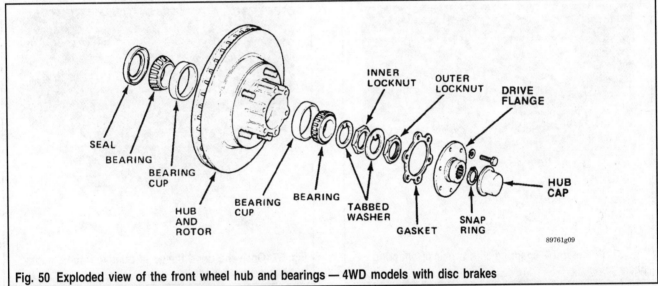

Fig. 50 Exploded view of the front wheel hub and bearings — 4WD models with disc brakes

Fig. 51 To remove the hub, first remove the front wheel

Fig. 52 Use a small prytool to get under the lip of the dust cap . . .

7-36 DRIVE TRAIN

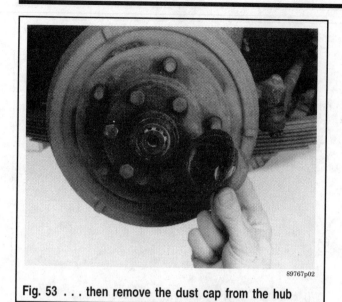
Fig. 53 ... then remove the dust cap from the hub

Fig. 56 ... then slide the flange off of the axle splines

Fig. 54 Remove the snapring with a pair of snapring pliers

Fig. 57 Once the drive flange is removed, the spindle nut can be accessed

Fig. 55 Remove all 6 drive flange retaining bolts ...

Fig. 58 If the spindle nut is difficult to remove, try using a chisel to get it started

DRIVE TRAIN 7-37

Remember to DO the following —
- Remove all outside dirt from the housing before exposing the bearing
- Treat a used bearing as gently as you would a new one
- Work with clean tools in clean surroundings
- Use clean, dry canvas gloves, or at least clean, dry hands
- Clean solvents and flushing fluids are a must
- Use clean paper when laying out the bearings to dry
- Protect disassembled bearings from rust and dirt. Cover them up
- Use clean rags to wipe bearings
- Keep the bearings in oil-proof paper when they are to be stored or are not in use
- Clean the inside of the housing before replacing the bearing

Do NOT do the following —
- Don't work in dirty surroundings
- Don't use dirty, chipped or damaged tools
- Try not to work on wooden work benches or use wooden mallets
- Don't handle bearings with dirty or moist hands
- Do not use gasoline for cleaning; use a safe solvent
- Do not spin-dry bearings with compressed air, otherwise they will be damaged
- Do not spin dirty bearings
- Avoid using cotton waste or dirty cloths to wipe bearings
- Try not to scratch or nick bearing surfaces
- Do not allow the bearing to come in contact with dirt or rust at any time

4-Wheel Drive Models

1. Raise the front of the vehicle and safely support the vehicle on jackstands.
2. Remove the wheel.
3. Remove the front hub grease cap and driving hub snapring. On models equipped with locking hubs, remove the retainer knob hub ring, agitator knob, snapring, outer clutch retaining ring and actuating cam body.
4. Remove the splined driving hub and the pressure spring. This may require slight prying with a prytool.
5. Remove the external snapring from the spindle shaft and remove the hub shaft drive gear.
6. Remove the wheel bearing locknut, lockring, adjusting nut and inner lockring.
7. On vehicles with drum brakes, remove the hub and drum assembly. This may require that the brake adjusting wheel be backed off a few turns. The outer wheel bearing and spring retainer will come off with the hub.
8. On vehicles with disc brakes, remove the caliper and suspend it out of the way by hanging it from a suspension or frame member with a length of wire. Do not disconnect the brake hose, and be careful to avoid stretching the hose. Remove the rotor and hub assembly. The outer wheel bearing and, on vehicles with locking hubs, the spring collar, will come off with the hub.
9. Carefully drive out the inner bearing and seal from the hub, using a wood block.
10. Inspect the bearing races for excessive wear, pitting or grooves. If they are cracked or grooved, or if pitting and excess wear is present, drive them out with a drift or punch.
11. Check the bearing for excess wear, pitting or cracks, or excess looseness.

➡ **If it is necessary to replace either the bearing or the race, replace both. Never replace just a bearing or a race. These parts wear in a mating pattern. If just one is replaced, premature failure of the new part will result.**

12. If the old parts are retained, thoroughly clean them in a safe solvent and allow them to dry on a clean towel. Never spin dry them with compressed air.
13. On vehicles with drum brakes, cover the spindle with a cloth and thoroughly brush all dirt from the brakes. Never blow the dirt off the brakes, due to the presence of asbestos in the dirt, which is harmful to your health when inhaled.
14. Remove the cloth and thoroughly clean the spindle.
15. Thoroughly clean the inside of the hub.
16. Pack the inside of the hub with EP wheel bearing grease. Add grease to the hub until it is flush with the inside diameter of the bearing cup.
17. Pack the bearing with the same grease. A needle-shaped wheel bearing packer is best for this operation. If one is not available, place a large amount of grease in the palm of your hand and slide the edge of the bearing cage through the grease to pick up as much as possible, then work the grease in as best you can with your fingers.
18. If a new race is being installed, very carefully drive it into position until it bottoms all around, using a brass drift. Be careful to avoid scratching the surface.
19. Place the inner bearing in the race and install a new grease seal.
20. Place the hub assembly onto the spindle and install the inner lockring and outer bearing. Install the wheel bearing nut and tighten it to 50 ft. lbs. (68 Nm) while turning the wheel back and forth to seat the bearings. Back off the nut about ¼ turn (90°) maximum.
21. Install the lockwasher with the tab aligned with the keyway in the spindle and turn the inner wheel bearing adjusting nut until the peg on the nut engages the nearest hole in the lockwasher.
22. Install the outer locknut and tighten it to 50 ft. lbs. (68 Nm).
23. Install the spring collar, drive flange, snapring, pressure spring, and hub cap.
24. Install the caliper over the rotor.

7-38 DRIVE TRAIN

2WD FRONT AXLE

♦ See Figure 59

➡Early production Utility models equipped with 4-134 engines were equipped with a Planar type, independent front suspension. All other 2WD Utility models are equipped with a solid I-beam type, reverse Elliot front suspension. Although not technically part of the drive train, the following 2WD front axle-related procedures have been included in this section. For additional information on the Steering Knuckle and Pivot Pins, please refer to Section 8.

Pivot Pins

REMOVAL & INSTALLATION

Solid I-Beam Front Axle

1. Raise and safely support the front end on jackstands.
2. Remove the hub and dust caps.
3. Remove the cotter pin, wheel retaining nut and washer.
4. Pull the wheel out slightly to free the outer bearing, remove the bearing and remove the wheel and hub assembly.
5. Disconnect the brake line at the wheel cylinder and cap the end.
6. Remove the brake shoes and springs.
7. Remove the brake backing plate.
8. Remove the pivot pin lock.
9. Remove the top expansion plug and drive out the pin through the bottom with the lower plug.

➡There is a shim between the upper face of the axle and the spindle. Do not lose it!

10. Remove the thrust bearing and bushings.
11. If new bushings are being installed, they must be reamed for a running fit with the pivot pins. Be sure that the oil holes in the bushings are aligned with their lubrication fittings.
12. If the thrust bearing shows any signs of wear, replace it.
13. Install the pivot pin, aligning the notch with the pin hole.
14. When assembling the knuckle, check for play between the axle and inner face of the knuckle. If play seems excessive, use a different size shim. Shims were available in 0.011 in. (0.279mm), 0.033 in. (0.838mm) and 0.035 in. (0.889mm).
15. Install the top expansion plug and drive out the pin through the bottom with the lower plug.
16. Install the pivot pin lock.
17. Install the brake backing plate.
18. Install the brake shoes and springs.
19. Connect the brake line at the wheel cylinder.
20. Install the wheel and hub assembly.
21. Install the outer bearing.
22. Install the wheel retaining nut and washer.
23. While turning the wheel, tighten the nut until the wheel binds, then back off the nut $1/6$-$1/4$ turn (60-90°) to free the bearing.
24. Install the cotter pin.
25. Install the hub and dust caps.
26. Bleed the brakes.
27. Lower the front end.

Planar Front Suspension

1. Raise and safely support the front end on jackstands.
2. Remove the hub and dust caps.
3. Remove the cotter pin, wheel retaining nut and washer.
4. Pull the wheel out slightly to free the outer bearing, remove the bearing and remove the wheel and hub assembly.
5. Disconnect the brake line at the wheel cylinder and cap the end.
6. Remove the brake shoes and springs.
7. Remove the brake backing plate.
8. Remove the pivot pin lock.
9. Use a sharp drift to remove the pivot pin lower expansion plug.
10. Drive the pivot pin upward until the needle bearing assembly can be removed.
11. Drive the pivot pin out through the bottom.
12. Remove the bushings from the lower part of the spindle.
13. If new bushings are being installed, they must be reamed for a running fit with the pivot pins. Be sure that the oil holes in the bushings are aligned with their lubrication fittings.
14. If the thrust bearing shows any signs of wear, replace it.
15. Drive the pivot pin in through the bottom.
16. Drive the pivot pin upward until the needle bearing assembly can be installed.
17. Install the pivot pin lower expansion plug.
18. Install the pivot pin lock.
19. Install the brake backing plate.
20. Install the brake shoes and springs.
21. Connect the brake line at the wheel cylinder.
22. Install the wheel and hub assembly.
23. Install the outer bearing.
24. Install the wheel retaining nut and washer.
25. While turning the wheel, tighten the nut until the wheel binds, then back off the nut $1/6$-$1/4$ turn (60-90°) to free the bearing.
26. Install a new cotter pin.
27. Install the hub and dust caps.
28. Bleed the brakes.
29. Lower the front end.

DRIVE TRAIN 7-39

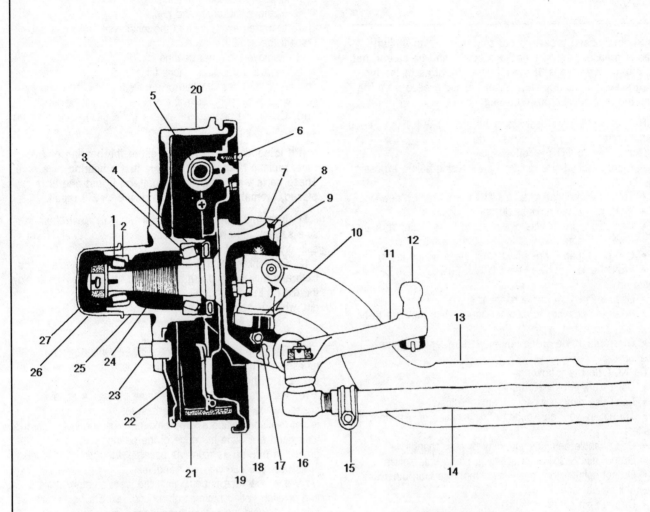

1. Outer front wheel bearing cone & rollers
2. Outer front wheel bearing race
3. Inner front wheel bearing cone & rollers
4. Inner front wheel bearing race
5. Wheel brake cylinder
6. Wheel brake cylinder bleeder screw
7. Pivot bolt expansion plug-upper
8. Pivot bolt
9. Steering knuckle bushing
10. Pivot bolt thrust bearing
11. Steering knuckle arm
12. Steering arm ball
13. Front axle I-beam
14. Steering tie rod
15. Steering tie rod clamp
16. Steering tie rod socket assembly
17. Lubrication fitting
18. Lower pivot bolt expansion plug
19. Brake backing plate
20. Brake drum
21. Brake shoe assembly
22. Brake shoe retainer plate
23. Wheel hub bolt
24. Steering knuckle assembly
25. Front wheel hub
26. Hub dust cap
27. Front axle spindle nut

Fig. 59 Cutaway view of the solid I-beam, reverse Elliot type front suspension, used on some Jeep models

7-40 DRIVE TRAIN

Front Hub and Wheel Bearings

ADJUSTMENT

➡ Sodium-based grease is not compatible with lithium-based grease. Read the package labels and be careful not to mix the two types. If there is any doubt as to the type of grease used, completely clean the old grease from the bearing and hub before replacing.

Before handling the bearings, there are a few things that you should remember to do and not to do.

Remember to DO the following —
- Remove all outside dirt from the housing before exposing the bearing
- Treat a used bearing as gently as you would a new one
- Work with clean tools in clean surroundings
- Use clean, dry canvas gloves, or at least clean, dry hands
- Clean solvents and flushing fluids are a must
- Use clean paper when laying out the bearings to dry
- Protect disassembled bearings from rust and dirt. Cover them up
- Use clean rags to wipe bearings
- Keep the bearings in oil-proof paper when they are to be stored or are not in use
- Clean the inside of the housing before replacing the bearing

Do NOT do the following —
- Don't work in dirty surroundings
- Don't use dirty, chipped or damaged tools
- Try not to work on wooden work benches or use wooden mallets
- Don't handle bearings with dirty or moist hands
- Do not use gasoline for cleaning; use a safe solvent
- Do not spin-dry bearings with compressed air, otherwise they will be damaged
- Do not spin dirty bearings
- Avoid using cotton waste or dirty cloths to wipe bearings
- Try not to scratch or nick bearing surfaces
- Do not allow the bearing to come in contact with dirt or rust at any time

2-Wheel Drive Models

1. Raise the front of the vehicle and safely support it on jackstands.
2. Remove the wheel.
3. Remove the front hub grease cap.
4. Remove the cotter pin and locknut.
5. Pull out on the brake drum slightly to free the outer bearing and remove the bearing.
6. Remove the drum and hub.
7. Using an awl, puncture the inner seal and pry it out. Discard the seal.
8. Remove the inner bearing.
9. Inspect the bearing races for excessive wear, pitting or grooves. If they are cracked or grooved, or if pitting and excess wear is present, drive them out with a drift or punch.
10. Check the bearing for excess wear, pitting or cracks, or excess looseness.

➡ If it is necessary to replace either the bearing or the race, replace both. Never replace just a bearing or a race. These parts wear in a mating pattern. If just one is replaced, premature failure of the new part will result.

11. If the old parts are retained, thoroughly clean them in a safe solvent and allow them to dry on a clean towel. Never spin dry them with compressed air.
12. On vehicles with drum brakes, cover the spindle with a cloth and thoroughly brush all dirt from the brakes. Never blow the dirt off the brakes, due to the presence of asbestos in the dirt, which is harmful to your health when inhaled.
13. Remove the cloth and thoroughly clean the spindle.
14. Thoroughly clean the inside of the hub.
15. Pack the inside of the hub with EP wheel bearing grease. Add grease to the hub until it is flush with the inside diameter of the bearing cup.
16. Pack the bearing with the same grease. A needle-shaped wheel bearing packer is best for this operation. If one is not available, place a large amount of grease in the palm of your hand and slide the edge of the bearing cage through the grease to pick up as much as possible, then work the grease in as best you can with your fingers.
17. If a new race is being installed, very carefully drive it into position until it bottoms all around, using a brass drift. Be careful to avoid scratching the surface.
18. Place the inner bearing in the race and install a new grease seal.
19. Place the hub assembly onto the spindle and install the outer bearing. Install the wheel bearing nut and tighten it until the hub binds while turning. Back off the nut about $1/6$-$1/4$ turn (60-90°) to free the bearings. Install a new cotter pin.
20. Install the grease cap.
21. Install the wheel.
22. Lower the vehicle and install the hub cap.

FRONT AND REAR SUSPENSIONS
  FRONT END ALIGNMENT 8-7
  FRONT STABILIZER BAR 8-5
  LEAF SPRINGS 8-2
  SHOCK ABSORBERS 8-3
  STEERING KNUCKLE AND PIVOT
    PINS 8-5
  STEERING KNUCKLE OIL SEAL 8-6
  UPPER CONTROL ARM 8-6
SPECIFICATIONS CHARTS
  TROUBLESHOOTING BASIC
    STEERING AND SUSPENSION
    PROBLEMS 8-15
  TROUBLESHOOTING THE MANUAL
    STEERING GEAR 8-20
  TROUBLESHOOTING THE STEERING
    COLUMN 8-16
  TROUBLESHOOTING THE TURN
    SIGNAL SWITCH 8-18
  WHEEL ALIGNMENT
    SPECIFICATIONS 8-8
STEERING
  MANUAL STEERING GEAR 8-10
  STEERING COLUMN 8-10
  STEERING LINKAGE 8-11
  STEERING WHEEL 8-9
  TURN SIGNAL SWITCH 8-9
WHEELS
  WHEELS 8-2

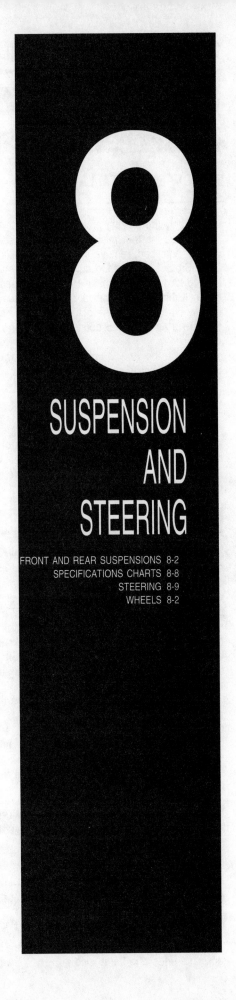

8

SUSPENSION AND STEERING

FRONT AND REAR SUSPENSIONS 8-2
SPECIFICATIONS CHARTS 8-8
STEERING 8-9
WHEELS 8-2

SUSPENSION AND STEERING

WHEELS

Wheels

REMOVAL & INSTALLATION

1. Apply the parking brake and block the opposite wheel.
2. Place the transmission shifter in Reverse.
3. If equipped, remove the wheel cover or hub cap.
4. Break loose the lug nuts. If a nut is stuck, never use heat to loosen it or damage to the wheel and bearings may occur. If the nuts are seized, one or two heavy hammer blows directly on the end of the bolt head usually loosens the rust. Be careful as continued pounding will likely damage the brake drum or rotor.
5. Raise the vehicle until the tire is clear of the ground. Support the vehicle safely using jackstands.
6. Remove the lug nuts, then remove the tire and wheel assembly.

To install:

7. Make sure the wheel and hub mating surfaces, as well as the wheel lug studs, are clean and free of all foreign material. Always remove rust from the wheel mounting surfaces and the brake rotors/drums. Failure to do so may cause the lug nuts to loosen in service.
8. Position the wheel on the hub or drum and hand-tighten the lug nuts. Make sure that the coned ends face inward.
9. Tighten all the lug nuts, in a crisscross pattern, until they are snug.
10. Remove the supports, if any, and lower the vehicle. Tighten the lug nuts, in a crisscross pattern. Always use a torque wrench to achieve the proper lug nut torque and to prevent stretching the wheel studs.
11. Repeat the torque pattern to assure proper wheel tightening.
12. If equipped, install the hub cab or wheel cover.

INSPECTION

Check the wheels for any damage. They must be replaced if they are bent, dented, heavily rusted, have elongated bolt holes, or have excessive lateral or radial run-out. Wheels with excessive run-out may cause a high-speed vehicle vibration.

Replacement wheels must be of the same load capacity, diameter, width, offset and mounting configuration as the original wheels. Using the wrong wheels may affect wheel bearing life, ground and tire clearance, or speedometer and odometer calibrations.

FRONT AND REAR SUSPENSIONS

All springs should be examined periodically for broken or shifted leaves, loose or missing clips, angle of the spring shackles, and position of the springs on the saddles. Springs with shifted leaves do not retain their normal strength. Missing clips may permit the spirit leaves to fan out or break on rebound. Broken leaves may make the vehicle hard to handle or permit the axle to shift out of line. Weakened springs may break causing difficulty in steering. Spring attaching clips or bolts must be tight. It is suggested that they be checked at each vehicle inspection.

CJ-2A, CJ-3A, CJ-3B and Utility models are equipped with shackles at the front of the front leaf springs. CJ-5 models up to serial No. 44437 and CJ-6 models up to serial No. 11981 have shackles at the rear of the front leaf springs, and pivot bolts at the front.

All rear leaf springs have shackles at the rear and pivot bolts at the front.

Leaf Springs

REMOVAL & INSTALLATION

♦ See Figure 1

Except Early Utility Models With Planar Front Suspension

1. Raise the vehicle with a jack under the axle and place a jackstand under the frame side rail. Then lower the axle jack so that the load is relieved from the spring and the wheels rest on the floor.
2. Remove the nuts which secure the spring clip bolts. Remove the spring plate and clip bolts. Free the spring from the axle by raising the axle jack.
3. Remove the pivot bolt nut and drive out the pivot bolt. Disconnect the shackle either by removing the lower nuts and bolts on the rubber bushed shackles, or by removing the threaded bushings on the U-shackles.

To install:

4. To replace, first install the pivot bolt. Then, connect the shackle using the following procedures.
5. On bronze-bushed pivot bolts, install the bolt and nut and tighten the nut. Then back it off two cotter pin slots and install the cotter pin. The nut must be drawn up tightly but must be sufficiently loose to allow the spring to pivot freely. Otherwise the spring might break.
6. On rubber-bushed pivot bolts and locknuts (or lockwasher and nut) only tighten the bolt enough to hold the bushings in position until the vehicle is lowered from the jack.
7. Connect the shackle. On rubber bushed shackles install the bolts as in Step 6. For U-shackles, insert the shackle through the frame bracket and eye of the spring. Holding the U-shackle tightly against the frame, start the upper bushing on the shackle, taking care that when it enters the thread in the frame it does not crossthread. Screw the bushing on the shackle tightly against the spring eye, and thread the bushing in approximately half way. Then, alternately from top bushing to lower bushing, turn them in until the head of the bushing is snug against the frame bracket and the bushing in the spring

SUSPENSION AND STEERING   8-3

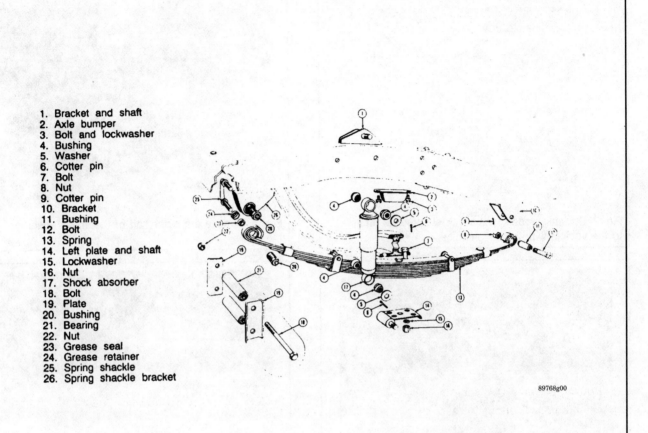

1. Bracket and shaft
2. Axle bumper
3. Bolt and lockwasher
4. Bushing
5. Washer
6. Cotter pin
7. Bolt
8. Nut
9. Cotter pin
10. Bracket
11. Bushing
12. Bolt
13. Spring
14. Left plate and shaft
15. Lockwasher
16. Nut
17. Shock absorber
18. Bolt
19. Plate
20. Bushing
21. Bearing
22. Nut
23. Grease seal
24. Grease retainer
25. Spring shackle
26. Spring shackle bracket

Fig. 1 Exploded view of the front suspension components utilized on the 2WD solid I-beam front axle

eye is 1/32 in. (0.794mm) away from the spring as measured from the inside of the hexagon head in the spring. Lubricate the bushing and then try the flex of the shackle, which must be free. If a shackle is tight, rethread the bushings on the shackle.

8. Move the axle into position on the spring by lowering or raising the axle jack. Install the spring clip bolts, spring plate, lockwashers, and nuts. Tighten the nuts to 50-55 ft. lbs. (68-75 Nm). Avoid overtightening. Be sure the spring is free to move at both ends.

9. Remove both jacks. On rubber bushed shackles and pivot bolts, allow the weight of the vehicle to seat the bushings in their operating positions. Then torque the nuts to 27-30 ft. lbs. (37-41 Nm).

Early Utility Models With Planar Front Suspension

1. Raise the front of the vehicle with a floor jack under the front axle, then safely support the fame of the vehicle on jackstands.

2. Slowly lower the front axle until the spring tension is relieved, then position 2 additional jackstands under the axle assembly. At this point both the vehicle's frame and the front axle assembly should be supported by jackstands.

3. Support the spring and disconnect the spring eyes at the knuckle supports.

4. Remove the spring from the vehicle.

5. Installation is the reverse of removal. Centralize the spring eye in the lower end of the knuckle support before starting the threaded pin. Tighten the pivot bolts to 35 ft. lbs. (48 Nm).

Shock Absorbers

REMOVAL & INSTALLATION

♦ See Figures 2, 3, 4, 5, 6 and 7

1. Remove the locknuts and washers. Utility, CJ-2A, CJ-3A and CJ-3B models have cotter pins instead of locknuts. Remove the cotter pins and washers on these models.

8-4 SUSPENSION AND STEERING

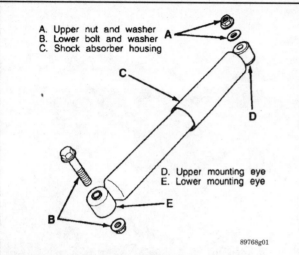

A. Upper nut and washer
B. Lower bolt and washer
C. Shock absorber housing
D. Upper mounting eye
E. Lower mounting eye

Fig. 2 On later models, the shock absorber is mounted to the vehicle with 2 through-bolts

Fig. 3 On early models, remove the shock absorber's upper retaining cotter pin . . .

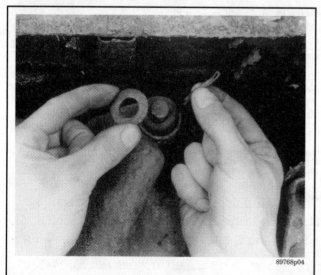

Fig. 4 . . . and remove the outer flat washer

Fig. 5 Remove the outer half of the shock absorber bushing

Fig. 6 Slide the shock absorber off of the mounting stud and remove the inner half of the bushing

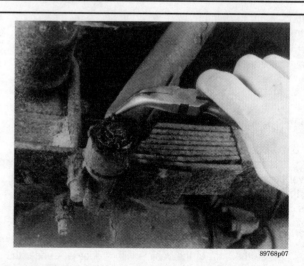

Fig. 7 Perform the same removal steps on the lower end of the shock absorber

SUSPENSION AND STEERING

2. Pull the shock absorber eyes and rubber bushings from the mounting pins.

3. Install the shocks in reverse order of the removal procedure. Tighten the upper bolt to 35 ft. lbs. (48 Nm) and the lower bolt to 45 ft. lbs. (61 Nm).

➡ Squeaking usually occurs when movement takes place between the rubber bushings and the metal parts. The squeaking may be eliminated by placing the bushings under greater pressure. This is accomplished either by adding additional washers where the cotter pins are used or by tightening the locknuts. Do not use mineral lubricant to stop the squeaking as it will deteriorate the rubber.

Front Stabilizer Bar

REMOVAL & INSTALLATION

▶ See Figure 8

1. Raise and safely support the front end on jackstands.
2. Unbolt the stabilizer bar from the vertical links.
3. Unbolt the stabilizer bar from the frame brackets.
4. Replace any worn or damaged rubber parts.

To install:

5. Install the stabilizer bar at the links first, hand-tightening the fasteners.
6. Install the frame brackets, hand-tightening the fasteners.
7. Make sure everything is aligned and tighten the frame bracket bolts to 35 ft. lbs. (48 Nm).
8. Tighten the link nuts to 55 ft. lbs. (75 Nm) on CJ-5 and CJ-6 models.

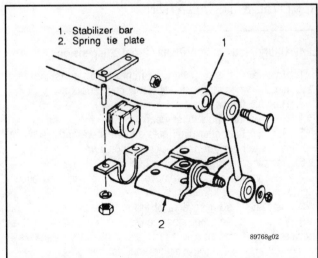

Fig. 8 Exploded view of stabilizer bar mounting on all models

Steering Knuckle and Pivot Pins

REMOVAL & INSTALLATION

4-Wheel Drive Models

1. Raise and safely support the front end of the vehicle on jackstands, then remove the wheels.
2. Remove the front brake drum and brake shoes, as described in Section 9.
3. Remove the 8 screws that hold the oil seal retainer in place.
4. Remove the 4 screws which secure the lower pivot pin bearing cap.
5. Remove the 4 screws which hold the upper bearing cap in place. On CJ-2A models before serial No. 22972, the nuts also hold the steering arm in place.
6. Remove the bearing cap. On CJ-2A and 3A models, remove the brake hose shield.
7. The steering knuckle can now be removed from the axle.

To install:

8. Wash all of the parts in cleaning solvent.
9. Replace any worn or damaged parts. Inspect the bearings and races for scores, cracks, or chips. Should the bearing cups be damaged, they may be removed and installed with a driver.
10. Installation is the reverse the removal procedure. When reinstalling the steering knuckle sufficient shims must be installed under the top bearing cap to obtain the correct preload on the bearing. Shims are available in 0.003 in. (0.0762mm), 0.005 in. (0.127mm), 0.010 in. (0.254mm), and 0.030 in. (0.762mm). thicknesses. Install only one shim of the above thicknesses at the top only. Install the bearing caps, lockwashers, and screws, and tighten securely.

You can check the preload on the bearings by hooking a spring scale in the hole in the knuckle arm for the tie rod sprocket. Take the scale reading when the knuckle has just started its sweep.

The pivot pin bearing preload should be 12-16 lbs. (26-35 kg) with the oil seal removed. Remove or add shims to obtain a preload within these limits. If all shims are removed and adequate preload is still not obtained, a washer may be used under the top bearing cap to increase preload. When a washer is used, shims may have to be reinstalled to obtain proper adjustment.

2-Wheel Drive Models

WITH SOLID I-BEAM FRONT AXLE

1. Raise and safely support the front end on jackstands.
2. Remove the hub and dust caps.
3. Remove the cotter pin, wheel retaining nut and washer.
4. Pull the wheel out slightly to free the outer bearing, remove the bearing and remove the wheel and hub assembly.
5. Disconnect the brake line at the wheel cylinder and cap the end.
6. Remove the brake shoes and springs.
7. Remove the brake backing plate.
8. Remove the pivot pin lock.

8-6 SUSPENSION AND STEERING

9. Remove the top expansion plug and drive out the pin through the bottom with the lower plug.

➡ There is a shim between the upper face of the axle and the spindle. Do not lose it!

10. Remove the thrust bearing and bushings.

To install:

11. If new bushings are being installed, they must be reamed for a running fit with the pivot pins. Be sure that the oil holes in the bushings are aligned with their lubrication fittings.
12. If the thrust bearing shows any signs of wear, replace it.
13. Install the pivot pin, aligning the notch with the pin hole.
14. When assembling the knuckle, check for play between the axle and inner face of the knuckle. If play seems excessive, use a different size shim. Shims were available in 0.011 in. (0.279mm), 0.033 in. (0.838mm) and 0.035 in. (0.889mm).
15. Install the top expansion plug and drive out the pin through the bottom with the lower plug.
16. Install the pivot pin lock.
17. Install the brake backing plate.
18. Install the brake shoes and springs.
19. Connect the brake line at the wheel cylinder.
20. Install the wheel and hub assembly.
21. Install the outer bearing.
22. Install the wheel retaining nut and washer.
23. While turning the wheel, tighten the nut until the wheel binds, then back off the nut $1/6$-$1/4$ turn to free the bearing.
24. Install the cotter pin.
25. Install the hub and dust caps.
26. Bleed the brakes.
27. Lower the front end.

WITH PLANAR FRONT SUSPENSION

1. Raise and safely support the front end on jackstands.
2. Remove the hub and dust caps.
3. Remove the cotter pin, wheel retaining nut and washer.
4. Pull the wheel out slightly to free the outer bearing, remove the bearing and remove the wheel and hub assembly.
5. Disconnect the brake line at the wheel cylinder and cap the end.
6. Remove the brake shoes and springs.
7. Remove the brake backing plate.
8. Remove the pivot pin lock.
9. Use a sharp drift to remove the pivot pin lower expansion plug.
10. Drive the pivot pin upward until the needle bearing assembly can be removed.
11. Drive the pivot pin out through the bottom.
12. Remove the bushings from the lower part of the spindle.
13. If new bushings are being installed, they must be reamed for a running fit with the pivot pins. Be sure that the oil holes in the bushings are aligned with their lubrication fittings.
14. If the thrust bearing shows any signs of wear, replace it.
15. Drive the pivot pin in through the bottom.
16. Drive the pivot pin upward until the needle bearing assembly can be installed.
17. Install the pivot pin lower expansion plug.
18. Install the pivot pin lock.
19. Install the brake backing plate.
20. Install the brake shoes and springs.
21. Connect the brake line at the wheel cylinder.
22. Install the wheel and hub assembly.
23. Install the outer bearing.
24. Install the wheel retaining nut and washer.
25. While turning the wheel, tighten the nut until the wheel binds, then back off the nut $1/6$-$1/4$ turn to free the bearing.
26. Install a new cotter pin.
27. Install the hub and dust caps.
28. Bleed the brakes.
29. Lower the front end.

Steering Knuckle Oil Seal

REMOVAL & INSTALLATION

Remove the old steering knuckle oil seal by removing the 8 screws which hold it in place. Earlier production vehicles have two piece seals. Later production vehicles have a split oil seal and backing ring assembly, an oil seal felt, and two seal retainer plate halves.

Examine the spherical surface of the axle for scores or scratches which could damage the seal. Smooth any roughness with emery cloth.

Before installing the oil seal felt, make a diagonal cut across the top side of the felt so that it may be slipped over the axle. Install the oil seal assembly in the sequence mentioned above, making sure the backing ring (of the oil seal and backing ring assembly) is toward the wheel.

After driving in wet, freezing weather swing the front wheels from side to side to remove moisture adhering to the oil seal and the spherical surface of the axle housing. This will prevent freezing with resultant damage to the seals. Should the vehicle be stored for any period of time, coat the surfaces with light grease to prevent rusting.

Upper Control Arm

REMOVAL & INSTALLATION

Early Utility Models With Planar Front Suspension

1. Raise and safely support the front end on jackstands.
2. Let the wheels hang to relieve spring tension.
3. Remove the wheels.
4. Remove the shock absorbers.
5. Remove the cotter pins, nuts and washers and disconnect the control arm at the knuckle support arm.
6. Remove the control arm pin bushing.
7. Remove the nuts and remove the control arm and bushings from the frame brackets
8. Installation is the reverse of the removal procedure.
9. When mounting the upper control arm pin bushing in the knuckle support, tighten it to 175 ft. lbs. (238 Nm). Centralize the control arm assembly over the knuckle support before starting the threaded pin. This will provide the proper caster and equalize the clearance on each side for the dust seals.

SUSPENSION AND STEERING   8-7

Front End Alignment

GENERAL INFORMATION

♦ See Figures 9, 10 and 11

If the tires are worn unevenly, if the vehicle is not stable on the highway or if the handling seems uneven in spirited driving, wheel alignment should be checked. If an alignment problem is suspected, first check tire inflation and look for other possible causes such as worn suspension and steering components, accident damage or unmatched tires. Repairs may be necessary before the wheels can be properly aligned. Wheel alignment requires sophisticated equipment and can only be performed at a properly equipped shop.

The most important factors of front wheel alignment are wheel camber, axle caster and wheel toe-in.

Wheel toe-in is the distance by which the wheels are closer together at the front than at the rear.

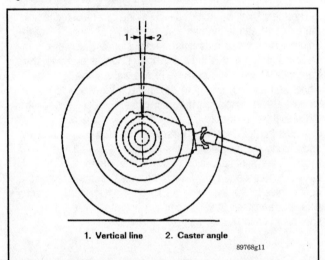

1. Vertical line
2. Caster angle

Fig. 9 Caster is the angle that the steering pivot pins are tilted toward the rear of the vehicle

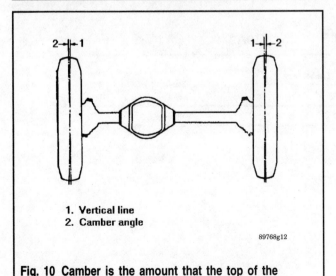

1. Vertical line
2. Camber angle

Fig. 10 Camber is the amount that the top of the wheels are tilted toward the outside of the vehicle

1. Vertical line
2. Toe-in angle

Fig. 11 Toe-in is the amount that the wheels are closer at the front than at the rear

Wheel camber is the amount the top of the wheels incline outward from the vertical plane.

Front axle caster is the amount in degrees that the steering pivot pins are tilted toward the rear of the vehicle. Positive caster is inclination of the top of the pivot pin toward the rear of the vehicle.

These points should be checked at regular intervals, particularly when the front axle has been subjected to a heavy impact. When checking wheel alignment, it is important that wheel bearings and knuckle bearings (through 1971) be in proper adjustment. Loose bearings will affect instrument readings when checking the camber, pivot pin inclination, and toe-in.

Front wheel camber on 4WD models, and solid I-beam 2WD models is preset. Some alignment shops can correct camber to some extent by installing special tapered shims between the steering knuckle and the spindle.

Camber on early Utility models, with the Planar front suspension is controlled by a shim pack installed on each side, between the frame and the upper control arm support bracket. Shim thicknesses of 0.060 in. (1.524mm) and 0.120 in. (3.05mm) were used.

Caster is also preset, but can be altered by use of tapered shims between the axle pad and the springs. Wheel toe-in is adjustable.

Turning Angle

To avoid damage to the U-joints, it is advisable to check the turning angle periodically. An adjustment turntable is advisable for properly determining the angle. Correct turning angles are:

- All CJ-2A and CJ-3A models, CJ-3B models before serial No. 57348-35326, CJ-5 models before serial No. 57548-48284, and CJ-6 models before serial No. 57748-12497 — 23 degrees maximum
- CJ-3B models after and including No. 57348-35326, CJ-5 models after and including No. 57548-48284, and CJ-6 models after and including No. 57748-12497 — 27.5 degrees maximum

To adjust the turning angle, loosen the locknut (on some early models, a securing weld will have to be broken) and turn the adjusting screw. The adjusting screw is located on the axle

8-8 SUSPENSION AND STEERING

tube near the knuckle on early models, and on the knuckle, just below the axle centerline on later models.

Caster Adjustment

Caster angle is established in the axle design by tilting the top of the kingpins forward so that an imaginary line through the center of the kingpins would strike the ground at a point ahead of the point of the contact.

The purpose of caster is to provide steering stability which will keep the front wheels in the straight-ahead position and also assist in straightening up the wheels when coming out of a turn.

If the angle of caster, when accurately measured, is found to be incorrect, correct it to the specification given in this section by either installing new parts or installing caster shims between the axle pad and the springs.

If the camber and toe-in are correct and it is known that the axle is not twisted, a satisfactory check may be made by testing the vehicle on the road. Before road testing, make sure all tires are properly inflated, being particularly careful that both front tires are inflated to exactly the same pressure.

If the vehicle turns easily to either side but is hard to straighten out, insufficient caster for easy handling of the vehicle is indicated. If correction is necessary, it can usually be accomplished by installing shims between the springs and axle pads to secure the desired result.

Camber Adjustment

EXCEPT EARLY UTILITY MODELS WITH PLANAR FRONT SUSPENSIONS

The purpose of camber is to more nearly place the weight of the vehicle over the tire contact patch on the road to facilitate ease of steering. The result of excessive camber is irregular wear of the tires on the outside shoulders and is usually caused by bent axle parts.

The result of excessive negative or reverse camber will be hard steering and possibly a wandering condition. Tires will also wear on the inside shoulders. Negative camber is usually caused by excessive wear or looseness of the front wheel bearings, axle parts or the result of a sagging axle.

Unequal camber may cause any or a combination of the following conditions: unstable steering, wandering, kickback or road shock, shimmy or excessive tire wear. The cause of unequal camber is usually a bent steering knuckle or axle end.

Correct wheel camber is set in the axle at the time of manufacture. It is important that the camber be the same on both front wheels.

EARLY UTILITY MODELS WITH PLANAR FRONT SUSPENSIONS

Camber is set by changing the shim pack thickness, located between the upper control arm bracket and the frame. Follow the procedure for Upper Control Arm removal and installation, and change the shims as required.

Toe-In Adjustment

The toe-in may be adjusted with a line or straightedge, as the vehicle tread is the same in the front and rear. To set the adjustment, both tie rods must be adjusted as follows: Set the tie rod end of the steering bell crank at right angles with the front axle. Place a straightedge or line against the left rear wheel and left front wheel to determine if the wheel is in a straight-ahead position. If the front wheel tire does not touch the straightedge at both the front and rear, it will be necessary to adjust the left tie rod by loosening the clamps on each end and turning the rod until the tire touches the straightedge.

Check the right-hand side in the same manner, adjusting the tie rod if necessary making sure that the bell crank remains at right angles to the axle. When it is determined that the front wheels are in the straight-ahead position, set the toe-in by shortening each tie rod approximately ½ turn.

Wheel Alignment Specifications

Year	Caster (deg.) Range	Caster (deg.) Pref.	Camber (deg.) Range	Camber (deg.) Pref.	Toe-in (in.)	King Pin Incl. (deg.)
1945–70	2½P to 3½P	3P	1P to 2P	1½P*	3/64 to 3/32	7½

*2-WD Utility Models: 1P

SUSPENSION AND STEERING 8-9

STEERING

Steering Wheel

REMOVAL & INSTALLATION

▶ See Figures 12, 13 and 14

1. Disconnect the negative battery cable.
2. Set the front tires in a straight-ahead position.
3. Pull the horn button from the steering wheel.
4. Remove the steering wheel nut and horn button contact cup.
5. Scribe a line mark on the steering wheel and steering shaft if there is not one already. Release the turn signal assembly from the steering post and install a puller.

Fig. 12 After removing the horn button, remove the retaining nut . . .

Fig. 13 . . . then remove the retaining nut washer/spacer from the steering column shaft

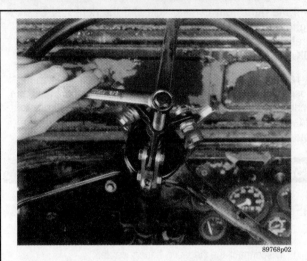

Fig. 14 Use a gear puller to draw the wheel off of the column shaft

6. Remove the steering wheel and spring.

To install:

7. Align the scribe marks on the steering shaft with the steering wheel and secure the steering wheel spring, steering wheel, and horn button contact cup with the steering wheel nut.
8. Install the horn button.
9. Connect the battery cable and test the horn.

Turn Signal Switch

REMOVAL & INSTALLATION

The turn signal switch is attached to the steering column; the whole unit is mounted externally. To remove the switch assembly, perform the following:

1. Disconnect the negative battery cable.
2. Remove the attaching screws.
3. Unfasten the wires.
4. Remove the unit from the steering column.
5. Installation is the reverse of the removal procedure.

INSPECTION

The most frequent causes of failure in the directional signal system are loose connections and burned out bulbs. A flashing rate of approximately twice normal usually indicates a burned out bulb in the circuit. When trouble in the signal switch is suspected, it is advisable to make a few checks to definitely locate the trouble before going tot he effort of removing the signal switch. First check the fuse. There is an inline fuse located between the ignition switch and the turn signal flasher. If the fuse checks out OK, next eliminate the flasher unit by substituting a known good flasher. If a new flasher does not

8-10 SUSPENSION AND STEERING

cure the trouble, check the signal system wiring connections at the fuse and at the steering column connector.

➡ **If the right front parking light and the right rear stop light are inoperative, switch failure is indicated. If the brake lights function properly, the rear signal lights are OK.**

To check the switch, first put the control lever in the neutral position. Then disconnect the wire to the right side circuit and bridge it to the "L" terminal, thus bypassing the signal switch. If the right side circuit lights, the signal switch is inoperative and must be replaced.

Steering Column

REMOVAL & INSTALLATION

1. Disconnect the negative battery cable.
2. Remove the column cover plate at the floorboards.
3. On early CJ-2A and CJ-3A with remote control, remove the two screws attaching the remote control housing to the steering column.
4. On later models, remove the column-to-dash lower bezel.
5. Remove the column-to-dash bracket and lower the column.

➡ **Later models have breakaway capsules in the bracket. Remove the bracket and put it in a safe place to avoid damage to the capsules.**

6. Disconnect any wiring attached to column components.
7. Remove the steering column-to-gear shaft coupling and pull the column out of the Jeep.
8. On models with energy absorbing columns, it is extremely important that only specified fasteners be used. Fasteners which are not of the exact length or hardness may impair the energy absorbing action of the column. Bolts securing the column mounting bracket to the dash must be tightened exactly.
9. Connect the column to the gear shaft and tighten the coupling pinch bolt to 45 ft. lbs. (61 Nm).
10. Connect all wiring.
11. Install the toe plates, but do not fully tighten the fasteners.
12. Install the bracket on the column and tighten the bolts to 20 ft. lbs. (27 Nm).
13. Align the bracket and dash and loosely install the mounting bolts.
14. While applying a constant upward pressure on the column, tighten the bracket-to-dash bolts to 20 ft. lbs. (27 Nm).
15. Tighten the toe plate bolts to 121 inch lbs. (13.6 Nm).
16. Install the bezel.
17. Connect the transmission linkage and check its operation.

Manual Steering Gear

REMOVAL & INSTALLATION

The steering gear must be removed down through the floor pan.
1. Remove the left front fender.
2. On early CJ-2A and Utility models with remote control steering linkage, disconnect the control rods at the transmission.
3. Remove the steering wheel.
4. Unbolt the steering column bracket from the instrument panel.
5. Disconnect the exhaust pipe at the manifold.
6. Remove the steering column cover plate from the floorboard.
7. On early CJ-2A and Utility models, remove the two screws holding the shift control rods housing to the steering column.
8. On CJ-2A models, remove the horn wire contact. On all other models, disconnect the horn wire.
9. On early CJ-2A and Utility models, lower the shift linkage through the floor.
10. Remove the drag link from the steering gear arm ball.
11. Unbolt the steering gear housing from the frame.
12. Lower the steering gear through the floor pan and over the outside of the frame rail.

To install:
13. Lift the steering gear through the floor pan and into position on the frame rail.
14. Install the bolts attaching the steering gear housing to the frame. Tighten the 3/8 in. diameter bolts to 40 ft. lbs. (54 Nm) and the 7/16 in. diameter bolts to 55 ft. lbs. (75 Nm).
15. Install the drag link on the steering gear arm ball.
16. On early CJ-2A and Utility models, install the shift linkage.
17. On CJ-2A models, install the horn wire contact. On all other models, Connect the horn wire.
18. On early CJ-2A and Utility models, install the two screws holding the shift control rods housing to the steering column.
19. Install the steering column cover plate on the floorboard.
20. Connect the exhaust pipe at the manifold.
21. Bolt the steering column bracket to the instrument panel.
22. Install the steering wheel.
23. On early CJ-2A and Utility models with remote control steering linkage, connect the control rods at the transmission.
24. Install the left front fender.
25. Adjust the shifting linkage on early CJ-2A and Utility models.

ADJUSTMENTS

➡ **Adjustments must be made in the order given. Failure to following sequence could result in damage to the gear.**

Before adjusting, remove all load from the system by disconnecting the drag link from the steering arm and loosening the instrument panel bracket bolts and the steering gear-to-frame bolts.

SUSPENSION AND STEERING 8-11

Steering Shaft Play

1. Remove the shims installed between the steering gear housing and the upper cover.
2. Loosen the housing side cover adjusting screw.
3. Loosen the housing cover to cut and remove one or more shims as required. Proper adjustment allows a slight drag and free operation.
4. Tighten the cover.

Backlash

1. Loosen the adjusting screw locknut.
2. Turn the adjusting screw in until a very slight drag is felt through the mid-point in steering wheel travel. This procedure is done with the wheels in the straight-ahead position.
3. Tighten the adjusting screw locknut.

Steering Linkage

♦ See Figures 15 and 16

REMOVAL & INSTALLATION

Tie Rod Ends

♦ See Figures 17, 18, 19, 20 and 21

➡ Early production CJ models and early production 2WD Utility models with 4-134 engines are equipped with 2-piece tie rods. All other models are equipped with 1-piece tie rods.

1. Raise and safely support the front end on jackstands.
2. Remove the cotter pin and nut and disconnect the right tie rod section from the bell crank.
3. Remove the cotter pins and nuts, and, using a puller or separator, disconnect the outer ends from the knuckles.
4. Where applicable, the left and right tie rod sections can now be separated.
5. The tie rod ends can be removed by loosening the clamps and unscrewing the ends. Before unscrewing the ends, note the exact number of threads visible, as an installation reference.
6. All seals that show any sign of wear should be replaced. New tie rod ends should be installed if the old ones show any play or roughness of movement.

To install:

7. Install the new tie rod ends, leaving the exact number of threads exposed, as previously noted. On CJ models, tighten all nuts to 38-42 ft. lbs. (52-57 Nm). On Utility models, tighten the $5/16$ in. diameter clamp bolts to 121-182 inch lbs. (14-20 Nm) and the $7/16$ in. diameter clamp bolts to 35-45 ft. lbs. (48-61 Nm).

Center Link/Connecting Rod/Drag Link

♦ See Figure 22

1. Raise and safely support the front end on jackstands.
2. Remove the cotter pins from each end of the link.
3. Remove the adjusting plugs, ball seats and spring from each end.
4. Disconnect the link and remove the dust cover and dust shield.
5. Replacement kits are available which contain all the above parts. It is best to replace all these parts at once.
6. Install the dust cover and shield at each end and connect the link at the steering arm and bell crank.
7. Install the ball seat and spring at each end and turn the adjusting plugs in until they firmly contact the ball. At the front end, back off the adjusting plug $1/2$ turn and insert a new cotter pin. At the steering arm end, back off the plug one full turn and insert a new cotter pin.

Steering Damper

1. Raise and safely support the front end on jackstands.
2. Place the wheels in a straight-ahead position.
3. Remove the attaching nut at each end of the damper and remove the damper.
4. Install the damper, making sure that the wheels are still in the straight-ahead position. Tighten the $3/8$ in. nuts to 22 ft. lbs. (30 Nm) and the $7/16$ nuts to 30 ft. lbs. (41 Nm).

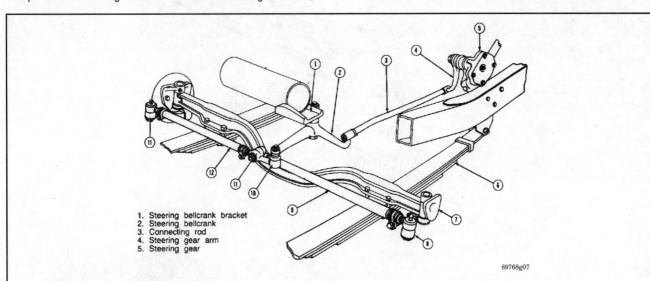

1. Steering bellcrank bracket
2. Steering bellcrank
3. Connecting rod
4. Steering gear arm
5. Steering gear

Fig. 15 Identification of the steering system components used on 2WD models with I-beam front suspension

8-12 SUSPENSION AND STEERING

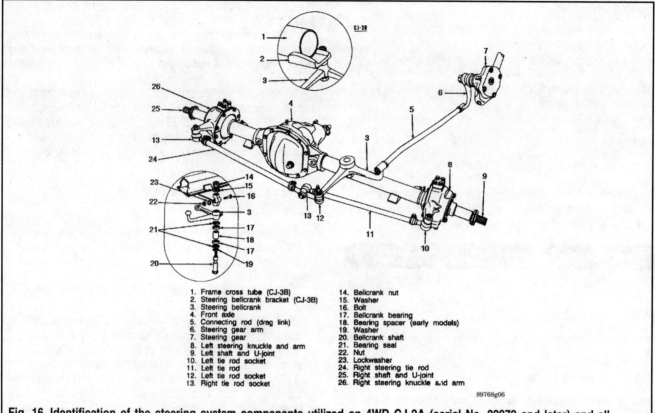

Fig. 16 Identification of the steering system components utilized on 4WD CJ-2A (serial No. 22972 and later) and all CJ-3A, CJ-3B, CJ-5 and CJ-6 models

1. Frame cross tube (CJ-3B)
2. Steering bellcrank bracket (CJ-3B)
3. Steering bellcrank
4. Front axle
5. Connecting rod (drag link)
6. Steering gear arm
7. Steering gear
8. Left steering knuckle and arm
9. Left shaft and U-joint
10. Left tie rod socket
11. Left tie rod
12. Left tie rod socket
13. Right tie rod socket
14. Bellcrank nut
15. Washer
16. Bolt
17. Bellcrank bearing
18. Bearing spacer (early models)
19. Washer
20. Bellcrank shaft
21. Bearing seal
22. Nut
23. Lockwasher
24. Right steering tie rod
25. Right shaft and U-joint
26. Right steering knuckle and arm

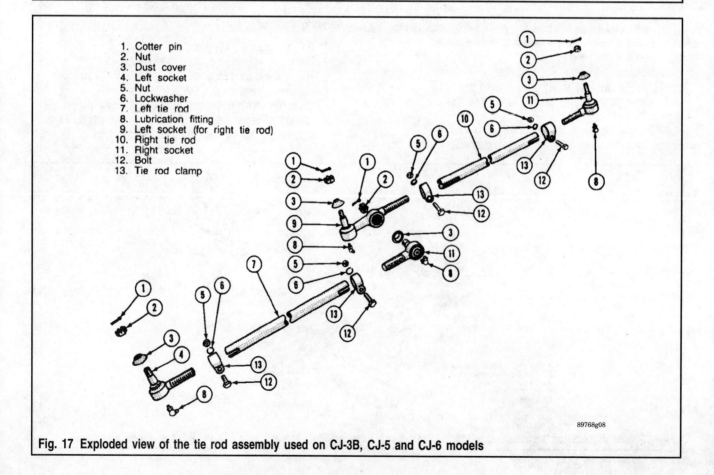

Fig. 17 Exploded view of the tie rod assembly used on CJ-3B, CJ-5 and CJ-6 models

1. Cotter pin
2. Nut
3. Dust cover
4. Left socket
5. Nut
6. Lockwasher
7. Left tie rod
8. Lubrication fitting
9. Left socket (for right tie rod)
10. Right tie rod
11. Right socket
12. Bolt
13. Tie rod clamp

SUSPENSION AND STEERING 8-13

Fig. 18 Remove the tie rod end cotter pin . . .

Fig. 20 Separate the tie rod end from the steering knuckle arm using a special puller

Fig. 19 . . . then remove the tie rod end's castle nut

Fig. 21 After the tie rod end is separated, make certain to retain the spring

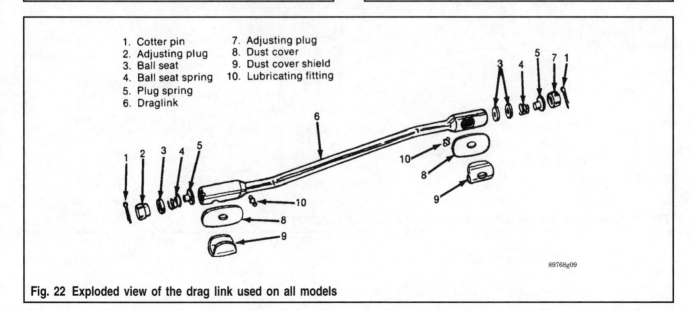

1. Cotter pin
2. Adjusting plug
3. Ball seat
4. Ball seat spring
5. Plug spring
6. Draglink
7. Adjusting plug
8. Dust cover
9. Dust cover shield
10. Lubricating fitting

Fig. 22 Exploded view of the drag link used on all models

SUSPENSION AND STEERING

Pitman Arm

1. Raise and safely support the front end on jackstands.
2. Place the wheels in a straight-ahead position.
3. Matchmark the Pitman arm and gear housing.
4. Disconnect the connecting rod/drag link from the arm or, on Utility models, the knuckle.
5. Matchmark the Pitman arm and shaft.
6. Remove the Pitman arm nut and washer.
7. Using a puller, remove the Pitman arm from the gear. Never hammer on the arm or use a wedge tool to remove it!

To install:

8. Install the Pitman arm aligning the matchmarks on the arm and shaft.
9. Install the washer and nut. Tighten the nuts as follows:
   - Ross gear, except Utility models — 70-90 ft. lbs. (95-122 Nm)
   - Ross gear, Utility models — 95-115 ft. lbs. (129-156 Nm)
   - Saginaw gear — 120-160 ft. lbs. (163-218 Nm)
10. Attach the connecting rod/drag link, or knuckle, to the Pitman arm.
11. Tighten the Pitman arm-to-knuckle nut to 65 ft. lbs. (88 Nm). Tighten the Pitman arm-to-link nut to 70 ft. lbs. (95 Nm) on models.

Bell Crank

▶ See Figure 23

The L-shaped component termed "Bell Crank" is a predecessor of the current idler arm. The bell crank attaches the connecting rod (the other end of which is connected to the steering gear) and the tie rod assembly together, and pivots around a shaft/bracket unit mounted onto the front frame member.

1. Raise and safely support the front end on jackstands.
2. Place the wheels in a straight-ahead position.
3. Detach the connecting rod and tie rod from the bell crank.
4. Remove the bell crank-to-support bracket nut and washers.
5. Remove the bell crank from the support bracket. It may be necessary to drive it out of the bracket with a soft drift.
6. To disassemble the bell crank, drive out the pin and remove the parts. Service kits are available for rebuilding the bell crank. CJ-2A models, starting with serial No. 199079, and all CJ models using bell cranks after that, utilize a new bell crank assembly. Most notably, the pin size was increased from ¾ in. diameter (19.05mm) to ⅞ in. diameter (22.225mm), a floating hardened sleeve was installed between the pin and needle bearings, and a new arm, with upward facing bearings was used.
7. When assembling the parts, make sure that the new bearings in the bell crank are installed ⅛ in. (3mm) below the surface of the bell crank face. When installing the washers, make sure that the chamfer on the washers face the bell crank.
8. After assembling the parts, install the bell crank in the Jeep, but do not connect the linkage. Tighten the bell crank pin nut to the following values:
   - CJ-2A models before serial No. 199079, and all Utility Models — 70-90 ft. lbs. (95-122 Nm)
   - All other models — 14-19 ft. lbs. (19-26 Nm)
9. Loosen the ⁷⁄₁₆ in. diameter clamp bolt and adjust the locknut on the end of the bell crank shaft until the bell crank just rotates freely, without binding.
10. Tighten the ⁷⁄₁₆ in. diameter clamp nut to 50-70 ft. lbs. (68-95 Nm).
11. Connect the tie rod to the bell crank and tighten the nut to 38-45 ft. lbs. (52-61 Nm).
12. Attach the connecting rod to the bell crank and adjust it as explained earlier in this section.

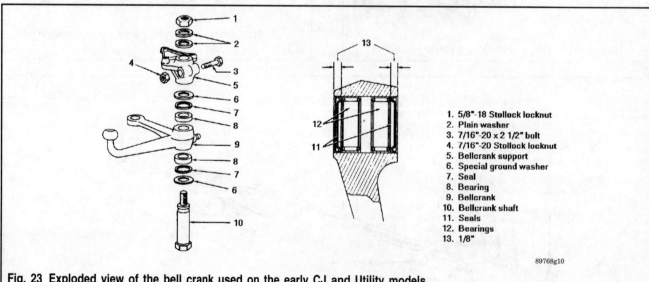

Fig. 23 Exploded view of the bell crank used on the early CJ and Utility models

1. 5/8"-18 Stollock locknut
2. Plain washer
3. 7/16"-20 x 2 1/2" bolt
4. 7/16"-20 Stollock locknut
5. Bellcrank support
6. Special ground washer
7. Seal
8. Bearing
9. Bellcrank
10. Bellcrank shaft
11. Seals
12. Bearings
13. 1/8"

SUSPENSION AND STEERING

Troubleshooting Basic Steering and Suspension Problems

Problem	Cause	Solution
Hard steering (steering wheel is hard to turn)	• Low or uneven tire pressure	• Inflate tires to correct pressure
	• Incorrect front end alignment	• Have front end alignment checked/adjusted
	• Defective power steering pump	• Check pump
	• Bent or poorly lubricated front end parts	• Lubricate and/or replace defective parts
Loose steering (too much play in the steering wheel)	• Loose wheel bearings	• Adjust wheel bearings
	• Loose or worn steering linkage	• Replace worn parts
	• Faulty shocks	• Replace shocks
	• Worn ball joints	• Replace ball joints
Car veers or wanders (car pulls to one side with hands off the steering wheel)	• Incorrect tire pressure	• Inflate tires to correct pressure
	• Improper front end alignment	• Have front end alignment checked/adjusted
	• Loose wheel bearings	• Adjust wheel bearings
	• Loose or bent front end components	• Replace worn components
	• Faulty shocks	• Replace shocks
Wheel oscillation or vibration transmitted through steering wheel	• Improper tire pressures	• Inflate tires to correct pressure
	• Tires out of balance	• Have tires balanced
	• Loose wheel bearings	• Adjust wheel bearings
	• Improper front end alignment	• Have front end alignment checked/adjusted
	• Worn or bent front end components	• Replace worn parts
Uneven tire wear	• Incorrect tire pressure	• Inflate tires to correct pressure
	• Front end out of alignment	• Have front end alignment checked/adjusted
	• Tires out of balance	• Have tires balanced

8-16 SUSPENSION AND STEERING

Troubleshooting the Steering Column

Problem	Cause	Solution
Will not lock	• Lockbolt spring broken or defective	• Replace lock bolt spring
High effort (required to turn ignition key and lock cylinder)	• Lock cylinder defective • Ignition switch defective • Rack preload spring broken or deformed • Burr on lock sector, lock rack, housing, support or remote rod coupling • Bent sector shaft • Defective lock rack • Remote rod bent, deformed • Ignition switch mounting bracket bent • Distorted coupling slot in lock rack (tilt column)	• Replace lock cylinder • Replace ignition switch • Replace preload spring • Remove burr • Replace shaft • Replace lock rack • Replace rod • Straighten or replace • Replace lock rack
Will stick in "start"	• Remote rod deformed • Ignition switch mounting bracket bent	• Straighten or replace • Straighten or replace
Key cannot be remove in "off-lock"	• Ignition switch is not adjusted correctly • Defective lock cylinder	• Adjust switch • Replace lock cylinder
Lock cylinder can be removed without depressing retainer	• Lock cylinder with defective retainer • Burr over retainer slot in housing cover or on cylinder retainer	• Replace lock cylinder • Remove burr
High effort on lock cylinder between "off" and "off-lock"	• Distorted lock rack • Burr on tang of shift gate (automatic column) • Gearshift linkage not adjusted	• Replace lock rack • Remove burr • Adjust linkage
Noise in column	• One click when in "off-lock" position and the steering wheel is moved (all except automatic column) • Coupling bolts not tightened • Lack of grease on bearings or bearing surfaces • Upper shaft bearing worn or broken • Lower shaft bearing worn or broken • Column not correctly aligned • Coupling pulled apart • Broken coupling lower joint • Steering shaft snap ring not seated • Shroud loose on shift bowl. Housing loose on jacket—will be noticed with ignition in "off-lock" and when torque is applied to steering wheel.	• Normal—lock bolt is seating • Tighten pinch bolts • Lubricate with chassis grease • Replace bearing assembly • Replace bearing. Check shaft and replace if scored. • Align column • Replace coupling • Repair or replace joint and align column • Replace ring. Check for proper seating in groove. • Position shroud over lugs on shift bowl. Tighten mounting screws.
High steering shaft effort	• Column misaligned • Defective upper or lower bearing • Tight steering shaft universal joint • Flash on I.D. of shift tube at plastic joint (tilt column only) • Upper or lower bearing seized	• Align column • Replace as required • Repair or replace • Replace shift tube • Replace bearings

SUSPENSION AND STEERING 8-17

Troubleshooting the Steering Column (cont.)

Problem	Cause	Solution
Lash in mounted column assembly	• Column mounting bracket bolts loose • Broken weld nuts on column jacket • Column capsule bracket sheared • Column bracket to column jacket mounting bolts loose • Loose lock shoes in housing (tilt column only) • Loose pivot pins (tilt column only) • Loose lock shoe pin (tilt column only) • Loose support screws (tilt column only)	• Tighten bolts • Replace column jacket • Replace bracket assembly • Tighten to specified torque • Replace shoes • Replace pivot pins and support • Replace pin and housing • Tighten screws
Housing loose (tilt column only)	• Excessive clearance between holes in support or housing and pivot pin diameters • Housing support-screws loose	• Replace pivot pins and support • Tighten screws
Steering wheel loose—every other tilt position (tilt column only)	• Loose fit between lock shoe and lock shoe pivot pin	• Replace lock shoes and pivot pin
Steering column not locking in any tilt position (tilt column only)	• Lock shoe seized on pivot pin • Lock shoe grooves have burrs or are filled with foreign material • Lock shoe springs weak or broken	• Replace lock shoes and pin • Clean or replace lock shoes • Replace springs
Noise when tilting column (tilt column only)	• Upper tilt bumpers worn • Tilt spring rubbing in housing	• Replace tilt bumper • Lubricate with chassis grease
One click when in "off-lock" position and the steering wheel is moved	• Seating of lock bolt	• None. Click is normal characteristic sound produced by lock bolt as it seats.
High shift effort (automatic and tilt column only)	• Column not correctly aligned • Lower bearing not aligned correctly • Lack of grease on seal or lower bearing areas	• Align column • Assemble correctly • Lubricate with chassis grease
Improper transmission shifting—automatic and tilt column only	• Sheared shift tube joint • Improper transmission gearshift linkage adjustment • Loose lower shift lever	• Replace shift tube • Adjust linkage • Replace shift tube

SUSPENSION AND STEERING

Troubleshooting the Turn Signal Switch

Problem	Cause	Solution
Turn signal will not cancel	• Loose switch mounting screws • Switch or anchor bosses broken • Broken, missing or out of position detent, or cancelling spring	• Tighten screws • Replace switch • Reposition springs or replace switch as required
Turn signal difficult to operate	• Turn signal lever loose • Switch yoke broken or distorted • Loose or misplaced springs • Foreign parts and/or materials in switch • Switch mounted loosely	• Tighten mounting screws • Replace switch • Reposition springs or replace switch • Remove foreign parts and/or material • Tighten mounting screws
Turn signal will not indicate lane change	• Broken lane change pressure pad or spring hanger • Broken, missing or misplaced lane change spring • Jammed wires	• Replace switch • Replace or reposition as required • Loosen mounting screws, reposition wires and retighten screws
Turn signal will not stay in turn position	• Foreign material or loose parts impeding movement of switch yoke • Defective switch	• Remove material and/or parts • Replace switch
Hazard switch cannot be pulled out	• Foreign material between hazard support cancelling leg and yoke	• Remove foreign material. No foreign material impeding function of hazard switch—replace turn signal switch.
No turn signal lights	• Inoperative turn signal flasher • Defective or blown fuse • Loose chassis to column harness connector • Disconnect column to chassis connector. Connect new switch to chassis and operate switch by hand. If vehicle lights now operate normally, signal switch is inoperative • If vehicle lights do not operate, check chassis wiring for opens, grounds, etc.	• Replace turn signal flasher • Replace fuse • Connect securely • Replace signal switch • Repair chassis wiring as required
Instrument panel turn indicator lights on but not flashing	• Burned out or damaged front or rear turn signal bulb • If vehicle lights do not operate, check light sockets for high resistance connections, the chassis wiring for opens, grounds, etc. • Inoperative flasher • Loose chassis to column harness connection • Inoperative turn signal switch • To determine if turn signal switch is defective, substitute new switch into circuit and operate switch by hand. If the vehicle's lights operate normally, signal switch is inoperative.	• Replace bulb • Repair chassis wiring as required • Replace flasher • Connect securely • Replace turn signal switch • Replace turn signal switch

SUSPENSION AND STEERING 8-19

Troubleshooting the Turn Signal Switch (Cont.)

Problem	Cause	Solution
Stop light not on when turn indicated	• Loose column to chassis connection • Disconnect column to chassis connector. Connect new switch into system without removing old. Operate switch by hand. If brake lights work with switch in the turn position, signal switch is defective. • If brake lights do not work, check connector to stop light sockets for grounds, opens, etc.	• Connect securely • Replace signal switch • Repair connector to stop light circuits using service manual as guide
Turn indicator panel lights not flashing	• Burned out bulbs • High resistance to ground at bulb socket • Opens, ground in wiring harness from front turn signal bulb socket to indicator lights	• Replace bulbs • Replace socket • Locate and repair as required
Turn signal lights flash very slowly	• High resistance ground at light sockets • Incorrect capacity turn signal flasher or bulb • If flashing rate is still extremely slow, check chassis wiring harness from the connector to light sockets for high resistance • Loose chassis to column harness connection • Disconnect column to chassis connector. Connect new switch into system without removing old. • Operate switch by hand. If flashing occurs at normal rate, the signal switch is defective.	• Repair high resistance grounds at light sockets • Replace turn signal flasher or bulb • Locate and repair as required • Connect securely • Replace turn signal switch
Hazard signal lights will not flash—turn signal functions normally	• Blow fuse • Inoperative hazard warning flasher • Loose chassis-to-column harness connection • Disconnect column to chassis connector. Connect new switch into system without removing old. Depress the hazard warning lights. If they now work normally, turn signal switch is defective. • If lights do not flash, check wiring harness "K" lead for open between hazard flasher and connector. If open, fuse block is defective	• Replace fuse • Replace hazard warning flasher in fuse panel • Conect securely • Replace turn signal switch • Repair or replace brown wire or connector as required

SUSPENSION AND STEERING

Troubleshooting the Manual Steering Gear

Problem	Cause	Solution
Hard or erratic steering	• Incorrect tire pressure	• Inflate tires to recommended pressures
	• Insufficient or incorrect lubrication	• Lubricate as required (refer to Maintenance Section)
	• Suspension, or steering linkage parts damaged or misaligned	• Repair or replace parts as necessary
	• Improper front wheel alignment	• Adjust incorrect wheel alignment angles
	• Incorrect steering gear adjustment	• Adjust steering gear
	• Sagging springs	• Replace springs
Play or looseness in steering	• Steering wheel loose	• Inspect shaft splines and repair as necessary. Tighten attaching nut and stake in place.
	• Steering linkage or attaching parts loose or worn	• Tighten, adjust, or replace faulty components
	• Pitman arm loose	• Inspect shaft splines and repair as necessary. Tighten attaching nut and stake in place
	• Steering gear attaching bolts loose	• Tighten bolts
	• Loose or worn wheel bearings	• Adjust or replace bearings
	• Steering gear adjustment incorrect or parts badly worn	• Adjust gear or replace defective parts
Wheel shimmy or tramp	• Improper tire pressure	• Inflate tires to recommended pressures
	• Wheels, tires, or brake rotors out-of-balance or out-of-round	• Inspect and replace or balance parts
	• Inoperative, worn, or loose shock absorbers or mounting parts	• Repair or replace shocks or mountings
	• Loose or worn steering or suspension parts	• Tighten or replace as necessary
	• Loose or worn wheel bearings	• Adjust or replace bearings
	• Incorrect steering gear adjustments	• Adjust steering gear
	• Incorrect front wheel alignment	• Correct front wheel alignment
Tire wear	• Improper tire pressure	• Inflate tires to recommended pressures
	• Failure to rotate tires	• Rotate tires
	• Brakes grabbing	• Adjust or repair brakes
	• Incorrect front wheel alignment	• Align incorrect angles
	• Broken or damaged steering and suspension parts	• Repair or replace defective parts
	• Wheel runout	• Replace faulty wheel
	• Excessive speed on turns	• Make driver aware of conditions
Vehicle leads to one side	• Improper tire pressures	• Inflate tires to recommended pressures
	• Front tires with uneven tread depth, wear pattern, or different cord design (i.e., one bias ply and one belted or radial tire on front wheels)	• Install tires of same cord construction and reasonably even tread depth, design, and wear pattern
	• Incorrect front wheel alignment	• Align incorrect angles
	• Brakes dragging	• Adjust or repair brakes
	• Pulling due to uneven tire construction	• Replace faulty tire

BRAKE OPERATING SYSTEM
    ADJUSTMENTS 9-4
    BASIC OPERATING PRINCIPLES 9-2
    BLEEDING THE BRAKES 9-10
    BRAKE HOSES AND LINES 9-8
    MASTER CYLINDER 9-5
    POWER BRAKE BOOSTER 9-7
    PROPORTIONING VALVE 9-7
    STOP LIGHT SWITCH 9-10

DRUM BRAKES
    BRAKE DRUM 9-11
    BRAKE SHOES 9-13
    WHEEL CYLINDERS 9-16

SPECIFICATIONS CHARTS
    BRAKE SPECIFICATIONS 9-20
    TROUBLESHOOTING THE BRAKE
     SYSTEM 9-21

TRANSMISSION (PARKING) BRAKE
    BRAKE SHOES 9-17
    CABLE(S) 9-17

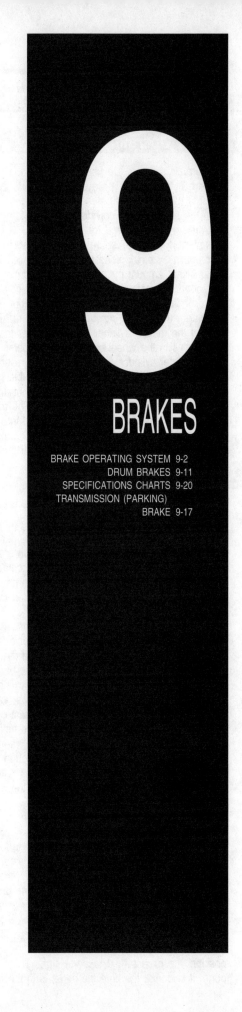

9
BRAKES

BRAKE OPERATING SYSTEM 9-2
DRUM BRAKES 9-11
SPECIFICATIONS CHARTS 9-20
TRANSMISSION (PARKING)
BRAKE 9-17

BRAKES

BRAKE OPERATING SYSTEM

Basic Operating Principles

Hydraulic systems are used to actuate the brakes of all modern automobiles. The system transports the power required to force the frictional surfaces of the braking system together from the pedal to the individual brake units at each wheel. A hydraulic system is used for two reasons.

First, fluid under pressure can be carried to all parts of an automobile by small pipes and flexible hoses without taking up a significant amount of room or posing routing problems.

Second, a great mechanical advantage can be given to the brake pedal end of the system, and the foot pressure required to actuate the brakes can be reduced by making the surface area of the master cylinder pistons smaller than that of any of the pistons in the wheel cylinders or calipers.

The master cylinder consists of a fluid reservoir along with a double cylinder and piston assembly. Double type master cylinders are designed to separate the front and rear braking systems hydraulically in case of a leak. The master cylinder coverts mechanical motion from the pedal into hydraulic pressure within the lines. This pressure is translated back into mechanical motion at the wheels by either the wheel cylinder (drum brakes) or the caliper (disc brakes).

Steel lines carry the brake fluid to a point on the vehicle's frame near each of the vehicle's wheels. The fluid is then carried to the calipers and wheel cylinders by flexible tubes in order to allow for suspension and steering movements.

In drum brake systems, each wheel cylinder contains two pistons, one at either end, which push outward in opposite directions and force the brake shoe into contact with the drum.

In disc brake systems, the cylinders are part of the calipers. At least one cylinder in each caliper is used to force the brake pads against the disc.

All pistons employ some type of seal, usually made of rubber, to minimize fluid leakage. A rubber dust boot seals the outer end of the cylinder against dust and dirt. The boot fits around the outer end of the piston on disc brake calipers, and around the brake actuating rod on wheel cylinders.

The hydraulic system operates as follows: When at rest, the entire system, from the piston(s) in the master cylinder to those in the wheel cylinders or calipers, is full of brake fluid. Upon application of the brake pedal, fluid trapped in front of the master cylinder piston(s) is forced through the lines to the wheel cylinders. Here, it forces the pistons outward, in the case of drum brakes, and inward toward the disc, in the case of disc brakes. The motion of the pistons is opposed by return springs mounted outside the cylinders in drum brakes, and by spring seals, in disc brakes.

Upon release of the brake pedal, a spring located inside the master cylinder immediately returns the master cylinder pistons to the normal position. The pistons contain check valves and the master cylinder has compensating ports drilled in it. These are uncovered as the pistons reach their normal position. The piston check valves allow fluid to flow toward the wheel cylinders or calipers as the pistons withdraw. Then, as the return springs force the brake pads or shoes into the released position, the excess fluid reservoir through the compensating ports. It is during the time the pedal is in the released position that any fluid that has leaked out of the system will be replaced through the compensating ports.

Dual circuit master cylinders employ two pistons, located one behind the other, in the same cylinder. The primary piston is actuated directly by mechanical linkage from the brake pedal through the power booster. The secondary piston is actuated by fluid trapped between the two pistons. If a leak develops in front of the secondary piston, it moves forward until it bottoms against the front of the master cylinder, and the fluid trapped between the pistons will operate the rear brakes. If the rear brakes develop a leak, the primary piston will move forward until direct contact with the secondary piston takes place, and it will force the secondary piston to actuate the front brakes. In either case, the brake pedal moves farther when the brakes are applied, and less braking power is available.

All dual circuit systems use a switch to warn the driver when only half of the brake system is operational. This switch is usually located in a valve body which is mounted on the firewall or the frame below the master cylinder. A hydraulic piston receives pressure from both circuits, each circuit's pressure being applied to one end of the piston. When the pressures are in balance, the piston remains stationary. When one circuit has a leak, however, the greater pressure in that circuit during application of the brakes will push the piston to one side, closing the switch and activating the brake warning light.

In disc brake systems, this valve body also contains a metering valve and, in some cases, a proportioning valve. The metering valve keeps pressure from traveling to the disc brakes on the front wheels until the brake shoes on the rear wheels have contacted the drums, ensuring that the front brakes will never be used alone. The proportioning valve controls the pressure to the rear brakes to lessen the chance of rear wheel lock-up during very hard braking.

Warning lights may be tested by depressing the brake pedal and holding it while opening one of the wheel cylinder bleeder screws. If this does not cause the light to go on, substitute a new lamp, make continuity checks, and, finally, replace the switch as necessary.

The hydraulic system may be checked for leaks by applying pressure to the pedal gradually and steadily. If the pedal sinks very slowly to the floor, the system has a leak. This is not to be confused with a springy or spongy feel due to the compression of air within the lines. If the system leaks, there will be a gradual change in the position of the pedal with a constant pressure.

Check for leaks along all lines and at wheel cylinders. If no external leaks are apparent, the problem is inside the master cylinder.

DISC BRAKES

➡ Although disc brakes are not available on any 1945-70 CJ, Utility or Military model Jeep vehicle, and since the method by which disc brakes function is essentially the same regardless of make or model of an automobile, the description of basic disc brake operation is included for added understanding about this automotive system.

BRAKES

Instead of the traditional expanding brakes that press outward against a circular drum, disc brake systems utilize a disc (rotor) with brake pads positioned on either side of it. An easily-seen analogy is the hand brake arrangement on a bicycle. The pads squeeze onto the rim of the bike wheel, slowing its motion. Automobile disc brakes use the identical principle but apply the braking effort to a separate disc instead of the wheel.

The disc (rotor) is a casting, usually equipped with cooling fins between the two braking surfaces. This enables air to circulate between the braking surfaces making them less sensitive to heat buildup and more resistant to fade. Dirt and water do not drastically affect braking action since contaminants are thrown off by the centrifugal action of the rotor or scraped off the by the pads. Also, the equal clamping action of the two brake pads tends to ensure uniform, straight line stops. Disc brakes are inherently self-adjusting. There are three general types of disc brake:

1. A fixed caliper.
2. A floating caliper.
3. A sliding caliper.

The fixed caliper design uses two pistons mounted on either side of the rotor (in each side of the caliper). The caliper is mounted rigidly and does not move.

The sliding and floating designs are quite similar. In fact, these two types are often lumped together. In both designs, the pad on the inside of the rotor is moved into contact with the rotor by hydraulic force. The caliper, which is not held in a fixed position, moves slightly, bringing the outside pad into contact with the rotor. There are various methods of attaching floating calipers. Some pivot at the bottom or top, and some slide on mounting bolts. In any event, the end result is the same.

DRUM BRAKES

Drum brakes employ two brake shoes mounted on a stationary backing plate. These shoes are positioned inside a circular drum which rotates with the wheel assembly. The shoes are held in place by springs. This allows them to slide toward the drums (when they are applied) while keeping the linings and drums in alignment. The shoes are actuated by a wheel cylinder which is mounted at the top of the backing plate. When the brakes are applied, hydraulic pressure forces the wheel cylinder's actuating links outward. Since these links bear directly against the top of the brake shoes, the tops of the shoes are then forced against the inner side of the drum. This action forces the bottoms of the two shoes to contact the brake drum by rotating the entire assembly slightly (known as servo action). When pressure within the wheel cylinder is relaxed, return springs pull the shoes back away from the drum.

Most modern drum brakes are designed to self-adjust themselves during application when the vehicle is moving in reverse. This motion causes both shoes to rotate very slightly with the drum, rocking an adjusting lever, thereby causing rotation of the adjusting screw. Some drum brake systems are designed to self-adjust during application whenever the brakes are applied. This on-board adjustment system reduces the need for maintenance adjustments and keeps both the brake function and pedal feel satisfactory.

POWER BOOSTERS

▶ See Figure 1

Some later model Jeep vehicles may be equipped with a vacuum assisted power brake system to multiply the braking force and reduce pedal effort. Since vacuum is always available when the engine is operating, the system is simple and efficient. A vacuum diaphragm is located on the front of the master cylinder and assists the driver in applying the brakes, reducing both the effort and travel he must put into moving the brake pedal.

The vacuum diaphragm housing is normally connected to the intake manifold by a vacuum hose. A check valve is placed at the point where the hose enters the diaphragm housing, so that during periods of low manifold vacuum brakes assist will not be lost.

Depressing the brake pedal closes off the vacuum source and allows atmospheric pressure to enter on one side of the diaphragm. This causes the master cylinder pistons to move and apply the brakes. When the brake pedal is released, vacuum is applied to both sides of the diaphragm and springs return the diaphragm and master cylinder pistons to the released position.

If the vacuum supply fails, the brake pedal rod will contact the end of the master cylinder actuator rod and the system will apply the brakes without any power assistance. The driver will notice that much higher pedal effort is needed to stop the car and that the pedal feels harder than usual.

Vacuum Leak Test

1. Operate the engine at idle without touching the brake pedal for at least one minute.
2. Turn off the engine and wait one minute.
3. Test for the presence of assist vacuum by depressing the brake pedal and releasing it several times. If vacuum is present in the system, light application will produce less and less pedal travel. If there is no vacuum, air is leaking into the system.

System Operation Test

1. With the engine **OFF**, pump the brake pedal until the supply vacuum is entirely gone.
2. Put light, steady pressure on the brake pedal.
3. Start the engine and let it idle. If the system is operating correctly, the brake pedal should fall toward the floor if the constant pressure is maintained.

9-4 BRAKES

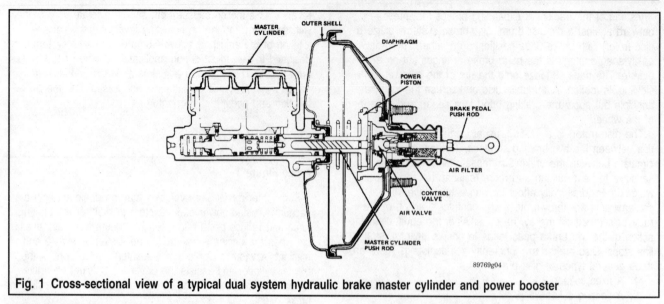

Fig. 1 Cross-sectional view of a typical dual system hydraulic brake master cylinder and power booster

Power brake systems may be tested for hydraulic leaks just as ordinary systems are tested.

✱✱CAUTION

Brake linings may contain asbestos. Asbestos is a known cancer-causing agent. When working on brakes, remember that the dust which accumulates on the brake parts and/or in the drum contains asbestos. Always wear a protective face covering, such as a painter's mask, when working on the brakes. NEVER blow the dust from the brakes or drum! There are solvents made for the purpose of cleaning brake parts. Use them!

✱✱WARNING

Clean, high quality brake fluid is essential to the safe and proper operation of the brake system. You should always buy the highest quality brake fluid that is available. If the brake fluid becomes contaminated, drain and flush the system, then refill the master cylinder with new fluid. Never reuse any brake fluid. Any brake fluid that is removed from the system should be discarded.

Adjustments

BRAKE SHOES

The method of brake adjustment varies depending on whether the vehicle is equipped with cam adjustment brakes or star wheel adjustment brakes with self-adjusters. When the brake linings become worn, effective brake pedal travel is reduced. Adjusting the brake shoes will restore the necessary travel.

Before adjusting the brakes, check the spring nuts, brake dust shield-to-axle flange bolts, and wheel bearing adjustments. Any looseness in these parts will cause erratic brake operation. Also make sure that the brake pedal has the correct amount of free travel without moving the master cylinder piston (free-play). There should be about ½ in. (13mm) of free-play at the master cylinder eye bolt. Turn the eye bolt to adjust the free-play.

Release the parking brakes and centralize the brake shoes in the drums by depressing the brake pedal hard and then releasing it. It is best to have all four wheels off the ground when the brakes are adjusted so that you can go back to each wheel to double check your adjustments.

Initial Brake Shoe Adjustment

If the brake assemblies have been disassembled, an initial adjustment must be made before the drum is installed. It may also be necessary to back off the adjustment to remove the drums.

When the brake parts have been installed in their correct position, adjust the adjusting screw assemblies to a point where approximately ⅜ in. (9.5mm) of threads are exposed between the star wheel and the star wheel nut.

Brake Adjustment

CAM EQUIPPED

▶ See Figures 2 and 3

1. Raise up the vehicle until all of the wheels, or at least the one to be adjusted first, are off the ground. Support the vehicle safely on jackstands.
2. Turn the forward shoe adjusting cams on the left side of the vehicle clockwise until the shoes are tight against the drums. Then turn the cams in the opposite direction until the wheels rotate freely without brake drag.
3. Turn the rear adjusting cams on the left side counterclockwise until the shoes are tight against the drums. Then turn the cams in the opposite direction until the wheels rotate freely without brake drag.
4. Repeat the two steps given above on the right side of the vehicle, turning the forward shoe adjusting cams counterclockwise and the rear shoe adjusting clockwise to tighten.

BRAKES 9-5

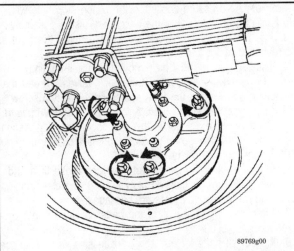

Fig. 2 Locations of the adjusting cam bolts on CJ-2A and CJ-3A models

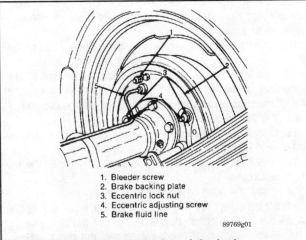

1. Bleeder screw
2. Brake backing plate
3. Eccentric lock nut
4. Eccentric adjusting screw
5. Brake fluid line

Fig. 3 Identification and location of the brake adjustment bolts, bleeder valve and fluid line on CJ-3B, CJ-5 and CJ-6 models with cam adjusters

5. On CJ-2A and CJ-3A models, if additional adjustment is required or when installing new brakes, reset the anchor pins as follows:

    a. With the brakes installed and the drum in place, loosen the anchor pin locknuts at the bottom of the backing plate.

    b. Turn the anchor pins in toward each other until the brake shoe-to-drum clearance is 0.005 in. (0.127mm) at the lower end of the shoe and 0.008 in. (0.203mm) at the upper end. On early models, a slot in the brake drum was provided to measure this clearance. The slot was eliminated on later models.

STAR WHEEL EQUIPPED

▶ See Figure 4

1. Raise and support the vehicle on jackstands.
2. Remove the access slot cover and using a brake adjusting tool or screwdriver, rotate the star wheel until the wheel is locked and can't be turned in the clockwise direction.
3. Back off the star wheel until the wheel rotates freely. To back off the star wheel on the brake, insert an ice pick or thin screw driver in the adjusting screw slot to hold the automatic adjusting lever away from the star wheel. Do not attempt to back off on the adjusting screw without holding the adjusting lever away from the star wheel as the adjuster will be damaged.

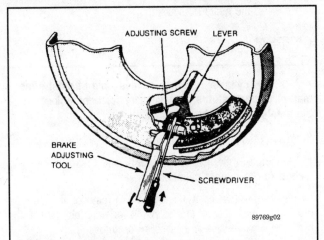

Fig. 4 To loosen the brake shoe adjustment, the adjusting lever must be held away from the star wheel while it is being rotated

Master Cylinder

✱✱CAUTION

Brake linings may contain asbestos. Asbestos is a known cancer-causing agent. When working on brakes, remember that the dust which accumulates on the brake parts and/or in the drum contains asbestos. Always wear a protective face covering, such as a painter's mask, when working on the brakes. NEVER blow the dust from the brakes or drum! There are solvents made for the purpose of cleaning brake parts. Use them!

✱✱WARNING

Clean, high quality brake fluid is essential to the safe and proper operation of the brake system. You should always buy the highest quality brake fluid that is available. If the brake fluid becomes contaminated, drain and flush the system, then refill the master cylinder with new fluid. Never reuse any brake fluid. Any brake fluid that is removed from the system should be discarded.

REMOVAL & INSTALLATION

1. Disconnect and plug the brake lines.
2. Disconnect the wires from the brake light switch.
3. Disconnect the master cylinder pushrod at the brake pedal (non-power brakes only).
4. Remove all attaching bolts and nuts, then lift the assembly from the vehicle.
5. Installation is the reverse of the removal procedure. Tighten the mounting bolts to 30 ft. lbs. (41 Nm).

9-6 BRAKES

6. Bleed the hydraulic system.

OVERHAUL

➡ A master cylinder bleeding kit, available at most after market or parts stores, is necessary for bench-bleeding the master cylinder before installation.

Single System

➡ The single brake system has only one brake line attached to the master cylinder.

1. After the master cylinder has been removed it should be dismantled and washed in alcohol. Never wash any part of the hydraulic braking system in gasoline or kerosene.
2. After all the parts have been thoroughly cleaned with alcohol, make a careful inspection, replacing those parts which show signs of deterioration.
3. Inspect the cylinder bore. If it is rough, it should be honed out or a new cylinder installed.
4. Clean out the cylinder with alcohol. Pass a wire through the ports that open from the supply reservoir into the cylinder bore to make sure that these passages are free of any foreign matter.
5. Install a new piston, primary cup, valve, and valve seat when rebuilding the master cylinder.
6. When reassembling the master cylinder, dip all internal parts in clean brake fluid. Install the valve seat in the end of the cylinder with the flat surface toward the valve.
7. Install the valve assembly.
8. Install the return spring and primary cup. The flat side of the cup goes toward the piston.
9. Install the piston and the piston stop snapring.
10. Install the fitting connection.
11. Fill the reservoir half full with brake fluid and operate the piston with the piston rod until fluid is ejected at the fitting.
12. Install the master cylinder to the firewall or in position under the floor pan. Fill it to a level 1/2 in. (13mm) below the top of the fill hole.
13. Make the necessary connections and adjust the pedal clearance.
14. Bleed the brake lines.
15. Recheck the entire hydraulic brake system to make sure there are no leaks.

Dual System

▶ See Figure 5

➡ The dual brake system utilizes 2 brake lines leading from the master cylinder, and the master cylinder reservoir is comprised of 2 separate fluid sections.

1. Remove the filler cap and empty all the fluid.
2. The stop light switch and primary piston stop, located in the stop light switch outlet hole, must be removed before removing the snapring from the piston bore. Remove the snapring, pushrod assembly and the primary and secondary piston assemblies. Air pressure applied in the piston stop hole will help facilitate the removal of the secondary piston assembly.
3. The residual check valves are located under the front and rear fluid outlet tube seats.
4. The tube seats must be removed with self-tapping screws to permit the removal of the check valves. Thread the self-tapping screws into the tube seats and place two screw driver tips under the screw head and force the screw upward.
5. Remove the expander in the rear secondary cup, secondary cups, return spring cup protector, primary cup, and washer from the secondary piston.
6. Immerse all of the metal parts in clean brake fluid and clean them. Use an air hose to blow out dirt and cleaning solvent from recesses and internal passages.
7. After cleaning, place all of the parts on clean paper or in a clean pan.
8. Inspect all parts for damage or excessive wear. Replace any damaged, worn, or chipped parts. Inspect the hydraulic cylinder bore for signs of scoring, rust, pitting, or etching. Any of these will require replacement of the hydraulic cylinder.
9. Prior to assembling the master cylinder, dip all of the components in clean brake fluid and place them on clean paper or in a clean pan.
10. Install the primary cup washer, primary cup, cup protector, and return spring in the secondary position.
11. Install the piston cups in the double groove end of the secondary piston, so the flat side of the cups face each other (lip of the cups away from each other). Install the cup expander in the lip groove of the end cup.
12. Coat the cylinder bore and piston assemblies with clean brake fluid before installing any parts in the cylinder.
13. Install the secondary piston assembly first, then the primary piston.
14. Install the pushrod assembly, which includes the pushrod, boot, and rod retainer, and secure with the snapring. Install the primary piston stop and stop light switch.
15. Place new rubber check valves over the check valve springs and install in the outlet holes, spring first.
16. Install the tube seats, flat side toward the check valve, and press in with tube nuts or the master cylinder brake tube nuts.
17. Before the master cylinder is installed on the vehicle it must be bled as follows:
    a. Support the cylinder assembly upright in a soft-jawed vise and fill both fluid reservoirs with new, clean brake fluid.
    b. Install one of the brake bleeding kit nipples into each of the master cylinder outlet ports and tighten them snugly.
    c. Attach one end of the plastic or rubber hoses from the bleeding kit to the outlet port nipples previously installed.
    d. Insert each of the other ends of the bleeding kit hoses into the brake fluid in the 2 reservoirs so that the front nipple hose is installed in the front reservoir and the rear nipple hose is installed in the rear reservoir.
    e. Depress the master cylinder pushrod until ALL air bubbles cease to appear in the brake fluid.
18. Install the master cylinder in the vehicle and bleed all the hydraulic lines at the wheel cylinders.

BRAKES 9-7

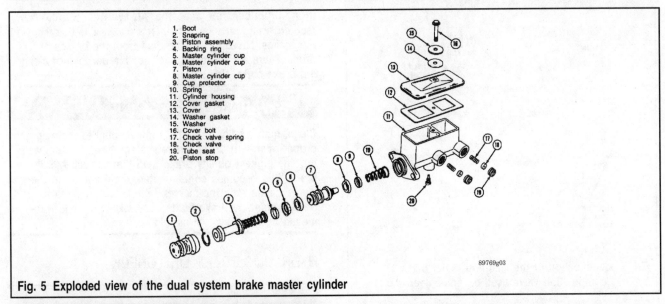

Fig. 5 Exploded view of the dual system brake master cylinder

Power Brake Booster

✱✱CAUTION

Brake linings may contain asbestos. Asbestos is a known cancer-causing agent. When working on brakes, remember that the dust which accumulates on the brake parts and/or in the drum contains asbestos. Always wear a protective face covering, such as a painter's mask, when working on the brakes. NEVER blow the dust from the brakes or drum! There are solvents made for the purpose of cleaning brake parts. Use them!

✱✱WARNING

Clean, high quality brake fluid is essential to the safe and proper operation of the brake system. You should always buy the highest quality brake fluid that is available. If the brake fluid becomes contaminated, drain and flush the system, then refill the master cylinder with new fluid. Never reuse any brake fluid. Any brake fluid that is removed from the system should be discarded.

REMOVAL & INSTALLATION

1. Disconnect the power unit pushrod at the pedal.
2. Disconnect the vacuum line at the power unit check valve.
3. Unbolt the master cylinder from the power unit and push the master cylinder aside carefully.
4. Unbolt the power unit bell crank at the dash panel and remove the power unit and bell crank as an assembly. If the power unit is being discarded, save the bell crank for the new unit.
5. Installation is the reverse of removal. Tighten the bell crank-to-dash panel bolts to 35 ft. lbs. (48 Nm), the master cylinder-to-power unit bolts to 30 ft. lbs. (41 Nm), and the pushrod-to-pedal bolt and nut to 35 ft. lbs. (48 Nm).

Proportioning Valve

▶ See Figures 6 and 7

Some later Jeep models may be equipped with a proportioning valve, which is a three part unit containing a metering valve, pressure differential valve and brake pressure warning switch. If any of these functions fails, the unit must be replaced. It is not repairable.

Fig. 6 View of a Type D combination valve used on some Jeep models

9-8 BRAKES

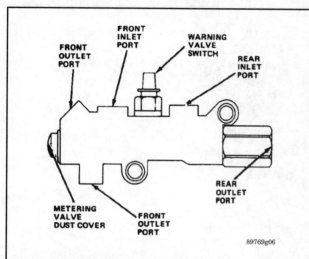

Fig. 7 Identification of the inlet and outlet ports of a Type W combination valve used on some Jeep models

The valve is located on the frame rail, directly under the driver's position, if equipped.

✱✱CAUTION

Brake linings may contain asbestos. Asbestos is a known cancer-causing agent. When working on brakes, remember that the dust which accumulates on the brake parts and/or in the drum contains asbestos. Always wear a protective face covering, such as a painter's mask, when working on the brakes. NEVER blow the dust from the brakes or drum! There are solvents made for the purpose of cleaning brake parts. Use them!

✱✱WARNING

Clean, high quality brake fluid is essential to the safe and proper operation of the brake system. You should always buy the highest quality brake fluid that is available. If the brake fluid becomes contaminated, drain and flush the system, then refill the master cylinder with new fluid. Never reuse any brake fluid. Any brake fluid that is removed from the system should be discarded.

REMOVAL & INSTALLATION

1. Disconnect the brake lines at the valve and plug them.
2. Unbolt and remove the valve.
3. Installation is the reverse of removal. Bleed the system.

Brake Hoses and Lines

✱✱CAUTION

Brake linings may contain asbestos. Asbestos is a known cancer-causing agent. When working on brakes, remember that the dust which accumulates on the brake parts and/or in the drum contains asbestos. Always wear a protective face covering, such as a painter's mask, when working on the brakes. NEVER blow the dust from the brakes or drum! There are solvents made for the purpose of cleaning brake parts. Use them!

✱✱WARNING

Clean, high quality brake fluid is essential to the safe and proper operation of the brake system. You should always buy the highest quality brake fluid that is available. If the brake fluid becomes contaminated, drain and flush the system, then refill the master cylinder with new fluid. Never reuse any brake fluid. Any brake fluid that is removed from the system should be discarded.

HYDRAULIC BRAKE LINE CHECK

The hydraulic brake lines and brake linings are to be inspected at the recommended intervals in the maintenance schedule. Follow the steel tubing from the master cylinder to the flexible hose fitting at each wheel. if a section of the tubing is found to be damaged, replace the entire section with tubing of the same type, size, shape and length.

✱✱CAUTION

Copper tubing should never be used in the brake system. Use only SAE J526 or J527 steel tubing.

When installing anew section of brake tubing, flush clean brake fluid or denatured alcohol through to remove any dirt or foreign material from the line. Be sure to flare both ends to provide sound, leak-proof connections.

✱✱CAUTION

Double-flare brake lines; never install a new line with only a single flare.

When bending the tubing to fit the underbody contours, be careful not to kink or crack the line.

Check the flexible brake hoses that connect the steel tubing to each wheel cylinder. Replace the hose if it shows any signs of softening, cracking or other damage. When installing a new front brake hose, position the hose to avoid contact with other chassis parts. Place a new copper gasket over the hose fitting and thread he hose assembly into the front wheel cylinder. A new rear brake hose must be positioned clear of the exhaust pipe or shock absorber. Thread the hose into the rear brake tube connector. When installing either a new front or rear brake hose, engage the opposite end of the hose to the bracket on the frame. Install the horseshoe retaining clip and connect the tube to the hose with the tube fitting nut.

Always bleed the system after hose or line replacement. Before bleeding, make sure that the master cylinder is topped up with high-temperature, extra heavy duty fluid of at least SAE 70R3 (DOT 3) quality.

REMOVAL & INSTALLATION

Brake Hose

1. Raise the end of the vehicle which contains the hose to be repaired, then support the vehicle safely using jackstands.
2. If necessary, remove the wheel for easier access to the hose.
3. Disconnect the hose from the wheel cylinder or caliper and plug the opening to avoid excessive fluid loss or contamination.
4. Disconnect the hose from the brake line and plug the openings to avoid excessive fluid loss or contamination.

To install:

5. Install the brake hose to the brake line and tighten to 14 ft. lbs. (19 Nm) for rear brakes or 18 ft. lbs. (24 Nm) for front brakes.
6. If installing a front brake hose, make sure the hose is routed properly, with the loop to the rear of the vehicle.
7. Install the hose to the wheel cylinder or caliper using NEW washers, then tighten the retainer to 36 ft. lbs. (49 Nm).
8. Properly bleed the brake system, then check the connections for leaks.
9. Remove the supports and carefully lower the vehicle.

Brake Line

There are 2 options available when replacing a brake line. The first, and probably most preferable, is to replace the entire line using a line of similar length which is already equipped with machined flared ends. Such lines are usually available from auto parts stores and usually require only a minimum of bending in order to properly fit then to the vehicle. The second option is to bend and flare the entire replacement line (or a repair section of line) using the appropriate tools.

Buying a line with machined flares is usually preferable because of the time and effort saved, not to mention the cost of special tools if they are not readily available. Also, machined flares are usually of a much higher quality than those produced by hand flaring tools or kits.

1. Raise the end of the vehicle which contains the hose to be repaired, then support the vehicle safely using jackstands.
2. Remove the components necessary for access to the brake line which is being replaced.
3. Disconnect the fittings at each end of the line, then plug the openings to prevent excessive fluid loss or contamination.
4. Trace the line from one end to the other and disconnect the line from any retaining clips, then remove the line from the vehicle.

To install:

5. Try to obtain a replacement line that is the same length as the line that was removed. If the line is longer, you will have to cut it and flare the end, or if you have decided to repair a portion of the line, see the procedure on brake line flaring, later in this section.
6. Use a suitable tubing bender to make the necessary bends in the line. Work slowly and carefully; try to make the bends look as close as possible to those on the line being replaced.

➡ **When bending the brake line, be careful not to kink or crack the line. If the brake line becomes kinked or cracked, it must be replaced.**

7. Before installing the brake line, flush it with brake cleaner to remove any dirt or foreign material.
8. Install the line into the vehicle. Be sure to attach the line to the retaining clips, as necessary. Make sure the replacement brake line does not contact any components that could rub the line and cause a leak.
9. Connect the brake line fittings and tighten to 18 ft. lbs. (24 Nm), except for the rear line-to-hose fitting which should be tightened to 14 ft. lbs. (19 Nm).
10. Properly bleed the brake system and check for leaks.
11. Install any removed components, then remove the supports and carefully lower the vehicle.

BRAKE LINE FLARING

Use only brake line tubing approved for automotive use; never use copper tubing. Whenever possible, try to work with brake lines that are already cut to the length needed. These lines are available at most auto parts stores and have machine made flares, the quality of which is hard to duplicate with most of the available inexpensive flaring kits.

When the brakes are applied, there is a great amount of pressure developed in the hydraulic system. An improperly formed flare can leak with resultant loss of stopping power. If you have never formed a double-flare, take time to familiarize yourself with the flaring kit; practice forming double-flares on scrap tubing until you are satisfied with the results.

The following procedure applies to the SA9193BR flaring kit, but should be similar to commercially available brake-line flaring kits. If these instructions differ in any way from those in your kit, follow the instructions in the kit.

1. Determine the length necessary for the replacement or repair and allow an additional $1/8$ in. (3.2mm) for each flare. Select a piece of tubing, then cut the brake line to the necessary length using an appropriate saw. Do not use a tubing cutter.
2. Square the end of the tube with a file and chamfer the edges. Remove burrs from the inside and outside diameters of the cut line using a deburring tool.
3. Install the required fittings onto the line.
4. Install SA9193BR, or an equivalent flaring tool, into a vice and install the handle into the operating cam.
5. Loosen the die clamp screw and rotate the locking plate to expose the die carrier opening.
6. Select the required die set (4.75mm DIN) and install in the carrier with the full side of either half facing clamp screw and counter bore of both halves facing punch turret.
7. Insert the prepared line through the rear of the die and push forward until the line end is flush with the die face.
8. Make sure the rear of both halves of the die rest against the hexagon die stops, then rotate the locking plate to the fully closed position and clamp the die firmly by tightening the clamp screw.

9-10 BRAKES

9. Rotate the punch turret until the appropriate size (4.75mm DIN) points towards the open end of the line to be flared.

10. Pull the operating handle against the line resistance in order to create the flare, then return the handle to the original position.

11. Release the clamp screw and rotate the locking plate to the open position.

12. Remove the die set and line, then separate by gently tapping both halves on the bench. Inspect the flare for proper size and shape. Dimension A should be 0.272-0.286 in. (6.92-7.28mm).

13. If necessary, repeat Steps 2-12 for the other end of the line or for the end of the line which is being repaired.

14. Bend the replacement line or section using SA91108NE, or an equivalent line bending tool.

15. If repairing the original line, join the old and new sections using a female union and tighten.

Bleeding the Brakes

▶ See Figure 8

✳✳CAUTION

Brake linings may contain asbestos. Asbestos is a known cancer-causing agent. When working on brakes, remember that the dust which accumulates on the brake parts and/or in the drum contains asbestos. Always wear a protective face covering, such as a painter's mask, when working on the brakes. NEVER blow the dust from the brakes or drum! There are solvents made for the purpose of cleaning brake parts. Use them!

✳✳WARNING

Clean, high quality brake fluid is essential to the safe and proper operation of the brake system. You should always buy the highest quality brake fluid that is available. If the brake fluid becomes contaminated, drain and flush the system, then refill the master cylinder with new fluid. Never reuse any brake fluid. Any brake fluid that is removed from the system should be discarded.

➡It will be necessary to have the help of an assistant during this procedure.

The hydraulic brake system must be bled whenever a fluid line has been disconnected because air gets into the system. A leak in the system may sometimes be indicated by a spongy brake pedal. Air trapped in the system is compressible and does not permit the pressure applied to the brake pedal to be transmitted solidly to the brake shoe and drum surfaces. The system must be absolutely free from air at all times. When bleeding brakes, bleed at the wheel most distant from the master cylinder first, the next most distant second, and so on. During the bleeding operation the master cylinder must be kept at least ¾ full of brake fluid; if the fluid level falls too low air can get into the system through the master cylinder.

To bleed the brakes:

1. Carefully clean all dirt from around the master cylinder filler cap.

➡If a bleeder tank is to be used, follow the manufacturer's instructions.

2. Remove the filler cap and fill the master cylinder to within ¼ in. (6mm) of the top of the master cylinder.

3. Clean off the bleeder valve nipples at all four wheel cylinders.

4. Attach a clear plastic bleeder hose to the right rear wheel cylinder bleeder screw and place the other end of the tube in a glass jar, submerged in brake fluid.

5. Open the bleeder valve ½-¾ of a turn while keeping the other end of the bleeder hose submerged in the brake fluid in the jar.

6. Have an assistant depress the brake pedal SLOWLY and allow it to return. Continue this pumping action to force any air out of the system.

7. When bubbles cease to appear at the end of the bleeder hose submerged in the brake fluid, close the bleeder valve and remove the hose.

8. Check the level of fluid in the master cylinder reservoir and replenish as necessary.

9. Proceed to the left rear wheel cylinder and repeat Steps 3-8.

10. After bleeding the left rear wheel cylinder, move on to the right front wheel cylinder and repeat Steps 3-8 once again.

11. Finally move on to the left front wheel cylinder and bleed it as with the other three wheels (Steps 3-8).

12. After the bleeding operation at each wheel cylinder is complete, fill the master cylinder reservoir and replace the filler plug.

13. Dispose of the brake fluid in the jar, used during the bleeding process, because it is contaminated with air bubbles and dirt.

Stop Light Switch

Two types of switches have been used on Jeep vehicles. One type is attached to the brake pedal rod end of the pushrod, and cannot be adjusted. The other type is mounted on a flange attached to the brake pedal support bracket and is

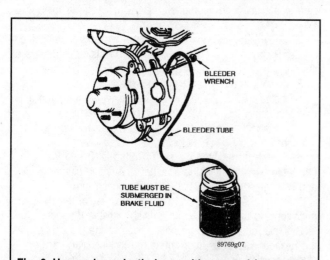

Fig. 8 Use a clear plastic hose with one end immersed in a jar of clean brake fluid and the other end attached to the bleeder valve when bleeding the brake system

BRAKES 9-11

held in the OFF position by the brake pedal resting in its released position. Upon depressing the brake pedal, the switch plunger is allowed to move outward and contact is made within the switch to allow current to pass and operate the stop lights.

ADJUSTMENT

1. Hold the brake pedal in the applied position.
2. Push the stop light switch through the mounting bracket until it stops against the brake pedal bracket. Release the pedal to set the switch in the proper position.
3. Check the position of the switch. The switch plunger should be in the ON position and activate the brake lights after brake pedal travel of $3/8$-$5/8$ in. (9.5-16mm).

DRUM BRAKES

Brake Drum

REMOVAL & INSTALLATION

> **✱✱CAUTION**
>
> Brake linings may contain asbestos. Asbestos is a known cancer-causing agent. When working on brakes, remember that the dust which accumulates on the brake parts and/or in the drum contains asbestos. Always wear a protective face covering, such as a painter's mask, when working on the brakes. NEVER blow the dust from the brakes or drum! There are solvents made for the purpose of cleaning brake parts. Use them!

> **✱✱WARNING**
>
> Clean, high quality brake fluid is essential to the safe and proper operation of the brake system. You should always buy the highest quality brake fluid that is available. If the brake fluid becomes contaminated, drain and flush the system, then refill the master cylinder with new fluid. Never reuse any brake fluid. Any brake fluid that is removed from the system should be discarded.

Front

The front brake drums are attached to the wheel hubs by five bolts. These bolts are also used for mounting the wheels on the hub. Press or drive out the bolts to remove the drum from the hub.

When placing the drum on the hub, make sure that the contacting surfaces are clean and flat. Line up the holes in the drum with those in the hub and put the drum over the shoulder on the hub. Insert five new bolts through the drum and hub and drive the bolts into place solidly. Place a round piece of stock approximately the diameter of the head of the bolt, in a vise. Next place the hub and drum assembly over it so that the bolt head rests on it. Then flatten the bolt head into the countersunk section of the hub with a punch.

The run-out of the drum face should be within 0.030 in. (0.762mm). If the run-out is found to be greater than 0.030 in. (0.762mm), it will be necessary to reset the bolts to correct the condition.

The left-hand hub bolts have an L stamped on the head of the bolt. The left-hand threaded nuts may have a groove cut around the hexagon faces, or the word LEFT stamped on the face.

Hubs with left-hand threaded hub bolts are installed on the left-hand side of the vehicle. Late production vehicles are equipped with right-hand bolts and nuts on all four bolts.

Rear
▶ See Figures 9, 10, 11, 12, 13 and 14

The rear brake drums are held in position by spring clip type locknuts, a central axle nut and cotter pin or by three drum-to-hub retaining screws, depending on the model and year. After the spring-type locknuts or retaining screws are removed, the drum can be slid off the axle shaft or hub and brake shoes. It may be necessary to back off the brake shoe adjustment so that any lip on the inside of the brake drum clears the brake shoes.

For models equipped with central axle nuts and cotter pins:
1. Position wheel blocks around the wheels which will stay on the ground to keep the vehicle from rolling. Raise and safely support the vehicle on jackstands.
2. Remove the wheels.
3. Straighten the cotter pin ends and pull it out of the castellated axle nut. Discard the old cotter pin and make certain to get new cotter pins for reassembly.
4. Remove the castellated axle nut and flat washer from the axle shaft.

Fig. 9 After removing the rear wheel, access can be gained to the rear brake drum

9-12 BRAKES

Fig. 10 Remove the cotter pin from the castellated axle nut . . .

Fig. 11 . . . then remove the axle nut itself

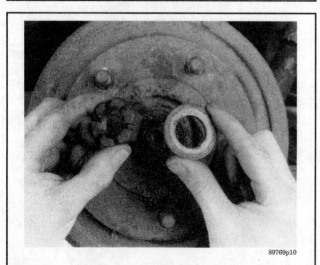

Fig. 12 Remove the flat washer from the end of the axle shaft

Fig. 13 It may be necessary to use a drum puller to remove the drum

Fig. 14 While removing the drum, make sure to keep track of the axle shaft key

5. Pull the brake drum off of the axle shaft. It may be necessary to use a hub puller to loosen the drum from the axle shaft.

➡While removing the brake drum, make certain to keep track of the axle shaft key.

To install:

6. Make sure that the key is installed in the key groove in the axle shaft, then slide the brake drum onto the axle shaft so that the key groove in the drum is aligned with the key in the axle shaft.

7. Tap the drum onto the axle shaft with a soft-faced hammer until the castellated axle nut can be threaded onto the axle shaft.

8. Slowly tighten the axle nut to draw the drum completely onto the axle shaft.

9. Once the drum is completely drawn onto the axle shaft tighten the axle nut to 150 ft. lbs. (204 Nm).

BRAKES 9-13

10. After tightening the axle nut to 150 ft. lbs. (204 Nm), continue to tighten it until one of the castellated grooves is aligned with the cotter pin hole in the axle.
11. Install a new cotter pin through the axle nut and the hole in the axle shaft, then bend the ends of the cotter pin so that it cannot work its way out during use.
12. Adjust the brake shoes, if necessary.
13. Install the wheels and tighten the lug nuts until snug.
14. Lower the vehicle and finish tightening the lug nuts.

INSPECTION

Using a brake drum micrometer, check all drums. Should a brake drum be scored or rough, it may be reconditioned by grinding or turning on a lathe. Do not remove more than 0.030 in. (0.762mm) thickness of metal.

Use a clean cloth to clean dirt from the brake drums. If further cleaning is required, use soap and water. Do not use brake fluid, gasoline, kerosene or any other similar solvents.

Brake Shoes

✱✱CAUTION

Brake linings may contain asbestos. Asbestos is a known cancer-causing agent. When working on brakes, remember that the dust which accumulates on the brake parts and/or in the drum contains asbestos. Always wear a protective face covering, such as a painter's mask, when working on the brakes. NEVER blow the dust from the brakes or drum! There are solvents made for the purpose of cleaning brake parts. Use them!

✱✱WARNING

Clean, high quality brake fluid is essential to the safe and proper operation of the brake system. You should always buy the highest quality brake fluid that is available. If the brake fluid becomes contaminated, drain and flush the system, then refill the master cylinder with new fluid. Never reuse any brake fluid. Any brake fluid that is removed from the system should be discarded.

REMOVAL & INSTALLATION

◆ See Figures 15, 16, 17, 18, 19, 20, 21, 22, 23, 24, 25, 26 and 27

1. Raise and safely support the vehicle on jackstands so that all four wheels are off the ground.
2. On vehicles equipped with cam adjustment brakes, turn all eccentric cams to the lower side of the cam. On vehicles equipped with star wheel adjustment, turn the star adjuster all the way in.
3. Remove the wheels and the hubs and drums to give access to the brake shoes.
4. Install wheel cylinder clamps on the wheel cylinder to retain the wheel cylinder pistons in place and prevent leakage of brake fluid while replacing the shoes.
5. Remove the return springs with a brake spring removal tool.
6. On models with self-adjusters, remove the adjuster cable, cable guide, adjuster lever and adjuster springs.
7. Remove the hold-down clips or springs and remove the brake shoes.
8. Before installing the new shoes, now would be a good time to inspect the oil seals in the hubs. If the condition of the seals is doubtful, replace them. Also check the wheel cylinders for leakage. Pull back the dust covers. If there is fluid present behind the dust cover, the wheel cylinder must be rebuilt or replaced.
9. Clean the backing plate with a brush or cloth. Place a dab of molybdenum disulfide grease on each raised pad where the shoes rub the backing plate.

➡Always replace brake shoes in axle sets. Never replace linings on only one side or just on one wheel.

To install:
10. Install the parking brake cable and lever on the secondary shoe. Secure the lever with a washer and new U-clip.
11. Install the guide and self-adjuster cable on the anchor pin.
12. Install the shoes, one at a time, on the backing plate and secure them with the hold-down springs, pins and retainers.
13. Install the cross-strut and spring.
14. Install the star wheel adjuster, spring and lever.
15. Install the return springs.
16. Make sure that the brake shoe surfaces are clean and free from any contamination.
17. Perform the initial brake shoe adjustment, outlined at the beginning of this section.
18. Install the drums and wheels, lower the truck and check brake operation. On Jeep vehicles without self-adjusters, refer to the Adjustment procedures at the beginning of this section. On vehicles with self-adjusters, drive the Jeep in a series of alternating forward and reverse stops. Usually 10-15 full stops in reverse are sufficient.

9-14 BRAKES

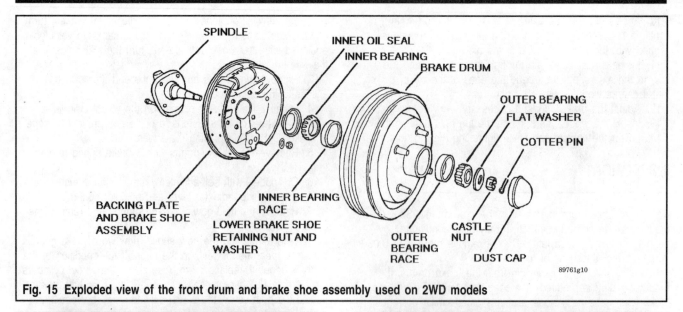

Fig. 15 Exploded view of the front drum and brake shoe assembly used on 2WD models

Fig. 16 Remove the brake drum to gain access to the brake shoes — rear brakes shown

Fig. 18 . . . then unhook the return spring from the rear (trailing) shoe

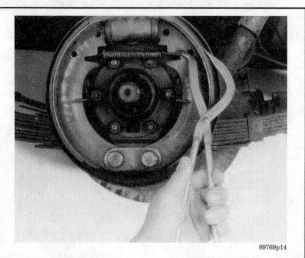

Fig. 17 Detach the return spring from the front (leading) brake shoe . . .

Fig. 19 Allow both shoes to hang from the bottom pivot bolts

BRAKES 9-15

Fig. 20 Remove the bottom front pivot bolt to remove the front brake shoe

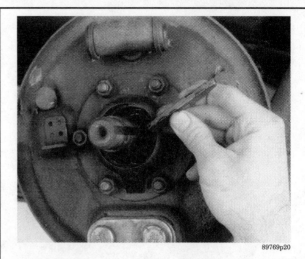

Fig. 23 If removing the backing plate, first remove the axle shaft key . . .

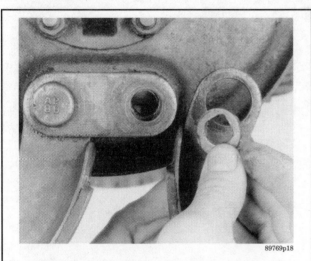

Fig. 21 When removing the front shoe, retain the cam washer for reassembly . . .

Fig. 24 . . . then remove the 6 backing plate retaining bolts

Fig. 22 . . . then remove the pivot bolt plate and rear shoe from the backing plate

Fig. 25 If necessary, use a small prytool to loosen the backing plate flange . . .

9-16 BRAKES

Fig. 26 . . . then remove the backing plate from the axle tube flange

Fig. 27 The front brakes are of similar design, and are removed in the same manner as rear brakes

Wheel Cylinders

✱✱CAUTION

Brake linings may contain asbestos. Asbestos is a known cancer-causing agent. When working on brakes, remember that the dust which accumulates on the brake parts and/or in the drum contains asbestos. Always wear a protective face covering, such as a painter's mask, when working on the brakes. NEVER blow the dust from the brakes or drum! There are solvents made for the purpose of cleaning brake parts. Use them!

✱✱WARNING

Clean, high quality brake fluid is essential to the safe and proper operation of the brake system. You should always buy the highest quality brake fluid that is available. If the brake fluid becomes contaminated, drain and flush the system, then refill the master cylinder with new fluid. Never reuse any brake fluid. Any brake fluid that is removed from the system should be discarded.

REMOVAL & INSTALLATION

▶ See Figures 28 and 29

1. Raise and safely support the vehicle on jackstands and remove the wheel, hub, and drum.
2. Loosen, but do not remove, the screws or nuts which hold the wheel cylinder to the backing plate.
3. Disconnect the brake line at the fitting on the brake backing plate.
4. Remove the brake assemblies, as described earlier in this section.
5. Remove the wheel cylinder retaining fasteners, then remove the wheel cylinder from the backing plate.

Fig. 28 Loosen, but do not yet remove, the wheel cylinder retaining fasteners . . .

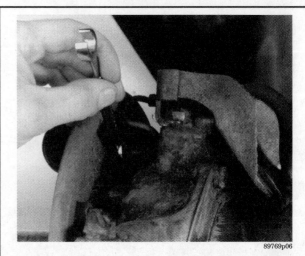

Fig. 29 . . . then detach the brake line from the wheel cylinder

BRAKES 9-17

6. Installation is the reverse of the removal procedure. Tighten the wheel cylinder-to-backing plate fasteners to 18 ft. lbs. (25 Nm) and the brake line-to-wheel cylinder connection to 160 inch lbs. (18 Nm).

OVERHAUL

▶ See Figure 30

Wheel cylinder rebuilding kits are available for reconditioning wheel cylinders. The kits usually contain new cup springs, cylinder cups and, in some cases, new boots. The most important factor to keep in mind when rebuilding wheel cylinders is cleanliness. Keep all dirt away from the wheel cylinders when you are reassembling them.

1. Remove the wheel cylinder, as described earlier in this section.
2. Remove the rubber dust covers on the ends of the cylinder.
3. Remove the pistons and piston cups and the spring.
4. Remove the bleeder screw and make certain that it is not plugged.
5. Discard all of the parts that the rebuilding kit will replace.
6. Examine the inside of the cylinder. If it is severely rusted, pitted or scratched, then the cylinder must be replaced as the piston cups will not be able to seal against the walls of the cylinder.
7. Using emery cloth or crocus cloth, polish the inside of the cylinder. Do not polish in a lengthwise direction. Polish by rotating the wheel cylinder around the polishing cloth supported on your fingers. The purpose of this is to put a new surface on the inside of the cylinder. Keep the inside of the cylinder coated with brake fluid while polishing.

➡ **Honing the wheel cylinders is not recommended due to the possibility of removing too much material from the bore, making it too large to seal.**

8. Wash out the cylinder with clean brake fluid after polishing.
9. When reassembling the cylinder dip all of the parts in clean brake fluid.
10. Reassemble the wheel cylinder in the reverse order of removal.
11. Install the wheel cylinder.

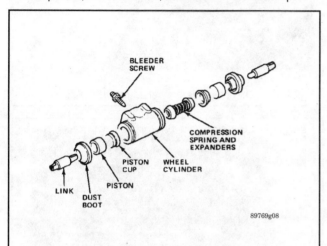

Fig. 30 Exploded view of the wheel cylinder used on all Jeep models

TRANSMISSION (PARKING) BRAKE

Cable(s)

REMOVAL & INSTALLATION

1. Fully release the hand brake.
2. Disconnect the cable at the hand brake lever.
3. Disconnect the hook from the spring at the actuating lever.
4. Installation is the reverse of removal.

Brake Shoes

REMOVAL & INSTALLATION

▶ See Figures 31, 32, 33, 34, 35, 36, 37, 38, 39, 40, 41, 42 and 43

✱✱CAUTION

Brake linings may contain asbestos. Asbestos is a known cancer-causing agent. When working on brakes, remember that the dust which accumulates on the brake parts and/or

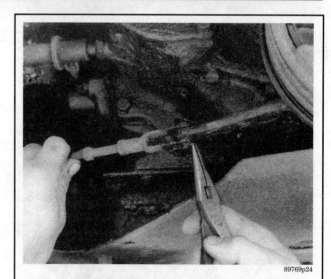

Fig. 31 Detach the brake cable from the actuating lever

9-18 BRAKES

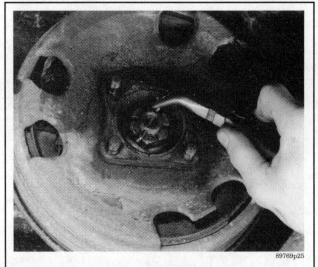

Fig. 32 Straighten the cotter pin ends . . .

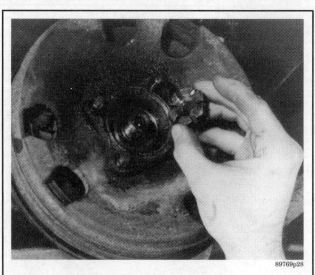

Fig. 35 . . . then remove the retaining nut

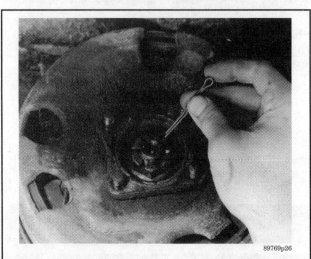

Fig. 33 . . . then remove the cotter pin from the castellated retaining nut

Fig. 36 Use a small prytool to work the driveshaft flange loose . . .

Fig. 34 Use a large ratchet wrench and socket to loosen the retaining nut . . .

Fig. 37 . . . then remove the driveshaft flange and seal from the drum

BRAKES 9-19

Fig. 38 Slide the transmission brake drum off of the brake shoes

Fig. 41 . . . and remove the upper transmission brake shoe

Fig. 39 Once the drum is removed, access to the brake shoes is possible

Fig. 42 The brake cable pulls on the actuating cam lever to apply braking force

Fig. 40 Disconnect the return spring, then remove the lower shoe and spring together . . .

Fig. 43 Pull the cable spring back and disconnect the cable from the rod

9-20 BRAKES

in the drum contains asbestos. Always wear a protective face covering, such as a painter's mask, when working on the brakes. NEVER blow the dust from the brakes or drum! There are solvents made for the purpose of cleaning brake parts. Use them!

✱✱WARNING

Clean, high quality brake fluid is essential to the safe and proper operation of the brake system. You should always buy the highest quality brake fluid that is available. If the brake fluid becomes contaminated, drain and flush the system, then refill the master cylinder with new fluid. Never reuse any brake fluid. Any brake fluid that is removed from the system should be discarded.

1. Remove the driveshaft.
2. Remove the retracting spring clevis pin and the spring clip.
3. Remove the hub locknut, the nut and washer from the transfer case output shaft.
4. Using a puller, remove the brake drum and companion flange.
5. Remove the retracting springs and shoes from the backing plate.
6. Clean all parts with a safe solvent.
7. Installation is the reverse of the removal procedure. Replace any weak springs and clean the adjuster threads. Coat the threads with a LIGHT film of oil. It will be necessary to back off the adjusting screw wheels to allow drum installation.
8. Adjust the brake, as described later in this section.

ADJUSTMENT

Make sure that the brake handle on the instrument panel is fully released. Check the operating linkage and the cable to make sure that they do not bind. If necessary, free the cable and lubricate it. Rotate the brake drum, located on the back end of the transmission assembly, until one pair of the three sets of holes are over the shoe adjusting screw wheels in the brake drum. Use the edge of the holes in the brake drum as a fulcrum for the brake adjusting tool or a prytool. Rotate each notched adjusting screw by moving the handle of the tool away from the center of the driveshaft until the shoes are snug against the drum. Back off seven notches on the adjusting screw wheels to secure the proper running clearance between the shoes and the drum.

Brake Specifications

Years	Master Cyl. Bore	Brake Disc				Brake Drum		Wheel Cyl. or Caliper Bore	
		Original Thickness	Minimum Thickness	Maximum Run-out	Diameter	Orig. Inside Dia.	Max. Wear Limit	Front	Rear
1945–71 CJ models	1.000	—	—	—	—	9.000	9.060	1.000	0.750
1947–64 Utility	1.000	—	—	—	—	11.000	11.060	1.125	1.000

Troubleshooting the Brake System

Problem	Cause	Solution
Low brake pedal (excessive pedal travel required for braking action.)	• Excessive clearance between rear linings and drums caused by inoperative automatic adjusters	• Make 10 to 15 alternate forward and reverse brake stops to adjust brakes. If brake pedal does not come up, repair or replace adjuster parts as necessary.
	• Worn rear brakelining	• Inspect and replace lining if worn beyond minimum thickness specification
	• Bent, distorted brakeshoes, front or rear	• Replace brakeshoes in axle sets
	• Air in hydraulic system	• Remove air from system. Refer to Brake Bleeding.
Low brake pedal (pedal may go to floor with steady pressure applied.)	• Fluid leak in hydraulic system	• Fill master cylinder to fill line; have helper apply brakes and check calipers, wheel cylinders, differential valve tubes, hoses and fittings for leaks. Repair or replace as necessary.
	• Air in hydraulic system	• Remove air from system. Refer to Brake Bleeding.
	• Incorrect or non-recommended brake fluid (fluid evaporates at below normal temp).	• Flush hydraulic system with clean brake fluid. Refill with correct-type fluid.
	• Master cylinder piston seals worn, or master cylinder bore is scored, worn or corroded	• Repair or replace master cylinder
Low brake pedal (pedal goes to floor on first application—o.k. on subsequent applications.)	• Disc brake pads sticking on abutment surfaces of anchor plate. Caused by a build-up of dirt, rust, or corrosion on abutment surfaces	• Clean abutment surfaces
Fading brake pedal (pedal height decreases with steady pressure applied.)	• Fluid leak in hydraulic system	• Fill master cylinder reservoirs to fill mark, have helper apply brakes, check calipers, wheel cylinders, differential valve, tubes, hoses, and fittings for fluid leaks. Repair or replace parts as necessary.
	• Master cylinder piston seals worn, or master cylinder bore is scored, worn or corroded	• Repair or replace master cylinder
Decreasing brake pedal travel (pedal travel required for braking action decreases and may be accompanied by a hard pedal.)	• Caliper or wheel cylinder pistons sticking or seized	• Repair or replace the calipers, or wheel cylinders
	• Master cylinder compensator ports blocked (preventing fluid return to reservoirs) or pistons sticking or seized in master cylinder bore	• Repair or replace the master cylinder
	• Power brake unit binding internally	• Test unit according to the following procedure: (a) Shift transmission into neutral and start engine (b) Increase engine speed to 1500 rpm, close throttle and fully depress brake pedal (c) Slow release brake pedal and stop engine (d) Have helper remove vacuum check valve and hose from power unit. Observe for backward movement of brake pedal. (e) If the pedal moves backward, the power unit has an internal bind—replace power unit

Troubleshooting the Brake System (cont.)

Problem	Cause	Solution
Spongy brake pedal (pedal has abnormally soft, springy, spongy feel when depressed.)	· Air in hydraulic system · Brakeshoes bent or distorted · Brakelining not yet seated with drums and rotors · Rear drum brakes not properly adjusted	· Remove air from system. Refer to Brake Bleeding. · Replace brakeshoes · Burnish brakes · Adjust brakes
Hard brake pedal (excessive pedal pressure required to stop vehicle. May be accompanied by brake fade.)	· Loose or leaking power brake unit vacuum hose · Incorrect or poor quality brakelining · Bent, broken, distorted brakeshoes · Calipers binding or dragging on mounting pins. Rear brakeshoes dragging on support plate. · Caliper, wheel cylinder, or master cylinder pistons sticking or seized · Power brake unit vacuum check valve malfunction · Power brake unit has internal bind · Master cylinder compensator ports (at bottom of reservoirs) blocked by dirt, scale, rust, or have small burrs (blocked ports prevent fluid return to reservoirs). · Brake hoses, tubes, fittings clogged or restricted · Brake hoses, tubes, fittings clogged or restricted · Brake fluid contaminated with improper fluids (motor oil, transmission fluid, causing rubber	· Tighten connections or replace leaking hose · Replace with lining in axle sets · Replace brakeshoes · Replace mounting pins and bushings. Clean rust or burrs from rear brake support plate ledges and lubricate ledges with molydisulfide grease. **NOTE:** If ledges are deeply grooved or scored, do not attempt to sand or grind them smooth—replace support plate. · Repair or replace parts as necessary · Test valve according to the following procedure: (a) Start engine, increase engine speed to 1500 rpm, close throttle and immediately stop engine (b) Wait at least 90 seconds then depress brake pedal (c) If brakes are not vacuum assisted for 2 or more applications, check valve is faulty · Test unit according to the following procedure: (a) With engine stopped, apply brakes several times top exhaust all vacuum in system (b) Shift transmission into neutral, depress brake pedal and start engine (c) If pedal height decreases with foot pressure and less pressure is required to hold pedal in applied position, power unit vacuum system is operating normally. Test power unit. If power unit exhibits a bind condition, replace the power unit. · Repair or replace master cylinder **CAUTION:** Do not attempt to clean blocked ports with wire, pencils, or similar implements. Use compressed air only. · Use compressed air to check or unclog parts. Replace any damaged parts. · Use compressed air to check or unclog parts. Replace any damaged parts. · Replace all rubber components, combination valve and hoses. Flush entire brake system with

Troubleshooting the Brake System (cont.)

Problem	Cause	Solution
	components to swell and stick in bores	DOT 3 brake fluid or equivalent.
	· Low engine vacuum	· Adjust or repair engine
Grabbing brakes (severe reaction to brake pedal pressure.)	· Brakelining(s) contaminated by grease or brake fluid	· Determine and correct cause of contamination and replace brakeshoes in axle sets
	· Parking brake cables incorrectly adjusted or seized	· Adjust cables. Replace seized cables.
	· Incorrect brakelining or lining loose on brakeshoes	· Replace brakeshoes in axle sets
	· Caliper anchor plate bolts loose	· Tighten bolts
	· Rear brakeshoes binding on support plate ledges	· Clean and lubricate ledges. Replace support plate(s) if ledges are deeply grooved. Do not attempt to smooth ledges by grinding.
	· Incorrect or missing power brake reaction disc	· Install correct disc
	· Rear brake support plates loose	· Tighten mounting bolts
Dragging brakes (slow or incomplete release of brakes)	· Brake pedal binding at pivot	· Loosen and lubricate
	· Power brake unit has internal bind	· Inspect for internal bind. Replace unit if internal bind exists.
	· Parking brake cables incorrrectly adjusted or seized	· Adjust cables. Replace seized cables.
	· Rear brakeshoe return springs weak or broken	· Replace return springs. Replace brakeshoe if necessary in axle sets.
	· Automatic adjusters malfunctioning	· Repair or replace adjuster parts as required
	· Caliper, wheel cylinder or master cylinder pistons sticking or seized	· Repair or replace parts as necessary
	· Master cylinder compensating ports blocked (fluid does not return to reservoirs).	· Use compressed air to clear ports. Do not use wire, pencils, or similar objects to open blocked ports.
Vehicle moves to one side when brakes are applied	· Incorrect front tire pressure	· Inflate to recommended cold (reduced load) inflation pressure
	· Worn or damaged wheel bearings	· Replace worn or damaged bearings
	· Brakelining on one side contaminated	· Determine and correct cause of contamination and replace brakelining in axle sets
	· Brakeshoes on one side bent, distorted, or lining loose on shoe	· Replace brakeshoes in axle sets
	· Support plate bent or loose on one side	· Tighten or replace support plate
	· Brakelining not yet seated with drums or rotors	· Burnish brakelining
	· Caliper anchor plate loose on one side	· Tighten anchor plate bolts
	· Caliper piston sticking or seized	· Repair or replace caliper
	· Brakelinings water soaked	· Drive vehicle with brakes lightly applied to dry linings
	· Loose suspension component attaching or mounting bolts	· Tighten suspension bolts. Replace worn suspension components.
	· Brake combination valve failure	· Replace combination valve
Chatter or shudder when brakes are applied (pedal pulsation and roughness may also occur.)	· Brakeshoes distorted, bent, contaminated, or worn	· Replace brakeshoes in axle sets
	· Caliper anchor plate or support plate loose	· Tighten mounting bolts
	· Excessive thickness variation of rotor(s)	· Refinish or replace rotors in axle sets

Troubleshooting the Brake System (cont.)

Problem	Cause	Solution
Noisy brakes (squealing, clicking, scraping sound when brakes are applied.)	• Bent, broken, distorted brakeshoes • Excessive rust on outer edge of rotor braking surface • Brakelining worn out—shoes contacting drum of rotor • Broken or loose holdown or return springs • Rough or dry drum brake support plate ledges • Cracked, grooved, or scored rotor(s) or drum(s) • Incorrect brakelining and/or shoes (front or rear).	• Replace brakeshoes in axle sets • Remove rust • Replace brakeshoes and lining in axle sets. Refinish or replace drums or rotors. • Replace parts as necessary • Lubricate support plate ledges • Replace rotor(s) or drum(s). Replace brakeshoes and lining in axle sets if necessary. • Install specified shoe and lining assemblies
Pulsating brake pedal	• Out of round drums or excessive lateral runout in disc brake rotor(s)	• Refinish or replace drums, re-index rotors or replace

EXTERIOR
  DOORS 10-2
  FENDERS 10-6
  FRONT BUMPER 10-5
  FRONT CROSSMEMBER
    COVER 10-7
  GRILLE 10-5
  HARDTOP 10-6
  HOOD 10-2
  LIFTGATE 10-4
  REAR BUMPER 10-5
  SOFT TOP 10-6
  SWING-OUT SPARE TIRE
    CARRIER 10-7
  TAILGATE 10-4
INTERIOR
  DOOR GLASS 10-9
  DOOR HINGES 10-8
  DOOR LOCK 10-8
  DOOR TRIM PANEL 10-8
  LIFTGATE GLASS 10-13
  SEATS 10-13
  STATIONARY WINDOW GLASS 10-12
  STRIKER PLATE 10-9
  WINDOW REGULATOR 10-10
  WINDSHIELD FRAME 10-10
  WINDSHIELD GLASS 10-10
SPECIFICATIONS CHARTS
  HOW TO REMOVE STAINS FROM
    FABRIC INTERIOR 10-15

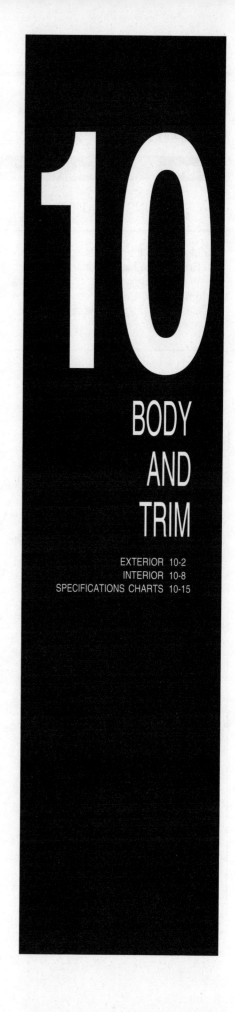

10
BODY AND TRIM

EXTERIOR 10-2
INTERIOR 10-8
SPECIFICATIONS CHARTS 10-15

10-2 BODY AND TRIM

EXTERIOR

► See Figures 1, 2 and 3

Doors

REMOVAL & INSTALLATION

1. Matchmark the hinge-to-door position.
2. Remove the hinge-to-door screws and lift off the door.
3. When installing the door, install the fasteners but don't fully tighten them. Move the door to obtain a satisfactory fit when closed, then tighten the screws.

Hood

REMOVAL & INSTALLATION

► See Figure 4

1. Matchmark the hinges and mounting panels.
2. Disconnect the underhood light wire.
3. Unbolt the hood from the hinges.
4. Remove the hood prop rod, prop rod retainer clip, side catch brackets, windshield bumpers and footman loop.
5. Assembly and installation is the reverse of removal and disassembly. Check hood alignment

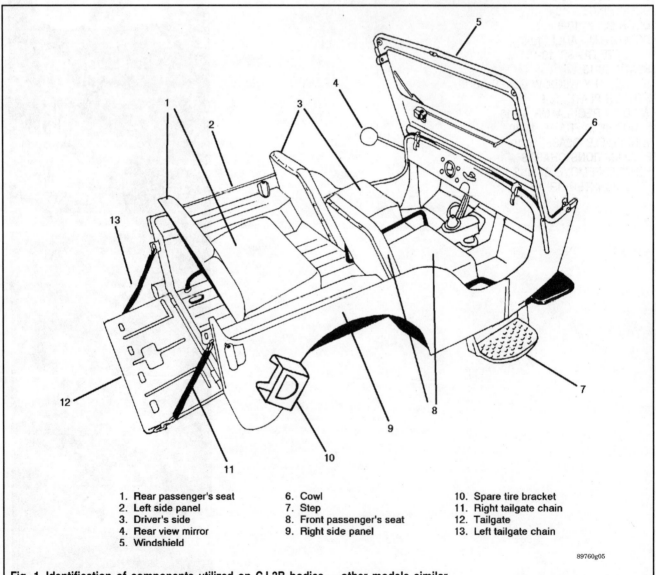

1. Rear passenger's seat
2. Left side panel
3. Driver's side
4. Rear view mirror
5. Windshield
6. Cowl
7. Step
8. Front passenger's seat
9. Right side panel
10. Spare tire bracket
11. Right tailgate chain
12. Tailgate
13. Left tailgate chain

Fig. 1 Identification of components utilized on CJ-3B bodies — other models similar

A-B: 44.31" (1125.474mm)
C-D: 48.48" (1231.392mm)
Front Width: 29.25" (742.95mm)
Rear Width: 29.25" (742.95mm)
E: 3.21875" (81.756mm)
F: 4.15625" (130.989mm)
Overall Length: 122.65625" (3115.4687mm)

89760g19

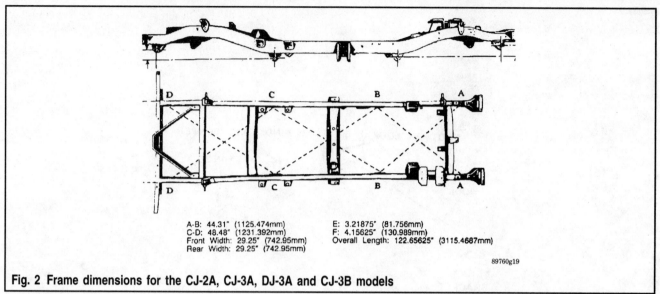

Fig. 2 Frame dimensions for the CJ-2A, CJ-3A, DJ-3A and CJ-3B models

A: 12.51" (317.754mm)
B: 17.50" (444.500mm)
C: 5.20" (132.080mm)
D: 12.19" (309.626mm)
E: 15.73" (399.542mm)
F: 14.57" (370.078mm)
G: 40.61" (1031.494mm)
H: 46.16" (1172.464mm)
J: 43.50" (1104.900mm)
K: 31.26" (794.004mm)
M: 41.52" (1054.608mm)
N: 37.84" (961.136mm)
P: 9.39" (238.506mm)
Q: 13.75" (349.250mm)
R: 27.50" (698.500mm)
S: 39.06" (992.124mm)

89760g20

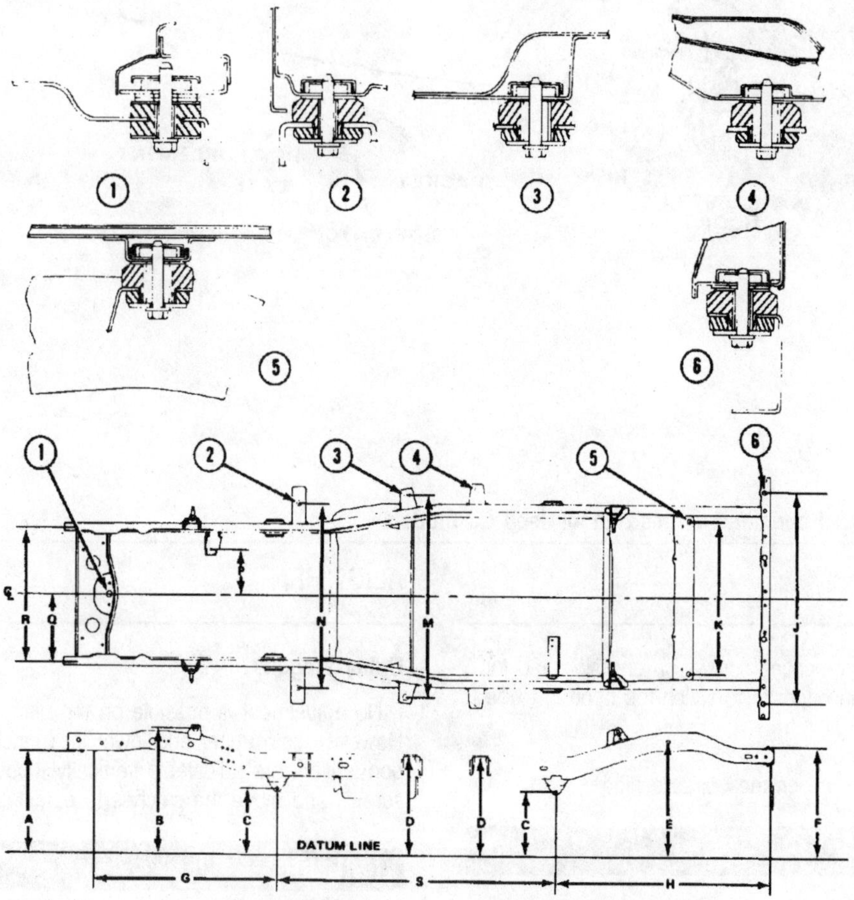

Fig. 3 Frame dimensions for late CJ-5 models

10-4 BODY AND TRIM

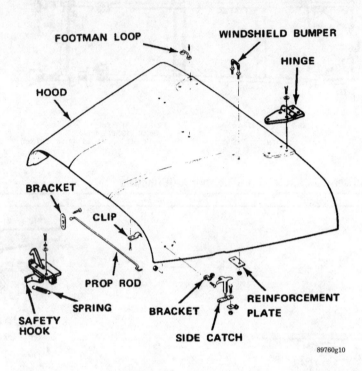

Fig. 4 Hood and related components used on all Jeep CJ models

ALIGNMENT

1. Loosen the hinge mounting screws on one side and tap the hinge in the direction opposite to which the hood is to be moved.
2. Tighten the screws.
3. Repeat this procedure on the opposite hinge.

Liftgate

REMOVAL & INSTALLATION

Utility Wagons

1. Matchmark the support prop-to-liftgate position.
2. Unbolt the support props from the liftgate.
3. Unbolt the liftgate hinge from the body.
4. Installation is the reverse of removal.

ALIGNMENT

Utility Wagons

No adjustment is possible on the piano-type liftgate hinges. However, both upper and lower lock catches mounted on the body pillars are adjustable vertically. Loosen the mounting screws and move the catches to obtain a satisfactory fit.

Tailgate

REMOVAL & INSTALLATION

Except Utility Wagons
▶ See Figure 5

1. Open the tailgate to the 45° position and disengage the right hinge.
2. Open it a bit more and disengage the left hinge.

BODY AND TRIM   10-5

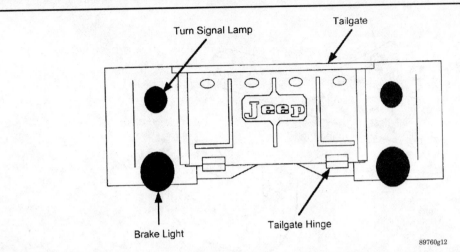

Fig. 5 The tailgate used on late CJ-5 and CJ-6 models is fastened to the body by 2 hinges on the bottom — this tailgate differs very little from that used on earlier models

3. Installation is the reverse of removal. Alignment is accomplished by moving the hinges.

Utility Wagons

1. Matchmark the support prop-to-tailgate position.
2. Unbolt the support props from the liftgate.
3. Unbolt the liftgate hinge from the body.
4. Installation is the reverse of removal. Alignment is accomplished by loosening the catches and moving them to obtain a satisfactory fit.

Front Bumper

REMOVAL & INSTALLATION

Except Utility Models
♦ See Figure 6

1. Remove any auxiliary lighting.

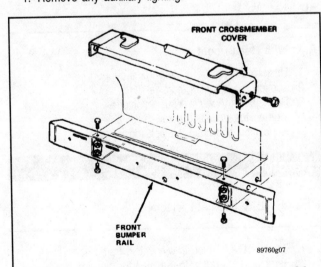

Fig. 6 Typical mounting for front bumpers used on CJ models

2. Remove the bolts and nuts attaching the bumper to the frame extensions.
3. Remove the bumper.
4. Installation is the reverse of removal.

Rear Bumper

REMOVAL & INSTALLATION

Except Utility Models
♦ See Figure 7

1. Remove the nuts and bolts attaching the bumper(s) to the frame.
2. Remove the bumper(s).
3. Installation is the reverse of removal.

Grille

REMOVAL & INSTALLATION

Except Utility Models
♦ See Figure 8

1. Remove the front crossmember cover, if so equipped.
2. Remove the screws securing the radiator and shroud to the radiator grille guard panel.
3. Remove the bolts securing the guard panel to the fenders.
4. Remove the grille-to-frame crossmember hold-down assembly, keeping track of the sequence of parts.
5. Loosen the radiator support rods-to-grille guard support bracket nuts.
6. Remove the rods from the brackets.
7. Tilt the grille panel forward and disengage the electrical wiring at the headlamp sealed beam unit and parking lamp assembly wiring harness at the connectors.
8. Lift the grille from the vehicle.

10-6 BODY AND TRIM

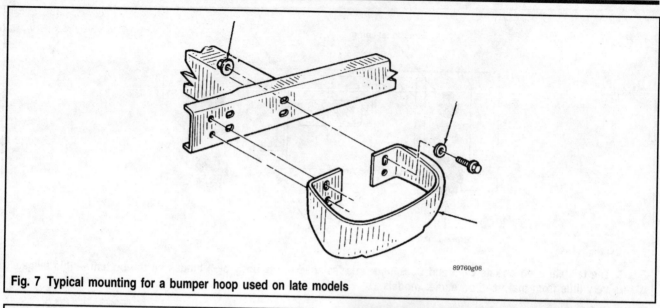

Fig. 7 Typical mounting for a bumper hoop used on late models

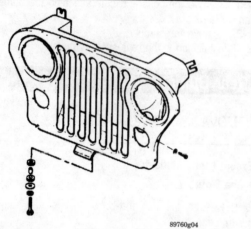

Fig. 8 The front grille is mounted with small screws around the side and top perimeter, and with a larger bolt on the bottom

To install:
9. Position the grille panel and attach the electrical wiring at the headlamp sealed beam unit and parking lamp assembly wiring harness at the connectors.
10. Install the rods on the brackets.
11. Tighten the radiator support rods-to-grille guard support bracket nuts.
12. Install the grille-to-frame crossmember hold-down assembly.
13. Install the bolts securing the guard panel to the fenders.
14. Install the screws securing the radiator and shroud to the radiator grille guard panel.
15. Install the front crossmember cover, if so equipped.

Fenders

REMOVAL & INSTALLATION

Except Utility Models

1. Remove or disconnect all items attached to the fender apron.
2. Disconnect the wiring at the marker light.
3. Remove the rocker panel molding.
4. Remove the bolts attaching the fender and brace to the firewall.
5. Remove the bolts attaching the fender to the grille panel.
6. Pull the fender out and lift it from the Jeep.
7. Installation is the reverse of removal.

Soft Top

ADJUSTMENT

Tops With Metal Doors

1. Unsnap the top from the vertical support blade.
2. Loosen the adjusting screws.
3. Reposition the vertical support blade.
4. Tighten the adjusting screws.
5. Reposition and snap the soft top into place.

Hardtop

REMOVAL & INSTALLATION

1. Remove the hardtop-to-windshield frame screws.
2. Remove the hardtop-to-rear quarter panel bolts.
3. Disconnect the dome lamp.

BODY AND TRIM 10-7

4. Lift the top from the Jeep, being careful to avoid damage to the foam seals.
5. Installation is the reverse of removal.

Front Crossmember Cover

REMOVAL & INSTALLATION

Except Utility Models

1. Remove the nuts and bolts attaching the crossmember to the frame.
2. Remove the crossmember.
3. Installation is the reverse of removal.

Swing-Out Spare Tire Carrier

REMOVAL & INSTALLATION

▶ See Figure 9

1. Remove the tire from the carrier.
2. Remove the hinge pin nuts and bolts.
3. Support the carrier. Unlatch the handle from the latch bracket and remove the carrier and hinge spacer washers.
4. Remove the pin attaching the latch handle to the carrier and remove the handle, spring and washer.
5. Installation is the reverse of removal.

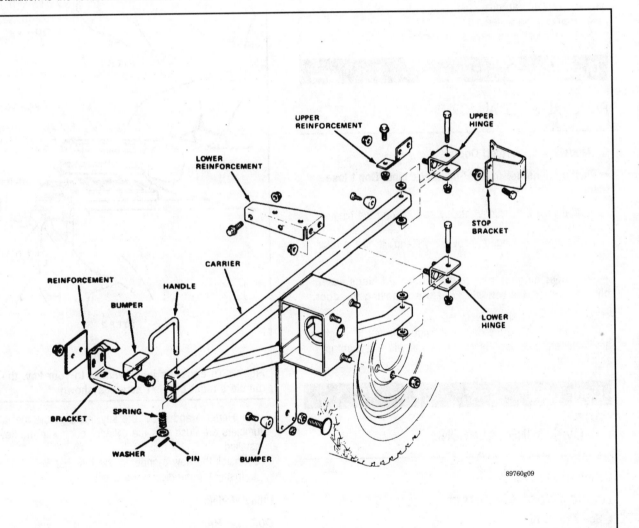

Fig. 9 Exploded view of the swing-out spare tire carrier

10-8 BODY AND TRIM

INTERIOR

Door Trim Panel

REMOVAL & INSTALLATION

Utility and CJ Hardtop Models

1. Remove the door handle.
2. Remove the window crank handle.
3. Carefully pry the trim panel clips from the door. Be very careful! It's very easy to tear the trim panel or tear loose the clip from the panel. Inexpensive tools are made for this job and are available at most auto parts stores.
4. Remove the watershield.
5. Installation is the reverse of removal.

Door Hinges

REMOVAL & INSTALLATION

CJ Models with Hardtop Doors

➡ Plastic shims are used at the hinge pins. Don't lose them!

1. Matchmark the hinge-to-body position and the hinge-to-door position.
2. Remove the hinge-to-body screws and lift off the door assembly.

➡ The upper hinge is part of the windshield hinge assembly, so support the windshield before removing the door.

3. Remove the hinges from the door.
4. When installing the door and hinges, do not fully tighten any fasteners until door, hinge and windshield alignment is satisfactory.

Door Lock

REMOVAL & INSTALLATION

CJ Hardtop

LOCK CYLINDER AND OUTSIDE HANDLE

♦ See Figure 10

➡ Replacement outside handles come without the lock cylinder. Replacement lock cylinders come uncoded, without keys.

1. Unbolt and remove the handle from the door.
2. To code your existing key to a replacement cylinder:
   a. Insert your key in the new cylinder.
   b. File the tumblers until they are flush with the cylinder body.

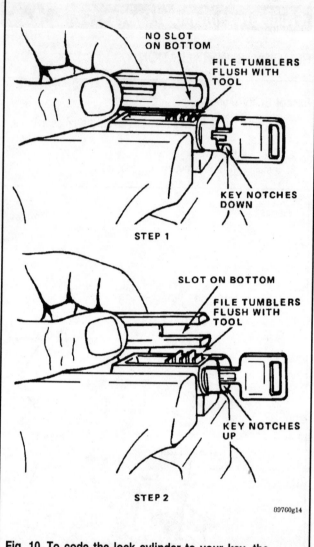

Fig. 10 To code the lock cylinder to your key, the tumblers must be filed down as shown

   c. Remove and install the key, making sure that all the tumblers are flush with the cylinder body with the key installed.
3. Install the new cylinder in the new handle.
4. Install the handle on the door.

Utility Models

OUTSIDE HANDLE

1. Remove the handle retaining screw from the door edge.
2. Raise the glass to the full up position.
3. Unsnap the door trim panel from the corner of the door, just enough to reach behind it and remove the retaining nut.
4. Remove the handle.
5. Installation is the reverse of removal.

LOCK CYLINDER

1. Raise the glass to the full up position.

BODY AND TRIM 10-9

2. Press inward on the window handle trim ring and remove the handle retaining pin.
3. Remove the crank handle.
4. Remove the arm rest.
5. Unsnap the trim panel. Be very careful! The trim panel is easily torn when prying at the retaining snaps.
6. Unscrew the lock button.
7. Remove the two lower glass channel screws from the door edge.
8. Lock the door by turning the forked latch to the vertical position.
9. Remove the 3 lock control attaching screws from the door panel.
10. Remove the 4 lock assembly-to-door edge screws and remove the lock assembly.
11. Installation is the reverse of removal.

DOOR LOCK ADJUSTMENT

Utility Models
♦ See Figure 11

Should the outside door handle fail to release the lock easily, it is usually due to the trigger in the handle failing to release the lock until it is nearly flush with the handle. This is due to wear or a bent release lever on the lock assembly. To correct this problem, perform the following:
1. Remove the door trim panel.
2. Remove the outside door handle.
3. Close and lock the door with the button.
4. Working through the door handle hole, measure the distance from the outside face of the sheet metal to the lock release lever.
5. On the door handle, measure the distance from the edge of the handle casing to the tip of the boss on the trigger striker lever.
6. Subtract the two measurements. The result will be the amount that the lever boss must be built up. Brazing is an acceptable way to restore the lost metal. Add slightly more than necessary and file it down to the correct dimension.

7. Lubricate the working parts, install the handle and check lock operation.

Striker Plate

ADJUSTMENT

♦ See Figure 12

To prevent the door's opening in the safety latched position, the door striker wedge must be properly positioned in relation to the cam surface of the lock toggle. Improper safety latch positioning will permit the toggle to override the striker pin, causing the door to open. The striker must be positioned so that the door lock toggle will be held securely in engagement with the striker pin.
1. Position a brass drift against the upper inside edge of the striker plate.
2. Using a heavy hammer, drive the striker plate outward until the wedge end of the plate firmly contacts the cam surface of the lock toggle, exerting enough pressure to prevent the toggle from over-riding the striker pin.
3. Make several checks of the safety latch operation until it is satisfactory.
4. Securely tighten the striker plate-to-pillar screws after the adjustment.

Door Glass

REMOVAL & INSTALLATION

CJ Hardtop Models
1. Remove the door handle.
2. Remove the window crank handle.
3. Carefully pry the trim panel clips from the door. Be very careful! It's very easy to tear the trim panel or tear loose the clip from the panel. Inexpensive tools are made for this job and are available at most auto parts stores.

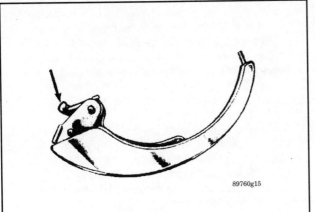

Fig. 11 When adjusting the door lock, measure the distance from the edge of of the handle casing to the tip of the boss on the trigger striker lever (arrow)

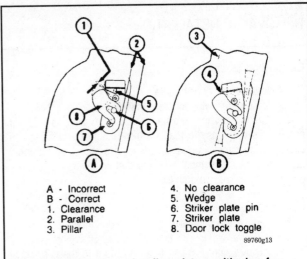

A - Incorrect
B - Correct
1. Clearance
2. Parallel
3. Pillar
4. No clearance
5. Wedge
6. Striker plate pin
7. Striker plate
8. Door lock toggle

Fig. 12 Lock toggle and striker plate positioning for Utility models

10-10 BODY AND TRIM

4. Remove the watershield.
5. Remove the glass down-stop.
6. Remove the guide panel-to-plastic fastener screws.
7. Remove the guide channel and plastic fasteners.
8. Remove the division channel upper attaching screw and lower adjusting screw.
9. Disengage the front 3 in. (76mm) of weatherstripping from the upper door frame.
10. Remove the division channel.
11. Tilt the glass toward the hinge side of the door and disengage it from the rear channel.
12. Pull the glass up and out of the door.

To install:
13. Insert the glass into the door with the front tilted down, while engaging the rear channel.
14. Install the plastic fasteners on the glass.
15. Lower the glass to the bottom of the door.
16. Lower the division channel into the door and position the glass in the channel.
17. Install the upper attaching screw and lower adjusting screw.
18. Install the weatherstripping.
19. Slide the guide channel on the regulator arm and position the channel on the glass. Install the screws.
20. Install the glass down-stop.
21. Make sure that the window works properly.
22. Install the watershield.
23. Install the trim panel and handles.

Utility Models

1. Remove the door trim panel.
2. Remove the garnish molding from around the glass.
3. Loosen the glass run channel and remove the regulator control arms from the channel., mounted on the bottom of the glass, by removing the two hair pin type locks which retain the control arm buttons.
4. Remove the glass and runway as an assembly, through the window opening.
5. Installation is the reverse of removal.

Window Regulator

REMOVAL & INSTALLATION

CJ Hardtop Models

1. Remove the door handle.
2. Remove the window crank handle.
3. Carefully pry the trim panel clips from the door. Be very careful! It's very easy to tear the trim panel or tear loose the clip from the panel. Inexpensive tools are made for this job and are available at most auto parts stores.
4. Remove the watershield.
5. Lower the glass to gain access to the guide channel fasteners.
6. Remove the fasteners and guide channel.
7. Raise the window to thew full up position and secure it in position by using masking tape to tape it to the door frame.
8. Remove the division channel lower adjusting screw.
9. Remove the regulator attaching screws.
10. Push the division channel outward and remove the regulator through the access hole.
11. Installation is the reverse of removal.

Windshield Frame

REMOVAL & INSTALLATION

1. On early models, disconnect the wiper vacuum hose from the vacuum motor.
2. On later models, disconnect the wiring from the electric wiper motor.
3. Unlatch the clamps on each side of the windshield.
4. Tilt the windshield forward until the slot in each hinge aligns with the flat side of the pin in the body hinges.
5. Pull the windshield frame off the pins and remove it from the body.
6. Installation is the reverse of the removal procedure.

Windshield Glass

REMOVAL & INSTALLATION

Utility Models

WITH TWO-PIECE WINDSHIELD

➡ To replace either side of the glass or both glass sections, their common frame must first be removed.

1. Remove the cover plate from the center bar garnish molding.
2. Remove the mirror bracket plate.
3. Remove the center bar.
4. Remove the outer cover panel.
5. Remove the two garnish moldings.
6. Have an assistant support the windshield assembly from the inside, while you, working on the outside, force the rubber molding off the body flange with a wooden spatula. Start at the top center and press inward while prying off the molding, to prevent it from slipping back over the flange.
7. Remove the pane of glass to be replaced, by working the rubber channel over the edge of the glass. It may be necessary to break the cement seal with a prytool.

To install:
8. Thoroughly clean and inspect the weatherstripping. Replace it if it is worn, cracked or brittle.
9. Apply a $1/16$ in. (1.6mm) bead of 3M Auto Bedding and Glazing Compound, or equivalent, completely around the weatherstripping in the glass cavity.
10. Install the weatherstripping on the glass.
11. Install the glass in the frame, working the rubber weatherstripping into position.
12. Mix a soap and water solution and thoroughly coat the body flange and the rubber weatherstripping with it.
13. Place a $1/16$-$1/8$ in. (1.580-3.175mm) diameter cord in the flange cavity of the weatherstripping, completely around the circumference. You will need at least 8 ft. (2.43m) of string.

BODY AND TRIM 10-11

Let the ends of the cord hang outside the glass at the upper center.

14. Position the glass frame and weatherstripping in the opening. Pull on the ends of the cord to pull the lip of the weatherstripping over the body flange.

15. Use a wood spatula to lock the weatherstripping.

16. Apply a bead of 3M Windshield Sealer, or equivalent, between the weatherstripping and the body flange, around its entire perimeter. Clean off the excess.

WITH ONE-PIECE WINDSHIELD

♦ See Figure 13

1. Unscrew and remove the garnish molding covers.
2. Remove the garnish moldings.
3. If the vehicle is equipped with a heater, there are rubber plugs under the garnish molding at each side of the defroster openings. Save the plugs.
4. Using a wood spatula, unlock the rubber weatherstripping.
5. Carefully remove the windshield and discard the weatherstripping.

6. Apply a 1/16 in. (1.58mm) bead of 3M Auto Bedding and Glazing Compound, or equivalent, completely around hem flange groove of the new weatherstripping.

7. Install the weatherstripping on the hem flange with the weatherstripping lock facing outside.

8. Install the filler tubing beneath the weatherstripping lip, facing inside. Locate the 6 in. (15.2cm) long piece of tubing at the top center of the windshield opening. Locate the 32 in. (81.3cm) long piece of tubing along the bottom edge of the windshield opening with the ends of the tubing extending beyond the defroster openings in the instrument panel. Install these pieces of tubing **before** installing the windshield glass.

9. With the weatherstripping unlocked, install the windshield glass in the glass groove of the weatherstripping. Fill the glass groove with a 1/16 in. (1.58mm) bead of 3M Auto Bedding and Glazing Compound, or equivalent.

10. Lock the weatherstripping into place with a wood spatula. Remove all excess sealer.

11. Install the garnish moldings, molding covers and defroster rubber plugs. The 1½ in. long screws are used along the top; the 1¼ in. long screws along the sides and bottom.

12. If a different type of garnish molding was used, new garnish molding screw holes must be drilled before the molding can be installed. Use the new moldings as templates as follows:

    a. Position the moldings on the door pillars with the moldings as far as possible to the rear.
    b. Drill three 1/8 in. (3mm) diameter holes into each pillar and loosely attach the moldings with the screws.
    c. Position the ends of the moldings at both the top and bottom center of the windshield opening with dimension A, in the accompanying illustration, 1/8-3/16 in. (3-5mm).
    d. Drill seven 1/8 in. (3mm) diameter holes in the header rail and nine 1/8 in. (3mm) diameter holes in the instrument panel.
    e. Install the garnish moldings as instructed in Step 11.

CJ Models

1945-52 VEHICLES

1. Remove the screws on each side of the windshield adjusting bracket at the top.
2. Bend down the lip on the left-hand outer end of the hinge at the top.
3. Open the windshield just enough to clear the frame and slide the assembly out of the hinge to the left.
4. Unbolt the upper glass channel from the frame and remove it.
5. Remove the glass from the frame.
6. Installation is the reverse of removal. Use new tape on the glass.

1953-70 VEHICLES

♦ See Figures 14, 15 and 16

1. Cover all adjoining painted surfaces.
2. Remove the wiper arms.
3. Remove the rear view mirror from its bracket.
4. Remove the sun visors.
5. Disconnect the defroster ducts.
6. Have someone support the glass from the outside. Starting at the top, pull the weatherstripping away from the flange

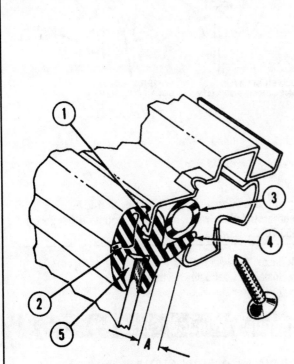

1. Hem flange groove
2. Weatherstripping lock
3. Filler tubing
4. Weatherstripping lip
5. Glass groove

Fig. 13 Cross-section of the weatherstripping, windshield and mounting flange used on Utility models equipped with one-piece windshields

10-12 BODY AND TRIM

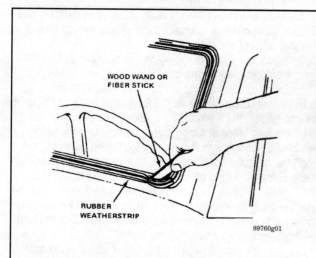

Fig. 14 It may be necessary to use a wooden tool to break the old windshield weatherstripping seal

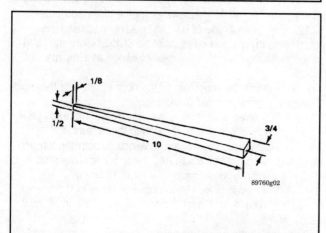

Fig. 15 The wooden tool used to break the windshield weatherstripping seal can be fashioned from a piece of wood to the dimensions shown

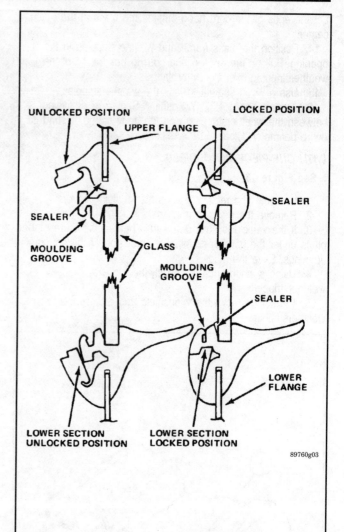

Fig. 16 Cross-section of the upper and lower weatherstripping, windshield and mounting flange on 1953-70 CJ models

while gently pushing out on the glass. It may be necessary to break the sealer by prying with a wood spatula.

  7. Work the entire weatherstripping from the flange to remove the glass.
  8. Thoroughly clean and inspect the weatherstripping. Replace it if it is worn, cracked or brittle.

To install:

  9. Apply a ¹⁄₁₆ in. (1.5mm) diameter bead of 3M Auto Bedding and Glazing Compound, or equivalent, completely around the weatherstripping in the flange cavity.
  10. Install the weatherstripping on the glass. The split should be at the bottom center.
  11. Position the glass and weatherstripping in the frame, and, beginning at the bottom, work the weatherstripping over the flange with a wood spatula or fiber stick.
  12. When the glass is installed, apply a bead of 3M Windshield Sealer, or equivalent, between the glass and the weatherstripping on the outside. Clean off the excess.
  13. Install the mirror.
  14. Install the wiper arms.
  15. Install the defroster ducts.
  16. Install the sun visors.

Stationary Window Glass

REMOVAL & INSTALLATION

Utility and CJ Hardtop Models

  1. Unlock the weatherstripping from the hardtop with a wood spatula or fiber stick.
  2. Using a fiber stick, break the seal between the glass and weatherstripping.
  3. Push the glass and weatherstripping outward and remove it.
  4. Inspect the weatherstripping. Replace it if cracked or otherwise damaged. Clean all old sealer from the glass and weatherstripping.

5. Apply a ⁹⁄₁₆ in. (5mm) bead of 3M Auto Bedding and Glazing Compound, or equivalent, in the weatherstripping glass cavity, using a pressure applicator.

6. Install the glass in the weatherstripping.

7. Place a ¼ in. (6mm) cord in the flange cavity of the weatherstripping, completely around the circumference. Let the ends of the cord hang outside the glass at the upper center.

8. Position the glass and weatherstripping in the opening. Pull on the ends of the cord to pull the lip of the weatherstripping over the hardtop flange.

9. Use a wood spatula to lock the weatherstripping.

10. Apply a bead of 3M Windshield Sealer, or equivalent, between the weatherstripping and the glass, around its entire perimeter. Clean off excess sealer.

Liftgate Glass

REMOVAL & INSTALLATION

Utility Hardtop Models

1. Unlock the weatherstripping from the hardtop with a wood spatula or fiber stick.

2. Using a plastic or wooden stick, break the seal between the glass and weatherstripping.

3. Push the glass and weatherstripping outward and remove it.

4. Inspect the weatherstripping. Replace it if cracked or otherwise damaged. Clean all old sealer from the glass and weatherstripping.

5. Apply a ⁹⁄₁₆ in. (5mm) bead of 3M Auto Bedding and Glazing Compound, or equivalent, in the weatherstripping glass cavity, using a pressure applicator.

6. Install the glass in the weatherstripping.

7. Place a ¼ in. (6mm) cord in the flange cavity of the weatherstripping, completely around the circumference. Let the ends of the cord hang outside the glass at the upper center.

8. Position the glass and weatherstripping in the opening. Pull on the ends of the cord to pull the lip of the weatherstripping over the hardtop flange.

9. Use a wood spatula to lock the weatherstripping.

10. Apply a bead of 3M Windshield Sealer, or equivalent, between the weatherstripping and the glass, around its entire perimeter. Clean off any excess sealer.

Seats

REMOVAL & INSTALLATION

Front and Rear
▶ See Figures 17, 18, 19 and 20

1. Unbolt the seat frame from the floor pan.

2. Remove the seat.

3. Installation is the reverse of removal. Tighten the bolts to 15 ft. lbs. (20 Nm).

➡ The seat pivot bolts on Utility models may work loose unless they are properly installed. Proper installation is with the bolt head next to the seat leg, not the pivot bracket. The flat washer should be next to the seat leg.

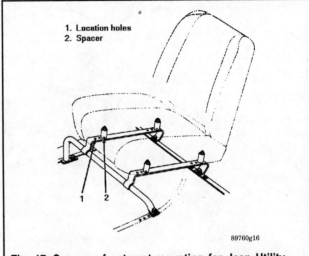

Fig. 17 Common front seat mounting for Jeep Utility models

Fig. 18 Common mounting for rear seats used on CJ models

10-14 BODY AND TRIM

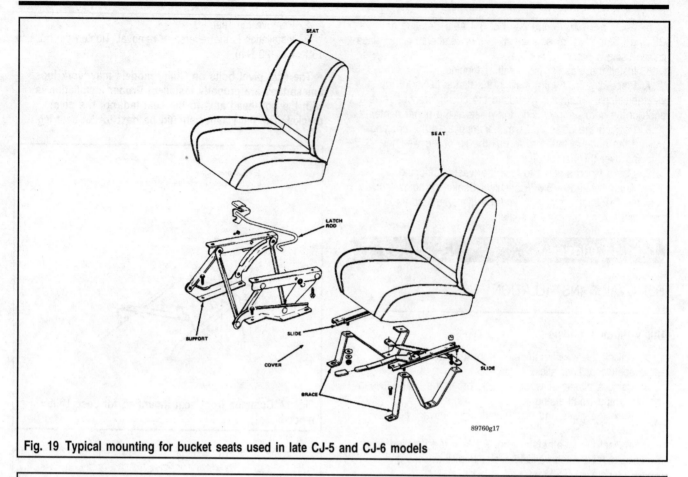

Fig. 19 Typical mounting for bucket seats used in late CJ-5 and CJ-6 models

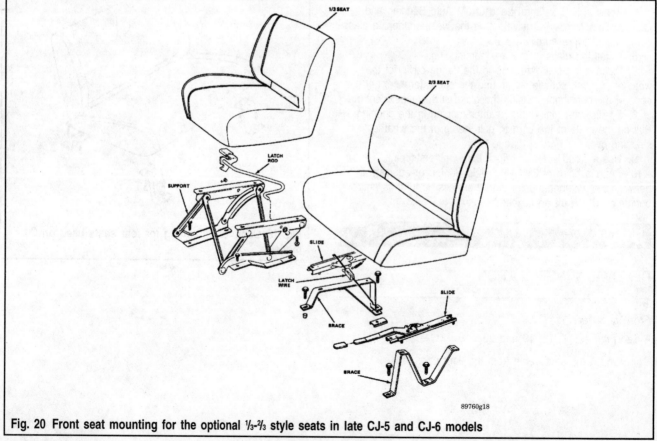

Fig. 20 Front seat mounting for the optional ⅓-⅔ style seats in late CJ-5 and CJ-6 models

BODY AND TRIM

How to Remove Stains from Fabric Interior

For rest results, spots and stains should be removed as soon as possible. Never use gasoline, lacquer thinner, acetone, nail polish remover or bleach. Use a 3' x 3" piece of cheesecloth. Squeeze most of the liquid from the fabric and wipe the stained fabric from the outside of the stain toward the center with a lifting motion. Turn the cheesecloth as soon as one side becomes soiled. When using water to remove a stain, be sure to wash the entire section after the spot has been removed to avoid water stains. Encrusted spots can be broken up with a dull knife and vacuumed before removing the stain.

Type of Stain	How to Remove It
Surface spots	Brush the spots out with a small hand brush or use a commercial preparation such as K2R to lift the stain.
Mildew	Clean around the mildew with warm suds. Rinse in cold water and soak the mildew area in a solution of 1 part table salt and 2 parts water. Wash with upholstery cleaner.
Water stains	Water stains in fabric materials can be removed with a solution made from 1 cup of table salt dissolved in 1 quart of water. Vigorously scrub the solution into the stain and rinse with clear water. Water stains in nylon or other synthetic fabrics should be removed with a commercial type spot remover.
Chewing gum, tar, crayons, shoe polish (greasy stains)	Do not use a cleaner that will soften gum or tar. Harden the deposit with an ice cube and scrape away as much as possible with a dull knife. Moisten the remainder with cleaning fluid and scrub clean.
Ice cream, candy	Most candy has a sugar base and can be removed with a cloth wrung out in warm water. Oily candy, after cleaning with warm water, should be cleaned with upholstery cleaner. Rinse with warm water and clean the remainder with cleaning fluid.
Wine, alcohol, egg, milk, soft drink (non-greasy stains)	Do not use soap. Scrub the stain with a cloth wrung out in warm water. Remove the remainder with cleaning fluid.
Grease, oil, lipstick, butter and related stains	Use a spot remover to avoid leaving a ring. Work from the outside of the stain to the center and dry with a clean cloth when the spot is gone.
Headliners (cloth)	Mix a solution of warm water and foam upholstery cleaner to give thick suds. Use only foam—liquid may streak or spot. Clean the entire headliner in one operation using a circular motion with a natural sponge.
Headliner (vinyl)	Use a vinyl cleaner with a sponge and wipe clean with a dry cloth.
Seats and door panels	Mix 1 pint upholstery cleaner in 1 gallon of water. Do not soak the fabric around the buttons.
Leather or vinyl fabric	Use a multi-purpose cleaner full strength and a stiff brush. Let stand 2 minutes and scrub thoroughly. Wipe with a clean, soft rag.
Nylon or synthetic fabrics	For normal stains, use the same procedures you would for washing cloth upholstery. If the fabric is extremely dirty, use a multi-purpose cleaner full strength with a stiff scrub brush. Scrub thoroughly in all directions and wipe with a cotton towel or soft rag.

GLOSSARY

AIR/FUEL RATIO: The ratio of air-to-gasoline by weight in the fuel mixture drawn into the engine.

AIR INJECTION: One method of reducing harmful exhaust emissions by injecting air into each of the exhaust ports of an engine. The fresh air entering the hot exhaust manifold causes any remaining fuel to be burned before it can exit the tailpipe.

ALTERNATOR: A device used for converting mechanical energy into electrical energy.

AMMETER: An instrument, calibrated in amperes, used to measure the flow of an electrical current in a circuit. Ammeters are always connected in series with the circuit being tested.

AMPERE: The rate of flow of electrical current present when one volt of electrical pressure is applied against one ohm of electrical resistance.

ANALOG COMPUTER: Any microprocessor that uses similar (analogous) electrical signals to make its calculations.

ARMATURE: A laminated, soft iron core wrapped by a wire that converts electrical energy to mechanical energy as in a motor or relay. When rotated in a magnetic field, it changes mechanical energy into electrical energy as in a generator.

ATMOSPHERIC PRESSURE: The pressure on the Earth's surface caused by the weight of the air in the atmosphere. At sea level, this pressure is 14.7 psi at 32°F (101 kPa at 0°C).

ATOMIZATION: The breaking down of a liquid into a fine mist that can be suspended in air.

AXIAL PLAY: Movement parallel to a shaft or bearing bore.

BACKFIRE: The sudden combustion of gases in the intake or exhaust system that results in a loud explosion.

BACKLASH: The clearance or play between two parts, such as meshed gears.

BACKPRESSURE: Restrictions in the exhaust system that slow the exit of exhaust gases from the combustion chamber.

BAKELITE: A heat resistant, plastic insulator material commonly used in printed circuit boards and transistorized components.

BALL BEARING: A bearing made up of hardened inner and outer races between which hardened steel balls roll.

BALLAST RESISTOR: A resistor in the primary ignition circuit that lowers voltage after the engine is started to reduce wear on ignition components.

BEARING: A friction reducing, supportive device usually located between a stationary part and a moving part.

BIMETAL TEMPERATURE SENSOR: Any sensor or switch made of two dissimilar types of metal that bend when heated or cooled due to the different expansion rates of the alloys. These types of sensors usually function as an on/off switch.

BLOWBY: Combustion gases, composed of water vapor and unburned fuel, that leak past the piston rings into the crankcase during normal engine operation. These gases are removed by the PCV system to prevent the buildup of harmful acids in the crankcase.

BRAKE PAD: A brake shoe and lining assembly used with disc brakes.

BRAKE SHOE: The backing for the brake lining. The term is, however, usually applied to the assembly of the brake backing and lining.

BUSHING: A liner, usually removable, for a bearing; an anti-friction liner used in place of a bearing.

CALIPER: A hydraulically activated device in a disc brake system, which is mounted straddling the brake rotor (disc). The caliper contains at least one piston and two brake pads. Hydraulic pressure on the piston(s) forces the pads against the rotor.

CAMSHAFT: A shaft in the engine on which are the lobes (cams) which operate the valves. The camshaft is driven by the crankshaft, via a belt, chain or gears, at one half the crankshaft speed.

CAPACITOR: A device which stores an electrical charge.

CARBON MONOXIDE (CO): A colorless, odorless gas given off as a normal byproduct of combustion. It is poisonous and extremely dangerous in confined areas, building up slowly to toxic levels without warning if adequate ventilation is not available.

CARBURETOR: A device, usually mounted on the intake manifold of an engine, which mixes the air and fuel in the proper proportion to allow even combustion.

CATALYTIC CONVERTER: A device installed in the exhaust system, like a muffler, that converts harmful byproducts of combustion into carbon dioxide and water vapor by means of a heat-producing chemical reaction.

CENTRIFUGAL ADVANCE: A mechanical method of advancing the spark timing by using flyweights in the distributor that react to centrifugal force generated by the distributor shaft rotation.

GLOSSARY 10-17

CHECK VALVE: Any one-way valve installed to permit the flow of air, fuel or vacuum in one direction only.

CHOKE: A device, usually a moveable valve, placed in the intake path of a carburetor to restrict the flow of air.

CIRCUIT: Any unbroken path through which an electrical current can flow. Also used to describe fuel flow in some instances.

CIRCUIT BREAKER: A switch which protects an electrical circuit from overload by opening the circuit when the current flow exceeds a predetermined level. Some circuit breakers must be reset manually, while most reset automatically.

COIL (IGNITION): A transformer in the ignition circuit which steps up the voltage provided to the spark plugs.

COMBINATION MANIFOLD: An assembly which includes both the intake and exhaust manifolds in one casting.

COMBINATION VALVE: A device used in some fuel systems that routes fuel vapors to a charcoal storage canister instead of venting them into the atmosphere. The valve relieves fuel tank pressure and allows fresh air into the tank as the fuel level drops to prevent a vapor lock situation.

COMPRESSION RATIO: The comparison of the total volume of the cylinder and combustion chamber with the piston at BDC and the piston at TDC.

CONDENSER: 1. An electrical device which acts to store an electrical charge, preventing voltage surges. 2. A radiator-like device in the air conditioning system in which refrigerant gas condenses into a liquid, giving off heat.

CONDUCTOR: Any material through which an electrical current can be transmitted easily.

CONTINUITY: Continuous or complete circuit. Can be checked with an ohmmeter.

COUNTERSHAFT: An intermediate shaft which is rotated by a mainshaft and transmits, in turn, that rotation to a working part.

CRANKCASE: The lower part of an engine in which the crankshaft and related parts operate.

CRANKSHAFT: The main driving shaft of an engine which receives reciprocating motion from the pistons and converts it to rotary motion.

CYLINDER: In an engine, the round hole in the engine block in which the piston(s) ride.

CYLINDER BLOCK: The main structural member of an engine in which is found the cylinders, crankshaft and other principal parts.

CYLINDER HEAD: The detachable portion of the engine, usually fastened to the top of the cylinder block and containing all or most of the combustion chambers. On overhead valve engines, it contains the valves and their operating parts. On overhead cam engines, it contains the camshaft as well.

DEAD CENTER: The extreme top or bottom of the piston stroke.

DETONATION: An unwanted explosion of the air/fuel mixture in the combustion chamber caused by excess heat and compression, advanced timing, or an overly lean mixture. Also referred to as "ping".

DIAPHRAGM: A thin, flexible wall separating two cavities, such as in a vacuum advance unit.

DIESELING: A condition in which hot spots in the combustion chamber cause the engine to run on after the key is turned off.

DIFFERENTIAL: A geared assembly which allows the transmission of motion between drive axles, giving one axle the ability to turn faster than the other.

DIODE: An electrical device that will allow current to flow in one direction only.

DISC BRAKE: A hydraulic braking assembly consisting of a brake disc, or rotor, mounted on an axle, and a caliper assembly containing, usually two brake pads which are activated by hydraulic pressure. The pads are forced against the sides of the disc, creating friction which slows the vehicle.

DISTRIBUTOR: A mechanically driven device on an engine which is responsible for electrically firing the spark plug at a predetermined point of the piston stroke.

DOWEL PIN: A pin, inserted in mating holes in two different parts allowing those parts to maintain a fixed relationship.

DRUM BRAKE: A braking system which consists of two brake shoes and one or two wheel cylinders, mounted on a fixed backing plate, and a brake drum, mounted on an axle, which revolves around the assembly.

DWELL: The rate, measured in degrees of shaft rotation, at which an electrical circuit cycles on and off.

ELECTRONIC CONTROL UNIT (ECU): Ignition module, module, amplifier or igniter. See Module for definition.

ELECTRONIC IGNITION: A system in which the timing and firing of the spark plugs is controlled by an electronic control unit, usually called a module. These systems have no points or condenser.

END-PLAY: The measured amount of axial movement in a shaft.

10-18 Glossary

ENGINE: A device that converts heat into mechanical energy.

EXHAUST MANIFOLD: A set of cast passages or pipes which conduct exhaust gases from the engine.

FEELER GAUGE: A blade, usually metal, of precisely predetermined thickness, used to measure the clearance between two parts.

FIRING ORDER: The order in which combustion occurs in the cylinders of an engine. Also the order in which spark is distributed to the plugs by the distributor.

FLOODING: The presence of too much fuel in the intake manifold and combustion chamber which prevents the air/fuel mixture from firing, thereby causing a no-start situation.

FLYWHEEL: A disc shaped part bolted to the rear end of the crankshaft. Around the outer perimeter is affixed the ring gear. The starter drive engages the ring gear, turning the flywheel, which rotates the crankshaft, imparting the initial starting motion to the engine.

FOOT POUND (ft. lbs. or sometimes, ft.lb.): The amount of energy or work needed to raise an item weighing one pound, a distance of one foot.

FUSE: A protective device in a circuit which prevents circuit overload by breaking the circuit when a specific amperage is present. The device is constructed around a strip or wire of a lower amperage rating than the circuit it is designed to protect. When an amperage higher than that stamped on the fuse is present in the circuit, the strip or wire melts, opening the circuit.

GEAR RATIO: The ratio between the number of teeth on meshing gears.

GENERATOR: A device which converts mechanical energy into electrical energy.

HEAT RANGE: The measure of a spark plug's ability to dissipate heat from its firing end. The higher the heat range, the hotter the plug fires.

HUB: The center part of a wheel or gear.

HYDROCARBON (HC): Any chemical compound made up of hydrogen and carbon. A major pollutant formed by the engine as a byproduct of combustion.

HYDROMETER: An instrument used to measure the specific gravity of a solution.

INCH POUND (inch lbs.; sometimes in.lb. or in. lbs.): One twelfth of a foot pound.

INDUCTION: A means of transferring electrical energy in the form of a magnetic field. Principle used in the ignition coil to increase voltage.

INJECTOR: A device which receives metered fuel under relatively low pressure and is activated to inject the fuel into the engine under relatively high pressure at a predetermined time.

INPUT SHAFT: The shaft to which torque is applied, usually carrying the driving gear or gears.

INTAKE MANIFOLD: A casting of passages or pipes used to conduct air or a fuel/air mixture to the cylinders.

JOURNAL: The bearing surface within which a shaft operates.

KEY: A small block usually fitted in a notch between a shaft and a hub to prevent slippage of the two parts.

MANIFOLD: A casting of passages or set of pipes which connect the cylinders to an inlet or outlet source.

MANIFOLD VACUUM: Low pressure in an engine intake manifold formed just below the throttle plates. Manifold vacuum is highest at idle and drops under acceleration.

MASTER CYLINDER: The primary fluid pressurizing device in a hydraulic system. In automotive use, it is found in brake and hydraulic clutch systems and is pedal activated, either directly or, in a power brake system, through the power booster.

MODULE: Electronic control unit, amplifier or igniter of solid state or integrated design which controls the current flow in the ignition primary circuit based on input from the pick-up coil. When the module opens the primary circuit, high secondary voltage is induced in the coil.

NEEDLE BEARING: A bearing which consists of a number (usually a large number) of long, thin rollers.

OHM:(Ω) The unit used to measure the resistance of conductor-to-electrical flow. One ohm is the amount of resistance that limits current flow to one ampere in a circuit with one volt of pressure.

OHMMETER: An instrument used for measuring the resistance, in ohms, in an electrical circuit.

OUTPUT SHAFT: The shaft which transmits torque from a device, such as a transmission.

OVERDRIVE: A gear assembly which produces more shaft revolutions than that transmitted to it.

OVERHEAD CAMSHAFT (OHC): An engine configuration in which the camshaft is mounted on top of the cylinder head and operates the valve either directly or by means of rocker arms.

OVERHEAD VALVE (OHV): An engine configuration in which all of the valves are located in the cylinder head and the camshaft is located in the cylinder block. The camshaft operates the valves via lifters and pushrods.

GLOSSARY 10-19

OXIDES OF NITROGEN (NOx): Chemical compounds of nitrogen produced as a byproduct of combustion. They combine with hydrocarbons to produce smog.

OXYGEN SENSOR: Used with the feedback system to sense the presence of oxygen in the exhaust gas and signal the computer which can reference the voltage signal to an air/fuel ratio.

PINION: The smaller of two meshing gears.

PISTON RING: An open-ended ring which fits into a groove on the outer diameter of the piston. Its chief function is to form a seal between the piston and cylinder wall. Most automotive pistons have three rings: two for compression sealing; one for oil sealing.

PRELOAD: A predetermined load placed on a bearing during assembly or by adjustment.

PRIMARY CIRCUIT: The low voltage side of the ignition system which consists of the ignition switch, ballast resistor or resistance wire, bypass, coil, electronic control unit and pick-up coil as well as the connecting wires and harnesses.

PRESS FIT: The mating of two parts under pressure, due to the inner diameter of one being smaller than the outer diameter of the other, or vice versa; an interference fit.

RACE: The surface on the inner or outer ring of a bearing on which the balls, needles or rollers move.

REGULATOR: A device which maintains the amperage and/or voltage levels of a circuit at predetermined values.

RELAY: A switch which automatically opens and/or closes a circuit.

RESISTANCE: The opposition to the flow of current through a circuit or electrical device, and is measured in ohms. Resistance is equal to the voltage divided by the amperage.

RESISTOR: A device, usually made of wire, which offers a preset amount of resistance in an electrical circuit.

RING GEAR: The name given to a ring-shaped gear attached to a differential case, or affixed to a flywheel or as part of a planetary gear set.

ROLLER BEARING: A bearing made up of hardened inner and outer races between which hardened steel rollers move.

ROTOR: 1. The disc-shaped part of a disc brake assembly, upon which the brake pads bear; also called, brake disc. 2. The device mounted atop the distributor shaft, which passes current to the distributor cap tower contacts.

SECONDARY CIRCUIT: The high voltage side of the ignition system, usually above 20,000 volts. The secondary includes the ignition coil, coil wire, distributor cap and rotor, spark plug wires and spark plugs.

SENDING UNIT: A mechanical, electrical, hydraulic or electro-magnetic device which transmits information to a gauge.

SENSOR: Any device designed to measure engine operating conditions or ambient pressures and temperatures. Usually electronic in nature and designed to send a voltage signal to an on-board computer, some sensors may operate as a simple on/off switch or they may provide a variable voltage signal (like a potentiometer) as conditions or measured parameters change.

SHIM: Spacers of precise, predetermined thickness used between parts to establish a proper working relationship.

SLAVE CYLINDER: In automotive use, a device in the hydraulic clutch system which is activated by hydraulic force, disengaging the clutch.

SOLENOID: A coil used to produce a magnetic field, the effect of which is to produce work.

SPARK PLUG: A device screwed into the combustion chamber of a spark ignition engine. The basic construction is a conductive core inside of a ceramic insulator, mounted in an outer conductive base. An electrical charge from the spark plug wire travels along the conductive core and jumps a preset air gap to a grounding point or points at the end of the conductive base. The resultant spark ignites the fuel/air mixture in the combustion chamber.

SPLINES: Ridges machined or cast onto the outer diameter of a shaft or inner diameter of a bore to enable parts to mate without rotation.

TACHOMETER: A device used to measure the rotary speed of an engine, shaft, gear, etc., usually in rotations per minute.

THERMOSTAT: A valve, located in the cooling system of an engine, which is closed when cold and opens gradually in response to engine heating, controlling the temperature of the coolant and rate of coolant flow.

TOP DEAD CENTER (TDC): The point at which the piston reaches the top of its travel on the compression stroke.

TORQUE: The twisting force applied to an object.

TORQUE CONVERTER: A turbine used to transmit power from a driving member to a driven member via hydraulic action, providing changes in drive ratio and torque. In automotive use, it links the driveplate at the rear of the engine to the automatic transmission.

TRANSDUCER: A device used to change a force into an electrical signal.

GLOSSARY

TRANSISTOR: A semi-conductor component which can be actuated by a small voltage to perform an electrical switching function.

TUNE-UP: A regular maintenance function, usually associated with the replacement and adjustment of parts and components in the electrical and fuel systems of a vehicle for the purpose of attaining optimum performance.

TURBOCHARGER: An exhaust driven pump which compresses intake air and forces it into the combustion chambers at higher than atmospheric pressures. The increased air pressure allows more fuel to be burned and results in increased horsepower being produced.

VACUUM ADVANCE: A device which advances the ignition timing in response to increased engine vacuum.

VACUUM GAUGE: An instrument used to measure the presence of vacuum in a chamber.

VALVE: A device which control the pressure, direction of flow or rate of flow of a liquid or gas.

VALVE CLEARANCE: The measured gap between the end of the valve stem and the rocker arm, cam lobe or follower that activates the valve.

VISCOSITY: The rating of a liquid's internal resistance to flow.

VOLTMETER: An instrument used for measuring electrical force in units called volts. Voltmeters are always connected parallel with the circuit being tested.

WHEEL CYLINDER: Found in the automotive drum brake assembly, it is a device, actuated by hydraulic pressure, which, through internal pistons, pushes the brake shoes outward against the drums.

2WD FRONT AXLE
  FRONT HUB AND WHEEL BEARINGS
    ADJUSTMENT 7-40
  PIVOT PINS
    REMOVAL & INSTALLATION 7-38
4WD FRONT DRIVE AXLE
  AXLE SHAFT, BEARING AND SEAL
    REMOVAL & INSTALLATION 7-31
  FRONT AXLE UNIT
    REMOVAL & INSTALLATION 7-34
  FRONT HUB AND WHEEL BEARINGS
    ADJUSTMENT 7-34
  PINION SEAL AND YOKE
    REMOVAL & INSTALLATION 7-34
AIR POLLUTION
  AUTOMOTIVE POLLUTANTS
    HEAT TRANSFER 4-3
    TEMPERATURE INVERSION 4-2
  INDUSTRIAL POLLUTANTS 4-2
  NATURAL POLLUTANTS 4-2
AUTOMOTIVE EMISSIONS
  CRANKCASE EMISSIONS 4-5
  EVAPORATIVE EMISSIONS 4-5
  EXHAUST GASES
    CARBON MONOXIDE 4-4
    HYDROCARBONS 4-3
    NITROGEN 4-4
    OXIDES OF SULFUR 4-4
    PARTICULATE MATTER 4-4
BASIC ELECTRICAL THEORY
  BATTERY, STARTING AND CHARGING SYSTEMS
    BASIC OPERATING PRINCIPLES 3-4
  UNDERSTANDING ELECTRICITY
    BASIC CIRCUITS 3-2
    TROUBLESHOOTING 3-3
BASIC FUEL SYSTEM DIAGNOSIS 5-2
BRAKE OPERATING SYSTEM
  ADJUSTMENTS
    BRAKE SHOES 9-4
  BASIC OPERATING PRINCIPLES
    DISC BRAKES 9-2
    DRUM BRAKES 9-3
    POWER BOOSTERS 9-3
  BLEEDING THE BRAKES 9-10
  BRAKE HOSES AND LINES
    BRAKE LINE FLARING 9-9
    HYDRAULIC BRAKE LINE CHECK 9-8
    REMOVAL & INSTALLATION 9-9
  MASTER CYLINDER
    OVERHAUL 9-6
    REMOVAL & INSTALLATION 9-5
  POWER BRAKE BOOSTER
    REMOVAL & INSTALLATION 9-7
  PROPORTIONING VALVE
    REMOVAL & INSTALLATION 9-8
  STOP LIGHT SWITCH
    ADJUSTMENT 9-11
CARBURETED FUEL SYSTEM
  CARBURETORS
    ADJUSTMENTS 5-4
    OVERHAUL 5-10
    REMOVAL & INSTALLATION 5-8
  FUEL PUMP
    REMOVAL & INSTALLATION 5-2
    TESTING 5-2
  GOVERNOR
    ADJUSTMENT 5-14
CIRCUIT PROTECTION
  FUSES 6-22
  FUSIBLE LINKS 6-22

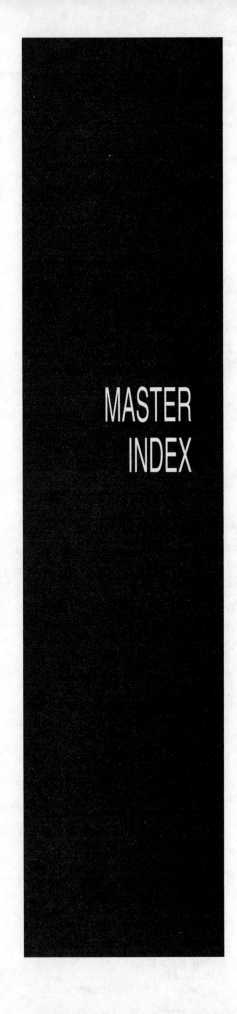

MASTER INDEX

INDEX

CLUTCH
  ADJUSTMENTS
    CLUTCH LINKAGE 7-12
  DRIVEN DISC AND PRESSURE PLATE
    REMOVAL & INSTALLATION 7-13
  UNDERSTANDING THE CLUTCH 7-12

DRIVE AXLES
  DETERMINING AXLE RATIO 7-27
  UNDERSTANDING DRIVE AXLES 7-27

DRIVELINE
  FRONT AND REAR DRIVESHAFTS
    REMOVAL & INSTALLATION 7-23
  U-JOINTS
    OVERHAUL 7-24

DRUM BRAKES
  BRAKE DRUM
    INSPECTION 9-13
    REMOVAL & INSTALLATION 9-11
  BRAKE SHOES
    REMOVAL & INSTALLATION 9-13
  WHEEL CYLINDERS
    OVERHAUL 9-17
    REMOVAL & INSTALLATION 9-16

EMISSION CONTROLS
  AIR INJECTION SYSTEM
    MAINTENANCE & SERVICE 4-9
    OPERATION 4-6
    REMOVAL & INSTALLATION 4-9
  CARBURETOR 4-6
  ELECTRICALLY ASSISTED CHOKE
    OPERATION 4-9
  EMISSION CONTROL CHECKS
    AIR PUMP 4-10
    ANTI-BACKFIRE DIVERTER VALVE 4-10
    CHECK VALVE 4-10
  FUEL RETURN SYSTEM 4-10
  FUEL TANK VAPOR EMISSION CONTROL SYSTEM
    OPERATION 4-10
  POSITIVE CRANKCASE VENTILATION (PCV) SYSTEM
    OPERATION 4-6
    REMOVAL & INSTALLATION 4-6
    TESTING 4-6

ENGINE ELECTRICAL
  ALTERNATOR/GENERATOR
    ALTERNATOR PRECAUTIONS 3-10
    BELT TENSION ADJUSTMENT 3-10
    GENERAL INFORMATION 3-9
    REMOVAL & INSTALLATION 3-10
  BATTERY
    REMOVAL & INSTALLATION 3-19
  DISTRIBUTOR
    INSTALLATION 3-8, 3-9
    REMOVAL 3-7
  IGNITION COIL
    REMOVAL & INSTALLATION 3-5
  REGULATOR
    CURRENT LIMITING REGULATOR 3-11
    REMOVAL & INSTALLATION 3-12
    VOLTAGE REGULATOR 3-11
    VOLTAGE TESTS & ADJUSTMENTS 3-11
  STARTER
    REMOVAL & INSTALLATION 3-12
    SOLENOID OR RELAY REPLACEMENT 3-14
    STARTER DRIVE REPLACEMENT 3-14
    STARTER OVERHAUL 3-15

ENGINE MECHANICAL
  CAMSHAFT
    REMOVAL & INSTALLATION 3-66

  COMPRESSION TESTING 3-22
  CRANKSHAFT PULLEY (VIBRATION DAMPER)
    REMOVAL & INSTALLATION 3-56
  CRANKSHAFT
    INSPECTION 3-75
    INSTALLATION 3-75
    REMOVAL 3-74
  CYLINDER HEAD
    REMOVAL & INSTALLATION 3-41
  DESIGN
    4-134 F-HEAD ENGINE 3-19
    4-134 L-HEAD ENGINE 3-19
    6-226 L-HEAD ENGINE 3-20
    6-230 ENGINE 3-20
    V6-225 ENGINE 3-19
  ENGINE OVERHAUL TIPS
    INSPECTION TECHNIQUES 3-20
    OVERHAUL TIPS 3-20
    REPAIRING DAMAGED THREADS 3-21
    TOOLS 3-20
  ENGINE
    REMOVAL & INSTALLATION 3-25
  EXHAUST MANIFOLD
    REMOVAL & INSTALLATION 3-36
  FLYWHEEL/FLEXPLATE AND RING GEAR
    REMOVAL & INSTALLATION 3-75
  INTAKE MANIFOLD
    REMOVAL & INSTALLATION 3-33
  OIL PAN
    REMOVAL & INSTALLATION 3-53
  OIL PUMP
    REMOVAL & INSTALLATION 3-53
  PISTONS AND CONNECTING RODS
    CHECKING CYLINDER BORE 3-72
    CYLINDER HONING 3-71
    INSPECTION 3-69
    PISTON ASSEMBLY & INSTALLATION 3-72
    PISTON PIN REPLACEMENT 3-69
    PISTON RING REPLACEMENT 3-72
    REMOVAL 3-67
    RING TOLERANCES 3-72
  RADIATOR
    REMOVAL & INSTALLATION 3-37
  REAR MAIN OIL SEAL
    REPLACEMENT 3-73
  ROCKER SHAFTS AND ROCKER STUDS
    REMOVAL & INSTALLATION 3-28
  THERMOSTAT
    REMOVAL & INSTALLATION 3-31
  TIMING CHAIN AND TENSIONER
    REMOVAL & INSTALLATION 3-60
  TIMING CHAIN/GEAR COVER AND OIL SEAL
    REMOVAL & INSTALLATION 3-57
  TIMING GEARS
    REMOVAL & INSTALLATION 3-62
  VALVE GUIDES
    REMOVAL & INSTALLATION 3-52
  VALVE SEATS
    INSPECTION & REFACING 3-52
  VALVE TIMING
    L4-134 ENGINES AFTER ENGINE NO. 175402 AND ALL F4-134 ENGINES 3-65
    L4-134 ENGINES BEFORE NO. 175402 IN CJ-2A MODELS 3-64
  VALVES AND SPRINGS
    INSPECTION & REFACING 3-48
    INSTALLATION 3-51
    LAPPING 3-51

INDEX 10-23

REFACING 3-51
REMOVAL 3-48
VALVE SPRING TESTING 3-51
WATER PUMP
REMOVAL & INSTALLATION 3-37
EXHAUST SYSTEM
CATALYTIC CONVERTER
REMOVAL & INSTALLATION 3-78
FRONT EXHAUST PIPE (HEAD PIPE)
REMOVAL & INSTALLATION 3-77
GENERAL INFORMATION 3-76
MUFFLER
REMOVAL & INSTALLATION 3-76
REAR EXHAUST PIPE OR TAILPIPE
REMOVAL & INSTALLATION 3-77
EXTERIOR
DOORS
REMOVAL & INSTALLATION 10-2
FENDERS
REMOVAL & INSTALLATION 10-6
FRONT BUMPER
REMOVAL & INSTALLATION 10-5
FRONT CROSSMEMBER COVER
REMOVAL & INSTALLATION 10-7
GRILLE
REMOVAL & INSTALLATION 10-5
HARDTOP
REMOVAL & INSTALLATION 10-6
HOOD
ALIGNMENT 10-4
REMOVAL & INSTALLATION 10-2
LIFTGATE
ALIGNMENT 10-4
REMOVAL & INSTALLATION 10-4
REAR BUMPER
REMOVAL & INSTALLATION 10-5
SOFT TOP
ADJUSTMENT 10-6
SWING-OUT SPARE TIRE CARRIER
REMOVAL & INSTALLATION 10-7
TAILGATE
REMOVAL & INSTALLATION 10-4
FASTENERS, MEASUREMENTS AND CONVERSIONS
BOLTS, NUTS AND OTHER THREADED RETAINERS 1-8
STANDARD AND METRIC MEASUREMENTS 1-13
TORQUE
TORQUE ANGLE METERS 1-13
TORQUE WRENCHES 1-10
FIRING ORDERS 2-11
FLUIDS AND LUBRICANTS
AUTOMATIC TRANSMISSION
DRAIN, FILTER SERVICE AND REFILL 1-44
FLUID LEVEL CHECK 1-43
BODY LUBRICATION AND MAINTENANCE
BODY DRAIN HOLES 1-53
DOOR HINGES AND HINGE CHECKS 1-53
LOCK CYLINDERS 1-53
TAILGATE 1-53
BRAKE AND CLUTCH MASTER CYLINDERS 1-49
CHASSIS GREASING 1-50
COOLING SYSTEM
DRAINING, FLUSHING AND REFILLING 1-48
LEVEL CHECK 1-47
DRIVE AXLES
DRAIN & REFILL 1-45
FLUID LEVEL CHECK 1-45
ENGINE
OIL AND FILTER CHANGE 1-40

OIL LEVEL CHECK 1-40
FUEL AND OIL RECOMMENDATIONS
ENGINE OIL 1-39
FUEL 1-39
MANUAL STEERING GEAR
FLUID LEVEL CHECK 1-49
MANUAL TRANSMISSION
FLUID CHANGE 1-43
FLUID LEVEL CHECK 1-43
POWER STEERING PUMP
FLUID LEVEL CHECK 1-49
STEERING KNUCKLE
FLUID LEVEL CHECK 1-50
TRANSFER CASE
DRAIN & REFILL 1-45
FLUID LEVEL CHECK 1-45
FRONT AND REAR SUSPENSIONS
FRONT END ALIGNMENT
GENERAL INFORMATION 8-7
FRONT STABILIZER BAR
REMOVAL & INSTALLATION 8-5
LEAF SPRINGS
REMOVAL & INSTALLATION 8-2
SHOCK ABSORBERS
REMOVAL & INSTALLATION 8-3
STEERING KNUCKLE AND PIVOT PINS
REMOVAL & INSTALLATION 8-5
STEERING KNUCKLE OIL SEAL
REMOVAL & INSTALLATION 8-6
UPPER CONTROL ARM
REMOVAL & INSTALLATION 8-6
FUEL TANK
TANK ASSEMBLY
REMOVAL & INSTALLATION 5-15
HEATER
BLOWER MOTOR
REMOVAL & INSTALLATION 6-12
HEATER CORE
REMOVAL & INSTALLATION 6-13
HISTORY AND MODEL IDENTIFICATION 1-15
HOW TO BUY A USED VEHICLE
TIPS
ROAD TEST CHECKLIST 1-58
USED VEHICLE CHECKLIST 1-57
HOW TO USE THIS BOOK
AVOIDING THE MOST COMMON MISTAKES 1-2
AVOIDING TROUBLE 1-2
MAINTENANCE OR REPAIR? 1-2
WHERE TO BEGIN 1-2
IDLE SPEED AND MIXTURE ADJUSTMENTS
IDLE MIXTURE 2-21
IDLE SPEED 2-21
IGNITION TIMING
TIMING
GENERAL INFORMATION 2-16
INSPECTION AND ADJUSTMENT 2-17
INSTRUMENTS AND SWITCHES
IGNITION LOCK CYLINDER
REMOVAL & INSTALLATION 6-15
IGNITION SWITCH
REMOVAL & INSTALLATION 6-15
INSTRUMENT CLUSTER
REMOVAL & INSTALLATION 6-15
SPEEDOMETER CABLE REPLACEMENT 6-15
INTERIOR
DOOR GLASS
REMOVAL & INSTALLATION 10-9

INDEX

DOOR HINGES
  REMOVAL & INSTALLATION 10-8
DOOR LOCK
  DOOR LOCK ADJUSTMENT 10-9
  REMOVAL & INSTALLATION 10-8
DOOR TRIM PANEL
  REMOVAL & INSTALLATION 10-8
LIFTGATE GLASS
  REMOVAL & INSTALLATION 10-13
SEATS
  REMOVAL & INSTALLATION 10-13
STATIONARY WINDOW GLASS
  REMOVAL & INSTALLATION 10-12
STRIKER PLATE
  ADJUSTMENT 10-9
WINDOW REGULATOR
  REMOVAL & INSTALLATION 10-10
WINDSHIELD FRAME
  REMOVAL & INSTALLATION 10-10
WINDSHIELD GLASS
  REMOVAL & INSTALLATION 10-10
JACKING AND HOISTING 1-56
JUMP STARTING A DEAD BATTERY
  JUMP STARTING PRECAUTIONS 1-55
  JUMP STARTING PROCEDURE 1-56
LIGHTING
  HEADLIGHTS
    REMOVAL & INSTALLATION 6-17
  TURN SIGNALS
    REMOVAL & INSTALLATION 6-18
MANUAL TRANSMISSION
  ADJUSTMENTS
    SHIFT LINKAGE 7-2
  BACK-UP LIGHT SWITCH
    REMOVAL & INSTALLATION 7-3
  OVERDRIVE UNIT
    REMOVAL & INSTALLATION 7-11
  T-86AA 3-SPEED OVERHAUL
    ASSEMBLY 7-6
    DISASSEMBLY 7-6
  T-90C 3-SPEED OVERHAUL
    ASSEMBLY 7-6
    DISASSEMBLY 7-6
  T-98A 4-SPEED OVERHAUL
    CASE ASSEMBLY 7-11
    DISASSEMBLY 7-9
  TRANSMISSION
    REMOVAL & INSTALLATION 7-3
  UNDERSTANDING THE MANUAL TRANSMISSION 7-2
POINT TYPE IGNITION
  BREAKER POINTS AND CONDENSER
    ADJUSTMENT 2-15
    INSPECTION 2-12
    REMOVAL & INSTALLATION 2-13
POWER TAKE-OFF (PTO) UNIT
  PULLEY DRIVE UNIT
    DISASSEMBLY & ASSEMBLY 7-22
    REMOVAL & INSTALLATION 7-22
  SHAFT DRIVE UNIT
    DISASSEMBLY & ASSEMBLY 7-21
    REMOVAL & INSTALLATION 7-21
  SHIFT ASSEMBLY
    DISASSEMBLY & ASSEMBLY 7-21
    REMOVAL & INSTALLATION 7-21
REAR AXLE
  AXLE SHAFT BEARING
    REMOVAL & INSTALLATION 7-29
  AXLE SHAFT
    REMOVAL & INSTALLATION 7-29
  PINION OIL SEAL
    REMOVAL & INSTALLATION 7-27
  REAR AXLE UNIT
    REMOVAL & INSTALLATION 7-30
ROUTINE MAINTENANCE
  AIR CLEANER
    OIL BATH TYPE 1-17
    PAPER ELEMENT TYPE 1-18
  BATTERY
    BATTERY FLUID 1-20
    CABLES 1-21
    CHARGING 1-23
    GENERAL MAINTENANCE 1-19
    REPLACEMENT 1-23
  BELTS
    ADJUSTING 1-28
    INSPECTION 1-28
    REMOVAL & INSTALLATION 1-29
  EVAPORATIVE CANISTER 1-19
  FRONT HUB AND WHEEL BEARINGS
    REMOVAL, REPACKING AND INSTALLATION 1-31
  FUEL FILTER
    REPLACEMENT 1-18
  HEAT RISER 1-19
  HOSES
    INSPECTION 1-30
    REMOVAL & INSTALLATION 1-31
  PCV VALVE 1-19
  TIRES AND WHEELS
    CARE OF SPECIAL WHEELS 1-39
    INFLATION & INSPECTION 1-37
    TIRE DESIGN 1-36
    TIRE ROTATION 1-35
    TIRE STORAGE 1-37
  WINDSHIELD WIPERS
    ELEMENT (REFILL) CARE AND REPLACEMENT 1-23
SERIAL NUMBER IDENTIFICATION
  DRIVE AXLE 1-17
  ENGINE
    4-134 1-15
    6-225 1-16
    6-226 1-16
    6-230 1-16
  TRANSFER CASE 1-17
  TRANSMISSION 1-16
  VEHICLE 1-15
SERVICING YOUR VEHICLE SAFELY
  DO'S 1-6
  DON'TS 1-7
SPECIFICATIONS CHARTS
  ALTERNATOR AND REGULATOR SPECIFICATIONS 3-5
  BRAKE SPECIFICATIONS 9-20
  CAMSHAFT SPECIFICATIONS 3-23
  CAPACITIES 1-61
  CARBURETOR SPECIFICATIONS 5-16
  CRANKSHAFT AND CONNECTING ROD SPECIFICATIONS 3-24
  DRIVELINE NOISE DIAGNOSIS 7-26
  ENGINE IDENTIFICATION 1-15
  FRONT AND REAR DRIVE AXLE APPLICATIONS 1-17
  FUSE APPLICATIONS 6-22
  GENERAL ENGINE SPECIFICATIONS 3-23
  GENERATOR AND REGULATOR SPECIFICATIONS 3-5
  HOW TO REMOVE STAINS FROM FABRIC INTERIOR 10-15
  LIGHT BULB APPLICATIONS 6-19
  MAINTENANCE INTERVALS 1-59
  MANUAL TRANSMISSION APPLICATIONS 7-2, 1-16

PISTON AND RING SPECIFICATIONS 3-24
POWER TAKE-OFF GEAR AND SPEED SPECIFICATIONS 7-22
REAR AXLE APPLICATIONS 7-27
STANDARD (ENGLISH) TO METRIC CONVERSION
 CHARTS 1-62
STARTER SPECIFICATIONS 3-5
TORQUE SPECIFICATIONS 3-24
TROUBLESHOOTING BASIC CHARGING SYSTEM
 PROBLEMS 3-80
TROUBLESHOOTING BASIC DASH GAUGE PROBLEMS 6-16
TROUBLESHOOTING BASIC FUEL SYSTEM PROBLEMS 5-16
TROUBLESHOOTING BASIC LIGHTING PROBLEMS 6-20
TROUBLESHOOTING BASIC STARTING SYSTEM
 PROBLEMS 3-80
TROUBLESHOOTING BASIC STEERING AND SUSPENSION
 PROBLEMS 8-15
TROUBLESHOOTING BASIC TURN SIGNAL AND FLASHER
 PROBLEMS 6-21
TROUBLESHOOTING BASIC WINDSHIELD WIPER
 PROBLEMS 6-15
TROUBLESHOOTING ENGINE PERFORMANCE 2-21
TROUBLESHOOTING THE BRAKE SYSTEM 9-21
TROUBLESHOOTING THE HEATER 6-14
TROUBLESHOOTING THE IGNITION SYSTEM 2-2
TROUBLESHOOTING THE MANUAL STEERING GEAR 8-20
TROUBLESHOOTING THE MANUAL TRANSMISSION AND
 TRANSFER CASE 7-18
TROUBLESHOOTING THE STEERING COLUMN 8-16
TROUBLESHOOTING THE TURN SIGNAL SWITCH 8-18
TUNE-UP SPECIFICATIONS 2-2
USING A VACUUM GAUGE 3-79
VALVE SPECIFICATIONS 3-23
VEHICLE IDENTIFICATION 1-15
WHEEL ALIGNMENT SPECIFICATIONS 8-8
STEERING
 MANUAL STEERING GEAR
  ADJUSTMENTS 8-10
  REMOVAL & INSTALLATION 8-10
 STEERING COLUMN
  REMOVAL & INSTALLATION 8-10
 STEERING LINKAGE
  REMOVAL & INSTALLATION 8-11
 STEERING WHEEL
  REMOVAL & INSTALLATION 8-9
 TURN SIGNAL SWITCH
  INSPECTION 8-9
  REMOVAL & INSTALLATION 8-9
TOOLS AND EQUIPMENT
 SPECIAL TOOLS 1-6
TOWING THE VEHICLE 1-53
TRAILER TOWING
 COOLING
  ENGINE 1-54
  TRANSMISSION 1-54
 HANDLING A TRAILER 1-54
 HITCH (TONGUE) WEIGHT 1-53
 TRAILER WEIGHT 1-53
TRAILER WIRING 6-22
TRANSFER CASE
 ADJUSTMENTS
  SHIFT LINKAGE 7-20
 TRANSFER CASE
  REMOVAL & INSTALLATION 7-20
TRANSMISSION (PARKING) BRAKE
 BRAKE SHOES
  ADJUSTMENT 9-20
  REMOVAL & INSTALLATION 9-17
 CABLE(S)
  REMOVAL & INSTALLATION 9-17
TUNE-UP PROCEDURES
 SPARK PLUGS
  INSPECTION & GAPPING 2-5
  REMOVAL & INSTALLATION 2-2
  SPARK PLUG CABLES 2-5
  SPARK PLUG HEAT RANGE 2-2
**UNDERSTANDING AND TROUBLESHOOTING ELECTRICAL
 SYSTEMS**
 ADD-ON ELECTRICAL EQUIPMENT 6-12
 SAFETY PRECAUTIONS 6-2
 TROUBLESHOOTING
  BASIC TROUBLESHOOTING THEORY 6-4
  TEST EQUIPMENT 6-4
  TESTING 6-7
 UNDERSTANDING BASIC ELECTRICITY
  AUTOMOTIVE CIRCUITS 6-3
  CIRCUITS 6-3
  SHORT CIRCUITS 6-3
  THE WATER ANALOGY 6-2
 WIRING HARNESSES
  WIRING REPAIR 6-9
VALVE LASH
 ADJUSTMENT
  PROCEDURE 2-18
WHEELS
 WHEELS
  INSPECTION 8-2
  REMOVAL & INSTALLATION 8-2
WINDSHIELD WIPERS
 WIPER BLADES AND ARMS
  REMOVAL & INSTALLATION 6-14
 WIPER LINKAGE
  REMOVAL & INSTALLATION 6-14
 WIPER MOTOR
  REMOVAL & INSTALLATION 6-14
WIRING DIAGRAMS 6-23

Don't Miss These Other Important Titles From NP/CHILTON'S

TOTAL CAR CARE MANUALS
The ULTIMATE in automotive repair manuals

Features:
- Based on actual teardowns
- Each manual covers all makes and models (unless otherwise indicated)
- Expanded photography from vehicle teardowns
- Actual vacuum and wiring diagrams—not general representations
- Comprehensive coverage
- Maintenance interval schedules
- Electronic engine and emission controls

ACURA
Coupes and Sedans 1986-93
PART NO. 8426/10300

AMC
Coupes/Sedans/Wagons 1975-88
PART NO. 14300

BMW
Coupes and Sedans 1970-88
PART NO. 8789/18300
318/325/M3/525/535/M5 1989-93
PART NO. 8427/18400

CHRYSLER
Aspen/Volare 1976-80
PART NO. 20100
Caravan/Voyager/Town & Country 1984-95
PART NO. 8155/20300
Caravan/Voyager/Town & Country 1996-99
PART NO. 20302
Cirrus/Stratus/Sebring/Avenger 1995-98
PART NO. 20320
Colt/Challenger/Conquest/Vista 1971-89
PART NO. 20340
Colt/Vista 1990-93
PART NO. 8418/20342
Concorde/Intrepid/New Yorker/LHS/Vision 1993-97
PART NO. 8817/20360
Front Wheel Drive Cars-4 Cyl 1981-95
PART NO. 8673/20382
Front Wheel Drive Cars-6 Cyl 1988-95
PART NO. 8672/20384
Full-Size Trucks 1967-88
PART NO. 8662/20400
Full-Size Trucks 1989-96
PART NO. 8166/20402
Full-Size Vans 1967-88
PART NO. 20420
Full-Size Vans 1989-98
PART NO. 8169/20422
Neon 1995-99
PART NO. 20600
Omni/Horizon/Rampage 1978-89
PART NO. 8787/20700
Ram 50/D50/Arrow 1979-93
PART NO. 20800

FORD
Aerostar 1986-96
PART NO. 8057/26100
Aspire 1994-97
PART NO. 26120
Contour/Mystique/Cougar 1995-99
PART NO. 26170
Crown Victoria/Grand Marquis 1989-94
PART NO. 8417/26180
Escort/Lynx 1981-90
PART NO. 8270/26240
Escort/Tracer 1991-99
PART NO. 26242
Fairmont/Zephyr 1978-83
PART NO. 26320
Ford/Mercury Full-Size Cars 1968-88
PART NO. 8665/26360
Full-Size Vans 1961-88
PART NO. 26400

Full-Size Vans 1989-96
PART NO. 8157/26402
Ford/Mercury Mid-Size Cars 1971-85
PART NO. 8667/26580
Mustang/Cougar 1964-73
PART NO. 26600
Mustang/Capri 1979-88
PART NO. 8580/26604
Mustang 1989-93
PART NO. 8253/26606
Mustang 1994-98
PART NO. 26608
Pick-Ups and Bronco 1976-86
PART NO. 8576/26662
Pick-Ups and Bronco 1987-96
PART NO. 8136/26664
Pick-Ups/Expedition/Navigator 1997-00
PART NO. 26666
Probe 1989-92
PART NO. 8266/26680
Probe 1993-97
PART NO. 8411/46802
Ranger/Bronco II 1983-90
PART NO. 8159/26686
Ranger/Explorer/Mountaineer 1991-97
PART NO. 26688
Taurus/Sable 1986-95
PART NO. 8251/26700
Taurus/Sable 1996-99
PART NO. 26702
Tempo/Topaz 1984-94
PART NO. 8271/26720
Thunderbird/Cougar 1983-96
PART NO. 8268/26760
Windstar 1995-98
PART NO. 26840

GENERAL MOTORS
Astro/Safari 1985-96
PART NO. 8056/28100
Blazer/Jimmy 1969-82
PART NO. 28140
Blazer/Jimmy/Typhoon/Bravada 1983-93
PART NO. 8139/28160
Blazer/Jimmy/Bravada 1994-99
PART NO. 8845/28862
Bonneville/Eighty Eight/LeSabre 1986-99
PART NO. 8423/28200
Buick/Oldsmobile/Pontiac Full-Size 1975-90
PART NO. 8584/28240
Cadillac 1967-89
PART NO. 8587/28260
Camaro 1967-81
PART NO. 28280
Camaro 1982-92
PART NO. 8260/28282

Camaro/Firebird 1993-98
PART NO. 28284
Caprice 1990-93
PART NO. 8421/28300
Cavalier/Sunbird/Skyhawk/Firenza 1982-94
PART NO. 8269/28320
Cavalier/Sunfire 1995-00
PART NO. 28322
Celebrity/Century/Ciera/6000 1982-96
PART NO. 8252/28360
Chevette/1000 1976-88
PART NO. 28400
Chevy Full-Size Cars 1968-78
PART NO. 28420
Chevy Full-Size Cars 1979-89
PART NO. 8531/28422
Chevy Mid-Size Cars 1964-88
PART NO. 8594/28440
Citation/Omega/Phoenix/Skylark/XII 1980-85
PART NO. 28460
Corsica/Beretta 1988-96
PART NO. 8254/28480
Corvette 1963-82
PART NO. 28500
Corvette 1984-96
PART NO. 28502
Cutlass RWD 1970-87
PART NO. 8668/28520
DeVille/Fleetwood/Eldorado/Seville 1990-93
PART NO. 8420/28540
Electra/Park Avenue/Ninety-Eight 1990-93
PART NO. 8430/28560
Fiero 1984-88
PART NO. 28580
Firebird 1967-81
PART NO. 28600
Firebird 1982-92
PART NO. 8534/28602
Full-Size Trucks 1970-79
PART NO. 28620
Full-Size Trucks 1980-87
PART NO. 8577/28622
Full-Size Trucks 1988-98
PART NO. 8055/28624
Full-Size Vans 1967-86
PART NO. 28640
Full-Size Vans 1987-97
PART NO. 8040/28642
Grand Am/Achieva 1985-98
PART NO. 8257/28660
Lumina/Silhouette/Trans Sport/Venture 1990-99
PART NO. 8134/28680
Lumina/Monte Carlo/Grand Prix/Cutlass Supreme/Regal 1988-96
PART NO. 8258/28682

Metro/Sprint 1985-99
PART NO. 8424/28700
Nova/Chevy II 1962-79
PART NO. 28720
Pontiac Mid-Size 1974-83
PART NO. 28740
Chevrolet Nova/GEO Prizm 1985-93
PART NO. 8422/28760
Regal/Century 1975-87
PART NO. 28780
Chevrolet Spectrum/GEO Storm 1985-93
PART NO. 8425/28800
S10/S15/Sonoma Pick-Ups 1982-93
PART NO. 8141/28860
S10/Sonoma/Blazer/Jimmy/Bravada Hombre 1994-99
PART NO. 8845/28862

HONDA
Accord/Civic/Prelude 1973-83
PART NO. 8591/30100
Accord/Prelude 1984-95
PART NO. 8255/30150
Civic, CRX and del SOL 1984-95
PART NO. 8256/30200

HYUNDAI
Coupes/Sedans 1986-93
PART NO. 8412/32100
Coupes/Sedans 1994-98
PART NO. 32102

ISUZU
Amigo/Pick-Ups/Rodeo/Trooper 1981-96
PART NO. 8686/36100
Cars and Trucks 1981-91
PART NO. 8069/36150

JEEP
CJ 1945-70
PART NO. 40200
CJ/Scrambler 1971-86
PART NO. 8536/40202
Wagoneer/Commando/Cherokee 1957-83
PART NO. 40600
Wagoneer/Comanche/Cherokee 1984-98
PART NO. 8143/40602
Wrangler/YJ 1987-95
PART NO. 8535/40650

MAZDA
Trucks 1972-86
PART NO. 46600
Trucks 1987-93
PART NO. 8264/46602
Trucks 1994-98
PART NO. 46604
323/626/929/GLC/MX-6/RX-7 1978-89
PART NO. 8581/46800
323/Protege/MX-3/MX-6/626 Millenia/Ford Probe 1990-98
PART NO. 8411/46802

MERCEDES
Coupes/Sedans/Wagons 1974-84
PART NO. 48300

MITSUBISHI
Cars and Trucks 1983-89
PART NO. 7947/50200

3P1VerB

"...and even more from CHILTON"

System-Specific Manuals

Guide to Air Conditioning Repair and Service 1982-85
PART NO. 7580

Guide to Automatic Transmission Repair 1984-89
PART NO. 8054

Guide to Automatic Transmission Repair 1984-89
Domestic cars and trucks
PART NO. 8053

Guide to Automatic Transmission Repair 1980-84
Domestic cars and trucks
PART NO. 7891

Guide to Automatic Transmission Repair 1974-80
Import cars and trucks
PART NO. 7645

Guide to Brakes, Steering, and Suspension 1980-87
PART NO. 7819

Guide to Fuel Injection and Electronic Engine Controls 1984-88
Domestic cars and trucks
PART NO. 7766

Guide to Electronic Engine Controls 1978-85
PART NO. 7535

Guide to Engine Repair and Rebuilding
PART NO. 7643

Guide to Vacuum Diagrams 1980-86
Domestic cars and trucks
PART NO. 7821

Multi-Vehicle Spanish Repair Manuals

Auto Repair Manual 1992-96
PART NO. 8947

Import Repair Manual 1992-96
PART NO. 8948

Truck and Van Repair Manual 1992-96
PART NO. 8949

Auto Repair Manual 1987-91
PART NO. 8138

Auto Repair Manual 1980-87
PART NO. 7795

Auto Repair Manual 1976-83
PART NO. 7476

SELOC MARINE MANUALS

OUTBOARDS

Chrysler Outboards, All Engines 1962-84
PART NO. 018-7(1000)

Force Outboards, All Engines 1984-96
PART NO. 024-1(1100)

Honda Outboards, All Engines 1988-98
PART NO. 1200

Johnson/Evinrude Outboards, 1.5-40HP, 2-Stroke 1956-70
PART NO. 007-1(1300)

Johnson/Evinrude Outboards, 1.25-60HP, 2-Stroke 1971-89
PART NO. 008-X(1302)

Johnson/Evinrude Outboards, 1-50 HP, 2-Stroke 1990-95
PART NO. 026-8(1304)

Johnson/Evinrude Outboards, 50-125 HP, 2-Stroke 1958-72
PART NO. 009-8(1306)

Johnson/Evinrude Outboards, 60-235 HP, 2-Stroke 1973-91
PART NO. 010-1(1308)

Johnson/Evinrude Outboards, 80-300 HP, 2-Stroke 1992-96
PART NO. 040-3(1310)

Mariner Outboards, 2-60 HP, 2-Stroke 1977-89
PART NO. 015-2(1400)

Mariner Outboards, 45-220 HP, 2 Stroke 1977-89
PART NO. 016-0(1402)

Mercury Outboards, 2-40 HP, 2-Stroke 1965-91
PART NO. 012-8(1404)

Mercury Outboards, 40-115 HP, 2-Stroke 1965-92
PART NO. 013-6(1406)

Mercury Outboards, 90-300 HP, 2-Stroke 1965-91
PART NO. 014-4(1408)

Mercury/Mariner Outboards, 2.5-25 HP, 2-Stroke 1990-94
PART NO. 035-7(1410)

Mercury/Mariner Outboards, 40-125 HP, 2-Stroke 1990-94
PART NO. 036-5(1412)

Mercury/Mariner Outboards, 135-275 HP, 2-Stroke 1990-94
PART NO. 037-3(1414)

Mercury/Mariner Outboards, All Engines 1995-99
PART NO. 1416

Suzuki Outboards, All Engines 1985-99
PART NO. 1600

Yamaha Outboards, 2-25 HP, 2-Stroke and 9.9 HP, 4-Stroke 1984-91
PART NO. 021-7(1700)

Yamaha Outboards, 30-90 HP, 2-Stroke 1984-91
PART NO. 022-5(1702)

Yamaha Outboards, 115-225 HP, 2-Stroke 1984-91
PART NO. 023-3(1704)

Yamaha Outboards, All Engines 1992-98
PART NO. 1706

STERN DRIVES

Marine Jet Drive 1961-96
PART NO. 029-2(3000)

Mercruiser Stern Drive Type 1, Alpha, Bravo I, II, 1964-92
PART NO. 005-5(3200)

Mercruiser Stern Drive Alpha 1 Generation II 1992-96
PART NO. 039-X(3202)

Mercruiser Stern Drive Bravo I, II, III 1992-96
PART NO. 046-2(3204)

OMC Stern Drive 1964-86
PART NO. 004-7(3400)

OMC Cobra Stern Drive 1985-95
PART NO. 025-X(3402)

Volvo/Penta Stern Drives 1968-91
PART NO. 011-X(3600)

Volvo/Penta Stern Drives 1992-93
PART NO. 038-1(3602)

Volvo/Penta Stern Drives 1992-95
PART NO. 041-1(3604)

INBOARDS

Yanmar Inboard Diesels 1988-91
PART NO. 7400

PERSONAL WATERCRAFT

Kawasaki 1973-91
PART NO. 032-2(9200)

Kawasaki 1992-97
PART NO. 042-X(9202)

Polaris 1992-97
PART NO. 045-4(9400)

Sea Doo/Bombardier 1988-91
PART NO. 033-0(9000)

Sea Doo/Bombardier 1992-97
PART NO. 043-8(9002)

Yamaha 1987-91
PART NO. 034-9(9600)

Yamaha 1992-97
PART NO. 044-6(9602)

FOR THE TITLES LISTED, PLEASE VISIT YOUR LOCAL CHILTON RETAILER

For a FREE catalog of Chilton's complete line of Automotive Repair Manuals, or to order direct
Call toll-free 877-4CHILTON

1020 Andrew Drive, Suite 200 • West Chester, PA 19380-4291
www.chiltononline.com

Total Car Care, continued

Eclipse 1990-98
PART NO. 8415/50400

Pick-Ups and Montero 1983-95
PART NO. 8666/50500

NISSAN
Datsun 210/1200 1973-81
PART NO. 52300

Datsun 200SX/510/610/710/810/Maxima 1973-84
PART NO. 52302

Nissan Maxima 1985-92
PART NO. 8261/52450

Maxima 1993-98
PART NO. 52452

Pick-Ups and Pathfinder 1970-88
PART NO. 8585/52500

Pick-Ups and Pathfinder 1989-95
PART NO. 8145/52502

Sentra/Pulsar/NX 1982-96
PART NO. 8263/52700

Stanza/200SX/240SX 1982-92
PART NO. 8262/52750

240SX/Altima 1993-98
PART NO. 52752

Datsun/Nissan Z and ZX 1970-88
PART NO. 8846/52800

RENAULT
Coupes/Sedans/Wagons 1975-85
PART NO. 58300

SATURN
Coupes/Sedans/Wagons 1991-98
PART NO. 8419/62300

SUBARU
Coupes/Sedan/Wagons 1970-84
PART NO. 8790/64300

Coupes/Sedans/Wagons 1985-96
PART NO. 8259/64302

SUZUKI
Samurai/Sidekick/Tracker 1986-98
PART NO. 66500

TOYOTA
Camry 1983-96
PART NO. 8265/68200

Celica/Supra 1971-85
PART NO. 68250

Celica 1986-93
PART NO. 8413/68252

Celica 1994-98
PART NO. 68254

Corolla 1970-87
PART NO. 8586/68300

Corolla 1988-97
PART NO. 8414/68302

Cressida/Corona/Crown/MkII 1970-82
PART NO. 68350

Cressida/Van 1983-90
PART NO. 68352

Pick-ups/Land Cruiser/4Runner 1970-88
PART NO. 8578/68600

Pick-ups/Land Cruiser/4Runner 1989-98
PART NO. 8163/68602

Previa 1991-97
PART NO. 68640

Tercel 1984-94
PART NO. 8595/68700

VOLKSWAGEN
Air-Cooled 1949-69
PART NO. 70200

Air-Cooled 1970-81
PART NO. 70202

Front Wheel Drive 1974-89
PART NO. 8663/70400

Golf/Jetta/Cabriolet 1990-93
PART NO. 8429/70402

VOLVO
Coupes/Sedans/Wagons 1970-89
PART NO. 8786/72300

Coupes/Sedans/Wagons 1990-98
PART NO. 8428/72302

General Interest / Recreational Books

We offer specialty books on a variety of topics including Motorcycles, ATVs, Snowmobiles and automotive subjects like Detailing or Body Repair. Each book from our General Interest line offers a blend of our famous Do-It-Yourself procedures and photography with additional information on enjoying automotive, marine and recreational products. Learn more about the vehicles you use and enjoy while keeping them in top running shape.

ATV Handbook
PART NO. 9123

Auto Detailing
PART NO. 8394

Auto Body Repair
PART NO. 7898

Briggs & Stratton Vertical Crankshaft Engine
PART NO. 61-1-2

Briggs & Stratton Horizontal Crankshaft Engine
PART NO. 61-0-4

Briggs & Stratton Overhead Valve (OHV) Engine
PART NO. 61-2-0

Easy Car Care
PART NO. 8042

Motorcycle Handbook
PART NO. 9099

Snowmobile Handbook
PART NO. 9124

Small Engine Repair (Up to 20 Hp)
PART NO. 8325

Total Service Series

These innovative books offer repair, maintenance and service procedures for automotive related systems. They cover today's complex vehicles in a user-friendly format, which places even the most difficult automotive topic well within the reach of every Do-It-Yourselfer. Each title covers a specific subject from Brakes and Engine Rebuilding to Fuel Injection Systems, Automatic Transmissions and even Engine Trouble Codes.

Automatic Transmissions/Transaxles Diagnosis and Repair
PART NO. 8944

Brake System Diagnosis and Repair
PART NO. 8945

Chevrolet Engine Overhaul Manual
PART NO. 8794

Engine Code Manual
PART NO. 8851

Ford Engine Overhaul Manual
PART NO. 8793

Fuel Injection Diagnosis and Repair
PART NO. 8946

Collector's Hard-Cover Manuals

Chilton's Collector's Editions are perfect for enthusiasts of vintage or rare cars. These hard-cover manuals contain repair and maintenance information for all major systems that might not be available elsewhere. Included are repair and overhaul procedures using thousands of illustrations. These manuals offer a range of coverage from as far back as 1940 and as recent as 1997, so you don't need an antique car or truck to be a collector.

Auto Repair Manual 1993-97
PART NO. 7919

Auto Repair Manual 1988-92
PART NO. 7906

Auto Repair Manual 1980-87
PART NO. 7670

Auto Repair Manual 1972-79
PART NO. 6914

Auto Repair Manual 1964-71
PART NO. 5974

Auto Repair Manual 1954-63
PART NO. 5652

Auto Repair Manual 1940-53
PART NO. 5631

Import Car Repair Manual 1993-97
PART NO. 7920

Import Car Repair Manual 1988-92
PART NO. 7907

Import Car Repair Manual 1980-87
PART NO. 7672

Truck and Van Repair Manual 1993-97
PART NO. 7921

Truck and Van Repair Manual 1991-95
PART NO. 7911

Truck and Van Repair Manual 1986-90
PART NO. 7902

Truck and Van Repair Manual 1979-86
PART NO. 7655

Truck and Van Repair Manual 1971-78
PART NO. 7012